Conceptual Foundations of Radical Behaviorism

Jay Moore

University of Wisconsin—Milwaukee

2008
Sloan Publishing
Cornwall-on-Hudson, NY 12520

Library of Congress Control Number: 2007921516

Moore, Jay
  Conceptual Foundations of Radical Behaviorism
    p. cm.
  Includes bibliographic references and index.
  ISBN 1–59738-011-3

Cover design by Amy Rosen, K&M Design, Inc.

© 2008
Sloan Publishing, LLC
220 Maple Road
Cornwall-on-Hudson, NY 12520

Printed in the United States of America

ISBN 10: 1-59738-011-3

Table of Contents

13 Scientific Verbal Behavior: Explanations   289

Section Three: Comparison and Contrast with Alternative Viewpoints   313

14 Opposition to Mentalism   315

15 The Challenge of Cognitive Psychology   336

16 The Challenge of Psycholinguistics   354

17 Radical Behaviorism and Traditional Philosophical Issues-1   377

Preface

This book is about the conceptual foundations of radical behaviorism. Radical behaviorism is the underlying philosophical perspective of behavior analysis, an approach to the science of behavior and its application associated with B. F. Skinner.

The initial chapter outlines the four domains of behavior analysis: the experimental analysis of behavior, applied behavior analysis, service delivery, and radical behaviorism. The next 17 chapters are divided into three sections.

The first section is concerned with the foundations of behavior analysis. Chapters in this section deal with the history of behaviorism and behavior analysis, behavior as a subject matter in its own right (and as distinct from the subject matter of such other disciplines as neuroscience), the categories and concepts that are deployed in behavior analysis, and an examination of selection by consequences as a causal mode across the three levels of phylogeny, ontogeny, and culture.

The second section is concerned with the realization of the radical behaviorist program in areas traditionally regarded as important in psychology. Chapters in this section deal with verbal behavior, private behavioral events, methods in a science of behavior, and the nature, origin, and validity of scientific language, such as found in theories and explanations.

The third section compares and contrasts radical behaviorism with alternative viewpoints. Chapters in this section deal with mentalism, cognitive psychology, psycholinguistics, and selected traditional issues in philosophy, including a position known generically as "methodological behaviorism," which by some accounts is the orthodox position in contemporary psychology.

The final chapter is concerned with radical behaviorism as epistemology. This chapter reviews how the perspective of radical behaviorism allows one to profitably engage the question of knowledge in light of the concept of operant behavior and within human operant behavior, verbal behavior.

The chapters are not specifically concerned with research issues in the experimental analysis of behavior (e.g., research on schedules of reinforcement), applied behavior analysis (e.g., research on the best way to teach language to autistic children), or the delivery of behavior analytic professional services (e.g., case histories in education, developmental disabilities, or business). Rather, the chapters present the radical behaviorist perspective on an important theoretical, philosophical, or conceptual topic in a science of behavior, and then contrast the radical behaviorist perspective with that of other forms of behaviorism, as well as other forms of psychology. Also included for each chapter is a brief study guide to focus student attention on relevant issues. The book is intended for advanced undergraduate or beginning graduate students, in courses within behavior analytic curricula dealing with conceptual foundations and radical behaviorism as a philosophy.

This book is dedicated to the memory of Willard F. Day, Jr.

1

Radical Behaviorism as a Philosophy of Science

Synopsis of Chapter 1: This book is about radical behaviorism as the philosophy of science underlying behavior analysis, the science of behavior and its application. Chapter 1 considers some implications of the radical behaviorist perspective for the science of behavior, contrasting it with traditional perspectives. An important goal of radical behaviorism is to foster effective explanations of behavior, so that others may act productively on the basis of the explanation. For radical behaviorism, to explain behavior is to specify the functional relation between behavior and the environmental circumstances in which it occurs. The elements of such explanations are all part of the one dimension in which behavior takes place. Radical behaviorism typically objects to explanations of behavior that appeal to causal powers and forces in other dimensions, such as the mental because they interfere with explanations in terms of environmental relations. In the final analysis, radical behaviorism is interested in providing comprehensive explanatory statements about the causes of anyone's behavior, and especially instances when individuals are said to "know" something. This interest includes instances when scientists are said to know something in a way that enables them to explain an event. Thus, radical behaviorism is ultimately an epistemological statement.

Behavior analysis is the science of behavior and its application. As a science, it has a two-fold goal: (a) to increase the scientific understanding of behavior as a subject matter in its own right, and (b) to promote the application of science-based behavioral principles to improve the quality of human life. Behavior analysis is based on ideas developed by B. F. Skinner (1904–1990) early in his professional career, and then extended by Skinner during the remainder of his professional career, as well as by many others. Individuals who work in behavior analysis are known as "behavior analysts," and because of their association with Skinner's ideas, sometimes by such other names as "Skinnerians" or "operant conditioners."

WHAT ARE THE DOMAINS OF BEHAVIOR ANALYSIS?

There are four domains of behavior analysis: (1) the experimental analysis of behavior, (2) applied behavior analysis, (3) behavior-analytic service delivery, and (4) radical behaviorism. Many behavior analysts work in more than one domain during their careers, and a few work in all four (Hawkins & Anderson, 2002).

Behavior analysts who work in the experimental analysis of behavior conduct basic research. This research elucidates fundamental principles of behavior. In the early years of the field, the experimental analysis of behavior was concerned mainly with basic laboratory research examining the behavior of relatively uncomplicated nonhuman animals, such as white rats and pigeons. In recent years, the experimental analysis of behavior has become increasingly concerned with complex questions, such as those involving human behavior and the role of language. In all cases, the experimental analysis of behavior is concerned with the extensive, intensive laboratory-based analysis of basic, fundamental processes (e.g., reinforcement, punishment, avoidance, escape, discrimination, generalization, acquisition, extinction) influencing the behavior of individual organisms. Questions of generality and reliability are addressed by the careful demonstration of the control of behavior, such as through a series of repeated exposures to experimental conditions that replicate data. The research does not usually entail aggregating data across groups of subjects and conducting tests of statistical inference on the aggregated data. In addition, the research is typically concerned with understanding the effects of various environmental relations on behavior, rather than with cataloging the derived, actuarial effects of those relations within a population.

Behavior analysts who work in applied behavior analysis conduct applied research. This research develops and evaluates practices aimed at remedying problems associated with socially significant behavior. In the process, new principles for applications are sometimes discovered. Consequently, applied behavior analysis is sometimes close to the experimental analysis of behavior by virtue of its concern with research and discovering new ideas, and sometimes close to service delivery by virtue of its concern with strengthening socially significant behavior. Nevertheless, the primary emphasis in applied behavior analysis remains with developing and evaluating a technology that seeks to solve problems related to socially significant behavior, rather than with deriving new principles of behavior. The technology may focus on many different kinds of behavioral problems, ranging from: (a) those occurring in particular settings, such as an institution or classroom; to (b) those associated with particular populations, such as children with autism or eating disorders; to (c) those embedded in a broader social context, such as a community recycling program or an energy conservation program. The technology may also take the form of clinical behavior analysis and assess ways to alleviate anxiety disorders, mood disorders, or one of the other standard classifications of psychopathology.

Behavior analysts who work in service delivery earn their living in professional practice. They deploy behavioral technologies to effect changes in socially significant behavior in the world outside the laboratory. Typically, the changes involve increasing the rate of some beneficial behavior or decreasing the rate of some maladaptive behavior. Many of the areas in which service providers work follow from those of applied behavior analysis. However, in service delivery the emphasis is on solving problems in the world at large for clients. Although data-based decision making clearly plays an important role in service delivery, the activity remains focused on delivering behavior-analytic services to clients, rather than on research activity aimed at developing new technologies, identifying best practices, or communicating results to an audience via the process of peer review.

Behavior analysts who work in radical behaviorism seek to clarify the philosophical implications of the behavioristic approach to experimental research, applied research, and service delivery. When addressing scientific matters, radical behaviorism is concerned with the nature and purpose of a scientific analysis of behavior and the critical examination of traditional approaches to the subject matter and methods of a science of behavior (Skinner, 1974/college edition, p. xiii). Hence, radical behaviorism is particularly concerned with verbal behavior, the relation between verbal behavior and knowledge, and the nature of the intellectual activity that underlies science and its application.

Figure 1 presents an overview of the four domains and shows the continuity of behavior-analytic activity across the experimental analysis of behavior, applied behavior

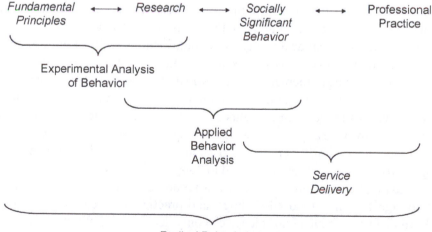

Figure 1.1   The domains of radical behaviorism: experimental analysis of behavior, applied behavior analysis, service delivery, and radical behaviorism.

analysis, and professional practice. The experimental analysis of behavior focuses on fundamental principles of behavior; the research it conducts is basic research. Applied behavior analysis focuses on socially significant behavior; the research it conducts is applied research. Service delivery also focuses on socially significant behavior. However, it provides services to clients regarding socially significant behavior; it does not carry out research concerning that behavior. Radical behaviorism guides behavior analysts as they carry out experimental and applied analyses of behavior, or as they deliver professional services to clients.

RADICAL BEHAVIORISM AS THE PHILOSOPHY OF SCIENCE UNDERLYING BEHAVIOR ANALYSIS

This book is about radical behaviorism as the philosophy of science underlying behavior analysis, the science of behavior and its application. Skinner (1989) explicitly emphasized the relation between his ideas and the philosophy of science when he defined radical behaviorism in the following way:

> I don't believe I coined the term radical behaviorism, but when asked what I mean by it, I have always said, "the philosophy of a science of behavior treated as a subject matter in its own right apart from internal explanations, mental or physiological." (p. 122)

Several phrases within this definition may now be more closely examined.

Behavior as a Subject Matter in Its Own Right

One important phrase in Skinner's definition is "behavior treated as a subject matter in its own right." However, the grounds for this position need to be clearly understood, as the position differs a great deal from a more traditional view. In a traditional view, the subject matter of psychology is assumed to be mental life. According to this traditional view, an understanding of mental life, such as an understanding of how the mind works, provides the basis for understanding the human condition in all its complexities, where those complexities range from thoughts and beliefs to ideas, feelings, and emotions. Importantly, answers to any questions concerning the causes of behavior are also to be found in mental life. Early versions of psychology sought to investigate mental life through introspection, or looking inward to "observe" what one was feeling or thinking. Eventually, however, this approach was regarded as unsatisfactory. Many people could not agree on its supposed findings, and practical applications were limited at best. Further, critics argued that science can only deal with a publicly observable subject matter. Mental life is not publicly observable. How can psychology become an effective science if it focuses on introspective statements about mental life? Interestingly, the answer was not to re-examine the fundamental assumption that psychology was the science of mental life, but rather to downplay introspection and develop new methods to investigate mental life. How, then, can mental life be respectably engaged? Traditionally, the answer was that mental life could be engaged inferentially, on the basis of "evidence" provided by behavior. In sum, the assumption remained that mental life was what was really important. Mental phenomena caused behavior, such that behavior was regarded as only an expression or manifestation of mental life, necessary to validate inferences about it.

For radical behaviorism, this matter is extraordinarily complex. An important principle for radical behaviorism is that behavior is a subject matter in its own right. At issue is what counts as behavior. Radical behaviorism does accept that individuals have important experiences that are personal and private and to which they alone have access. Thus, radical behaviorism recognizes the relevance to an understanding of behavior of both independent and dependent variables "within an organism's skin" and not accessible to anyone other than the person who is behaving. However, the way these variables are relevant, even though they are not publicly observable, distinguishes radical behaviorism from other approaches. It views these variables and the relations in which they participate as part of the behavioral dimension, rather than part of a supposed mental dimension. Their importance arises from the way they are linked with the environment. Consequently, radical behaviorism does not accept the traditional view that events going on inside the skin are of a dimension that supposedly differs qualitatively from a dimension outside the skin. The net result for radical behaviorism is that behavior, whether inside or outside the skin, may be usefully regarded as a phenomenon directly related to the circumstances in which it occurs, rather than as merely an expression or manifestation of an inner or mental life.

In sum, radical behaviorism emphasizes the study of behavior because it is a legitimate subject matter in its own right, irrespective of how many persons have contact with it or with the variables that influence it. The study of behavior is not emphasized because it is evidence of events somewhere else, in some other dimension, and for which behavior is merely evidence to justify inferences about those events. This point is visited extensively throughout this book.

Internal Explanations, Causes, and Dimensions

A second important phrase in Skinner's definition of radical behaviorism is "apart from internal explanations, mental or physiological." Again, the topic of explanation is complex. Different forms of psychology take different approaches to the nature of explanation. For some, an event is explained when some internal mechanism or entity with some sort of inferred causal power is proposed. The internal mechanism or entity and its inferred powers could be mental, conceptual, or at the level of physiology. For others, an event is explained when its features can be described as a specific instance of a mathematical expression. For still others, an event is explained when it is deduced from an existing law or theory. For radical behaviorism, explanation means specifying functional relations between behavior and the environmental circumstances in which it occurs. However, more needs to be said about the implications of the radical behaviorist approach to explanation.

For example, related to explanation is the topic of causation. Radical behaviorism is explicitly concerned with identifying the causes of behavior. For radical behaviorism, then, one important sense of the causes of behavior is the totality of the variables and relations of which the behavior is a function. A sense of cause to which radical behaviorism objects is that of push-pull causation, in which the postulation of a presumed antecedent causal entity with a set of presumed mechanical causal powers is held to be sufficient to explain the event in question.

Related in turn to causation is the dimension in which the causes are taken to reside. Radical behaviorism is concerned about the dimension of an explanation when the explanation includes elements that are not expressed in the same terms and cannot be confirmed with the same methods of observation and analysis as the facts they are said to address (e.g., Catania & Harnad, 1988, p. 88). In particular, Skinner's definition raises concerns about explanations that appeal to "internal" or "inner" causes and dimensions. As discussed in the section above in which behavior is regarded as a subject matter in its own right, one sense of "internal" is mental, or psychic, or spiritual. Radical behaviorism is concerned about talk of mental causes and dimensions because it is fanciful to think there is such a qualitatively different dimension with qualitatively different causes. To state the matter somewhat starkly, there is no such dimension and there are no such causes. They are fictions, talk of which is a product of nonscientific influences. The properties with which the mental causes are supposedly endowed ultimately sidetrack more effective analyses in terms of causal relations in the one dimension in which behavior takes place.

Again, the grounds for concern about explanations appealing to causal entities from a supposed different dimension need to be clearly understood. Radical behaviorism argues that these explanations are attributable to mischievous and deceptive cultural traditions and linguistic practices. Hence, radical behaviorism rejects these sorts of explanations because they are not primarily based on anything factual, and do not ultimately lead to effective prediction and control. In light of their origin, such explanations represent an unwarranted diversion from more effective concerns. It is not merely that an explanation should only include certain features (e.g., those that are publicly observable) and not others (e.g., those that are mental and unobservable) to be respectable. Rather, the rejection of mental causes is directly related to the view that the appropriate subject matter of psychology is behavior, as opposed to mental life. There is no mental life in the sense implied by traditional psychology because there is no mental dimension that differs from a behavioral dimension.

Of course, another sense of "internal" is physiological, as Skinner's definition suggests. Hence, radical behaviorism is also concerned about the way some explanations of behavior appeal to physiological variables. As before, the grounds for this concern need to be clearly understood. From the perspective of radical behaviorism, a knowledge of underlying physiology is clearly relevant in a science of behavior. After all, an organism's physiology participates in every behavioral event, and the nature of the participation by that physiology in the event is something that can be known about. Thus, one can predict an organism's behavior by knowing either (a) the history of the organism's interaction with features of the environment, or (b) the physiological state that those interactions have produced. Moreover, a knowledge of the underlying physiology may yield new possibilities for interventions that will control the behavior. Nevertheless, the radical behaviorist perspective differs greatly from a traditional view, in which physiological variables are endowed with some sort of intrinsic power or force to cause the behavior in question. Radical behaviorism objects to this traditional sense of physiological variables as exerting some kind of internal power or force, even though the variables appear to be legitimate because they are physiological. A common example in everyday language is when someone cites the brain as causing a given instance of behavior. The brain is obviously involved in a great deal of behavior. However, radical behaviorists become concerned when physiological structures are invoked in explanations because they are assumed to have some internal power that causes behavior. Such a viewpoint distorts the legitimate role of physiological variables in explanations. It also deflects attention away from other variables, such as environmental, that participate in the event.

In addition, radical behaviorism is concerned about the appeal to physiological variables in explanations because those variables are sometimes taken as evidence to legitimize inferences about mental causes. Accordingly, just because an explanation happens to appeal to physiology in some fashion doesn't automatically mean the explanation is going to be useful or effective. An appeal to physiology could be just a surrogate for an appeal to a mental cause, and therefore just as troublesome.

Finally, radical behaviorism is concerned about the appeal to physiological variables in some explanations because of reductionism. Reductionism is roughly the position that something is held to be explained when it is reduced to the subject matter of a science at a lower level. With regard to a science of behavior, reductionism is the position that a behavioral event can only be considered to be genuinely explained when some underlying physiological mechanism, structure, or pathway with some sort of causally effective power or force has been identified. Radical behaviorism rejects this interpretation of reductionism because it violates the concern with the dimensional question, in addition to raising questions about the nature of causation. Suppose one accepts the proposition that behavior is only properly explained in terms of physiology. Wouldn't one then have to explain physiology in terms of biology, chemistry in terms of physics, and so on? At the very least, reductionism creates an infinite regress of explanations. Again, the way that physiology is relevant in a science of behavior is an important topic, and is dealt with later in this book, as is the topic of explanation. Clearly, knowledge of physiology is important in a science of behavior, but traditional approaches have miscast the contribution of physiology to causal knowledge and explanations, with the result that researchers and theorists have neglected the larger picture regarding the causal analysis of behavior.

The emphasis that radical behaviorism places on explanations that identify causes at a consistent level of observation and analysis is not simply a matter of style or preference. Even the briefest survey of Western culture reveals that it generally favors explanations of human psychological phenomena that appeal to causes from a dimension that supposedly differs from the one in which observation and analysis take place. For example, when psychology began to be distinguished as a relatively independent science in the late nineteenth and early twentieth centuries, its practitioners accepted the fundamental premise that the appropriate subject matter for psychology was in another dimension: the content and structure of mental life. Because the mental was presumed to be in another dimension, it had to be studied according to introspective methods, and researchers then had to make inferences about mental life.

Many concerns were raised at the time about the reliability and validity of introspection and inferences about mental life, with or without presumed physiological correlates of that life, and in many ways these concerns contributed to the development of behaviorism. Early versions of behaviorism sought to clarify and refine both the subject matter and methods of psychology, so that a genuine science of behavior could be realized and contribute to improving the human condition. A fundamental concern of these early versions was practical: What could be manipulated in time and space to predict and control behavior as a subject matter? Hence, early versions of behaviorism came to be viewed as a significant departure from introspective approaches, and correctly so. Radical behaviorism continues this trend.

In its endeavors, radical behaviorism therefore seeks answers to questions about the causes of behavior in terms of behavioral processes in the behavioral dimension, rather than in terms of supposed mental processes in a supposed mental dimension. As noted earlier in this chapter, however, radical behaviorism can include variables within the skin. Thus, in certain instances radical behaviorism is not restricted to the consideration of publicly observable variables. Nevertheless, when radical behaviorism does consider variables inside the skin, it conceives of their origin, nature, and function in behavioral events quite differently from traditional psychology, and even from other versions of psychology nominally identified as behavioral. They are behavioral variables, not mental. Consequently, radical behaviorism does not invest them with originating or initiating mechanical power to cause behavioral events. Rather, it regards them as a function of events in the world outside the skin, but in their current form accessible to only the behaving individual. Others may have to be dealt with inferentially, but for the behaving individual, they are no inference.

Radical Behaviorism as Epistemology

A final comment concerns the initial phrase in Skinner's definition, namely, that radical behaviorism is "a philosophy of a science of behavior." The philosophy of science is the branch of philosophy that critically examines the philosophical foundations, assumptions, and implications of activity and findings in both the natural sciences, like physics, chemistry, and biology, and the social sciences, like psychology, sociology, and economics. It addresses such topics as: (a) the nature, origin, and validity of scientific language (e.g., scientific terms, concepts, statements, laws, theories, and other sorts of knowledge claims); (b) the nature of scientific explanation and prediction; (c) the means by which science mediates the harnessing of nature; (d) the means by which the validity of scientific information is determined; (e) the types of reasoning used to arrive at scientific conclusions; and (f) the implications of scientific methods and models for the sciences, as well as for society at large. The philosophy of science is closely linked with epistemology, or the study of the nature and limits of knowledge, as well as with ontology, or the critical examination of the nature of what exists, though some philosophers of science disparage the latter as unfounded metaphysical speculation.

Skinner's phrase highlights that as a philosophy of science, radical behaviorism is also an epistemological statement. As discussed throughout this book, radical behaviorism is interested in providing comprehensive explanatory statements about the causes of anyone's behavior, and especially instances when individuals are said to "know" something. This interest includes instances when scientists are said to know something in a way that enables them to explain an event. As an epistemological statement, radical behaviorism is therefore intimately concerned with explaining the behavior of the observing individuals—the scientists themselves. As a result, radical behaviorism is intimately concerned with how scientists talk about behavioral events, and why they talk as they do. By virtue of its fundamental concern with verbal behavior and knowledge claims, radical behaviorism is in a unique position: It is based on the science for which it stands as a foundation. Importantly, then, radical behaviorism admits no discontinuity between the behavior being explained and the behavior of explaining it. Neither is caused by mental states or other forms of internal entities from another dimension.

To be sure, radical behaviorism is concerned with how to make sense out of a wide variety of knowledge claims on the part of observing scientists. Nevertheless, appeals to such phenomena as mental states in knowledge claims are not regarded as identifying anything that is literally mental, because there is literally no mental dimension. As suggested earlier in this chapter, talk of a mental dimension is regarded as a function of social practices, rather than anything having to do with an actual dimension that is realized apart from the behavioral dimension. Consequently, a particular emphasis for radical behaviorism is the analysis of verbal behavior, the relation between verbal behavior and knowledge, the nature of the intellectual activity that underlies science, and the application of science-based principles to phenomena outside the laboratory for the benefit of humankind. Skinner (1957) addressed this very important point in the following way:

> The verbal processes of logical and scientific thought deserve and require a more precise analysis than they have yet received. One of the ultimate accomplishments of a science of verbal behavior may be an empirical logic, or a descriptive and analytical scientific epistemology, the terms and practices of which will be adapted to human behavior as a subject matter. (p. 431)

Clearly, then, just as radical behaviorism conceives of the causes of the "to-be-explained" behavior on the part of the observed individual in behavioral terms, so also does it conceive of the causes of the "explanatory" behavior on the part of the observing individual in comparable and compatible terms, at a comparable and compatible level. In the final analysis, not only are mental variables rejected as causes for the behavior of the subject or participant; they are also not readmitted in a formulation of the scientist's scientific behavior, as scientists seek to explain the basis of their knowledge. Zuriff (1985) describes this relation well in the following passage, when he speaks of behaviorism as a "philosophy of mind"(to use a currently popular descriptor) as well as a philosophy of science:

> [B]ehaviorism is also a philosophy of mind with certain assumptions about human nature.... . This philosophy of mind is interdependent with behaviorist philosophy of science; each justifies the other. Given the assumptions of the behaviorist philosophy of mind, the kinds of methods, theories, and explanations favored by behaviorist philosophy of science appear most appropriate. Conversely, the behaviorist philosophy of science supports its philosophy of mind. (p. 2)

THE SENSE OF "RADICAL" IN RADICAL BEHAVIORISM

What, then, is the sense of the term "radical" in radical behaviorism? Sometimes radical behaviorism is taken as an "extreme" or even "fanatical" form of behaviorism, wherein only publicly observable stimuli and responses are allowed, and direct consideration of a purported internal phenomenon is rejected because it is unobservable or cannot be agreed upon by two or more people. Some early versions of behavioral psychology did in fact adopt this perspective, but radical behaviorism is not extreme in the limiting or restricting sense of the word *radical*. Rather, a more appropriate synonym for radical is "thoroughgoing." Radical behaviorism argues for a thoroughgoing, comprehensive explanation of behavior at the descriptively consistent level of behavior.

Behavior and the variables of which it is a function may be inside or outside the skin of the behaving organism, but they are all in the behavioral dimension. In short, radical behaviorism rejects the all too common distinction between mental and behavioral, within or across the behavior of either the subject, the research scientist, the service provider, or the client. It formulates answers to questions about behavior in thoroughgoing behavioral terms. Behavior-analytic approaches run decidedly contrary to well-established intellectual traditions in Western culture, and are often disparaged as merely descriptive or even as dangerously aberrant. Behavior analysts, of course, take exception to the disparaging treatments by others, and point to the effectiveness of their approach: If behavior-analytic approaches work so well, and traditional approaches based on an assumption of mental life do not, behavior analysts ask on what basis are behavior analytic approaches so lightly dismissed, and traditional mentalistic approaches so heavily embraced? The present book explores answers to this question as well.

SUMMARY

In summary, the main function of radical behaviorism is to monitor and analyze the nature of knowledge claims in a science of behavior and its technological applications. Radical behaviorism is the domain that underlies the other domains of behavior analysis, and that makes behavior analysis a coherent whole. The present book also takes the position that although behavior analysis and radical behaviorism are often classified as variants of traditional behaviorism, an examination of the conceptual foundations of radical behaviorism reveals that it differs enough from other forms of psychology, including many of those traditionally identified as behavioral, that it is usefully regarded as an unique and independent perspective. This book explores those foundations. The first section of the book consists of six chapters outlining the basic features of radical behaviorism. Chapters 2 and 3 present some historical background.

TABLE 1–1

Radical Behaviorism

---

1. Critical examination of subject matter, methods, and knowledge claims of behavioral science, as well as the application of its findings

2. Theoretical, philosophical, or conceptual questions asked by radical behaviorists:
   a. Why do scientists examine and explore a given subject?
   b. What rate of discovery will sustain their behavior in doing so?
   c. What precurrent behaviors will improve their chances of success and extend the adequacy and scope of their descriptions?

> d. What steps do they take in moving from protocol to general statement?
> e. What aspects of behavior are significant?
> f. Of what variables are changes in these aspects a function?
> g. How are the relations among behavior and its controlling variables to be brought together in characterizing the organism as a system?
> h. What methods are appropriate in studying such a system experimentally?
> i. Under what conditions does such an analysis yield a technology of behavior, and what issues arise in its application to socially significant behavior? (e.g., Skinner, 1969, pp. x, xii)

REFERENCES

Catania, A. C., & Harnad, S. (Eds.). (1988). *The selection of behavior: The operant behaviorism of B. F. Skinner: Comments and controversies*. Cambridge: Cambridge University Press.

Hawkins, R. P., & Anderson, C. M. (2002). In response: On the distinction between science and practice: A reply to Thyer and Adkins. *The Behavior Analyst, 25*, 115–119.

Skinner, B. F. (1957). *Verbal behavior*. New York: Appleton-Century-Crofts.

Skinner, B. F. (1969). *Contingencies of reinforcement*. New York: Appleton-Century-Crofts.

Skinner, B. F. (1974). *About behaviorism* (college edition). New York: Knopf.

Skinner, B. F. (1989). *Recent issues in the analysis of behavior*. Columbus, OH: Merrill.

Zuriff, G. E. (1985). *Behaviorism: A conceptual reconstruction*. New York: Columbia University Press.

STUDY QUESTIONS

1. In one sentence, define behavior analysis.

2. In one or two sentences each, describe the four domains of radical behaviorism

3. In one or two sentences, state or paraphrase Skinner's definition of radical behaviorism.

4. In three or four sentences, describe the nature of radical behaviorism's concerns with explanations that appeal to causes of behavior from the mental dimension.

5. In three or four sentences, describe the nature of radical behaviorism's concerns with explanations that appeal to physiological causes of behavior.

6. Describe the sense of "radical" in radical behaviorism.

Section 1

The Foundations of Radical Behaviorism

Chapters 2 through 7 make up Section 1 of this book. These chapters lay out the foundations of radical behaviorism. Chapters 2 and 3 examine the historical context for the development of radical behaviorism. Chapter 4 looks to a principal thesis of radical behaviorism—behavior as a subject matter in its own right—and distinguishes the analysis of behavior from neuroscience. Chapter 5 outlines a taxonomy of behavior, based on the environmental conditions of which a given instance of behavior is a function. Chapter 6 presents a vocabulary for the analysis of behavior, emphasizing the function of consequences. Chapter 7 examines selection by consequences as the appropriate causal mode for radical behaviorism.

2

History of Behaviorism and Behavior Analysis: 1800–1930

Synopsis of Chapter 2: Chapter 2 is the first of two chapters that examine the historical development of behaviorism. It seeks to identify the major trends in the development of psychology generally, and then moves to the development of classical S – R behaviorism specifically, from roughly 1800 to 1930. It is intended as a brief review of relevant milestones, rather than as a comprehensive history of psychology during this period. The chapter argues that behaviorism developed in two phases. The first phase was that of classical S – R behaviorism, which emerged from influences in functionalism, animal psychology, and reflexology. A convenient date by which to mark the advent of classical behaviorism is 1913. Classical behaviorism attempted to be objective, empirical, reliable, and to generate agreement by accounting for all forms of behavior in terms of immediate antecedent causation and the generalized S – R reflex model. However, despite its early claims of success, by around 1930 classical behaviorism was revealed as inadequate. For example, it couldn't convincingly account for the variability and apparent spontaneity of behavior. Consequently, behaviorism was poised to enter a second phase of its development.

The intellectual context in the early nineteenth century is difficult to compare to that of today. Psychology had not yet emerged as an independent scientific discipline. To be sure, philosophers and other scholars were intensely concerned with a wide variety of topics that are thematically linked to psychology, ranging from moral conduct to the phenomena of subjective, conscious experience. However, the "scientific" status of these concerns was problematic. Science was usually assumed to involve the empirical investigation of a physical subject matter. Even then, the conventionally accepted test of whether the subject matter of a science is physical was whether it was publicly observable, such that it could be counted, measured, or recorded. Subjective, conscious experience was regarded as mental, not physical. By definition, it was not publicly observable, and could not be counted, measured, or recorded, at least not in the same way as the subject matter of chemistry or physics. Consequently, scholars in the early nineteenth century tended to pursue their concerns about mental or conscious or subjective experience according to some form of rational inquiry, rather than according to some understanding of the scientific method. A particularly influential figure in this regard was the philosopher Immanuel Kant (1724–1804), who argued that psychology, construed as a science of the mental, could never be an actual science with a status comparable to, say, the physics of his time because its presumed subject matter—conscious experiences—resisted mathematization. Rather, mental phenomena and the nature of the conscious mind had to be analyzed by reason alone.

Similarly, other scholars in the early nineteenth century were concerned with the mechanics of the physical movements of the body. Again, however, these scholars regarded those movements as a subject matter of a different science—physiology—rather than psychology. A common assumption among scholars of the time was that if individuals were really concerned about behavior as a subject matter, an appropriate understanding of behavior would come about once philosophical inquiry revealed how the conscious mind worked.

PSYCHOLOGY AND THE SCIENCE OF THE "MENTAL"

As the nineteenth century progressed, however, scholars began to discover that a great array of fundamental human activities actually did exhibit an impressive degree of orderliness. In particular, scholars accumulated a great deal of knowledge about basic physiology (e.g., research by Bell and Magendie on the spinal cord, knowledge of reflex mechanisms, research on the speed of neural conduction and reaction time by Helmholtz, laboratory synthesis of urea by Wohler) and the orderly functioning of the sensory end organs (e.g., in color vision). Similarly, scholars had found that subjects' judgments in basic sensory discrimination tasks produced relatively orderly data (e.g., psychophysical research by Helmholtz, Weber, and Fechner). Psychophysics in particular came to be regarded as a sort of "window to the mind" (Hilgard, 1987). Consequently, by the third quarter of the nineteenth century, scholars began to assume: (a) that mental events must be correlated with and underlie these fundamental activities; and (b) the underlying mental events must be at least as orderly as the functioning of the associated physiology. In light of these developments, some scholars, first in Europe and then in the United States, began to argue unselfconsciously that a scientific investigation of these mental events must in fact be possible, given the appropriate methods.

Voluntarism and Structuralism

In Europe the way was led by Wilhelm Wundt (1832–1920), a German philosopher, physician, physiologist, and ultimately psychologist. Wundt is often called the founder of experimental psychology by virtue of his establishing the first psychological laboratory at the university in Leipzig, Germany, in 1879. Wundt was fundamentally concerned with the "empirical" study of the conscious human mind and the laws that govern it. He proposed an elaborate system of psychology that incorporated reaction time experiments as well as "introspection," which was defined as the rigorous, contemplative description of one's private experience. He referred to this branch of psychology as an experimental "physiological psychology," in the sense that the conscious phenomena he held to be the objects of study were ultimately to be linked to their physiological substrates. He extended his efforts to a kind of social anthropology, believing that the historical study of humans and their cultures would promote further understanding of the human mind. Wundt called his position "Voluntarism," and his development of the "new science" became so influential that many scholars from the United States and elsewhere in Europe came to Leipzig to visit, observe, or study under Wundt, then go out and found their own laboratories at other universities. Benjamin, Durkin, Link, Vestal, and Acord (1992) report that by 1900, there were 42 psychology laboratories in U.S. colleges and universities; 13 of those laboratories had been founded by ten graduates from Leipzig, and eight were from the United States.

Notable among the Americans who either visited Leipzig or studied with Wundt were James McKeen Cattell (1860–1944), G. Stanley Hall (1844–1924), E. W. Scripture (1864–1945), Charles Judd (1843–1902), Frank Angell (1857–1939), and Lightner Witmer (1867–1956), all of whom were extraordinarily influential in the development of psychology in the United States, joining fledgling programs or establishing new ones at such universities as Pennsylvania, Johns Hopkins, Yale, Chicago, Columbia, and Stanford. Hugo Munsterberg (1863–1916) was European but studied with Wundt and came to the United States in the 1890s, helping to establish psychology at Harvard as well as to establish applied psychology more generally. Although Wundt was a towering intellectual figure and the Americans clearly learned in Leipzig to appreciate empirical research methods and a scientific attitude, many of the programs established in the US reflected the idiosyncratic interests of their founders, rather than the specifics of Wundt's approach to either philosophy or psychology.

Also studying with Wundt was the Englishman E. B. Titchener (1867–1927). Titchener emigrated to the United States in the early 1890s and established a psychology program at Cornell that came to be labeled "Structuralism." Titchener's structuralism resembled Wundt's voluntarism in some respects but differed in others. For example, it resembled voluntarism in that it emphasized "descriptions" of the contents and structure of consciousness based on reaction times and introspective reports. It differed in that it included nothing akin to Wundt's cultural anthropology. In addition, it wanted a place for the explanation of mental phenomena beyond their description. In certain respects, structuralism resembled the chemistry of the time. Just as the chemistry of the time sought to determine the "elements" that made up the natural world and how they combined, so did structuralism seek to determine the "elements" that made up mental life, and then how the mind worked to connect these elements into more complex mental phenomena.

Structuralism came into prominence at a time when many other forms of science, such as physics, chemistry, and biology, consisted of observing and then carefully describing what were presumed to be nature's mechanisms at work. Structuralism applied this basic approach to psychology by arguing that subjects could "observe" the mental by looking inward to critically examine their mental processes at work when they were engaged in some act of perception, cognition, discrimination, choice, judgment, insight, or ratiocination. Introspective reports on sensations, images, and feelings then provided the basis for making inferences about what was presumed to be the content, structure, and connections of mental life, again as that mental life was presumed to be correlated with underlying physiological processes. The sum total of these introspective inferences constituted an approach to psychology as a new, independent, and empirical discipline.

Given this general orientation, structuralists earnestly set about validating their new discipline. Things did not always go smoothly, however. For example, structuralists debated with others about: (a) how well trained a subject needed to be (structuralists argued that at least 10,000 training trials were necessary); (b) whether "imageless thought" was possible (yes, argued some of Wundt's students; no, argued Wundt and Titchener themselves, but for different reasons); and (c) whether the "stimulus error" had been committed (structuralists argued that subjects should simply describe the conscious sensation of the stimulus, rather than interpret its meaning; if subjects correctly described the sensation, they might be able to report as many as 42,415 different sensations). For example, subjects would commit the stimulus error if they looked at a square table top at an angle and reported it as a square, rather than describing the visual image as a trapezoid. They were interpreting the sensation, rather than describing the sensation when the stimulus was projected on the retina. Nevertheless, despite a few such controversies and technicalities, many scholars of the time accepted the structuralist position that subjective experience was the appropriate subject matter of their new discipline, and introspection was an appropriate methodology. Behavior was an incidental concern at best.

Functionalism

Despite its generally favorable reception, concerns about structuralism remained. For example, Charles Darwin (1809–1882) had proposed certain ideas about evolution and the origin of species by means of natural selection. Some concerns about structuralism arose because it did not incorporate a Darwinian evolutionary perspective into its theories, even though Darwin's ideas were becoming increasingly influential in the scientific community. In this regard, structuralism did not incorporate data from nonhumans; for example, by showing how certain processes in nonhumans might be a lower-level approximation of those in humans. Similarly, structuralism didn't adopt a developmental approach for dealing with an individual organism; for example, by examining the processes that took place as a child matured into an adult. In fact, it explicitly avoided issues pertaining to children, declining even to use children as research subjects.

Another concern about structuralism was even more telling: Structuralism had little if any room for practical applications, such as improving educational practices or dealing with those deemed mentally ill. These concerns were particularly significant in the United States, with its generally progressive orientation. In light of these concerns, scholars in the 1890s began to develop alternative approaches to psychology. Most prominent among the alternatives that became popular in the United States during this time was a viewpoint called "Functionalism."

Individuals from many different backgrounds were called functionalists. Consequently, functionalism had many different manifestations. William James (1842–1910) of Harvard is often described as having anticipated functionalism, although he left professional psychology in favor of philosophy during the 1890s. James was followed by those with a more focused pragmatic orientation in education and psychology, such as John Dewey (1859–1952), James Rowland Angell (1869–1949), and Harvey Carr (1873–1954). James Mark Baldwin (1861–1934), although not a functionalist in the same sense as the others, wrote extensively on the relation between evolutionary theory, development, and psychology. Especially influential was G. Stanley Hall (1844–1924), who studied at Harvard with William James and then went to Leipzig to study with Wundt. He returned to the United States in the early 1880s, taking a position at Johns Hopkins, where founded the first psychological laboratory in the United States. From Hopkins, Hall moved to become the first president of Clark University in Worcester, Massachusetts. At Clark, he continued to be professionally active, founding the American Psychological Association in 1892. Hall's varied interests ranged from philosophy, to religion, to child development, to education. The strain of functionalism with which Hall is associated is generally known as "genetic psychology," where the term "genetic" implies the developmental nature of psychological processes (as in "genesis"), rather than anything pertaining to constituents of chromosomes involved in the mechanics of inheritance.

Despite these diverse backgrounds and manifestations, functionalism nevertheless adopted many of the same principles as did structuralism, including the reliance on mental life as the principal subject matter and on introspection as a standard method. However, functionalism emphasized these matters differently from structuralism. For example, structuralism emphasized the study of the elements of conscious experience through introspection. In contrast, functionalism adopted a more developmental viewpoint and emphasized the factors of which conscious experience was a function, how conscious experience functioned in everyday life, and how conscious experience functioned to aid adaptation. In sum, whereas structuralism was concerned with simply the "What" of conscious experience, functionalism was concerned with both the "How" and "Why."

Consistent with Darwin's ideas, most functionalists also emphasized the continuity of psychological processes, both (a) within a species, as members developed from young into old individuals, as well as (b) between species, from nonhumans to humans, although functionalists recognized that humans might exhibit some unique features in light of their lofty developmental status. In addition, most functionalists tended to emphasize the utility and practical value of psychological processes as organisms developed. With regard to practical matters, many functionalists of the time had two broad classes of interests. The first concerned such matters of personal development as "moral philosophy," "mental hygiene," and the development of ethical behavior. To some extent these interests followed from the tradition of "Scottish realism" that had been extraordinarily influential earlier in the nineteenth century in the United States. The second class of interests concerned educational practices. Functionalists sought through introspective, observational, and quasi-experimental methods to construct a normative picture of development. When complete, the picture would yield the content of a child's mind at various ages, as well as information about which psychological processes were innate and which were the result of adaptation. Child rearing and pedagogical practices could then be brought into conformity with what was viewed as the natural process of development. In addition, more would be known about how a child's psychological processes were modified as it adapted to the demands imposed by the environment.

A dispute that arose in the 1890s between structuralists and functionalists in the United States illustrates the differences between them. The general topic of the dispute was the role of various mental processes in adaptation. The specific topic was whether reaction times were slower when subjects concentrated on the stimulus, rather than on the response. When structuralists performed such experiments, they declared that subjects' reaction times were about 100 ms (milliseconds) slower when the subjects concentrated on the stimulus. Exceptions were discounted as failures of technique or the results of inadequate training. When functionalists performed the same experiments, they found that the reaction times of some subjects were indeed slower when the subjects concentrated on the stimulus, as had the structuralists. However, functionalists also found that the reaction times of other subjects were reliably slower when the subjects concentrated on the response. This latter finding, of course, was in direct contrast to the structuralists.

The difference between the results of these experiments was critical because the results were central to the psychological perspectives of structuralism and functionalism. Structuralists believed that reaction times should be slower when subjects concentrated on the stimulus because that arrangement involved a complex rather than simple form of the perception of the stimulus. This complex form of perception took longer than simple perception, and consequently yielded a slower reaction time.

In contrast, functionalists did not accept that reaction time was always slower when subjects concentrated on the stimulus. Instead, functionalists argued that the reaction-time experiments yielded different results because there were both sensory and motor types of people who served as subjects for the experiments. For example, functionalists hypothesized that sensory persons got better results when they concentrated on the stimulus than when they concentrated on the response because the response was already a habit and was already at its peak efficiency. For sensory persons, concentrating on the response would only interfere with the act and slow them down. Common examples were musicians trying to think of each finger movement as they play, or sharpshooters thinking of their finger on the trigger as they aim.

The dispute was partially resolved when J. R. Angell and A. W. Moore, two functionalists, proposed a compromise position that allowed each side to be somewhat correct. Angell and Moore proposed that there were indeed two different types of people, as the functionalists had suggested. Angell and Moore also proposed that different amounts of training would affect the types differently. Structuralists gave their subjects extensive training, whereas functionalists gave their subjects only a minimum amount of training. Subjects with extensive training tended to respond faster when they concentrated on the response. Some subjects with less training responded faster when they concentrated on the stimulus; others with less training responded faster when they concentrated on the response. These results depended on whether the subjects were sensory or motor types. Thus, the results that each side obtained were correct, as far as those results went, but the larger picture each offered was somewhat restricted.

The dispute strikes contemporary readers as curious, and understandably so. It involves questions and issues that are no longer current, and methods of analysis that seem inconclusive at best. The important point for present purposes is that both structuralists and functionalists regarded conscious mental experience as the appropriate subject matter for psychology, and regarded introspection as an appropriate method to investigate that subject matter. Behavior was not regarded as a subject matter in its own right. If anything, behavior was only loosely regarded as a basis for drawing inferences about purported events going on in the mental dimension, but the purported mental events remained of principal importance.

EMERGING CONCERNS WITH MENTAL EXPERIENCE AS A SUBJECT MATTER AND INTROSPECTION AS A METHOD

Despite the acceptance of first structuralism and then functionalism in the late nineteenth and early twentieth centuries, many scholars of the time continued to have serious reservations about the reliability and validity of a science based on what was regarded as a special technique—introspection—for dealing with a subject matter that was not publicly observable—mental events. For example, Turner (1967, p. 11) summarizes the following concerns that nineteenth-century scholars had about a psychology based on introspection:

1. By focusing upon itself, by its rendering the introspective state static, introspection falsifies its own subject matter. As explicitly stated by Kant and Comte, one cannot introspect the act of introspection.

2. There is little agreement among introspectionists.

3. Where agreement does occur, it can be attributed to the fact that introspectionists must be meticulously trained, and thereby have a bias built into their observations.

4. A body of knowledge based on introspection cannot be inductive. No discovery is possible from those who are trained specifically on what to observe.

5. Due to the extent of the pathology of mind, self-report is hardly to be trusted.

6. Introspective knowledge cannot have the generality we expect of science. It must be restricted to the class of sophisticated, trained adult subjects.

7. Much of behavior occurs without conscious correlates.

8. Mind and consciousness are not coextensive.

9. Introspection and consciousness cannot give an adequate explanation of memory.

10. The arousal of a conscious image is not itself introspectible.

11. The brain records unconsciously. Its response is a function of organic states which themselves are not introspectible.

12. Emphasis on introspection minimizes attention given to physiological processes without which there would be no mental states.

In addition, as American society developed in the late nineteenth and early twentieth centuries, it began to impatiently demand a psychology that would make a greater practical contribution. Matters pertaining to managing the work force were surfacing; but especially critical in light of compulsory education and land-grant colleges were contributions in the area of education and pedagogy, following from questions about human development. Just how any form of a science purporting to examine esoteric questions related to the structure of mental or subjective or conscious experience was going to make a practical contribution in any area was not immediately clear. As noted earlier, functionalists were intimately concerned with developmental processes, and they did seek to pave the way for a deeper understanding of child rearing, educational practices, or even abnormal behavior. However, the writing of many functionalists tended to digress at the earliest opportunity into arcane philosophical speculations concerned with the relation between consciousness and development, within and across species. Moreover, functionalism lacked a concrete technology by which to implement its findings. Overall, a kind of vague uneasiness was emerging with respect to whether any psychology of the time could actually deliver what it advertised, regardless of whether it was the psychology of the structuralists or the functionalists.

THE CONTRIBUTION OF POST-DARWINIAN COMPARATIVE PSYCHOLOGY: "ANIMAL PSYCHOLOGY"

Interestingly, other movements were growing in psychology at just about this time. One of these movements was comparative, animal psychology (Boakes, 1984). This movement had its roots in the late-nineteenth-century post-Darwinian era in which scholars were concerned about the continuity of "mental" development across species, and was decidedly evolutionary and developmental. These comparative, animal psychologists did not rely on introspection to support their conclusions. Rather, they relied on the observation of behavior and one or another form of experimentation, however primitive that experimentation was by contemporary standards. Thus, the question was given morphological continuity across species: Was there a corresponding behavioral, emotional, and mental continuity? Can researchers make observations or perform experiments to support the inference that animals have emotions and consciousness? The experiments that were performed involved imitation, delayed response procedures, multiple choice procedures, double and triple alternation, and insight or detour problems. Notable figures in this movement were G. J. Romanes (1848–1894), a devoted disciple of Darwin given to anthropomorphism and the "anecdotal method"; C. Lloyd Morgan (1852–1936), who urged caution: "In no case may we interpret the action as the outcome of the exercise of a higher psychical faculty, if it can be interpreted as the outcome of the exercise of one which stands lower in the psychological scale" (Morgan, 1903, p. 53); and L. T. Hobhouse (1864–1929), who manipulated antecedent conditions in empirical efforts to compare the "intelligence" of various species, notably dogs, cats, monkeys, an elephant, and even an otter.

A particular concern during this period was identifying the extent to which an organism's repertoire consisted of innate or "instinctive" responses, and then how those responses were modified during the organism's lifetime. Unfortunately, the immediate relevance of working with nonhuman animals wasn't always apparent to a general population who expected sciences to make practical contributions to human concerns, such as mental hygiene or education or mental testing. Nevertheless, the comparative, animal psychologists did focus on an observable subject matter—learned behavior—and did offer a technology—various pieces of apparatus and an associated set of methods. These developments emphasized the measurement of behavioral changes over time. Together, they suggested that the empirical and objective study of behavior was possible.

THE CONTRIBUTION OF REFLEXOLOGY

Overlapping to some extent with animal psychology was the physiological study of reflex processes. Europe had a long and distinguished tradition of reflex physiology, and knowledge was rapidly accumulating that showed instances of behavior could be understood in terms of physical, chemical processes, rather than mysterious powers and forces or vital spirits. In central Europe, the German Hermann von Helmholtz (1821–1894) was enormously influential, conducting experiments elucidating the biological processes underlying reflexes and training new researchers. In Russia, Ivan Sechenov (1829–1905) emphasized inhibitory influences on behavior, and generally established the tradition from which would arise the next generation of researchers, which included Vladimir Bechterev (1867–1927) and Ivan Pavlov (1849–1936).

Another important figure was Jacques Loeb (1859–1924), a German-born biologist who departed from certain features of the European tradition. For Loeb, the brain was important not as a conscious instigator of action with faculties localized in particular cortical regions, but rather as a place where protoplasm bridged gaps between stimulus and response and conveyed neural impulses. Consciousness was nothing but the processes of associative memory, and these processes could be reduced further to physical and chemical processes taking place in the brain. Instinctive and even voluntary behavior could be understood as a series of mechanical reactions to external stimuli, transmitted through the nervous system and requiring no appeal beyond that to physical and chemical processes in irritability, conductivity, and contraction. Particularly important for Loeb was the concept of a *tropism*, or the movement of the whole body of an organism to fields of physical force in the environment. In one of his canonical examples, he noted that leaves of plants grow toward the sun. A butterfly might lay its eggs close to the ground, but then as the plant grows, the developing caterpillar evidences *heliotropism*, or an attraction to the sun, by climbing up the developing leaves. As the caterpillar continues to develop, it loses its heliotropism and descends downward, finding new leaves to eat. The whole life cycle could be described in terms of simple physical and chemical processes in response to fields of external stimulation. Overall, Loeb sought to reduce the phenomena of life to basic processes involving irritable sensory tissue, contracting muscles, and chains of reflexes. This approach emphasized the idealized possibility of engineering life processes for the betterment of the human condition. Loeb laid out the foundation of his approach in several books, two of the most important of which were *Comparative Physiology of the Brain and Comparative Psychology* (Loeb, 1900) and *The Organism as a Whole* (Loeb, 1916). Loeb moved from Germany to the United States in the early 1890s, taking a position at the University of Chicago in 1892, where he continued his research and writing. While at Chicago, Loeb had a talented, ambitious, and equally iconoclastic graduate student named John B. Watson (1878–1958) in his classes, the significance of which would emerge some ten years later.

Viewed as a whole, reflexology suggested physical and chemical processes discovered in the study of reflexes could be systematically applied to explain behavior in its entirety, without appeal to consciousness and other mental processes. Many reflexologists also studied animal behavior, so there was a natural kinship between the two movements as an alternative to introspective psychology. The foundations of an objective approach to the study of behavior were gradually emerging.

THE FIRST PHASE OF THE BEHAVIORAL MOVEMENT: CLASSICAL S-R BEHAVIORISM

In the last decade of the nineteenth century and the first decade of the twentieth, individuals with a wide variety of interests called themselves psychologists. Some were interested in studying observable behavior. Some of these individuals studied observable behavior from the standpoint of the generalized S – R reflex model, with or without a knowledge of physiology and underlying reflex processes. Others studied observable behavior from the standpoint of animal behavior, intent on making comparisons within and across species. Other individuals were interested in making inferences about what was presumed to be mental life rather than behavior, with or without a knowledge of any physiology that was supposedly correlated with that mental life. Clearly psychology was very heterogeneous.

Early in the second decade of the twentieth century, societal uncertainty about the contributions of psychology as a science, as well as the continuing concerns among the psychologists themselves about the heterogeneous nature of psychology, helped to bring together a number of the movements reviewed in this chapter. From functionalism came a focus on society's practical concerns, especially in the area of human development and education. From comparative, animal psychology came a technology for systematically examining how behavior changed over time. From reflexology came a relevant set of nonmentalistic analytic concepts. As these movements came together, they significantly changed the face of psychology in the United States, and constituted the source of behaviorism as a new movement in psychology. In broad perspective, the behavioral movement took place across two phases. This section of Chapter 2 describes the first.

John B. Watson

The figure most associated with the first phase of the behavioral movement is John B. Watson. Watson was born and raised in rural circumstances in South Carolina. After receiving his undergraduate degree and a master's degree at Furman University, and after working for a year as a principal at a private school, he enrolled at the University of Chicago, intending to study the philosophy underlying educational psychology from such notable figures as John Dewey, G. H. Mead, and J. R. Angell. However, early in his time at Chicago Watson found he simply could not understand what Dewey was talking about. As a result, Watson changed the focus of his graduate work to what would today be called developmental psychobiology. He received his Ph. D. in 1903 for a project in which he investigated whether myelinization of neurons in rats' brains was related to their learning ability; he found that it wasn't. He was the youngest to receive the Ph.D. in the history of Chicago, although that history was relatively short. Subsequently, Watson remained at the University of Chicago and embarked on a series of other research projects, becoming a well-known figure in the field of animal behavior.

   A move to Johns Hopkins University in 1908 solidified his professional standing in the field. However, he had long been concerned about the nature of psychology as a science, and after his move to Hopkins, these concerns could no longer be held in check. How could psychology be a science if it persisted in thinking consciousness was an appropriate subject matter? In 1913, Watson's views had crystallized to the point where, in a series of lectures at Columbia University, he could publicly proclaim his new standpoint. A modified version of one lecture, titled "Psychology as the Behaviorist Views It" (Watson, 1913), was published shortly thereafter in the influential journal *Psychological Review*, and is now termed his "behavioral manifesto." The article opens with the following passage:

> Psychology as the behaviorist views it is a purely objective experimental branch of natural science. Its theoretical goal is the prediction and control of behavior. Introspection forms no essential part of its methods, nor is the scientific value of its data dependent upon the readiness with which they lend themselves to interpretation in terms of consciousness. The behaviorist, in his efforts to get a unitary scheme of animal response, recognizes no dividing line

between man and brute. The behavior of man, with all of its refinement and complexity, forms only a part of the behaviorist's total scheme of investigation. (Watson, 1913, p. 158)

Thus, the year 1913 is often taken as the starting date for behaviorism as a new movement in psychology and the date for the beginning of the "behavioral revolution." Whether the emergence of the new movement was actually rapid and widespread enough to merit being called a "revolution" is a question of considerable historical debate (Leahey, 1992). Not everyone was convinced. Nevertheless, at least some of the discipline was clearly reorienting itself away from the introspective study of the contents and structure of conscious experience, and toward the study of observable behavior.

Watson is generally credited as the first to use terms such as *behaviorism* and *behaviorist*. The behaviorism Watson launched is appropriately termed *classical S – R behaviorism*, to distinguish it from other versions that followed. Watson strongly desired to overcome the ambiguities of both structuralism and functionalism, and to make psychology comparable to the natural sciences. His classical behaviorism emphasized that psychology should be empirical, in the sense that its data base should come through the senses; for example, through careful observation of behavior rather than through introspection. His classical behaviorism also emphasized that psychology should be objective, in the sense that it is independent of individual prejudices, tastes, and private opinions of its practitioners. Finally, it emphasized that psychologists should be able to agree on important analytical terms and concepts. Given these emphases, classical S – R behaviorism argued that the subject matter of psychology should be behavior, rather than mental or subjective or conscious experience. In Watson's (1913) words, "The time seems to have come when psychology must discard all reference to consciousness; when it need no longer delude itself into thinking that it is making mental states the object of observation.... . In a system of psychology completely worked out, given the response the stimuli can be predicted; given the stimuli the response can be predicted" (pp. 163, 167). Watson was even bolder a few years later, when the United States was in the throes of a eugenics movement. Here he explicitly rejected prevailing ideas about inborn instincts and traits in a famous passage:

> I should like to go one step further now and say, "Give me a dozen healthy infants, well-formed, and my own specified world to bring them up in and I'll guarantee to take any one at random and train him to become any type of specialist I might select—doctor, lawyer, artist, merchant-chief, and yes, even beggar-man and thief, regardless of his talents, penchants, tendencies, abilities, vocations, and race of his ancestors. I am going beyond my facts and I admit it, but so have the advocates of the contrary and they have been doing it for many thousands of years. Please note that when this experiment is made up I am allowed to specify the way the children are to be brought up and the type of world they have to live in. (Watson, 1925, p. 82)

Leahey (2000) has pointed out that Watson argued for his approach on empirical, philosophical, and practical grounds. Empirically, Watson emphasized the conspicuous lack of agreement on data or concepts of a psychology based on introspection: "I firmly believe that two hundred years from now, unless the introspective method is discarded, psychology will still be divided on the question as to whether auditory sensations have the quality of 'extension,' whether intensity is an attribute which can be applied to color, whether there is a difference in 'texture' between image and sensation and upon many hundreds of others of like character" (Watson, 1913, p. 164). Philosophically, Watson repudiated "centrally initiated processes" (e.g., Watson, 1913, p. 174) and pointed out the origin of mental concepts in religious doctrines: "Behaviorism claims that 'consciousness' is neither a definable nor a usable concept; that it is merely another word for the 'soul' of more ancient times. The old psychology is thus dominated by a kind of subtle religious philosophy.... All psychology except behaviorism is dualistic.... All that Wundt and his students really accomplished was to substitute for the word 'soul' the word 'consciousness'" (Watson, 1925, pp. 3–5). Practically, Watson argued that introspective psychology did not lend itself to application, whereas behaviorism did:

> All the way through this course I have attempted to show that while there is a science of psychology independent, interesting, worthwhile in itself, nevertheless to have a right to existence it must serve in some measure as a foundation for reaching out into human life. I think behaviorism does lay a foundation for saner living. It ought to be a science that prepares men and women for understanding the first principles of their own behavior. It ought to make men and women eager to rearrange their own lives, and especially eager to prepare themselves to bring up their own children in a healthy way.... I am trying to dangle a stimulus in front of you, a verbal stimulus which, if acted upon, will gradually change this universe" (Watson, 1925, pp. 247–248).

In short, behaviorism could be applied to personality, psychopathology, and even the ethics of living.

Watson's early writing actually reads somewhat ambiguously when it comes to consciousness and other mental phenomena: "Imagery becomes a mental luxury (even if it really exists) without any functional significance whatever" (Watson, 1913, p. 174); "Psychology as behavior will, after all, have to neglect but few of the really essential problems with which psychology as an introspective science now concerns itself" (Watson, 1913, p. 177). On the basis of such passages, Watson is sometimes viewed as suggesting that he didn't care whether individuals had minds or mental phenomena; all he wanted was to predict and control publicly observable behavior on the basis of publicly observable environmental variables. Whatever the validity of this impression from Watson's early writings, his later writings were more decisive. There was no such thing as the mental; it was a fiction. Rather, the subject matter of psychology was behavior, because that was all there was to study, and behaviorists were all anyone could be, though some were better than others. To hold the mental was something more simply indicated how people had been warped by mentalistic thinking. Watson (1925) had his reader posing the rhetorical question of whether something was being left out, such as sensations, perceptions, conceptions, and images. Watson confidently reassured the reader that a behavioristic treatment would answer appropriately framed questions about such phenomena "in a perfectly satisfactory natural science way" (Watson, 1925, p. 10).

Watson was ultimately concerned with the process of human adjustment—a process that involved the whole of the human: "Behaviorism… is, then, a natural science that takes the whole field of human adjustments as its own…. Behaviorism … while it is intensely interested in all of the functioning of these parts, is intrinsically interested in what the whole animal will do from morning to night and from night to morning" (Watson, 1925, p. 11). Adjustment was defined as "the momentary point where the individual by his action has quieted a stimulus or has gotten out of its range" (Watson, 1925, p. 162). Watson continued: "If, when he gets into the same situation again, he can accomplish the one or the other of these results more rapidly and with fewer movements, then we say that he has learned or has formed a habit" (Watson, 1925, p. 162). Just a few years earlier Watson had stated:

> At the present time there is no satisfactory way of giving an account of the formation of a habit in terms of cause and effect…. We cannot state in detail what the course of events is in the inception of any individual habit. Habits start, as we have seen, with the so-called random movements (if the object fails to arouse either positive or negative reaction tendencies no habit can be formed). Among those random movements is one group or combination which completes the adjustment, the "successful" one. All others, from a superficial standpoint, seem to be unnecessary…. The formation of a habit is an enormously complicated affair. (Watson, 1919, p. 293)

Habit, then, as the observed S – R relation, became the fundamental unit of analysis.

Watson was aware at a relatively early stage of conditioning experiments done largely in Russia by Pavlov and Bechterev, but he initially saw them as suitable more for determining sensory capabilities than for studying behavior:

> While properly belonging among physiological methods, Pawlow's salivary secretion method has been widely used in animal behavior, by Russian students especially. This method is used to determine the efficiency of animals' receptors…. It is quite clear that Pawlow's method, in theory at least, is designed to give the behavior student the same set of facts as the 'discrimination method' … now so widely used. As a matter of fact, it has nothing like the general range of usefulness of the method first described…. These reflexes have not the precision-like character which the students of Pawlow at first maintained. (Watson, 1914, pp. 65–68)

Watson's own initial investigations of the conditioned reflex were not productive, perhaps contributing to his cautious assessment of the method. However, those of a colleague, Karl Lashley (1890–1958), did seem to bear fruit, although even Lashley's attempts were not 100 percent successful. Nevertheless, Watson was sufficiently influenced by work in conditioning that his APA Presidential Address was on the place of the conditioned reflex in psychology (Watson, 1916). Subsequently, Watson (1919) featured coverage of both the conditioned salivary reflex made popular by Pavlov and conditioned motor reflex made popular by Bechterev. Watson (1925) expanded the discussion of conditioned reflexes in comparison to earlier sources, noting the contribution of conditioning to emotional and visceral responses through stimulus substitution, habits ("the conditioned reflex is the unit out of which the whole habit is formed," p. 166), and even language ("After conditioned word responses have become partly established, phrase and sentence habits begin to form. Naturally single word conditioning does not stop. All types of word, phrase and sentence habits develop simultaneously," p. 183). For Watson, the relevant principles were quite simple and based on temporal contiguity: Responses made most frequently and most recently in the presence of a stimulus will tend to be repeated when the stimulus is next presented. This treatment would replace the mentalistic treatments involving long lists of instincts by William James and William McDougall (1871–1938). Also to be rejected was the appeal to consequences on the basis of their emotionally satisfying aftereffects; for example, as represented in the work of Watson's contemporary, E. L. Thorndike:

> Most of the psychologists, it is to be regretted, have even failed to see that there is a problem. They believe habit formation is implanted by kind fairies. For example, Thorndike speaks of pleasure stamping in the successful movement and displeasure stamping out the unsuccessful movements. Most of the psychologists talk, too, quite volubly about the formation of new pathways in the brain, as though there were a group of tiny servants of Vulcan who run through the nervous system with hammer and chisel digging new trenches and deepening old ones. (Watson, 1925, p. 166)

In sum, classical behaviorism formally and explicitly defined psychology as the science of behavior. Introspection and a concern with the mental dimension, such as a concern with consciousness, played no part in the new viewpoint. Classical behaviorism emphatically embraced the generalized S – R reflex model. It sought to explain behavioral events in terms of an antecedent stimulus (S) that called forth the response (R) in question. Classical behaviorism unselfconsciously borrowed some of its fundamental concepts from reflex physiology. Indeed, the early notions of stimuli as forms of physical energy impinging on the response system, responses as the contractions of a muscle or gland, of excitation and inhibition, and so on, all had their origins in reflex physiology. Classical behaviorism further stated that its goal was the prediction and control of publicly observable behavior. Given the stimulus, the task of the psychologist was to predict the response; and given the response, the task was to determine the stimulus that had produced it. No appeal to mental phenomena was appropriate, as it was not necessary.

Watson was a central figure in American psychology generally, and in the launching of classical S – R behaviorism specifically. In some ways, his contributions can be identified as much by what he was against as by what he was for. The list below, set up in contrasting pairs where possible, is intended to provide some flavor of his position.

AGAINST	FOR
Introspection	Observation, conditioning, testing, verbal report
Consciousness	Generalized S - R reflex model of behavior
Subjective	Objecctive, empirical, observable
Centralism	Peripheralism
Dualism	Monism
Religion; free-will	Science; determinism
Molarism	Molecular, mechanistic, associationistic
Statis	Dynamic, developmental
Large numbers of instincts; nature > nurture	Small number (3) of instincts (fear, love, rage); nurture > nature
Human behavior qualitively different from animals	Human behavior qualitatively similar to animals (except for language)
Thinking as mental process	Thinking as involving response systems of the whole organism
Emotion as mental process	Emotion as response of peripheral organs (e.g., lust as tingling in the genitals
	Planned society based on behaviorist principles, especially concerning child rearing and marriage

There is, of course, much more to Watson's story than can be covered in this space. Readers are referred to Boakes (1984) or Buckley (1989) for their excellent coverage of his career and contributions. Indeed, there are many others who made important contributions in the era of classical behaviorism, and whose stories round out a complete understanding of the development of psychology in the United States.

Recapitulation

In summary, Watson's classical S – R behaviorism advocated the study of stimulus-response relations, in part as a rejection of both structuralism and functionalism and their attendant concerns with consciousness. However, by the early 1930s, psychologists began to see at least three problems with the validity of classical behaviorism. The first problem was that publicly observable stimuli and responses just weren't always correlated with each other in the way that classical behaviorism required. In particular, there were concerns about both the variability and apparent spontaneity of behavior. The term *variability* here means that often the expected form of behavior did not appear, given the stimulus, or a given form of behavior could appear across a range of stimuli. The apparent spontaneity of behavior means that often behavior would occur in the absence of some eliciting stimulus. If the S - R model was adequate for the explanation of behavior, behavior should exhibit neither variability nor spontaneity. For example, although Mateer (1918) and Cason (1922) reported some success in carrying out conditioning experiments with eyeblink and pupillary responses, Lashley (1916) was unsuccessful when he tried to condition a salivary response with humans. Liddell (1926) had conditioned leg flexion in sheep, but Hamel (1919) had found that results with a conditioned finger withdrawal preparation in humans were confounded by what would now be called the "voluntary characteristics" of the response, making them unsystematic and difficult to interpret when viewed from the perspective of the generalized S - R reflex model. Hilgard (1987) states that "For the most part, the investigators were pleased that they could obtain conditioned reflexes at all, a far cry from Watson's bold attempt to substitute the conditioned reflex method for the other laboratory methods according to which habit formation and discrimination could be investigated" (p. 818).

The second problem was that the S – R model does not easily accommodate how individuals come to use subjective terms to describe various conditions inside their bodies. Don't people have feelings, sensations, aches, pains, thoughts, and personal experiences that they talk about and that are important in their conduct? Are psychologists denying or ignoring the relevance of these phenomena when they make psychology the science of publicly observable behavior? To be sure, Watson did put forth primitive accounts of how to deal with certain phenomena that weren't publicly observable, such as emotions, images, and thinking, but many scholars questioned the adequacy of these accounts. Although introspective psychology was no longer in vogue, individuals were still capable of making introspective reports, at least to some approximation. How could they do so? Were psychologists mistaken to assume that certain phenomena must be mental because they aren't publicly observable, and then to argue that these phenomena shouldn't be included in a science of behavior?

The third problem was that other sciences seemed to be making progress by postulating unobservables (e.g., physics with relativity theory and quantum mechanics). Was psychology handcuffing itself by emphasizing publicly observable phenomena? Again, Watson had appealed to implicit responses, which were internal and often unobservable to others, but did psychology need to incorporate unobservables even more?

During this same period, an additional influence on the development of behavioral psychology was the work of E. L. Thorndike (1874–1949). Thorndike received his doctoral degree in 1898, five years before Watson. Thorndike's research concerned the process of learning, first with nonhumans and then with humans. His early research with nonhumans dealt with some of the same issues as the functionalists and animal psychologists, in the sense of how was it that animals could be said to have learned something. Unlike many of the animal psychologists, who talked in terms of mental concepts even with nonhumans, Thorndike (1911) emphasized the law of effect:

Of several responses made to the same situation, those which are accompanied or closely followed by satisfaction to the animal will, other things being equal, be more firmly connected with the situation, so that, when it recurs, they will be more likely to recur; those which are accompanied or closely followed by discomfort to the animal will, other things being equal, have their connections with that situation weakened, so that, when it recurs, they will be less likely to recur. The greater the satisfaction or discomfort, the greater the strengthening or weakening of the bond. (p. 244)

This law emphasized the consequences of a response, as Herbert Spencer (1820–1903) and Alexander Bain (1818–1903) had done earlier (Boakes, 1984). Thorndike believed this law was responsible for a wide variety of behavior, including that viewed as reflexive in the tradition of S – R classical behaviorism. His later research also concerned learning, with continued emphasis on the law of effect, but focused more on humans, without invoking mental concepts as functionalists were inclined to do. Although a question has been raised as to whether the appeal to such emotional events as pleasure or satisfaction and discomfort or annoyance was fundamentally mentalistic, Thorndike himself believed he was being objective and empirical, if not mechanical. Pavlov even appreciated Thorndike's work. As mentioned earlier in this chapter, Watson did not.

Thorndike was massively productive during his career, publishing over 500 books, monographs, and articles. As a result he was extraordinarily influential in the development of psychology in the United States. However, he doesn't fit neatly into the category of either functionalist or classical S – R behaviorism. He was given to objectivity, empiricism, and experimentation in a way that distinguished him from functionalism. In addition, he emphasized the role of the consequences of a response in a way that distinguished him from classical S – R behaviorism. Accordingly, he stood apart from the influences of functionalism, animal psychology, and reflexology identified above, and exerted an effect on behavioral psychology in a different way.

Overall, the shortcomings of classical S – R behaviorism with respect to variability, spontaneity, "subjective" terms, and unobservables provided the impetus for the second phase of the behavioral movement. The second phase is the subject of Chapter 3.

TABLE 2.1
Definitions

Voluntarism
Wundt's approach to psychology, emphasizing research into mental laws as they affected human phenomena ranging from consciousness to culture.

Structuralism
Titchener's approach to psychology, emphasizing the content and structure of conscious, mental experience.

Functionalism
American approach to psychology, emphasizing the function of conscious, mental experience

Introspection
A research method emphasizing "observing inward" to assess conscious, mental experience. An important part of voluntarism, structuralism, and functionalism.

Post-Darwinian comparative psychology: Animal psychology
Research seeking to determine behavioral continuity across species. Particularly concerned with how experience modified instinctive responses. Methodology often employed problem-solving tasks, but involved measuring changes in responding over time.

Reflexology
Application of concepts from reflex physiology to behavioral processes.

Classical S – R behaviorism
Interpretation of behavior in terms of S – R relations. Launched by John B. Watson in 1913, it flourished until around 1930. Problems leading to its diminished influence were: variability and spontaneity of behavior, use of subjective terms, role of unobservables.

REFERENCES

Benjamin, L., Durkin, M., Link, M., Vestal, M., & Acord, J. (1992). Wundt's American doctoral students. *American Psychologist, 47*, 121–131.

Boakes, R. A. (1984). *From Darwin to behaviourism.* Cambridge, England: Cambridge University Press.

Buckley, K. W. (1989). *Mechanical man: John B. Watson and the beginnings of behaviorism.* New York: Guilford Press.

Cason, H. (1922). The conditioned pupillary reaction. *Journal of Experimental Psychology, 5*, 108–146.

Hamel, I. A. (1919). A study and analysis of the conditioned reflex. *Psychological Monographs, 27* (whole number 118).

Hilgard, E. R. (1987). *Psychology in America: A historical survey.* San Diego, CA: Harcourt Brace Jovanovich.

Lashley, K. (1916). The human salivary reflex and its use in psychology. *Psychological Review, 23*, 446–464.

Leahey, T. (1992). The mythical revolutions of American psychology. *American Psychologist, 47*, 308–318.

Leahey, T. (2000). *A history of psychology,* 5th ed. Upper Saddle River, NJ: Prentice Hall.

Liddell, H. S. (1926). A laboratory for the study of conditioned motor responses. *American Journal of Psychology, 37*, 418–419.

Loeb, J. (1900). *Comparative physiology of the brain and comparative psychology.* New York: G.P. Putnam's Sons.

Loeb, J. (1916). *The organism as a whole.* New York: G.P. Putnam's Sons.

Mateer, F. (1918). *Child behavior, a critical and experimental study of young children by the method of conditioned reflexes*. Boston, MA: Badger.

Morgan, C.L. (1903). *Introduction to comparative psychology* (2nd edition, revised). London: Walter Scott.

Thorndike, E. L. (1911). *Animal intelligence*. New York: Macmillan.

Turner, M. B. (1967). *Philosophy and the science of behavior*. New York: Appleton-Century-Crofts.

Watson, J. B. (1913). Psychology as the behaviorist views it. *Psychological Review, 20,* 158–177.

Watson, J. B. (1914). *Behavior: An introduction to comparative psychology*. New York: Henry Holt.

Watson, J. B. (1916). The place of the conditioned reflex in psychology. *Psychological Review, 23,* 89–116.

Watson, J. B. (1919). *Psychology from the standpoint of a behaviorist*. Philadelphia: Lippincott.

Watson, J. B. (1925). *Behaviorism*. New York: Norton.

STUDY QUESTIONS

1. List any three phenomena that were thematically linked to psychology and that were of interest to philosophers and other scholars at the beginning of the nineteenth century.

2. List any three phenomena related to human activities that by the third quarter of the nineteenth century had been shown to have an impressive degree of orderliness.

3. Briefly describe Wilhelm Wundt's role in the development of psychology in the late nineteenth century. List any three individuals who studied with Wundt and then established or joined with fledgling psychology programs in the United States.

4. Briefly describe E. B. Titchener's role in the development of psychology in the late nineteenth century. Use the terms *structuralism* and *introspection* knowledgeably in your answer.

5. In one or two sentences, describe the functionalist school of thought. Indicate how it differed from structuralism, and list any three individuals who were influential in functionalism.

6. State or paraphrase any three concerns that scholars in the late nineteenth and early twentieth century had about a psychology based on introspection.

7. List any three practical contributions that American society in the late nineteenth and early twentieth centuries thought psychology should be making.

8. Describe the principal contribution of post-Darwinian comparative, animal psychology to the first phase of the "Behavioral Revolution."

9. Name the year that is conventionally set for the beginning of the first phase of the behavioral revolution. Name the publication and author that is typically associated with this date.

10. Describe any three characteristics of classical behaviorism.

11. In three to four sentences each, describe two problems that led to the second phase of the behavioral revolution.

3

History of Behaviorism and Behavior Analysis: 1930–1980

Synopsis of Chapter 3: Chapter 3 continues to examine the historical development of behaviorism. The chapter begins with the second phase of the development of behaviorism around 1930, after classical behaviorism was revealed as inadequate, and traces developments up to around 1980. The hallmark of the second phase was the emergence of the position here called mediational S – O – R neobehaviorism. This newer form of behaviorism perpetuated the tradition of linear, S – R antecedent causation begun previously under classical behaviorism. However, in this newer form organismic entities were inferred to mediate the relation between stimulus and response. The organismic entities gained credibility through operational definitions. Chapter 3 relates many developments in philosophy during this time to developments in behavioral psychology because of a presumed parallelism between them. Of particular interest in the chapter is the treatment of these inferred organismic entities or other unobservables as theoretical terms. The chapter further points out that mediational neobehaviorism has now gained widespread recognition as the defining exemplar of behaviorism, such that it is regarded as orthodox in the field. The chapter concludes by tracing the career and some of the contributions of B. F. Skinner. Skinner never embraced the mediational neobehaviorist approach as he developed his own point of view. Similarly, he wasn't influenced by developments in the philosophy of the time. Indeed, he often criticized mediational neobehaviorism and its ostensible philosophical support just as strenuously as he did more outwardly mentalistic approaches. The result is that uncritical attempts to link Skinner's radical behaviorism with traditional forms of behaviorism, such as mediational neobehaviorism, are in error.

Classical behaviorism flourished from 1913 to the early 1930s. As suggested in Chapter 2, however, by the early 1930s some shortcomings of classical behaviorism had become apparent. Consequently, researchers and theorists began to abandon classical S – R behaviorism in favor of a new form of behaviorism. In this new form, appeals to unobservables were explicitly readmitted. They were regarded as internal, "organismic" variables that mediated the relation between stimulus and response. According to this new point of view, publicly observable stimuli (S) affect mediating, unobservable internal variables (i.e., O: acts, states, mechanisms, processes, entities), and these variables in turn affect publicly observable responses (R). The new form of behaviorism is here called mediational S – O – R neobehaviorism. The use of mediating variables allowed this new form of behaviorism to address the three problems that had previously been noted with classical S – R behaviorism: (a) the variability of behavior, (b) the apparent spontaneity of some forms of behavior, and (c) the use of unobservables, for example, concerning subjective terms. Importantly, the emergence of mediational neobehaviorism meant that the behavioral movement had entered its second phase.

THE SECOND PHASE OF THE BEHAVIORAL MOVEMENT: MEDIATIONAL S – O – R BEHAVIORISM

An early representative of this mediational approach was Woodworth (1929), who explicitly proposed an S – O – R formulation. The "O" was meant precisely to accommodate a wide variety of "organic states"—motives, response tendencies, and purposes—which were presumed to determine the effects of environmental stimuli. Other theorists of the time mentioned moods, attitudes, and "sets," meaning predispositions. Thorndike was aware of the rise of neobehaviorism as an alternative to classical S – R behaviorism, and his approach also involved some of the same concepts that the neobehaviorists labeled as mediators. However, his continued emphasis on consequences and the law of effect meant that he remained independent of the neobehaviorists and their commitment to antecedent causation.

An important concern of the mediational neobehaviorists in the 1930s was how to remain scientifically respectable in the process of proposing these organismic variables. How could one be sure that researchers and theorists weren't just making something up that was unscientific, particularly when they invoked "mental states" as mediating organismic variables? How could agreement be reached on the important concepts? Although the entire story is quite complicated, suffice it to say that during the 1930s, at the same time that mediational neobehaviorism was developing, philosophers of science and research scientists in both the natural and social sciences were seeking to work through problems associated with the meaning and logical status of scientific concepts.

Logical Positivism

The various groups developed somewhat similar positions, and although their concerns overlapped, the groups did not necessarily interact or cooperate as they worked through those concerns. The position that developed in the philosophy of science is called *logical positivism*. Logical positivism emerged out of positions taken by members of the Vienna Circle and the Berlin Society for Empirical Philosophy, beginning in the 1920s. The members of these groups were primarily logicians, mathematicians, and physical scientists who sought to reaffirm the fundamentally empirical nature of science in light of such developments as quantum mechanics and relativity theory in physics. Their goal was nothing less than to rationally reconstruct all knowledge claims in all sciences on a secure, empirical foundation, using the techniques of formal, symbolic logic. The logical positivists took their cues regarding empiricism from various sources, but emphasized the contributions of such figures as Auguste Comte, David Hume, J. S. Mill, Henri Poincaré, Pierre Duhem, and Ernst Mach. As with more general forms of empiricism, they took their cues regarding formal logic from various sources, but emphasized the contributions of Gottfried Leibniz, Gottlob Frege, Bertrand Russell, and Ludwig Wittgenstein (Ayer, 1959). Wittgenstein's first book, the *Tractatus Logico-Philosophicus* (Wittgenstein, 1922/1974), was especially influential in the early discussions of the Vienna Circle as they sought to apply logic to the analysis of language. Although Wittgenstein did meet informally with members of the Vienna Circle and others to discuss his ideas, particularly those concerning the application of mathematical logic to more general philosophical problems, the meetings were irregular and he was never a member of the Circle as such.

The generally empirical stance of the logical positivists meant that philosophy was to be construed as an analytical activity focusing upon the use of language, rather than as a matter of advancing doctrine or even theoretical speculation about the ultimate constituents of nature. Metaphysical discussions about "reality" were to be avoided at all costs, as unproductive. Science was an activity concerned with developing talk about cause and effect relations in nature. In contrast, philosophy was an activity concerned with analyzing that talk, rather than the cause and effect relations themselves, although in the process of analyzing that talk philosophers might reveal something of interest about nature to scientists. The logical positivists distinguished between statements that are true necessarily, called *analytic*, and statements that are true contingently, called *synthetic*. The statement that a bachelor is an unmarried man is an analytic statement, true by definition and tautological. The statement that the man named Smith is a bachelor is a synthetic statement, given that it can be empirically determined whether Smith is married. The analysis of science consists in the analysis of its synthetic statements to assess their truth value, and then in the rational reconstruction of those statements, to put them in appropriate logical form. Similarly, the logical positivists distinguished between the context of justification and the context of discovery. The context of justification concerned the logical evaluation of the proposition in question that determined its validity. The context of discovery concerned the source of the proposition. The context of justification was held to be a rational process and appropriate for philosophy. It superseded the context of discovery, which was held to be a psychological process and appropriate for history, sociology, or psychology, rather than philosophy.

In short, philosophy would serve science by helping to clarify scientific concepts. Language was conceived of as essentially a logical activity, and the requisite clarification would come via logical analysis of scientific concepts. Importantly, the vocabulary of science included three sorts of terms: (a) logical terms, (b) observational terms, and (c) theoretical terms. Logical terms refer to the logical operators of symbolic logic (conjunction, disjunction, etc.). These terms show the essential syntax that relates elements of the scientific statement or theory. Observational terms refer to variables, mechanisms, and structures that can be directly observed and agreed upon by at least two persons, through either the natural sensory organs or relatively unsophisticated observational instruments. Theoretical terms refer to variables, mechanisms, and structures that are unobserved and hence inferred. Theoretical terms must be defined with respect to observations on counters, dials, meters, and pointers. The various concepts in physics that appealed to unobservables were therefore to be treated as theoretical terms.

One important principle for the logical positivists was verification, later amended to confirmation. In simple terms, *verification* means to give either (a) the publicly observable conditions, or (b) the conditions that were logically related to public conditions under which a proposition is true and those under which it is false. Thus, to understand the meaning of a proposition is to know what directly, publicly observable facts or what logical extensions of publicly observable facts will verify it. In short, propositions for which no acceptable method of verification had been or could be proposed, such as those from traditional metaphysics or theology, were dismissed as meaningless and without cognitive significance.

A second important principle for the logical positivists was physicalism. Formally stated, the doctrine of *physicalism* as applied to psychology holds that for every sentence P in a psychological (i.e., mental) language there must be a sentence Q in a physical thing language, such that P and Q can be logically deduced from each other without remainder. The directly and publicly observable, physicalistic measures provided the needed verification or confirmation. As shall be seen, this statement was not necessarily an ontological commitment to materialism and a rejection of dualism, but rather only a statement regarding the preferred data language of science.

In addition to verification, the logical positivists were also interested in bringing a new unity to intellectual endeavors, based on their linking of empiricism and logic.

Thus, a third important principle for the logical positivists was the unity of science, broadly conceived to consist of three aims:

1. *Establishing the unity of scientific concepts.* The concepts would be empirical, derived from direct public observations or else logically constructed from public observations. Of prime importance was the commitment to the thesis of physicalism: Any concept in any branch of science could be expressed in the language of physics.

2. *Establishing the unity of scientific laws.* The laws would be hierarchically arranged, building up from physics and the natural sciences to biology and the life sciences and ultimately to psychology and the social sciences. The laws in any branch of science would therefore be ultimately reducible to the laws of physics.

3. *Establishing the unity of scientific methods.* The hypothetico-deductive method would be the standard. This method would consist of proposing laws, deducing implications of the laws in terms of publicly observable measures, and subjecting the implications to experimental test to see whether the implications obtained. Explanations were to be accommodated as logically valid conclusions in a deductive argument with a covering law as one premise and a statement of antecedent conditions as another. The logical positivists eventually expressed tolerance for different languages within the various branches of science, so long as the three aims were observed.

Philosophy would serve psychological science by clarifying "mental" concepts. Certain versions of psychology, such as Titchener's structuralism and one form or another of functional or genetic psychology, were popular in various arenas prior to the 1900s in the United States, and their influence lingered into at least the 1920s and 1930s, when logical positivism began to ascend to prominence. During this same time frame in Austria and Germany, Gestalt psychology was popular and Freudian psychology was noteworthy for its clinical applications. Watson's behaviorism had emerged as a rival to structuralism and functionalism in the United States, and the logical positivists were familiar with Watson's behaviorism from Bertrand Russell's treatment of it in his publications. Mediational S – O – R neobehaviorism began to rise during the 1930s. What was necessary was to bring some sense of order to the diverse vocabularies and concepts in the discipline. For the logical positivists, the way to do that was to embrace a position called "logical behaviorism," which is discussed in Chapter 17. For now, suffice it to note that the logical positivists resolutely believed their principles of verification, physicalism, and the unity of science, coupled with their view of language, would more or less resolve the critical questions, and all that remained was to mop up a few details.

Operationism

Similar events were taking place in the natural sciences, but again these events were not necessarily identical or even a subset of those in philosophy. For example, in 1927 the physicist P. W. Bridgman proposed a principle he called "operationism." According to this principle, the meaning of a scientific concept was entirely synonymous with the corresponding set of operations (e.g., by which it is measured). Thus, the meaning of the term "length" was determined by the operation of measuring the distance in question. Operationism therefore was able to generate agreement about a scientific concept and promote both communication and scientific advance.

The operational point of view became increasingly influential in psychology during the 1930s, and especially so for mediational neobehaviorism. The unobserved, mediating, organismic terms were regarded as inferred, logical, or theoretical constructions. Although such terms were not directly observable through the use of any known scientific instrument, they were permissible to the extent that scientists could "operationally define" them by specifying a set of operations by which they were measured. The operational definition allowed mediational neobehaviorists to secure agreement, and to circumvent any problems arising because they had included direct appeals to phenomena of an uncertain ontology.

THEORETICAL TERMS AS INTERVENING VARIABLES OR HYPOTHETICAL CONSTRUCTS?

One further matter needs to be clarified. This matter concerns the definition of the mediating theoretical term and the implication of that definition for the question of whether the theoretical term referred to something that actually existed. An operational definition specified the publicly observable phenomena (i.e., operations by which a given phenomenon was thought to be observed and measured) that established the meaning of the theoretical term, so that theorists could agree on their concepts. In its original sense, the definition was exhaustive. That is, the term that was operationally defined in terms of observables had no further meaning beyond its systematizing role in a single equation or statement. Exhaustively defined terms did not imply existence, which would mean other, perhaps as-yet-unobserved properties, and certainly other functions in other situations. This position was consistent with that of the logical positivists, who during the early 1930s had embraced the position that meaning should be exhaustively expressed in terms of observables in a physical-thing language, without implying that the theoretical term referred to anything that actually existed.

By the mid-1930s, however, Rudolf Carnap and other logical positivists realized a doctrine advocating that theoretical terms be exhaustively defined caused several problems. One problem revolved around the logical status of the inferred entity when the test conditions were not in effect (for further discussion of the problem of the "counterfactual conditional," see Zuriff, 1985). A second problem was that scientific concepts were dynamic and probabilistic, not static in the sense implied by exhaustive definitions. A third problem came to be known as the "theoretician's dilemma" (Hempel, 1958). One horn of the dilemma is that if the theoretical term does not help to provide an accurate and valid explanation of the event in question, it obviously should not be used. The other horn is that even if an exhaustively defined theoretical term does help, its exhaustive definition means it is totally reducible to the observable variables entailed in its measurement; therefore, it adds nothing beyond that which is already known. A fourth problem was more pertinent to the practicing scientist. If the operationally defined theoretical term had meaning in only one specific situation, namely, the one in which it was invoked, how could general (e.g., cross-situational) theories be developed? Couldn't other observations be a measure of the same concept? Taken together, such problems posed a significant challenge to the "rational reconstruction" of scientific activity that philosophers of science were trying to provide.

In recognition of these problems, Carnap (1936, 1937) worked out "partial definitions" and "reductive chains." These moves freed the interpretation of theoretical terms from the confines of exhaustive definitions and required simply that theoretical terms be linked through logic to public observables. The moves were so revolutionary that many feel the movement after this time should formally be redesignated as "logical empiricism," rather than remain known as logical positivism, to officially recognize the significant shift in position (see Smith, 1986).

In any case, mediational neobehaviorists (and particularly those who embraced the conventional interpretation of operationism) faced essentially the same problems in their theorizing that the logical positivists had a few years earlier: Were operational definitions actually exhaustive? And what was the existential status of the terms that were operationally defined? In a highly influential article, the psychologists Kenneth MacCorquodale and Paul Meehl (1948) recognized that psychologists used more and more "theoretical" terms that were not exhaustively defined, and that psychologists often used those terms that did and those that did not require exhaustive definition interchangeably. As a result, MacCorquodale and Meehl proposed a linguistic convention in an effort to sort things out. They proposed that theorists recognize they used two varieties of theoretical terms, and implicitly suggested that either variety of theoretical term was acceptable. They then proposed the identifying characteristics of each variety. The first variety involved theoretical terms that simply served a systematizing function in an equation or scientific statement. These terms involved no hypothesis as to the existence of unobserved entities or the occurrence of unobserved processes. The terms had no surplus meaning, or meaning beyond the immediate symbolic application. MacCorquodale and Meehl proposed that this first variety be called "intervening variables." This treatment was consistent with the original sense of operationism and logical positivism. (Note that some writers, including

MacCorquodale and Meehl, may also use "intervening variable" to refer to any theoretical term; to avoid terminological confusion, this chapter uses "theoretical term" as the overarching, generic term; it then uses "intervening variable" as the first of two specific varieties of theoretical terms.)

MacCorquodale and Meehl (1948) then proposed a second variety of theoretical term. These terms referred to a possibly existing, but at the moment unobserved, entity or process. If the existence of a process or entity was entertained, then presumably the process or entity has another property as well; this property might be observed at some time in the future. Thus, because such terms are thought to refer to processes or entities that possibly existed, these terms do allow surplus meaning, or meaning beyond the set of publicly observable operations from which they are derived. MacCorquodale and Meehl proposed that this second variety be called "hypothetical constructs." (Again, to avoid terminological confusion, this chapter refers to a "hypothetical construct" as the second of two specific varieties of theoretical terms.) MacCorquodale and Meehl regarded appeals to both intervening variables and hypothetical constructs as permissible in theoretical statements, so long as the usage was consistent.

The upshot was that such moves as Carnap (1936, 1937) and MacCorquodale and Meehl (1948) liberalized the principle of operationism substantially, and theorists once again felt reassured their verbal-theoretical practices coincided with their experimental practices. For example, Tolman (1949), who was one of the first researchers and theorists to introduce theoretical terms to psychology, was quite explicit as he abandoned his original intervening variable interpretation and embraced the hypothetical construct interpretation:

> I am now convinced that "intervening variables" to which we attempt to give merely operational meaning by tying them through empirically grounded functions either to stimulus variables, on the one hand, or to response variables, on the other, really can give us no help unless we can also embed them in a model from whose attributed properties we can deduce new relationships to look for. That is, to use Meehl and MacCorquodale's distinction, I would abandon what they call pure "intervening variables" for what they call "hypothetical constructs," and insist that hypothetical constructs be parts of a more general hypothesized model or substrate. (p. 49)

In fact, most mediational neobehaviorists followed Tolman and came to favor the hypothetical construct interpretation, primarily because it afforded greater latitude in theory construction.

RECAPITULATION

The historical record indicates that the grand learning theorists of 1930s, 1940s, and 1950s developed a large set of mediating theoretical terms, no longer necessarily related to Woodworth's original sense of "organic states." For example, the neobehaviorist and learning theorist E. C. Tolman (e.g., 1948) introduced such organismic variables as expectancies and cognitive maps, which were couched in the language of cognition. C. L. Hull (e.g., 1943) introduced habit strength and reaction potential in his system, and then suggested the possible locus, structure, or functioning of his variables in the nervous system, although his suggestions were unsubstantiated by any direct observation of physiology. K. W. Spence (e.g., 1956), a collaborator with the logical positivist Gustav Bergmann and in many ways an ardent disciple of the Hullian approach, differed with Hull and advocated a purely quantitative meaning of theoretical terms as intervening variables, on the basis of their systematizing contribution. O. H. Mowrer (e.g., 1947, 1960a, 1960b) talked in terms of the "diffuse emotional responses" of fear, relief, disappointment, and hope, and the increments or decrements to responding associated with onsets and offsets of mediating emotional states following a response. Most of these new approaches to psychological theorizing were regarded as forms of behaviorism, in that they drew their strength, either implicitly or explicitly, from the study of S - R relations rather than introspection. Nevertheless, they are properly regarded as neobehavioral positions because they included theoretical mediating variables and sought to anchor the theoretical entities to publicly observable data at the stimulus end, the response end, or both ends.

In any case, mediational neobehaviorism has proved exceptionally popular and influential, and to a large extent, the history of psychology since the advent of mediational neobehaviorism in the 1930s is the history of various sets of unobserved, mediating, organismic variables that theorists have proposed. One theorist might emphasize variables associated with physiology, either directly or metaphorically, whereas another theorist might emphasize those associated with supposed "cognitive" processes, either directly or metaphorically, but in any case, the underlying theme is one of mediation. Moreover, the general tendency has been to give existence to the mediating terms, in the sense of hypothetical constructs.

THE CONTRIBUTIONS OF B. F. SKINNER

The last section of Chapter 2 and the first section of the present chapter presented an abbreviated version of how conventional behaviorism developed in the United States over a nearly fifty-year period that began slightly before World War I and ended slightly after the middle of the twentieth century. Classical behaviorism was initially popular, but problems developed with its generality. Mediational neobehaviorism then succeeded classical behaviorism and has remained influential. B. F. Skinner began his scientific career when the era of classical behaviorism ended and that of neobehaviorism began. However, his contributions differed significantly from those of the neobehaviorists. To understand the contributions of B. F. Skinner to behaviorism and behavior analysis, one needs to return to the era of classical S – R behaviorism and examine certain biographical details in Skinner's life.

B. F. Skinner was born on March 20, 1904, in Susquehanna, Pennsylvania, and died of leukemia on August 18, 1990, in Cambridge, Massachusetts. As Skinner described in the three volumes of his autobiography (Skinner, 1976, 1979, 1984), his life was rich and eventful. As a child, he was inquisitive and inventive, finding numerous creative activities to engage his attention. Skinner went through elementary and high school in the same building, graduating second in his high school class of eight students. Skinner's father was an attorney, and the same year Skinner graduated from high school, Skinner's father took a position in Scranton, Pennsylvania, and the family moved there.

Skinner attended Hamilton College in Clinton, New York, and received his undergraduate degree in 1926. He majored in English literature while at Hamilton, with a minor in Romance languages. He also took a few courses in biology and public speaking. In the summer of 1925, before his senior year at Hamilton, he met Robert Frost at a writing workshop in Vermont. Frost subsequently gave Skinner some encouraging feedback on some short stories, so when Skinner graduated in June of 1926, he decided to try his hand at writing something substantial, perhaps even a novel. He was particularly interested in writing "objectively" about the human condition and the meaning of life as revealed through the behavior of his characters. He tried for about a year to write while living with his parents in Scranton, but he failed to produce anything of merit. He despaired at his lack of progress and mystified his parents, who wondered what people would think about their son's hanging around home, seemingly not interested in getting a real job. During that year, he read a great deal, including progressive social criticism, modernist literature, and the philosopher Bertrand Russell. Through this reading, Skinner finally decided that he should study behavior, directly and scientifically, rather than simply write about it. After reading John B. Watson, Ivan Pavlov, and more of Russell, he then applied to and was accepted in the graduate program in psychology at Harvard, even though he had not had any psychology courses as an undergraduate.

Skinner entered Harvard in the fall of 1928. Given that he had finally reached a decision about his future after more than a year of frustration and uncertainty, he was looking forward to immersing himself in the empirical, objective study of behavior. Unfortunately, the study of behavior was not held in high regard in the Harvard department, which was institutionally subordinated under philosophy in a combined academic department and remained under the lingering influence of structuralism and concerns with mental life. However, the direct study of behavior did hold center stage in Harvard's Department of General Physiology, in the Division of Biology. On the basis of his few undergraduate courses in biology, Skinner proceeded to establish an intellectual home in a physiology laboratory while nominally a psychology student, studying with William J. Crozier (1892–1955). In the physiology laboratory, he studied various environmental conditions that affected the elicitation of certain reflexes, taking his doctoral degree in early 1931. He remained at Harvard in a series of post-doctoral appointments until 1936, when he assumed a position at the University of Minnesota. In 1938 he published his first book, *The Behavior of Organisms* (Skinner, 1938). This book presented the results of his research to that point, but more importantly argued the case for a particular, systematic approach to the study of behavior as a subject matter in its own right, rather than as an index to physiology or the mental. Although the book received a generally favorable reception, it did not sell particularly well. During World War II, Skinner assisted in the war effort by seeking to develop a guidance system whereby pigeons in the nose cone of a descending bomb would guide the bomb to its target. A laboratory simulation was quite functional, but the device was never tested in actuality. Funding for the project was terminated toward the end of the war, perhaps because of the development of the atomic bomb, and Skinner then returned to the University of Minnesota. He moved to Indiana University in 1945, and ultimately returned to Harvard as a faculty member in 1948. He worked on instructional technology during the 1950s, focusing on both hardware (developing a mechanical teaching machine) and software (programmed instruction to use in such a machine). He made advances in each area, but he ultimately moved on to other interests. He received a career award in 1964 that allowed him to concentrate on writing, although he did keep an office in the Harvard department for several more years, teaching an occasional course, meeting intermittently with students, and conducting a few experiments in the laboratory.

During his graduate school years, Skinner adopted the conceptual framework for the study of behavior that was dominant at the time: All behavior was properly analyzed in terms of a generalized S – R reflex model. This framework was essentially that of classical S – R behaviorism. His dissertation was somewhat polemical, arguing that the term *reflex* was more properly understood as: (a) a law of behavior describing an observed correlation between stimulus and response, rather than (b) a explanation of behavior in terms of hypothetical physiological events taking place inside the organism. He used the data from his various research projects on the "eating reflex" to buttress his theoretical arguments. Skinner was so vigorous in expounding the principal argument of his dissertation that one of his professors jokingly asked, "Who do you think you are—Helmholtz?"

However, as noted in Chapter 2 and earlier in this chapter, various problems loomed large for theorists who embraced the generalized S – R reflex model. The first problem concerned variability and spontaneity. Regarding the problem of variability, Skinner gradually came to realize during his post-doctoral years that stimuli and responses were related to each other as members of classes, rather than in a one-to-one basis. In addition, he realized that reflexes were influenced by various environmental conditions that could modify them; he referred to these conditions as "third variables." Regarding the problem of spontaneity, he came to realize that although some forms of behavior were indeed elicited by antecedent environmental conditions according to the S – R model, not all were. Other forms were a function of their consequences. Hence, unlike Pavlov, Watson, or other S – R theorists, Skinner did not try to reinterpret all behavior according to S – R reflex processes. In addition, unlike Thorndike, Skinner did not try to reinterpret all behavior in relation to its consequences. Rather, he admitted both forms of behavior, and distinguished between them on the basis of the processes that caused them. He called the first category of behavior "respondent" behavior, to distinguish it from the second category, which he called "operant" behavior. Neither was a special case of the other, but rather the two were a function of different environmental circumstances.

These developments in Skinner's thought took place at about the same time that many other psychologists were turning to mediational S – O – R neobehaviorism as an alternative to S – R classical behaviorism, as recounted earlier in this chapter. Even though others were turning in the direction of mediational behaviorism, Skinner held his course for his own independent viewpoint, and explicitly rejected the entire mediational program. Thus, Skinner never embraced any of the S – O – R approach, the distinction between observational and theoretical terms, and the distinction between the intervening variable and hypothetical construct interpretation of theoretical terms that so occupied the rest of psychology. The reasons for his rejection are examined in greater detail in Chapter 12.

In any event, while Skinner was working out these problems in the research laboratory during the 1930s, he continued to pursue his interests in theoretical, philosophical, and conceptual issues, particularly having to do with an objective approach to verbal behavior and its contribution to epistemology. He traced his interest to several sources. An early influence was the work of Francis Bacon (1561–1626), which he read in eighth grade when he pondered whether Bacon had actually written the works of Shakespeare and encountered again in college. Another was the work of Bertrand Russell (1872–1970), which he read in the period after his graduation from Hamilton but before he entered Harvard for graduate study. Yet another was the work of Ernst Mach (1838–1916), to whom he was introduced in a class on the history and philosophy of science while a graduate student. Still other work that influenced Skinner was that of the physicist Percy Bridgman (1882–1961), for his principle of operationism, and the French philosophers Henri Poincaré (1854–1912) and Pierre Duhem (1861–1916), for their observations that scientific statements are more properly regarded as having a certain time-bound conventional character, rather than an ontological absoluteness. While Skinner was a post-doctoral fellow, the famous philosopher Alfred North Whitehead (1861–1947) challenged him to account for an instance of verbal behavior in objective-empirical terms, and Skinner began a book that he described as his most important. The book, which would ultimately appear over 20 years later, was titled simply *Verbal Behavior* (Skinner, 1957). The topic of verbal behavior is taken up in Chapters 8 and 9.

Further problems for behavioral psychology of the time were explaining the use of subjective terms and coming to grips with unobservables in psychological theorizing. In his contribution to a symposium, Skinner (1945) proposed a way that speakers learn how to describe events and conditions inside their bodies, or to be influenced by other factors that aren't publicly observable, all within the framework of an objective and empirical approach to behavior. This paper was the first time Skinner used the term "radical behaviorism" in print. As mentioned in Chapter 1, the term was used in the sense of a "thoroughgoing" behaviorism. That is, radical behaviorism was a behaviorism that fully embraced all aspects of human functioning. It did not deny or ignore important aspects of human functioning that were not publicly observable; it did not seek to explain those aspects inferentially by labeling them as "theoretical"; it did not pursue explanations of behavior using hypothetical constructs. Rather, the phenomena in question were treated as behavioral. They were explained as other forms of behavior were explained, even though they weren't publicly observable. Although Skinner didn't use the term "philosophy of mind" at the time, presumably because it had not yet become a significant term in the scientific or philosophical lexicon, what Skinner had proposed was exactly that. His contribution to the 1945 symposium was in fact part of the book *Verbal Behavior*. More details on Skinner's approach to the question of how speakers learn to use subjective terms are found in Chapter 10 of this book.

Skinner's form of behaviorism began to attract more followers when he returned to Harvard in 1948, although the followers resonated more to the experimental control demonstrated in the laboratory analysis of behavior than to the implications of radical behaviorism as a philosophy of science. A colleague from Skinner's graduate school days at Harvard, Fred S. Keller (1899–1996), developed a behavioral curriculum at Columbia University in New York City, initially making great use of *The Behavior of Organisms*. In addition, the faculty and students in the program began to hold focused research meetings in which they could discuss their research; the first was at Indiana University in 1947 (Dinsmoor, 1987). By the mid-1950s Skinner had developed an extensive program of laboratory research, working with C. B. Ferster (1922–1981) and a new generation of graduate students. A common pattern was for students to take their undergraduate degrees at one university, either Harvard or Columbia, and to take their graduate degrees at the other. When research reports were not readily accepted into professional journals controlled by mainstream academic psychology, researchers began to publish their own journal in 1958: the *Journal of the Experimental Analysis of Behavior* (abbreviated as *JEAB*), which was situated at Indiana. The journal was primarily for the original publication of experiments relevant to the behavior of individual organisms, but also published review articles and theoretical papers.

The experimental domain of behavior analysis was not the only domain that was developing, however. The fundamental principles of behavior identified in the experimental analysis of behavior gave rise to a new wave of application formally linked to

Skinner's approach. Much of the early work took place in educational settings, presumably because of the important contribution that could be made there. Skinner himself worked on a teaching machine that could be used to supplement standard classroom instructional practices. The application took the form of not only arranging the content and programming of instructional material in a way that expedited a student's academic behavior, but also for managing student nonacademic behavior in the classroom. Other applications centered on rehabilitating or enhancing the repertoires of institutionalized individuals. The individuals may have been institutionalized for developmental disabilities, psychopathology, or any number of other reasons. Applications eventually ranged from education, to developmental disabilities, to occupational safety. A second journal, the *Journal of Applied Behavior Analysis* (abbreviated as *JABA*), was launched in 1968 to publish reports on the application of behavioral principles to behavioral matters of social significance. The University of Kansas was particularly influential in the development of applied behavior analysis. As the field progressed, academic programs producing both applied researchers and professionals who delivered behavior analytic services became more numerous.

The discipline of behavior analysis took another step forward with the founding of the Midwest Association for Behavior Analysis in 1974. Just as traditional disciplinary journals balked at accepting behavior-analytic research for publication, resulting in the formation of *JEAB* in the late 1950s and *JABA* in the late 1960s, so also did traditional disciplinary learned societies balk at accepting behavior-analytic presentations at their conventions. The result was that basic researchers, applied researchers, and service providers launched their own learned society and sponsored their own convention. Both the Association, now known as the Association for Behavior Analysis-International, and its convention have grown exponentially since 1974, as the intellectual and social contributions of the discipline have become better known.

TWO WAYS OF REPRESENTING THE RELATION BETWEEN RADICAL BEHAVIORISM AND OTHER FORMS OF PSYCHOLOGY

Figure 3–1 outlines the historical development of radical behaviorism reviewed in Chapters 2 and 3. Along the horizontal axis is a timeline from approximately 1860 to 1980. Along the vertical axis is a listing of important positions in psychology, physiology, and philosophy. In psychology, voluntarism, structuralism, and functionalism were prominent leading up to the early twentieth century. The influence of Darwin led to the movement in animal, comparative psychology and the work of Romanes, Lloyd Morgan, and Hobhouse. In physiology, there was the enduring tradition of reflexology and concerns with sensory physiology. In philosophy, there was the robust tradition of empiricism and positivism in Europe, and of pragmatism in the United States. The influences in psychology and physiology led to classical S – R behaviorism in the second

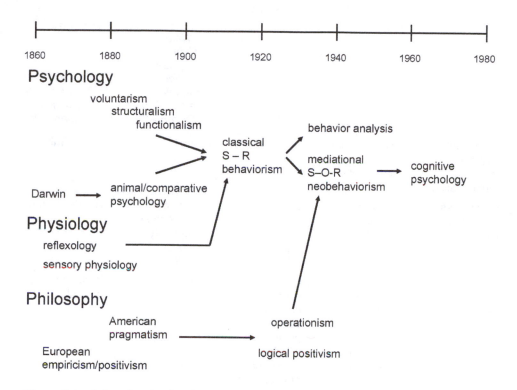

Figure 3.1   A time line for the development of behaviorism, showing influences from psychology, physiology, and philosophy.

decade of the twentieth century. As reviewed earlier in this chapter, when classical S – R behaviorism was found wanting in the third decade, mediational S – O – R neobehaviorism took its place as the modal position. The largely American movement of operationism and to a much lesser extent logical positivism influenced the development of neobehaviorism. Skinner's form of behaviorism—behavior analysis—arose at about the same time as neobehaviorism but differed entirely. As is discussed in Chapter 15 later in this book, cognitive psychology followed from many of the developments in neobehaviorism, particularly the interpretation of theoretical terms as hypothetical constructs rather than intervening variables.

Table 3–1 summarizes some of the principal features of radical behaviorism and compares those features with other forms of psychology and behaviorism. According to Table 3–1, for the various forms of introspective psychology (e.g., structuralism, functionalism), the principal subject matter was the structure and content of mental life in another dimension. This subject matter was engaged by the method of introspection. In sum, introspective psychology advocated the direct appeal to mental processes and phenomena as independent and dependent variables.

TABLE 3.1

Position	Subject Matter	Methods	Nature of Explanatory Appeal to Independent Variables That Are Not Publicly Observable	Admit Variables That Are Not Publicly Observable
Introspective psychology (structuralism, functionalism)	Structure and content of mental life	introspection	direct	Yes, admit as mental
Early classical S – R behaviorism	Publicly observable S – R relations	Observational methods of natural science	Ignore, deny, or reject mental; accept only publicly observable stimuli	No, don't admit
Mediational S – O – R neobehaviorism	S – O – R relation; operating characteristics of O (mediating organismic variable)	Observational methods of natural science, supplemented with logical constructions or inferences	indirect	Yes, admit as mental
Radical behaviorism	Behavioral relations with environment at phylogenic, ontogenic, and cultural levels	Observational methods of natural science, supplemented with interpretive techniques	direct	Yes, admit but as behavioral and as resulting from publicly observable relations

Chapter 2 suggested that early forms of behaviorism ignored, denied, or rejected unobservable mental processes as acceptable subject matter. These early forms argued that mental concepts were unnecessary, and favored instead the direct study of publicly observable behavior. The science consisted of descriptions of the publicly observable relation between stimulus and response. Thus, these early forms abandoned introspection as a method in favor of observational methods of natural science. They further advocated the direct appeal to publicly observable stimulus and response variables. If something wasn't publicly observable, it was regarded as not in the behavioral dimension and had to be rejected.

This chapter describes later forms of behaviorism as instances of mediational S – O – R neobehaviorism. These forms of behaviorism admitted unobservable mental processes as theoretical concepts, given that they could be operationally defined. The processes were inferred and were held to mediate the relation between publicly observable stimuli and responses. Advocates of this form of behaviorism argued that they retained the observational methods of natural science, but supplemented them with logical constructions or inferences. Thus, an important element of this mediational approach is that it indirectly admitted unobservable mental processes through inference, rather than directly through what was held to be introspective observation.

Radical behaviorism stands in contrast to the other approaches. It embraces behavioral relations at the level of phylogeny, ontogeny, and the culture. It employs the observational methods of natural science, supplemented with interpretive extensions based on demonstrated behavioral principles. It can directly consider phenomena that aren't publicly observable, but regards them as behavioral rather than mental. Hence, radical behaviorism is appropriately regarded as a thoroughgoing behaviorism. One of its foremost principles is that behavior is a subject matter in its own right. This principle is the topic of Chapter 4.

Table 3.2
Definitions

Introspective psychology
It appealed directly to consciousness and mental processes in another dimension as both independent and dependent variables, and sought to examine these phenomena through introspection. Examples were Wundt's voluntarism, Titchener's structuralism, and much of American functionalism.

Early forms of behaviorism (Classical S – R behaviorism)
Early forms of behaviorism ignored, denied, or otherwise rejected mental processes as a suitable subject matter and introspection as a suitable method for psychology. In place of the introspective study of consciousness, they favored the study of publicly observable behavior. Of primary concern was a description of the relation between publicly observable stimuli and responses, according to the observational methods of natural science.

Later forms of behaviorism (mediational S – O – R neobehaviorism)
Unobservable mental processes were admitted, but as theoretical concepts, given that they could be operationally defined; they were taken to mediate the relation between publicly observable stimuli and responses. This move allowed theorists to retain observational methods of natural science, but supplement them with logical constructions or inferences. It represented an indirect appeal to unobservable mental processes, rather than direct.

REFERENCES

Ayer, A. J. (Ed.). (1959). *Logical positivism*. Glencoe, IL: Free Press.

Carnap, R. (1936). Testability and meaning. *Philosophy of Science, 3*, 419–471.

Carnap, R. (1937). Testability and meaning—continued. *Philosophy of Science, 4*, 1–40.

Dinsmoor, J. A. (1987). A visit to Bloomington: The first conference on the experimental analysis of behavior. *Journal of the Experimental Analysis of Behavior, 48*, 441–445.

Hempel, C. G. (1958). The theoretician's dilemma. In H. Feigl, M. Scriven, & G. Maxwell (Eds.), *Minnesota studies in the philosophy of science, Vol. 2,* pp. 37–98. Minneapolis, MN: University of Minnesota Press.

Hull, C. L. (1943). *Principles of behavior*. New York: Appleton-Century-Crofts.

MacCorquodale, K., & Meehl, P. (1948). On a distinction between hypothetical constructs and intervening variables. *Psychological Review, 55*, 95–107.

Mowrer, O. H. (1947). On the dual nature of learning—a re-interpretation of "conditioning" and "problem-solving." *Harvard Educational Review, 17*, 102–148.

Mowrer, O. H. (1960a). *Learning theory and behavior*. New York: Wiley.

Mowrer, O. H. (1960b). *Learning theory and the symbolic processes*. New York: Wiley.

Skinner, B. F. (1938). *The behavior of organisms*. New York: Appleton-Century.

Skinner, B. F. (1945). The operational analysis of psychological terms. *Psychological Review, 52*, 270–277, 291–294.

Skinner, B. F. (1957). *Verbal behavior*. New York: Appleton-Century-Crofts.

Skinner, B. F. (1976). *Particulars of my life*. New York: Knopf.

Skinner, B. F. (1979). *The shaping of a behaviorist*. New York: Knopf.

Skinner, B. F. (1984). *A matter of consequences*. New York: New York University Press.

Smith, L. D. (1986). *Behaviorism and logical positivism*. Stanford, CA: Stanford University Press.

Spence, K. W. (1956). *Behavior theory and conditioning*. New Haven, CT: Yale University Press.

Tolman, E. C. (1948). Cognitive maps in rats and men. *Psychological Review, 55*, 189–208.

Tolman, E. C. (1949). Discussion: Interrelationships between perception and personality: A symposium. *Journal of Personality, 18*, 48–50.

Wittgenstein, L. (1974). *Tractatus Logico-Philosophicus*. New York: Routledge. (Original edition published in 1922; trans. by D. F. Pears and B. F. McGuiness)

Woodworth, R. S. (1929). *Psychology: A study of mental life*. New York: Henry Holt.

Zuriff, G. (1985). *Behaviorism: A conceptual reconstruction*. New York: Columbia University Press.

STUDY QUESTIONS

1. In a short paragraph, describe the new form of behaviorism that was embraced in the second phase of the behavioral movement. Use the terms "organismic variable" and "mediation" knowledgeably in your answer.

2. Describe an important concern of the mediational neobehaviorists in the 1930s as they proposed their organismic variables.

3. In a short paragraph, describe the position in philosophy of science known as logical positivism. Mention the sorts of terms they argued should be included in a philosophy of science, and the three important unifying principles they espoused. Indicate whether the logical positivists thought the role of a philosophy of science

was to: (a) clarify the language of science through logical analysis, or (b) offer metaphysical speculation about the ultimate constituents of the universe.

4. Describe what is meant by the principle of operationism. Name two things that operational definitions allowed mediational neobehaviorists to claim they had done.

5. Describe MacCorquodale and Meehl's (1948) distinction between intervening variables and hypothetical constructs as forms of theoretical terms. Name the form that has come to predominate.

6. Name the subject in which Skinner majored as an undergraduate.

7. Name the department in which Skinner established his intellectual home while in graduate school.

8. Name the subject matter of Skinner's first book.

9. Name the important philosopher who prompted Skinner to begin to study verbal behavior while Skinner was a post-doctoral fellow.

10. Name the year in which Skinner first used the term radical behaviorism in print.

11. Name the colleague at Harvard with whom Skinner collaborated in an extensive program of laboratory research in the 1950s.

12. Name the colleague at Columbia who established a behavioral curriculum in the Psychology Department at Columbia University in New York City in the 1950s.

13. Describe the events that led to the founding of JEAB.

14. Describe the events that led to the founding of JABA.

15. Name the behavior-analytically oriented professional society that was founded in 1974.

16. List the three levels at which radical behaviorism embraces behavioral relations.

4

Behavior as a Subject Matter in Its Own Right

Synopsis of Chapter 4: Chapter 4 takes up one of the central principles of radical behaviorism: behavior as a subject matter in its own right. According to the radical behaviorist view, behavior is one form of interaction between organism and environment. The chapter argues that the study of this interaction is usefully undertaken in its own terms, rather than as an index to causal events supposedly taking place in another dimension. In a traditional view, the other dimension is variously called mental, cognitive, conceptual, or sometimes even neural or physiological. Behavior is merely evidence to justify inferences about causal factors in this other dimension. Radical behaviorist concerns about physiology are that physiological data are often used to justify inferences about inner causes. The legitimate contribution of neuroscience is to reveal the means through which an organism is able to behave as it does in a given context. Behavioral neuroscience is therefore complementary to behavior analysis. Behavioral neuroscience provides the information regarding the physiology within a behavioral event, from stimulus to response, and between behavioral events, from one event to its effects as measured in the future.

One of the central principles of radical behaviorism is that behavior is a subject matter in its own right. Thus, radical behaviorists do not call for the study of behavior because it is an index to unobservable causes in other dimensions (e.g., neural, cognitive, mental, conceptual), which are regarded as the true causes of behavior and for which behavior is merely publicly observable evidence that justifies explanations in terms of those causes. Rather, radical behaviorists call for the study of behavior because behavior is one of the principal characteristics of living organisms. Consequently, the study of behavior may be meaningfully construed as one of the life sciences and a branch of biology. In almost every way imaginable, the behavior of an organism has an impact on the world in which it lives, including an impact on other organisms.

ETYMOLOGY OF "BEHAVIOR"

According to the etymology in the *Oxford English Dictionary*, the word *behavior* is derived from the Latin *habere*, meaning to hold or to have, as in to possess. It is also related to the French *avoir*, meaning to have; to the Old and Middle English *haver*, meaning also to have; as well as to various Germanic and Teutonic cognates. The prefix be-, used in the sense of being all over or being all around, became attached in such words as the old English *behabban*. Through usage and the influence of the French, the old English -b- was gradually dropped in favor of the -v- as the middle phoneme. Consistent with the sense of having or possessing, the word *behavior* was originally concerned with how one held oneself, and was closer to the sense of comportment or demeanor than to the now more customary sense of movement or activity. The word *behavior* is also indirectly linked to the words habit, inhibit, and ability, which are derived from the past participle of the Latin *habere*.

Contemporary English has a number of other terms that are often used in connection with behavior. Among the more common of such terms are acts, actions, activities, conduct, and movements, although each term carries a slightly different shade of meaning. Interestingly, definitions of behavior are plentiful, but a conceptually consistent definition of behavior is surprisingly hard to come by. A common definition of behavior is "anything an organism does," but Catania (2007) suggests this definition may be too broad to be especially useful. Below are some other representative definitions of behavior.

SOME REPRESENTATIVE DEFINITIONS OF BEHAVIOR

John B. Watson

John B. Watson was the first to use the term *behaviorism*, as well as cognate terms such as behaviorist and behavioristic. In his initial book-length treatment titled *Behavior*, Watson (1914) suggested that there were three kinds of behavior: (a) that of the sense organs, (b) inherited or instinctive, and (c) learned habits. Moreover, behavior could be either explicit or implicit. Explicit behavior was overt and could occur either immediately after the stimulus or after a delay. Implicit behavior was covert and occurred during the time that intervened between stimulus and response in cases of delayed explicit behavior. Perhaps the most famous example of implicit behavior is Watson's rendering of "thinking" as involving small-scale elements of three response systems: subvocal speech, visceral, and motor.

Watson (1919) subsequently defined behavior as: "We should mean by response the total striped and unstriped muscular and glandular changes which follow upon a given stimulus" (p. 14). Here, he de-emphasized the behavior of sense organs from his 1914 treatment, and talked instead of: (a) explicit habit responses, (b) implicit habit responses, (c) explicit hereditary responses, and (d) implicit hereditary responses. Explicit habit responses were such things as unlocking a door or playing tennis. Implicit habit responses were thinking, as well as conditioned salivary reflexes. Explicit hereditary responses were observable human instinctive or emotional responses, as in fear, rage, or love. Examples of implicit hereditary responses were found in the whole system of glandular secretions. Watson's responses, including implicit ones, involved the whole organism. To cast behavior as exclusively a product of one or another component of an organism's physiology was to risk invoking the mind or soul as the initiator of behavior, rather than to view behavior as an ongoing pattern of adjustment and adaptation to the environment.

Watson (1925) continued this approach by again distinguishing between external, overt and internal, covert forms of response, which could be either learned or unlearned. As noted in Chapter 2, Watson talked about behavior as the total adjustment of the organism to its environment. Ultimately, Watson (1925) was to say: "Behaviorism..., is, then, a natural science that takes the whole field of human adjustments as its own" (p. 11). Because verbal, visceral, and motor systems were all interconnected, subdividing the organism's behavior for anything other than convenience of study was inappropriate.

Significant in Watson's (1919) definition is the phrase "changes which follow upon a given stimulus." In other words, behavior was a form of interaction between the organism and environment. Of concern in the nascent science of behavior was the relation between the stimulus features of the environment and the resulting response. Moreover, for Watson (1925) the world of stimuli—the environment—was inclusive:

> The whole group of visual, tactual, temperature, smell and taste stimuli (so-called objects of the external world) constitutes what most people think of as environment. I want you to think of this as merely part of man's environment, namely his external environment (more or less common to groups). The whole group of visceral, temperature, muscular and glandular stimuli, both conditioned and unconditioned, present inside the body, are just as truly objects of stimulation as are chairs and tables. They constitute the other part of man's (each man's) environment—his internal environment, an environment not shared by others.... The organism, being stimulated always by both environments simultaneously, naturally never is responding at any one time just to the inside or just to the outside. (p. 160)

Watson attempted to deal with the apparent variability of behavior in terms of the influence of the internal environment. If behavior wasn't consistently related to the stimuli in the external environment, he reasoned it must then be related to stimuli in the internal environment. However, his attempts were not entirely successful, in that they were mostly post-hoc efforts to maintain the generalized S – R reflex model. Others began to appeal to drives as elements of the internal environment, which would seem to be consistent with Watson's notions, but Watson would have none of it, arguing that appeals to drives amounted to vitalism.

Overall, Watson repeated the central thesis of his behaviorism—that psychology was the study of stimulus and response relations—many times. To show the continuity, the statement from Watson (1913) is repeated, and then followed with succeeding statements:

> In a system of psychology completely worked out, given the response the stimuli can be predicted; given the stimuli the response can be predicted. (Watson, 1913, p. 167)

> [W]e may say that the goal of psychological study is the *ascertaining of such data and laws that, given the stimulus, psychology can predict what the response will be; or, on the other hand, given the response, it can specify the nature of the effective stimulus.* (Watson, 1919, p. 10, italics in original)

> [B]ehavioristic psychology has as its goal *to be able, given the stimulus, to predict the response—or, seeing the reaction take place to state what the stimulus is that has called out the reaction.* (Watson, 1925, p. 16, italics in original)

However, as noted in Chapter 2, despite his vigorous arguments in favor of psychology as a science of behavior, rather than mental life, Watson's thesis never became pre-eminent in the discipline.

B. F. Skinner

In *The Behavior of Organisms*, Skinner (1938) offered the following definition:

> Behavior is what an organism is doing—or more accurately, what it is observed by another organism to be doing.... It is more to the point to say that behavior is that part of the functioning of an organism which is engaged in acting upon or having commerce with the outside world....

> By behavior, then, I mean simply the movement of an organism or of its parts in a frame of reference provided by the organism itself or by various external objects or fields of force. It is convenient to speak of this as the action of the organism upon the outside world, and it is often desirable to deal with an effect rather than with the movement itself as in the case of the production of sounds.... It will be seen, then, that ... the term 'stimulus' must refer to a *class* of events, the members of which posses some property in common, but otherwise differ rather freely, and the term 'response' to a similar class showing a greater freedom of variation but also defined rigorously with respect to one or more properties.... The members of the class are quantitatively mutually replaceable in spite of their differences. (pp. 6, 34, 37)

This passage is from Skinner's first book-length treatment of how behavior was usefully regarded as a subject matter in its own right. At the time his first book was published, Skinner was a junior faculty member, seeking to establish himself in the discipline by developing a "system." His writing was conformist, in that he was embracing the physicalist, positivist trends of the time. The idea that behavior was responsive to fields of force is presumably derived from Skinner's work with his graduate mentor at Harvard, W. J. Crozier, who was a student of the physiologist Jacques Loeb at the University of Chicago. Loeb and Crozier conceived of behavior in terms of tropisms, with mechanical movements of the whole body in response to physical sources of energy in the environment, such as light, heat, or gravity. Also relevant is the work on reflexes by Pavlov, Sir Charles Sherrington (1852–1957), and Rudolf Magnus (1873–1927). Skinner eventually moved well beyond this position, of course, but his early work was clearly grounded in the traditional notion of the reflex.

An especially noteworthy portion of Skinner's statement is that "Behavior is what an organism is doing—or more accurately, what it is observed by another organism to be doing…." Ironically, the linking of behavior to public observation was in keeping with the very approach he would come to reject some years later. For example, Skinner later took the position that events within the skin, inaccessible to anyone but the individual in question, could count as behavior, even though another organism could not directly observe them.

A further important feature of Skinner's definition is the generic nature of stimuli and responses. Skinner argued as early as 1935 that stimuli and responses weren't always independent entities, unrelated to other stimuli and responses. Rather, stimuli and responses could be grouped into classes according to the environmental circumstances of which they were a function. For example, responses that were a function of one set of environmental conditions belonged to one class, whereas responses that were a function of another set of conditions belonged to another class. The topography or form of the responses might vary, but so long as the responses were caused by the same environmental conditions, the responses belonged to the same class. Thus, Skinner emphasized that one member of an operant class is equivalent to any other, hence the phrase "quantitatively mutually replaceable." As reviewed earlier in the present book, Skinner sought to come to grips with the apparent variability and spontaneity of behavior that troubled classical S-R behaviorism. The generic nature of stimuli and responses allowed him to do so, provide an orderly arrangement of facts, and escape the thankless task of botanizing reflexes (Skinner, 1938, p. 10).

In *Science and Human Behavior*, Skinner (1953) provided a slightly different wording:

> The term [operant] emphasizes the fact that the behavior *operates* upon the environment to generate consequences…. In this sense an operant is defined by an effect which may be specified in physical terms… (p. 65)

The interesting feature of this definition is not so much a distinction between operants and respondents, but rather with the way the particular kind of behavior, an "operant," is defined. Of particular significance is the use of the term "physical." A reasonable question is whether the term *physical* means publicly observable, or physical in principle, so that if observers had the right kind of measuring instruments they could detect that energy had been expended in some sense. The answer is not clear. In any case, this definition elaborates on the earlier definition, but with the continued development of the notion of operant behavior, the definition relies on a more functional, less mechanical conception of antecedent causation.

Somewhat later, Skinner stated: "I would define behavior as the movement of an organism in space with respect to itself or any other useful frame of reference" (Skinner in Evans, 1976, p. 84). This definition revisits the physicalistic tendencies of the definition offered in 1938, but it also continues the theme that behavior is with respect to its surrounding circumstances. Thus, all along Skinner has had the sense of the unit of study in a science of behavior as being distinct from the simple study of the physiology of movement or action.

Johnston and Pennypacker

In a highly regarded textbook on research methods in behavior analysis, Johnston and Pennypacker (1993) define behavior as follows:

> The behavior of an organism is that portion of the organism's interaction with its environment that is characterized by detectable displacement in space through time of some part of the organism and that results in a measurable change in at least one aspect of the environment. (p. 23)

This definition, characterized as a working definition for its practical benefits, is laudable in that it emphasizes the interactive character of behavior. Nevertheless, it still contains the physicalist elements of Skinner's earlier definitions, by virtue of its appeal to detectable displacements and measurable changes. In some cases, such as events within the skin, the authors acknowledge that the technological sophistication may be required to extend the sensitivity of the observational process.

ISSUES RAISED BY THE ABOVE DEFINITIONS

To their credit, the definitions reviewed above emphasize the interactive nature of behavior, involving a real organism as it lives and interacts with a real environment. Prototypical cases in behavior analysis are: rats that press levers in experimental chambers and produce 45–mg food pellets, or pigeons that peck keys in experimental chambers and get access to an elevated food hopper filled with mixed grain for 3 s. Other cases may now be considered.

Physiological Responses

Is a heartbeat an instance of behavior? Is digestion? They are both certainly instances of an organism's activity.

One way of talking about these instances is to say that they do not become cases that interest radical behaviorists until they are shown to be functionally related to environmental circumstances in some way. For example, events associated with noxious stimuli may make the heart beat faster or impede digestion, in which case it is useful to conceive of these aspects of an organism's functioning as behavior.

Novel Behavior

The term *behavior* is also used to characterize novel activity. For example, porpoises have been trained to emit a series of jumps, flips, and turns that had not been previously observed (Pryor, Haag, & O'Reilly, 1969). Similarly, rats and pigeons have been trained to emit a sequence of responses on two response devices that differs from some number of prior sequences (Bryant & Church, 1974; Page & Neuringer, 1985). In addition, humans have learned to type numbers at a computer keyboard that are as "random" as those produced by the computer's random number generator (Neuringer, 1986). At issue is how to define such responses, as there does not seem to be a common physical property across the various instances that defines class membership.

One way to make sense out of such cases is to understand that behavior at one time becomes part of the environment that contributes to the determination of behavior at some future time. For example, a subject can easily be trained to make one of two responses on one trial, and then the opposite response on the next trial. In this case, given that one response is made at time $(T-1)$, that response enters into the determination of the next response, such that a different response is made at time T. Novel behavior is defined by its relation to one or more instances of prior behavior. In the case of responding in a sequence of randomly varying responses (i.e., responding on the left but not the right of two response devices) or typing a sequence of random numbers, the responses are novel in the sense that the environment requires that any given response differ in some specified way from some number of prior responses, not just one, and the number is usually fairly large. Worth noting, however, is that when subjects are required to type random numbers, the environment isn't so accommodating that typing letters counts as an acceptable response, even though typing letters rather than numbers is surely novel.

Perceptual Behavior

The relation between perception and various definitions of behavior is particularly important. Consider the following passages from Skinner's writings:

Do we see red as a property of an object, as a retinal response to a given frequency of radiation, as nerve impulses in the optic tract, or as activity in the occipital cortex? As a behaviorist, I must reply that what is happening in retina, optic tract, and occipital cortex are part of seeing red. As a behaviorist, I leave that to the physiologist, who has more appropriate instruments and methods. As a behaviorist, I am concerned only with the way in which a discriminative response (whether it be key press, saying "red," or stepping on the brake of a car) is brought under the control of red objects. As a behaviorist, I am concerned with how a person learns to say "I see red" in both the presence and absence of red objects. (Skinner in Catania & Harnad, 1988, p. 206)

Behaviorists often say that perceiving is behaving. But that is not quite right. Perceiving is only part of behaving. Seeing a tree is a common part of what happens when we respond to trees in many different ways. Whatever it is physiologically (and only a physiologist will be able to tell us that), it cannot have been strengthened by reinforcing consequences until behavior followed. But it can occur whether action follows or not. In other words, seeing is responding up to the point of specific action; it is the product of many instances in which action has followed. (Skinner, 1985, p. 76)

Is the eyeball analogous in a mysterious way to some kind of musculature that presses a lever in the optic tract? Presumably, seeing red when red is actually present is something that the visual system does, just as absorbing oxygen is something that the lungs do, or absorbing nutrients from food is something that the digestive system does. At issue is the extent to which this sort of process is modified by behavioral contact with the environment, at which point it becomes of interest to behaviorism. For example, direction of gaze and accommodation (i.e., focus) require experience that involves consequences. Similarly, instances of perception, such as seeing red, clearly become of interest when they are followed by other instances of behavior, such as stepping on the brake of a car. They also become of interest when other stimuli control the "perception of red." Individuals shown a playing card that has the shape of the suit called a "heart" but is actually colored black might say they see red. In this latter example, the behavior of seeing red was initially established by seeing a red heart. The same behavior was later occasioned by simply the shape of a heart, independently of the actual color of the object present in the visual field. Many optical illusions can be understood in this same way.

In more complex examples, individuals might well be able to see something that is not actually there, given an appropriate history. An experienced chess player may be able to look at the arrangement of pieces on a board and imagine what would happen if a pawn were moved here or a rook there. This behavior develops after a lengthy history of actually seeing chess boards with the pieces in various positions, and then experiencing the consequences of moving the pieces to different positions. Again, the behavior of seeing in the absence of things seen is a function of environmental circumstances.

Covert Behavior

Interestingly, various other forms of activity, such as thinking or imagining, may be referred to as private or covert forms of behavior. Private behavior is taken up in greater detail in Chapter 10, but relevant at this point is the sense in which private events like thinking or imagining involve producing effects on the environment that may be specified in physical terms, such as movements or displacements of the body in space and time. What is the physical effect when one listens selectively to the strings during a symphony? What is the physical effect when thinking is defined as "behaving which automatically affects the behaver and is reinforcing because it does so" (Skinner, 1957, p. 438).

A first concern here is just how physicalistic one wants to be when one talks about behavior that involves detectable movement in space and time. A second concern is how to define "effects on the environment," such as environmental consequences, in physicalistic terms. A response inevitably has a consequence, if only because the environment after the response differs from the environment before the response. The environment before the response did not include the response, because it hadn't yet been made. The environment after the response does include the response. The implication is that it is presumably not necessary to be as physicalistic as many definitions seem inclined to be. Nevertheless, the behavior analyst must take care to specify the functional relation between response and environment; other stimuli in an organism's environment might also change after the response, although those stimuli might not influence the response.

ANALYSIS OF THE ISSUES

Some consideration of the factors that led to the framing of the formal definitions of behavior cited earlier in this chapter may help analyze the issues associated with those definitions. After all, the definitions are instances of verbal behavior. That is, they are behavioral products of real people acting with respect to a particular set of factors. Presumably, the definitions served some purpose.

Chapter 2 pointed out that early behaviorists such as Watson were concerned with establishing a genuine science of behavior, in contrast to the prevailing attempts to establish a science of mental life by making inferences about consciousness on the basis of introspective reports and reaction times. The early behaviorists chose to make their case by emphasizing a subject matter that was publicly observable. Behavior was publicly observable, whereas conscious experience was not. Only if their subject matter was publicly observable could it be considered scientific. By this criterion, the introspective study of conscious experience could not be regarded as a science.

For Skinner, stimuli and responses were generic, rather than isolated instances. That is, stimuli and responses were members of classes. Importantly, the classes were defined functionally, rather than in terms of their topographical properties. Thus, an operant was a class of responses that had the same effect on the environment. Despite tendencies toward physicalistic definitions, the members of that class did not necessarily have the same physical topography. The operant class of a lever press is defined as "whatever depresses the lever sufficiently to operate the microswitch," given that operation of the microswitch then produced a food pellet. The operant class was not defined in terms of a contraction of specific musculature. Of course, if whatever was required to produce a food pellet was the contraction of specific musculature, so be it, but the response class was still defined in terms of what was required to produce reinforcement. A remaining question is whether the boundaries of a class of responses are determined by events during the lifetime of the species ("phylogenic") or during the lifetime of the individual organism ("ontogenic") . Presumably, that question is to be answered empirically, through the analysis of many different responses within and between species.

Must an event be publicly observable for it to count as an instance of behavior? To be sure, in most cases behavior analysts are interested in publicly observable behavior, if only from a pragmatic perspective. In addition, behavior analysts subscribe enough to the philosophical thesis of physicalism to believe that something is physically or physiologically different after a response than before, even though one may not be able to provide a publicly observable measure of it. However, not all behavior involves a publicly observable movement, and not all publicly observable movements count as behavior (e.g., Catania, 2007, p. 11).

In any case, regardless of whether the boundaries of a class of behavior are phylogenic or ontogenic, it seems reasonable that a definition of behavior retain language that specifies interaction with the environment. In this view, the term *behavior* is an abstraction that concerns a particular sort of functional relation between the activity of an organism and its environment. The task is not to specify a Platonic or metaphysical "essence" that when present means some activity counts as behavior, and when absent means it does not. The task does not mean that the job of the behavioral scientist is to divine whether such an essence is present or absent. Is a heartbeat behavior? It depends. Changes in the beating of the heart as a function of coming into contact with some biologically relevant stimulus such as a shock would seem to count as behavior. As Skinner said, seeing what is there when it is there is part of many instances of behavior. In addition, seeing modifications of what is there, as in an optical illusion, or seeing in the absence of the thing seen, as an image, would presumably count as behavior, when the seeing is a function of the environment.

The cases mentioned above suggest the definition of the term *behavior* might be usefully interpreted to reflect the wide range of circumstances in which it is used. In particular, certain aspects of existing definitions, such as public observability and specification of its physical dimensions, are less important in today's intellectual climate than relatively early in the twentieth century, when Watson and Skinner first advocated behavior as a subject matter in its own right. Indeed, Skinner said: "I see no reason why we should not also call the action of efferent nerves behavior if no muscular response is needed for reinforcement" (Skinner in Catania & Harnad, 1988, p. 485). Are muscles necessary? Probably not, if one wants to count perceptual responses as behavior. Is movement necessary? Again, probably not. For that matter, standing still could conceivably count as behavior: "It is sometimes necessary ... to regard doing nothing as a response if it has identifiable reinforcing consequences" (Skinner, 1957, p. 379). As suggested earlier, not all movements need be instances of behavior, and not all instances of behavior need be movements. What matters is whether a specific instance of behavior is with respect to the environmental circumstances, given the broad interpretation of environment that behaviorists use. Behavioral scientists have distinguished among a number of categories of behavior, which will be discussed in Chapter 5. The categories are distinguished by the nature of the interaction between organism and environment.

In sum, behavior is one of the primary characteristics of life. It consists of an organism's interactions that are with respect to, and influenced by, the environment in particular ways. In this view, the organism is understood as a complex life form that carries on the functions of life by means of the functioning of its separate but interdependent organs and systems (Johnston & Pennypacker, 1993, p. 28). The environment consists of the sum total of objects, circumstances, and stimulus properties that constitute the occasion to which behavior is functionally related. The environment can be past or present. It can be inside the skin, accessible to only the behaving individual, or outside the skin, accessible to others. It can be exteroceptive, interoceptive, proprioceptive, hormonal, and so on. The environment of which a response is a function is outside of the response at the time the response occurs, but not necessarily outside of the skin. Moreover, behavior and its consequences at a given time are part of the environment that can enter into a functional relation with subsequent behavior. Analysis determines the nature of the functional relation between behavior and environment. Implicit in this view is that the organism is in "contact" with the environment. This contact is a necessary but not sufficient condition for an organism to respond with respect to it. To cite a common example, given that the upper range of human hearing is 20,000 Hz, an auditory stimulus of 30,000 Hz is not a feature of the environment with which a human's behavior is in contact.

In this view, behavior may be viewed as an event wherein a causal relation exists between (a) the functioning of one or more of an organism's neural or muscular systems responsible for movement or posture (including standing still); and (b) the environment. The functioning of the systems can be at any point along the continuum labeled central to peripheral. In addition, the environment with respect to which the functioning is causally related can be inside or outside the skin. The environment is that which is outside behavior (Hayes, 1984). Behavior is, then, an event that occurs when many different variables come together. The organism's genetics are to be included because they determine the receptivity to the environment with respect to which the organism responds, and the systems that do the responding. The behaving organism is the locus or the host of this entire process (Baer, 1976).

Some behavior analysts apply the "Dead Man's Test" to determine whether an event is behavior. By this test is meant that behavior should be regarded as something active or present; if something is passive or absent, such that a dead man could do it, then it isn't behavior. To be sure, such a conception can be valuable, as it focuses on the interactive sense of behavior. However, one might also take care that the conception doesn't limit practical action. For example, if individuals are troubled because they bite their fingernails and can't seem to stop, then presumably the goal of a therapeutic intervention is to get the individuals to not bite their fingernails. Clearly, dead men don't bite their fingernails. Nevertheless, it would seem that getting live individuals to not bite their fingernails is a meaningful objective. One can salvage an active sense of behavior implied by the Dead Man's Test by stating the objective of the therapeutic intervention in an alternative and positive way, as "growing one's fingernails." Presumably, the fingernails of dead men don't grow, but then what is useful is some specification of how long they must grow for the live individual, in what time frame, and so on.

What, then, about the nature of the functional relations between behavior and environment? A response is an event that has taken place in a particular setting at a particular time. The event involves an interaction between the organism and its stimulating environment. A variety of descriptors may be applied to characterize events as behavioral events, rather than events appropriate for other sciences (e.g., Kantor & Smith, 1975).

1. Behavioral events are variable and differential, as a function of the occasion on which they occur. That is, they are conditional on and modifiable by the properties of the environment to which they are related.

2. Behavioral events are developmental and integrative. That is, they represent adjustments that have taken place over the lifetime of the species or the lifetime of the individual organism to its environment, and they have served the species or the organism as it adapts to its environment.

Given these considerations, how does behavior as conceived by radical behaviorists differ from events studied in other sciences?

Consider the following simple example: Person A pushes person B, who then falls down. When person B falls down, is this event behavior? A radical behaviorist would say the movement of person B is not behavior. Rather, this event would be the subject matter of physics. Consider what would happen if A pushed B harder: Presumably, B would fall faster. This event entails a kind of commutative and mechanical interaction involving the transfer of energy that causes matter to be in motion. As such, the event is the subject matter of physics. The falling doesn't develop over the history of the species or the individual, and is conditional only in the sense that it depends on the transfer of energy by the push. Adjectives such as differential, integrative, variable, delayable, and even inhibitive don't meaningfully apply to falling down. If person B extended a hand to break the fall, the movement of the hand would be behavior, but not the fall itself.

Thus, the sense of behavior that is relevant to radical behaviorism is that it is an interaction between organism and environment that has particular properties as a result of certain functional relations that obtain between the features of the behavior and features of the environment. The interaction may have developed phylogenically or ontogenically, and represents a central characteristic of the organism as it progresses through its life cycle.

THE RELATION BETWEEN BEHAVIOR ANALYSIS AND NEUROSCIENCE

As stated above, behavior is an event that involves the functional relation between the movement or posture of the organism and certain features of the environment. Importantly, the study of behavior is not simply the study of the physiological mechanisms underlying movement. If the study of behavior were simply physiological mechanics, behavior analysis would reduce to something like kinesiology, or the study of the actual physiological interchange between muscles, joints, tendons, and sensory systems, as the study of the motion of the body or body segments around a joint in space and time and nothing else, such as what caused that motion.

With regard to physiology, then, do the above statements mean that physiological events inside the skin are irrelevant to the science of behavior? The answer here is no, but it is important to reconcile the distinctions at hand.

A comprehensive science of behavior is presumably concerned with two interrelated questions:

1. How is an organism's behavior functionally related to its environment?

2. How do the organism's neural, muscular, and hormonal systems participate in those functional relations?

Radical behaviorism is concerned with the first question and the relation between environmental circumstances and organism called behavior. These relations exist at many different levels in an organism's life (Catania & Harnad, 1988).

However, the second question differs from the first. Skinner (1974, p. 221) has pointed out that in a sense, there are two "gaps" in a behavior analytic account of a behavioral event. The first gap is within a behavioral event itself, as the organism comes in contact with the relevant environmental circumstances and eventually responds to them. Here, stimuli and responses are separated both temporally and spatially. The second gap is between the events of one occasion and the effect of those events on the organism's behavior, as measured on a future occasion. Here, contact with the environment on one day may cause a response to increase or decrease in similar circumstances on a subsequent day.

A science that differs from behavior analysis is needed to deal with the second question and fill the two gaps (Donahoe, 1996; Reese, 1996). Behavioral neuroscience is just that different science. It is concerned with the operating characteristics of the underlying neural, muscular, and hormonal systems (a) within a behavioral event and (b) between one behavioral event and the next. For example, within a behavioral event, behavioral neuroscientists might be interested in how an organism's neural, muscular, and hormonal systems provide continuity from the time the organism comes into contact with an antecedent stimulus through the time the response occurs. Alternatively, between behavioral events, behavioral neuroscientists might be interested in how an organism's neural, muscular, and hormonal systems provide continuity from one event to the effects of that event as measured in the future.

In this regard, readers may note that Skinner (1974) suggested that a different science is needed to "make the picture of human action more nearly complete" (p. 221). For the moment, it is important to emphasize that events providing the neural, muscular, and hormonal continuity spoken of above are not stimuli in the behavioral sense. If the events are construed as stimuli, the analysis remains at the behavioral level. The subject matter identified by the second question above is not environmental stimulation and therefore requires a categorically different science to address it. Moreover, the sophisticated scans and images (e.g., fMRI) that are much in vogue are therefore on the dependent variable side of things, rather than independent. They reveal physiological structures that are activated by the environment, or how those structures have been changed by interaction with the environment. They do not reveal machinery that is operated by entities from other dimensions.

Contributions of Behavioral Neuroscience to Causal Explanations of Behavioral Events

Given the distinction above between behavior analysis and neuroscience, the information that neuroscience provides may be summarized in the following way:

1. how neural, muscular, and hormonal systems provide continuity between stimulus and response within a behavioral event

2. how neural, muscular, and hormonal systems are changed by experience

3. how the changes in neural, muscular, and hormonal systems persist through time and influence future behavioral events

4. how a changed organism behaves differently in the future

5. how the internal biochemical context modulates stimulating action of the environment

Comparable contributions hold true for allied disciplines, such as behavioral pharmacology and behavioral toxicology, which study the effects of various substances on an organism's physiological and behavioral systems. The substances examined in such disciplines change the organism, by selectively affecting: (a) sensory systems permitting input or responsiveness to environmental stimulation, or (b) motor systems permitting output, or (c) links between sensory and motor systems, but the information provided in the allied disciplines remains the same as other branches of neuroscience.

A further contribution of neuroscience is heuristic. That is, the physiological information that fills the two gaps may suggest new possibilities for prediction and control. To be sure, techniques for behavioral control can be identified independently of any knowledge of physiology, and in any case their effectiveness as interventions can be determined independently of any knowledge of physiology. Moreover, if the resulting interventions and manipulations are effective, physiology will not disprove them, but rather reveal the mechanisms inside the skin by which they work.

Clearly, then, behavior analysis and neuroscience are complementary disciplines. Use of the term *complementary* implies that the more that is known of one factor, the less needs to be known of the other factor to predict or control behavior adequately. Thus, the term implies a sense of cooperative rather than competitive, mutually supportive rather than mutually exclusive, and reciprocal rather than restricting, but a sense that stops short of reductionism.

"Interaction" Between Nature and Nurture?

Sometimes nature and nurture are spoken of as "interacting," where by "nature" one means the biological factors one has inherited, and by "nurture" one means the environmental factors one has experienced during one's lifetime. This sort of language may now be critically examined. Behavior was earlier treated as an aspect of the interaction between organism and environment. For behavior to be a subject matter in its own right, the assumption is that the resulting behavior is orderly. The traditional albeit informal term that applies in such cases is that behavior is "caused."

However, the term *cause* has a variety of different meanings. The ancient Greek philosopher Aristotle proposed four senses of the word *cause*: efficient, formal, final, and material. The efficient cause is the mechanical action or force by which something is caused. The formal cause is the guiding principle according to which it is caused. The final cause is the purpose according to which it is caused. The material cause is the substance out of which something is realized. Aristotle's treatment is actually quite complex, but the common illustration is that of a statue: The efficient cause is the hand of the sculptor, the formal cause is the smaller model according to which the eventual life-sized statue is created, the final cause is the purpose of honoring a distinguished figure, and the material cause is the material out of which the statue is constructed, say bronze, marble, or clay.

Aristotle's categories can be interpreted in an abstract sense to apply to behavior analysis. Although Winston (1987) has argued persuasively against the present interpretation, perhaps the interpretation presented in Table 4–1 will nevertheless be useful for the purpose of illustration. This table seeks to interpret the sense of efficient, formal, final, and material causes in the language of behavior analysis. Accordingly, efficient causes may be interpreted in an abstract sense as the relation among environmental conditions that determine the response, formal causes as the occasion upon which the response occurs, final causes as the consequence of the response, and material causes as the physiology of the sentient and behaving organism. The table, then seeks to reflect the varied sense of the term cause, when questions dealing with why an object or event is what it is are addressed.

The term *interaction* implies a relation between two or more causes. Clearly, nature does interacts with nurture. In the same sense that the consistency of a lump of clay (a material cause) interacts with the forces created by hands of the sculptor (an efficient cause), so does the genetic endowment of the sentient, behaving organism (a material cause) interact with the forces created by the environment (an efficient cause). Indeed, it could not be otherwise. The lump of clay cannot form itself into a statue; the hands of the sculptor are necessary. Similarly, the organism necessarily lives in a stimulating environment, with respect to which it behaves. Features of the environment may activate or deactivate genes, resulting in quite different organisms, even though their genetics are ostensibly similar. Nevertheless, the point is the notion of interaction does not imply that the causes are necessarily of the same type. The clay of the statue is a material

TABLE 4.1

Aristotle's 4 causes	Ordinary language meaning	Statue	Behavior-analytic interpretation
efficient	That by the action of which	sculptor	Relation among environmental conditions
formal	That according to which	Design of small statue	occasion
final	That for the sake of which	To honor distinguished person	consequence
material	That from which	Bronze or clay	Physiology of sentient, behaving organism

cause, and not the same type of cause as the hands of the sculptor, which is an efficient cause. The physiology of the behaving organism is a material cause, and not the same type of cause as the environment, which is an efficient cause. Thus, neuroscience and behavior analysis deal with different kinds of causes.

Recall the two sciences address two different questions. In the present view, one must take care when using the term *interaction*, so that one does not imply that nature is the same type of cause as nurture. For example, one would not want to say that genetics and physiology are the same type of causes as those of the environment. Some of Skinner's objections to early explanations of behavior, which may be found in his definition of radical behaviorism in Chapter 1, revolved around the uncritical use of physiological factors as efficient causes. Skinner's point was that explanations need to take into account "the natural lines of fracture along which behavior and environment actually break" (Skinner, 1938, p. 33), and should not equate physiological factors with efficient causes.

Explanation and Physiological Reductionism?

The preceding section pointed out that Skinner talked of two "unavoidable gaps" in a behavioral analysis. The first is within a behavioral event. This gap starts with the time that a stimulus impinges on an individual and ends with a response that is a function of that same stimulus. The second is between behavioral events. This gap starts with a behavioral event at a given time and ends with the effect of that event as measured in the future. It is important to critically examine this and other instances of Skinner's language, because as noted in Chapter 1, that language is potentially very troublesome if not properly understood.

Given that behavior is a subject matter in its own right (Skinner, 1938, p. 440), then presumably explanations of behavior do not have to engage it at a different level to be valid. Indeed, readers will recall that Skinner's definition of radical behaviorism in Chapter 1 explicitly cautioned against internal explanations of behavior, both mental and physiological. Elsewhere, however, Skinner said:

> Eventually, we may assume, the facts and principles of psychology will be reducible not only to physiology but through biochemistry to physics and subatomic physics. (Skinner, 1972, p. 303)

and

> I agree that "only an account of the machinery within the skin can explain behavior." (Skinner in Catania & Harnad, 1988, p. 334)

The use of such terms as "reducible" and "only," as well as the entire "gaps" argument is potentially troubling because such language implies that a behavioral account is necessarily limited in principle, and that it can never identify all the relevant factors that are necessary to secure an adequate explanation. Ironically, Skinner might appear to be guilty of some version of reductionism here, by saying that explanations in behavior analysis are really limited in principle, because they don't identify underlying physiological mechanisms, and that behavior analysis is just something clever to do until a sufficiently sophisticated neuroscience comes along and provides the "ultimate" and "complete" explanations for behavior in terms of those mechanisms.

One way to resolve the problem of reductionism and reconcile Skinner's apparently divergent language is to recognize that neurophysiology is concerned with how underlying systems participate in functional relations between the organism and environment (Skinner, 1969, p. 283). As suggested in Chapter 1, if the current neural, muscular, or hormonal states of an organism are known, those states may be used as a basis for prediction, manipulation, and control of the organism's behavior, instead of a possibly inadequate specification of the history of interaction between the organism and environment. In this view, behavior analysis and neuroscience provide mutual and reciprocal support for each other; neuroscience does not provide the logical grounds for validating explanations of behavior. Behavior analysis and a theoretical behavioral neuroscience may therefore be regarded as complementary sciences, in the pragmatic sense of mutually supporting. In a more practical vein, physiological information, such as how an organism has been changed by interactions with its environment during its lifetime, can compensate for a possibly inadequate specification of behavioral interactions as a basis for making predictions or taking direct action. Overall, behavior analysis gives neuroscience one of its directions, in the same sense that Mendel's studies of the numerical relations among the traits of successive generations of pea plants gave the study of the gene one of its directions (e.g., Catania & Harnad, 1988, p. 470).

Pragmatic Basis

More formally, then, if a primary goal of behavioral science is to predict, influence, manipulate, or control behavior, or to provide a sufficient data base that makes such actions possible, then the following conclusions are appropriate:

1. In principle, knowledge from either behavior analysis or neuroscience can serve as adequate basis for attempts to predict, influence, manipulate, or control behavior.

2. If knowledge from one domain is limited, attempts to predict, influence, manipulate, or control behavior on the basis of that knowledge might be made more effective if they are informed by the other science.

3. Neuroscience is not necessary to provide the logical or empirical grounds for validating behavior-analytic theories, explanations, or technological advances.

The link between behavior analysis and either genetics or neuroscience is therefore pragmatic. Each science can inform the other in its characteristic way, but genetics and neuroscience are not necessary to validate behavior-analytic explanations, any more than behavior analysis is necessary to validate explanations in genetics or neuroscience.

The Charge of the "Empty Organism"

One of the common charges against the adequacy of behavior analysis is that it deals with an "empty organism" or with the organism as a "black box." The charge usually comes about when critics hold that behavior analysis deals only with publicly observable variables and relations, and that restricting an analysis to publicly observable variables and relations is inadequate. The charge goes that variables or relations inside the organism need to be taken into account, and behavior analysis doesn't do that. The variables and relations inside the organism are expressly held to not be behavioral because they are not publicly observable. Consequently, the charge goes, they need to be taken into account as either physiological or "mental" in nature. The charge of an empty organism was made early on by E. G. Boring, one of Skinner's graduate school mentors in the Harvard department, when Boring responded to drafts of Skinner's dissertation in the late fall of 1930. In his dissertation, Skinner was seeking to rehabilitate the concept of the reflex by stripping it of any reference to hypothesized neural events, and Boring questioned Skinner about his tactics.

Radical behaviorism rejects the entire line of reasoning that underlies the charge of an empty organism. Radical behaviorism is explicitly concerned with variables and relations that are inside the organism, although it views these variables and relations differently from traditional psychology. The way that radical behaviorism takes into account behavioral variables that are not publicly observable is taken up in Chapter 10 on private behavioral events. The pragmatic, complementary way that physiological variables are taken into account in radical behaviorism was reviewed earlier in the present chapter. Again, the important explanatory relation is not reductionism. Radical behaviorists reject the reductionistic assertion that behavior cannot be considered to be explained until the physiological mechanism involved in the behavior has been identified. Rather, radical behaviorists hold that neuroscience and behavior analysis each deals with a unique subject matter in its own terms, at a descriptively consistent level. Indeed, it is mentalistic to attribute homuncular causal efficacy to any sort of variables inside the skin, whether they are presumed to be physiological or "mental" or "theoretical." The following passage from Skinner (1972) is representative:

> This does not mean, of course, that the organism is conceived of as actually empty, or that continuity between input and output will not eventually be established. The genetic development of

the organism and complex interchanges between organism and environment are the subject matters of appropriate disciplines. Some day we shall know, for example, what happens when a stimulus impinges upon the surface of an organism, and what happens inside the organism after that, in a series of stages the last of which is the point at which the organism acts upon the environment and possibly changes it.... But all these inner events will be accounted for with the techniques of observation and measurement appropriate to the physiology of the various parts of the organism, and the account will be expressed in terms appropriate to that subject matter. It would be a remarkable coincidence if the concepts now used to refer inferentially to inner events were to find a place in that account.... A comprehensive set of causal relations stated with the greatest possible precision is the best contribution which we, as students of behavior, can make in the co-operative venture of giving a full account of the organism as a biological system. (pp. 269–270)

In short, an organism's physiology necessarily participates in every behavioral event. A behavioral event wouldn't have occurred without the participation of the organism's physiology, in some fashion and at some level. Knowledge of the physiology that has participated is information about the event that is available for the purposes of prediction and control. However, the full formulation of the behavioral event as an event would also properly include the environmental circumstances of which the behavior is a function. Restricting the formulation to simply physiological factors inside the skin necessarily limits the scope of the explanation and restricts the possibilities for prediction and control.

SUMMARY AND CONCLUSIONS: THE COMPLEMENTARITY OF BEHAVIOR ANALYSIS AND BEHAVIORAL NEUROSCIENCE

Behavior analysis and neuroscience support each other by virtue of their respective contributions to direct action, as opposed to any supposed logical connection. Direct, effective action with respect to behavior (prediction, influence, manipulation, control) can be predicated on knowledge of: (a) environmental history, and (b) neural, muscular, or hormonal states produced through a history of interactions with the environment. The former is the scope of behavior analysis, whereas the latter is the scope of neuroscience.

An independent science of behavior as a function of environmental circumstances is therefore appropriate for at least three reasons. First, individuals may not know how to control a given instance of behavior through direct neural, muscular, or hormonal interventions, but they would be able to control behavior by manipulating environmental circumstances. Second, even if individuals do know how to control behavior through direct neural, muscular, or hormonal interventions, implementing these interventions may not always be practical in a given instance. Third, a behavioral technology is propaedeutic to discovering the functional relevance of information about the current neural, muscular, or hormonal state of the behaving organism, where that state has been produced through interactions with the environment or through neural, muscular, or hormonal interventions that have modified the organism, such that it responds differently from otherwise to stimulation in its environment. Skinner (1938) quoted Ernst Mach (1914) to support his point:

> It often happens that the development of two different fields of science goes along side by side for long periods, without either of them exercising an influence on the other. On occasion, again, they may come into closer contact, when it is noticed that unexpected light is thrown on the doctrines of the one by the doctrines of the other. In that case a natural tendency may even be manifested to allow the first field to be completely absorbed in the second. But the period of buoyant hope, the period of over-estimation of this relation which is supposed to explain everything, is quickly followed by a period of disillusionment, when the two fields in question are once more separated, and each pursues its own aims, putting its own special questions and applying its own methods. But on both of them the temporary contact leaves abiding traces behind. Apart from the positive addition to knowledge, which is not to be despised, the temporary relation between them brings about a transformation of our conceptions, clarifying them and permitting of their application over a wider field than that for which they were originally formed. (Skinner, 1938, p. 432)

The possibilities of such an effective interchange between the life sciences are just beginning to be realized. Given that behavior is a function of interaction with the environment, different categories of that interaction give rise to different categories of behavior. Those categories are the subject of Chapter 5.

TABLE 4.2

Definitions

Etymology of Behavior
from Latin habere, French avoir, old English behabban. The original sense was as a possession, rather than as movement, activity, or conduct.

Watson (1919)
"We should mean by response the total striped and unstriped muscular and glandular changes which follow upon a given stimulus" (p. 14).
Categories: (a) external, overt, explicit; (b) internal, covert, implicit; (c) learned, habit; (d) innate, hereditary

Skinner
Behavior is what an organism is doing—or more accurately what it is observed by another organism to be doing.... It is more to the point to say that behavior is that part of the functioning of an organism which is engaged in acting upon or having commerce with the outside world.... By behavior, then, I mean simply the move-

ment of an organism or of its parts in a frame of reference provided by the organism itself or by various external objects or fields of force. (Skinner, 1938, pp. 6, 34)

Skinner
"I would define behavior as the movement of an organism in space with respect to itself or any other useful frame of reference" (Skinner in Evans, 1976, p. 84).

Johnston and Pennypacker (1993)
The behavior of an organism is that portion of the organism's interaction with its environment that is characterized by detectable displacement in space through time of some part of the organism and that results in a measurable change in at least one aspect of the environment. (p. 23)

Two questions in a science of behavior
1. How is an organism's behavior functionally related to its environment?
2. How do the organism's neural, muscular, and hormonal systems participate in those functional relations?

Two gaps in which information from neuroscience is relevant
1. Within a behavioral event, from stimulus to response
2. Between behavioral events, from one event to its effects as measured in the future

Contributions of neuroscience to a science of behavior
1. How neural, muscular, and hormonal systems provide continuity between stimulus and response within a behavioral event
2. How neural, muscular, and hormonal systems are changed by experience
3. How the changes in neural, muscular, and hormonal systems persist through time and influence future behavioral events
4. How a changed organism behaves differently in the future
5. How the internal biochemical context modulates stimulating action of the environment

Aristotle's four causes
   efficient: that by the action of which;
   formal: that according to which;
   final: that for the sake of which;
   material: that from which

Complementarity between behavior analysis and behavioral neuroscience
Effective action with respect to behavior (prediction, influence, manipulation, control) can be predicated on knowledge of either (a) environmental history or (b) neural, muscular, or hormonal states produced through a history of interactions with the environment, during the lifetime of the species or that of an individual organism. Behavior analysis provides the first category of information. Neuroscience provides the second. The more of either is known, the less of the other is needed for direct, effective action.

REFERENCES

Baer, D. M. (1976). The organism as host. *Human Development, 19,* 87–98.

Bryant, D., & Church, R. M. (1974). The determinants of random choice. *Animal Learning & Behavior, 2,* 245–248.

Catania, A. C. (2007). *Learning* (4th interim ed.). Cornwall-on-Hudson, NY: Sloan Publishing.

Catania, A. C., & Harnad, S. (Eds.). (1988). *The selection of behavior: The operant behaviorism of B. F. Skinner: Comments and controversies.* Cambridge: Cambridge University Press.

Donahoe, J. (1996). On the relation between behavior analysis and biology. *The Behavior Analyst, 19,* 71–73.

Evans, R. I. (1976). *The making of psychology.* New York: Knopf.

Hayes, S. C. (1984). But whose behaviorism is it? A review of Barry Schwartz and Hugh Lacey, *Behaviorism, Science, and Human Nature. Contemporary Psychology, 29,* 203–206.

Johnston, J., & Pennypacker, H. (1993). *Strategies and tactics of behavioral research (2nd edition).* Hillsdale, NJ: Erlbaum.

Kantor, J. R., & Smith, N. (1975). *The science of psychology.* Chicago, IL: Principia Press.

Mach, E. (1914). *The analysis of sensations* (English translation). Chicago, IL: Open Court.

Neuringer, A. (1986). Can people behavior "randomly"? The role of feedback. *Journal of Experimental Psychology: General, 115,* 62–75.

Page, S., & Neuringer, A. (1985). Variability is an operant. *Journal of Experimental Psychology: Animal Behavior Processes, 11,* 429–452.

Pryor, K., Haag, R., & O'Reilly, J. (1969). The creative porpoise: Training for novel behavior. *Journal of the Experimental Analysis of Behavior, 12,* 653–661.

Reese, H. W. (1996). How is physiology relevant to behavior analysis? *The Behavior Analyst, 19,* 61–70.

Skinner, B. F. (1938). *The behavior of organisms.* New York: Appleton-Century-Crofts.

Skinner, B. F. (1953). *Science and human behavior.* New York: Macmillan.

Skinner, B. F. (1957). *Verbal behavior.* New York: Appleton-Century-Crofts.

Skinner, B. F. (1969). *Contingencies of reinforcement.* New York: Appleton-Century-Crofts.

Skinner, B. F. (1972). *Cumulative record.* New York: Appleton-Century-Crofts.

Skinner, B. F. (1974). *About behaviorism.* New York: Knopf.

Skinner, B. F. (1985). Reply to Place: "Three senses of the word 'tact'." *Behaviorism, 13,* 75–76.

Watson, J. B. (1913). Psychology as the behaviorist views it. *Psychological Review, 20,* 158–177.

Watson, J. B. (1914). *Behavior: An introduction to comparative psychology.* New York: Henry Holt.

Watson, J. B. (1919). *Psychology from the standpoint of a behaviorist.* Philadelphia, PA: Lippincott.

Watson, J. B. (1925). *Behaviorism.* New York: Norton.

Winston, A. S. (1987). The use and misuse of Aristotle's four causes in psychology: A case of obscurum per obscurius. In S. Bem & H. Rappard (Eds.), *Studies in the history of psychology and the social sciences: Vol. 4. Proceedings of the 1985 conference of CHEIRON, the European Society for the History of the Behavioral and Social Sciences,* pp. 90–103. Leiden, Netherlands: Psychologish Instituut van de Rijksuniversiteit Leiden.

STUDY QUESTIONS

1. List one Latin, one French, and one old English cognate to which the English term behavior is etymologically related.

2. List any three terms in the contemporary English language that are synonymous with behavior.

3. State or paraphrase Watson's (1919) definition of behavior.

4. State or paraphrase Skinner's (1938) definition of behavior.

5. State or paraphrase Johnston and Pennypacker's (1993) definition of behavior.

6. State or paraphrase the definition of behavior offered on p. 66, beginning with the words "In this view, behavior may be viewed as an event ..."

7. State or paraphrase what is meant by the Dead Man's Test.

8. Describe why radical behaviorists do not regard person B's falling down after being pushed by person A as behavior.

9. Describe how radical behaviorists subsume novel behavior under the definition of behavior.

10. Describe how radical behaviorists subsume perceptual behavior under the definition of behavior.

11. Describe how radical behaviorists subsume covert behavior under the definition of behavior.

12. State or paraphrase the two interrelated questions with which a comprehensive science of behavior is presumably concerned.

13. Describe the two gaps that Skinner believes pertain to a behavior-analytic account of a behavioral event. Indicate which gap is filled by neuroscience, and which by behavior analysis. Indicate why behavior analysis is not a reductionistic position.

14. Describe five kinds of information that neuroscience provides to an understanding of a behavioral event.

15. Describe why it is troublesome to talk of an interaction between nature and nurture.

16. Describe how Aristotle's concept of four causes relates to the distinction between neuroscience and behavior analysis.

17. State or paraphrase three conclusions that support a pragmatic, complementary relation between neuroscience and behavior analysis.

18. State or paraphrase the radical behaviorist response to the charge that behavior analysis deals with an empty organism.

5

Categories of Behavior

Synopsis of Chapter 5: The chapters in this first section review the foundation of radical behaviorism. To this end, Chapters 2 and 3 examined the history of behavior analysis. These chapters argued that the behavioral revolution occurred over two successive phases: classical behaviorism and mediational neobehaviorism. Behavior analysis began at approximately the same time as mediational neobehaviorism, but differed in a number of ways. Chapter 4 examined the principle that behavior is a subject matter in its own right. It examined various definitions of behavior, and sought to clarify the important relation between behavioral neuroscience and behavior analysis. Chapter 5 continues to develop the thesis that behavior is a subject matter in its own right by examining various categories of behavior and the criteria for distinguishing them. Radical behaviorism uses a conceptually consistent system to distinguish these categories. The system is based on the environmental conditions of which the behavior is a function: stimulus presentation operations, consequential operations, signaling operations. The chapter examines both innate and learned behavior, but gives particular attention to conditioned respondent behavior and operant behavior.

Sciences often categorize their subject matter so that they can deal more effectively with it. Behavior analysts categorize their subject matter—behavior—on the basis of the environmental variables and relations responsible for its origin, as well as those of which the behavior is a function in a given instance. Moreover, behavior analysts recognize those variables and relations may have acquired their functional significance at the phylogenic level, during the evolutionary history of the species, and at the ontogenic level, during the lifetime of the individual organism. One of the benefits of these various forms of analytical efforts is the development of a set of terms and concepts that are appropriate to the prediction and control of the behavior in question. The present chapter explores the taxonomy of behavior from the perspective of behavior analysis and radical behaviorism.

The analytical efforts that underlie a taxonomy of behavior take place in three phases. Although behavior analysts do not necessarily conduct a controlled laboratory analysis in each phase, behavior analysts still proceed in accordance with known principles throughout. The first phase is to assess what variables and relations are in effect in the current environment. It is useful to describe these variables and relations by noting that three operations could conceivably be influencing the organism: (a) a stimulus presentation operation (also called an eliciting operation), (b) a consequential operation, or (c) a signaling operation related to the eliciting or consequential operations (Catania, 2007). Stimulus presentations involve presenting a stimulus to an organism. The stimulus then elicits one or another form of behavior. The terms stimulus and stimulus presentation are used here in a generic sense, to indicate the numerous ways organisms can come into contact with features of the environment. These features range from a broad complex of antecedent environmental circumstances having many individual features, including temperature, humidity, and sun position, to particular or discrete stimuli, such as food or loud noises or electric shocks. Consequential operations involve arranging for a response to have some consequence. The temporal sequence is relevant here, if only as the necessary property of the consequential operation: The response occurs, and the correlated consequence follows. Sometimes the term consequence implies a discrete event, such as the presentation of food or the cessation of shock. At other times, consequences entail broader changes in the environment, such as the opportunity to engage in a form of behavior. Signaling operations involve correlating a characteristic antecedent stimulus with one of the other two operations, namely, by signaling that the state of the environment on that occasion is such that: (a) an eliciting stimulus is forthcoming, or (b) a response customarily has a particular consequence.

The second phase is to observe whether instances of the target behavior become more or less probable, given the operations noted above.

The third phase is to determine that the change in the probability of the target behavior is a function of contact with the relevant relation in the environment, and not because some other environmental relation is involved and has been overlooked.

The nature of the operations of which the change in probability of behavior is a function then determines the category of that behavior and the vocabulary appropriate to it.

STIMULUS PRESENTATIONS AND INNATE BEHAVIOR

One of the most common distinctions pertaining to the analysis of behavior is between innate and learned behavior. Innate behavior is a function of the stimulus presentation operation. Again, for purposes of exposition, this operation may be described as involving unitary discrete stimuli. However, in the world at large, organisms may come into contact with combinations or patterns of stimuli in particular settings or contexts. Behavior analysts regard an organism's behavior as innate when the environmental circumstances of which it is a function are related more to the lifetime of the species of which the organism is a member, rather than repeated, specific experiences over the lifetime of the individual organism. Allowing for maturational or other forms of developmental changes, innate behavior is further recognized by its relatively uniform, stereotyped topography across a species in response to contact with specific stimuli or environmental situations.

To use birds as an example, birds fly when they leave the nest, they mate, they build nests, and they sing songs for a variety of different reasons, ranging from attracting mates to proclaiming themselves present in a particular territory. When birds do so, their behavior is not necessarily acquired piecemeal over a long series of exposures involving interactions with the environment during their lifetime. The behavior is a function of contact with a large set of complex environmental conditions and relations. Conditions in the external environment, such as ambient air temperature and position of the sun, play a role. There obviously has to be material available in the environment out of which to build a nest. Hearing a conspecific sing its song at a critical time is relevant to the bird's being able to sing the song itself. In addition, conditions in the internal environment are significant: One of the important factors that contributes to nest building is the presence of certain levels of reproductive hormones. Nevertheless, these forms of behavior are appropriately understood as having developed in particular circumstances over the evolutionary history of the species, rather than over the lifetime of the individual organism, and their ultimate appearance is a function of the prevailing circumstances in the environment.

The various forms of innate behavior are more often the subject matter for ethologists than behavior analysts. Often ethologists describe the behavior as having been released by contact with stimuli. The common examples of innate behavior are unconditioned reflexes, tropisms, kineses, and taxes. There are also sequences of innate behavior. A common example here is the fixed action pattern. Finally, there are reaction chains, which are further sequences of behavior but involving both innate and learned behavior. Again, these definitions do not specify some essence of the behavior being defined. Rather, the definitions simply reflect the behavior being talked about and the conditions of which it is a function. In each case the important conditions are the antecedent conditions in the environment.

Reflex

A reflex is a class of responses in an isolated muscle, gland, or single behavioral system that is elicited by the presentation of a specific stimulus. In the middle 1930s, Skinner developed a set of slightly different terms for the analysis of behavior, one of which was the term "respondent" instead of "reflex"; accordingly, the term *respondent* is used in this chapter. If the stimulus reliably elicits the response in question without any unique post-natal experiences, the stimulus is called an unconditioned stimulus (US) and the response is called an unconditioned respondent. Characteristically, a respondent occurs reliably and with a short latency after the presentation of the relevant stimulus. The topography of a given respondent is determined by the stimulus involved, and ordinarily does not vary widely from instance to instance within a species when a given stimulus is used. Common examples are salivation to food in the mouth, or increased heart rate, breathing, or perspiration to an electric shock.

Tropism

A tropism is a change in the orientation of an organism in response to external fields of force. A common example is geotropism: Organisms that are manually inverted by a researcher will right themselves in response to gravity. Many researchers further distinguish between two kinds of tropisms: kineses and taxes.

Kinesis

A kinesis is an instance of behavior in which a stimulus produces a change in movement or orientation, irrespective of the direction of that movement. The movement involves the whole organism. A common example is that of a wood louse, which prefers dark, humid areas. If placed in a dry area, the louse simply begins to move about. It stops when it reaches a dark, moist area.

Taxis

A taxis is an instance of behavior in which a stimulus produces guided, oriented movements carried out with respect to an eliciting stimulus. The response is guided by feedback, which is to say the nature and extent of continuing contact with the eliciting stimulus. A common example is that of egg retrieval by a goose. If an egg rolls away from its nest, the goose will extend its neck toward the egg and roll it back toward the nest with the underside of its bill. It constantly adjusts the way it maintains contact with the egg, based on the terrain and how the irregular shape of the egg is causing it to roll.

Fixed Action Pattern (FAP)

A FAP is a pattern of behavior in which the response is:

1. stereotyped within a species

2. released via a specific stimulus (often called the "releasing stimulus"), after which it is relatively independent of immediate environmental context and feedback In addition, there can be some variability in the releasing stimuli, and there is a refractory period after the response is released. Ethologists sometimes refer to the releasing stimuli as sign stimuli, in the sense that the stimuli are signs that release the response in question. FAPs can be embedded in a sequence of other actions, which may be either innate or learned.

3. innate

Common examples of FAPs are the major components in:

1. Feeding

2. Mating and reproduction

3. Nesting

4. Social activities, rituals

5. Fighting, attack, aggression

The stimuli that release the behavior in question are critical. The ability of the stimuli to release the behavior can depend on the internal or hormonal environment, the external or contextual environment, as well as particular features of the stimuli. Sometimes relational features or configurations of the stimulus are important. For example, when parent birds bring food to nestling birds, the nestlings will open their beaks ("gape") at the sight of the parents' bills with the food, and the parents will then deliver the food to the nestlings. Research has investigated what features will release the gaping by manipulating various features of models of the parents' beaks, such as length, thickness, and coloration. This research has shown that the nestlings will gape at models based on their proportions to other elements, rather than their absolute properties. However, sometimes artificially exaggerated features of a stimulus, well beyond anything that occurs naturally, will release and control more behavior than the natural stimulus it models. Such stimuli are called supernormal stimuli. Research has shown that when a bird is presented with two eggs, one of which is artificially enlarged and the other of which is normal-sized, the bird will incubate the enlarged egg.

Two curious forms of innate behavior are vacuum activity and displacement activity. Vacuum activity is a FAP released in the apparent absence of the usual sign stimuli. An example would be a predator that performs a complete sequence of movements, such as is involved in hunting and attacking prey, even though no prey seems to be present. Displacement activity is when a conflict between two innate behaviors results in a third, qualitatively different (and perhaps even paradoxical) form of behavior. A dog that meets another dog and is in conflict between dominant and submissive postures may scratch itself.

Reaction chains are sequences or combinations of innate and environmentally determined responses in which progression from one response to the next depends on an appropriate external stimulus. Reaction chains are similar to FAPs, but each response requires an appropriate stimulus to release it. Portions of the chain may even be skipped if the appropriate releasing stimuli are not present. Mazur (2002) describes the reaction chain of a hermit crab searching for and selecting a new shell in which to live. The hermit crab does not live in its own shell. Rather, it lives in shells abandoned by others. After growing too large for its previous shell, the crab begins searching for a new one. Upon encountering a new shell, the crab follows a fixed pattern of behavior as it examines its features, inspects the opening, removes debris, and positions the shell for occupancy. The sequence may cease at any point if the stimulus setting for the next step does not occur, and some steps in the sequence may be omitted if a future stimulus occurs.

A Closer Look at Unconditioned Respondents: Contact with an Eliciting Stimulus

In preparation for a discussion of learning based on elicited behavior, an unconditioned respondent may be analyzed as follows:

1. An identifiable target response is observed in one or more of the organism's response systems when the organism comes into contact with a particular stimulus.

2. The probability of the target response increases when the organism has come into contact with the stimulus.

3. The increased probability of the target response is a function of the contact with the stimulus, rather than some other environmental relation.

The "other environmental relation" is that there could be instances in which the response is followed by the stimulus, rather than elicited by the contact with the stimulus per se. To use Pavlov's dogs as an example, they could be salivating because salivating is occasionally followed by food, even if after a delay, rather than because the food is eliciting the salivation. To determine if responding is a function of the temporal sequence of response-stimulus instead of the antecedent eliciting contact with the stimulus, one would explicitly control contact with the stimulus. For example, one could arrange for the target response to prevent the stimulus from occurring for some designated period of time. In the case of Pavlov's dogs above, if responding continues when it prevents contact with the food, then presumably the responding is not a function of the response-stimulus temporal sequence.

SIGNALING OPERATIONS, CONSEQUENTIAL OPERATIONS, AND LEARNED BEHAVIOR

In contrast to innate behavior is learned behavior. A common definition of learning comes from a textbook of some years ago:

> Learning is a relatively permanent change in response potentiality which occurs as a result of reinforced practice. (Kimble, 1961, p. 481)

Interestingly, this definition posits learning as an intervening internal state or entity (response potentiality), often hypothetical, that mediates the relation between stimulus events and the ensuing behavior. It specifies the stimulus events in terms of reinforced practice, to distinguish changes in behavior that might occur from simple maturation, injury, fatigue, or drugs.

As described in Chapter 3, radical behaviorism typically avoids appealing to mediational processes. Therefore, an alternative definition of learning is as follows: Learning is the name used to describe changes in behavior that occur as a result of particular post-natal experiences. The changes in behavior are changes in the topography of a response, the properties of a response, or in the circumstances in which a given response occurs. The post-natal experiences involve contact with stimulus events and relations in the environment, rather than events that involve tissue damage or chemical intervention. The study of learning is concerned with identifying the manner in which particular post-natal experiences are effective, and with formulating the processes by which the change of behavior occurs.

This alternative definition treats learning as simply a label for a change in the topography of behavior, the properties of behavior (e.g., force, duration, tempo, rate), or in the circumstances in which a given class of behavior occurs. A further distinction that some researchers make is between nonassociative and associative learning. Examples of nonassociative learning are habituation and sensitization. Habituation is diminished responding elicited by a stimulus after repeated contact with a stimulus. Sensitization is enhanced responding elicited by a stimulus after repeated contact with a stimulus. In these two cases, the change in behavior is a change in the topography of the response, and is brought about by a single experimental operation—the repeated presentation of a stimulus. Whether one observes habituation or sensitization after repeated presentations of a stimulus depends on the specific stimulus and the specific response system being stimulated. Nonassociative learning is often regarded as the simplest form of behavioral adjustment. Associative learning involves experimental operations in which stimulus events in the environment are correlated either with each other or with behavior. Given this distinction, two of the most commonly studied forms of learned behavior are conditioned respondents and operants.

More is said in the next section of this chapter about conditioned respondents and operants. At this point, some follow-up questions may now be asked about learning, and answers supplied:

1. Why does behavior change? Because the organism finds itself in changed environmental circumstances. Organisms whose behavior doesn't change when environmental circumstances change probably won't survive.

2. What aspects of the changed environmental circumstances are functionally related to the changes in behavior? Answers to this question come from a science of behavior. Indeed, this question virtually sets the program for a science of behavior.

3. Why do changed circumstances produce changes in behavior? Given that questions 1 and 2 have been answered as above, the answer to this question comes from neuroscience. When an organism's behavior changes, its physiology has presumably changed. Organisms whose physiology doesn't change when environmental circumstances change won't survive.

4. What physiological changes take place in an organism's body when it is said to have learned? As before, answers to these questions come from neuroscience. Indeed, this question virtually sets the program for neuroscience.

In sum, in this series of rhetorical questions, questions 1 and 2 concern behavior analysis. Questions 3 and 4 are related, but as discussed in Chapter 4, in light of the sense of "Why ...?" and "What ...?" in questions 1 and 2, those questions concern neuroscience.

Traditional treatments often distinguish between learning and performance. Learning is regarded as the process of acquisition, related to change in the intervening, hypothetical mediator, and performance is regarded as merely the evidence supporting inferences that learning has taken place. According to this traditional treatment, learning may not involve motivation, whereas performance surely does. Radical behaviorism does not observe this distinction in the same way as traditional approaches. In particular, learning is not regarded as some intervening, internal, hypothetical state, process, or entity about which inferences are made, in the sense of Kimble's (1961) definition. At issue for radical behaviorism is how the subject's current repertoire relates to the eventual repertoire. What environmental conditions facilitate the development of the eventual repertoire? What current elements of the subject's repertoire interfere with that development? What conditions are necessary to maintain the eventual repertoire? Have any unanticipated events taken place, either in the transition between current and eventual repertoires, or once the eventual repertoire is established, that have facilitated or interfered with the behavior? These questions are all practical ones, to be answered empirically on the basis of observations. To be concerned with a distinction between learning and performance as is traditional psychology is to be misled by unwarranted assumptions about the nature of behavior.

CONDITIONED RESPONDENT BEHAVIOR

The Signaling Operation in Combination with a Stimulus Presentation Operation

As suggested earlier in this chapter, the experimental operations can also be combined. One talks of a conditioned respondent when a signaling operation is combined with the stimulus presentation operation. In a conditioned respondent, a stimulus (call it stimulus A) doesn't originally elicit the response in question. However, it comes to do so when it signals an increased probability that another stimulus (call it stimulus B, or the US), which already elicits the response, will be presented. Stimulus A is then called a conditioned stimulus (CS). Some other terms or phrases that are often used to denote the relation between the signaling operation involving the CS and the stimulus presentation operation involving the US are "paired," "associated," "correlated," or "presented in conjunction with." One can also say an explicit elicitation contingency is an effect that involves two terms: (a) the CS, and (b) the US. The notion of a contingency implies an "if-then and not otherwise" relation. According to an elicitation contingency, if the CS is present, then the US will follow and the US will not be presented otherwise.

The topography of a conditioned respondent is determined by the nature of stimuli involved, and does not vary widely from instance to instance when a given stimulus elicits it. Nevertheless, conditioned respondents are defined functionally, rather than structurally or topographically. That is, all responses produced by a given stimulus or set of stimuli are considered to be members of the same conditioned respondent class. Classical conditioning and Pavlovian conditioning may be regarded as synonymous terms for respondent conditioning.

In summary, given the operations described above, a conditioned respondent may be analyzed as follows:

1. A signaling operation and a stimulus presentation operation are in effect. In other words, the state of the environment is such that a characteristic antecedent stimulus (the CS) is correlated with the impending presentation of the US.

2. The probability of the target response in the presence of the CS increases when the CS-US elicitation contingency is in effect: that is, when the CS is correlated with the US.

3. The increased probability of the target response is a function of the CS-US elicitation contingency, rather than some other environmental relation.

ASSESSING CONDITIONED RESPONDENT FUNCTIONAL RELATIONS

The simplest way to address the third matter above and to determine whether responding is functionally related to the presentation of the US is to alter the relation between the CS and US, and see what happens to behavior. This relation could be altered in either of two ways. One is to withhold the US for a series of trials. The second is to present the US independently of the CS, sometimes when the CS is present, and sometimes when it is not. If responding decreases in each case, then the way is clear to label the behavior as conditioned respondent behavior.

Nevertheless, in situations when the US is presented, there is another environmental relation that is implicit in the setting that could conceivably be involved. That is, responding could be a function of instances in which responding in the presence of the CS is followed by the US in a manner similar to a consequential operation, rather than elicited by virtue of the CS-US contingency per se. To return to Pavlov's dogs as an example, they could be salivating in the presence of the CS because of some adventitious temporal correlation between the salivation and food at the end of the trial. This adventitious temporal correlation is superficially similar to the temporal relations that are explicitly arranged when a consequential operation is in effect. Hence, the behavior may be occurring because of this superficial similarity, rather than the CS-US elicitation contingency.

To determine whether responding is a function of the adventitious temporal sequence of response-stimulus instead of the CS-US elicitation contingency, one would make some form of a consequential operation explicit in the setting. For example, one would arrange for the target response to prevent the US from occurring on that trial, as mentioned earlier in this chapter. The technical name for this manipulation is the omission procedure. The procedure gains its name because the US is omitted if the target response occurs. Note that on trials when the response does not occur, the US is presented, reinstating the CS-US relation. If responding continues when it prevents the US, then one concludes the responding is not a function of the response-stimulus temporal sequence. If responding is eliminated when it prevents the US, then one concludes the responding is a function of the temporal sequence of response-stimulus.

Another way to investigate whether the response occurring to the CS is being influenced by an adventitious temporal sequence of response-stimulus is to explicitly arrange for the response to modify the US. For example, if shock is the US, one might arrange for the response to reduce the intensity of the shock. Across different conditions in which the intensity of the shock is reduced to increasingly greater degrees, if responding becomes increasingly stronger, then presumably the responding is a function of an adventitious correlation between responding and food. If responding is relatively stable and consistent, even though properties of the US are modified as a consequence of the response, then presumably the responding is a function of the CS-US relations.

The field of respondent conditioning is concerned with identifying the many ways the CS can be correlated with the US to produce conditioning. Moreover, conditioning operations can in principle be applied to the other forms of innate behavior. One might investigate conditioning involving a taxis or fixed action pattern, for example. Of course, not every form of innate behavior is going to be susceptible to a conditioning operation. However, whether a given form is susceptible can clearly be determined empirically.

OPERANT BEHAVIOR

The Signaling Operation in Combination with a Consequential Operation

Operant behavior is defined as behavior that occurs because of its consequences. In other words, operant behavior is a function of a consequential operation. Instances of a given operant are members of a class. Membership in the class is defined by a common functional property, which is that they produce the same consequence. As Skinner (1938) noted, the various instances are quantitatively mutually replaceable. The term *operant* stands in contrast to the term *respondent* in the analysis of behavior. Operants are said to be "emitted," rather than "elicited." The topography of a given operant is a function of the environmental operations that are necessary to produce the consequence and is not dictated by the nature of the stimuli involved, as for a respondent. Thus, the specific topography of an operant could conceivably vary from instance to instance. Again, operants are defined functionally, rather than structurally or topographically. That is, all responses that produce the same consequence are considered to be members of the same operant class, even though their topographies may differ. (Of course, an arrangement can exist where a given consequence is produced only when the response is of the same, prescribed topography.) Instrumental learning (or instrumental conditioning) and Skinnerian or Thorndikian conditioning may be regarded as synonymous terms for operant conditioning.

Signaling operations may also be combined with the consequential operation to produce an operant, and typically are. For example, if a particular stimulus is present, then the response will produce a given consequence, but if the stimulus is absent or if a different stimulus is present, then the response will not produce the consequence. This stimulus is called a discriminative stimulus (S^D). Responding comes to occur in the presence of such a stimulus, and not in its absence. Thus, it is incorrect to say such things as "an operant occurs independently of the prior stimulus," or "an operant is unrelated to the prior stimulus," or "an operant is uncaused." It simply is not caused by an eliciting stimulus. Thus, the causal role of the S^D differs from that of the CS. The S^D is said to set the occasion upon which the response will be successful in producing the consequence in question, rather than to elicit a response.

The Three-term Operant Contingency

When a signaling operation is combined with a consequential operation, one can say an explicit operant contingency is in effect that involves three terms: (a) the discriminative stimulus; (b) the response; and (c) the consequence. As before, the notion of a contingency implies an "if-then and not otherwise" relation. According to this operant contingency, if the response occurs (in the presence of the discriminative stimulus), then the consequence will follow and not otherwise. For radical behaviorists, the three-term contingency is the fundamental analytical unit of operant behavior. The three-term operant contingency is schematically depicted as follows:

$$S^D : R => \text{consequence}$$

The simplest way to state this relation is to say that a discriminative stimulus [S^D] sets the occasion [:] for a response [R] to produce [=>] a consequence.

Note that the vocabularies of respondent and operant behavior are asymmetrical. A respondent is elicited by an eliciting stimulus, and an operant is emitted, but the prior stimulus in operant behavior is not designated as an emitting stimulus. In addition, note that an internal condition (hunger, pain, etc.) that exists prior to the response is not an S^D. The internal condition is regarded as part of the motivational complex for the behavior. It makes the prior stimulus and consequence relevant, but it is not an S^D itself.

The categories of behavior called respondent and operant are defined functionally, in terms of the environmental variables and relations that cause them. In respondent conditioning, the response is caused by the presentation of stimuli. One says the response is elicited. The response is not ordinarily caused by any explicitly arranged consequence, in any robust sense of the term *cause*. Even if the response does have some implicit consequence, that consequence does not substantially affect whether the response occurs again, independently of the eliciting relation.

As discussed earlier in this chapter, some researchers have taken to using the term contingency in conjunction with the relations of which respondent behavior is a function. In this sense, the contingency in respondent conditioning is between the CS and the US. As reviewed earlier, one can say that if the CS is presented, then the US will follow, and not otherwise. Importantly, one notes that using the term *contingency* in conjunction with the environmental conditions that cause respondent conditioning implies a causal relation between operations involving the CS and US, rather than between a response and its consequences. In particular, the response is not necessary for the US to be presented.

In operant conditioning, the response does have an explicitly arranged consequence: The response is necessary for the consequence to occur. That consequence does affect whether the response occurs again, independently of the eliciting relation. In such a case, one can say that operant conditioning is caused by a contingency among the three elements of the contingency. Importantly, one notes that using the term *contingency* in conjunction with operant conditioning implies a causal relation between a response and its consequences, rather than between a CS and US.

In addition, there are at least two common statements that appear to deal with the distinction between respondent and operant behavior. However, even though the statements appear to be definitive, they are not, and should be used only with great caution. The reason for caution is that the statements do not reflect the environmental conditions that cause each category of behavior, which is the basis by which radical behaviorists distinguish categories of behavior. The first statement is that respondent conditioning involves the autonomic nervous system and smooth muscles, whereas operant conditioning involves skeletal muscles and the peripheral nervous system. Empirically, the statement is not accurate because respondent conditioning can clearly affect skeletal muscles. At this writing, the extent to which operant relations affect the autonomic nervous system is unclear. In any case, the statement is not consistent with the means by which radical behaviorists categorize behavior: It says nothing about the causal relations.

The second statement is that respondent conditioning involves involuntary, reflexive responses, whereas operant conditioning involves voluntary, purposive responses. The statement may presumably be traced back at least as far as René Descartes, who offered a similar distinction 350 years ago. However, the statement assumes the terms voluntary and involuntary are scientifically meaningful. In the present view, the terms are not. Although the terms may be a common part of everyday discourse, they reflect a conceptual scheme associated with pre-scientific views of the human condition and behavior. Hence, they are not part of the behavior-analytic technical vocabulary.

Worth noting is that an operant conditioning experiment that involves purely operant relations, with no respondent relations, is probably impossible to perform. Some respondent relations will presumably intrude into the experimental situation. After all, whatever precedes the consequence, if only in the temporal or chronological sense, may result in respondent relations that influence behavior to some degree. Similarly, a respondent conditioning experiment that involves purely respondent relations, with no operant relations, is probably impossible to perform. Some operant relations will presumably intrude into the experimental situation. After all, whatever follows the occurrence of a response, if only in the temporal or chronological sense, may result in operant relations that influence behavior to some degree. Most contemporary theorists suggest that the important issue is to recognize that when talking about one process, the contribution of the other process has been at least identified or (better yet) minimized. One may then be reasonably confident one is dealing predominantly with the one process in question. The present chapter subscribes to this view. Other theorists argue that the distinction should be abandoned because it is too difficult to maintain in light of the complexity of the environmental circumstances in which behavior occurs, so why bother. The present chapter doesn't accept this view.

As with respondents, whether a given form of behavior will reliably come under the control of a particular set of environmental circumstances and consequential operations is an empirical question that is addressed in the research laboratory. In the case of respondent conditioning, not every instance of respondent behavior is equally conditionable to every CS. Similarly, in the case of operant conditioning, not every instance of operant behavior is equally conditionable to every consequence, or can be brought under the control of the particular stimulus used in a signaling operation. Most instances can, to be sure, but not all. Nevertheless, the ubiquity of experimental control by signaling operations in conjunction with stimulus presentation or consequential operations clearly testifies to the validity of the causal processes.

In summary, given the operations described above, operant behavior may be analyzed as follows:

1. A consequential operation is in effect, and also probably a signaling operation. In other words, the state of the environment is such that some stimulus or event is the consequence of the response, and a characteristic antecedent stimulus serves to signal that this state of affairs exists.

2. The probability of the target response when the operant contingency is in effect differs from when it is not in effect.

3. The different probability of the target response is a function of the operant contingency, rather than some other environmental relation.

Assessing Operant Functional Relations

The simplest way to determine whether responding is functionally related to the consequential operation is to modify the response-consequence relation and see what happens to behavior. This can be done in either of two ways. One is to withhold the consequence entirely for a series of trials. The other is to present the event that otherwise would be the consequence independently of a response. This second way also allows one to judge whether any change in responding is a function of the mere presentation of the stimulus, without regard to whether the stimulus is actually contingent on the response. In either case, if responding decreases, then behavior can be judged to be a function of its consequences.

SOURCES OF OPERANT BEHAVIOR

A response must occur in one form or another, however fragmentary, for some other reason before it can be an operant. That is, a behaving organism must make a response before the organism makes contact with the contingency, and the response produces a consequence. A response might be labeled an operant the second time it occurs, but not the first. What is the source of the earlier response? Three sources of operant behavior are (a) random behavior, (b) shaping, and less frequently (c) respondents.

Random behavior becomes involved when uncommitted behavior is followed by consequences. Certain consequences make the responses that produced them more likely, and hence gave rise to an operant class. In the first part of the twentieth century, the distinguished learning psychologist E. L. Thorndike (e.g., 1911) designated the source of learned behavior as "trial-and-error" followed by "accidental success." In Thorndike's view, the organism comes to the situation with a multitude of responses, and simply starts engaging in them. When one response happens to be followed by an emotionally satisfying aftereffect, the connection between the situation and response gets stamped in incrementally and mechanically over trials through some hypothetical physiological process called a "confirming reaction." For Thorndike the organism has no preconceived idea about what response will produce which outcome. Rather, the organism simply acts ("trial-and-error") and experiences consequences ("accidental success"). Thorndike's approach has the virtue of recognizing the importance of consequences in the acquisition of new forms of behavior and the maintenance of existing forms. However, radical behaviorism conceives of the important events a bit differently. The uncommitted behavior may be emitted in fragmentary form, and then the relevant properties of the response are gradually strengthened, such that the ultimate form may not look anything like the initial form, except for the sharing of the properties necessary for the consequences to follow. Moreover, the consequence produces both the change in behavior and the aftereffect. Any strengthening of the response is due to the consequence that produces the emotional aftereffect, rather than the emotional aftereffect itself.

Shaping is a process whereby another agent, say a human, delivers a consequence for responses that come progressively closer to some final, desired form. A synonymous phrase is "differential reinforcement of successive approximations." As with uncommitted behavior, the form of the response at the start of the shaping process may differ significantly from its form at the conclusion. The terms "progressively closer" and "successive approximations" suggest each response comes closer and closer to satisfying the criteria that are necessary for the consequence to be presented at the end of the progression. The standard metaphor follows from the nontechnical word "shaping." Consider a sculptor who is creating a statue from an undifferentiated lump of clay. The sculptor gradually applies pressure on the clay with hands here or tools there in a straightforward progression to shape the final, desired form of the object. The undifferentiated lump of clay corresponds to the initial, uncommitted repertoire of the organism. Thus, a behavior analyst would apply pressure in the form of particular consequences. The behavior analyst would continue in a straightforward progression to shape the final, desired form of the response.

An operant might evolve from a respondent over a series of experiences with the environment. A baby might cry, for example, as an unconditioned respondent elicited by a wet diaper. A caregiver might change the diaper. Although the crying originated as an unconditioned respondent, it was followed by a consequence: the caregiver putting on a dry diaper. In the future, the baby might cry when its diaper was wet and a caregiver was within earshot because in the past such crying had resulted in a dry diaper. In principle, operants could develop from such processes, working singly or in combination with other processes. Teitelbaum (1977) used additional examples to argue that many responses began as respondents, and then were transformed into motivated operants as the organism matured and encountered continued forms of environmental stimulation.

SOME FURTHER COMMENTS ON UNDERSTANDING WHEN BEHAVIOR IS OPERANT BEHAVIOR

For behavior analysts, the most important category of behavior is operant behavior. Yet, the concept of operant behavior is often misunderstood. For example, how specifically can it be determined that a change in responding is controlled by its consequences, in keeping with the second and third phases of analytical activity mentioned at the beginning of this chapter? According to the analysis of operant behavior above in terms of experimental operations, Catania (1973, 2007) suggests that the term *operant* is appropriate when the actual distribution of responses generated by a consequential operation becomes stable and corresponds fairly closely to the idealized class of responses required to produce a consequence. Again, this definition is a conceptually sophisticated treatment of the definition of an operant and merits further discussion.

Suppose a hungry pigeon is placed into an operant experimental chamber. The chamber has a slot, say 20 cm long and 1 cm high, into which the pigeon can peck with its beak. Suppose also that there are a series of 20 sensors (e.g., photocells) evenly spaced along the slot. The photocells are transducers that send an electronic signal to some control apparatus (e.g., a computer) regarding when and where the pigeon has broken one of the beams of the photocells. At issue is whether presenting food as a consequence of pecking into some arbitrarily chosen locus, say locus #8, makes the pigeon do so more often. If it does, then the term *operant* may be applied to the resulting category of behavior.

Prior to imposing this consequential operation, the pigeon's behavior is observed, and a standard frequency distribution is constructed of the frequency with which the pigeon pecks into each of the various locations along the slot. This frequency distribution reveals what is called the operant level, which is to say, the rate before pecking at locus #8 produces food. One possibility is that the pecking will be uniformly distributed along the length of the slot. The pecking needn't be, of course, as there may be some reason why the pecking favors one location over another. For example, the pigeon may have a phylogenic tendency to peck at one location, or it may have had some sort of prior experience that results in its favoring one locus. Thus, another possibility is that there will be a mode at one or another locus. For simplicity, the present treatment assumes the pigeon pecks into the slot somewhat uniformly along the length of the slot. Then, the consequential operation of delivering food every time it pecks into locus #8 is imposed, and a new frequency distribution is constructed.

A first thing that happens is that the frequency of pecking increases all along the slot. In other words, the pigeon pecks into the slot everywhere along its length, and not just in a certain locus. This effect is called *induction*.

However, after a brief period of time, the frequency distribution begins to show a mode at locus #8, and pecking at other loci decreases substantially. Perhaps in an ideal sense, given that the pigeon is being maximally efficient, all pecks might come to occur at locus #8, and none at any other locus. However, organisms simply aren't this idealized. Although clearly many responses will be made at locus #8, fewer will be made at locus #7 and locus #9, on either side of the locus designated for producing a consequence. Perhaps still fewer pecks will be made at locus #6 and locus #10.

It is appropriate to speak of operant behavior when the consequential operation has produced a shift in the distribution of responses, from the prior flat distribution across loci to the mode at the locus that has produced a consequence. Hence, Catania (1973, 2007) speaks of the observed distribution of responses coming to correspond "fairly closely" with a distribution that is correlated with the consequence. Thus, an operant is a class of responses that are functionally related to their consequences. Each response is a member of the class because it has the common property of producing food. The shift of the distribution of responses brought about by the consequential operation is the criterion that indicates to behavior analysts that the response in question is in fact an operant.

Again, an operant is not defined by its topography. That is, given the present example, all that is necessary for the pigeon to produce food is to break the beam of the photocell. Technically, whether the pigeon does so with its beak or tip of its wing doesn't matter. However, a researcher could require a response of a particular topography as part of the contingency. Thus, a researcher could require that the pigeon break the beam with only its beak, or only the tip of its wing, in order to produce food. The researcher could require that the pigeon break the beam with only its upper beak, or only its lower beak. It could require that it break the beam with its left wing, or right. In principle, the consequence could be made contingent on virtually any property of the response, such as its timing, its force, or its duration. The important consideration is that the environment sets the requirements, and the pigeon's behavior changes because of the consequences of its behavior. The different instances are members of the same class and are quantitatively mutually replaceable.

A signaling operation may be conjoined with this consequential operation by arranging for a light to be illuminated whenever pecking into locus #8 will produce food. When the light is off, pecking into locus #8 will not produce food. After a period of time, the pigeon pecks into the slot, predominantly at locus #8, when the light is on, but does something else when the light is off. In sum, the rate of a designated class of responses (i.e., the pecks at locus #8) varies with respect to a feature of the antecedent environment, namely, the presence or absence of the light, because the presence of the light signals that the consequence of responding is food.

STIMULUS CONTROL

The relation called stimulus control pertains to the effect of the signaling operation. Stimulus control is said to exist when the probability of a response varies with respect to some property of the antecedent setting. Stimulus control applies equally to conditioned respondent and operant behavior. For example, suppose the salivary response had been conditioned in Pavlov's dogs with an auditory CS having a frequency of 1000 Hz. If a tone of slightly lower (e.g., 900 Hz) or higher (e.g., 1100 Hz) frequency was presented to the dog on a test trial, the degree of salivation might differ slightly from that observed when the CS is 1000 Hz. In this case, the response varies with respect to the frequency of the tone, and stimulus control is said to exist. The 1000 Hz tone is termed the CS+.

Similarly, suppose a pigeon's pecking response at locus #8 on the slot when a yellow-green light of 560 nm was illuminated inside the chamber has previously produced food. If a light of slightly different color was presented to the pigeon on a test trial, the pigeon might respond more slowly. In this case, the response varies with respect to the color of the light, and stimulus control is said to exist. As recounted earlier in this chapter, the light is termed a discriminative stimulus, or S^D. A discriminative stimulus is ordinarily defined as a stimulus in whose presence a response is more probable than in its absence because a particular consequence for a response is more probable in its presence than in its absence. An older and less technical term for a discriminative stimulus is cue.

Stimulus control is a very important concept in the understanding of respondent and operant behavior. In controlled laboratory research, the stimulus is typically one that the experimenter can conveniently manipulate, such as a light or a tone. Often, the stimuli belong to a continuous dimension, such as frequency, wavelength, intensity, size, or duration. However, in principle the stimulus can be virtually any feature of the situation, or even combinations of elements in a situation. Sometimes the stimulus that exerts control is something unintended by the experimenter. For example, in the late nineteenth century, a horse in Germany was called "Clever Hans" because of its apparent ability to solve mathematical problems. When asked to indicate the sum of two numbers, it would stamp its hoof some number of times to express its answer. Subsequent investigation revealed that the horse was responding to inadvertent and very subtle facial and postural cues from its handler when it came close to the correct number. In other words, the horse would simply start stamping, and stop when the facial expression of its handler changed, as the horse neared the correct answer. The facial expression of the handler was a discriminative stimulus that controlled stamping.

Two important terms in the discussion of stimulus control are generalization and discrimination. These terms describe behavior as it relates to the prevailing stimulus conditions, rather than an internal response on the part of an organism that is somehow responsible for the degree of overt responding that is observed.

One speaks of generalization in respondent conditioning when an organism responds similarly to stimuli that are similar to the CS+. In other words, if a dog salivates say, 10 drops of saliva on a trial with a 1000 Hz tone as the CS+, one speaks of generalization when the dog salivates say, 7 drops of saliva on a trial with 900 or 1100 Hz tone, 9 drops with 975 or 1125 Hz, 5 drops with 800 or 1200 Hz, and so on.

One speaks of generalization in operant conditioning when an organism responds similarly to stimuli that are similar to the discriminative stimulus. In other words, if a pigeon responds at, say, 50 responses per minute in the presence of a 560 nm light as a discriminative stimulus, one speaks of generalization when the pigeon responds at, say, 40 responses per minute in the presence of a 550 nm or 570 nm light, 45 responses per minute in the presence of a 555 or 565 nm light, 30 responses per minute in the presence of a 540 or 580 nm light, and so on. In the conventional illustration of generalization, the pigeon has not previously received training with such other stimuli as the 550 nm or 570 nm lights, and they are presented in probe trials, in which responding does not produce a consequence. The stimuli are related to the training stimulus—the 560 nm light—by being part of the continuous dimension of wavelength.

One speaks of discrimination in respondent conditioning when an organism responds differently to stimuli that differ from the CS+. In other words, if a dog salivates at, say, 10 drops of saliva on a trial with a 1000 Hz tone as the CS+, one speaks of discrimination when the dog salivates at, say, 1 drop of saliva on a trial with a 100 Hz tone. In the standard example, discrimination comes about because the dog has experienced several trials in which the 100 Hz tone has been presented alone, without an unconditioned stimulus. Thus, the dog has typically had some sort of contact with the other stimuli. A stimulus that has been correlated with the absence of the unconditioned stimulus is termed a CS-.

One speaks of discrimination in operant conditioning when an organism responds differently to stimuli that differ from the discriminative stimulus, typically as a result of experiencing different response-consequence relations in the presence of other stimuli.

In other words, if a pigeon responds at, say, 50 responses per minute in the presence of a 560 nm light, one speaks of discrimination when the pigeon responds at, say, 2 responses per minute in the presence of a 460 nm light. In the standard example, discrimination comes about because the pigeon has made responses in the presence of the 460 nm light that have not produced food. A stimulus in the presence of which responses have not produced a consequence is termed an S-delta (S^Δ).

An important matter concerning the usage of such terms as generalization and discrimination is that they are the names for relations between antecedent stimuli and behavior. They do not refer to processes presumed to be going on inside the skin of the organism. Thus, appropriate usage is to talk of generalization or discrimination in terms of whether a pattern of responding exists across a range of stimuli. One does not talk of the subject generalizing or discriminating.

The terms *concept* and *abstraction* refer to matters of stimulus control. A concept is defined as generalization within a class of stimuli, and discrimination between classes. That is, all instances or a given class of stimuli are responded to as equivalent, and all instances are treated differently from stimuli in other classes. One labels all instances of bounded figures with three sides as triangles, not rectangles, even though isosceles triangles, right triangles, and equilateral triangles look different. Abstraction refers to stimulus control by one feature of a stimulus, say its color, even though the stimulus has many other properties that could potentially exert stimulus control, say its size or shape. One labels a color as red, even though the object that is colored red may be a stoplight, an apple, or a fire hydrant. As with other terms in the vocabulary of stimulus control, concepts and abstractions describe behavior as it relates to the prevailing stimulus conditions, rather than an internal response on the part of an organism that is somehow responsible for the degree of overt responding that is observed.

The everyday word "attention" is often used in nontechnical discussions of stimulus control, such as in discussion of what stimulus a subject is "paying attention to." However, like many everyday words, attention suffers from ambiguity. As with concepts and abstractions, attention is often thought to imply an internal and unobservable mediating or filtering process on the part of the organism. From the point of view of radical behaviorism, such talk is not helpful. The difficulty is not that such talk appeals to something unobservable, but rather that there is no such process. Subjects may well engage in a precurrent behavior of orienting toward a stimulus that is present in its environment, but use of the term attention implies more. It implies a controlling relation, such that some property of responding, such as rate, varies when some property of the antecedent stimulus is manipulated. In most instances, the term *attention* is simply synonymous with the fact that stimulus control exists.

The common question then is: What training conditions are necessary to produce the varying demonstrations of stimulus control with various stimulus modalities? This question is the topic of much research in the experimental analysis of behavior (Catania, 2007).

MOLAR AND MOLECULAR ANALYSES OF BEHAVIOR

A time-honored question in the analysis of behavior concerns the level of analysis. Theorists in the past have debated this question for many years. In some cases the terms *global* and *local* are used in conjunction with the debate. In others, the terms *molar* and *molecular* are used. The latter pair of terms is used here.

Worth noting, however, is that the meanings of the terms molar and molecular have changed over the years. An early sense of the distinction was that molar analyses involved behavioral variables that were external and had been directly observed, whereas molecular analyses involved inferred or perhaps even physiological variables that were internal and unobserved. A somewhat later sense of the distinction was that molar analyses involved an operant response with a series of functionally integrated movements across time, whereas molecular analyses involved chains of discrete responses, each individually conditioned and linked to the next through respondent processes. The debate remains lively, and the recent sense of the distinction turns on the time frames across which both the independent and dependent variables are formulated to reveal order in behavior. When the independent and dependent variables are formulated in terms of large-scale relations, across relatively extended periods of time in ways that transcend local relations between the behavioral unit and the environment, the contemporary tendency is to speak of a molar level of analysis. In contrast, when the independent and dependent variables are formulated in terms of smaller-scale relations, across relatively circumscribed periods of time in ways that emphasize local relations between the behavioral unit and the environment, the contemporary tendency is to speak of a molecular level of analysis.

Molar and Molecular Analyses of the Dependent Variable

The molar versus molecular controversy began well over 100 years ago. Psychologists of the time began to note the orderly relations that would come to be known as the reflex, and then apply it to the analysis of more complex, temporally extended forms of behavior. A classic reference to molecular and molar levels of analysis in the history of behavioral theory is from E. B. Holt's (1914) article titled "The Freudian Wish and Its Place in Ethics":

> This is very evident in the case of the bee. We may grant ... that the bee is only, in the last analysis, a reflex mechanism. But it is a very complex one, and when we are studying the bee's behavior we are studying an organism which by means of integrated reflexes has become enabled to respond specifically to the objects of its environment.... To study the behavior of the bee is of course to put the question, "What is the bee doing?" This is a plain scientific question.... [One answer] would probably be: "it is doing of course a great many things; now its visual organ is stimulated and it darts toward a flower; now its olfactory organ is stimulated and it goes for a moment to rub antennae with another bee of its own hive; and so forth" But this is not an answer. We

ask, "What is the bee doing?" And we are told, "Now its visual... and now its olfactory, ..." etc. With a little persistence, we could probably get Bethe to say, "Why the *bee* isn't doing anything." Whereas an unbiased observer can see plainly enough that "The bee is laying by honey in its home."…. Many biologists shy at such a description; ... they themselves deem it safer to deal with the bee's olfactory and visual organs. They will not describe the bee's behavior as a whole, will not observe what mere reflexes when cooperating integrally in one organism can accomplish, because they fear, at bottom, to encounter that bogy which philosophers have set in their way, the 'subjective' or the 'psychic.' They need not be afraid of this, for all that they have to do is to describe in the most objective manner possible what the bee is doing. (pp. 77–80)

An important later reference is a chapter on serial processes in behavior by Lashley (1951). Lashley critically examined the thesis that all complex forms of behavior consist of individual S – R respondent movements that are concatenated, with each stage evoking the next, ultimately producing the final act. Historically, this thesis was a popular one, as researchers embraced the idea of the reflex as the objective behavioral unit underlying all forms of behavior, including temporally extended, complex forms.

In short, Lashley found no empirical support for the thesis that complex acts may be decomposed into smaller, reflex units. For example, consider the movements of the skilled pianist or typist. One kind of a molecular analysis might hold that when an individual plays the piano or types, one finger movement produces kinesthetic stimulation that elicits the next finger movement, and so on. Lashley pointed out that the individual responses take place so rapidly that the necessary sensory feedback couldn't take place. Another example is language. A molecular analysis of language might argue that speaking a sentence is just a chain of responses in which saying one word acts as a stimulus to elicit saying the next, and so on. According to Lashley, this argument is all wrong. The essential feature of language is its inherent organization, resulting in multiple forms of sentences, rather than a strictly linear process where one word evokes the succeeding word, as beads occur on a chain. In sum, Lashley argued that complex behavior isn't necessarily organized in the mechanistic, sequential fashion, and analyses shouldn't seek to decompose it into smaller, molecular reflex-like units.

A more reasonable point of view is that the nature of the dependent variable is a function of the prevailing contingencies in the environment, within the boundaries established by innate considerations. Sometimes the contingencies force the dependent variable to be rather small, as in a discrete-trial procedure. At other times, the dependent variable may drift, and even change across time. Some research has explicitly manipulated contingencies by requiring the passage of a certain amount of time between consecutive responses, called the inter-response time, or IRT. In this research, the behavioral unit is actually defined in terms of three parameters: (a) the first response, which initiates the IRT; (b) the duration of the time before the next response; and (c) the last response, which terminates the IRT. Thus, the behavioral unit is not simply a single response, but rather a molar pattern of responding. The research has shown that this rather molar response unit has a certain integrity when it is considered as a whole, in the sense that it varies in orderly ways when contingencies are applied to it.

Molar and Molecular Analyses of the Independent Variable

A great deal of research indicates that a range of factors (independent variables), from short to long term, can control behavior. Often the independent variables that control behavior depend on the procedure. A great deal of laboratory research has shown that behavior is more strongly controlled by local variables like immediacy of a consequence than by large-scale variables like the overall rate of the consequence. Indeed, many studies over the years have emphasized the important role of temporal contiguity in learning and behavior. For example, when given a choice between two situations, pigeons may choose the situation in which there is a shorter delay to the first food presentation, even if it is a small amount, showing the strength of the short term relation, even though the other situation provides more food presentations or a larger amount in the long run (McDiarmid & Rilling, 1965; Shull, Spear, & Bryson, 1981).

However, other data show that remote or distal variables can have an effect. For example, Lattal and Gleeson (1990) have shown that a rat learned to press a lever even when the consequence of a response, a food pellet, was delayed as long as 30 s after the response. Clearly, immediate or proximal events are highly important, but ruling out the possibility that distal events can have an impact appears unwise. The question is ultimately empirical. The pivotal consideration for behavior analysts interested in the molar versus molecular question is of what variables and relations is the response in question a function. Once those variables and relations have been identified, they are available in attempts to manipulate contingencies and deliberately control behavior. In a practical or pragmatic sense, individuals often want to control how often an organism does something. There are other properties of responding on which a consequence might be made contingent—latency, force, etc., but the modal concern is presumably rate.

To some extent, the question concerning the control of behavior is: At what level of analysis is order found? The answer is not one that can be legislated a priori. As with many other scientific questions, the question may actually be much more complex and not resolvable as one and not the other, as molar but not molecular or as molecular but not molar. At present, the twin questions of (a) whether the dependent variable is momentary or temporally extended, and (b) whether the independent variables that control behavior are local (i.e., immediate) or distal (i.e., remote), remain to be answered by research data on a case-by-case basis. It is conceivable that for one species but not necessarily for another, the form of response may be controlled by one set of variables when food is the consequence, and by another when avoidance of shock is the consequence. Indeed, the same form of behavior may be controlled by one set of variables when an organism of a given species is hungry and food is the consequence, and by another set of variables when the organism is thirsty and water is the consequence. It appears fundamentally incorrect to make attributions about the "proper" level of analysis. Doing so represents an ontological or metaphysical commitment that history suggests is not useful.

SUMMARY

Chapter 5 showed that a conceptually consistent taxonomy of behavior can be established by examining the functional relations between behavior and environment. The resulting categories of behavior are a function of stimulus presentation operations, consequential operations, and signaling operations. Table 5–1 presents some key terms relating to innate behavior and the modification of innate behavior. This behavior is elicited by the presentation of a stimulus. The common example is the elicitation of a reflex by (a) a US or (b) a CS that has been correlated with a US. The table gives the term, and then describes the relation to ongoing behavior, the nature of the experimental operation that affects the behavior, and the resulting effect on behavior. Table 5–2 summarizes the relations of which unconditioned respondents, conditioned respondents, and operants are a function.

Chapter 6 continues the theme of Chapter 5 by developing a conceptually consistent vocabulary for the functional role of consequences in the regulation of behavior.

TABLE 5–1
Some terms relating to innate behavior or the modifications of innate behavior via experimental operations that affect the function of antecedents

Term	Relation to ongoing behavior	Experimental operation	Effect on behavior
habituation	without regard	repeated presentations of US	decreased responding elicited by US (exact effect of repeated presentations depends on underlying response system)
sensitization	without regard	repeated presentations of US	increased responding elicited by US (exact effect of repeated presentations depends on underlying response system)
pseudo-conditioning	without regard	repeated presentations of US combination	increased responding elicited by another stimulus that has not been correlated with US
extinction–1	without regard	CS but not US presented during experimental session	decreased responding elicited by CS

TABLE 5.1 (cont.)

Term	Relation to ongoing behavior	Experimental operation	Effect on behavior
extinction–2	without regard	CS and US presented randomly during experimental session	decreased responding elicited by CS
omission training	contingent on occurrence of elicited response	withhold US	slight reduction of responding elicited by CS and possible emergence of cyclic pattern across trials, but not total cessation
spontaneous recovery	n/a	CS-US training followed by extinction trials, followed by removal of subject from experimental apparatus, followed by reintroduction of subject to apparatus	temporary increase in responding immediately after reintroduction to apparatus

---

TABLE 5–2

Definitions: Unconditioned respondents, conditioned respondents, and operants

Unconditioned respondent
A class of innate behavior that is elicited by a stimulus presentation operation. The behavior is typically that of a single response system (gland, organ, muscle, or muscle group) activated by contact with the stimulus. The response occurs relatively soon after the presentation of the stimulus, and the topography of the response is relatively stable from instance to instance, and across the species.

Conditioned respondent
A class of behavior that is acquired during the lifetime of the organism. A signaling operation is combined with a stimulus presentation operation to elicit a conditioned respondent. The response is in the same system as that activated by the US.

Operant
A class of behavior that occurs because previous instances of the class have produced certain consequences. There is a contingency between the response and its consequence, such that if the response occurs, then a consequence is produced. The response is said to be emitted. Often, a characteristic antecedent stimulus

condition is in effect when the response will produce the consequence. The antecedent stimulus is referred to as a discriminative stimulus, and is said to set the occasion for the response. Hence, a signaling operation is often combined with a consequential operation to produce an operant. When all three terms are present and interrelated (a discriminative stimulus, a response, a consequence), the relation is called a three-term contingency. Operant behavior is the predominant form of behavior that is of interest in the analysis of the human condition. A contingency involving operant behavior is therefore the predominant unit in the analysis of human behavior.

REFERENCES

Catania, A. C. (1973). The concept of the operant in the analysis of behavior. *Behaviorism, 1*, 103–116.

Catania, A. C. (2007). *Learning* (4th interim ed.). Cornwall-on-Hudson, NY: Sloan Publishing.

Holt, E. B. (1914). *The Freudian wish and its place in ethics*. New York: Holt.

Kimble, G. (1961). *Hilgard and Marquis' conditioning and learning* (2nd ed.). New York: Appleton.

Lashley, K. (1951). The problem of serial order in behavior. In L. A. Jeffress (Ed.), *Cerebral mechanisms in behavior*, pp. 112–146. New York: Wiley.

Lattal, K. A., & Gleeson, S. (1990). Response acquisition with delayed reinforcement. *Journal of Experimental Psychology: Animal Behavior Processes, 16*, 27–39.

Mazur, J. E. (2002). *Learning and behavior*. Upper Saddle River, NJ: Prentice Hall.

McDiarmid, C., & Rilling, M. (1965). Reinforcement delay and reinforcement rate as determinants of schedule preference. *Psychonomic Science, 2*, 195–196.

Shull, R., Spear, D., & Bryson, A. (1981). Delay or rate of food delivery as a determiner of response rate. *Journal of the Experimental Analysis of Behavior, 35*, 129–143.

Skinner, B. F. (1938). *The Behavior of Organisms*. New York: Appleton-Century.

Teitelbaum, P. (1977). Levels of integration of the operant. In W. K. Honig & J. E. R. Staddon (Eds.), *Handbook of operant behavior*, pp. 7–27. Englewood Cliffs, NJ: Prentice-Hall.

Thorndike, E. L. (1911). *Animal Intelligence*. New York: Macmillan.

STUDY QUESTIONS

1. State or paraphrase how behavior analysts approach the question of innate behavior.

2. Define the following instances of innate behavior: reflex, tropism, kinesis, taxis, fixed action pattern.

3. State or paraphrase Kimble's (1961) definition of learning.

4. State or paraphrase the alternative definition of learning presented in the current chapter.

5. State or paraphrase four follow-up questions regarding the process called learning, and supply answers for the questions.

6. Summarize the way radical behaviorists treat the traditional distinction between learning and performance.

7. Define a conditioned respondent.

8. Define an operant.

9. Define a discriminative stimulus.

10. Define a three-term operant contingency.

11. Describe the three sources of operants mentioned in the chapter.

12. Describe the definitive basis for the distinction between respondents and operants.

13. Describe how it can be determined that a response is controlled by its consequences, according to Catania (2007).

14. Define stimulus control.

15. Distinguish between generalization and discrimination.

16. Distinguish between molar and molecular levels of analysis.

6

Consequences and Concepts in the Analysis of Behavior

Synopsis of Chapter 6: Chapter 4 made the case for behavior as a subject matter in its own right. Chapter 5 examined how radical behaviorists analyze the environment to categorize behavior and achieve a useful taxonomy. The result is that the various categories of behavior are distinguished by the environmental variables and relations of which they are a function, rather than any supposed essence or quality of the behavior. Chapter 6 continues the analysis by developing a consistent vocabulary concerning the effects of consequences on behavior. The chapter uses the framework and language of a three-phase process, parallel to that of Chapter 5, to secure conceptually consistent and conceptually valid definitions of the terms that relate to consequential operations. The initial portion of the chapter focuses on the terms reinforcement and punishment, both positive and negative. The analyses employ parallel language to show the interrelatedness of the vocabulary of consequences. The chapter then examines whether the definition of reinforcement is circular, the conceptual status of "self-reinforcement," extinction, superstition, and finally, motivative operations.

The notion that the consequences of a response can affect its future probability is not new. For example, it was an element of classical hedonism in the third century B.C., the Spencer-Bain principle in the nineteenth century, and Thorndike's Law of Effect in the twentieth century. Radical behaviorism formalizes the role of consequences in the determination of behavior by noting that some consequences make a response more likely, whereas other consequences make the response less likely. This chapter reviews basic conceptual and definitional issues related to the functions of consequences.

TO REINFORCE: THE ROOT TERM AND ITS COGNATES

The format that was employed in Chapter 5 to identify operant behavior may now be extended to provide a consistent treatment of the vocabulary of consequences (Catania, 2007). Readers will recall that operant behavior is behavior that occurs because of its consequences. Accordingly, one speaks of operant behavior when the following three conditions are satisfied:

1. The response produces a consequence.
2. The probability of the response changes when it produces the consequence.
3. The different probability is a function of the consequence.

With respect to these three conditions, the root term *reinforce* and its cognates are used when the consequences of operant behavior produce an increase in responding (#2 above). Therefore, in keeping with the analysis of Chapter 5 and Catania (2007), the standard usage for reinforce and its cognates is when the following three conditions are satisfied:

1. The response produces a consequence.
2. The probability of the response increases.
3. The increased probability is a function of the consequence.

As alluded to above, the vocabulary of consequences includes the various verb forms of "to reinforce," as well as the gerundival "reinforcing." Other cognates of the root term *reinforce* include reinforcer and reinforcement. The terms *reinforcer* and *reinforcement* are often used in conjunction with modifiers, such as unconditioned, conditioned, positive, and negative. In addition, some terms like reinforcement have usages as both a process and an operation. Usage as a process emphasizes the increase in behavior that occurs when a response has certain consequences (#2 above). Usage as an operation emphasizes the actual manner in which the consequences are arranged, such that an organism comes into contact with them (#1 above). Finally, in many cases the consequence involves a manipulation of a discrete stimulus, although other ways of arranging a response to have a consequence are possible (Catania, 2007). This section of the chapter reviews uses of the root term *reinforce* and its cognates.

Reinforce and its cognates are generally used in the perhaps metaphorical sense of strengthening the response, as evidenced by its becoming more frequently observed or occurring at a higher rate because of its consequence. Technically, a consequence doesn't strengthen the response that produced it. That response has already occurred. Rather, the consequence increases the probability of future responses in the operant class. To avoid tiresome repetition, many of the reviews in this chapter assume the third condition above is satisfied, and dispense with noting in each and every case that the increase in behavior occurs because of the consequence. Worth emphasizing is that in standard usage, the response is reinforced, rather than the organism. Thus, standard usage is to say that "the pigeon's pecking response was reinforced," rather than "the pigeon was reinforced for pecking." A moment's reflection suggests the pigeon wasn't made stronger or more frequent by the consequence of a response.

To Reinforce as a Verb

Verb forms of *to reinforce* may be used as a process or an operation. Usage as a process emphasizes an increase in responding produced by the consequence. An illustration is "The experiment was designed to find out whether gold stars would reinforce cooperative play among first-graders" (Catania, 2007). Usage as an operation emphasizes the delivery of the consequence contingent on a response. An illustration is "When a period of free play was used to reinforce the child's completion of class assignments, the child's grades improved" (Catania, 2007).

Reinforcing as an Adjective

As an adjective, the term *reinforcing* refers to a property of a stimulus. An illustration is "Three seconds access to mixed grain was used as a reinforcing stimulus for the pigeon's pecking."

Reinforcer as a Noun: Unconditioned, Conditioned, Positive, Negative

As a noun, the term *reinforcer* generally refers to a consequence that increases responding via a consequential operation. An unconditioned reinforcer exerts its effect without any special training. Common examples are food for a hungry organism, water for a thirsty organism, warmth for a cold organism, and so on. The relation is empirically determined: Food might not be a reinforcer for an anorexic. Moreover, the criterion is functional: Ice cream would be called a reinforcer because it produces an increase in responding when involved in a consequential operation, not because it contains a certain percentage of sugar.

A conditioned reinforcer is a stimulus that exerts a reinforcing effect because it has been correlated during the lifetime of the organism with other stimuli that already are reinforcers. Common examples of conditioned reinforcers in the experimental laboratory are lights and tones that have been correlated with food or water for hungry or thirsty organisms. For humans in the world outside the laboratory, gold stars, awards, certificates, status symbols, designer labels, etc., that have been correlated with other consequences, such as interpersonal attention, are often conditioned reinforcers. A generalized conditioned reinforcer is a conditioned reinforcer that has been correlated with many unconditioned reinforcers. For humans, money is an example of a generalized conditioned reinforcer, as it is correlated with a wide variety of both unconditioned and conditioned reinforcers.

A positive reinforcer is a stimulus whose response contingent presentation increases the rate at which similar responses are later emitted. With respect to the three conditions for reinforcement, the concept of a positive reinforcer pertains to the first condition: The consequential operation involves added something to the environment. An illustration is "Three seconds access to mixed grain is a positive reinforcer for a pigeon's pecking." The three seconds of mixed grain is the stimulus that when added to the environment as a consequence of the response results in an increase in behavior. Many of the examples in this chapter involve positive reinforcers, either unconditioned or conditioned.

A negative reinforcer is a stimulus whose response contingent removal increases the rate at which similar responses are later emitted. With respect to the three conditions for reinforcement, the concept of a negative reinforcer pertains to the first: The consequential operation involves removing or terminating something from the environment. An illustration is "The research demonstrated that the loud noise directed toward the subject was a negative reinforcer because when a response terminated it, the response increased in frequency." The loud noise is the stimulus that when terminated as a consequence of the response results in an increase in behavior.

Reinforcement: A Process and an Operation

Like verb forms of to reinforce, the noun form *reinforcement* may be used as a process—the name for the increase in behavior when the response has a particular consequence—or as an operation—the name for an arrangement between the response and a particular consequence. Unconditioned reinforcement means either the operation of delivering an unconditioned reinforcer, or the increase in responding produced by that operation. Conditioned reinforcement means either the operation of delivering a conditioned reinforcer, or the increase in responding produced by that operation.

The modifier *positive* denotes an increase in responding when the consequence of the response is to add something to the environment. The "something" is the positive reinforcer. An illustration of usage involving both unconditioned and positive as modifiers is "The experiment demonstrated unconditioned positive reinforcement by arranging for a response to produce three seconds' access to mixed grain." The introduction of three seconds of mixed grain as a consequence of the response is an increase in stimulation in the environment, and the behavior was subsequently observed to increase because of this operation.

The modifier *negative* denotes an increase in behavior when the consequence of the response is the removal of something. The "something" is the negative reinforcer. If the negative reinforcer is present at the time the response is made, the procedure is called "escape." If the negative reinforcer will occur at some future time, and the consequence of the response is to prevent the negative reinforcer from occurring, the procedure is called "avoidance."

To further illustrate the vocabulary of negative reinforcers and negative reinforcement, suppose that the ambient temperature in the pigeon's chamber is much warmer than normal. The consequence of a pigeon pecking into locus #8 is to produce a brief burst of cool air from an air conditioner. Assume that under these conditions, the pigeon's responses at locus #8 increase. This case of negative reinforcement is called "escape." The consequence of the response is to remove heat from the chamber, where heat is the negative reinforcer, and responding increases. The situation would not be called positive reinforcement, through the introduction of cool air, because energy is being removed, rather than added. Cool air has less energy than warm air.

An alternative situation is to suppose the ambient temperature in the pigeon's chamber is in the normal range, but the temperature will become much warmer for some period of time unless the pigeon occasionally pecks into locus #8. When the pigeon does so, the consequence of the response is to prevent the temperature from increasing in the box for some specified period of time. If the pigeon fails to peck into the slot again during that period of time, the temperature will increase when that time has elapsed. Assume that under these conditions, the pigeon's responses at locus #8 increase. An analysis of the situation reveals that in the absence of the response, some form of environmental stimulation would occur: the temperature would increase from the introduction of the heat energy associated with the warm air. The response prevented this occurrence. This case of negative reinforcement is called "avoidance."

Note that "reinforcer" is the stimulus, and "reinforcement" is either the operation of presenting the reinforcer or the increase in responding produced by that operation. That is, "reinforcer" and "reinforcement" are not interchangeable. Thus, to say that "Access to mixed grain for three seconds served as [unconditioned positive] reinforcement for the pigeon's pecking" is incorrect. One would have to say either "The grain served as the [unconditioned positive] reinforcer for the pecking," or "The delivery of three seconds of mixed grain served as the [unconditioned positive] reinforcement for the pecking."

A Further Consideration

In its most general sense, the term *reinforcement* suggests the operation of presenting a stimulus of primary biological significance in a way that strengthens a response that has occurred in the presence of another stimulus that didn't previously evoke the response. Thus, one might say that presenting food reinforces the response that occurs in the presence of a light. However, further examination of this wording indicates it is ambiguous, in that it fails to distinguish between the respondent and operant cases.

For example, one could be talking about the operation of presenting food in a respondent conditioning trial. Reflecting older usages, some texts talk of the food presentation in this case as "reinforcement." They might also talk of the "reinforced stimulus," meaning a CS in the presence of which a US is presented, or of a "reinforced trial," meaning a trial on which the US has been presented. For present purposes, note that the important relation is between the light and the food presentation. The CS-US contingency underlies salivation, and the response is elicited. The present chapter does not use the term *reinforcement* in this way.

Alternatively, one could be talking about the operation of presenting food contingent on a lever press in the presence of the light. In this alternative case, the consequential operation of presenting food is again called the reinforcement, but the light bears an entirely different relation to the response with which it is correlated: the lever press. No elicitation is involved. The response-reinforcer contingency underlies the lever press, and the response is emitted. The present chapter uses the term *reinforcement* in only this way.

In any event, without recognizing such a difference, one might not appreciate that elicited responses differ from emitted, and think that the job of the experimental analyst of behavior is to devise some common hypothetical mechanism that underlies both cases. Indeed, the history of learning theory is a powerful illustration of how important it is to distinguish between these two usages. To be sure, some theorists don't feel there is a difference between these two forms of conditioning. Accordingly, they don't feel a need to differentiate between them. The present chapter is written from the point of view that it is useful to differentiate between them.

TO PUNISH: THE ROOT TERM AND ITS COGNATES

The examples considered to this point involve the term reinforcement and increases in operant responding as a function of its consequences. Consequences can also produce a decrease in operant responding. With respect to the three conditions of operant behavior noted earlier in this chapter, the root term *punish* and its cognates are used when the consequences of operant behavior produce a decrease in responding. Therefore, in keeping with the analysis of Chapter 5 and Catania (2007), the standard usage for punish and its cognates is when the following three conditions are satisfied:

1. The response produces a consequence.

2. The probability of the response decreases.

3. The decreased probability is a function of the consequence.

As with reinforce, there are various verb forms of *to punish*, as well as the gerundival *punishing*. Other cognates of the root term *punish* include punisher and punishment. The terms *punisher* and *punishment* are also used in conjunction with modifiers, such as unconditioned, conditioned, positive, and negative. In addition, some terms like punishment have usages as both a process and an operation. Usage as a process emphasizes the decrease in behavior that occurs when a response has certain consequences (#2 above). Usage as an operation emphasizes the actual manner in which the consequences are arranged, such that an organism comes into contact with them (#1 above). Finally, in many cases the consequence involves a manipulation of a discrete stimulus, although as with reinforcement, other ways of arranging a response to have a consequence are possible (Catania, 2007). This section of the chapter reviews uses of the root term *punish* and its cognates.

Technically, a consequence doesn't weaken the response that produced it. That response has already happened. Rather, the consequence decreases the probability of future responses in the operant class. As with the review of *reinforce*, the review here assumes the third condition mentioned at the outset of the chapter is always satisfied, and that the decrease in behavior is attributable to the consequence. In standard usage, the response is punished, rather than the organism. Thus, standard usage is to say that "The pigeon's pecking response was punished," rather than "The pigeon was punished for pecking." A moment's reflection suggests the pigeon wasn't made weaker or less frequent by the consequence of a response.

To Punish as a Verb

Verb forms of *punish* may be used as a process or an operation. Usage as a process emphasizes the decrease in responding produced by the consequence. An illustration is "The delivery of an air blast after each response punished the response." Usage as an operation emphasizes the delivery of the consequence contingent on a response. An illustration is "The delivery of an air blast after each response was used to punish the response."

Punishing as an Adjective

As an adjective, the term *punishing* refers to a property of a stimulus. An illustration is "An air blast served as the punishing stimulus."

Punisher as a Noun: Unconditioned, Conditioned, Positive, Negative

As a noun, the term *punisher* refers to a consequence that reduces responding via a consequential operation. An unconditioned punisher exerts a punishing effect without any special training. Common examples are air blasts, shocks, loud noises, a spanking, and so on. The relation is empirically determined: a spanking might not be a punisher for a masochist. A conditioned punisher is a consequence that exerts a punishing effect because of certain experiences with other stimuli that already are punishers during the lifetime of the organism. Common examples are verbal threats, reprimands, and criticism.

A positive punisher is a stimulus whose response contingent presentation decreases the rate at which similar responses are later emitted. An illustration is "A blast of air was used as a punisher for a pigeon's pecking." The air blast is the stimulus that when arranged as a consequence of the response results in a decrease in behavior.

A negative punisher is a stimulus whose response contingent removal decreases the rate at which similar responses are later emitted. In effect, many positive reinforcers would function as negative punishers. However, this terminology can be confusing in many cases, as the use of a common term cuts across different processes. For that reason it is not be used in this chapter.

Punishment: A Process and an Operation

Like verb forms of *to punish*, the noun form *punishment* may be used as a process—the decrease in behavior when the response has a consequence—or as an operation—the arrangement between response and the consequence. Unconditioned punishment means either the operation of delivering an unconditioned punisher, or the decrease in responding produced by that operation. Conditioned punishment means either the operation of delivering a conditioned punisher, or the decrease in responding produced by that operation. The modifier *positive* denotes a decrease in responding when the consequence of the response is to add something to the environment. In this case, the "something" is a positive punisher. In contrast, the modifier *negative* denotes a decrease in behavior when the consequence of the response is the removal of something. In this case, the "something" is a negative punisher.

An example using the pigeon pecking into slot #8 and getting food illustrates the difference between positive and negative punishment. Suppose that the pigeon's pecking occasionally produces food, but that also, a brief puff of compressed air is occasionally injected into the chamber in the vicinity of the pigeon when the pigeon pecks. Again, the pigeon will continue to receive food occasionally, but it will also receive the air puff occasionally . Assume that under these conditions, the pigeon is observed to peck into locus #8 less often than when responding doesn't produce the air puff. This procedure is called positive punishment in a sense that is analogous to positive reinforcement. The response produces an increase in something in the environment—in this case, the increase is the appearance of the air puff—and the rate of responding decreases.

Suppose now a slightly different situation is arranged, in which the apparatus is occasionally turned off and the opportunity to receive food is suspended for some specified period of time as a consequence of the pigeon's response. Assume that under these conditions, the pigeon is observed to peck into locus #8 less often than when responding doesn't have this consequence. This arrangement is called negative punishment in a sense that is analogous to negative reinforcement. The response produces a decrease in something in the environment—in this case the possibility of food—and the response decreases in frequency. In everyday language, the terms "penalty" and "time-out" are applied to this arrangement.

Note that "punisher" is the stimulus, and "punishment" is either the operation of presenting the punisher or the behavioral effect, a decrease in responding produced by that operation. That is, "punisher" and "punishment" are not interchangeable. Thus, to say that "An air blast served as punishment for the pigeon's pecking" is incorrect. One would have to say either "An air blast served as the punisher for the pecking," or "The delivery of an air blast served as the punishment for the pecking."

Two Further Considerations

There are two further considerations pertaining to the conceptual status of punishment. The first consideration involves a procedure called "Differential Reinforcement of Other" behavior, or DRO. This procedure is often used in applied settings to decrease troublesome behavior and correspondingly increase constructive behavior. In this procedure, an organism's behavioral repertoire is divided into two exhaustive and mutually exclusive classes: (a) some target response, and (b) all other responses. Reinforcers are delivered if the target response is not emitted, but withheld if the target response is emitted. Should this procedure be called a positive reinforcement procedure, because positive reinforcers are delivered for engaging in any other response than the target behavior? Alternatively, should it be called a negative punishment procedure, because the reinforcers are removed as a consequence of engaging in the target response? To some extent, the decision is arbitrary, as in deciding whether to call a glass of water capable of holding 8 ounces but currently holding only 4 ounces half full or half empty. Conventional usage favors the terminology of a reinforcement procedure, as in DRO. However, perhaps talking of the procedure in terms of a negative punishment procedure is conceptually more consistent, because the response class involved in the contingency is smaller.

The second consideration is that punishment takes place in a context of reinforcement. Suppose punishment is implemented for a response, but reinforcement isn't simultaneously maintained for the response. Rate of responding might well decrease in such circumstances. However, one can't be sure that if responding did decrease, the decrease was a function of the punishment, rather than the absence of reinforcement. In sum, in order for a response to be made and punished, the response must also be simultaneously related to or have a history of some form of reinforcement. If reinforcement is not involved, no response is present to be punished. As a result, when one talks about punishment, one is always talking about the effects of a punishment operation superimposed on a reinforcement operation.

OVERVIEW OF REINFORCEMENT AND PUNISHMENT

Figure 6.1 summarizes the relations called reinforcement and punishment.

1. The effect on the environment is whether the response increases or decreases a given form of stimulation.

2. The effect on behavior is whether the response increases or decreases in frequency.

3. Note that nothing is said about the "feeling" (e.g., pleasantness or unpleasantness, satisfaction or discomfort) produced by the stimulus, although the consequences may definitely produce feelings. Thus, the feeling produced by the consequence does not cause the effect on behavior. The consequence causes both the change in behavior and the feeling.

4. In correct usage, responses are reinforced or punished, not organisms.

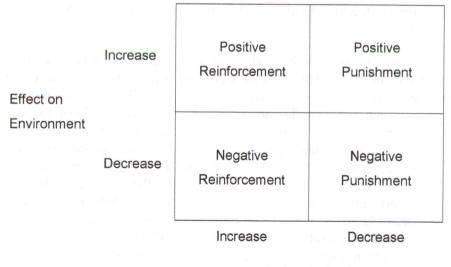

Figure 6.1   The Relations Called Reinforcement and Punishment

A single core sentence may be developed for the definitions, with appropriate selection of terms:

> (Positive/negative) (reinforcement/punishment) is the name for the (increase/decrease) in responding produced by a response dependent (increase/decrease) in a given form of stimulation.

OTHER COMBINATIONS AND CATEGORIES INVOLVING CONSEQUENCES

To be sure, the world of behavior is very complex. Chapter 5 began by trying to simplify several categories of behavior—various forms of innate behavior as well as two prominent forms of learned behavior, conditioned respondent and operant. Innate behavior emphasized stimulus presentations, where the term "presentation" is broadly conceived to include many forms of contact with stimuli. Learned behavior emphasized other environmental operations that are typically responsible for the various forms. For conditioned respondents, a signaling operation is combined with a stimulus presentation operation. For operant behavior, a signaling operation is combined with a consequential operation. The preceding section of the present chapter developed a consistent vocabulary for the function of consequences. In light of these distinctions, it is important to recognize that other possibilities exist for imposing the experimental operations.

Stimulus Presentation in Explicit Combination with Consequential Operations

When Chapter 5 analyzed conditioned respondent behavior, one technique suggested to identify the causal role of the CS-US contingency was to arrange for the response to prevent the occurrence of the US on a trial. As noted in Chapter 5, this procedure is called the omission procedure. The preparation chosen to illustrate the omission procedure was conditioned salivary responding. Other preparations and manipulations may now be considered. For example, one common preparation that is used to study respondent conditioning in the laboratory is eyeblink conditioning. In this procedure, a US of a puff of air to the eye or a mild electrical stimulation to the cheek below the eye is administered shortly after the onset of a visual or auditory CS. After a few such trials, a subject such as a human or a rabbit will come to blink in the presence of the CS.

At issue is whether the subject is blinking because of the negative reinforcement involved with avoiding or otherwise reducing the aversiveness of the US. One way to examine whether this relation is controlling behavior is to explicitly arrange for the response to reduce the intensity of the US. If the responding is being controlled by its consequences, then one would expect the response to become more probable, because one has explicitly arranged for the response to be beneficial. Alternatively, if the response is elicited, the situation reduces to that of intermittent US presentation. One would then expect the response to be somewhat less probable. The results of such research indicate that responding is not more probable (Mackintosh, 1974). This result supports the integrity of elicitation as a separate process.

To be sure, sometimes consequences can modify elicited behavior. Consider a preparation involving the punishment of shock-elicited aggression. In this research, subjects (e.g., monkeys) occasionally received a shock. The shock functioned as a US to elicit an aggressive response (a UR) toward an inanimate object in the subject's chamber. A consequential operation was then imposed whereby a second shock was administered contingent on the aggressive response. The research showed that the aggressive behavior decreased appreciably, although the monkeys did exhibit unfortunate side effects; they became difficult to manage and engaged in self-injurious behavior, biting and scratching themselves. In any case, the point remains that the target behavior of attacking the inanimate object did decrease, demonstrating that in some circumstances, consequences can modify even elicited behavior (Azrin, 1970).

Intermingling of Categories of Behavior

In addition to situations in which consequential operations are linked with stimulus presentations, there are situations in which conditioned respondent relations are involved in operant behavior. A common example is conditioned reinforcement. For present purposes, suppose that the stimulus-stimulus relations that produce a conditioned reinforcer are isomorphic with those that produce a CS. To be sure, the effectiveness of a stimulus as a conditioned reinforcer is measured differently than the effectiveness of a CS. The effectiveness of a conditioned reinforcer is measured in terms of how much emitted behavior it maintains when it is a consequence of a response, whereas the effectiveness of a CS is measured in terms of how much behavior it elicits.

Conditioned reinforcers are often used to train target responses. For example, an auditory stimulus, produced by, say, a toy hand-held clicker, might be established as a conditioned reinforcer by correlating it with food. The clicker can be sounded immediately after a target response as part of the training procedure to strengthen the response of a hungry subject. The rationale is that reinforcers work best when they occur as soon as possible after the target response. The sound of the clicker can be given immediately, rather than after a subject emits a response and moves to where it might receive a food reinforcer. Having to move to a particular location to receive the unconditioned reinforcer involves a delay, however brief, and such a delay might slow down the acquisition of the behavior. To be sure, the unconditioned reinforcer will need to be delivered, but much research has shown that presenting a conditioned reinforcer to "bridge" the gap between the response and the unconditioned reinforcer facilitates the acquisition of the desired response (Pryor, 1985; Skinner, 1951). Conditioned reinforcement is also involved to some degree in the controlled situation of the operant laboratory, where the sound of the food-dispensing mechanism occurs immediately after an appropriate response, contributing to the strengthening of the response. Comparable effects can be noted with conditioned punishment.

A second case involves another effect on operant behavior of a stimulus that has acquired behavioral significance through conditioned respondent relations. Suppose a hungry rat in an experimental chamber is presented with an operant discrimination task. If the rat presses a lever when a 1000 Hz tone is on, it will receive food. If the rat presses a lever when a 100 Hz tone is on, it will not receive food. The rat will readily learn to press when the 1000 Hz tone is on, but not when the 100 Hz tone is on. However, research has shown that the acquisition of the operant discrimination is facilitated if the rat receives prior conditioned respondent training in which the 1000 Hz tone is correlated with food, and the 100 Hz tone is presented alone. In addition, suppose that after the operant discrimination is acquired, it is reversed. Food is now produced by responding in the presence of 100 Hz tone, rather than the 1000 Hz tone. As with acquisition, research has shown that the reversal of the operant discrimination is facilitated if the rat receives prior conditioned respondent training in which the 100 Hz tone is correlated with food, and the 1000 Hz tone is presented alone. Clearly, behavior can be influenced by many different combinations of experimental operations (Mackintosh, 1974).

A final case is when a stimulus that has acquired behavioral significance through conditioned respondent relations is superimposed onto ongoing operant behavior. Suppose a hungry rat in an experimental chamber is pressing a lever and is occasionally producing food. Then a 1000 Hz tone that has previously been correlated with an electric shock in a conditioned respondent relation is superimposed onto the ongoing operant behavior. The presentation of the tone is independent of the rat's behavior. Research has shown that the rat's rate of lever pressing decreases in the presence of the tone, perhaps even to a zero level. A conditioned respondent process has affected the rate of an ongoing operant response, even though the operant relations haven't changed.

Now suppose the situation is changed slightly. Suppose the rat's lever pressing in an experimental chamber is maintained by negative reinforcement; lever pressing avoids electric shocks that will occasionally occur in the absence of responding. If the same 1000 Hz tone that has previously been correlated with an electric shock in a conditioned respondent relation is presented, research has shown that the rat's rate of lever pressing in the presence of the tone will increase substantially. As before, a conditioned respondent process has affected the rate of an ongoing operant response. However, even though the conditioned respondent relation between tone and shock is the same as with operant behavior maintained by positive reinforcement, and even though the same response—lever pressing—is being measured as with positive reinforcement, the opposite effect of the conditioned respondent relation is observed: When positive reinforcement maintains the ongoing operant behavior, the operant behavior decreases during the tone, but when negative reinforcement maintains the ongoing operant behavior, the operant behavior increases during the tone (Rescorla & Solomon, 1967). The point is that the total setting in which an organism is living needs to be examined to understand its behavior.

Molar and Molecular Analyses of Behavior Maintained by Negative Reinforcement

The terms *molar* and *molecular* were introduced in Chapter 5. These terms relate largely to the level of analysis, such as the time scope in an analysis of behavior. Analyses in terms of large-scale relations, spread across some relatively lengthy period of time, are conventionally referred to as molar analyses. Analyses in terms of small-scale relations, spread across some relatively brief or local period of time, are conventionally referred to as molecular analyses. Interestingly, certain of the avoidance work in the area of negative reinforcement might be regarded as one of the last vestiges of a molecular approach to operant behavior that incorporates respondent conditioning, albeit not as chains of S – R units. This work is typically cited as the "two-process theory" of avoidance. Here, however, the respondent conditioning component was responsible for motivation, not the behavior itself viewed as a series of S – R units. Suppose a procedure called the "discriminated avoidance procedure" is in effect. In this procedure as it might be used with a rat, a stimulus (say, a light) comes on in the rat's chamber. The light is often labeled a "warning stimulus." If the rat fails to run to the other end of its chamber after a short period of time, say 15 seconds, the rat receives a shock through the floor bars of the end of the chamber in which it remained. If the rat does run to the other end of its chamber, the warning stimulus terminates when the rat crosses the midline of the chamber and the shock is canceled on that trial. An analysis of this procedure according to two-process theory holds that the light is a conditioned aversive stimulus that has motivative properties, by virtue of its respondent conditioning relation with the US of the shock. The light generates fear, just as the shock generates fear, and the rat responds to escape from the conditioned fear of the light, just as it responds to escape from the unconditioned fear of the shock. Just as the rat's response concerning the shock is reinforced through negative reinforcement, so also is the rat's response concerning the light reinforced through negative reinforcement. The "avoidance" response is considered an escape response moved forward in time.

The contrary view is that responding in avoidance situations is a function of only one process, which is the operant reduction in shock frequency brought about by responding. Thus, this view emphasizes the direct operant relation between responding and reduction in the frequency of shocks received, rather than the control of responding being mediated by a hypothetical emotional, motivating state produced by classical conditioning. A state of fear may be said to exist, and no doubt one can specify physiological indicants of such an inner state. However, the causal explanation consists in specifying the relation between responding and the environmental context that produces the fear, not between responding and a hypothetical inner state.

Research has examined two important experimental questions: (a) Will any condition associated with fewer shocks serve as a reinforcer? and (b) How literally should "frequency reduction" be interpreted? Data have shown that when rats are given a choice between two conditions, their responding is often a function of molecular contingencies. They prefer the condition associated with the longer delay to the first shock, even though that same condition may be associated with a greater number of shocks in the long run (Gardner & Lewis, 1976). These data indicate that the temporal patterning of events is important, in addition to their frequency, and that literal interpretations of such parameters as frequency should be made with great caution. As with other research issues, debate is lively, and experimental analysts of behavior are conducting research aimed at putting the information together into a coherent picture (Catania, 2007).

IS THE DEFINITION OF REINFORCEMENT CIRCULAR?

Over the years, one of the most persistent criticisms of behavioral theory is that the definition of reinforcement is logically circular. That is, some people claim that since there is no a priori way to identify a reinforcer, the concept of reinforcement cannot be used in an explanation. The criticism often takes the following form:

The Circular Treatment

A. *Question*: Why did stimulus X produce an increase in responding?
   Answer: Because it was a reinforcer.

B. *Question*: How is it known that stimulus X was a reinforcer?
   Answer: Because it produced an increase in responding.

C. *Circularity*: Stimulus X is called a reinforcer because it produces an increase in responding, but then it is said to increase the responding because it is a reinforcer.

One prominent treatment suggested that the way out of this apparent problem involves transsituationality. That is, something may legitimately be labeled a reinforcer in one situation if it has previously functioned as a reinforcer in another situation (Meehl,

1950; Schnaitter, 1978). However, radical behaviorism has another approach to the matter.

The Non-circular Treatment

The above treatment is based on certain assumptions about the nature of language, namely that terms must have a sort of logical status that somehow permit predictions to be made. According to this view, transsituationality solves the problem because one can predict whether stimulus X will be a reinforcer in one situation by whether it is a reinforcer in another.

Radical behaviorists take a very different approach. In particular, the view that terms must have a logical status to be used in explanations is regarded as mischievous. The view presupposes a kind of reification, in which it is assumed that because a name can be applied to something, the "thing" so named must exist in the world at large and must have the status and properties ascribed to it via the naming process. Rather, for radical behaviorists reinforcement is simply the name for a relation brought about when certain conditions obtain in the environment. It is not the cause of the relation. In addition, that the concept of transsituationality is taken to solve the problem of circularity is also regarded as mischievous, and not a genuine solution at all. For example, if one wants to go this route, one has not specified why the reinforcer has the effect it does in the other situation. One has only deferred the question, not answered it.

A non-circular treatment follows from different assumptions about the nature of language. This treatment begins by re-casting question A above into three less complex questions:

1. Why is it said that responding increased? It occurred more often; for instance, as measured by the apparatus.

2. Why did it occur more often? A certain antecedent stimulus was present, and responding had previously produced a certain consequence in the presence of this antecedent stimulus. That is, a specified contingency was in effect. This is the level appropriate for a science of behavior, and it is the level at which behavior analysis operates.

3. Why did this contingency have this effect; that is, of producing the observed increase in responding? Given that question #2 has been asked and answered as above, question #3 is most meaningfully interpreted as a question about neuroscience and genetics. So interpreted, its answer will presumably be provided by neuroscientists and geneticists, rather than by psychologists per se. The assumption is that an organism's physiology inherits a genetic susceptibility to being changed by the consequences of prior actions. Organisms whose genetic endow-

ment is such that they are responsive to operant contingencies have presumably been selected during the lifetime of the species, as that species has evolved. Organisms that are susceptible to operant contingencies presumably have an increased chance of survival, in contrast to those organisms that are not sensitive to the consequences of prior actions.

Given that question A has been addressed differently, question B above may in turn be recast:

4. How is it that such a consequence is called a reinforcer? That's the term that is conventionally used to describe consequences that have the effect of producing an increase in responding when presented in the context of a contingency of reinforcement. Consequences that do not have this effect are not called reinforcers.

Indeed, in one of his early statements, Skinner (1938) pointed out that:

> A reinforcing stimulus is defined as such by its power to produce the resulting change. There is no circularity about this; some stimuli are found to produce the change, others not, and they are classified as reinforcing and non-reinforcing accordingly. A stimulus may possess the power to reinforce when it is first presented (when it is usually the stimulus of an unconditioned respondent) or it may acquire the power through conditioning. (p. 62)

In one of his last statements, Skinner stated: "Could anything be more factual than the effect of reinforcement, either in a single instance or when scheduled? What is hypothetical about it...? There is nothing circular in learning about the power of a reinforcer from observing its effect" (Skinner in Catania & Harnad, 1988, pp. 484, 486).

SELF-REINFORCEMENT?

An interesting conceptual issue regarding the function of consequences is self-reinforcement (Catania, 1975). Setting aside the terminological issue of whether consequences can make oneself stronger or more frequent, the question is whether individuals can reinforce their own responses in some sense. Suppose an individual has an itchy nose and scratches the itch. The response of scratching the itch is reinforced by the consequence of removing the itch, and the individual who has the itch is the same individual who has scratched and removed it. Does this state of affairs validate the sense of self-reinforcement, and that an individual is an agent? Worth noting is that the same itch would have been removed if someone else had scratched. Thus, there is no sense of unique or intrinsic self-reinforcement.

Related to self-reinforcement is automatic reinforcement (Vaughan & Michael, 1982). This term refers to a process in which an individual's verbal product, say a vocalized sound, resembles that produced by others and associated with reinforcement. The individual then repeatedly engages in behavior that produces this form of stimulation. A common example would be a child's babbling. The sounds are reinforcing because they are acoustically similar to sounds made by caregivers when attending to the child. The sounds will be even more reinforcing when they become even more acoustically similar to caregivers' vocalizations, in a process that contributes to the development of language. Another example would be singing a favorite song to oneself. The song was reinforcing, and singing the song is automatically strengthened because of the reinforcing nature of the song. Comparable analyses may be made of such activities as day-dreaming or fantasizing. One ordinarily day-dreams or fantasizes about events that are reinforcing in one's life. The reinforcement may be positive or negative. The point is that such phenomena may be understood in virtue of their relation to the environment. They do not reveal an autonomous or initiating influence over behavior.

As Catania (2007) has discussed, an alternative to speaking of self-reinforcement is to speak of self-regulation or self-management. Self-regulation is the process whereby individuals arrange their environment so that effective behavior results. There are two classes of response at issue: (a) the regulating behavior, and (b) the regulated behavior. Setting an alarm clock is one convenient example. Studying for an hour before watching a television program is another. Setting the alarm clock is the regulating behavior, and getting up on time is the regulated behavior. Watching television is the regulating behavior, and studying is the regulated behavior. Analysis of these situations indicates that getting up on time or receiving a good grade in the subject being studied is already important and reinforcing. In self-regulation, individuals take steps (in the form of the regulating behavior) to make responses (the regulated behavior) leading to particular consequences more probable. The regulating and regulated responses are contingently related and occur in a sequence. As before, the outcome of the regulated response would be just as reinforcing if someone else had set the alarm, or if someone else had compelled an individual to study before watching television. The history necessary to produce the self-regulating behavior and the parameters that affect the self-regulating behavior may be analyzed in the experimental laboratory (Rachlin & Green, 1972).

EXTINCTION

As with other terms, extinction has usage as both a noun and a verb, in the sense of an operation and a process. In its usage as an operation, extinction refers to carrying out certain operations not involving punishment that decrease the probability of a response. In its usage as a process, extinction refers to the decrease in responding produced by an extinction operation. In addition, extinction has both a respondent and operant usage.

With regard to conditioned respondent behavior, recall that a conditioned respondent is produced by the contingency between a CS and a US. One can degrade the contingency by conducting either of two operations. First, one can withhold the US after the CS. Second, one can present the US randomly with respect to the CS. In both cases, the conditioned respondent elicited by the CS decreases.

With regard to operant behavior, recall that an operant is a function of the contingency between a response and a consequence. Again, one can degrade the contingency by conducting either of two operations. First, one can withhold the consequence entirely after a response. Second, one can present the consequence randomly with respect to the response. In both cases, the probability of behavior changes. The review below is phrased in terms of extinction and positive reinforcement, and therefore concerns a decrease in responding. Analogous statements apply to extinction and negative reinforcement, and to extinction and punishment.

It is appropriate to use the term *extinction* when the following three conditions are satisfied:

1. A response formerly produced some consequence; the response now no longer produces that consequence. Thus, it could be that the consequence the response formerly produced now (a) no longer occurs, or (b) occurs regardless of whether the response has been made. In this second case, the event is not contingent upon responding. That is, the event happens independently of responding, and randomly with respect to responding.

2. The response decreases in frequency or probability.

3. The decrease in frequency or probability occurs because the response no longer produces the consequence it formerly did, and not as an artifact of other experimental operations.

In conventional usage, the response is extinguished, not the organism. Thus, standard usage is to say "The pigeon's pecking response was extinguished," rather than "The pigeon was extinguished for pecking." A moment's reflection suggests the pigeon wasn't made weaker or less frequent by the extinction operation.

SUPERSTITION

In certain instances, the mere presentation of a stimulus that might otherwise function as a reinforcer may produce an increase in behavior based simply on the adventitious temporal correlation between the response and the stimulus. This effect is called "superstition." To illustrate superstition, consider a hungry pigeon in an operant experimental chamber. Food is presented to the pigeon, independently of a response, every 30 seconds. The first time food is presented, the pigeon has just been stretching its neck upwards. During the next few minutes, the pigeon is observed stretching its neck upwards more frequently. Although food wasn't contingent upon neck stretching (i.e., the neck stretching didn't cause food to be delivered), the response nevertheless increased in frequency during the observation period, purely as a function of the adventitious correlation between neck stretching and food. As a result, behavior analysts have applied the term *superstition* from the everyday vocabulary to this change in behavior.

It is appropriate to use the term *superstition* when the following conditions are satisfied:

1. Some event that under other circumstances has been observed to function as a reinforcer occurs independently of a response.

2. There is an increase in the frequency or probability of one class of behavior that is temporally correlated with the event (i.e., a change in the level of stimulation).

3. The increase in the frequency or probability of the response occurs because of the adventitious temporal correlation between responding and the change in the level of stimulation.

The example above describes how superstition may apply to the adventitious development of a response. In addition, superstition may also apply to incidental features of an existing response. For example, when the pigeon is first learning to peck into locus #8 on the slot, it may have just turned in a circle, or it may be standing with a particular posture, before pecking and producing the reinforcer. In future occasions, the pigeon is observed turning a circle before pecking, or standing with a particular posture before pecking. What has happened?

Note that for the pigeon to receive food, all that is necessary is a peck into the slot. The pigeon's prior behavior or posture when it is pecking is incidental. Nevertheless, the delivery of food strengthens a wide variety of features of the pigeon's behavior. It strengthens the pecking itself, because pecking is required to produce the food, but it also strengthens turning in a circle or standing with a particular posture, even though these features are not required. Many aspects of behavior, such as "body English" of bowlers or golfers, develop in this way.

The examples above illustrate superstition involving an increase in some form of response. Other effects may involve a decrease in some form of response, analogous to punishment.

Finally, it should be noted that the effect is usually transient or temporary. That is, because there is no contingency between the response and the adventitious delivery of the stimulus that might otherwise be a reinforcer, as time progresses there are going to be instances in which the response occurs and the stimulus doesn't follow, and the stimulus occurs when the response hasn't preceded it. These variations typically result in the disappearance of an early form, perhaps to be replaced by another form. Again, athletes who continually cycle from one pattern of superstitious behavior to another are a common example.

MOTIVATIVE OPERATIONS

What, then, about "motivation?" The concept of motivation in operant behavior is accommodated by the concept of "motivative operation," formerly known as an "establishing operation." As defined by Michael (1993), a motivative operation is an environmental event, operation, or stimulus condition that affects an organism's repertoire by momentarily altering: (a) the reinforcing effectiveness of particular consequences and the discriminative relevance of antecedent stimuli correlated with those reinforcing consequences, and (b) the frequency of occurrence of that part of the organism's repertoire relevant to those consequences.

Imagine again a hungry pigeon in an experimental chamber with a slot into which it can peck and produce food. Suppose food is available to the pigeon when it pecks into locus #8 of its experimental chamber. Another feature is now added: A light is illuminated when the response will have this consequence but is off when it will not. Use of the light in this way is an example of Catania's signaling operation. An example of an motivative operation is deprivation. The pigeon might be deprived of food for 24 hours, or it might be deprived until it weighs about 80% of what it would weigh if it had unlimited access to food. The pigeon will rapidly come to peck when the light is on but not when it is off. The withholding of food has two effects. The first effect is to increase the behavioral relevance of: (a) the food itself, which functions as a reinforcer; as well as (b) the light, which functions as a discriminative stimulus. In the absence of the deprivation, the food and light would not be meaningful to the pigeon. Although food would be produced if the pigeon pecked into locus #8 when the light is on, if the pigeon is not deprived the pigeon does not engage in the response.

The second effect is to increase the rate at which the pigeon engages in any responses reinforced with food. For example, if the pigeon had previously received food when it pulled a chain, when the pigeon was deprived, the pigeon would begin pulling the chain more than it had when it was not deprived.

Why then is the hunger not considered a discriminative stimulus? To answer this question, it is useful to formalize the definition of a discriminative stimulus. A discriminative stimulus is an environmental event or condition in the presence of which responses are more probable than in its absence. The follow-up question may then be asked: Why are responses more probable in its presence than absence? The answer is that reinforcement is correlated with the presence and not the absence of the discriminative stimulus. In the example above, food would be produced if the pigeon pecked into locus #8 when the light was on, even if it wasn't hungry. The motivative operation doesn't determine whether the food is available; the state of the environment is what determines whether food is available. The motivative operation makes the contingency involving environmental discriminative stimuli, responses, and reinforcers relevant.

Importance of Motivative Operations

A proper analysis of motivative functions is of course vitally necessary to anyone who seeks a causal understanding of behavior. To illustrate the necessity, consider the following case involving positive reinforcement. Suppose that a hungry pigeon's pecking response to locus #8 on a slot in its experimental chamber will produce three seconds' access to mixed grain. Under these conditions the pigeon learns to peck the slot and will continue to do so. Next, the food dispenser is turned off. The pigeon responds numerous times but eventually stops. The pecking response has extinguished. If the pigeon was satiated prior to the experimental session and the rate of the pigeon's responding was observed to decrease to a comparably low level, use of the term *extinction* would not be correct. Extinction involves a decrease in responding brought about by discontinuing the response-reinforcer relation, not by altering motivation. In the present example, the response-reinforcer relation was discontinued by not presenting the mixed grain as a consequence of a response. The response-reinforcer relation could have been discontinued in another way, of course. The mixed grain could have been presented independently of a response.

In any case, both extinction and satiation reduce responding. However, what happens if the satiated pigeon is again deprived? If the decrease in responding was brought about by extinction, the pigeon would not respond, even if hungry. However, if the decrease in responding was brought about by satiation, the rat resumes responding when it is again hungry. The process that was used to decrease responding has different effects.

Parallel with Negative Reinforcement

Now consider the case of negative reinforcement. Suppose a pigeon's pecking response to locus #8 cancels an air blast that would otherwise be delivered to the pigeon. As before, assume that under these conditions the pigeon learns to peck the slot and will continue to do so. Avoidance is occurring. Now suppose the air compressor is turned off. The pigeon responds numerous times but eventually stops. Is it correct to say that the avoidance response has extinguished? After all, a piece of apparatus that is concerned with the development of the pigeon's responding has been turned off, and the pigeon's responding has decreased. Isn't that the same as the extinction of a response maintained through positive reinforcement?

The argument here is that it is not. The rationale for this answer is to be found in an analysis of the motivative relations. In the case of positive reinforcement, the hungry pigeon remains hungry, even though the food dispenser has been turned off, or even though food has been delivered independently of a response. The response is emitted, but it no longer has the original consequence. It decreases in frequency because of the extinction operation: The relation between the response and its consequence has been discontinued.

Does a comparable state of affairs exist in the case of negative reinforcement, for the pigeon that has avoided air blasts in the past but for which at present the air compressor is turned off? The argument here is that the state of affairs is not comparable. When the air compressor has been turned off, the procedure is the same as satiating the pigeon prior to the experimental session. The pigeon would presumably stop responding, but the operation affects the motivation to respond, not the environmental relations involved in the conditioning process. The pigeon is not motivated to respond if the air compressor is turned off. If the intent is to extinguish the avoidance response, the relation between the response and its consequence must be discontinued, but the motivating operation must be left in effect. Michael (1993) has correctly emphasized that doing something like turning off the air compressor in the example above is behaviorally neutral, much like making food reinforcement unavailable for a food-satiated rat.

How could the relation in negative reinforcement between the response and its consequence be discontinued, but the motivating operation left in effect? Suppose an arrangement is implemented in which if the pigeon doesn't respond, air blasts would be administered every n seconds. If the pigeon does respond, the blast is postponed for t seconds, where t is longer than n. The response could then be extinguished in either of two ways. The first way to extinguish the response is to administer air blasts every n seconds, even if the pigeon does respond. This manipulation corresponds to keeping the pigeon hungry but turning off the food dispenser. The second way to extinguish the response is to arrange for air blasts to be administered every t seconds, irrespective of the pigeon's response. This manipulation corresponds to giving the pigeon food independently of a response.

The point is that without recognizing the importance of the motivative operation, one might mistakenly assume that if avoidance responding decreases after the air compressor is turned off, the avoidance response has extinguished, when all that has happened is that one has manipulated the motivation to respond. Something directly related to the response-reinforcer relation needs to be manipulated, while keeping motivation constant.

Is an Air Blast an S^D for Negative Reinforcement?

The answer here is no, with reasoning analogous to why hunger is not an S^D for positive reinforcement. For purposes of illustration, consider an escape procedure in which the aversive stimulus—the air blast—comes on independently of any response and remains on until the designated response terminates it. As Michael (1993) has pointed out, the air blast is not regarded as an S^D because its absence has not been a condition in which an effective form of reinforcement was unavailable for a particular type of behavior. In the absence of the air blast, there is no effective consequence that could have failed to follow the response in an analog to the extinction responding that occurs in the absence of an S^D. In the absence of the air blast, the relevant motivative operation is absent. The fact that the key peck does not turn off the non-present air blast is in no sense extinction, but is rather like the unavailability of food when the pigeon is satiated. The absence of the air blast is more like the absence of food deprivation than like the absence of the S^D.

To be sure, Michael (1993) has pointed out that one could have a discriminated escape procedure. One might arrange for pecking to terminate an air blast only when a light was on. The light would then be an S^D in a meaningful sense of the term. Negative reinforcement (i.e., the termination of the air blast) is relevant when the light is off, because the air blast is on, but the negative reinforcement is unavailable.

SUMMARY

Table 6–1 presents some key terms relating to operant behavior and its modification. This behavior is emitted by the subject, and is acquired during the lifetime of the subject. Two common examples are the emission of a lever press by a rat, or of a key peck by a pigeon. The table gives the term, and then describes the relation to ongoing behavior, the nature of the experimental operation that affects the behavior, and the resulting effect on behavior. The analyses of Chapter 6 have emphasized a conceptually consistent treatment of the vocabulary of consequences. These analyses point to a further central feature of radical behaviorism: the thesis of selection by consequences as a causal mode. Chapter 7, the final chapter of the initial section of the book dealing with the foundations of radical behaviorism, addresses this important topic.

Table 6.1

Some terms having to do with operant behavior and the modification of operant behavior via experimental operations that affect consequences

Term	Relation to ongoing behavior	Experimental operation	Effect on behavior
positive reinforcement	contingent on target response	target response produces new stimulus or condition	increased behavior (because of contingency between target response and consequence)

Term	Relation to ongoing behavior	Experimental operation	Effect on behavior
negative reinforcement: escape	contingent on target response	target response terminates ongoing stimulus or condition	increased behavior (because of contingency between target response and consequence)
negative reinforcement: avoidance	contingent on target response	target response postpones or cancels stimulus or condition that is not present but in the absence of response would occur at some time in the future	increased behavior (because of contingency between target response and consequence)
positive punishment	contingent on target response (which is concurrently producing reinforcers or maintaining a condition in which reinforcers are delivered)	target response produces new stimulus or condition	decreased behavior (because of contingency between target response and consequence)
Negative punishment: penalty, time out, omission training, DRO	contingent on target response (which is concurrently producing reinforcers or maintaining a condition in which reinforcers are delivered)	target response terminates ongoing stimulus or condition, or postpones or cancels stimulus or condition that is not present but in the absence of response would occur at some time in the future	decreased behavior (because of contingency between target response and consequence)
extinction–1	contingent on target response	response no longer produces reinforcer	decreased behavior (because of degraded contingency between target response and consequence)
extinction–2	contingent on target response	former reinforcer delivered randomly, independent of a response	decreased behavior (because of degraded contingency between targed response and consequence)
spontaneous recovery	n/a	response-reinforcer training, followed by extinction trials, followed by removal of subject	temporary increase in behavior immediately after reintroduction to apparatus

Term	Relation to ongoing behavior	Experimental operation	Effect on behavior
Spontaneous recovery (continued)		from apparatus, followed by reintroduction of subject to apparatus	
satiation	independent of response	allowing relatively unrestricted contact with reinforcer prior to or during an experimental session for the purpose of decreasing motivation, rather than degrading the contingency between a target response and consequence	decreased behavior
deprivation	independent of response	restricting contact with a reinforcer prior to or during an experimental session for the purpose of increasing motivation, rather than strengthening the contingency between a target response and consequence	increased behavior
establishing operation (generic term, also known as motivative operation; satiation and deprivation are two specific types of motivative operations: a third type is imposing an aversive stimulus as antecedent condition	independent of response	imposing an aversive stimulus as an antecedent condition or controlling contact with reinforcers prior to experimental session for purpose of altering motivation, rather than altering response-reinforcer contingency	(a) momentary effectiveness of reinforcers supporting operant behavior is altered ("establishing" increases the effectiveness; "abolishing" decreases the effectiveness) (b) the momentary probability of operants that have produced such reinforcement is altered ("evocative effect": an increase in the probability; "abative effect: a decrease in the probability)

REFERENCES

Azrin, N. H. (1970). Punishment of elicited aggression. *Journal of the Experimental Analysis of Behavior, 14*, 7–10.

Catania, A. C. (1975). The myth of self-reinforcement. *Behaviorism, 3*, 192–199.

Catania, A. C. (2007). *Learning* (4th interim ed.). Cornwall-on-Hudson, NY: Sloan Publishing.

Catania, A. C., & Harnad, S. (Eds.) (1988). *The Selection of Behavior: The Operant Behaviorism of B. F. Skinner: Comments and Controversies*. Cambridge: Cambridge University Press.

Gardner, E., & Lewis, P. (1976). Negative reinforcement with shock frequency increase. *Journal of the Experimental Analysis of Behavior, 25*, 3–14.

Mackintosh, N. J. (1974). *The psychology of animal learning*. New York: Academic Press.

Meehl, P. E. (1950). On the circularity of the law of effect. *Psychological Bulletin, 47*, 52–75.

Michael, J. (1993). Establishing operations. *The Behavior Analyst, 16*, 191–206.

Pryor, K. (1985). *Don't shoot the dog*. New York: Bantam.

Rachlin, H., & Green, L. (1972). Commitment, choice, and self-control. *Journal of the Experimental Analysis of Behavior, 17*, 15–22.

Rescorla, R. A., & Solomon, R. L. (1967). Two-process learning theory: Relationships between Pavlovian conditioning and instrumental learning. *Psychological Review, 74*, 151–182.

Schnaitter, R. (1978). Circularity, trans-situationality, and the law of effect. *Psychological Record, 28*, 353–362.

Skinner, B. F. (1938). *Behavior of organisms*. New York: Appleton-Century.

Skinner, B. F. (1951). How to teach animals. *Scientific American, 185*, 26–29.

Vaughan, M. E., & Michael, J. L. (1982). Automatic reinforcement: An important but ignored concept. *Behaviorism, 10*, 217–227.

STUDY QUESTIONS

1. Describe the three conditions that must prevail in order to speak of the reinforcement relation, according to Catania (2007).

2. Distinguish between reinforcer and reinforcement.

3. Distinguish between positive and negative reinforcement. Distinguish between escape and avoidance as instances of negative reinforcement.

4. Describe the three conditions that must prevail in order to speak of the punishment relation, according to Catania (2007).

5. Distinguish between punisher and punishment.

6. Distinguish between positive and negative punishment.

7. Describe the criticism that the definition of reinforcement is circular. Describe the non-circular treatment of the definition of reinforcement.

8. Describe the three conditions that must prevail in order to speak of extinction, following from Catania (2007).

9. Describe the three conditions that must prevail in order to speak of superstition, following from Catania (2007).

10. Define establishing operation, according to Michael (1993).

11. Describe why hunger is not considered a discriminative stimulus for negative reinforcement.

12. Describe why turning off a device that supplies an aversive stimulus to a subject is not the same as the extinction of a response maintained by positive reinforcement.

13. Describe why an ongoing aversive stimulus is not considered a discriminative stimulus for negative reinforcement.

14. Distinguish between molar and molecular analysis of behavior maintained by negative reinforcement.

15. Describe why the following definition is incorrect: "Positive reinforcement is presenting something pleasant after a response."

16. Describe why the following definition is incorrect: "Positive reinforcement is presenting something and the response increases."

17. Describe why the following definition is incorrect: "Positive punishment is presenting something unpleasant after a response."

18. Describe why the following definition is incorrect: "Positive punishment is presenting something and the response decreases."

19. Describe why the following definition is incorrect: "Negative reinforcement is removing something unpleasant after a response."

20. Describe why the following definition is incorrect: "Negative reinforcement is removing something and the response increases."

21. Describe why the following definition is incorrect: "Negative punishment is removing something pleasant after a response."

22. Describe why the following definition is incorrect: "Negative punishment is removing something and the response decreases."

7

Selection by Consequences

Synopsis of Chapter 7: The preceding three chapters have examined behavior as a subject matter in its own right, categories of behavior, and the development of a systematic vocabulary that recognizes the function of consequences. Chapter 7 addresses the relevant causal mode for radical behaviorism: selection by consequences. Selection as a causal mode has long been recognized in biology, as exemplified by Darwin's ideas about the evolution of species by means of natural selection. For radical behaviorism, the environment selects behavioral characteristics of organisms, just as it selects their morphological characteristics. Behavior is selected at the phylogenic level when the environment creates a repertoire of innate behavior. Behavior is selected at the ontogenic level when the environment creates new or modifies existing repertoires of learned behavior. Behavior is selected at the cultural level when the environment creates new or modifies existing cultural practices. Just as the survival of organisms is at risk if they are not sensitive to the consequences of their behavior, so also is the survival of cultures at risk if they are not sensitive to the consequences of their practices. As in prior chapters, the review of the three levels employs parallel language, to show the parallels in the selection process.

As a science pertaining to the behavior of organisms, behavior analysis is one of the life sciences and ultimately a branch of biology. Selection by consequences is an important causal mode in biology, and it is just as important in behavior analysis as it is the rest of biology.

SELECTION BY CONSEQUENCES: CYCLES OF VARIATION, INTERACTION, AND DIFFERENTIAL REPLICATION

In its general sense, the term *selection* may be understood as the name for the process in which repeated cycles occur of: (a) variation, (b) interaction with the environment, and

136

(c) differential replication as a function of the interaction. Charles Darwin proposed the idea of evolution by natural selection in his book *On the Origin of Species by Means of Natural Selection* (Darwin, 1859). Darwin had read the work of Thomas Malthus (1766–1834), an English political economist, who noted that organisms produce many more offspring than can be reasonably expected to survive in a particular environment. Among these organisms and their offspring, those who have some advantage over others are "favored" and will survive. Those who don't have an advantage will perish. Consequently, all organisms are in a life-long struggle to survive, typically involving other organisms that are similar to themselves. The struggle to survive takes many forms. One is avoiding predators. Prey don't necessarily need to run faster than the predator to survive. It is fine if they do, but at the very least they have to run faster than other prey. A second is gaining preferential access to life-sustaining resources. Organisms have an increased chance of survival if they can get more food and water than other organisms. A third is gaining preferential reproductive access to mates. Organisms who reproduce are the ones who have their genes expressed in the next generation.

The variation that enters into the struggle concerns the distribution of a given characteristic in a population of organisms. It is convenient to talk of the characteristic as randomly varying in the population, and to talk of a particular mean of the characteristic in the population. The term fitness refers to how well organisms with their characteristics meet whatever demands are posed by the environment in the struggle to survive or reproduce at any point during the repeated cycles. Important to note is that the fitness of organisms is judged relative to the environment that poses the demands on the organisms, based on their characteristics. If that environment changes significantly, perhaps the characteristics that had previously favored the organisms no longer stand the organisms in good stead, and the organisms will perish, to be replaced by other organisms with other characteristics. Fitness is conditional and does not necessarily imply improvement in any absolute sense. The term *lineage* refers to the entire history or line of descent of the characteristic as a consequence of the selection process, starting with the original distribution of characteristics and extending across time to its currently existing form or iteration.

NATURAL SELECTION

Natural selection is one kind of Darwinian selection process. In natural selection, the interaction with the environment concerns survival of the individual organism. As described above, the survival of an organism is contingent on one or more of the aforementioned characteristics because the characteristics afford favorable access to life-sustaining resources or escape from predators. If a bird's beak is stout enough to allow it to crack open a particular kind of seed in its environment, the bird will have an advantage over other birds whose beaks are thinner. However, if the environment changes and a different kind of seed begins to grow, the bird with a thinner beak may be able to reach the new kind of seed, which the bird with the stout beak cannot. Similarly, organisms who are faster than others of the same species will escape a predator. In such cases, organisms with particular characteristics will survive, and organisms that lack the characteristics will not. The organisms of the next generation are the offspring of those that possessed the characteristics upon which survival was contingent. Differential replication concerns the biological mechanisms and processes by which the characteristic can be transmitted to and expressed in future generations of organisms. That only particular organisms with particular characteristics survive implies that the mean of the future distribution may be expected to shift in the direction that the surviving organisms and their characteristics are from the original mean. Again, this shift does not necessarily imply a purposeful improvement, but rather only an adaptation to prevailing conditions.

Thus, at any given time, the living organisms that are the objects of study stand at the end of a lineage that has been selected through interaction with the environment. Other organisms from other lineages may have lived previously, but they did not survive because they lacked important characteristics, or because the ones they did possess did not serve them well in the struggle for survival, for example, if the environment changed in some way. They perished, and left no line of descent.

Sexual Selection

Sexual selection is a second kind of Darwinian selection process. In sexual selection, the interaction with the environment concerns reproduction. Some organisms are better able to attract mates, by virtue of having particular bodily characteristics. The organisms that attract mates are the organisms that reproduce and transmit their genes to the next generation. A female bird may grant reproductive access to a male with brightly colored feathers and not to a male with drab feathers. A lioness may grant reproductive access to a large alpha male lion but not a small male. In such cases, genes for males with bright feathers or large size are differentially replicated by being differentially transmitted and expressed in the offspring.

To be sure, in some cases sexual selection may well be correlated with natural selection and an accompanying competitive survival advantage in the environment. In the case of the lions, the large alpha male lion may be so physically imposing it will keep away predators or other rivals that will interfere with the upbringing of the cubs. It may intimidate and keep away other rivals from food sources, increasing the chances of the survival of the cubs in which the lioness has invested her maternal resources. A human female may select her mate on the basis of his power and status for related reasons. Similarly, a human male may select his mate on the basis of her physical proportions (e.g., ratios involving shoulders to waists to hips) and symmetrical characteristics of her body (e.g., in the facial structure), which are presumed to be correlated with her fertility, ability to nurture offspring, resistance to disease, and general good health.

In any event, sexual selection involves the same elements of the selection process as natural selection: variation, interaction, differential replication. There is variation in the characteristics, interaction in the form of reproductive access, and a resulting differential replication when only some organisms produce offspring. The result is that the next generation has characteristics inherited from only some of the prior generation. The difference between natural and sexual selection is that the characteristics are not necessarily related to the survival of the individual organism, although certainly the survival of a line of descent may be said to be contingent on the characteristics.

"SELECTION FOR" VERSUS "SELECTION OF"

A further point may now be made concerning evolutionary processes and selection. This point completes the story of how organisms come to possess the characteristics they do, and concerns the distinction between "selection for" and "selection of." Organisms that are living today stand at the end of a long evolutionary history, and they possess a wide variety of characteristics as a consequence of this history. Some of these organisms and their characteristics have been directly selected through interaction with the environment in the form of natural or sexual selection. In conventional parlance, there is said to be "selection for" these organisms on the basis of their characteristics. Other characteristics are present in these organisms because the characteristics have simply been correlated with those characteristics that were selected for, without being necessary elements of the selection process itself. In conventional parlance, there is said to be "selection of" these characteristics. Selection for denotes the causes of the selection process, whereas selection of denotes the effects (Sober, 1984).

In "selection for" organisms, and using natural selection as the example, the survival of an organism, and hence the differential replication of its characteristics in the population, are a direct function of interaction with the environment. A frequently cited example of "selection for" organisms with particular morphological characteristics via repeated cycles of variation, interaction with the environment, and differential replication is that of the peppered moth, *biston betularia*. This species of moth lives near industrial cities in England. It gets its common name from the scattered dark markings on its wings and body. The process of natural selection involves its coloration. In the early to mid-nineteenth century, light colored lichens lived on the trunks of the trees. The moths flew at night but rested during the days on the trees. The lighter-colored moths in the population were virtually the same color as the lichens, so they were hard to spot during the day. In contrast, the darker-colored moths stood out. Consequently, birds preyed on the darker-colored moths. In this case, the lighter-colored moths had an obvious survival advantage, and lighter-colored moths started to become more prevalent in the population of moths.

However, as coal burning increased during the later nineteenth century and continued into the twentieth, the environment changed. Atmospheric soot began to kill the light-colored lichens on the trees, and the dark bark of the trees was unmasked. The darker-colored moths in the population were now virtually the same color as the dark tree bark, so they were now hard to spot during the day. In contrast, the lighter-colored moths stood out. Consequently, birds now preyed on the lighter-colored moths. In this case, the darker-colored moths had an obvious survival advantage, and darker-colored moths started to become more prevalent in the population of moths. However, as pollution control increased in the latter half of the twentieth century, soot was reduced, the lichens returned to the tree trunks, and the lighter-colored form is making a comeback. In other words, the environment was selecting for certain organisms from a population of organisms based on their morphological characteristics, with the result that subsequent generations of the organisms reflected those characteristics.

In "selection of" organisms, the concern is with those characteristics that are present in organisms living today but upon which survival was not directly contingent in the evolutionary past. That is, these characteristics simply accompanied the characteristics upon which survival was directly contingent. These characteristics may remain unrelated to fitness, or they may become directly related to fitness in the evolutionary future, if the environment changes. To be sure, these characteristics may be traced to the genetics of the organism, as indeed everything related to the structure of the living organism may be traced to its genetics. Nevertheless, regardless of whether these characteristics become significant, they are part of the organism's genetic endowment, and they would not be present in the population if the ancestors of the organism had not survived long enough to reproduce.

An example may be used to illustrate the distinction between selection for and selection of (Sober, 1984). Suppose there are two sorts of balls mixed together in an urn. One sort of ball is 5 cm in diameter; these balls are colored red. The other sort of ball is 10 cm in diameter; these balls are colored green. Now suppose all balls from the urn are subjected to a filtering device that has holes 5.1 cm in diameter drilled in it. The smaller balls will in fact pass through the device, whereas the larger balls will not. The result of the filtering process would be two populations of balls, one large and one small. The balls have been selected for size, but accompanying the selection for size is the selection of color, because the characteristic of color happens to accompany the characteristic of size. The distinction is relevant because if an observer who was not informed of the selection criterion before the process began examined the two populations of balls after the fact, the observer would not be able to determine what the selection criterion was. Indeed, an observer might speculate that the balls were selected on the basis of color, rather than size. Of course, if there were any 5 cm balls that were a color other than red, they would have been selected along with all the 5 cm red balls, but the process just wasn't presented with any 5 cm balls that were a color other than red.

A further example of the distinction between selection for and selection of is the spandrel in certain forms of architecture (Gould & Lewontin, 1979). Spandrels are somewhat triangular vacant spaces formed when the curve of an arch meets a horizontal support element in a building. Spandrels may be understood as artifacts of a prevalent construction process, rather than anything upon which the structural integrity of the buildings is contingent. When many buildings were constructed with arches and horizontal elements, resulting in spandrels, artisans set about decorating the spandrels. The result was that fashionably decorated spandrels became very prominent architectural features in the design of buildings (e.g., San Marco in Venice). The decorated spandrels weren't selected for, in the sense of being a deliberate or essential structural design feature. Rather, the arches joined by horizontal elements were the design features. The decorated spandrels simply accompanied the design feature and became prominent.

REVIEW

The driving forces behind natural and sexual selection are: (a) differential success in gaining or avoiding contact with specific forms of environmental stimulation, and (b) differential success in mating and reproduction. Each outcome leads ultimately to survival of the line of descent of organisms having certain characteristics. In addition, the selection process entails a mechanism for replicating the characteristic in question by transmitting and expressing it in the future. Notably, each step in the selection process produces a new distribution with respect to which the selection process plays out over time. In this way, selection may produce a systematic change across evolutionary time in the mean of the distribution of characteristics with which the environment interacts.

The term *genome* and its cognate *genotype* refer to the entire set of information carried in the genes of the organism. The term *phenome* and its cognate *phenotype* refer to the actual outward expression in structural and indeed behavioral characteristics of the organism. Of additional importance is that selection processes can produce organisms with a wide variety of characteristics. Some characteristics were selected because they contributed to survival, but not all characteristics that end up being present are so because they have contributed to survival in the past. When viewed in the context of a reproductively isolated lineage that produces offspring that can themselves reproduce, the result of the selection process is the biological entity called a species. Organisms that can't meet the demands of the environment, for example, because they don't possess the relevant characteristics, perish. If those organisms existed as members of a species, the species then becomes extinct.

THE EVOLUTION OF BEHAVIOR: SELECTION BY CONSEQUENCES AS A CAUSAL MODE

Radical behaviorists find it useful to analyze the evolution of behavior using concepts that are similar to those of natural and sexual selection. For example, not only do contingencies in the environment across time select organisms with particular bodily characteristics, but contingencies also select particular behavioral characteristics, based on the fitness of the behavioral characteristics. Radical behaviorists suggest that there are three levels of the analysis: phylogenic, ontogenic, and cultural. At the phylogenic level, the contingencies in the environment select innate forms of behavior during the lifetime of the species. In a metaphorical extension of the concept of selection, at the ontogenic level the contingencies in the environment select or modify forms of behavior during the lifetime of the individual organism. In a further metaphorical extension, at the cultural level the contingencies in the environment select or modify cultural practices during the lifetime of the culture. It is useful to look more closely at the contingencies that apply to each level of the analysis.

The Phylogenic Level

The phylogenic level concerns the selection of innate behavior by the environment during the evolutionary history of the species. The relevant sciences at this level are behavioral genetics and ethology. Assume there is initially a distribution of innate behavior across some population of organisms in response to forms of environmental stimulation. Examples of these forms of innate behavior were discussed in Chapter 5. The environment at a given time favors organisms having particular forms of innate behavior, as those forms concern, for instance, behavior with respect to food, water, or predators lurking nearby. Those organisms possessing certain forms of innate behavior (i.e., behavioral phenotypes) are able to survive and reproduce. A behavioral counterpart of sexual selection recognizes that organisms having particular forms of innate behavior related to mating and reproduction have differential reproductive success.

Thus, the fitness of innate behavior is judged in terms of its consequences: (a) differential success in gaining or avoiding contact with specific forms of environmental stimulation, and (b) differential success in mating and reproduction. Each outcome leads ultimately to survival of a line of descent, if not also of the individual organism at least to the point it reproduces. As the organism reproduces, the genes responsible for the behavioral characteristics replicate themselves across time, resulting in the transmission and expression of the relevant behavioral characteristics to future generations and the evolution of innate behavior. Analogous to the way they inherit bodily characteristics, subsequent generations of organisms inherit the innate behavior in question. The lineage is the development of the innate behavior, traced from its initial to its current form. When viewed in the context of a reproductively isolated population of organisms, the result is the behavioral entity called a repertoire of species-specific innate behavior. Organisms that don't possess the necessary forms of innate behavior perish. If those organisms existed as members of a species, the species then becomes extinct.

One can meaningfully use the phrase "selection by consequences" to describe the important relations. There is variation, interaction, and differential replication. The variation is in the behavioral characteristics of the population. The interaction consists in differential access to resources, differential avoidance of predators, or differential reproductive success. The differential replication is when organisms with a given behavioral phenotype survive and reproduce, as compared with other organisms from the population. When the behavioral characteristics contribute to the survival of the organism, the organism flourishes. When they don't, the organism perishes. Knowledge of the environment is critical to understanding the entire process because the contingency between: (a) the innate behavioral characteristics of the organism, and (b) differential survival or reproduction mediated by those behavioral characteristics is a result of the cycles of interaction with the environment.

The Ontogenic Level

The ontogenic level concerns the selection of behavior by the environment during the lifetime of the individual organism. The relevant science at this level is behavior analysis. Assume that a given organism initially engages in some amount of behavior. After all, behavior is one of the characteristics of a living organism. The behavior could simply be randomly varying, uncommitted behavior, or it could even be behavior that is already a function of some form of environmental stimulation. At some point, these instances of behavior may begin to produce consequences that were not previously produced. For example, the behavior may produce access to food or water, or it may avoid predators.

If an organism engages in particular forms of behavior, and particular consequences follow, the organism may be affected by those consequences such that the forms of the behavior begin to occur more frequently in the future. Clearly, behavior that produces access to food is beneficial to the organism, and organisms whose behavior is sensitive to its consequences have an increased chance of survival. If particular antecedent stimuli are correlated with the response having those consequences, the antecedent stimuli may also enter into the relation that controls the behavior in question. As analyzed in Chapters 5 and 6, when consequences control behavior, the environmental relations are called operant relations, and the behavior in question is called operant behavior. The operant behavior is then available to the organism as it encounters future, related situations in the environment. Responses that don't possess the relevant characteristics decrease in frequency, analogous to extinction of a species. In fact, if the environment does not (for whatever reason) select a sufficient number of suitable responses in other, genetically similar organisms, then that species of organism might become extinct as well.

Appropriate to emphasize is that the environmental consequences of the behavior select the behavior having particular characteristics from a population of behavior that has various characteristics, in the same way that natural selection may select an organism having particular characteristics from a population of organisms that has various characteristics. In addition, there can be the behavioral counterpart of selection *for* and selection *of*. The susceptibility to selection by consequences may contribute directly to survival, in the sense of selection for. Alternatively, the susceptibility in question may have simply accompanied natural or sexual selection, in the sense of selection of. The lineage is the development of the acquired operant behavior, traced from its initial to its current form. When viewed in the context of a collection of populations of responses, the result is the behavioral entity called a repertoire of operant behavior.

As with fitness at the phylogenic level, the fitness of the operant repertoire is ultimately judged relative to the environment that poses the demands on the repertoire. If that environment changes significantly, perhaps the responses that had previously mediated solutions to problems posed by the environment no longer stand the organism in good stead. Similarly, perhaps responses that had previously been strengthened through certain consequences are now counterproductive. In these cases, unless the responses are modified, the organism will perish.

For instance, in much of the evolutionary past of humans, their activities that resulted in procuring and consuming sweet food were reinforced by the sweet food. This relation was decidedly adaptive. Now, however, humans consume much more sweet food than is required for good health, resulting in tooth decay and obesity. A change in the environment, notably the ready availability of sweet food, has rendered formerly adaptive behavioral relations less adaptive, if not outright harmful.

Overall, one can meaningfully use the phrase "selection by consequences" to describe the important relations at the ontogenic level. There is variation, interaction, and differential replication. The variation is in the responses. At least in the short term, the interaction consists in the reinforcer that strengthens particular responses from a population of varying responses on the basis of the functional characteristics of the response. The differential replication is that these responses become a continuing part of the organism's repertoire. Knowledge of the environment is critical to understanding the entire process because the contingency between response and reinforcer is a result of the cycles of interaction with the environment. Behavior analysts become interested in the process when the various classes of responses develop into an operant repertoire over the lifetime of the individual organism.

The Cultural Level

The cultural level concerns the selection of cultural practices by the environment during the lifetime of the culture. The relevant science at this level is a behavior-analytically informed social or cultural anthropology. Assume for a given group that there is initially a distribution of social practices. Particular forms among those social practices are favored in some way: they are better able to promote the welfare if not ultimately the very survival of the group. These practices might pertain to how certain classes of individuals within the group are treated (e.g., the young, the old, the sick, the educationally, socially, or economically disadvantaged), how tools are made, how resources are acquired and consumed, how agriculture is practiced, how waste products are disposed of, or indeed how members are convinced to work collectively for the very survival of the group. The practices would be useful to the group even if there were no competition with other groups; the group would still be in competition with its environment. The practices themselves may be understood as forms of operant behavior, but metaphorically extending across the lifetime of the group, rather than simply across the lifetime of any individual member of the group. When the group engages in forms of behavior that are beneficial to its welfare or survival, the practices tend to occur more frequently in the future.

What, then, about future generations of the group? Some way of replicating the practices, such that they are transmitted and expressed in the future, is obviously beneficial. Thus, at the cultural level of analysis, not only are there important contingencies involving: (a) the degree to which various practices solve enduring problems related to the welfare and survival of the group as a whole; but there are also important contingencies involving (b) the actual practices of transmitting the practices to the members of the group, such that other members come in contact with them and end up actually engaging in them. These contingencies involve the more localized social reinforcers administered among the members of the group for instruction in and adherence to group practices. Future generations of the group acquire the practices because the members of an earlier time have modified the artifacts of the culture in such a way that the important practices are available in the future. Language is a particularly important medium for transmitting the relevant practices to future generations.

Overall, the lineage is the development of the group practices, traced from its initial to its current form. When viewed in the context of a collection of a population of practices and the artifacts involved in their replication, the result is the entity that from the behavioral perspective is called a culture. Given that cultural practices are forms of operant behavior, the evolution of these cultural practices is also similar to the evolution of the morphological characteristics of a species, such as particular forms of hearts, stomachs, eyes, ears, fins, legs, wings, and so on.

As with fitness at the phylogenic and ontogenic levels, the fitness of the culture is ultimately judged relative to the environment that poses the demands on the culture. That environment consists of geographic variables, but also competing practices from other cultures. If that environment changes significantly, perhaps the practices that had previously mediated solutions to problems posed by the environment no longer stand the culture in good stead. Similarly, perhaps practices that had previously been strengthened through the social contingencies of the culture are now counterproductive. In these cases, unless the cultural practices are modified, the culture will perish.

One can meaningfully use the phrase "selection by consequences" to describe the important relations. There is variation, interaction, and differential replication. The variation is in the practices of the culture. In the short term, the interaction consists in the social reinforcement, administered among the group, that strengthens particular practices that then become part of the culture. In the long term, the degree to which the practices provide solutions to enduring problems related to the welfare of the group, or at least do not interfere with providing those solutions, further selects practices by contributing to the survival of the culture. The replication is in the interlocking social contingencies and patterns of social reinforcement in the culture, generally through language, through which the practices are transmitted and expressed in the future. Knowledge of the environment is critical because the contingency between cultural practices and social reinforcement is a result of the cycles of interaction with the environment.

SOME FURTHER CONSIDERATIONS REGARDING SELECTION OF BEHAVIOR BY ITS CONSEQUENCES

Selection and the Contributions of Genetics and the Nervous System

Selection acts on organisms as a function of their characteristics, both bodily and behavioral. With respect to bodily characteristics, the genes of the selected organism provide the recipe for these characteristics, as well as for the extent to which these characteristics can be modified by experience. For example, an organism's genetic endowment provides it with a particular musculature, but its genetic endowment might also mean that the musculature can be modified through exercise. However, whether the musculature is actually modified is determined by the interaction with the environment. Similarly, an organism's genetic endowment might provide it with a variety of genetic mechanisms that can be switched on and off, producing a variety of different effects. The mechanisms may well be switched on and off by contact with certain variables in the environment, such as stimuli or even complex relations among stimuli.

With respect to innate behavioral characteristics (the phylogenic level), the genes of the selected organism provide the recipe for its nervous system. By virtue of this aspect of the recipe, its nervous system controls structures that may respond in relatively fixed ways, given relatively fixed forms of stimulation and conditions in the environment. For example, organisms might spin webs, build nests, sing songs, salivate when presented with food, retrieve eggs when they roll away from a nest, stay close to objects that are present in their immediate environment a few hours after hatching, and so on, given appropriate prior conditions. The genes responsible for the nervous system that determines the form of the innate behavior are replicated across time, resulting in the transmission and expression of the innate behavior to future generations.

With respect to acquired behavioral characteristics (the ontogenic level), the process is a bit more complex. Again, the genes of the selected organism provide the recipe for its nervous system. In this case, however, by virtue of a different aspect of the recipe, the nervous system is such that it can be modified by environmental relations. In a science of behavior, the modified nervous system is the replicator that transmits the form of the acquired behavior across time, resulting in the expression of the acquired behavior in similar situations in the future. Whether the nervous system is actually modified, with the result that behavior is actually acquired, is determined by the interaction with the environment.

Three other genetically based features of the nervous system are of service to organisms at the ontogenic level. First, it was previously noted that consequences select operant behavior from the population of randomly varying, uncommitted responses. It follows that organisms that are genetically predisposed to engage in greater amounts of uncommitted behavior have an increased chance of survival, because there are more instances of behavior on which consequences can exert an effect. Second, it follows that organisms that are genetically more susceptible to modification by a greater range of: (a) antecedent stimuli that can serve as discriminative stimuli in the operant relations in question, and (b) consequences that can serve as reinforcers or punishers in the operant relations in question, have increased chances of survival. Third, it follows that organisms that possess a nervous system that is genetically susceptible to modification by conditioned respondent relations in addition to operant relations have a survival advantage. Conditioned respondents are not selected by environmental relations in the same way that operant behavior is, but the nervous system that can be modified by conditioned respondent relations is. Accordingly, the ability of the nervous system to be modified by conditioned respondent confers a survival advantage; for example, in adapting to new environments.

Selection For versus Selection Of in the Evolution of Behavior

Worth repeating is that selection *of* organisms based on their behavioral characteristics at each of the three levels accompanies selection *for* organisms. In selection *for* organisms, the outcome is directly contingent on the behavioral characteristics. In selection *of* organisms, some behavioral characteristics are present in an organism simply because they have accompanied selection for other characteristics, rather than because the outcome is contingent on characteristics in question. Moreover, through normal variation, these subsidiary behavioral characteristics may also be modified across evolutionary time.

CONTINGENCIES OF SURVIVAL

An umbrella phrase that encompasses the selection for organisms with certain morphological and behavioral characteristics is "contingencies of survival." In its general sense, the term selection describes contingent relations. It means that if organisms possess a genetic endowment that provides a certain morphology as well as sensory, motor, and nervous systems that function in certain ways, then those organisms will survive, because they will meet the demands of the environment. Importantly, for many species including humans their nervous systems have evolved to function in both fixed and modifiable ways. When the functioning of an organism's nervous system is fixed, its nervous system mediates fixed ("innate") forms of behavior in response to the environment. These fixed forms of behavior are directly selected at the phylogenic level and directly contribute to survival with respect to demands posed by unchanging features of the environment. When the functioning of an organism's nervous system is modifiable, its nervous system mediates the acquisition and maintenance of operant behavior and behavior engendered by conditioning operations affecting innate behavior, such as conditioned respondent behavior. These forms of behavior contribute to survival with respect to demands posed by changing features of the environment at ontogenic levels. The phrase "contingencies of survival" emphasizes these several contingent relations as elements of the selection process.

SELECTION BY CONSEQUENCES: DARWINIAN OR LAMARCKIAN?

At the phylogenic level, the selection processes are Darwinian processes of either natural or sexual selection. That is, only genetically based characteristics are differentially replicated across the history of the species. No characteristics acquired during the lifetime of an organism enter into the selection process. The genes of the organism are the replicators at the phylogenic level, in the sense that they are what are carried forward to the future of the species and produce the effect in question, such as the repertoire of species-specific innate behavior.

In contrast, at the ontogenic and cultural levels, the selection of behavior is Lamarckian. Jean-Baptiste Lamarcke (1744–1829) was a French biologist who proposed an early version of evolution. In Lamarcke's version, characteristics acquired during the lifetime of an organism are transmitted and expressed in future generations.

Although initially attractive, even to Darwin, the idea of inherited characteristics was discredited, but it is occasionally resurrected in discussions of mechanisms of evolution. The way that Lamarckian processes are involved is as follows. In the evolution of behavior at the ontogenic level, the environment modifies the nervous system of the organism during its lifetime, so that it is better adapted to its environment. The acquired modifications are then transmitted to the future in the form of a modified organism with a modified behavioral repertoire. The modified nervous system is the replicator at the ontogenic level, in the sense that it is what is carried forward to future behavioral events in the lifetime of the individual organism and produces the effect in question, namely the repertoire of operant behavior. The operant doesn't have to be relearned every day. Moreover, organisms with nervous systems that aren't changed by environmental relations, say by not having some consequence of a particular response produce an increased probability of the response, don't have the benefit of that response to aid in their adaptation.

At the cultural level, the acquired modifications are transmitted to the future in the form of modified cultural traditions, for example, via language. Language is the replicator at the cultural level, in the sense that it is what is carried forward to future cultural events in the lifetime of the culture and produces the effect in question, namely the evolved set of cultural practices. As with ontogenic selection, the cultural practices don't have to be re-established every generation. Skinner (1971) described this relation in the following way:

> The fact that a culture may survive or perish suggests a kind of evolution, and a parallel with the evolution of species has, of course, often been pointed out. It needs to be stated carefully. A culture corresponds to a species. We describe it by listing many of its practices, as we describe a species by listing many of its anatomical features. Two or more cultures may share a practice, as two or more species may share an anatomical feature. The practices of a culture, like the characteristics of a species, are carried by its members, who transmit them to other members. In general, the greater the number of individuals who carry a species or culture, the greater its chance of survival.

> A culture, like a species, is selected by its adaptation to an environment: to the extent that it helps its members get what they need and avoid what is dangerous, it helps them to survive and transmit the culture. The two kinds of evolution are closely interwoven. The same people transmit both a culture and a genetic endowment—though in very different ways and for different parts of their lives. The capacity to undergo the changes in behavior which make a culture possible was acquired in the evolution of the species, and, reciprocally, the culture determines many of the biological characteristics transmitted. Many current cultures, for example, enable individuals to survive and breed who would otherwise fail to do so. Not every practice in a culture, or every trait in a species, is adaptive, since nonadaptive practices and traits may be carried by adaptive ones, and cultures and species which are poorly adaptive may survive for a long time.

> New practices correspond to genetic mutations. A new practice may weaken a culture—for example, by leading to an unnecessary consumption of resources or by impairing the health of its members—or strengthen it—for example, by helping its members make a more effective use of resources or improve their health. Just as a mutation, a change in the structure of a gene, is

unrelated to the contingencies of selection which affect the resulting trait, so the origin of a practice need not be related to its survival value….

The parallel between biological and cultural evolution breaks down at the point of transmission. There is nothing in the chromosome-gene mechanism in the transmission of a cultural practice. Cultural evolution is Lamarckian in the sense that acquired practices are transmitted. To use a well-worn example, the giraffe does not stretch its neck to reach food which is otherwise out of reach and then pass on a longer neck to its offspring; instead, those giraffes in whom mutation has produced longer necks are more likely to reach available food and transmit the mutation. But a culture which develops a practice permitting it to use otherwise inaccessible sources of food can transmit that practice not only to new members but to contemporaries or to surviving members of an earlier generation. More important, a practice can be transmitted through "diffusion" to other cultures—as if antelopes, observing the usefulness of the long neck in giraffes, were to grow longer necks. Species are isolated from each other by the nontransmissibility of genetic traits, but there is no comparable isolation of cultures. A culture is a set of practices, but it is not a set which cannot be mixed with other sets….

Although the parallel between biological and cultural evolution falters at the point of transmissibility, the notion of cultural evolution remains useful. New practices arise, and they tend to be transmitted if they contribute to the survival of those who practice them. We can in fact trace the evolution of a culture more clearly than the evolution of a species, since the essential conditions are observed rather than inferred and can often be directly manipulated. Nevertheless, as we have seen, the role of the environment has only begun to be understood, and the social environment which is a culture is often hard to identify. It is constantly changing, it lacks substance, and it is easily confused with the people who maintain the environment and are affected by it. (pp. 129–132)

The three levels of selection processes described above have been presented separately, but in most cases the contingencies are thoroughly intermingled. For example, a human might act aggressively because of phylogenic contingencies (e.g., aggressive organisms may have had a survival advantage in the evolutionary history of the species), ontogenic contingencies (e.g., persons may learn to act aggressively during their lifetimes), or cultural contingencies (e.g., persons may act aggressively because their culture encourages them to do so). If steps to deal with aggressive behavior are called for, then those steps must start with understanding and respecting the contingency or combination of contingencies that controls any particular instance.

MORE ON CULTURAL SELECTION

A First Example: Hunting Practices

Humans are social organisms, and further examination of selection at the cultural level is instructive. Two examples of cultural selection may be considered. The examples are taken from Glenn (2003, 2004). The first example concerns two members—A and B—of a society of hunters. Initially, each member hunts independently, but according to a somewhat different practice. A has developed a style of hunting that entails approaching prey from the left. B has developed a style of hunting that entails approaching prey from the right. When each hunts independently, each is able to capture only one of a band of prey, and the other prey escape in the opposite direction. Now, one day, say by chance, the two hunters end up hunting the same band of prey. The hunters follow their past practices. When A approaches from the left, the prey runs to the right, but this action brings them toward B. When B approaches, the prey runs to the left, but this action brings them toward A, and so on. As a result, the band of prey is trapped between the two hunters and can't escape. The hunters end up capturing more prey than either could have independently. Given this outcome, their hunting practices become transformed: they hunt together in the future. Moreover, others in the society observe that the cooperative hunting practice results in the outcome of more prey. Consequently, others try it with the same beneficial effect. Younger hunters then acquire the practice from older, not via simple observation but rather through language-mediated instruction. In addition, the practice of transmitting the hunting techniques is encouraged within the society, and becomes an integral part of the lifestyle of the society.

An analysis of this example reveals the important role of environmental contingencies. The original hunting practices of A and B are instances of operant behavior. The two practices have been shaped and maintained at the individual level by the success in getting prey. The next stage occurs when A and B happen to work together. This stage occurs by chance. It is followed by the consequence of more prey than if the hunters had acted independently. This outcome strengthens the practice of hunting together. One speaks of "interlocking contingencies" when the interactive nature of the hunting is identified: A moves, and the movements of A set the occasion for what B should do next; B moves, and the movements of B set the occasion for what A should do next. Others in the society observe the beneficial outcome, and they try it, too. Presumably, they experience the same beneficial effect, so the practice is strengthened in others. The cumulative beneficial effect in the society is greater for the society than if hunters continued to act independently. Depending on the language customs of the society, if still others are verbally instructed in the hunting practice, and the practice remains successful, it is further strengthened. Although imitation and observation may contribute to the acquisition of the hunting skills, the adoption and strengthening of the responses in others is presumably due to more than simple imitation or observation. First, the target responses probably develop gradually, rather than in an all-or-none, imitated fashion. Second, explicit verbal mediation and social reinforcement arising from other members of the group play a significant role.

Importantly, other practices might be transmitted to members of the group via language, in the same way that the hunting practices were. When these practices prove beneficial to the group, as more prey was, they too are strengthened. One speaks of "metacontingencies" when interlocking contingencies have been identified that promote behavior that becomes more or less probable across the group when the group is considered as a whole. The hunting practice that arises within the group in the example above is more than the simple sum of the independent practices of A and B, or indeed any two other members of the group. It has arisen within the group and when fostered (in the example above, verbally transmitted) among members of the group, resulted in a beneficial outcome for the group. It has become independent of which two members originated the hunting practice, or which members engage in it on any given day. The practice and the contingencies that promote it have themselves become an integrated unit that are continued within the unit because they have some benefit for the group as a whole.

A Second Example: Sharing a Resource

A second example, more complex than the hunting example above, concerns a society in which members commonly drive internal combustion engines powered by fossil fuels. Suppose each of two members of this society, X and Y, has a car and drives to work. Driving oneself to work has certain advantages: it is more convenient, it typically takes less time than other modes of transportation, and it fits in with the stereotype of rugged individualism and self-reliance that has developed in the society over more than 200 years. In any case, driving to work is individual operant behavior, maintained by its consequences: one gets to work and earns one's paycheck. However, driving oneself to work may also have certain disadvantages. It may well cost more than other modes of transportation. Not only is there an expense for gas and oil, but also for the maintenance of the car, parking fees, insurance, tolls, and the cost of the road itself, say through taxes. In addition, a single driver in a car contributes to air pollution, which is not good for the environment.

A moment's reflection suggests the complexity of this example, in addition to the considerations described above. Although "driving to work" is operant behavior, it is not a simple response, like pressing a lever or pecking a key. In one sense, it is a sequence of responses. Some elements of the sequence revolve around the car: putting the key in the ignition, starting the car, backing out of the garage and down the driveway, driving down the street, turning the corner, and so on. In another sense, it is nested in a very complex hierarchy of responses that define one's lifestyle. One has purchased a particular make of car, one performs maintenance on the car, one drives to the store to purchase food, one drives the car to leisure activities, and so on. One interacts with other drivers on the road at stop signs and traffic lights. One obeys speed limits and drives on the prescribed side of the road. The preferred route to any place may be under repair, with the result that the driver needs to take a detour. One has to find a parking place after arriving at work. All of these elements include important behavioral components, subject to their own contingencies. The point is that "driving to work" may usefully be considered as multiple responses, embedded both vertically and horizontally in a complex network of operant contingencies.

Importantly, one also needs to purchase gasoline. Suppose, for the sake of the example, that a gasoline shortage now develops in the society. X and Y might well try to drive to work in their own cars, but consider whether each can continue to do so. It is unlikely that if X or Y drives to work, that trip by itself is going to consume exactly an amount of gasoline in the society that means X or Y can't drive the next day. In other words, gasoline usage is spread among many users, and single users are not likely to cause themselves to be without gasoline the next day. In other words, the consequences of one's own gasoline use in a time of shortage are rarely punishing in an immediate sense for a single driver, and rarely produce a reduction of usage in a single driver.

Suppose next that X and Y share a ride, or "carpool." This form of cooperation is less convenient and takes more time. Importantly, it also means that about half as much gasoline is used per driver. Consequently, it costs less and produces less pollution. Overall, more gasoline is now available to the society as a whole. Perhaps the individuals will spend less of their budgets on gasoline, and more on health care. The advantages seem conspicuous.

However, recall the complexity of the lifestyle in this society. Suppose X and Y have now decided to carpool. The contingencies in their lives are now interlocking: X as a passenger has to be ready when Y as a driver arrives, and vice versa. Suppose that on a particular day, X wants to stop at the store on the way home to buy a loaf of bread. The problem is that Y needs to get home immediately so that the children in the family can get to an appointment with the dentist. The interlocking contingencies have now come into conflict.

Suppose further that X has been raised in a tradition in which one relies on oneself to get things done, and one takes pride in one's self-reliance. According to this tradition, not taking "responsibility" to prepare oneself to meet demands is punished by social consequences within the family unit. No doubt, this tradition is the result of such social-cultural factors as ethnic background and everything that comes along with that background. When X and Y begin to carpool, X comes face to face with other external demands, making it difficult to continue to live in the way in which X had been raised.

Nevertheless, regardless of the short-term circumstances that surround any particular trip, using less gasoline is better in the long run for society as a group: citizens spend less money for gas, leaving more for health care; there is less pollution; less tax money has to subsidize acquiring land and building roads and parking lots, and so on.

Clearly, the contingencies affecting X and Y are complex. There are contingencies that affect behavior at the individual level, and there are contingencies that affect behavior at the group level. Moreover, the contingencies are interlocking, in the sense that behavior engendered under the contingencies affecting X participate in the contingencies affecting Y, and vice versa. Often these contingencies seem to be associated with competing responses: X wants to stop at the store, but Y needs to get home. No doubt others in the society are faced with similar situations. One possibility that emerges from all the competing contingencies for all the individuals is for drivers to drive their own cars and meet halfway to the ultimate destination. Then, one driver could get into another's car to complete the trip, or the drivers might take a bus or commuter train. The drivers would then be free to deal with their own contingencies in the portion of travel in their own cars. If society sees such an arrangement as beneficial, society might formalize the arrangement by promoting "Park-N-Ride" or comparable commuter lots, to facilitate the process whereby drivers park and transfer. Indeed, society might take steps to encourage its members to follow the practice because of its large-scale benefit for society. The entire state of affairs may be described by saying that different but interlocking contingencies affect each individual. This interlocking set of contingencies creates new contingencies that in turn give rise to a new form of behavior in the society as a whole. This complex network of interlocking contingencies is called a metacontingency. Importantly for society as a whole, the metacontingencies that gave rise to the commuter lot are independent of whether any particular individuals avail themselves of the practice.

A macrocontingency is a single contingency that is applied in common to a large group of people. In connection with the example of the preceding paragraph, society could apply a macrocontingency by charging high tolls to single occupant vehicles, and low tolls to multiple occupant vehicles, to promote carpooling, taking a bus, taking a train, or other forms of commuting. Society would then presumably benefit from the resulting behavior. The behavior reduces pollution, not as many new roads have to be built, fossil fuels aren't profligately consumed, and so on. Again, this sort of cultural contingency exists without regard to how often X or Y practice it as individuals. As the responses engendered by the macrocontingency become more frequent, the culture has become more fit in some sense. Societies that analyze their practices in relation to the environment, promote the value of such analyses, and encourage their members to act accordingly, if only through contrived social mechanisms, are more likely to survive.

SUMMARY AND CONCLUSIONS

Chapter 7 concludes the initial section of the book—dealing with the foundations of radical behaviorism. In closing, three important stages in the development of the thesis of selection by consequences may be noted. These three stages seem to apply in a science of behavior just as in biology. In biology, the first stage was to replace the concept that species had been created or designed by some supernatural deity with the concept of selection. For example, in Darwin's time a common thesis was that when the Earth was created, so also were created prototypes or special designs for each species, with some degree of variation around each prototype. Darwin proposed an alternative, based on the principles of natural science. The second stage formulated the mechanisms and laws of genetics—the ways genes are combined and expressed in future generations. Darwin didn't have particularly well-formed ideas about the mechanisms underlying evolution, and it was Mendel and T. H. Morgan who provided information about these laws. The third stage was achieving an understanding of the underlying biochemistry and biophysics of the replicators—the genes themselves. The "Modern Synthesis" in the second quarter of the twentieth century, culminating in Watson and Crick's discovery of the Double Helix model of DNA in mid-century, provided this information.

In a science of behavior, the first stage was to replace creation and purpose with selection. The conception of the individual as an autonomous agent is gradually being replaced with that of the individual as a locus where many variables come together in a unique achievement: behavior. According to the new conception, the environment selects certain forms or classes of behavior, based on the functional consequences of those forms or classes. The second stage is to develop the laws of behavior analogous to the laws of genetics. These laws are coming from basic research in the behavioral laboratory, just as the laws of genetics came from basic research in biological laboratories. The third stage is to develop an understanding of the functioning of the nervous system when an organism is modified by experiences in its environment and acquires behavior, analogous to an understanding of the biochemistry and biophysics of the gene when an organism transmits its characteristics to its offspring.

Table 7–1 summarizes the relations called selection by consequences that are described in this chapter. The important levels are the phylogenic, ontogenic, and cultural levels, each with its respective science or sciences. At each level there is variation, interaction, differential replication, and a mechanism by which the replication takes place. Although selection at the phylogenic level is Darwinian, selection at the ontogenic and cultural levels is Lamarckian. Nevertheless, the thesis of selection by consequences applies throughout.

Worth emphasizing again is that language is generally the mechanism according to which practices that evolve at the cultural level are transmitted through metacontingencies, just as the gene is the mechanism through which characteristics and traits that evolve at the phylogenic level are transmitted through natural selection or sexual selection. Thus, understanding the development of language in human history, which is to say understanding the development of operant verbal behavior, is central to an understanding of the human condition. Skinner (1987) put it as follows:

The human species took a crucial step forward when its vocal musculature came under operant control in the production of speech sounds. Indeed, it is possible that all the distinctive achievements of the species can be traced to that one genetic change.... The crucial step in the evolution of verbal behavior appears, then, to have been the genetic change that brought them [vocal cords and pharynx] under the control of operant conditioning and made possible the coordination of all these systems in the production of speech sounds. (pp. 79–80)

The next section of the book deals with the realization of the radical behaviorist program. In keeping with the centrality of verbal processes in radical behaviorism, the first two chapters of the section, Chapters 8 and 9, address the topic of verbal behavior.

TABLE 7.1
The three levels pertaining to the thesis of selection by consequences

Nature of variation	*Nature of interaction*	*What is replicated?*	*Mechanism of replication*
Phylogenic level—behavioral genetics, ethology			
innate behavior	Natural/sexual selection	Species-specific repertoire of innate behavior	genetic (Darwinian)
Ontogenic level—behavior analysis			
amount of uncommitted behavior; susceptibility to reinforcers	reinforcement	operant repertoire	modified nervous system (Lamarckian)
Cultural level—social/cultural anthropology			
cultural practices	effective solution of problems at cultural level	set of practices called culture (special social contingencies involving interlocking operants)	language (Lamarckian)

REFERENCES

Darwin, C. (1859). *On the origin of species by means of natural selection*. London: Murray.

Glenn, S. S. (2003). Operant contingencies and the origin of cultures. In K. A. Lattal & P. N. Chase (Eds.), *Behavior theory and philosophy*, pp. 223–242. New York: Kluwer/Plenum.

Glenn, S. S. (2004). Individual behavior, culture, and social change. *The Behavior Analyst, 27*, 133–151.

Gould, S. J., & Lewontin, R. (1979). The spandrels of San Marco and the Panglossian paradigm: a critique of the adaptationist programme. *Proceedings of the Royal Society of London, B 205, 1161*, 581–598.

Skinner, B. F. (1971). *Beyond freedom and dignity*. New York: Knopf.

Skinner, B. F. (1987). *Upon further reflection*. New York: Appleton-Century-Crofts.

Sober, E. (1984). *The nature of selection: Evolutionary theory in philosophical focus*. Cambridge, MA: MIT Press.

STUDY QUESTIONS

1. Describe the three elements of the selection process.
2. Define and give an example of natural selection.
3. Define and give an example of sexual selection.
4. Distinguish between selection *for* and selection *of*.
5. Define and give an example of the selection of behavior at the phylogenic level.
6. Define and give an example of the selection of behavior at the ontogenic level.
7. Define and give an example of the selection of behavior at the cultural level.
8. Describe how the nervous system is the replicator at the ontogenic level, including the three genetically based features of the nervous system that are of service to organisms during their lifetimes.
9. Describe what is meant by the phrase "contingencies of survival."
10. Define the following terms: interlocking contingency, macrocontingency, metacontingency.
11. Distinguish between processes of natural selection and Lamarckian selection at each of the three levels of behavioral selection.
12. Describe the contribution of verbal behavior to the selection of cultural practices.
13. Compare and contrast the three stages of selection by consequences in biology with the three stages in a science of behavior.

Section 2

The Realization of the Radical Behaviorist Program

Chapters 8 through 13 make up Section 2 of this book. These chapters examine the realization of the radical behaviorist program. Chapters 8 and 9 examine elementary and complex verbal behavior. Chapter 10 reviews the radical behaviorist position on private events, which are defined as covert events accessible to only the individual who is behaving. Chapter 11 assesses radical behaviorist views on methodology and the nature of science. Chapters 12 and 13 then evaluate two forms of scientific verbal behavior that are significant for any scientific position, and especially so for radical behaviorism: theories and explanations.

8

Verbal Behavior 1:
Elementary Verbal Relations

Synopsis of Chapter 8: The chapters in the first section of this book established the foundations of radical behaviorism. Chapter 8 begins the second section of the book, which explores what radical behaviorism has to say about specific areas traditionally regarded as important in psychology. This chapter examines verbal behavior, using the same concepts as employed in the preceding analyses of operant behavior. From the point of view of radical behaviorism, verbal behavior is the most significant form of behavior in which humans can engage. Importantly, verbal behavior is operant behavior and amenable to analysis in terms of contingencies. The chapter outlines the nature of verbal behavior, some differences between verbal and nonverbal behavior, and some criticisms that have been leveled against a behavioral approach to verbal behavior. It closes with a review of the elementary forms of verbal behavior.

Following the receipt of his doctoral degree in 1931, B. F. Skinner remained at Harvard in a series of post-doctoral appointments, the last of which was a three-year term as a Junior Fellow in the newly formed and highly prestigious Society of Fellows. At a ceremonial dinner for the Society of Fellows on the Harvard campus in March of 1934, Skinner found himself seated next to Professor Alfred North Whitehead, the eminent English philosopher from whom Skinner had taken courses while a graduate student. As Skinner (1957) described events during the dinner, he and Whitehead began to discuss behaviorism, which was then still very much an "-ism," and of which Skinner was a zealous devotee. Here was an opportunity that Skinner could not overlook to strike a blow for the cause, and he began to enthusiastically set forth the principal arguments of behaviorism. Professor Whitehead earnestly tried to understand what Skinner was saying and how Skinner could possibly bring himself to say it. During the discussion, Whitehead agreed that a science of behavior might successfully account for much of human conduct, except for verbal behavior. Here, Whitehead insisted, something else must be at work. Skinner respectfully disagreed, and the next morning began to compose a book outlining a behavioral approach to verbal behavior. Competition from both personal (marriage, parenthood) and professional factors (getting himself established professionally; career moves; numerous scholarly articles, presentations, books, as well as one novel) delayed completion of the book for over twenty years. The book eventually appeared with the modest title of *Verbal Behavior* (Skinner, 1957). Skinner described the finished version as:

> an orderly arrangement of well-known facts, in accordance with a formulation of behavior derived from an experimental analysis of a more rigorous sort. The present extension to verbal behavior is thus an exercise in interpretation rather than a quantitative extrapolation of rigorous experimental results. (Skinner, 1957, p. 11)

Later, Skinner (1978) stated that he thought *Verbal Behavior* would prove to be his "most important work" (p. 122). Chapter 8 outlines the important features of Skinner's original approach to elementary verbal relations.

THE DEFINITION OF VERBAL BEHAVIOR

Operant behavior is behavior that occurs because of its reinforcing consequences. Many forms of operant behavior directly and mechanically produce a reinforcer. Verbal behavior is operant behavior, but differs from other forms of operant behavior in that it affects other persons, who then mediate reinforcement for the speaker's responses from the environment. More formally, verbal behavior may be defined as behavior that is reinforced through the mediation of other persons. Importantly, listeners mediate the reinforcement for speakers in such circumstances because they have been conditioned to do so.

Three relevant passages are from Skinner's (1957) book *Verbal Behavior*. In the first page Skinner laid out the basic definition of what counts as verbal behavior:

> Men act upon the world, and change it, and are changed in turn by the consequences of their action ... . Much of the time, however, a man acts only indirectly upon the environment from which the ultimate consequences of his behavior emerge. His first effect is on other men. Instead of going to a drinking fountain, a thirsty man may simply 'ask for a glass of water.'... The ultimate consequence, the receipt of water, bears no useful geometrical or mechanical relation to the form of the behavior of 'asking for water.' ... Behavior which is effective only through the mediation of other persons has so many distinguishing dynamic and topographical properties that a special treatment is justified and, indeed, demanded .... A definition of verbal behav-

ior as behavior reinforced through the mediation of other persons needs, as we shall see, certain refinements. (pp. 1-2)

Verbal behavior implies a listener as well. Somewhat after the passage above, Skinner extended his definition of verbal behavior by clarifying the role of the listener in verbal processes:

> Our definition of verbal behavior applies only to the speaker, but the listener cannot be omitted from our account.... Much of the behavior of the listener has no resemblance to the behavior of the speaker and is not verbal according to our definition. But the listener (and the reader as well) is reacting to verbal stimuli—the end products of the behavior here analyzed—and we are naturally interested in the fate of such stimuli.... The behavior of a man as listener is not to be distinguished from other forms of his behavior.... In a complete account of a verbal episode we need to show that the behavior of the listener does in fact provide the conditions we have assumed in explaining the behavior of the speaker. We need separate but interlocking accounts of the behavior of both speaker and listener if our explanation is to be complete. In explaining the behavior of the speaker we assume a listener who will reinforce his behavior in certain ways. In accounting for the behavior of the listener we assume a speaker whose behavior bears a certain relation to environmental conditions. The interchanges between them must explain all the conditions thus assumed. The account of the whole episode is then complete. (pp. 33–34)

In a third passage, which occurs later in the book, Skinner completed the previously promised refined definition of verbal behavior. The refined definition makes it clear that such forms of social behavior as an uppercut to the jaw by a boxer, or an appendectomy by a surgeon, do not count as instances of verbal behavior simply because they occur in a social context and affect another person. Hence, Skinner said:

> To say that we are interested only in behavior which has an effect upon the behavior of another individual does not go far enough, for the definition embraces all social behavior.... If we make the provision that the "listener" must be responding in ways which have been conditioned precisely in order to reinforce the behavior of the speaker, we narrow our subject to what is traditionally recognized as the verbal field. (pp. 224–225)

A graphic depiction of the status of verbal behavior is presented in Figure 8–1. In this figure, verbal behavior is a subset of human social behavior, which in turn is a subset of human operant behavior, which in turn is a subset of all human behavior.

As operant behavior, verbal behavior is a function of contingencies of reinforcement, and is to be explained and analyzed at that level. Notwithstanding Alfred North Whitehead's reservations, the radical behaviorist position is that a comprehensive account of verbal behavior can be developed that is based on a natural science approach and that is an extension of the account of nonverbal behavior. Thus, a qualitatively different account, appealing to mental or cognitive processes rather than behavioral processes, is not only unnecessary but harmful. In the preferred account, the term "language" is simply a name for the set of contingencies and conventional practices

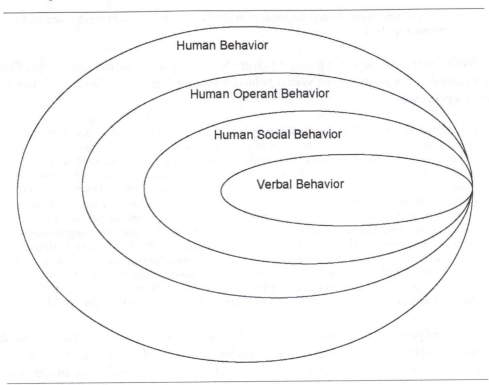

Figure 8.1   The relations among verbal behavior, human social behavior, and human operant behavior.

that prevail within a given verbal community, as opposed to some system of mental rules and representations according to which only humans are capable of functioning.

As noted in the preceding chapter, verbal behavior became possible with certain genetic changes in humans. Some genetic changes resulted in: (a) bipedalism and changes in the positioning of the head on the spinal column; (b) changes in the morphology of the skull that permitted cranial expansion and development; and (c) changes in the structure of the larynx, throat, jaw, tongue, sinus cavities, and nasal passages that afforded new articulatory and phonetic capabilities. Other genetic changes affected the nervous system associated with the vocal apparatus. These genetic changes meant that operant relations in the environment could modify the nervous system responsible for controlling and coordinating movements in the larynx, throat, jaw, and tongue. Whereas vocalization was previously related only to phylogenic contingencies, now vocalization could be controlled by operant relations during the lifetime of the individual organism. These new forms of vocalization could now function quite differently during the lifetime of the individual organism, and quite differently in the evolution of interactions in human social groups.

ELEMENTS OF A BEHAVIORAL APPROACH TO VERBAL BEHAVIOR

As discussed above, verbal behavior is operant behavior, and may be analyzed in terms of contingencies: the S^D, the verbal response, and the reinforcer. A classification system for different kinds of verbal behavior may be developed, where each category emphasizes an important feature of the contingency responsible for that classification. More is said about this classification system later. At this point, a few general features of the contingencies associated with verbal behavior may be examined.

Reinforcement

As with any kind of operant behavior, the reinforcer is tremendously important. Sometimes the reinforcer for verbal behavior is unconditioned, and sometimes conditioned. An unconditioned reinforcer is the physical, material reinforcer that exerts a reinforcing effect without any prior experience. If a speaker asks a listener to pass the salt, receiving the salt is the reinforcer for the speaker's request. In the case of much verbal behavior, however, the reinforcer is conditioned. The conditioned reinforcer supporting many instances of verbal behavior is perhaps best described as "generalized social attention." It may take the form of facial responsiveness, eye contact, what a listener says or does later, forms of social approval, or even contingent physical proximity as individuals interact in the verbal community. Sometimes the reinforcer occurs after each instance of a unit of verbal behavior, and sometimes it is intermittent. There may even be "multiple control," where verbal behavior is controlled by more than one contingency, which blends more than one discriminative stimulus and reinforcer.

The Antecedent Stimulus

Control by the antecedent stimulus (or occasion, or setting) is another important aspect of the behavioral approach to verbal behavior. In some cases, the antecedent stimulus may be an object or event, or some property or feature of an object or event. In other cases, an establishing operation (such as deprivation or aversive stimulation) joins with the presence of a receptive audience and other environmental circumstances to exert control over the verbal behavior.

In still other cases, the verbal behavior may be occasioned by other words. When speakers recite a poem learned "by heart," for example, early words set the occasion for later words. Not all verbal behavior takes this form, of course, but some does.

Some verbal behavior also functions by commenting on the antecedent relations responsible for that behavior or by modifying the effect of that behavior. This topic is complex and is discussed later in this chapter.

The Response

The topography of the response may be vocal, a gesture, or even a grimace on a face. An important issue is whether its reinforcement has been mediated by others like the speaker. From this point of view, the phrase "nonverbal communication" is not meaningful. All "communication" is by definition verbal (otherwise, it would not be called communication), although all communication may not be oral or vocal. Some might be gestural, etc. Perhaps the phrase "nonverbal communication" is better construed as "nonvocal," "nonoral," or "nonlinguistic" communication.

DIFFERENCES BETWEEN A "TRADITIONAL" ACCOUNT AND THAT OF RADICAL BEHAVIORISM

Mentalistic versus Nonmentalistic

Most traditional accounts of verbal behavior are mentalistic, in that they attempt to explain verbal behavior in terms of underlying mental causes and activities. Such accounts often suggest that persons use words in order to express themselves or to express a meaning. The word itself is regarded as a symbol. The meaning of a word is often determined by identifying something called the "referent" of the word. The meanings of words are stored in a "lexicon," which must be accessed prior to speech. Language is regarded as the output of various "cognitive mechanisms" that manipulate the symbols and generate the language according to rules. There are various parts of speech (nouns, verbs, adjectives, adverbs, prepositions, etc.), and various rules of grammar and syntax regarding the usage and manipulation of these parts of speech are said to be mental, if not innate. The deep structure of a sentence is an abstract representation of its underlying kernel, based on its grammatical constituents. The surface structure of a sentence is the form of the sentence that one actually sees or hears. It emerges when various rules are applied to the underlying grammatical constituents. The surface structure of a given sentence obviously differs across languages, but what is important is the deep structure, because analysis of it is said to reveal the innate, mental regularities underlying any human language.

   None of these characteristics find a place in a behavioral account. In a behavioristic view, such accounts misplace the causal origin of verbal behavior just as they would any other kind of behavior. The individual doesn't generate verbal behavior as an autonomous, initiating agent, any more than the individual generates any other kind of behavior as an autonomous, initiating agent. There is no dimension in which the various features of the mentalistic account are said to reside or take place. Rather, the individual is a unique locus, where a unique genetic endowment and unique history of experiences with the environment come together to result in an equally unique achievement: verbal behavior. An approach suggesting that the individual is an autonomous agent, and that the various mentalistic elements are necessary to explain the production of verbal behavior, is itself verbal behavior that is reinforced by way of adherence to various social and cultural preconceptions.

Structure versus Function

Traditional accounts often take a structural approach and divide speech into components of phonemes, morphemes, syllables, words, phrases, sentences, paragraphs, or portions thereof. Clearly, these sorts of verbal components do exist. At issue is whether the structural components should be regarded as having some sort of a priori or independent status, such that they should be viewed as the fundamental units of verbal behavior. The behavioral account says no. In contrast to a traditional or structural approach, a behavioral account adopts a functional approach. In a behavioral account, the verbal community shapes the fundamental unit from the stream that is verbal behavior. Thus, the fundamental unit in verbal behavior is whatever has emerged in the speaking organism's lifetime as the speaker interacts with the verbal community. To be sure, in many instances, what comes to be reinforced does correspond to one of the standard structural units, such as a word, but any correspondence with the structural unit is because of the conventional reinforcing practices of the verbal community, rather than because the word has a certain a priori or independent status as a fundamental unit.

Usage

A behavioristic account does emphasize usage, but differently from a traditional account. A traditional account might say that speakers use words to express themselves. In keeping with the point above about fundamental units, the problem is that the traditional account runs the risk of suggesting that words are independent things with a certain a priori status, like hammers or screwdrivers, that speakers use to accomplish a purpose. For a behaviorist, to say speakers use words to express themselves is like saying rats use lever presses to express themselves. Such statements are not ordinarily made about rats when they press levers, but are often made about people when they behave verbally. Lever presses are not ordinarily viewed as things, but words are. The case with which the statement is made about people shows the powerful seductiveness of the traditional account. Perhaps a more appropriate statement is that for both lever presses and verbal behavior the functional relations between instances of behavior and their surrounding circumstances need to be analyzed. For radical behaviorists, the conception of usage in verbal behavior does not imply the existence of a thing that is used, but simply of an act in context.

Meaning and Reference

The traditional notion of meaning is that it is a single entity that is formulated in the speaker's mind and then transmitted from the speaker to the listener, so that it gets into the listener's mind. For example, speakers are held to encode the meaning of an utterance during composition, and listeners are held to decode the meaning of an utterance from its structural properties. Radical behaviorism regards that approach, associated with information and communication theory, as comprehensively troublesome and to be avoided.

At the very least, it presupposes there is another dimension—a dimension of the "mind"—in which "meaning" and "information" exist, independently of human conduct. Unfortunately, a proposal of this sort of dimension does not answer questions about verbal behavior, any more than a proposal of a Greek god drawing the sun out of the ocean with a chariot answered questions about sunrise, or proposal of a magical substance called phlogiston answered questions about combustion. Rather, such proposals have the appearance of being answers, but in reality are no more than hollow statements devoid of any empirical content. The history of science reveals that seeming answers couched in appeals to other dimensions are quite prominent, but that they eventually give way to naturalistic answers dealing with functional relations in space and time.

What, then, can be said in a naturalistic sense about meaning? From the perspective of radical behaviorism, there are two senses of "meaning": (a) meaning for the speaker, and (b) meaning for the listener. Meaning for the speaker is found among the determiners, not the properties, of a verbal response. Thus, this sense of meaning is a function of the contingencies that control the speaker's verbal response. To ask what persons mean by their utterances is to ask nothing less than what causes them to speak as they do. The answer must specify contingencies. This perspective is captured in the colloquial question, "Where are you coming from?" when a listener asks what a speaker means. In this view, dictionaries don't give meanings; they give other words that mean the same thing.

The other sense of meaning is meaning for the listener. Meaning for the listener is found in the extent to which an utterance functions as a discriminative stimulus to occasion appropriate behavior in subsequent situations. When a listener says to a speaker, "I don't understand what you mean," or "What you say is not meaningful to me," the listener is saying that the utterance doesn't occasion an appropriate or effective response, leading to a reinforcer.

From the point of view of radical behaviorism, the "referent" of a given bit of verbal behavior is usually a matter of what exerts stimulus control over the response. In a loose sense, the nature of the stimulus control determines the meaning, but to say speakers refer to objects is troublesome and ultimately deceptive. To say that speakers' words refer to objects is just as odd as saying that rats' lever presses refer to objects. More appropriate is to say that speakers' words are under the control of features of the environment. Sometimes those features are objects in the environment, but the response is not "referring" to them.

As with appeals to communication, information theory, encoding, decoding, and so on, the appeal to reference is fundamentally misguided. The appeal presupposes another dimension in which the thing referred to, as well as the speaker's mind, are held to exist. Moreover, in what dimension does the referring take place? If a contemporary speaker says "Caesar," is the speaker referring to the long-dead Roman? How is the speaker in contact with Caesar, to refer to him? In what dimension does Caesar exist for a contemporary speaker, so that the contemporary speaker can refer to him? Is there a mental copy stored somewhere in the brain? If a contemporary speaker says "Unicorn," what organism is the speaker referring to? In what dimension does the unicorn exist? Such questions indicate the vast problems that come from characterizing verbal behavior as the product of a referential process. Words don't create different dimensions. Rather, they are instances of verbal behavior. As such, they are a function of the interaction with the environment, and may be analyzed at the descriptively consistent level of behavior.

Serial Processes

Traditional accounts often make two criticisms of any empirical, behavioral approach to verbal behavior. More is said about these two criticisms in Chapter 16, but these two criticisms may be briefly examined at this point. First, a traditional account assumes any behavioral approach is committed to the view that speech or language is a linear or serial process, in which the essential mechanism involves a speaker who emits words in a series or chain, like beads on a string. A serial process holds that word #1 is the stimulus for word #2, word #2 is the stimulus for word #3, and so on, with perhaps a reinforcer at the end. This first criticism is based on the undeniable finding that verbal behavior does not generally conform to serial processes in this sense. Since it does not, the first criticism goes, an empirical or behavioral account is wrong and must be rejected.

In response to this first criticism, radical behaviorism agrees that speech does not generally occur according to a linear or serial process. To be sure, some early behaviorists like Watson did adopt a linear or serial approach as a general model, as they sought to be objective and empirical, and radical behaviorists do acknowledge that some verbal behavior does occur according to a serial process. However, radical behaviorists do not argue that all verbal behavior does. For example, it is not the general model developed in Skinner's (1957) book *Verbal Behavior*. Thus, radical behaviorists argue that the first criticism doesn't apply, and individuals who disparage an operant approach on the basis of its supposed commitment to a serial process simply do not have sufficient knowledge of the actual tenets of the operant approach.

Developmental Processes, Underdetermination, and the Poverty of the Stimulus

A second criticism by a traditional account is that interaction with stimuli in the environment, for example, involving reinforcement, cannot explain the development of language in children. In particular, the second criticism goes, a behavioral approach cannot account for how children learn to speak a great many words in a very short period of time, and for how children learn to speak in grammatically and syntactically correct sentences that are novel. The argument is that these two features of language are acquired far too quickly for reinforcement to have acted on each one. Moreover, experiences with the environment are far too unsystematic to account for the many novel forms of verbal behavior that a child eventually exhibits, especially considering grammar and syntax. Hence, the criticism goes, verbal behavior cannot be completely "determined" through interaction with the environment. In fact, it is underdetermined by stimuli in the environment. Given that it is underdetermined, a behavioral explanation appealing to a history of interaction with stimuli in the environment is necessarily impoverished. Indeed, the criticism typically goes, a behavioral explanation is so impoverished it should be abandoned entirely.

In response to this second criticism, a behavioral approach holds that the analysis of many forms of a speaker's verbal behavior does start with understanding the effects of direct contact with a reinforcement contingency. Indeed, careful analysis of developmental data reveals that reinforcement principles do operate significantly in the development of language in children, particularly in interactions with their caregivers, despite claims to the contrary. Thus, understanding the nature of the interaction that takes place between a developing child and a caregiver can give insights into how verbal behavior does develop through interaction with the environment.

However, a behavioral approach doesn't end with the direct action of reinforcement. More specifically, a behavioral approach doesn't claim that all forms of verbal behavior (e.g., all words, all instances of grammatically and syntactically correct speech) are acquired through the direct action of reinforcement. Many other relations and processes are at work in the development, maintenance, and modification of verbal behavior. For example, verbal behavior can be shaped and subsequently modified as features of the environment are added or removed. One might identify the species of a bird by its size and the shape of its beak, and then, when the season changes, by the color of its plumage. A behavioral approach also emphasizes the complexity of stimulus control in which novel features of the environment may combine to occasion novel verbal responses. A child might identify a previously unencountered fuzzy caterpillar as a "Worm with thread." Contingencies producing novel verbal behavior can be directly implemented: "Say the first word that comes into your mind when I say _____ ." A behavioral approach further identifies the contributions of generalization and abstraction, based not only on observed features of the environment, but also on subtle relations among features of the environment and the speaker's own verbal behavior, both prior and ongoing. For example, computer programs might be said to possess a certain "architecture," and operate in a "host-client" relation.

Finally, speaking in syntactically and grammatically correct sentences is itself a superordinate form of behavior that is learned, although necessarily after speakers have come under the control of elementary verbal relations. The verbal community that teaches individuals to speak also teaches individuals to speak according to conventionally accepted syntactic and grammatical rules because doing so indicates the relation among elements of an utterance, giving further guidance to a listener. The practices thus learned may themselves generalize, without each and every utterance having to be made and reinforced. Consequently, according to radical behaviorism, it is true that not every verbal response or grammatically correct utterance occurs because it has been directly reinforced in the past. Clearly, other behavioral relations and processes in addition to direct reinforcement are at work. What is just as clear is that an appeal to nonbehavioral processes is mischievous and deceptive.

The Traditional Language of Science

Traditional accounts also presume that scientific verbal behavior and scientific knowledge are more valid and more certain than everyday knowledge, by virtue of having followed prescribed, logically validated methods. Meaning is achieved by ensuring the referents of important "theoretical" terms are established through operational definitions. Scientific concepts are then carefully constructed by means of logic, and as discussed in Chapter 3, given the status of either "intervening variables" or "hypothetical constructs." The meaning of an intervening variable consists entirely in the publicly observable relations to which it is linked; an intervening variable has no surplus meaning. The meaning of a hypothetical construct is carefully developed from logical manipulations of publicly observable measures; hypothetical constructs do admit surplus meaning.

The view of scientific verbal behavior based on radical behaviorism rejects much of the traditional analysis of the language of science. For radical behaviorism, the language of science is still verbal behavior, and should still be analyzed in terms of contingencies. Theories, explanations, hypotheses, predictions, constructs, and so on are all instances of verbal behavior. In the radical behaviorist view, the important questions pertain to the functional role of the verbal behavior in question, rather than its "logical status." Indeed, radical behaviorists hold that questions pertaining to logical status will eventually be embraced by a functional account of verbal behavior. The most important issues are: What contingencies control the scientific verbal behavior in question? How does the scientific verbal community exercise more precise control over the contingencies governing scientific verbal behavior, resulting in less ambiguity and greater effectiveness? What are the discriminative stimuli that occasion scientific verbal behavior? What reinforcers does scientific verbal behavior help to achieve? Sometimes the reinforcer is prediction and control of natural events, but often the reinforcer is even more subtle: alleviating confusion, resolving puzzlements, ordering confusing data, or otherwise helping to make sense out of the world. Ultimately, the value of scientific statements is in their discriminative control: They guide individuals as they seek to interact effectively with nature.

Recapitulation

Radical behaviorism does not include many elements of the traditional approach to verbal behavior, but not because they are beyond the reach of a behavioristic treatment. Rather, a behavioristic treatment regards much of the traditional account as fanciful. Much of a traditional account is itself a function of various mischievous, deceptive, and unwarranted preconceptions concerning the dimensions of human conduct.

DIFFERENCES BETWEEN VERBAL AND NONVERBAL BEHAVIOR

What is the difference between verbal and nonverbal behavior? Do nonhumans engage in verbal behavior and language? These questions are tricky, because they are often a matter of interpretation. The properties that define language have been a matter of controversy for centuries, and this chapter is not able to address the whole controversy. Suffice it to note that in a traditional point of view, the differences between verbal and nonverbal behavior are approached from an essentialist point of view. That is, a traditional point of view often assumes there is some essential quality, perhaps unobservable or "theoretical," that endows verbal behavior with properties that distinguish it from nonverbal behavior. As with the analysis of other instances of behavior, radical behaviorism does not seek to identify an essential quality when it defines anything, including any form of behavior. To search for essential qualities is the legacy of transcendental, dualistic ways of thinking. Rather, verbal behavior can be placed at the end of a continuum of development. In regard to this continuum, five relevant issues can be identified: innate or operant; instructional; modifiable; minimal units; and higher-order processes.

Innate or Operant?

The first issue is that some animals raise cries of alarm when predators are observed in the immediate area. Parrots imitate sounds they hear in the environment, including human vocalizations. Dogs beg for food. Do these examples count as instances of verbal behavior? Many of these instances appear to involve communication, broadly interpreted as instances in which vocalizations (or other forms of behavior) that are directed at other organisms yield changes in the behavior of those organisms. From the perspective of radical behaviorism, one important consideration is whether such instances of behavior have developed through reinforcement arising from others of the same species, as they have for humans. Cries of alarm and parrot imitations are presumably innate forms of behavior, selected by increased chances of survival for species rather than through operant reinforcement during the lifetime of the individual organism. To be sure, a dog that begs for food is engaging in operant behavior, but the begging of one dog has probably not been shaped through reinforcement mediated by a second dog, precisely because the second dog has been conditioned to reinforce the begging of the first dog. Of course, some animals might be explicitly trained to engage in interactions that have the same topography as verbal behavior, but an important consideration is whether that behavior has evolved through any sort of systematic interaction with others of its same species. If it has not, then one would presumably not label it as verbal behavior.

Instructional?

A second issue is whether vocalizations are in any sense involved in instruction. By means of language, one organism can change another's behavior, both verbal and nonverbal. In any case, once both organisms engage in verbal behavior, then one can instruct the other. Society and culture are based on systematic patterns of such exchanges, transmitted through time by means of verbal behavior. An important consideration is the extent to which anything like instruction, resulting in societies and culture with transmitted artifacts, is present in interactions among nonhuman species. If there is no instruction in the sense of the instructed organism providing reinforcement for the instructing organism, then presumably the behavior in question is not verbal.

Verbal Behavior That Modifies Other Verbal Behavior

A third issue is that some kinds of verbal behavior are occasioned by the relations that control other verbal behavior, and may even modify the ordinary effect of that verbal behavior. The function of this sort of verbal behavior is to modify the way listeners respond to the verbal behavior it accompanies; for example, by providing additional information about the contingencies that are responsible for it or about how an individual should respond to it. One might say "All swans are white," not because one has seen all swans, but to inform listeners that they can safely assume the color of any swan they encounter is going to be white. Importantly, verbal behavior that modifies the effect of other verbal behavior cannot occur unless there is a discrimination based on the conditions that control the original verbal behavior. The circumstances must be favorable for the establishment of the discrimination, through being promoted by others of the same species, and the practices of the verbal community must be sufficiently complex and differentiated to support this sort of discrimination. As noted above, nonverbal behavior does not appear to have this property. An important consideration is whether the nonhuman behavior under consideration as verbal exhibits this property. Although the behavior of a nonhuman has been brought under the discriminative control of topographical properties of its previous behavior, whether the behavior of a nonhuman can be brought under the discriminative control of very subtle functional or relational properties of its previous behavior is an open question.

Development from Minimal Units

A fourth issue is that verbal behavior develops from minimal units. As discussed in Chapter 5, in typical instances operant behavior does not initially appear in its final, mature form. Rather, it develops over time on the basis of the organism's interactions with the environment. So does it seem to be the case with verbal behavior. In other words, verbal behavior develops through the interaction with the social environment represented by the other members of the verbal community. The development starts with the reinforcement of minimal functional units, and then progresses to larger, more complex forms.

As noted earlier, verbal behavior is typically described in terms of structural units: syllables, phonemes, morphemes, words, parts of speech, etc. Discussion of these structural units hasn't played a role in the analysis of verbal behavior to this point. However, the behavioral view of language should not be reduced to the view that it simply involves reinforcement for emitting words.

In a behavioral view, the unit of behavior is determined functionally, by its relation to environmental circumstances and contingencies. The functional unit may appear to be similar to the structural unit, but readers should not make too much of the similarity. Phonemes concern simply the acoustic or physical properties of an utterance. Morphemes concern the correlation between utterances, individuated on the basis of acoustic properties, and the reinforcing practices of the verbal community in which the speaker lives. When morphemes appear singly or in succession, they are called words. When words appear singly or in succession, they are called phrases or sentences. When sentences appear singly or in succession, they are called paragraphs. And so on. The point is that verbal units develop during the lifetime of the speaker. In the infant, the verbal unit may simply be a very brief utterance, because that form of the utterance is what achieves a particular consequence in interactions with the verbal community. As the child develops, the verbal community demands increasingly more complex forms of verbal utterances before the consequence is achieved. Thus, the eventual form of an utterance has developed on the basis of an individual's interaction with the verbal community.

The dynamic, evolving nature of the verbal unit is one of the most important features of verbal behavior. In mature forms of verbal behavior, the size of the verbal unit has evolved over the course of the individual's linguistic history. To be sure, when the individual is an adult, the functional verbal unit may well conform to the structural unit called a word, but the functional unit was probably not always a word. It has become so, and in different situations might not continue to be a word, even for a competent adult speaker. In sum, the nature of the verbal unit depends on the contingencies of the verbal community, rather than any a priori considerations based on its structure. The functional verbal unit typically stands at the end of a line of development, and needs to be understood in the context of an interactive process.

Higher-order Processes: Derived Relations

A fifth issue concerns higher-order relations that seem to be inherent in verbal behavior. For example, suppose a normally developing individual is shown a picture of an arbitrary object and taught to select as correct a particular spoken word from among several spoken words. Much research indicates that if the individual is then presented with the spoken word, the individual will pick the correct picture from among several others. Alternatively stated, in this higher-order relation individuals recognize the reciprocal, reversible relation between a term and the circumstances that govern its use (if A => B then B => A). The early term in the research community for this bi-directional relation was *symmetry*.

In another higher-order relation, suppose as before that a normally developing individual is shown a picture of an arbitrary object and taught to select a particular spoken word. Suppose next the individual is presented with the spoken word, and is taught to choose a particular printed word from among several others. Much research has shown that if the individual is now presented with the picture, the individual will select the appropriate printed word from among several others. Alternatively stated, according to this relation individuals recognize that if one stimulus is related to a second in a particular way, and the second to a third, the first is also related to the third (i.e., if A => B and B => C, then A => C). The early term in the research community for this relation was *transitivity*. In fact, research has shown that if the individual is presented with the printed word, the individual is also able to select the appropriate picture (i.e., if A => B and B => C, then C => A). This second way of demonstrating the higher-order relation demonstrates both symmetry and transitivity.

The important consideration is that these higher-order relations appear in normally developing individuals in instances that haven't involved formal or direct training. For example, if a child learns that John is older than Sam, and Sam is older than Joe, the child will be able to state that John is older than Joe the very first time the question is asked, without a history of direct reinforcement for saying that John is older than Joe.

Thus, human verbal behavior seems to have a sort of "emergent" property, where speakers learn that some elements of verbalizations are related in certain ways to others. Nonverbal behavior does not appear to have this property. Some researchers believe that these derived relations are the single, essential feature that defines verbal behavior, and more is said in Chapter 9 on this topic. A further important consideration is whether nonhumans demonstrate these sorts of relations. Various experimenters are attempting to demonstrate derived relations in nonhumans, and discussion is lively on the topic.

EXTENSIONS

Further interesting cases are when verbal behavior, once learned through the verbal community, occurs when the speaker and listener are the same person. Awareness, thinking, reasoning, problem solving, and other "intellectual" processes may be studied as instances of verbal behavior in which speakers are their own listeners. The whole process may well be private, meaning only one person is involved. Nevertheless, the process is still behavioral, just as if someone other than the speaker had supplied the same stimulation. These cases are further examined in Chapter 10 of the present book.

CLASSIFICATION SYSTEM FOR ELEMENTARY VERBAL RELATIONS

As noted earlier, verbal behavior is operant behavior, maintained by contingencies of reinforcement. A classification system for verbal behavior may therefore be developed by examining contingencies involved in different instances of verbal behavior, and then by emphasizing particular features of the controlling relations. Some categories may emphasize the nature of the reinforcer, others may emphasize the antecedent conditions, still others may emphasize the relation between antecedent conditions and the form of the response, and so on. Several categories of elementary verbal relations may now be examined.

Mands

1. The category of verbal behavior called a "mand" (as in demand or command) emphasizes the controlling relation between response and reinforcer. A *mand* is defined as a verbal response that is under the functional control of one particular reinforcer. An establishing operation, such as deprivation or aversive stimulation, makes that reinforcer relevant to the speaker. The discriminative stimulus is typically just the presence of a listener. Common examples of mands are requests, asking questions, and raising one's hand for permission to speak.

2. With "pure" mands, there is a conventional correspondence between the response and the reinforcer. The verbal response often names or specifies the reinforcer. For example, a speaker might command a listener to give the time by saying, "Tell me the time!"

3. With "impure" mands, there is less conventional correspondence and more control from other sources. Often mands are "softened" by being turned into questions to avoid punishers, which actually blends in a second kind of manding. For example, a speaker who wants to know the time of day might ask a listener, "Do you know what time it is?" Presumably, the speaker is not really interested in finding out whether the listener knows what time it is and nothing more. Socialization, customs, manner, being polite, etc., are often cases of adopting conventional ways of softening mands within a particular verbal community.

4. A motivative operation potentiates the mand. As noted in Chapter 6, a motivative operation is some change in the environment that alters the effectiveness of some object or event as a reinforcer and correspondingly alters the effectiveness of an antecedent condition as a discriminative stimulus. As mentioned above, the two most common examples of motivative operations are (a) deprivation and (b) aversive stimulation. Note that the discriminative stimulus in manding is not the prevailing state of deprivation or aversive stimulation. In other words, the feeling of hunger is technically not the discriminative stimulus that occasions a request for food. Deprivation, aversive stimulation, and the resulting motivational state simply render relevant circumstances (e.g., the presence of another member of the verbal community who has the capability to administer food) behaviorally significant.

5. "Magical mands" are highly generalized mands, as when a speaker pleads to inanimate objects (or to no one in particular) for relief from the aversiveness or deprivation associated with current circumstances, as in "A horse, a horse, my kingdom for a horse!"

Tacts

1. The category of verbal behavior called a "tact" (as in contact) emphasizes the stimulus control relation between antecedent circumstances and response. A *tact* is defined as a verbal response that is under the functional control of an object, event, or situation, or some property of an object, event, or situation. The reinforcer is typically just generalized social attention, as in approval or confirmation of what was said. Speakers tact when they talk about the world.

2. With "pure" tacts, there is a conventional correspondence between the discriminative stimulus and the verbal response. The response often names, la-

bels, designates, or specifies what is being talked about. For example, a speaker would say "Apple" when shown an apple and asked what kind of fruit it is.

3. With "impure" tacts, there is less conventional correspondence and more control from other sources. For example, a mand may be blended in, as in fictional distortions or exaggeration. Children may say, "I saw a million stars in the sky last night." Typically, children are not reporting that they literally counted a million stars. Rather, they are commenting that a lot of stars were visible, and that they should be commended for being duly observant. They did see a lot of stars, but part of the control over their verbal behavior arises from the attention they receive from others for making statements involving large numbers of objects. These other forms of verbal behavior may be regarded as combinations of tacts and mands because they are at least partially under the control of the mand form of contingency. They get speakers something they couldn't get otherwise, such as attention, or allow them to avoid something they couldn't avoid otherwise, such as blame.

4. Abstraction is a special kind of tacting. In abstraction, a restricted or selected number of features of an event or object or property of an event or object (e.g., a single feature) controls the response, to the exclusion of other variables that are present. Higher-order scientific concepts, classification schemes, and rudimentary scientific laws are abstractions. Abstractions are not easily developed because of the difficulty in overcoming control exerted by other stimuli that are always present. In behavior analysis, the terms *respondent* and *operant* are abstract tacts, in that each is controlled by a special feature of an environmental relation, namely whether a stimulus-stimulus contingency (for a respondent) or a response-reinforcer contingency (for an operant) has caused the behavior. Beginning students have difficulty with these concepts and often identify an operant under discriminative stimulus control as a respondent, simply because an antecedent stimulus is present.

5. Lying is manding disguised as tacting (Moore, 2000). When a speaker lies, the speaker is exploiting the listener by saying something in a form that conventionally resembles that of a tact but is not actually a tact. Rather, a functional analysis of the speaker's behavior indicates that the speaker is manding the listener to deliver reinforcers that would otherwise not be forthcoming, or to refrain from delivering aversive stimulation that would otherwise be forthcoming. If the speaker was actually tacting, the verbal response would be incompatible with what was emitted. Boasting and exaggerating (stretching the facts, hyperbole) are manding, as are malingering, hypochondriasis, and the behavior of the neurotic that is reinforced through secondary gains. Often such statements appear to be tacts, which is how the speaker "gets away with it." However, if they were genuinely tacts under the control of a prevailing state of affairs, their form would necessarily be much different.

Intraverbals

1. The category of verbal behavior called an "intraverbal" emphasizes the relation between prior verbal behavior and response. An *intraverbal* is defined as a verbal response that is under the functional control of another verbal stimulus, where the relation between stimulus and response is an arbitrary one established by the verbal community. The reinforcer is typically just generalized social attention.

2. In many cases, intraverbals consist in just saying the next word in a previously acquired chain of responses. A common example is saying a "memorized" sequence of words, as in reciting the Pledge of Allegiance or singing a song. Intraverbal control can also be present in larger patterns of words, as in rhyming, alliteration, assonance, and meter.

3. A verbal response isn't usually an intraverbal the first time it is made. The response is ordinarily emitted for another reason first. It can be an intraverbal the second time and subsequently, however.

4. An extended verbal response, such as the memorized sequence of words in the Pledge of Allegiance or singing a song, is generally defined as an intraverbal because it consists largely of control by one word over the next. Technically, the first word isn't an intraverbal, but subsequent words may be. Once the intraverbal process begins, it is self-sustaining, in that the initial part occasions the intermediate part, and the intermediate part the terminal part. This classification is one instance where verbal behavior does take place according to a chained, serial process. To be sure, a relatively large portion of speech can be intraverbal in nature. Speakers do often say things they have said before.

5. In the current instance, an intraverbal can be a function of one's own immediately preceding verbal behavior or that of others. In an intraverbal, the speaker may simply pick up in sequence a previously learned chain of responses and finish it. Note that the speaker doesn't hear the entire sequence first and then repeat it in its entirety, and there is no point-to-point correspondence between the discriminative stimulus and response.

Verbal Behavior Involving "Formal Similarity"

1. Some verbal behavior may be classified in terms of the relation between the form of the discriminative stimulus (S^D) and the form of the verbal response (R_v). Four such classifications are presented below. There is a point-to-point correspondence between the S^D and the response. The reinforcers are typically generalized social attention.

2. An echoic is a verbal response in which an oral S ^{D} occasions a corresponding oral response. Unlike an intraverbal, an echoic is a verbal response where the speaker hears the entire sequence first, and then repeats it in its entirety.

3. Copying text (or transcription) is a verbal response in which a written S ^{D} occasions a corresponding written response.

4. A textual is a verbal response in which a written S ^{D} occasions a corresponding oral response. Textuals are the basic ingredients of what is called "reading" in everyday language, but reading is a broader category in that it involves supplemental control by word order, sentence construction, paragraph composition, etc.

5. Taking dictation is a verbal response in which an oral S ^{D} occasions a corresponding written response.

Classification	S ^{D}:	R $\lor$ =>	Reinforcer
Echoic	oral	oral	GSA (generalized
Copying text	written	written	GSA social
textual	written	oral	GSA attention)
Taking dictation	oral	written	GSA

Figure 8–2 is a graphic presentation of elementary verbal relations. It may be understood as a flow chart or decision tree for identifying the categories of verbal behavior reviewed in this chapter. One starts by asking whether a verbal response is controlled by antecedent conditions of deprivation or aversive stimulation. If it is, then the response is a mand. If it is not, then one asks further questions to determine whether the response is a tact, or whether it can be classified on the basis of formal similarity. As noted earlier in this chapter, verbal relations are classified in terms of their controlling relations, as opposed to the structure of the verbal response.

AUTOCLITIC ACTIVITY

Introduction

Some verbal behavior depends on the relations that produce other verbal behavior and modifies the effects of that verbal behavior. This kind of verbal behavior is called autoclitic, from the Greek words for "self" and "leaning back into." Some instances of autoclitic activity involve unique "words" themselves (examples are discussed below). Other instances involve fragments of words ('s, prefixes, suffixes, capital letters). Still others don't involve words or fragments at all (punctuation, underlining for emphasis, drawing arrows, putting items in parentheses or quotation marks). Basic features of lan-

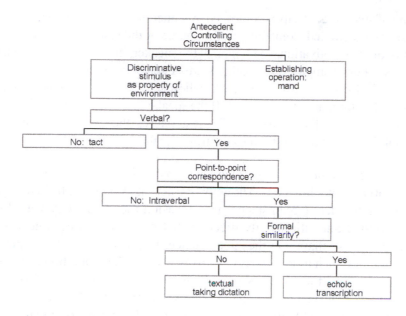

Figure 8.2 The elementary verbal relations.

guage, such as word order, syntax, and grammatical agreement in case, tense, and number, are also instances of autoclitic activity. Composition, rhetoric, constructing logical arguments, and so on may be understood as involving autoclitic activity. Nevertheless, autoclitic activity necessarily involves elementary verbal operants. If the basic verbal operants do not occur, there obviously can be no autoclitic activity regarding them.

The verbal community reinforces the development of such aspects of verbal behavior because some of the things that are indicated by autoclitics are generally useful to know. That is, the verbal community often encourages speakers to provide more precise information about what they are saying and why they are saying it. The verbal community may glean this sort of information from unique verbal responses that occur in conjunction with the elementary verbal responses that constitute the raw material of speech, and from the structure of a sequence of elementary verbal responses. Four kinds of autoclitic activity may be identified: descriptic autoclitics; quantifying autoclitics; qualifying autoclitics, relational autoclitics.

Four Kinds of Autoclitic Activity

1. *Descriptive autoclitics.* This kind of verbal activity may be designated as one sort of "autoclitic tact." The autoclitic activity here is controlled by properties of the antecedent circumstances that occasion the elementary verbal response. That is, this

kind of autoclitic activity is controlled by something of the circumstances in which a response is emitted, something of the source of the response, or something of the emotional or motivational condition of the speaker, including the strength of the response. For example, if a speaker starts a sentence with such phrases as "I am sure...," "I doubt...," "I think...," "I believe...," the speaker is tacting something about the strength of the response. If the speaker starts a sentence with "I heard...," "I see from ...," "To coin a phrase," "Presumably," the speaker is tacting something about the source of the stimulus control over the response.

2. *Quantifying autoclitics.*   This kind of verbal activity may be designated as a second sort of "autoclitic tact." The autoclitic activity here is controlled by properties of the antecedent circumstances that occasion the elementary verbal response. This kind of autoclitic activity affects the listener by indicating either a property of the speaker's behavior or the circumstances responsible for that property. Examples include such modifiers as few, many, some, all, all but, however, almost, always, perhaps, too. Articles such as the, this, that, and a are also quantifying autoclitics. Consider the statement "All swans are white." No one has ever seen all swans, so presumably the response is not a tact. Rather, according to a behavioral translation, the statement means that "100% of the time when I am asked what color a swan is, I will say white."

3. *Qualifying autoclitics.*   Perhaps it is meaningful to designate this kind of verbal activity as one sort of "autoclitic mand." The autoclitic activity here is reinforced when the listener behaves in a particular way after hearing the utterance. This kind of autoclitic activity qualifies an accompanying verbal response in such a way that the intensity or direction of the listener's behavior is modified. Examples include negation, assertion, certain adverbs, suffixes (-like, -less). For example, assertion ("yes!") involves attempting to persuade (mand) the listener to accept comments on a given state of affairs as relatively pure tacts. Negation involves adding "no" or "not" to verbal commentary to signal (mand) the listener that the commentary should not be construed as a tact. The negation indicates that the speaker is not emitting the verbal response under the same conditions as a tact would be emitted, and that the listener should understand this controlling relation for the verbal response.

4. *Relational autoclitics.*   Perhaps it is meaningful to designate this kind of verbal activity as a second sort of "autoclitic mand." The autoclitic activity here is reinforced when the listener behaves in a particular way after hearing the utterance. This kind of autoclitic activity is controlled by relations among elementary verbal operants. Sometimes the responses are unique words that in everyday language are called spatial prepositions: above, below, far, near. Other times they

are more complex: predication (use of "to be"), punctuation, syntactical word ordering, possessives and the use of 's, and grammatical agreement in tense, case, and number. Consider Roman numerals: Speakers will emit "IV," that is, one order of "I" and "V," when the listener is to take the response as being under the control of four units of something, and "VI," that is, a different order of "I" and "V," when the listener is to take the response as being under the control of six units of something.

In the case of syntactical word ordering, no unique "words" are involved. In addition, one presumably doesn't want to say that the person first covertly emits scrambled words, then covertly arranges them into a complete sentence that is grammatically and syntactically correct according to some mysterious mental editorial process involving mental "rules," and then finally emits audible speech. Rather, one simply acknowledges that early words in what will eventually be a complete utterance have some bearing on later words. The verbal community reinforces complex statements about events (or whatever) from speakers, but those statements must take forms that are conventionally acceptable to the verbal community. Given that early words in what will become a sentence have been emitted, later words will follow from the earlier according to the form acceptable to the verbal community, and according to the context of the speaker's utterances. (The term *context* here means both variables present and their functional role in contingencies.) The verbal community may even go so far as to condition "autoclitic frames," which are conventionally prescribed formats or sequences for emitting verbal behavior, as in subject-verb-object or actor-action-object sentences. These frames may become very generalized, such that they come to be applied in many other situations than the original. For example, if a speaker has learned to say "the boy's shoe," "the boy's coat," and "the boy's hat," the verbal frame "the boy's _____" has now become established, and the speaker may now be able to say "the boy's glove" when the boy acquires a glove, without the direct action of reinforcement connected with saying "the boy's glove."

Similarly, in predication, the speaker uses some form of the verb "to be" to indicate that there is an important relation between, say, two tacts, such that a tact specifying an object and a tact specifying a property are related in the sense that the speaker is signifying that the object has the tacted property. That is, the same physical object occasions both tacts. To illustrate, consider the statement "The apple is red." "The" is a quantifying autoclitic, designating one specific object. "Apple" is one tact concerning that object, and "red" is another. The verb "is" is a relational autoclitic of predication, indicating that the particular physical object that is being talked about is an apple, rather than a fire hydrant, and that the object is red, rather than green.

SUMMARY AND CONCLUSIONS

The behavior-analytic approach to verbal behavior is a functional approach; it emphasizes the causes of the behavior in question. As with other forms of operant behavior, behavior analysts do not look in other dimensions for those causes. In addition, it is not a structural approach, and does not infer causes from other dimensions on the basis of the structure or form of the dependent variable. Rather, behavior analysis looks to the contingencies that control the behavior. Skinner (1938) acknowledged that verbal behavior is clearly one of the most complex forms of behavior to be analyzed: "I may say that the only differences I expect to see between the behavior of rat and man (aside from enormous differences of complexity) lie in the field of verbal behavior" (p. 442). The verbal relations reviewed in this chapter represent the foundation of a behavioral approach. However, more complex forms of verbal behavior can also occur. These forms are addressed in Chapter 9.

TABLE 8.1
Definitions

Verbal behavior
Behavior reinforced through the mediation of other persons. "If we make the provision that the 'listener' must be responding in ways which have been conditioned precisely in order to reinforce the behavior of the speaker, we narrow our subject to what is traditionally recognized as the verbal field." (Skinner, 1957, p. 225)

Mand
A verbal response that is under the functional control of a particular reinforcer. An establishing operation, such as deprivation or aversive stimulation, makes that reinforcer relevant for the speaker.

Tact
A verbal response that is under the functional control of an object, event, or situation, or some property of an object, event, or situation.

Intraverbal
A verbal response that is under the functional control of another verbal stimulus, where the relation between stimulus and response is an arbitrary one established by the verbal community. Often the response continues a phrase or series of words.

Echoic
A verbal response in which an oral S^D occasions a corresponding oral response.

Taking dictation

A verbal response in which an oral S ^{D} occasions a corresponding written response.

Copying text (or transcription)

A verbal response in which a written S ^{D} occasions a corresponding written response.

Textual

A verbal response in which a written S ^{D} occasions a corresponding oral response.

Descriptive autoclitic

Autoclitic activity that is controlled by properties of the antecedent circumstances that occasion the elementary verbal response. This kind of autoclitic activity is controlled by something of the emotional or motivational condition of the speaker, or something of the conditions of which the response is a function, including the strength of the response.

Quantifying autoclitic

A second kind of autoclitic activity that is controlled by properties of the antecedent circumstances that occasion the elementary verbal response. This kind of autoclitic activity affects the listener by indicating either a property of the speaker's behavior or the circumstances responsible for that property.

Qualifying autoclitic

Autoclitic activity that is reinforced when the listener behaves in a particular way after hearing the utterance. This kind of autoclitic activity qualifies an accompanying verbal response in such a way that the intensity or direction of the listener's behavior is modified.

Relational autoclitic

A second kind of autoclitic activity that is reinforced when the listener behaves in a particular way after hearing the utterance. This kind of autoclitic activity is controlled by relations among elementary verbal operants.

REFERENCES

Moore, J. (2000). Words are not things. *The Analysis of Verbal Behavior, 17*, 143–160.

Skinner, B. F. (1938). *The behavior of organisms*. New York: Appleton-Century.

Skinner, B. F. (1957). *Verbal behavior*. New York: Appleton-Century-Crofts.

Skinner, B. F. (1978). *Reflections on behaviorism and society*. Englewood Cliffs, NJ: Prentice-Hall.

STUDY QUESTIONS

1. Describe how Skinner's "refined" definition of verbal behavior elaborates on the basic definition offered earlier in the book *Verbal Behavior*.

2. Describe the relation among verbal behavior, social behavior, and operant behavior depicted in Figure 8–1.

3. In one or two sentences, define language from the perspective of radical behaviorism.

4. List any three genetic changes that made verbal behavior possible in humans.

5. Describe the three elements of the verbal contingency: antecedent stimulus, response, reinforcer.

6. Describe the differences between the radical behaviorist account of verbal behavior and the traditional account with respect to: (a) mentalism, (b) structure versus function, (c) the concept of usage, (d) meaning versus reference.

7. In four to six sentences, describe the criticism involving serial processes that traditional accounts make of an empirical, behavioral approach to verbal behavior, and the radical behaviorist response to this criticism.

8. In four to six sentences, describe the criticism involving developmental processes, underdetermination, and the poverty of the stimulus that traditional accounts make of an empirical, behavioral approach to verbal behavior, and the radical behaviorist response to this criticism.

9. In about three to four sentences, contrast the radical behaviorist approach to scientific verbal behavior with the traditional account. Be sure to mention the different positions with respect to "theoretical terms," such as intervening variables and hypothetical constructs.

10. Describe five relevant issues according to which verbal behavior can be distinguished from nonverbal behavior.

11. Describe what is meant by an equivalence relation. Use the terms symmetry and transitivity knowledgeably in your answer.

12. Define (in terms of contingencies) and give an example of the following elementary verbal relation: mand.

13. Define (in terms of contingencies) and give an example of the following elementary verbal relation: tact.

14. Define (in terms of contingencies) and give an example of the following elementary verbal relation: intraverbal.

15. Describe (in terms of contingencies) the four classes of verbal behavior based on formal similarity.

16. Describe each of the four kinds of autoclitic activity.

9

Verbal Behavior 2: Complex Verbal Relations

Synopsis of Chapter 9: The chapters of the second section extend the foundations and concepts of radical behaviorism to additional topics. Chapter 8 used the concepts that were developed in the preceding analyses of operant behavior to focus on elementary verbal relations. Chapter 9 continues to examine verbal relations, but progresses to more complex forms of those relations. These forms involve derived relational responding, in which verbal behavior develops indirectly through interaction with the environment, rather than directly. The term indirect here implies that when these forms of verbal behavior appear, their history is not one of having been directly reinforced themselves, but rather only of being related in certain unique ways to other verbal behavior that was directly reinforced. The relations include mutual entailment, in which responding develops on the basis of the reciprocal relation between two stimuli, and combinatorial entailment, in which responding develops on the basis of the relation across three or more stimuli. A further feature of advanced forms of verbal behavior is transformation of function, in which a function nominally belonging to one stimulus spreads to other stimuli to which it is related. The chapter next considers instances of verbal regulation, or "rule-governed" behavior. The chapter closes with a discussion of awareness, or the influence of verbal stimuli, in which speakers sometimes are their own listeners, on subsequent behavior.

The terms, concepts, and relations identified in Chapter 8 emphasized the direct action of the environment on the development of verbal behavior. The term *direct* here means that analysis of the development of the verbal behavior in question reveals a history whereby the verbal behavior has produced a reinforcer after being emitted in the presence of an S^D . However, a moment's reflection suggests that some instances of verbal behavior are more complex, in that they seem to develop indirectly, rather than directly. The term *indirect* here means that when these forms of verbal behavior appear, their history is not one of having been reinforced themselves, but rather only of being related in certain unique ways to other verbal behavior that was directly reinforced. This chapter examines these more complex forms, as well as other complex ways that verbal behavior influences subsequent behavior, both verbal and nonverbal.

COMPLEX VERBAL RELATIONS: DERIVED RELATIONAL RESPONDING

Chapter 8 noted that the features identified as symmetry and transitivity illustrate verbal responding that develops even though the responding has no history of directly producing reinforcement in the presence of a discriminative stimulus. As an example, consider the verbal behavior that Skinner (1957) describes in the following passage:

> Thus *An amphora is a Greek vase with two handles* has at least three effects upon the listener. As a result of having heard this response he may (1) say *amphora* when asked *What is a Greek vase with two handles called?*, (2) say *A Greek vase having two handles* when asked *What is an amphora?*, and (3) may point appropriately when asked *Which of these is an amphora?* Again, these are not results which occur spontaneously in the naive speaker but rather as the product of a long history of verbal conditioning. Education is largely concerned with setting up the behavior necessary to permit these changes to occur. (p. 360)

In the passage above, being able to say "Amphora" wasn't directly taught as a response to the question of "What is a Greek vase with two handles called?" In addition, the response to the question does not seem in any obvious way to be a simple generalization of a previously learned tact. There was not a stimulus present from a particular dimension when the speaker learned to say "An amphora is a Greek vase with two handles," and then a related stimulus from the same dimension present when the speaker was asked "What is a Greek vase with two handles called?" Moreover, the response is not a simple intraverbal, because the term to be defined and its definition are reversed in the example. Nevertheless, the behavior Skinner identified occurs reliably in most competent speakers.

How to Account for Verbal Behavior That Develops Indirectly, Rather Than Through the Direct Action of Reinforcement

How is the indirect development of verbal behavior to be understood? Further reflection suggests that in most speakers, sometimes even in those who are very young, a great deal of verbal behavior seems to develop in this way. Clearly, people often see connections between things, or extensions from one state of affairs to another, purely through verbal statements. In the passage above, Skinner suggested this form of verbal behavior doesn't develop spontaneously, but rather as the result of a long history of verbal conditioning. What are the important elements of such a history, and what implications does the indirect development of verbal behavior have for our understanding of verbal behavior generally?

Although the process is not completely understood at present, it appears that as persons begin to interact with the verbal community, they learn through direct, first-order or elementary relations. As persons continue to develop, however, they also learn through higher-order relations. The terms "generalized operant" and "overarching operant class" have been used in conjunction with this sort of learning. Consider the non-verbal example of generalized imitation in a child (Baer, Peterson, & Sherman, 1967). A model raises her left arm. A child receives reinforcement for raising his left arm. The model raises her right arm. What does the child do? Perhaps some children will raise their left arms, since that response was the one that had previously been reinforced. However, and depending on the amount of experience a child has had, many children will raise their right arms, even though this response to this model had never previously been directly reinforced. At issue is why the children did so.

Clearly, some relations are at work beyond the direct effect of reinforcement administered for a response made in the presence of an antecedent discriminative stimulus. The example of generalized imitation above suggested that the response depended on the amount of the child's experience. In typically developing children, the response evidently develops at a fairly young age. Presumably, the response develops because of a history of something called "multiple exemplar training." That is, beginning at a very early age, children are taught to respond on the basis of the relation between their own response and the antecedent situation. If the model pats her head, reinforcement is delivered when the child pats his head. If the model pats a table, reinforcement is delivered when the child pats the table. If the model touches her knee, reinforcement is delivered when the child touches his knee. If the model rubs her stomach, reinforcement is delivered when the child rubs his stomach. And so on. The child has experience involving multiple examples.

In the case of generalized imitation, children are taught to respond in such a way that the topography of their response is related to the antecedent situation in a way called matching. The topography of the child's response wouldn't have to match or correspond to the model's response, of course. If the history of reinforcement were otherwise, when the model raised her left arm, the child might raise his right arm, and when the model raised her right arm, the child might raise his left. It may also be that some feature of the antecedent situation was correlated with whether reinforcement depended on matching or nonmatching. In the presence of one feature, matching the model would be reinforced. In the presence of another feature, doing something other than matching the model would be reinforced.

Relational Responding: Framing Events Relationally

To return to Skinner's verbal example of the amphora, when an individual initially learns that an amphora is a Greek vase with two handles, and subsequently is able to answer "Amphora" to the question "What is a Greek vase with two handles called?", the individual is engaging in relational verbal responding. As the individual interacted with the verbal community, the individual learned that a definition is conventionally expressed in a framework having two parts: (a) the word that is the term to be defined, and (b) the words of the definition itself. The individual presumably learned early in life that definitions are often framed in such a manner, and when they are, one part is equivalent to or is coordinated with the other.

Then, when the individual is presented with one part of the frame, on the basis of its past experiences involving multiple examples, the individual responds with the other, related part of the frame. The individual has framed events relationally. Through analogous experiences the individual may be able to engage in other forms of verbal behavior as well. When the individual learns someone's name and occupation, the individual may subsequently be able to name someone else who has the same occupation. In a perhaps more complex case, when the individual learns that snakes are fearful, and then learns that *crotalus cerastes* is a snake, the individual may be fearful when hearing the word *crotalus cerastes*, even though neither the snake itself nor the word has been directly associated with any unconditioned fear-evoking event. For example, the individual was never bitten by the snake, and at the same time told the snake was *crotalus cerastes*. The individual has learned a generalized tendency to frame events in relation to one another—in this case to frame them in a way that they are equivalent or coordinated—and one says that a relational frame has developed. The responding has developed through a history of reinforcement for responding based on relations between stimuli. It is not based solely on direct training in regard to the specific stimuli of interest, nor solely on the formal (i.e., physical) properties of either the stimuli or the relations between them.

Skinner coined the phraseology of "frames" and "responding relationally" in the following passage, when he talked about autoclitic behavior, as discussed in Chapter 8:

> Something less than full-fledged relational autoclitic behavior is involved when partially conditioned autoclitic "frames" combine with responses appropriate to a specific situation. Having responded to many pairs of objects with behavior such as *the hat and the shoe* and *the gun and the hat*, the speaker may make the response *the boy and the bicycle* on a novel occasion. If he has acquired a series of responses such as *the boy's gun*, *the boy's shoe*, and *the boy's hat*, we may suppose that the partial frame the boy's _____ is available for recombination with other responses. The first time the boy acquires a bicycle, the speaker can compose a new unit *the boy's bicycle*. This is not simply the emission of two responses separately acquired. The process resembles the multiple causation of Chapter 9. The relational aspects of the situation strengthen a frame, and specific features of the situation strengthen responses fitted into it. (Skinner, 1957, p. 336)

Framing Events Relationally: Mutual Entailment

In some cases, the relational frame obtains between two verbal elements. For example, if a speaker has learned that A weighs more than B, the speaker can also state that B weighs less than A. Thus, through their interactions with the environment, speakers learn to respond on the basis of the particular relations that exist between the two objects in the environment. When this sort of relation exists, one talks of a "mutually entailed relation," where "mutual" suggests the bidirectional relation between the two elements spoken about. In broader perspective, the relation initially labeled as symmetry may be seen as one form of a mutually entailed relation.

Framing Events Relationally: Combinatorial Entailment

In other cases, the relational frame obtains among three or even more verbal elements. For example, if a speaker has learned that A weighs more than B, and that B weighs more than C, the speaker can also state that A weighs more than C, and that C weighs less than A. Thus, through their interactions with the environment, speakers learn to respond to particular relations that exist among multiple objects in the environment on the basis of the words that are used to describe those relations. When this sort of behavior exists, one talks of a "combinatorially entailed relation," where the term "combinatorially" suggests the frame extends across the combination of the three elements spoken about. In broader perspective, the relations initially labeled as transitivity or as combining symmetry and transitivity may be seen as forms of combinatorially entailed relations.

In principle, speakers can learn to respond on the basis of a large number of these sorts of relations as a result of interactions with the verbal community. The examples above reflect a coordination among the elements. Speakers can also learn to derive relations of opposition, distinction, comparison, hierarchies, temporal relations, spatial relations, conditionality, causality, deictic relations, and many others, either singly or in complex interactions (Hayes, Barnes-Holmes, & Roche, 2001).

The relations may be described in terms of complex networks. As Skinner said, these sorts of relations do not appear spontaneously in the naive speaker, but only after a long history of conditioning. Education is often concerned with establishing relational networks of this sort, relating facts and principles to each other. Mathematics and logic represent abstract forms of the activity of responding to elements that are related to each other through their participation in networks of complex verbal frames.

Framing Events Relationally: Transformation of Function

Two important features of the relational framing process have been identified: mutual entailment and combinatorial entailment. A thorough treatment of higher-order verbal relations now needs to identify a third feature: transformation of function. This feature means that the effect of one verbal stimulus (e.g., in common parlance, a word or term) may be modified by the way it participates in a frame or a relational network. For example, some initially unknown term may become desirable through its participation in a frame or network with something else that already is desirable; direct experience or even being related as part of a common physical dimension is not necessary. Hence, suppose an individual likes a given make of car. The make of car then advertises that it comes with some new accessory. An individual might come to prize the new accessory, even though the individual doesn't know what it does, simply because it is related to the car.

Framing Events Relationally: Contextual Control

The relations may also come under contextual control. That is, there may be superordinate stimuli in the environment that are correlated with how a derived relation is transmitted through the network of stimuli. In one context, some superordinate feature of the environment may signal something positive about an aspect of the environment, whereas in another context, a different superordinate feature may signal something negative about an aspect of the environment. For example, a consumer may purchase item A instead of item B at store X, because store X is known to have a good purchasing agent who is aware of the variability in production lots of items A and B, and given this variability, that A is a better value from the lots available. Store X is the contextual stimulus. This control may then spread to the purchase of item C instead of D, under an assumption that C is likewise a better value.

Importantly, the forms of verbal behavior outlined above develop indirectly. That is, no relations have been directly trained. Although reinforcement in the past was provided directly for responding on the basis of the relation between one object and another, behavior in the current instance with respect to the stimuli has no comparable history of direct reinforcement. Moreover, there is no formal similarity between the two situations, in the sense that they do not share physical properties, such as being part of a common dimension, like size or wavelength. Thus, the behavior cannot simply be a case of stimulus generalization. It can only be understood in terms of the past pattern of reinforcement practices as those practices pertain to relations between and among stimuli.

THE CONDITIONAL DISCRIMINATION PROCEDURE AND REPRESENTATIVE RESEARCH

The bulk of the research on derived relational responding has been carried out using a procedure called a "conditional discrimination procedure," and it is useful to outline this procedure at this point. In this procedure, the subject is presented with one stimulus (typically called the "sample"), and then two or more subsequent stimuli (typically called the "comparisons"). The subject has to choose the correct comparison stimulus on the basis of the sample. The sample and comparison stimuli (for simplicity, two samples and comparisons are assumed) are often some sort of symbol, graphic, or nonsense set of characters or letters. Thus, a description might state that given sample stimulus A1, subjects must learn to choose comparison stimulus B1 rather than B2, but given A2, subjects must learn to choose B2 rather than B1. In probe trials, subjects might then be presented with B1 as a sample, to determine if they will choose A1 rather than A2 when those stimuli are presented as comparisons. If so, then one would say the A1 and B1 stimuli are equivalent, or coordinated. As described, this test would demonstrate the particular coordination of symmetry. The procedure can then be expanded to involve a third set of stimuli: C1 and C2. Given A1, subjects must now learn to choose C1 rather than C2, and given A2, C2 rather than C1. In probe trials, subjects might be presented with C1 as a sample and B1 and B2 as comparisons. At issue is whether subjects will now choose B1, since a network of relations involving A1, B1, and C1 has been established through the training procedure. If subjects do choose B1, then one would say that relations have been formed among the stimuli such that they have become equivalent. As described, this test demonstrates the coordination of both symmetry and transitivity. In briefer terms, one speaks of the existence of equivalence relations, or frames of coordination among the stimuli. Given the existence of such a frame or network, whatever stimulus function was associated with, say, A1 will now be acquired by B1 and C1, and one speaks of the transformation of stimulus function in the network.

To understand complex stimulus relations and transformation of function a bit better, some representative research may now be considered. A representative study showing complex stimulus relations and transformation of function in the area of respondent conditioning is Dougher, Augustson, Markham, Greenway, and Wulfert (1994). This article reported data from two experiments. In the first experiment, researchers conducted equivalence training using conditional discrimination procedures. In this training, participants were presented with A1 as a sample, and then, in different trials, trained to choose B1, C1, and D1. Similarly, participants were presented with A2 as a sample, and then, in different trials, trained to choose B2, C2, and D2. This training established stimuli A1, B1, C1, and D1 as members of one equivalence class, and A2, B2, C2, and D2 as members of a second equivalence class. Then, stimulus B1 was paired with shock, and stimulus B2 was presented alone, not paired with shock. B1 then came to elicit a conditioned response, whereas B2 did not. The researchers then tested stimuli C1, D1, C2, and D2. They found that in 6 of 8 participants, stimuli C1 and D1 elicited stronger conditioned responses than either stimulus C2 or D2. Thus, the eliciting function of B1 transferred to other stimuli that were part of the same class as stimulus B1, even though those stimuli had never been directly correlated with shock. That is, the stimulus function of C1 and D1 was transformed, such that they acquired the function of B1, through being in the same equivalence class as B1.

In their second experiment, Dougher, Augustson, Markham, Greenway, and Wulfert (1994) began by conducting the same kind of equivalence training as in the first experiment. This time, however, stimuli B1, C1, and D1 were all paired with shock. The next manipulation was to present stimulus B1 in respondent extinction trials, not paired with shock. When the researchers tested stimuli C1 and D1, they found that these stimuli failed to elicit a conditioned response. In a subsequent condition, stimulus B1, which had previously been presented in extinction, was reconditioned by pairing it again with shock. When the researchers tested stimuli C1 and D1, they found that these stimuli had regained their conditioned eliciting function. Thus, respondent stimulus functions transferred readily among equivalent stimuli, through tests of initial conditioning, extinction, and reconditioning, all without trials in which the association between the US and the relevant stimuli was altered. These results were consistent with other studies showing other sorts of transformation of function: discriminative control, contextual control, conditioned reinforcement, and conditioned punishment (see discussion in Hayes, 1994, p. 23). The research used arbitrary stimuli as A1, B1, C1, and so on. However, a moment's reflection suggests that much of our verbal behavior functions in analogous ways. That is, speakers learn the words dangerous, fearsome, poisonous, and so on, perhaps in relation to primary noxious events. The word snake may then come to be associated with such danger words, even though one has not had any direct dangerous experience with a snake. If one has not been informed that *crotalus cerastes* is a snake, *crotalus cerastes* may be a neutral stimulus. However, as soon as one is informed that *crotalus cerastes* is a snake, its function is transformed, such that it now elicits a fear response, even though it has itself never been directly associated with a dangerous event.

A representative study showing complex stimulus relations and transformation of function in operant conditioning is Steele and Hayes (1991). In this study, researchers first trained participants on conditional discrimination tasks to relate "same" stimuli (e.g., given a large square, pick a large square but not a small square) in the presence of one contextual cue, "opposite" stimuli (e.g., given a large square, pick a small square but not a large square) in the presence of a second contextual cue, and "distinct" stimuli (e.g., given a square, pick a cross but not a square) in the presence of a third contextual cue. Next, participants were taught an extensive network of additional conditional discriminations, with each conditional discrimination being made in the presence of one of the three contextual cues used in the earlier training. Thus, in the presence of the contextual stimulus for "opposite," suppose participants were given A1 and trained to pick B2 but not B1, and were given A1 and trained to pick C2 but not C1. In a test trial, the "opposite" contextual stimulus was again present, and participants were given B2, with a choice between C1 and C2. The important result was that participants chose C1.

The Steele and Hayes (1991) study shows the complex nature of the relations underlying verbal behavior. In the Steele and Hayes study, when participants were given B2 in the presence of the "opposite" contextual stimulus and asked to choose between C1 and C2, the participants chose C1, rather than C2, indicating that they were responding on the basis of the mutually entailed relation of "opposite." That is, participants responded on the basis of the derived relation by showing that if A1 is the opposite of both B2 and C2, then B2 and C2 must be the same. If this outcome were simply a function of first-order conditioning processes, participants should presumably have chosen C2, because they had been trained to pick B2 and C2 when given A1. Overall, the orderliness of the results implies that verbal stimuli can become related in rich and complex ways.

The results of these studies involving higher-order relations demonstrate clearly the indirect processes that underlie some forms of verbal behavior, as a result of a particular kind of interaction between the speaker and the verbal community. Hayes, Barnes-Holmes, and Roche (2001) have described the resulting process as that of framing events relationally. In fact, Hayes, Barnes-Holmes, and Roche have held the very strong position that "verbal" as a technical term is meaningfully used only when a speaker produces sequences of stimuli as a result of framing events relationally, and the verbal stimuli have their functions because they participate in those frames. Moreover, this entire process comes about through the influence of a listener who shares the frames, and the listener cannot be separated from the process. If the behavior in question has not come about through such a process, the implication is that it should not be regarded as verbal, but rather only some form of social behavior. Thus, for an instance of behavior to be called verbal, the behavior must involve the listener as well as the speaker, in the sense that the listener and speaker are bound together through their mutual participation in the relational frame. This position is called Relational Frame Theory, abbreviated as RFT.

The RFT definition of verbal behavior is therefore somewhat narrower than Skinner's. Skinner would acknowledge as verbal behavior all the same things that RFT does, but RFT does not acknowledge as verbal behavior some of the things that Skinner does. Skinner's (1957) book *Verbal Behavior* was written at a particular time, and sought to make a novel argument in favor of an objective, empirical, and behavioral approach to verbal behavior. Although Skinner clearly recognized that some verbal behavior can develop without the direct action of reinforcement, as the passage concerning the amphora shows, Skinner did not make a great deal of this process at the time. He simply stated that it was the result of a long history of conditioning, without going into any detail about what the important features of that history were. Clearly, further work was warranted. The RFT approach has championed itself as a "post-Skinnerian" account and has vigorously examined the role of indirect relations in complex human behavior, though it too has not examined in any comprehensive sense what experiences are necessary for the relations in question to develop. The present conclusion is that RFT is a continuation or extension of the approach launched in Skinner's book. At present, research and discussion continue in this most important area.

VERBAL REGULATION

Verbal antecedents can have a number of effects on the behavior that follows. This portion of the chapter reviews some of the more prominent examples of such effects.

Rules: What They Are, and What They Aren't

A conventional term for a verbal antecedent is a *rule*. Skinner began formally talking about rule-governed behavior in 1966 in connection with problem solving, although he had mentioned the topic occasionally in earlier writing (e.g., Skinner, 1957). He initially defined a rule as a contingency specifying (verbal) stimulus, and contrasted rule-governed behavior with contingency-shaped behavior. By contingency-shaped behavior Skinner meant operant behavior under the control of contingencies that didn't involve any verbal elements. The distinction was somewhat confusing because rule-governed behavior was also operant behavior and reinforced by its consequences. Nothing beyond an operant process was implied.

What, then, is the distinction between rule-governed and contingency-shaped behavior? The present treatment is that the distinction turns on the history of and discriminative stimulus involved in the contingency that governs the behavior in question. In the strictest sense, both forms of behavior are operant, and contingencies are always at the heart of operant behavior. At issue is whether the S^D in the contingency is verbal. A rule is a verbal S^D arising through interaction with others, and reinforcement for following the rule is initially social, rather than any material consequences achieved by following the rule. Reinforcement in subsequent instances may remain social, or it may eventually become material. Rule-governed behavior refers to the particular sequence or development of the stimulus control over the response, arising from verbal interactions with the verbal community. In contingency-shaped behavior, a history involving verbal interactions is largely absent.

Initially, research sought to examine whether the properties of rule-governed behavior differed from those of contingency-shaped behavior. One example is Shimoff, Catania, and Matthews (1981). In this research, college students' responses were occasionally reinforced by points later exchangeable for money. For some students, responding was established by shaping. For others, responding was established by demonstration and written instructions; that is, by rules. Initially, all students were exposed to a baseline condition in which responding was maintained by a special arrangement that prevented reinforcement after rapid responding. Later, this arrangement was modified, such that reinforcers could be earned by rapid responding. However, no exteroceptive stimulus change accompanied the modification. For the students whose responses had been shaped, rate of responding and rate of earning reinforcers did in fact increase. For the students whose responses had been established by instruction, the overall rate of responding usually continued at an unchanged low rate, even though there were instances in which reinforcers were produced by rapid responding. This latter result is important because it means that the insensitivity of instructed responding typically occurred despite contact with the modified arrangement. Thus, rule-governed behavior (the instructed behavior) persisted when researchers altered contingencies in an experiment, whereas the shaped behavior more readily conformed to the changed contingencies.

This effect was called the "insensitivity effect," in the sense that rule-governed behavior was thought to be insensitive (or at least less sensitive) to experimentally manipulated features of an operant task in the laboratory, or elsewhere. Such a label was probably inaccurate, as it risked promoting the idea that rule-governed behavior really was a qualitatively different process. Alternative analyses pointed out that participants in the experiments typically had 18 years or so of following verbal instructions, and that during the course of an experiment they may not have had sufficient experience with the nonverbal elements of the contingencies to counteract this history and adjust their behavior. In any case, recent analysis of verbal regulation has gone beyond this original designation by talking in terms of competing contingencies: the verbal contingencies of verbal regulation compete with the nonverbal contingencies of the nonverbal setting, often exerting stronger control.

Important to recognize is that verbal regulation occurs when a verbal antecedent actually exerts an effect. That is, a verbal stimulus is part of the antecedent setting that is actually responsible for the discriminative control over the response, either in the subject's history or in the current event. Hence, orderly behavior that can be described after the fact as "following a rule" or "obeying a rule" is not necessarily behavior that is verbally regulated. A verbal stimulus must literally be part or have been part of the antecedent setting. One might say that a pigeon trained to peck a green key and receive food is following the rule "If the key is green, then a peck produces food," but this statement is simply a post hoc description of the contingency, rather than a statement that the pigeon's behavior is rule governed.

Cognitive psychologists attribute human language to rule following, where the rules have to do with various structural components, grammar, and syntax. Radical behaviorists reject such treatments. At best, such treatments simply describe contingencies inherent in the conventional practices of the verbal community. At worst, such treatments are mentalistic appeals to events in some other dimension, in which the events are directed by some internal entity of dubious origin. The treatments induce people to neglect the role of environmental contingencies, and because they have a certain prestige—for instance, by claiming to be "theoretical"—they often carry unwarranted weight in scientific discussions.

Dynamics of Rule Following and Verbal Regulation

The verbal stimulus has to exist in some form before it can be included as part of the antecedent complex that regulates behavior. Where do verbal stimuli such as rules come from? From the perspective of radical behaviorism, they come from the verbal community, which encourages individuals to describe what they are doing and why as part of everyday interactions. The source of the verbal stimuli might be as echoics or textuals, when individuals hear others or read in books about particular courses of action. An example of such a process would be a saying used to determine how one should turn a wrench to tighten or loosen a nut on a bolt: "Right is tight and left is loose." According to this saying, if a tighter nut is reinforcing, one should turn the wrench to the right, and if a looser nut is reinforcing, one should turn the wrench to the left. Note that the rule takes advantage of the existing intraverbal relations involving (a) the rhyme "right-tight," and (b) the initial letter L in both words: "*l*eft-*l*oose." The verbal behaviors in question then come under intraverbal control and are available to the individual.

Several separate questions are associated with this process. The first concerns the accuracy or validity of the rule. There are contingencies that are responsible for this relation. Consider the disease of malaria. Taken literally, the word has its origin in "bad air." Many years ago, it was thought that if individuals wanted to avoid malaria, individuals followed the rule of keeping the windows closed, to keep out the bad air or miasma that was thought to be the vehicle of contagion. Such an action may have been partially helpful, as keeping the windows closed also tended to keep out the mosquitos that actually transmitted the disease. Although keeping the windows closed may have been better than leaving them open, the rule failed to specify the actual path of infection. The rule is clearly better than nothing, but an even more accurate rule would have the beneficial consequence of greater avoidance of disease.

A second question concerns following the rule, or the actual effect of the rule on the behavior of individuals who entertain the rule. Often individuals can state a rule, but it is an empirical question whether they are actually following the rule, and if so, what contingencies are responsible for them doing so. Consider the rule "If you want to avoid tooth decay, brush your teeth after every meal." Presumably, individuals who brush their teeth after every meal will have fewer cavities or other sorts of dental problems. Thus, fewer cavities is a consequence of tooth brushing. However, is a reduced number of cavities the actual consequence that maintains the behavior of tooth brushing? The answer is probably not, and almost certainly not in children, who are taught the rule at an early age in an effort to establish good dental hygiene. Consequences that are long delayed from a response tend not to be particularly effective. The negative reinforcement of not developing a cavity several weeks after brushing one's teeth is probably not strong enough to get 5-year-old children to brush their teeth regularly. A more immediate social consequence, such as praise from parents for regularly brushing one's teeth, or some contrived conditioned reinforcement system, such as gold stars backed up by a family outing, is likely to be more effective. Whether adults need comparable contrived systems so that they have regular preventive medical check-ups or health screenings is an open question. Often adults may flatter themselves by thinking they don't, but much research has shown that contrived systems facilitate coming in for check-ups and routine examinations. Dentists might give out free toothbrushes, or fee discounts for regular appointments. In any case, at least initially many circumstances that are responsible for rule following are social, rather than being related to the tangible benefits specified by the rule. The tangible benefits may be too remote from the action specified in the rule to be effective. Presumably, the behavior specified by the rule is adaptive in some sense, and the consequences specified in the rule may therefore contribute in some overall way to rule following, but the importance of more immediate consequences in rule following is important to recognize.

Establishing Operations and Augmentals

Schlinger and Blakely (1987) pointed out that some verbal antecedents exert their effect more through establishing operations than through a discriminative function. Hayes, Barnes-Holmes, and Roche (2001) have referred to these sorts of verbal antecedents as augmentals, and identified two sorts of augmentals: motivative and formative. Motivative augmentals alter the degree to which previously established consequences exert their characteristic effect. Formative augmentals establish consequences as reinforcers or punishers.

An example of a motivative augmental is advertising. Suppose a promotion for a brand of laundry detergent states: "Wash your clothes using Brand X laundry detergent to make them as clean as they can be!" Analysis suggests that the statement is not a simple discriminative stimulus, as it has little to do with going to the market and actually being able to purchase the detergent. Rather, it is a verbal manipulation designed to increase the reinforcing effectiveness of clean clothes, and then link clean clothes to Brand X laundry detergent. It suggests that if having your clothes as clean as they can be is reinforcing for you, then purchasing Brand X laundry detergent in which to wash your clothes will be reinforced by their subsequent cleanliness. The statement may take the form of a testimonial from a prestigious, credible representative or spokesperson, which is a further attempt to use social factors to manipulate consumer behavior.

An example of a formative augmental is when a teacher says, "All students who turn in their assignments on time will get a gold star and a chance to pick the game the class will play at the end of the day." If the gold stars reinforce turning in assignments on time, even before the stars are associated with being able to pick the class activity, the verbal statements have linked a particular behavior with a particular consequence. The gold stars may not have initially been reinforcing, but they acquire a reinforcing effectiveness through the verbal linkage.

Pliance

Some verbal regulation comes about more because of the immediate social consequences of engaging in the action specified in the rule, and less because of any nonsocial benefit of engaging in the action. Hayes, Zettle, and Rosenfarb (1989) have coined the term "pliance" (a neologism derived from socially reinforced "compliance") to designate these instances of verbal regulation. Thus, *pliance* is verbal regulation in which the actor engages in the form of behavior specified in the rule because of a history of coordination between that behavior and social consequences. Verbal antecedents having this function are referred to as "plys." The toothbrushing example reviewed earlier illustrates pliance. Children brush their teeth more because of the social reinforcement of parental social approval, rather than because tooth-brushing avoids cavities.

Tracking

Other verbal regulation comes about more because of the nonsocial benefit of engaging in the action specified in the rule, and less because of any immediate interpersonal consequences of engaging in the action. Hayes, Zettle, and Rosenfarb (1989) have coined the term *tracking* to designate these instances of verbal regulation, where tracking presumably implies that the regulated behavior tracks or conforms to the behavior verbally specified in the rule. Thus, tracking is verbal regulation in which an actor engages in the form of behavior specified in the rule because of a history of coordination between that behavior and the naturally occurring, nonsocial consequences of that behavior. Verbal antecedents having this function are referred to as "tracks." For example, an individual just learning to use a computer and a word processing program might read an instruction manual that to change the insertion point to the current location of the cursor, one has to click the left button on the mouse. The source of the rule was a textual in the manual, and left clicks then become routine in word processing.

INSTRUCTIONS

Respondent Conditioning

Instruction following is also a form of verbally regulated behavior. There are many examples in the research literature examining the effects of instructions on behavior. In the area of respondent conditioning, Dawson and Reardon (1969) conducted respondent conditioning trials with four groups of subjects. The CS was a tone and the US was a shock. Participants in one group, called the facilitory group, were told that the reasonable thing to do was to become conditioned. Participants in a second group, called the inhibitory group, were told the opposite. Participants in a third group, called the neutral group, received no instructions. Participants in a fourth group, called the pseudoconditioning group, were told that the tone and shock would be randomly presented. All participants then received the same number of trials in which the CS and US were paired. The results showed that the magnitude of the conditioned response was increased by the facilitory instructions and decreased by the inhibitory instructions. Participants in the pseudoconditioning group had the lowest response magnitude.

In two related studies, Grings, Schell, and Carey (1973) and McNally (1981) conducted autonomic conditioning trials in which one stimulus (i.e., a CS+) was positively correlated with a shock US and another (i.e., a CS–) was negatively correlated. They then instructed participants that the stimulus that was previously positively correlated with the US would no longer be paired with the US whereas the other stimulus, previously negatively correlated with the US, would now be paired with the US. The researchers observed that the previously negatively correlated stimulus now elicited a response, and that the previously positively correlated stimulus now did elicit a response. Moreover, this effect was observed on the very first presentation of the stimuli, before the US was encountered. Thus, the function of the stimuli changed, even though participants had not experienced any of the modified CS–US correlations. In a quest to control for ecological validity, McNally even used fear-relevant stimuli as CSs: pictures of snakes and spiders. The immediate and dramatic reversal of conditioning testifies to the effectiveness of the verbal instructions.

Operant Conditioning

In the area of operant conditioning, an experimental example showing the effect of instructions is Kaufman, Baron, and Kopp (1966). In this research, students in an introductory psychology class earned money by accumulating points on a button-pushing task. The schedule according to which they earned points was actually a time-based intermittent schedule in which a response would produce a point after a variable interreinforcement interval that averaged about 1 minute. The experimental manipula-

tion was to give participants a variety of different instructions about the relation between responding and points. The result was that the subjects' responding varied
according to the nature of the instructions they had been given, rather than the actual arrangement according to which their responses produced points.

The results of respondent and operant conditioning experiments in which instructions seem to have a greater effect on behavior than the nonverbal experimental conditions are often cited as supporting cognitive, mentalistic, mediational accounts of
behavior, as opposed to behavioral. However, the results do not necessarily do so. The
participants were verbally competent individuals. They had a lengthy history, say 18
years, of following instructions. Thus, instructions had become very powerful stimuli
in their lives by the time of the experiment. In the short time the individuals were exposed to the experimental procedure, the instructions were more powerful variables in
the control of their behavior than were the experimental conditions. One suspects that if
the participants in the respondent conditioning procedure were given trials for 18 years,
or in the operant conditioning procedure were allowed to earn points exchangeable for
food, water, clothes, and other items related to personal welfare for 18 years, their behavior would have come to conform to the actual conditions in effect.

AWARENESS

Over thirty years ago, a book chapter carried the provocative title: "There is no convincing evidence for classical or operant conditioning in humans" (Brewer, 1974). The
chapter argued that humans only evidenced a conditioning effect when they were
aware of the contingencies, and that what was important to understand about behavior
was how conscious mental processes mediated influences arising in the environment.

The present chapter disagrees with the fundamental premise of mediation by mental
processes. From the perspective of the present chapter, awareness can be interpreted as
a kind of self-instruction about the nature of the experimental procedure, and therefore
as an example of verbal regulation. To be sure, there are clearly many ways to assess
what is meant by awareness. The standard way is through a verbal protocol: subjects
would be considered to be aware when they could describe in words what the procedure
was about. Moreover, a relevant issue is what is the nature of the to-be-learned response. The bottom line is that as with instructions, there are many examples in the research literature examining the effects of awareness on behavior. A brief review of
representative experiments will shed some light on this topic and clarify whether humans only learn when they are aware.

One area of research in traditional experimental psychology is called *verbal learning*. A behavior analyst would view this area as a special case of operant conditioning,
but traditional researchers might view it as a separate category. In any case, in a common method (e.g., see Spielberger & DeNike, 1966), researchers decide on some

to-be-reinforced class of verbal behavior. Across different experiments, the class might be plural nouns, human nouns (e.g., architect, girl, protestants, Spaniard, uncle), opinion statements, or sentences starting with "I" or "We." The researchers then ask participants to simply start talking, or they might engage the participants in casual conversation, depending on the nature of the experiment and the definition of the reinforced class. The experimental manipulation is as follows. When the subject says words of a designated class, the experimenter says something positive, such as "Mmm-hmm." This verbalization on the part of the experimenters is presumed to function as a reinforcer and increase the rate at which participants will say words in that designated class. A frequently observed result is that the rate of saying words increases for some participants, but not all. In some of the research, for the participants that evidence an increased rate, the increase typically begins abruptly, rather than gradually. Post-conditioning interviews reveal that the only participants whose rates increased were participants who could state the relation between what they said and how the experimenters responded. Moreover, the point at which the rates increased was the point at which the participants were first able to describe the relation (see also Greenspoon, 1955, and Verplanck, 1955).

At first blush, such results seem to support Brewer's (1974) contention that awareness is a necessary mediating mental state for human learning. This matter is very complex and is examined in greater detail shortly. For the time being, suffice it to note that if awareness really is necessary, then there should not be any instance of human learning in which humans were unaware. This contention should hold for cases in which the to-be-learned response is a verbal response, as well as cases in which the to-be-learned response is a motor response.

Respondent Conditioning

Respondent conditioning is typically regarded as the simplest form of conditioning. As described in Chapter 5, given an unconditioned stimulus (US) that has been shown to elicit a respondent in a designated response system, respondent conditioning is said to have occurred when a previously neutral stimulus (CS) elicits a response in that same system because it has previously been presented in conjunction with the US.

Given that respondent conditioning is regarded as a reasonably simple form of conditioning, an important question is whether awareness of the CS–US contingency is necessary for conditioning. Assessing awareness of the various elements in the conditioning procedure is not simple, however. For example, is being able to specify the US sufficient to count as awareness? Is being able to specify the CS sufficient to count as awareness? Is being able to specify the relation between CS and US sufficient to count as awareness? Is being able to specify the target response sufficient to count as awareness? What overall pattern of statements about the conditioning procedure counts as awareness or lack thereof? How correct does the specification have to be to count as awareness? Does a partially correct specification count as awareness? Does the evidence taken to indicate awareness have to correlate with other behavior in the conditioning preparation? Do the results depend on the details of the preparation, such as the nature of CS and US? Do the results depend on the details of the procedure, such as whether trace conditioning or delay conditioning is employed? In a trace procedure, the CS comes on but then goes off before the US is presented. In a delay procedure, the CS remains on until the US is presented.

Not surprisingly, the evidence is quite mixed regarding these questions. The bulk of the evidence seems to indicate that participants who can't describe the relation between the CS and US don't acquire a conditioned response in a trace eyeblink conditioning procedure. More controversial is whether participants who can't describe the relation between the CS and US acquire a conditioned response in a delay eyeblink conditioning procedure. Clark and Squire (1998) assert yes. In this study, participants were judged to be aware when they answered at least 13 of 17 post-experimental questions in a particular way. Lovibond and Shanks (2002) critically examined the Clark and Squire study and argued that some participants may have been partially aware but were ruled out as unaware, thereby biasing the results in favor of showing that awareness is not a prerequisite for conditioning. Lovibond and Shanks then reviewed other studies that seem to indicate that awareness is necessary. However, Papka, Ivry, and Woodruff-Pak (1997) found that eyeblink conditioning in a delay procedure was equivalent among participants who were aware and unaware. In addition, Knight, Nguyen, and Bandettini (2003) found that participants exhibited conditioned responses mediated by the autonomic nervous system to a CS in a delay procedure when the CS was below perceptual threshold, such that they couldn't report the presence of the CS. Knight et al. conclude that the degree of conditioning is independent of awareness.

Operant Conditioning

Operant conditioning is ordinarily viewed as more complex than respondent conditioning. As noted in Chapter 5, in operant conditioning, a response is emitted more often in a given situation because the response has characteristically produced a particular consequence in that situation. In one operant conditioning experiment investigating awareness, Hefferline and Keenan (1963) had participants sit in a comfortable chair. The participants were then told they could earn money by being relaxed. In actuality, the participants could earn money when instruments detected that the electromyographic potential of a small muscle in their thumb was within a designated range. The potential was about half of the strength that would produce a visible contraction of the thumb. Thus, the response class actually associated with reinforcement was muscle contraction, rather than relaxation. The participants showed a reliable increase in the contraction of the thumb muscle when the operant reinforcement contingency was implemented, and a reliable decrease when the response was extinguished. In post-experimental questioning, no participant revealed the slightest idea that a muscle contraction was related to receiving money, and all participants expressed intense annoyance when the money stopped appearing. In a related and more recent study, Laurenti-Lions et al. (1985) also showed that imperceptibly small thumb-twitches can be controlled by the consequences of the response, in this case, by terminating or postponing aversive noise. Again, the participant was unaware of the nature of the response that produced the consequence.

Rosenfeld and Baer (1970) conducted a somewhat more involved study. They placed participants in a room, and then told the participants their room was connected with an intercom to another room in which a second person would be reading from a list of words. When the second person read a word fluently, that is, without stuttering or stammering, the participants were to award points. When the second person read a word disfluently, the participant was not to award points. After a word had been read, the participant would instruct the person in the other room to read the next word, until the list had been completed.

This arrangement was actually what is called a "deception." In reality, there was no second person in another room. There were only the experimenters playing a tape recording of the two kinds of spoken words, fluent and disfluent. The experimenters were trying to see if they could control the content of the subject's speech. The response class that they selected was the command that the subject gave to the presumed second person to continue; that is, to read the next word. For one subject, the command that was selected was "Next word." For another subject, the command that was selected was "O.K." Thus, the experiment was concerned with whether the participants' verbalizations could be modified by events during the experiment. In other words, could the experimenters manipulate events and get one subject to say "Next word" and the other subject "O.K." more often?

The relations that were manipulated during the experiment were as follows. When a subject issued a command to continue that was in the designated class, the experimenters played a fluent word. When a subject issued a command that was not of the designated class, the experimenters played a disfluent word. At issue was whether the commands in the designated class increased when they were followed by a fluent word, and decreased when they weren't. The results showed that the behavior did increase reliably when it was followed by one consequence, and did decrease when it was not followed by that consequence. A consequence that so functions satisfies the definition of a reinforcer. In everyday language, one might say that the participants felt comfortable when a fluent word was played, and uncomfortable when a disfluent word was played, although any reinforcing effects of a fluent word would be traced back to whatever history was responsible for the feeling, rather than the feeling itself.

Given that the behavior of the participants showed the effect of the reinforcement operation, the next question concerns awareness: Were the participants aware that their verbal behavior had been manipulated? The answer is no, they were not. Thus, this research showed not only that verbal behavior in humans can be manipulated through operant contingencies, but also that participants need not be aware for such effects to occur.

Clearly, the matter of awareness is complex. Perhaps the central issue is how awareness is measured. In most cases, researchers have measured it through a verbal report of a contingency between CS and US in a respondent conditioning procedure or between response and reinforcer in an operant conditioning procedure. In many situations involving either respondent or operant conditioning, it seems awareness is not necessary for conditioning to take place, in the sense that participants do not accurately report the contingency responsible for the behavior in question. This result suggests that awareness is not a mental state that mediates behavior, in the sense that mentalistic or cognitive theories imply. Nevertheless, subjects do exhibit stronger conditioning when they are able to describe the arrangements in the procedure involving stimuli, responses, and reinforcers. It follows that the verbal behavior occasioned by experimental protocols, even if that verbal behavior was only inchoate, exerts a discriminative effect that supplements the elements of the conditioning procedure, to yield stronger forms of behavior.

SELF-REPORTING

A final topic in keeping with the discussion of verbally regulated behavior and awareness is that of self-reporting. This term refers to instances in which participants seem to generate descriptions of events that affect their subsequent behavior.

In an operant conditioning experiment investigating the effect of self-reports, Critchfield and Perone (1990) measured the performance of adult human participants in a task that required both speed and accuracy. Correct responses made within a specified time limit earned points worth money that was awarded at the end of the session. In certain instances immediately after a response, participants were asked to report whether they thought their response had earned points. Thus, there were four possibilities, defined by whether or not their responses actually earned points, and by whether or not participants' reports of whether they had earned points was accurate. The results indicated that participants' reports did not correlate strongly with their performance on the task. One participant was strongly biased toward reporting that the response had earned points, even though it actually hadn't. For example, across about 400 trials, the participant reported that the response had earned points on over 300 trials, even though points were actually earned on only slightly fewer than 150 trials. A second participant was less biased toward reporting that the response earned points. Across about 375 trials, this participant reported that points had been earned on about 200 trials, when they had actually been earned on about 160 trials. In addition, this participant reported that points had not been earned on about 40 trials, when they actually had been earned. Thus, self-reports of the participants, usually taken to indicate awareness, were not closely related to task performance.

In a final study on self-reporting that can be reviewed, Hefferline and Perera (1963) used a thumb-twitch preparation, but differently from Hefferline and Keenan (1963). In the Hefferline and Perera study, right hand button presses within 2 seconds of left hand thumb contractions earned money. Thus, left hand thumb twitches in Hefferline and Perera served as the occasion for right hand responses to be reinforced; left hand thumb twitches did not produce reinforcers by themselves, as in Hefferline and Keenan. During baseline sessions, right hand button presses were no more likely following left thumb contractions than at other times. This pattern indicates that left thumb contractions were not functioning as a discriminative occasion for right hand button presses. Hefferline and Perera then introduced a tone that was correlated with the left thumb contractions, and over trials reduced its intensity. Soon, participants were differentially responding with their right hand after a left thumb contraction. This pattern of responding indicates that left thumb contractions had begun to function as a discriminative occasion for right hand button presses. Importantly, as in Hefferline and Keenan, participants were not able to report that a left thumb contraction was the occasion on which right hand button presses earned money. Thus, Hefferline and Keenan demonstrated that participants can respond reliably when they are unaware of the response, and Hefferline and Perera demonstrated that participants can produce their own discriminative stimulus and behave in orderly ways, even though they are not reporting to themselves that they are doing so.

SUMMARY AND CONCLUSIONS

Several questions are involved in a discussion of verbally regulated behavior. One question is "How accurate are the descriptions and rules that individuals generate?" This question pertains to the behavioral history of the individuals. The verbal community often questions individuals about what they are doing and why. Given that humans are pre-eminently verbal creatures, verbal stimuli typically come to be identified in the answers as governing elements, although there is considerable variation in the answers across individuals. A second question is "To what extent do the self-generated descriptions and rules enter into the regulation of behavior as verbal antecedents?" Again, this question pertains to the behavioral history of the individuals and their experiences with the verbal community. As before, there is considerable variation in the answers. A third question is "What is the nature of the contingency and target behavior to which the rules apply?" Given that the individual has a particular behavioral history and that the verbal rules are concerned with particular response systems, the rules may well function one way, whereas with other histories and with other response systems, the rules may function another way. In addition, making individuals aware of the contingencies will almost certainly increase the speed with which they acquire a response and the accuracy of their responding. Thus, there are presumably advantages when participants are aware of the contingencies associated with their responding. However, as with awareness, the overall pattern of results suggests that it is not useful to regard rules or verbal awareness as necessarily involved in every instance of human activity. To hold that every instance of human activity is verbally regulated is to return to traditional doctrines of autonomous mentalistic entities in human behavior. Overall, research indicates rules may come from other persons or after sufficient experience from oneself, and their effectiveness follows the same process regardless of the source. There is no inherent privilege or advantage of self-rules, self-instruction, or self-reports.

The discussions in Chapters 8 and 9 have focused on verbal interactions in the environment. Discussion of verbal interactions leads to the behavioral conception of private events. Private events are events that develop out of interaction with the environment, many of which are verbal. However, in their current state these events are not accessible to anyone other than the behaving individuals. Chapter 10 examines the nature and functional role of such events.

TABLE 9–1
Definitions

Mutual entailment
Interactions with the environment lead speakers to respond on the basis of the particular relations that exist between the two objects in the environment. When this sort of relation exists, one talks of a mutually entailed relation, where mutual suggests the bidirectional relation between the two elements spoken about.

Combinatorial entailment
Interactions with the environment lead speakers to respond to particular relations that exist among multiple objects in the environment on the basis of the words that are used to describe those relations. When this sort of behavior exists, one talks of a combinatorially entailed relation, where combinatorially suggests the frame extends across the combination of the three elements spoken about.

Transformation of function
The effect of one stimulus may be modified by the way it participates in a frame or a relational network.

Augmentals
Verbal antecedents having the form of rules or contingency-specifying stimuli that exert their effect more as establishing operations than through a discriminative function. Motivative augmentals alter the degree to which previously established consequences exert their characteristic effect. Formative augmentals establish consequences as reinforcers or punishers.

Plys
Verbal regulation in which the actor engages in the form of behavior specified in the rule because of a history of coordination between that behavior and social consequences.

Tracks
Verbal regulation in which an actor engages in the form of behavior specified in the rule because of a history of coordination between that behavior and the naturally occurring, nonsocial consequences of that behavior.

REFERENCES

Baer, D., Peterson, R., & Sherman, J. (1967). The development of imitation by reinforcing behavioral similarity to a model. *Journal of the Experimental Analysis of Behavior, 10*, 405–416.

Brewer, W. (1974). There is no convincing evidence for operant or classical conditioning in adult humans. In W. B. Weimer & D. S. Palermo (Eds.), *Cognition and the symbolic processes*, pp. 1–42. Hillsdale, NJ: Erlbaum.

Clark, R., & Squire, L (1998, April). Classical conditioning and brain systems: The role of awareness. *Science, 280*, 77–81.

Critchfield, T., & Perone, M. (1990). Verbal self-reports of delayed matching to sample by humans. *Journal of the Experimental Analysis of behavior, 53*, 321–344.

Dawson, M., & Reardon, P. (1969). Effects of facilitory and inhibitory sets on GSR conditioning and extinction. *Journal of Experimental Psychology, 82*, 462–466.

Dougher, M., Augustson, E., Markham, M., Greenway, D., & Wulfert, E. (1994). The transfer of respondent eliciting and extinction functions through stimulus equivalence classes. *Journal of the Experimental Analysis of Behavior, 62*, 331–351.

Greenspoon, J. (1955). The reinforcing effect of two spoken words on the frequency of two responses. *American Journal of Psychology, 68*, 409–416.

Grings, W., Schell, A., & Carey, C. (1973). Verbal control of an autonomic response in a cue reversal situation. *Journal of Experimental Psychology, 99*, 215–221.

Hayes, S. C. (1994). Relational frame theory: A functional approach to verbal events. In S. C. Hayes, L. J. Hayes, M. Sato, & K. Ono (Eds.), *Behavior analysis of language and cognition*, pp. 11–27. Reno, NV: Context Press.

Hayes, S. C., Barnes-Holmes, D., & Roche, B. (2001). *Relational frame theory: A post-Skinnerian account of human language and cognition.* New York: Plenum.

Hayes, S. C., Zettle, R., & Rosenfarb, I. (1989). Rule following. In S. C. Hayes (Ed.), *Rule-governed behavior: Cognition, contingencies and instructional control*, pp. 191–220. New York: Plenum.

Hefferline, R., & Keenan, B. (1963). Amplitude-induction gradient of a small-scale (covert) operant. *Journal of the Experimental Analysis of Behavior, 6*, 307–315.

Hefferline, R., & Perera, T. (1963). Proprioceptive discrimination of a covert operant without its observation by the subject. *Science, 139*, 834–835.

Kaufman, A., Baron, A. & Kopp, R. (1966). Some effects of instructions on human operant behavior. *Psychonomic Monograph Supplements, 1*, 243–250.

Knight, D., Nguyen, H., & Bandettini, P. (2003). Expression of conditional fear with and without awareness. *Proceedings of the National Academy of Science, 100*, 15280–15283.

Laurenti-Lions, L., Gallego, J., Chambille, B., Vardon, G., & Jacquemin, C. (1985). Control of myoelectrical responses through reinforcement. *Journal of the Experimental Analysis of Behavior, 44*, 185–193.

Lovibond, P., & Shanks, D. (2002). The role of awareness in Pavlovian conditioning: Empirical evidence and theoretical implications. *Journal of Experimental Psychology: Animal Behavior Processes, 28*, 3–26.

McNally, R. (1981). Phobias and preparedness: Instructional reversal of electrodermal conditioning to fear-relevant stimuli. *Psychological Reports, 48*, 175–180.

Papka, M., Ivry, R., & Woodruff-Pak, D. (1997). Eyeblink classical conditioning and awareness revisited. *Psychological Science, 8*, 404–408.

Rosenfeld, H., & Baer, D. (1970). Unbiased and unnoticed verbal conditioning: The double agent robot procedure. *Journal of the Experimental Analysis of Behavior, 14*, 99–105.

Schlinger, H., & Blakely, E. (1987). Function-altering effects of contingency-specifying stimuli. *The Behavior Analyst, 10*, 41–45.

Shimoff, E., Catania, A. C., & Matthews, B. (1981). Uninstructed human responding: Sensitivity of low rate performance to schedule contingencies. *Journal of the Experimental Analysis of Behavior, 36*, 207–220.

Skinner, B. F. (1957). *Verbal behavior.* New York: Appleton-Century-Crofts.

Spielberger, C., & DeNike, L. (1966). Descriptive behaviorism versus cognitive theory in verbal operant conditioning. *Psychological Review, 73*, 306–326.

Steele, D., & Hayes, S. (1991). Stimulus equivalence and arbitrarily applicable relational responding. *Journal of the Experimental Analysis of Behavior, 56*, 519–555.

Verplanck, W. (1955). The control of the content of conversation: Reinforcement of statements of opinion. *Journal of Abnormal and Social Psychology, 51*, 668–676.

STUDY QUESTIONS

1. Describe how behavior analysis accounts for verbal behavior that develops indirectly, rather than through the direct action of reinforcement. Use the term bidirectional knowledgeably in your answer.

2. Describe what is meant by the following three terms: mutual entailment, combinatorial entailment, transformation of function.

3. Describe the procedure, results, and implication of Dougher, Augustson, Markham, Greenway, and Wulfert (1994) for the question of complex stimulus relations and transformation of function in respondent conditioning.

4. Describe the procedure, results, and implication of Steele and Hayes (1991) for the question of complex stimulus relations and transformation of function in operant conditioning.

5. Distinguish between verbally regulated behavior and contingency shaped behavior.

6. Describe the procedure, results, and implication of Shimoff, Catania, and Matthews (1981) as it pertains to verbal regulation of operant behavior.

7. Describe two important questions that arise in the study of verbally regulated behavior.

8. Define and give examples of the following forms of verbal regulation: augmentals, pliance, tracking.

9. Describe an actual experiment involving respondent conditioning in which behavior was affected more by instructions given to the participants than by nonverbal procedural features of the experiment.

10. Describe an actual experiment involving operant conditioning in which behavior was affected by more by instructions given to the participants than by nonverbal procedural features of the experiment.

11. Describe an actual experiment involving either verbal learning, respondent conditioning, or operant conditioning that investigated the relation between participants' behavior and their awareness of features of the experiment.

12. Describe an actual experiment that investigated the relation between participants' behavior and their self-reports of features of the experiment.

10

Private Events

Synopsis of Chapter 10: The chapters of the second section apply the concepts of radical behaviorism to additional topics, so that those topics may be better understood. Chapter 8 began this section by using the concepts that were developed in the preceding analyses of operant behavior to examine elementary verbal relations. Chapter 9 continued by using the concepts to examine complex verbal relations. Chapter 10 examines the radical behaviorist position on private events. For radical behaviorists, private events are behavioral events that are not accessible to anyone other than the person who is behaving. Sometimes these events entail the influence of internal sensed conditions of the body. One common example is learning to describe the quality of the pains one is feeling, such as being able to describe a pain as sharp or dull. At other times these events entail the influence of covert operant behavior. A common example here is thinking. Much of traditional psychology argues that to be a science, psychology can comment directly only on things that are publicly observable. This stance is no doubt attributable to the legacy of introspection and the failure to reach agreement on certain important concepts. Sometimes traditional researchers and theorists remained silent on private events. At other times traditional researchers and theorists spoke only indirectly of them, for example, as "theoretical" entities. Nevertheless, people do describe the pains they are feeling, and they do think. This chapter develops an account of the processes underlying private events and how they come to influence behavior. Importantly, the account is based on consistent, natural science principles.

Behavior analysis is concerned with identifying the variables that control a given instance of an individual's operant behavior. In most instances, those variables are publicly observable and accessible to others. However, in certain instances some relevant variables are accessible only to the individual who is behaving. This chapter deals with the influence of those variables in those instances, called "private events." However, the way radical behaviorism incorporates the functional contribution of events that are only privately accessible deserves careful review because of its distinctiveness and how it avoids problems associated with traditional viewpoints.

J. B. WATSON ON IMPLICIT STIMULI AND RESPONSES

Historically, the founder of behaviorism, John B. Watson, recognized the importance of both independent and dependent variables that weren't publicly observable. Readers may recall from Chapter 4 that for Watson some stimuli and responses were internal and "implicit." Thus, Watson actually did have a lot to say about such phenomena as thinking, memory, and images. He removed the mental connotations from these phenomena and argued that certain events inside the skin could clearly be included within the behavioral dimension. However, the way that Watson sought to include these phenomena was only as stimuli and responses through the S – R model of classical behaviorism, rather than as operant behavior.

For Watson, thinking was primarily subvocal speech: "The behaviorist advances the view that what the psychologists have hitherto called thought is in short nothing but talking to ourselves" (Watson, 1925, p. 191). In this view, kinesthetic cues arising from small movements of the larynx, mouth, lips, and tongue joined with kinesthetic stimuli from other response systems to elicit the next response in the succession of responses responsible for the phenomenon called thinking. McComas (1916) had earlier suggested that if Watson's position (a variation on the motor theory of consciousness) was correct, it follows that a person whose larynx had been removed could no longer think. Watson then clarified his position by emphasizing that he never believed thinking consisted only of laryngeal movements. Rather, the whole organism was involved in thinking, just as it was in other forms of behavior. There were organizations of verbal, motor, and visceral responses, linked together by the internal or kinesthetic stimuli generated by engaging in these responses, showing "that we could still think in some sort of way even if we had no words" (Watson, 1925, p. 214). Overt speech becomes covert speech under the influence of society, which may rebuke individuals for being noisy and talking out loud, although when the individual is alone the talk may again become overt. Thus, thinking was a natural process, not a mental predecessor of overt action. Furthermore, memory was not conceived as a mental storage and retrieval process. Rather, it was the name for "the retention of a given habit in terms of how much skill has been retained and how much has been lost in the period of no practice. We do not need the term 'memory,' shot through as it is with all kinds of philosophical and subjective connotations" (Watson, 1925, p. 179).

Much the same could be said of images. Instead of being a ghostly apparition represented on some neurological screen in the theater of the mind, what was called an "image" could be understood as an organized system of implicit, learned responses. As Watson (1919) put it:

> We have learned to write words, sentences and paragraphs, to draw objects and to trace them with the eyes, hands, and fingers. We have done this so often that the process has become systematized and substitutive. In other words, they come to serve as stimuli substitutable for the object seen, drawn, written, or handled. These implicit processes may bring about a silent word (thought word), a spoken word (name of object or associated word), or an appropriate bodily set. (p. 324)

Again, Watson was engaging traditional topics, but seeking to make sense out of them from the perspective of a natural science as he understood it. He did not limit his attention to things that were publicly observable. He was willing to invoke kinesthetic and other implicit cues generated by the operation of physiological structures as the glue that linked portions of a sequence of responses together, even though he had no firm evidence that this approach was valid. For Watson, the principle underlying the various processes was akin to respondent conditioning, rather than that of operant conditioning, which Watson didn't recognize. In any case, his argument was that his approach was clearly more productive than an appeal to mental processes.

B. F. SKINNER AND PRIVATE EVENTS

The conception of private events is important, as it relates to mentalism, the radical behaviorist position on explanation, and the differences between radical behaviorism and traditional forms of psychology. If the influence of private stimulation is not appropriately formulated, the door is opened to either an incomplete or a mentalistic psychology. Skinner commented in numerous instances on the critical importance of getting the story straight on private events. Five representative sources are: (a) Skinner (1945), in a contribution to a symposium on operationism; (b) Skinner (1953), in a chapter explicitly dedicated to a discussion of private events; (c) Skinner's (1957) book on verbal behavior, reprising the argument from Skinner (1945) and Skinner (1953); (d) Skinner (1964), in another symposium presentation reflecting on the status of behaviorism in light of the 50 years since Watson's (1913) behaviorist manifesto; and (e) Skinner (1974), in a book for popular readership designed to clarify the main principles of the radical behaviorist position. For example, Chapter 17 in Skinner (1953) is on private events and opens in the following way:

> When we say that behavior is a function of the environment, the term "environment" presumably means any event in the universe affecting the organism. But part of the universe is enclosed within the organism's own skin. Some independent variables may, therefore, be related to behavior in a unique way. The individual's response to an inflamed tooth, for example, is unlike the response which anyone else can make to that particular tooth, since no one else can

make the same kind of contact with it. Events which take place during emotional excitement or in states of deprivation are often uniquely accessible for the same reason; in this sense our joys, sorrows, loves, and hates are peculiarly our own. With respect to each individual, in other words, a small part of the universe is private.

We need not suppose that events which take place within an organism's skin have special properties for that reason. A private event may be distinguished by its limited accessibility but not, so far as we know, by any special structure or nature. We have no reason to suppose that the stimulating effect of an inflamed tooth is essentially different from that of, say, a hot stove. The stove, however, is capable of affecting more than one person in approximately the same way. (pp. 257–258)

Given that traditional forms of psychology appeal to inner causes from another dimension, those forms tag the identification of those phenomena with the major burden of explanation. Radical behaviorism acknowledges that some important forms of stimulation are, in fact, private, meaning that they are accessible only to the behaving person. However, if these forms of stimulation are private, is Skinner being inconsistent, and admitting mentalism himself? No, for three reasons. First, the private forms of stimulation are still within the behavioral dimension. If Skinner was somehow confused and lapsing into mentalism, the stimulation would be proposed to lie within another dimension, such as the psychic, "mental," spiritual, subjective, conceptual, hypothetical, theoretical, or cognitive dimensions mentioned in Chapter 11 on mentalism. He would be talking of acts, states, mechanisms, processes, schemata, representations, memory traces, expectancies, or comparable sorts of mental or cognitive entities, collectively referred to as "explanatory fictions." These devices are typically organismic variables that mediate the relation between stimuli and responses, in the tradition of mediational $S - O - R$ neobehaviorism. Radical behaviorism does none of this, as there are no such other dimensions and no such other entities. Rather, talk of such other entities and dimensions is attributable to social-cultural factors, such as linguistic practices, unfortunate metaphors, and mentalistic if not outright dualistic assumptions.

Second, the private forms of stimulation are functionally related to the environment, by virtue of their belonging to the behavioral dimension. In other words, they arise because of a history of interaction with the environment. In contrast, for mentalism, mental phenomena are explicitly not held to be functionally related to the environment, by virtue of belonging to another dimension, such as that of the mind.

Third, the private forms of stimulation are only contingently effective, rather than necessarily effective. In other words, when the behavioral event occurs, private forms of stimulation may not even be functionally relevant to the behavior. If they are functionally relevant, radical behaviorists argue they contribute to discriminative control. In contrast, for traditional mentalistic viewpoints, mental phenomena are held to exert an independent causal contribution of the organism, without regard to the environment.

They are variously intrinsically mental (of which there is no such thing), innate, autonomous, or initiating. This important point is emphasized extensively in future sections of the current chapter.

To be sure, there are many events that take place within the body that can be known about. At issue is the functional role of these events in a science of behavior. For example, when one sees an object, there are clearly nerves firing in the optic tract. However, the firing of nerve cells in the optic tract is ordinarily not a private event with which radical behaviorism is concerned. Similarly, the brain obviously functions when an individual behaves, with many structures and pathways involved. Again, activity in these structures and pathways is not ordinarily a private event that radical behaviorism conceives of private events. Brain activity is simply part of the physiological processes according to which behavior can take place. As such, brain activity provides the continuity within a behavioral event, from environmental stimulation to behavior. It is part of neuroscience, rather than a science of behavior concerned with the relation between environment and behavior. Radical behaviorists are interested in private events whose contribution to subsequent behavior is a function of a specific history of environmental relations.

RADICAL BEHAVIORISM: FEELINGS AND SENSED CONDITIONS OF THE BODY

In general, two sorts of private events are at issue. The first is feelings or sensed conditions of the body. The second is covert operant activity. The functional role of stimulation from these two sorts of private events, such as how the stimulation exerts an effect on subsequent verbal and nonverbal behavior, may now be examined in some detail.

Functional Contribution

Just as individuals have an exteroceptive nervous system by means of which they contact publicly observable stimuli outside the skin, so also do individuals have an interoceptive nervous system by means of which they contact private stimulation inside the skin.

Consider "feelings." Pain and hunger are convenient examples. These forms of stimulation are typically brought about by establishing operations. What is critical to recognize is that the feelings of pain and hunger are themselves caused by something else. Pain is caused by, say, tissue damage from an injury or some form of inflammation by a pathogen. Hunger is caused by, say, the establishing operation of food deprivation. It is the cause of the injury or the inflammation that is the cause of the pain. It is the deprivation that is the cause of the feeling of hunger. By focusing only on the feeling, one does not go back far enough in the causal chain of events. Thus, a causal intervention is aimed at what causes the pain or hunger in the first place. To be sure, one can administer an anesthetic and block the contact with the tissue that has been affected by whatever is causing the pain. Surely anyone who has had a toothache is grateful for whatever relief can be gained from an anesthetic, however temporary. But the permanent relief is brought about by removing whatever has caused the pain of the toothache, say an infection. Similarly, the feeling called hunger is ordinarily resolved by eating.

A representative passage in which Skinner discusses the importance of going back far enough in the causal chain is as follows:

> The objection to inner states is not that they do not exist, but that they are not relevant in a functional analysis. We cannot account for the behavior of any system while staying wholly inside it; eventually we must turn to forces operating upon the organism from without. Unless there is a weak spot in our causal chain so that the second link is not lawfully determined by the first, or the third by the second, then the first and third links must be lawfully related. If we must always go back beyond the second link for prediction and control, we may avoid many tiresome digressions by examining the third link as a function of the first. Valid information about the second link may throw light upon this relationship but can in no way alter it. (Skinner, 1953, p. 35)

When Skinner discussed the epiphenomenal nature of feelings, and that feelings have no important causal relation to behavior, he simply emphasized that feelings are themselves caused by something else. The feelings aren't sources of "drive," as many traditional psychologists once formulated it, nor are interventions that are thought to be aimed at affecting the feelings and nothing else going to be ultimately productive. It is the environmental conditions that cause the feelings that are critical in causal interventions. To be sure, pain hurts. It is unpleasant, and one wants to escape from it. But the feeling is not something from another dimension. Rather, it is a condition of the body that is felt, and some event caused the condition. The intervention is aimed at the connection between (a) the event causing the condition and (b) the condition produced in the body.

What, then, about feelings of anxiety or depression, which typically play a major role in traditional forms of psychology? According to the traditional view of $S - O - R$ neobehaviorism, such internal states mediate the relation between stimuli and responses. The traditional argument is that one cannot understand the response that takes place without understanding the nature of the mediating internal state, and if one wants to modify the response, the mediating internal state has to be modified. In the case of human psychopathology, for example, one would presumably seek to modify the mediating internal state through a verbally oriented, "talking" form of psychotherapy.

From the perspective of radical behaviorism, an emphasis on a mediating role of feelings is misplaced. At issue when a person is anxious or depressed is what has caused those feelings. Is the person upset about home, work, or interpersonal relations, perhaps because of a history in which previously reinforced responses are now no longer reinforced, or perhaps even punished? Any intervention is aimed at correcting the circumstances that caused the feelings, rather than conceiving of the feelings as somehow autonomous mediating entities and then trying to verbally modify them.

Verbalizations about Feelings and Sensations

An accompanying question about feelings and sensations concerns being able to talk about them. How do persons come to do so? The question is not a trivial one, as answers may have important implications for the topic of mentalism. For example, the famous French philosopher René Descartes (1596–1650) argued that his ideas of himself were so clear and distinct that he could not possibly be mistaken about them or even his own existence, for that matter: "*Cogito ergo sum*"—"I think, therefore I am." A philosophical implication of this position is that humans just somehow know how to speak about things to which they alone have access. In other words, the philosophical implication is that one of the characteristics of humans with which humans are endowed is a so-called "private language," which does not owe its existence to interaction with others.

Chapters 8 and 9 argued that for radical behaviorists, language acquisition is regarded as a social phenomenon, involving an interaction in some sense between a speaker and listener. How does the speaker know which words to apply to the internal events, so that a listener knows what the speaker is talking about? Without the specification of a process by which a vocabulary descriptive of internal events is acquired and maintained, the answer lapses into mentalism and some magical Cartesian power of the mind to do so, but that is really no answer at all.

The present analysis begins with a review of the fundamentals of the operant model of verbal behavior. The operant model holds that in the presence of the appropriate discriminative stimulus, a response produces a reinforcer. In the case of verbal behavior, in the presence of the appropriate discriminative stimulus, a verbal response produces some form of reinforcement from the verbal community. As indicated in Chapter 8, the reinforcement in question may be loosely described as social reinforcement. At issue is how does the verbal community know whether to administer social reinforcement in the case of talking about such things as feelings and sensations. The verbal community does not even know whether the appropriate form of discriminative stimulation—the feeling or sensation—is actually present, and whether reinforcement should be administered for talking about it.

The problem of privacy.   The problem described immediately above is called the "problem of privacy." Consider the corresponding state of affairs in the public case.

Suppose someone wants to teach a hungry pigeon to peck a response key in the presence but not absence of a green light. In this case, note that the appropriate discriminative stimulus, the green light, is available to the individual who arranges this contingency, not just to the pigeon. When the individual sees the green light is present, the individual delivers the food after a response. When the individual sees the green light is absent, the individual does not deliver the food after a response. The differential reinforcement in the presence and absence of the discriminative stimulus produces the differential behavior of responding in the presence but not absence of green. The elements of the necessary relations are all public, in the sense that they are accessible to both the individual who is delivering the differential reinforcement and the pigeon who is acquiring the response.

Now consider the process by which speakers might learn to describe that they are in pain. In more general terms, this process concerns the extent to which an individual's behavior, in this case verbal and perhaps in other cases nonverbal, comes under the control of private stimulation. In principle, the pain is a discriminative stimulus for a speaker's verbal behavior. However, the pain is private, and not available to the verbal community in the same way that the discriminative stimulus of a green light was available to someone who differentially delivers reinforcers for responses in the presence but not absence of green. In short, the verbal community is not in contact with a speaker's pain in the same way it was in contact with a green light. This lack of contact limits the ability of the verbal community to differentially deliver reinforcers for talk of pain, and hence limits the extent to which speakers learn to come under the control of private stimulation. The problem is important, because parents want to teach their children to indicate when they are in pain, so that the parents can remedy the situation. Nevertheless, individuals obviously do learn to say they are in pain. Obviously, the verbal community does solve the problem somehow, else how could individuals learn to speak about stimulation to which they alone have access? The important question is: Given the problem of privacy, how is the verbal community involved in the process by which speakers learn to verbally report pain or other feelings and sensations?

Skinner (1945) outlined several ways that speakers come under the control of private stimulation. These ways are examined here. The first three ways concern the process by which speakers learn to describe internal feelings and sensations. In two of these three ways, the speaker learns on the basis of action taken by the verbal community, which works around the problem of privacy and generates verbal behavior under the control of private stimuli. In the third of the three ways, the verbal behavior in question is acquired in one situation and then transfers to the private case. The fourth way concerns covert operant activity, and the process by which private stimulation from covert behavior comes to exert discriminative control.

Collateral responses.   One way the verbal community solves the problem of privacy is by looking to publicly available correlates of the private stimulation. For example, individuals who are in pain might put their hands on the afflicted area, where there might be bleeding, swelling, or noticeable inflammation. The touching might be an elicited unconditioned respondent, or pressure from the touching might provide some measure of negative reinforcement. In any case, there is now publicly available stimulation—the individual's touching an area that is observed to be afflicted—and the verbal community will reinforce pain talk in the presence but not absence of this form of public stimulation. The process is the same as differentially reinforcing the pigeon's responding in the presence but not absence of green. In his writing, Skinner referred to this state of affairs as involving a "collateral response."

Public accompaniments.   The scenario above might help explain how individuals come to say they are in pain or not. However, when they are in pain, how do they come to say their pain is sharp or dull? Here, something further is involved, and the "something further" illustrates the second way the verbal community solves the problem of privacy. Skinner referred to this way as involving a "public accompaniment." This way involves the metaphorical practice of assigning a descriptive term from the object causing the pain to the quality of the pain itself. Thus, when a sharp object causes the pain, the verbal community will reinforce speaking of a sharp pain. When a dull object causes the pain, the verbal community will reinforce speaking of a dull pain. When a hot object causes the pain, the verbal community will reinforce speaking of a burning pain. Analogous metaphors apply to still other cases, like excruciating pains. As Skinner (1989) put it, "All words for feelings seem to have begun as metaphors, and it is significant that the transfer has always been from public to private. No word seems to have originated as the name of a feeling" (p. 8).

Stimulus generalization.   A third way that individuals come under the control of private stimulation is based on stimulus generalization. Consider how a speaker might come to say "I have a feeling of butterflies in my stomach." Presumably, a speaker learns to describe a sensation that occurs when a butterfly lands on one's skin, on the basis of the collateral response relations described above. The light and fluttering nature of the stimulation is pivotal. Now, when the properties of internal stimulation are similar to those of the external, the original response will also occur, through the process of stimulus generalization. One learns to say "I have a feeling of butterflies on my arm," and then when certain of the stimulus properties are similar, "I have a feeling of butterflies in my stomach."

The radical behaviorist argument is that as a result of these social processes, individuals learn to "know themselves" in an interesting and meaningful way, including the knowing of their own feelings and sensations. What, then, about the "awareness" of one's own feelings and sensations? In the sense that awareness is also something that depends on particular circumstances, individuals might not be aware that they are injured if the injury occurs in a life-or-death emergency, if a soldier is fighting on the battlefield, or if an athlete is involved in a competitive event. The demands of the current setting conflict with the awareness of the pain, such that the awareness comes only later, after the emergency or critical situation has passed.

Complicating the descriptions of feelings and sensations are the limitations of the nervous system itself. Human exteroceptive nervous systems are reasonably well developed, but consider the process of hearing. The typical range of human hearing is from 20 Hz to 20,000 Hz. Given these limits, individuals can't sense, let alone distinguish between auditory frequencies of 25,000 Hz and 30,000 Hz because their exteroceptive nervous system doesn't allow them to come in contact with that sort of stimulation. Similarly, with respect to the interoceptive nervous system, individuals often have trouble localizing pains, or giving other than metaphorical descriptions of pains. The interoceptive nervous system simply doesn't have enough nerves, or doesn't have nerves going to the right places, to allow individuals to come into contact with the precise nature of the stimulation. Individuals may well come up with elaborate descriptions of pains, but often those descriptions are based more on social convention or various metaphorical relations than actual contact with the pain itself. The result is that both the problem of privacy, mentioned earlier, and the inherent limitations of the nervous system restrict the accuracy of many self-reports. It follows that the elaborate introspective descriptions in older forms of psychology, as well as in current forms for that matter, are not as veridical as they claim.

To be sure, the processes described above don't always work in the way the verbal community intends. Sometimes individuals learn to hold an area and moan and groan, and by so doing evoke sympathy from others. They can pretend to be in pain by engaging in behavior that often is correlated with pain, but in the present case is actually not, and thereby avoid unpleasant tasks. The terms *hypochondria* and *malingering* are typically applied to these cases. The secondary gains of the neurotic are achieved by such actions. The importance of public relations in the discernment of pain by the verbal community is evidenced when malingerers are found out. Indeed, malingerers are typically discredited when, after complaining that they are too sick or too much in pain to be assigned to some demanding task, or even get out of bed, they then are discovered doing something equally vigorous but enjoyable. The collateral responses don't correlate with the verbal reports.

Overall, feelings and sensations are clearly adaptive. Organisms that don't ordinarily respond to environmental circumstances that cause tissue damage and pain don't ordinarily survive. But the important causal relation remains the circumstances that cause the tissue damage and pain in the first place.

COVERT OPERANT ACTIVITY

What, then, about private events that don't involve speaking about simple sensations and feelings? At issue here are such events as thinking and imaging. For radical behaviorism, these events entail covert operant behavior. The events are behavioral, although to take thinking as the example, in many instances they have receded in scope so that they are no longer publicly observable. They are not necessarily involved in every behavioral event. Even if they are present, it is an empirical question whether they have any functional contribution. When they do have a functional contribution, they contribute to discriminative control. But are there circumstances that are responsible for the activity being covert and coming to acquire discriminative control?

A fairly simple case may be analyzed: An individual reads a recipe "silently" and then bakes a cake. Often the process is described in mentalistic terms; the reading is characterized as a mental act, as opposed to the physical act of mixing the ingredients and putting the cake in the oven. For radical behaviorists, there are no such things as mental acts, so the whole process is a behavioral sequence.

Discriminative Control via Transfer from Public to Private Forms of Stimulation on the Basis of Common Properties

First, it is not idle to suggest one must account for how the individual has learned to read. The individual has learned to read via a public process. The individual was shown public stimuli of some sort—for instance the sort that are conventionally called "printed words"—and appropriate public vocalizations were reinforced in the presence of the words. If the individual's responses were not public, the necessary differential reinforcement could not be administered by the verbal community, and the individual would not have learned to read at all.

Second, one must account for why the reading has become silent. The silent reading is a form of private, covert operant activity. Behavior often becomes covert because of its relation to the public environment. If an individual persists in reading out loud in the presence of others, often others who are nearby may mildly rebuke the reader for being bothersome. In other words, public reading may be publicly punished. Thus, the individual comes to read in a successively softer voice until the reading recedes to a point it is detectable only to the individual. The reading may even involve only incipient or inchoate forms of responding. Indeed, there may even be an instrumental advantage in silent reading: It is faster. The relation between silent reading and its public origins becomes apparent if the individual encounters an unknown word. In this case, the individual may switch to public reading, to "sound out the word," in an effort to deal with it. In this history, the private form of the behavior acquires control because it shares some of the same properties as the public form. That is, silent reading is similar to, but probably less intense than public reading, and presumably supplies the same kind of discriminative stimulation, though in a weaker form. Watson (1925) offered a similar analysis, but as a generalized reflexive process, not an operant process involving discriminative control.

Third, the reading then contributes to the discriminative control over the eventual actions of mixing ingredients and putting the cake in the oven. If the individual makes a mistake, it is presumably because of the interference of some other sort of stimulation, such as from another recipe or a distraction.

Thinking

What, then, about thinking? The literature of radical behaviorism has addressed this topic in many different places. Here are some representative examples from Skinner's own writing:

> [B]ehavior may actually occur but on such a reduced scale that it cannot be observed by others—at least without instrumentation. This is often expressed by saying that the behavior is "covert." Sometimes it is said that the reduced form is merely the beginning of the overt form—that the private event is incipient or inchoate behavior. A verbal repertoire which has been established with respect to the overt case might be extended to covert behavior because of similar self-stimulation. The organism is generating the same effective stimuli, albeit on a much smaller scale.... Verbal behavior, however, can occur at the covert level because it does not require the presence of a particular physical environment for its execution. Moreover, it may remain effective at the covert level because the speaker himself is also a listener and his verbal behavior may have private consequences. The covert form continues to be reinforced, even though it has been reduced in magnitude to the point at which it has no appreciable effect on the environment. Most people observe themselves talking privately. A characteristic report begins "I said to myself..." where the stimuli which control the response "I said" are presumably similar, except in magnitude, to those which in part control the response, "I said to him ..." (Skinner, 1953, pp. 263–264, 279)

> There is no point at which it is profitable to draw a line distinguishing thinking from acting [on a continuum ranging from overt to covert forms of action] ... So far as we know, the events at the covert end have no special properties, observe no special laws, and can be credited with no special achievements.... A better case can be made for identifying thinking with behaving which automatically affects the behaver and is reinforcing because it does so. This can be either covert or overt. (Skinner, 1957, p. 438)

> So far as we know, the responses are executed with the same organs as observable responses but on a smaller scale. The stimuli they generate are weak but nevertheless of the same kind as those generated by overt responses.... Covert responses are not the causes of overt, both are the products of common variables. (Skinner, 1969, pp. 242, 258)

> Usually, however, the term [thinking] refers to completed behavior which occurs on a scale so small that it cannot be detected by others. Such behavior is called covert. The commonest examples are verbal, because verbal behavior requires no environmental support and because, as both speaker and listener, a person can talk to himself effectively; but nonverbal behavior may also be covert. Thus, what a chess player has in mind may be other moves he has made as he has played the game covertly to test the consequences.... Covert behavior is almost always ac-

quired in overt form and no one has ever shown that the covert form achieves anything which is out of reach of the overt. Covert behavior is also easily observed and by no means unimportant... It does not explain overt behavior: it is simply more behavior to be explained.

The present argument is this: mental life and the world in which it is lived are inventions. They have been invented on the analogy of external behavior occurring under external contingencies. Thinking is behaving. The mistake is in allocating the behavior to the mind. (Skinner, 1974, pp. 106–107)

To think, then, is to behave. In an interesting sense, an episode that involves thinking can be public or private or some mixture of the two. One calls behavior public thinking when it is a publicly observable activity that creates discriminative stimuli to guide subsequent behavior. An example is writing down a shopping list. The writing down of the items is publicly observable thinking. The items—the response products of the verbal behavior—are publicly observable discriminative stimuli that will occasion behavior when one is in the market. When the items are simply recited privately to oneself—"Bread, milk, cereal, eggs, vegetables, fruit, ..."—the recitation of the items is private thinking. Even though the words are spoken silently, they are private discriminative stimuli that will occasion purchasing the desired items when one gets to the market. The words are just as effective as when someone else speaks them.

As before, the relevant question is: Why would the speaking of the words become covert? As before, the answer is that the words were acquired in an overt form, and then something led to their becoming covert. It may be that the speaker's overt vocalizations ("talking to oneself out loud") were punished. It may be that the individual didn't have paper and pencil with which to write a list. Ultimately, however, the whole process is behavioral, and there need be no appeal to mental components. There are certainly private behavioral components, but no such things as mental components. It may also be that the individual generates the list privately, in the absence of paper and pencil, and then when paper and pencil do become available, writes down the items from the list. This would entail a chain of activity, with covert and overt components. As with following the recipe read silently, if there are "errors," they come about because of the intrusion of other discriminative stimuli, or competition from other contingencies.

The important thing to understand is that the whole process is related to environmental circumstances. One's cupboard is bare, and the market is the place where in the past, needed items have been obtained. The state of the environment then determines what form the behavior of thinking takes—covert or overt. The state of the environment determines the form of the discriminative stimulation produced by the responding in question—covert or overt. However, the same sort of processes are involved for the individual, regardless of whether the processes are called covert or overt. As Skinner (1953) put it:

The private event is at best no more than a link in a causal chain, and it is usually not even that. We may think before we act in the sense that we may behave covertly before we behave overtly, but our action is not an "expression" of the covert response or a consequence of it. The two are simply attributable to the same variables. (p. 279)

Thus, there are variables and relations that are responsible for the behavior in question to take place, and there are variables and relations that are responsible for the behavior called thinking to take place. And finally, there are variables and relations that are responsible for stimuli arising from the behavior called thinking to influence the behavior in question. The entire arrangement is contingent on the relations involved, rather than necessitarian and mechanical. Further, the way these relations develop and play out in the everyday lives of individuals is highly variable, accounting for why some people are better thinkers than others.

The subtle relations responsible for such activity are revealed when one compares the forms of behavior with and without an audience. Suppose an individual is presented with a task in which the individual must count a number of small items, such as dots scattered across a piece of paper. It is often faster and easier to simply scan and count, as a covert response. However, if the dots are very small and close together, the individual might become somewhat confused: Have I missed counting this dot? Have I counted this dot twice? The individual might then begin to engage in some overt activity, like nodding the head as each dot is counted. If a pencil is available, the individual might place a diagonal mark through each dot as it is counted. An overt response generates more interoceptive, proprioceptive, or even exteroceptive stimulation than the covert response of simply scanning, and the accuracy might increase with increased discriminative stimulation of this sort.

Now consider what might happen if the individual is alone. The individual probably has a history of auditory verbalizations such as counting being punished by others who are nearby. After all, overt auditory counting can be quite bothersome to others. However, if no one else is nearby, the individual's counting may revert to its overt form. The individual learned to count overtly before learning to count covertly, and now the overt counting returns, when there is little likelihood of punishment. As before, the increased discriminative stimulation from the overt form provides for a more accurate process.

The effect of the response-produced stimulation is the same as if the counting was performed by another person, who led the individual through a comparable enumeration of the items. If another person counts aloud, the stimulation is overt, but if only the single individual counts silently, the stimulation is private, but in each case the process is understandable through the discriminative control arising from the stimulation. The locus of the stimulation may differ, but not the process itself.

Imaging

A further associated term in the mental lexicon is imaging. In traditional parlance, individuals can form an image of something "in their mind's eye." Taken literally, such language seems to imply that an individual's visual system or brain forms a copy of an object, and that when individuals have an image, they see the copy. Not dealt with is the question of whether an infinite regress is formed. If one goes this route, wouldn't it imply that a second copy has to be formed of the first copy, and who sees the copy at the end of the process?

Nevertheless, most individuals have probably had an experience of closing their eyes and imagining some scene, or of being able to picture what some object looks like. How is one to make sense out of such events, from a behavioral point of view? The literature of radical behaviorism has addressed this topic by noting that individuals can often see an object even though the object isn't physically present to be seen.

One form of seeing in the absence of a thing to be seen is conditioned respondent seeing. Here the seeing is a function of the antecedent conditions. In this form, individuals see Y because X and Y have occurred in the past together, and individuals are currently in the presence of X. In a standard deck of playing cards, the red (X) suits are hearts (Y) and diamonds, and the black (X') suits are spades (Y') and clubs. If an individual is shown a red spade and asked what suit it is, the individual might see it as a heart, or if shown a black heart and asked what suit it is, the individual might see it as a black spade. The individual's visual perceptions are shaped by certain of their previous visual experiences, following the model of respondent conditioning.

Another form of seeing in the absence of an object to be seen is operant seeing. Seeing is a common and early part of many sequences of responses, but involves behavioral processes just as any other response of an organism to its environment. In operant seeing, the seeing is a function of the consequences. Suppose an individual is in a hurry to keep an appointment and is waiting for a bus to come down the street. In such circumstances, any large vehicle at the end of the street may be seen as the bus. It would be reinforcing if the vehicle seen actually is the bus, because one can then actually get on with getting to one's appointment, and hence "seeing a bus" is a function of the consequences. An individual who is an expert chess player can covertly move pieces on the board and "visualize" what happens after the move. The behavior of covert seeing is reinforced by the outcome, say of avoiding an unwise move or performing a wise one. The stimuli are not arising from a publicly available object, but rather interoceptively, from the behavior of seeing.

Because the stimuli involved are subtle, there are varying degrees to which they are effective, within the repertoire of the individual and across the repertoires of different individuals, depending on the personal histories involved. Some individuals are able to "imagine" many sorts of scenes, but the activity is always a behavioral process, rather than a supposed mental process that takes place in a mental dimension. As before, common versions of the mental formulation entail a representation that is "seen" by some "theoretical" entity. That this does not explain the problem is demonstrated by asking: Who sees the representation? Going the route of a representation is simply the start of a regress. Attempts to justify such language as "only theoretical" are ill-advised, as the language is little more than an excuse to engage in uncritical appeals to other dimensions.

Problem Solving

An important feature of problem solving is the generation of additional discriminative stimulation to guide effective behavior in an otherwise ambiguous situation. Sometimes the behavior generating the appropriate discriminative stimulation is in fact verbal. Suppose individuals want to memorize the seven principal colors of the visible spectrum. They might take advantage of intraverbal control and memorize a fanciful man's name in which each letter of each word gives the name of a color: "Roy G. Biv," in which R stands for red, O for orange, Y for yellow, G for green, B for blue, I for indigo, and V for violet. Suppose individuals want to memorize the names and order of the planets in the solar system, from the sun outward. They might take advantage of intraverbal control and memorize a short mnemonic in which the first letter (and in two instances the first and second letters) of each word gives the name of a planet: "Men Very Early Made Jars Stand Upright Nicely, Period," in which Me stands for Mercury, V for Venus, E for Earth, Ma for Mars, J for Jupiter, S for Saturn, U for Uranus, N for Neptune, and P for Pluto (although at this writing Pluto's status as a planet is being re-examined). Suppose individuals are taking a class on human anatomy and physiology and want to memorize the names of the 12 cranial nerves. They might take advantage of intraverbal control and memorize a short mnemonic in which the first letter of each word is the first letter of a nerve: "On old Olympus' towering top a Finn and German viewed a hop." In each case, the problem is solved by creating a necessary degree of discriminative stimulation, in this case verbally. The solution is neither mysterious nor mental. It is behavioral, and the self-supplied verbal discriminative stimuli have the same effect as if a second person provided the rhyme, or a book.

So-called "memory experts" have honed their skills to extraordinary levels in this regard. Seemingly extemporaneous speakers may glance around the room, receiving discriminative stimulation from particular objects. Waiters or waitresses in restaurants may associate spatial or personal characteristics of diners and remember what the diners have ordered without having to create a public stimulus by writing down the order. Again, the processes are all behavioral, rather than mental.

Suppose individuals want to be sure they have driven their cars far enough into the garage so that the garage door doesn't hit the trunk lid or bumper when the garage door is closed. They might suspend a tennis ball at a point where the car's windshield just meets the ball when the car is driven the appropriate distance into the garage. The problem is solved by creating the necessary degree of discriminative stimulation, in this case visually. As with memorizing cranial nerves or dinner orders, the problem is solved by recognizing the behavioral nature of the event, and creating discriminative stimulation that will make the appropriate response more likely.

Consciousness

The topic of consciousness has a time-honored place in the history of psychology. Traditionally, concerns with consciousness extend beyond simply being alive and reacting to environmental stimulation. Rather, consciousness is regarded as a mediating mental state that makes possible some sort of knowledge of oneself, as well as meta-knowledge, or knowing that one knows about oneself. Radical behaviorism holds that this entire orientation to the topic of consciousness is not useful. Rather, consciousness is better formulated in behavioral terms, as a relation that pertains to something that individuals do, not something that one has. The relation is that individuals respond on the basis of discriminative control arising from their own behavior and the variables that cause that behavior. More elaborately, consciousness is the conventional name for a state of affairs wherein an individual's behavior, properties of that behavior, or the variables of which that behavior is a function set the occasion for subsequent behavior. The behavior may be current behavior, potential behavior, or probable future behavior. The behavior may be covert, including incipient and inchoate forms, and provide a less intense form of the same stimulus as overt forms. The variables controlling this behavior may be public or private.

The crucial implication of this position is that "being conscious, as a form of reacting to one's own behavior, is a social product" (Skinner, 1945, p. 277). That is, being conscious is not a mental state that makes possible self-reflective behavior. It is the fact that self-reflective behavior occurs. What then causes this self-reflective behavior? For radical behaviorism, the answer is to be found in the contingencies that are experienced in social living. As self-reflective behavior, consciousness is acquired via the reinforcement supplied by the verbal community. Skinner (1945) continued:

> The hypothesis is equivalent to saying that it is only because the behavior of the individual is important to society that society makes it important to the individual. The individual becomes aware of what he is doing only after society has reinforced verbal responses with respect to his behavior as a source of discriminative stimuli. The behavior to be described (the behavior of which one is to be aware) may later recede to the covert level, and (to add a crowning difficulty) so may the verbal response. It is an ironic twist, considering the history of the behavioristic revolution, that as we develop a more effective vocabulary for the analysis of behavior we also enlarge the possibilities of awareness, so defined. The psychology of the other one is, after all, a direct approach to 'knowing thyself.' (p. 277)

In this view, the verbal community asks such questions as: 'What are you doing?" and "Why are you doing that?" It differentially reinforces correct answers, with the result that individuals develop self-descriptive repertoires. Skinner (1957) explored several possibilities, including responses occasioned by current overt behavior, covert behavior, past behavior, potential behavior, future behavior, the variables controlling behavior, and levels of the probability of behavior. The accuracy of the discriminative control, which is to say how conscious the individual is, is derived in large measure from how systematic the practices of the verbal community are with respect to the individual. No wonder that "As the philosophy of a science of behavior, behaviorism calls for probably the most drastic change ever proposed in our thinking about man. It is almost literally a matter of turning the explanation of behavior inside out" (Skinner, 1974, p. 256).

SENSATIONS AND TRADITIONAL EXPERIMENTAL PSYCHOLOGY

From a general point of view, sensations arise when individuals come in contact with significant and important stimuli. One has a sensation of loudness when one comes in contact with an auditory stimulus, or of brightness when one comes in contact with a light. In traditional experimental psychology, sensations are another form of mediating organismic entity. They are studied because they are thought to give some clue as to the operation of the mind. For example, the traditional field of psychophysics is concerned with trying to mathematically describe the relation between the psychological phenomenon created by the mind, such as a sensation, and the physical properties of the stimulus. Interestingly, this whole approach assumes that: (a) there is a mind or subjective, mental dimension in which the sensation is situated; (b) this dimension differs from the one in which observable behavior takes place; and (c) knowing about the sensation is necessary to be able to formulate how the eventual response is made. Much of the history of experimental psychology, particularly as concerned with the fields of psychophysics or sensation and perception, is based on such assumptions about human behavior, and the assumptions have proved troublesome, indeed. These mentalistic assumptions have led researchers and theorists to look for answers in other dimensions, which don't exist, and to neglect the role of variables and relations in the one dimension in which organisms live and interact with the environment.

Generally in psychophysical experiments, participants are first presented with a stimulus that has a particular physical property of interest, such as intensity or frequency. Sometimes researchers refer to this stimulus as the "standard." In one variation, the researcher might assign some numerical value to this stimulus. In another variation, the researcher might ask the participant to assign a value to it. This value is held to represent the magnitude of the psychological sensation created by the stimulus. In subsequent trials, participants are presented with a series of different stimuli, and asked to assign numerical values to those stimuli. Those values are held to represent an estimate of the magnitude of the psychological sensations created by those stimuli. The numerical values are assigned so as to preserve the perceived ratio of the sensations. For example, if an auditory stimulus is perceived as twice as loud as the standard, the participant would express the magnitude of the resulting sensation with a numerical value twice as large as that for the standard. If an auditory stimulus is perceived as half as loud as the standard, the participant would express the magnitude of the resulting sensation with a numerical value half as large as that for the standard. After many trials, a researcher might have a large data set consisting of many pairs of numbers. One number in each pair is the actual objective, physical property of the stimulus that was presented. The other number is held to represent the subjective strength of the sensation created by the stimulus. The researcher would then try to describe mathematically the relation between the actual physical magnitude of the stimulus, as represented across the various pairs of numbers, and the participant's estimate of the magnitude of the subjective sensation. One result that is claimed from all this research is the establishment of a psychological scale in which certain units of measure in the subjective world are held to correspond to other units of measure in the objective world.

Such research is often hailed as being consistent with the highest traditions of empiricism. After all, advocates claim, the only thing that is being described is the relation between two sets of numbers, in the spirit of Galileo, Newton, and the positivism of Comte and Mach. S. S. Stevens (1906–1973), a colleague of Skinner's from their graduate school days and later in the Harvard Department, was a particular advocate of this form of research.

Nevertheless, the whole enterprise is suspect, despite its time-honored place in experimental psychology. According to traditional psychophysics, the participants are necessarily reporting the magnitude of the subjective sensation, which is their response to the stimulus, rather than the magnitude of the stimulus itself, which is part of the environment. This view simply takes it for granted that the aim of the whole enterprise is to infer the nature of the causal events in another dimension—in this case, a "subjective" dimension. The view assumes that an external stimulus, which is in the behavioral dimension, causes events in the subjective dimension, which differs from a behavioral dimension, and that events in the subjective dimension in turn cause the subject's verbal report, which is back in the behavioral dimension. All this is mentalism. Skinner (1945) noted his objection in the following discussion of how verbal behavior descriptive of internal sensations is acquired and maintained:

> The older psychological view, however, was that the speaker was reporting not a property of the stimulus, but a certain kind of private event, the sensation of red. This was regarded as a later stage in a series beginning with the red stimulus. The experimenter was supposed to manipulate the private event by manipulating the stimulus. This seems like a gratuitous distinction, but in the case of some subjects a similar later stage could apparently be generated in other ways (by arousing an 'image'), and hence the autonomy of a private event capable of evoking the response 'red' in the absence of a controllable red stimulus seemed to be proved.... If the private events are free, a scientific description is impossible.... We can ac-

count for the response 'red' (at least as well as for the 'experience' of red) by appeal to past conditions of reinforcement. (p. 276)

Several important questions follow from the traditional view: How can the speaker describe the strength of the subjective sensation in the first place? Who is observing the magnitude of the sensation in the other dimension? How do events cross the dimensional boundary from objective to subjective and back again to objective? For radical behaviorists, speakers can describe their private events when they have histories that have enabled them to do so. Without this history, a self-descriptive repertoire is limited. As with other forms of behavior, there is no internal entity, agent, or homunculus from another dimension that observes private events and responds, and thus no boundaries between subjective and objective are crossed. The organism behaves, not some special mental entity within the organism. No wonder Skinner (1969) quipped that Stevens was not concerned with doing away with mentalism, but rather with trying to deal with mental events scientifically. Various degrees of mathematical sophistication, such as proposals of a logarithmic function to describe the relation between (a) the magnitude of the stimulus as measured by a physicist's instruments, and (b) participants' verbal reports ostensibly indicating the magnitude of their own internal (e.g., "subjective") sensations, do not alter the mentalistic nature of such activity.

With regard to the psychophysical task, participants' verbal reports may be under the discriminative control of either the properties of the stimulus or their own response to the stimulus. The latter case is a form of introspection, but an account needs to explain how such an introspective verbal report can come about. Thus, what is critical is the extent to which individuals have been provided with self-descriptive repertoires prior to the experimental session, according to the processes outlined in the earlier portion of this chapter. The sensation is not a necessary mediating entity from another dimension that is to be divined through some analytical process and then represented quantitatively according to some scaled value. Rather, it is simply part of the total response to external stimulation. An argument based on the traditional interpretation of operationism that a discrimination procedure may well yield better data than introspection is simply beside the point. If anything, the whole set of assumptions underlying traditional psychophysics misleads the experimental enterprise. These assumptions equate an operation performed by the experimenter—the presentation of a stimulus—with a response of the subject—the verbal report. As Skinner (1953) put it:

> Far from avoiding the traditional distinction between mind and matter, or between experience and reality, ... [the traditional] view actually encourages it. It assumes that there is, in fact, a subjective world, which it places beyond the reach of science. On this assumption the only business of a science of sensation is to examine the public events which may be studied in lieu of the private.

> The present analysis has a very different consequence. It continues to deal with the private event, even if only as an inference. It does not substitute the verbal report from which the in-

ference is made for the event itself. The verbal report is a response to the private event and may be used as a source of information about it. A critical analysis of the validity of this practice is of first importance. But we may avoid the dubious conclusion that, so far as science is concerned, the verbal report or some other discriminative response *is* the sensation. (p. 282, italics in original)

As traditionally interpreted, the principle of operationism implicitly assumed a subjective dimension. Indeed, the traditional interpretation sought to gain leverage on the subjective dimension by using observations in the objective dimension as a surrogate. However, in the radical behaviorist view, operationism has been misapplied for decades, resulting in the perpetuation of mentalism. Operationism means analyzing the environmental operations that cause the response in question, even if some stimuli and some features of the behavior are private, rather than asserting that the physical and objective can be used as proxies for the mental and subjective.

IDEAS

A further important term in the mentalistic lexicon is ideas. In traditional parlance, individuals are said to have an idea to do something. What does such language mean, from a behavioral point of view?

It clearly doesn't mean that some sort of mental phenomenon causes overt behavior. That is mentalism, and there are no mental phenomena of this sort. If someone is said to "have an idea," such statements presumably mean the individual has engaged in some form of operant behavior that exerts discriminative control over subsequent behavior. The operant behavior in question may be nonverbal, but more frequently consists of a set of interconnected verbalizations. One tends not to distinguish between covert and overt elements of the idea, as when an individual makes notes or fragmentary drawings that function as discriminative stimuli and guide development of the idea. In a good deal of conventional and traditional usage, the idea is at some point covert, according to the distinctions outlined above. The idea entails some relation between the object or plan of the idea, the behavior, and the consequence of the behavior. Behavioral relations are involved in every step, and they are effective because of their relation to the environment.

RADICAL BEHAVIORISM AND THE CHARGE OF THE "EMPTY ORGANISM"

Chapter 4 noted that one of the claims against the validity of radical behaviorism is that it considers the organism to be empty, or at least that certain events inside the skin can be safely ignored. That charge has previously been dealt with from the point of view of neuroscience and reductionism. Chapter 4 pointed out that radical behaviorism does recognize the contribution that neuroscience can make to the analysis of behavioral events. However, recognizing a contribution of neuroscience does not mean that the explanation of a behavioral event can be reduced to a specification of the structures and pathways that participate in the event, or that a behavioral event cannot be considered to be explained until the participating structures and pathways are specified. The event called a rat's lever press or a pigeon's key peck is not reducible in its entirety to synaptic biochemistry or the contraction of muscles.

The charge of an "empty organism" may now be addressed from the point of view of private behavioral events. One erroneous criticism of behaviorism is that it views individuals who are sitting in their seats at a concert enjoying an exquisite piece of music with their eyes closed no differently than it views individuals sitting in their seats at the same concert at the same time but sleeping.

Clearly, radical behaviorism does not consider the organism to be empty in the sense of either neuroscience or private behavior. Quite the contrary. A charge of the empty organism would be relevant if radical behaviorism restricted its analyses to publicly observable stimulus and response variables, but clearly it does not do so. Radical behaviorism can readily accommodate the private enjoyment of individuals listening to a piece of music, or watching a sunset, or a wide variety of personal experiences. In point of fact, it is better able than traditional psychology to understand the nature of these sorts of experiences and their roles in human life from the standpoint of a natural science. Traditional forms of psychology have sought to overcome the limitations of restricting analysis to publicly observable variables by inserting organismic variables of dubious ontology as mediators in behavioral processes. Traditional forms then claim that an operational definition safeguards the scientific integrity of the endeavor. For radical behaviorists, this entire orientation simply opens the door to mentalism. The important things to recognize when one raises the charge of an empty organism are: (a) the basis for raising the charge in the first place, and (b) the proposed solution to the problem. Traditional psychology raises the charge because it explicitly accepts the assumption of a mental dimension. When traditional psychology then proposes to use publicly observable variables as a measure of events and variables in the mental dimension, it institutionalizes the mental dimension, preserving and protecting it from critical analysis. In contrast, radical behaviorism argues that by recognizing private phenomena are just as much part of the behavioral dimension as public, and then by remaining in the behavioral dimension, one can achieve a thoroughgoing, consistent form of behavioral science.

In short, the analysis of behavior is ultimately concerned with identifying all the elements that participate in a behavioral event. In certain instances, some of those elements may be private. Private events are therefore just relevant to the analysis of behavior as it occurs in context as are public events. However, private behavior does not necessarily occur in every instance of behavior. Even when private behavior does occur, it may not be functionally related to subsequent behavior. Nevertheless, when private behavior does occur, and when it does influence subsequent behavior, its occurrence and influence need to be accounted for. Radical behaviorism does so in terms of ongoing operant processes, consistent with the principles of a natural science. The radical behaviorist orientation regarding private events gives rise to important views of several other aspects of behavioral science. One of these is scientific methodology, which is the subject of Chapter 11.

TABLE 10.1

Problem of privacy

Verbal behavior develops through the differential reinforcement supplied by the verbal community. In the presence of the appropriate discriminative stimulus, the verbal community reinforces the verbal behavior; in its absence, the verbal community does not. Thus, the discriminative stimulus ordinarily needs to be available to the verbal community, so that the verbal community can deliver the reinforcement differentially. In trying to establish verbal behavior under the discriminative control of feelings and internal sensations, the feelings and sensations are not available to the verbal community. Yet, individuals do learn to speak about their feelings and sensations, so differential reinforcement must have occurred somehow. On what basis does the verbal deliver the necessary differential reinforcement, such that a self-descriptive repertoire develops? The answer is that differential reinforcement is delivered on the basis of public stimuli, such that discriminative control is acquired by those events. The discriminative control then transfers to private stimuli that are correlated with the public stimuli.

Below are three ways that the verbal community can differentially reinforce verbal behavior about feelings and sensations, such that eventually the feelings or sensations themselves occasion appropriate verbal behavior:

1. *Public accompaniments*

The verbal community reinforces verbal behavior about sensations and feelings when that verbal behavior accompanies contact with public stimuli that cause sensations and feelings. The resulting verbal behavior is typically metaphorical, based on the nature of public stimulus. Individuals learn to describe pains as sharp when the pains are caused by contact with sharp objects; individuals learn to describe pains as dull when the pains are caused by contact with dull objects. In the future, the pains are described as sharp or dull based on the properties of the private stimulation, rather than the public stimulation that accompanied the private stimulation.

2. *Collateral public response*

The verbal community reinforces verbal behavior about sensations and feelings when the speaker engages in some collateral, pain-related response. Examples are holding an obviously afflicted area, or moaning and groaning. In future instances, the verbal behavior is occasioned by the private stimulation alone.

3. *Stimulus generalization*

The verbal community reinforces verbal behavior about sensations and feelings when that verbal behavior accompanies contact with public stimuli that cause sensations and feelings, as in #1 above. Stimulus generalization then occurs, such that the verbal behavior comes to be occasioned by feelings and sensations that are similar to the original. An example is a speaker who learns to describe the sensation of butterflies on the skin as fluttering, and then metaphorically describes a similar fluttering sensation as "butterflies in my stomach."

Below is one way on the basis of which stimuli arising from covert behavior come to exert discriminative control over subsequent behavior, either overt or covert, either verbal or nonverbal:

1. The verbal community reinforces verbal behavior about public, overt forms of behavior. Control may transfer to private, covert forms of behavior on the basis of private stimuli that coincide with the public form of the behavior. Covert forms, including incipient and inchoate forms, provide a less intense form of the same stimulus as overt forms. In future instances, the verbal behavior may be occasioned by current behavior, potential behavior, probable future behavior, or the variables controlling behavior. In each case, the variables may be public or private. The traditional topic of consciousness is accommodated by this analysis.

Reasons why overt behavior becomes covert

1. Overt form is punished.

2. Covert form is faster, more expedient, or more easily executed.

3. Environmental stimuli to support an overt form are present but only partially, with the result that only the covert and not overt form of response appears.

Reasons why the contingencies pertaining to private events may not always operate as desired

1. Multiple modes of reinforcement can be operating, resulting in lying, fictional distortions, malingering, hypochondriasis.

2. Even without problems caused by multiple modes of reinforcement, reinforcing practices are not as precise as with public stimuli. First, there are not enough nerves going to the right places, so the individual is often not going to be able to come into contact with important forms of stimulation. Second, the verbal community cannot differentially reinforce responses pertaining to private stimuli with the same degree of accuracy that it can with public stimuli, because it is not in contact with the private stimuli. There is, therefore, a necessary limitation on the accuracy of responses pertaining to private stimuli. The result is that self-reports are often inaccurate.

REFERENCES

McComas, H. C. (1916). Extravagances in the motor theory of consciousness. *Psychological Review, 23*, 397–406.

Skinner, B. F. (1945). The operational analysis of psychological terms. *Psychological Review, 52*, 270–277, 290–294.

Skinner B. F. (1953). *Science and human behavior.* New York: Macmillan.

Skinner, B. F. (1957). *Verbal behavior.* New York: Appleton-Century-Crofts.

Skinner, B. F. (1964). Behaviorism at fifty. In T. W. Wann (Ed), *Behaviorism and phenomenology*, pp. 79–108. Chicago: University of Chicago Press.

Skinner, B. F. (1969). *Contingencies of reinforcement.* New York: Appleton-Century-Crofts.

Skinner, B. F. (1974). *About behaviorism.* New York: Knopf.

Skinner, B. F. (1989). *Recent issues in the analysis of behavior.* Columbus, OH: Merrill.

Watson, J. B. (1913). Psychology as the behaviorist views it. *Psychological Review, 20*, 158–177.

Watson, J. B. (1919). *Psychology from the standpoint of a behaviorist.* Philadelphia, PA: Lippincott.

Watson, J. B. (1925). *Behaviorism.* New York: Norton.

STUDY QUESTIONS

1. Describe three reasons why Skinner's conception of private events is not mentalistic

2. Describe the radical behaviorist position on feelings.

3. Describe the "problem of privacy."

4. Describe how collateral responses contribute to the development of verbal behavior under the control of private stimuli.

5. Describe how public accompaniments contribute to the development of verbal behavior under the control of private stimuli.

6. Describe how stimulus generalization contributes to the development of verbal behavior under the control of private stimuli.

7. Describe how discriminative control transfers from public to private stimulation on the basis of common properties.

8. Describe the radical behaviorist position on thinking.

9. Describe the radical behaviorist position on images.

10. Describe the radical behaviorist position on problem solving.

11. Describe the radical behaviorist position on consciousness.

12. Compare and contrast the radical behaviorist view of sensations with the traditional view, such as found in a psychophysical task.

13. Describe how radical behaviorism responds to the claim that it advocates an empty organism.

11

Methods in a Science of Behavior

Synopsis of Chapter 11: The chapters in this second section of the book outline the realization of the radical behaviorist program. To this end, Chapters 8 and 9 addressed elementary and complex verbal relations, and Chapter 10 addressed the radical behaviorist position on private events. Chapter 11 continues this theme and addresses the nature of science and scientific research from the perspective of radical behaviorism. The plan of the chapter is to present the reasoning that underlies research practices. Thus, the chapter is not intended as a technical manual on what conditions serve as adequate controls, how best to carry out interventions or manipulations in basic or applied research, and so on. One topic concerns the use of single-subject designs instead of group designs in which aggregated data are evaluated by tests of statistical inference. Other topics are why scientists conduct research, the goals of research, modes of scientific reasoning, inferential processes, hypothesis testing, reliability and generality of data, and the use of nonhuman subjects in behavioral research. Throughout, the chapter contrasts the reasoning behind radical behaviorist practices with traditional practices.

As a philosophy of science, radical behaviorism guides the activities of behavioral scientists as they pursue their scientific goals. Even though the boundaries between basic research, applied research, and service delivery are not always distinct, the experimental analysis of behavior and applied behavior analysis may nevertheless be regarded as sciences rather than service delivery. Consideration of scientific methods and research practices in behavior analysis provides a further picture of the conceptual foundations of radical behaviorism.

THE NATURE OF SCIENCE AND SCIENTIFIC RESEARCH

From the perspective of radical behaviorism, what a science is may be defined in terms of what a science does. For example, Skinner (1969) suggested that:

> Scientific laws also specify or imply responses and their consequences.... As a culture produces maxims, laws, grammar, and science, its members find it easier to behave effectively without direct or prolonged contact with the contingencies of reinforcement thus formulated. ...The point of science ... is to analyze the contingencies of reinforcement found in nature and to formulate rules or laws which make it unnecessary to be exposed to them in order to behave appropriately. (pp. 141, 166)

The passage above characterizes science in terms of activity that leads to verbal products in the form of reports or statements of generalizable knowledge. The function of these products is to enable individuals who entertain them to act effectively without having to personally go through the same experiences as those who developed them. In many cases, the effective action entails prediction and control, although any form of effective action related to a desired outcome is clearly relevant. For example, astronomy is not a science in which the positions and movements of the planets and stars are controlled, but by knowing the positions and movements of the planets and stars, one can predict when the planting of crops will result in a bountiful harvest.

Given a distinction between science and practice, basic research in the experimental analysis of behavior is concerned with specification of fundamental behavioral principles, such as those pertaining to positive reinforcement, escape, avoidance, punishment, stimulus control, and so on. The knowledge produced by such endeavors is expressed at an abstract level, without necessarily being concerned with whether one is investigating the behavior of a rat, pigeon, or human. Research in applied behavior analysis typically examines the best practices for adapting fundamental behavioral principles to produce desired changes in concrete, socially significant behavior. Some forms of behavior may need to be increased, whereas others may need to be decreased. Reports of this research then inform others of how the problem has been solved, so that they may take appropriate steps themselves. Service delivery is the actual application of behavioral principles to the solving of problems relating to socially significant behavior. Communication to others of successful solutions, even if done extensively, is not a necessary element of this practice. Similarly, data-based decision making is good service delivery, but is not necessarily scientific research in the sense discussed here. To be sure, applied behavior analysis and service delivery may well be coordinated, in the sense of being concerned with similar classes of socially significant behavior, but they remain separate domains.

Goals of Science

Why, then, do scientists do science? For radical behaviorists, doing science is operant behavior It is occasioned by particular antecedent circumstances, and it is maintained by particular outcomes. Sidman (1960) identified several reasons why scientists conduct scientific research: (a) to evaluate hypotheses; (b) to indulge the investigator's curiosity about nature; (c) to try out a new method or technique; (d) to establish the existence of a phenomenon; and (e) to explore the conditions under which a phenomenon occurs. The scientific statements that eventually guide the behavior of others come out of the research activity stimulated by these reasons. Thus, the reasons that lead scientists to engage in doing science are empirical matters, to be examined on a case-by-case basis. To be sure, some science is done to critically examine hypotheses, but not all is or even needs to be. As Skinner (1974) once put it, "The behavior of the scientist is often reconstructed by scientific methodologists within a logical framework of hypothesis, deduction, and the testing of theorems, but the reconstruction seldom represents the behavior of the scientist at work" (p. 343).

In summary, the goals of a science of behavior according to radical behaviorism are as follows (Catania & Harnad, 1988, p. 104):

1. To search for order, for lawfulness, for general relations in behavior

2. To start with a description of simple cases and collect facts, then advance to larger systematic arrangements of those facts, where the arrangements include higher-order concepts that aid in organizing the facts

3. To identify what aspects of behavior are significant

4. To identify the variables of which changes in these aspects are a function

5. To identify how the relations among behavior and its controlling variables are to be brought together in a system

6. To identify what methods are appropriate to the study of such a system

Research is one way for experimenters to come under the control of variables participating in an event, and by so doing, formulate and refine principles that better inform the prediction and control of behavioral events. Research methods in a science are designed to promote effective scientific statements. They suggest manipulations that isolate the actions of relevant variables, so that their participation in events can be effectively understood (Johnston & Pennypacker, 1993; Sidman, 1960).

Methods in Science

John Stuart Mill (1806–1873) was a highly influential English philosopher and political economist of the nineteenth century whose works provide a suitable entry point for discussing scientific methods. Mill sought to develop a system of logical reasoning that was consistent with the way individuals drew conclusions on the basis of observed evidence. He was particularly concerned with the way individuals determined causation. In his *A System of Logic* (Mill, 1843/1956), he proposed five "canons," or Methods of Inductive Inference, by means of which one could investigate possible causes and lay the foundation for scientific explanations. These methods are the Method of Agreement, the Method of Difference, the Joint Method of Agreement and Difference, the Method of Residues, and the Method of Concomitant Variation. By following these Methods, one could identify the causes of an event and thereby explain it.

According to the Method of Agreement, one looks to see if some suspected causal factor is present when the effect in question occurs. According to the Method of Difference, one looks to see if some suspected causal factor is absent when the effect fails to occur. According to the Joint Method, one conducts both operations simultaneously. According to the Method of Residues, one eliminates factors when the effect occurs, and the last factor that remains when the effect in question occurs is the cause. According to the Method of Concomitant Variation, one manipulates the degree to which a presumed causal factor is present, and if the degree of the effect also varies, then one can conclude the factor is indeed causal. Across these methods, the chief manipulation is that of elimination. If one observes that a given event takes place, and then one eliminates some suspected causal factor, will the event take place as before? The factor is identified as causal when the event does not. Although these methods are over 150 years old, they still form the foundation of much scientific research.

If anyone believes Mill's Methods are of historical interest only, one might consider various manipulations used in psychological research, both traditional and behavior-analytic. Three examples may be reviewed here. One involves establishing an initial discrimination and then reversing it, which is a common control procedure in research investigating respondent conditioning and stimulus control. In this procedure, a response is first trained in the presence of one stimulus (stimulus A) but not another (stimulus B). Then, training conditions are reversed, such that the response is trained in B but not A. By gaining control of the response and producing it first in the presence of A and then B, one can then be reasonably sure that the training conditions one is manipulating are causing the response. The second is an A − B − A design that is familiar in much behavior-analytic research. In this design, some condition is put into effect (the A phase of training), then removed (the B phase), and then reinstated (another A phase). As before, by gaining control of the response and producing it first in A phase of training, not in B, and then again in A, one can then be reasonably sure that the training conditions one is manipulating are causing the response. The third involves parametric variations of independent variables. When variations in the dependent variable systematically track the variations in the independent variable, as in conventional dose-response curves, one can again infer the independent variable is causal. The discrimination and reversal and A − B − A manipulations follow from the Mill's Joint Method, and parametric variations follow from Mill's Method of Concomitant Variation.

In addition, many modern treatments of causation and explanation include some reference to "necessary and sufficient conditions." As in many research endeavors, the to-be-explained phenomenon is an event. One is said to have explained an event when one has identified the factors that cause the event, where causal factors are identified in terms of the necessary and sufficient conditions. P is said to be a necessary condition for event Q if Q never occurs in the absence of P (Copi, 1982). P is said to be a sufficient condition for event Q if Q always occurs whenever P occurs. As Copi (1982, pp. 409–410) has discussed, there may be several necessary conditions for the occurrence of an event, and the sufficient condition is the sum of all necessary conditions. In this regard, Mill's Method of Agreement is concerned with eliminating some factor as a necessary condition, and his Method of Difference is concerned with eliminating some factor as a sufficient condition.

The important point here is that Mill's Canons or the identification of necessary and sufficient conditions have the effect of creating additional discriminative control for manipulations designed to produce reinforcing outcomes in interactions with nature. Simply stated, the scientific method is a set of rules for researchers to follow if they want to determine the functional role of certain factors in an event.

A common distinction in scientific methodology is between an independent and dependent variable. A word that is sometimes used in everyday language for independent variable is *cause*. The independent variable is some manipulated property of the environment, such that the organism comes into contact with it. For humans, one can alter the frequency of an auditory stimulus from 25,000 Hz to 30,000 Hz, but a human is unlikely to contact this manipulation, as the upper range of human hearing is typically 20,000 Hz. One then seeks to codify the results of the various manipulations and put them in good order. The independent variable is often identified as simply a contingency, meaning some particular combination of antecedent circumstance, response, and reinforcing consequence.

A word that is sometimes used in everyday language for dependent variable is *effect*. In behavioral research, the dependent variable is some property of behavior, often rate of responding. Rate of responding is emphasized in behavioral research because it is generally the property that is most relevant to the issue of the control of behavior. If one can manipulate how often behavior occurs, other things being equal, one has clearly demonstrated control over the behavior in question. In principle, of course, the dependent variable can be virtually any other property of behavior, such as latency, duration, magnitude, or even its relation to other behavior.

Traditional Research Methods

A highly simplified description of the traditional experimental method, familiar to most individuals who have had conventional research methods courses in psychology, is as follows.

1. Define an experimental question to be asked, or a hypothesis to be tested.

2. Define independent and dependent variables.

3. Randomly assign subjects or participants to a control group and one or more experimental groups.

4. Expose the experimental group(s) to some level of the independent variable, and treat the control group the same except for the exposure to the independent variable; measure dependent variable for all subjects.

5. Compute a test statistic that pertains to the difference between the dependent variable of the control group and that of the experimental group(s); formulate a "null" hypothesis about that test statistic; for example, the null hypothesis might assume that the value of the test statistic has arisen by chance alone, from which one would infer that any difference between the ways the independent variable affects subjects in the groups is unsystematic; in contrast to the null hypothesis, formulate an alternative hypothesis that holds the observed value of the test statistic is unlikely to have arisen by chance, and reflects a systematic difference between experimental and control groups caused by the independent variable.

6. If the probability of obtaining the test statistic is greater than some conventionally acceptable level (e.g., .05 or .01), accept the null hypothesis; if the probability is less, reject the null hypothesis and accept the alternative hypothesis.

In this method, the experimental question is framed in such a way that it can be answered by data, or at least by the outcome of one or more comparisons. Similarly, the hypotheses are expressed in a way that is testable or falsifiable. The logic of this method is that if one has properly conducted the experiment (e.g., random assignment has made the groups equivalent at the start, and groups have been treated the same throughout), then any difference between the groups is likely to be attributable to the independent variable, although in principle one cannot rule out that any difference was actually an effect of chance.

Traditional Modes of Scientific Reasoning

In a traditional perspective, scientific reasoning often follows the form of deductive argument called a *syllogism*. In the form presented below, the syllogism has two premises and a conclusion or deduction. One premise is a conditional statement of the form "If P, then Q" (P ==> Q). The other premise is a statement of what is given as an antecedent condition (P, Q, ~P, ~Q). The symbol ~ indicates *not*. For example, ~P signifies not P. Then the conclusion or deduction is presented. At issue is whether the conclusion is valid, given the premise and the antecedent condition. In formal symbolic logic, the validity of the conclusion is technically determined by the development of a proof in terms of a "truth function" table, the details of which are beyond present concern.

Four modes of syllogistic reasoning are typically involved in discussions of traditional research methodology and scientific reasoning. The modes are described below in abbreviated format, and then in everyday language.

The first is called "affirming the antecedent," or "*modus ponens*":

1. $P \Longrightarrow Q$
P
___
Q

The second is called "denying the consequent," or "*modus tollens*":

2. $P \Longrightarrow Q$
~Q
___
~P

The third is called "affirming the consequent":

3. $P \Longrightarrow Q$
Q
___
P

The fourth is called "denying the antecedent":

4. $P \Longrightarrow Q$
~P
___
~Q

Suppose the premise $P \Longrightarrow Q$ is taken to mean, "If there is smoke, then there is fire." In the first form of reasoning, *modus ponens*, the given antecedent condition is P, that there is smoke. The conclusion is Q, that there is fire. According to most rules of logic, this argument is valid. Indeed, it represents probably the most common form of reasoning.

In the second form of reasoning, *modus tollens*, the given antecedent condition is ~Q, that there is no fire. The conclusion is ~P, that there is no smoke. This argument is also valid, and is discussed in greater detail below.

In the third form of reasoning, affirming the consequent, the given antecedent condition is Q, that there is fire. The conclusion is P, that there is smoke. This argument is not valid. Technically, a proof showing that the argument is not valid would be in terms of a truth function table. In everyday language, the argument is not valid because there could be a fire without smoke. The premise P ==> Q is only unidirectional, not bidirectional, in that it allows a fire without smoke, just not smoke without a fire.

In the fourth form of reasoning, denying the antecedent, the given antecedent condition is ~P, that there is no smoke. The conclusion is ~Q, that there is no fire. Again, this argument is not valid, as would be shown in a truth function table. In everyday language, the argument is not valid because there could be a fire without smoke. Not having smoke doesn't allow one to conclude that there is no fire.

With respect to scientific behavior, suppose P is taken to mean "If theory P is true (about the results we should observe when we perform an experiment)" and Q is taken to mean "Then when we perform that experiment, we should observe results Q."

> In everyday language, *modus ponens* states: "If P is true, we should observe results Q; P is true; therefore we should observe results Q."
>
> In everyday language, *modus tollens* states: "If P is true, we should observe results Q; we do not observe results Q; therefore P is false."
>
> In everyday language, affirming the consequent states: "If P is true, we should observe results Q; we do observe results Q; therefore P is true."
>
> In everyday language, denying the antecedent states: "If P is true, we should observe results Q; P is false; therefore we should not observe results Q."

Although the above forms of scientific reasoning preceded the formalities of hypothesis testing, in much contemporary reasoning the statement that "results Q are observed" should be taken to mean that they are observed with a sufficient degree of statistical significance, such as .05 or .01. In any event, recall that of these four forms of syllogistic reasoning, only the first and second are valid according to the rules of logic. Moreover, the validity of the reasoning is a matter of the form of the argument. The conclusion is true if the premise P ==> Q is assumed to be true. The premise need not necessarily be true when tested against the facts of experience. In any case, at issue is how the technicalities of logic map onto the realities of actual research and experimental practices.

Modus ponens is a valid form of reasoning, but it starts by assuming the theory is true. Typically, one performs an experiment to find out something new, such as whether a theory works. One wouldn't ordinarily perform an experiment to determine what one has already assumed to be true. Thus, the practical utility of *modus ponens* reasoning is suspect, despite its logical validity.

Modus tollens manifests the principle of falsifiability. However, in science one typically wants to find out how to control nature. Despite the logical validity of *modus tollens*, one ordinarily wants to archive successes at controlling nature, not failures. Again, what is valid according to logic seems inconsistent with practical action.

Affirming the consequent is logically fallacious. In everyday language, one might say that the results of the experiment could be observed for another reason, not necessarily because theory P is true. Nevertheless, affirming the consequent is "very nearly the life blood of science" (Sidman, 1960, p. 127). Despite its formal status as a fallacy, it is a way researchers document what controls nature. Indeed, it is the rare researcher who predicts the outcome of an experiment, and then discredits the prediction because it is not valid according to the rules of logic. The point is that again there is a substantial disconnect between the formal rules of logic and the behavior of doing science.

Denying the antecedent is also logically fallacious. Note that it assumes theory P is not true from the outset. That a scientist would take time to perform an experiment testing a theory that was already known to be false is unclear. Once again, the point is that the actual practices of researchers don't agree very well with the rational reconstructions provided by logicians and philosophers. As Skinner put it in one place:

> If it turns out that our final view of verbal behavior invalidates our scientific structure from the point of view of logic and truth value, then so much the worse for logic, which will also have been embraced by our analysis. (Skinner, 1945, p. 277)

The Hypothetico-deductive Approach

An approach to science that emphasizes the formal logic of hypothesis testing has an extensive history behind it. When the logical positivists sought to provide a rational reconstruction of science beginning in the 1930s, they argued for the primacy of verification and logic. All concepts had to be verified in (i.e., reduced to) the bedrock language of physics. Relations were then to be expressed in terms of logic. All sciences were assumed to follow what became known as the hypothetico-deductive method. General laws were conceived, and specific observations were regarded as explained when they could be framed as deductions from the laws. Explanation and prediction were symmetric, in that each had the same logical structure. Explanations differed by using the past tense in the logical argument, whereas predictions used the future tense. Experiments were often conceived by deducing implications (i.e., predictions) from general laws or theories ("covering laws") and then conducting the appropriate tests to see if the implications obtained. If they did not, the law or theory was disproved. If they did, the law or theory could not be said to be proven true, in light of the fallacy of affirming the consequent, but it could be said to have been corroborated or supported.

The support given to hypothesis testing by statistical inference is well described by Chiesa (1994). In the middle of the nineteenth century, the Belgian astronomer turned social statistician Adolphe Quetelet (1796–1874) developed the idea that statistical techniques could be applied to distributions of human physical and social characteristics, leading to the application of the normal curve to the world of human affairs. The mean of a population ("*l'homme moyen*") became an ideal, and variation around the mean was regarded as "error" and unavoidably bothersome. In light of these conceptions of means and variation, a further step was provided by R. A. Fisher, an agronomist, beginning in the 1930s. In what must surely be one of the most influential scientific publications of all time, Fisher (1935, and in subsequent editions) applied mathematical techniques of the laws of chance to comparisons between groups or populations. Fisher asserted that the appropriate comparisons could be made in terms of probability statements and sampling theory. By applying probability theory to experimental results, one can formulate a decision theory based on a process of mathematically rigorous inductive inference; namely, how likely the observed results were due to chance. Fisher further argued that inductive inference of the sort he formalized was the fundamental process according to which new knowledge comes into the world, and it was the responsibility of experimental science to validate its contributions to the data base of human knowledge, writ large in our culture. The result is the orthodox reliance on tests of statistical inference that is found today in psychological research.

Strong Inference

Nevertheless, some theorists remained concerned about the null hypothesis logic of inferential statistics. For example, the hypotheses rarely were formulated in a way that seemed a reasonable test of the question being examined (Lykken, 1968; Meehl, 1967). In recognition of these concerns, Platt (1964) published an influential article that proposed a four-step method of scientific inquiry called "strong inference." The four steps are:

1. Devise competing hypotheses (e.g., with differential predictions) as to why things are the way they are.

2. Devise one or more crucial experiments that will decide among the hypotheses.

3. Carry out the experiments.

4. Recycle and refine based on the outcomes of the experiments and their relation to the hypotheses, such that decisions about the adequacy of the hypotheses become apparent.

This method owes much to historical influences, ranging from Bacon to Galileo to Newton to Popper and to the formal hypothetico-deductive practices of the logical positivists in the twentieth century. The theories are stated in such a way that they generate different hypotheses about what will obtain, given particular experimental tests. The techniques of statistical inference are applied at step 4, to reach decisions about the hypotheses. Platt argued that in one form or another, this process has been the one by which the various sciences have progressed.

However, closer inspection reveals that the argument is not based on solid ground (O'Donohue & Buchanan, 2001). Numerous hypotheses can be formulated, but only some are tested—why? Crucial experiments are rarely as crucial as they seem. Most often, the data are quite variable. Moreover, when the data don't support a particular theory, auxiliary assumptions tend to be added in something like an ad hoc fashion, to accommodate disparate results. The recycling and refining of experiments is fine in principle, but analysis of the history of science suggests experimenters don't actually proceed in the way Platt described. In addition, it is not clear why step 4 is even required, in light of steps 1 and 2. Thus, an examination of actual sciences reveals that they don't progress in the logically sanitized manner described by such idealized reconstructions. The bottom line is that science is human behavior. It is often multiply controlled, or influenced by many factors, rather than simply logical, rational factors. Given the multiple control, science often cannot be neatly conceptualized in terms of one and only one method.

To be sure, many scholars both outside and inside behavior analysis have pointed out that the traditional hypothetico-deductive method aided by inferential statistics does not achieve what it claims, or at least that science does not operate in the way the conventional hypothetico-deductive method claims. A reasonable cross-section of those outside of behavior analysis would include Bakan (1966), Danziger (1990). Lykken (1968), Meehl (1967, 1970, 1978), and Rozeboom (1960). These sources go beyond challenges to Kuhn's (1970) concept of "normal science," such as by Feyerabend's (1970, p. 26) contention that "anything goes" in science, and Lakatos' (1970) argument that science advances through research programs instead of theories. In general, these sources express a wide variety of concerns about statistical hypothesis testing in experimental research, both in terms of its assumption and techniques. For example, Meehl (1967) points out that experimental procedures in the "soft" areas of psychology, such as personality and social psychology, often structure the hypotheses they are testing, so that the a priori probability of "confirming instances" from an experiment are in the neighborhood of 0.50. In contrast, experimental procedures in the physical sciences keep the a priori probability low. The disparity between sciences comes about because psychologists are often content with directions of effects, whereas physical sciences are concerned with specific point predictions. In addition, Meehl (1970, pp. 385 ff.) points out one of the problems with the logic of the traditional control group design. The import of traditional logic is that if the control subjects had been exposed to the independent variable, then they would have performed just as did the experimental subjects. Technically, this form of an "if-then" expression is known as the "counterfactual conditional" or the "contrary-to-fact conditional." According to logic, which is supposed to dictate experimental procedures, the truth value of such a conditional statement is actually undetermined. One footnote in Meehl's (1970) discussion is almost two pages in length, listing a large number of studies as references. An inescapable conclusion is that by their own hand, traditional methodologists can be inconsistent when applying their own principles.

A BEHAVIOR-ANALYTIC ASSESSMENT OF TRADITIONAL RESEARCH METHODS

To be sure, behavior-analytic research methods differ in emphasis from traditional methods relying on groups of subjects, the differences between which are evaluated using techniques of statistical inference. In any case, behavior analysts typically do not ordinarily conduct experimental research according to hypothetico-deductive methods and using tests of statistical inference. Behavior analysts have no particular objection to group designs and statistical inference, where appropriate. However, behavior analysts question whether they are in fact appropriate for behavioral research concerned with identifying fundamental principles of behavior. Statistical inference may well be appropriate for actuarial sorts of questions, such as determining the percentage of subjects in a population that might be expected to respond when a particular manipulation or intervention is applied, but the question of identifying fundamental principles of behavior is different. As Skinner (1972) put it, "No one goes to the circus to see the average dog jump through a hoop significantly oftener than untrained dogs raised under the same circumstances, or to see an elephant demonstrate a principle of behavior" (p. 114).

Variability and Error

As noted above, a central concern of traditional researchers is the concept of variability. A term that is related to variability is *error*. Three common sources are of variability are: (a) unintended discrepancies in procedure for different subjects; (b) failure to maintain consistent conditions in the apparatus throughout the experiment; and (c) experimenter mistakes in measuring the dependent variable for different subjects. In a traditional view, variability or error was thought to be intrinsic to the process of measurement or observation, and experimenters needed to adjust their methods to take it into account. As experimental error increases, so then does the probability that any difference between groups is due to chance, rather than the independent variable. For traditional researchers, one purpose of group designs and statistical inference is to minimize the possibility that experimenters will conclude that any observed difference between groups is attributable to the independent variable, when in fact it is simply due to error. Of course, mistakes are still possible, as technically one can never disprove the null hypothesis. When one incorrectly rejects the null hypothesis, one has committed a Type I error, or that of a "false positive." When one incorrectly accepts the null hypothesis, one has committed a Type II error, or that of a "false negative." By reducing the probability of making a Type I error, one unfortunately increases the probability of making a Type II error, and vice versa. Researchers set a conventional level of tolerance, say .05 or .01, as acceptable levels of risk of making such errors.

If variability is a problem, the behavior analyst looks to see what might be causing the variability. Can conditions be controlled better to reduce variability? Indeed, can something be identified in the experimental protocol that might itself be considered an independent variable, and manipulated such that its effects are better understood? The group statistical approach ends up maximizing the impact of uncontrolled factors on the dependent variable. Aggregating data ensures the experimenter remains uninformed about that impact by hiding it. This state of affairs seems contrary to what scientific research is all about, namely, producing scientific knowledge. Rather, it seems to be a matter of preventing researchers from becoming informed about the factors that affect the dependent variable. Moreover, the tactic encourages a passive approach of just waiting to see if something will happen consistent with a hypothesis, rather than an active approach of intervening to produce desired ends.

Reliability of Data

Further concerns for traditional researchers are reliability and generality. In a traditional view, the analysis of aggregated data from many subjects in a group design using techniques of statistical inference is thought to promote reliability and generality. But what do those two terms mean?

Radical behaviorists are just as concerned about reliability and generality as are traditional researchers. Clearly, scientific laws and the data on which they are based should be both reliable and general. For radical behaviorists, reliability is a matter of consistency: If one simply performs the experiment again, one expects to obtain the same result. Hence, radical behaviorists accommodate concern with reliability by replication. Sidman (1960) discusses a type of replication called "direct replication." In direct replication, the experiment or condition is simply repeated, with the same subjects, procedure, and apparatus.

Generality of Data

In principle, generality is a matter of how broadly applicable the results are. If the experimental procedures are performed again but with some differences, one would expect to observe similar results. The rationale of the traditional methodology is that by using groups of randomly assigned subjects, there is no internal bias, and the results of experimental research are presumed to apply to, or generalize to, larger populations of subjects. Only by using groups of representative subjects can the generality of the findings be assured.

As before, behavior analysts question the rationale for the group statistical approach. There is no assurance that simply conducting an experiment with a large number of subjects randomly assigned to different groups guarantees that the results are reliable and general. To some extent, the question is empirical. That is, whether the results of an experiment are reliable and general depends on how similar the subjects in subsequent experiments are to the original subjects, how similar the apparatus is, how similar the procedure is, how similar the independent variables are, how similar the dependent variable is, and so on.

Radical behaviorists accommodate generality through what Sidman (1960) called "systematic replication." Systematic replication is conducting the experiment again but with some variation: new subjects, new parameters, etc. But this sense of generality needs to be defined further. One can be concerned with generality "across" certain features of an experiment, or generality "of" certain features of an experiment. Group designs attempt to ensure generality, but at what cost? One aggregates data from many subjects. The argument is that one actually maximizes the variability by doing so, by not recognizing legitimate independent variables. For example, if the variability is too large, group designs encourage researchers to reduce the error term by "blocking" subjects in some fashion: gender, socioeconomic status, screening score on a paper and pencil personality inventory. The single subject design is the logical conclusion of this process. One is concerned with identifying the independent variables at work in the experiment, and for an elucidation of basic processes, that is best done at the level of the individual subject.

Group designs might well be suitable for actuarial questions, such as how many subjects in a given population might respond in a particular way to particular stimuli, but these aren't ordinarily questions about basic processes. At issue is how tolerant of variability does one need to be, as a practical question? If one is seeking to understand basic processes, one can't be very tolerant, because one wants to understand the process, and not how the contribution of other variables, many of them unknown, might mask or distort the effect of the variable or process in question. By including lots of other subjects, one introduces lots of other sources of influence over the behavior of the subjects or participants.

The bottom line is that single subject research requires reliability and generality, just as do group designs. However, it satisfies these requirements in different ways. Behavior is studied until it is stable, according to some criterion. Stability requires numerous instances of intrasubject direct replication. In addition, an experiment does typically involve several subjects (four is a common number), so intersubject replication is important. It would be an empirical question of whether the same effect would occur with water as a reinforcer in place of food, with a chain pull operant instead of a lever press or a key peck, with light instead of tone as a conditioned or discriminative stimulus, with negative instead of positive reinforcement, and so on. Conducting the experiment

TABLE 11.1
Radical Behaviorist Views of Generality

Generality across			
different subjects of same species	different subjects of different species	different response classes	different settings

Generality of		
Different variables	Different methods	different processes

with more subjects does not automatically yield generality in this sense. One does not collapse across the unrecognized effects of many independent variables or procedural features to understand the effect of a single process.

Table 11–1 summarizes the radical behaviorist view of generality, in the sense of generality *across* and generality *of* (Johnston & Pennypacker, 1993). Generality across is concerned with species, responses, and settings. Generality of is concerned with variables, methods, and processes. These forms of generality are accommodated by increased experimental control, and by replication, both direct and systematic.

Aggregating Data

In particular, the traditional methodology often exposes different groups of subjects to different treatments, calculates a mean or average performance of a group, and then draws conclusions based on a comparison of the means, where each mean is taken to represent the "ideal" case of subjects so treated. An important question is: To what extent does the mean correspond to an actual subject? If the mean doesn't represent an actual subject in the group, the results are suspect. The common example that illustrates the perils of aggregating data and using a mean is as follows (e.g., Estes, 1964):

1. Consider a procedure in which five subjects perform on some task, and the dependent variable score can range from 0 to 10.

2. Assume five trials are conducted.

3. Assume the data are as in Table 11.2.

What can be said about these results? If one considers the results in terms of the mean score, the results suggest a linear, gradually increasing function across trials. However, no individual subject actually shows such a linear, gradually increasing function. Rather, each subject shows an all-or-none or step function, where before a particular trial its score is 0, but after that trial its score is 10. The mean score on each trial gives a false sense of what an individual subject did, and if an experimenter considers the aggregate score, the experimenter is going to be misled.

TABLE 11.2

Subject	Trial				
	1	2	3	4	5
A	0	10	10	10	10
B	0	0	10	10	10
C	10	10	10	10	10
D	0	0	0	0	10
E	0	0	0	10	10
mean	2	4	6	8	10

BEHAVIOR-ANALYTIC RESEARCH METHODS

In contrast to group statistical approaches, behavior analysts typically study a small number of subjects for a long period of time, rather than a large number of subjects for a brief period of time. Questions of reliability and generality of findings are accommodated by replication and demonstrations of experimental control. The concerns raised by traditional methodology are important, but if large numbers of subjects are employed, the process of aggregating data from a group may only obscure, rather than reveal, the nature of the basic process. Behavior analysts tend to look instead for the asymptotic or steady-state behavior produced by a given manipulation or set of environmental conditions that is imposed on subjects. If the behavior is too variable from session to session, or if trends are evident across sessions, further sessions are conducted, until the variability and trends are eliminated or at least minimized. Transitions between steady states are relevant, but they also can be examined directly, as part of the experimental protocol. Moreover, transitions are themselves influenced by prior manipulations, so comprehensive knowledge involves identifying how any prior manipulations might have influenced transition states.

Of further concern is the magnitude of the effect, as measured in terms of the dependent variable. Statistical significance doesn't speak to that matter. If the test statistic isn't significant, traditional methodology often says to increase the number of observations by increasing the number of subjects. Traditional methodology doesn't tell researchers how to increase control, such that they obtain a greater effect in absolute terms. It tells them how to manipulate data, not behavior. Traditional methodology can claim to have a reliable effect at some level of statistical significance, but it is important to remember that many times statistical significance is achieved because the number of subjects in the groups is large, rather than because the difference between control and experimental groups is large in any practical sense.

Conducting the behavioral experiment could be described in terms of the following steps:

1. Select subjects. The subjects could be selected for any of several reasons. With what question is the research focused? What resources are available to support the research? If one is interested in studying verbal behavior, then presumably humans are the subjects of choice. However, if a representative response is all that is required, perhaps nonhuman subjects are suitable. Any question of extrapolation of results from nonhumans is an empirical question, as the extrapolation would be from one group of humans to another.

2. Determine how the environmental conditions will be controlled. What apparatus will be employed? What response system will be studied? What motivational system or reinforcement parameters will be used? What stimuli will be used?

3. Determine whether the research is concerned with the asymptotic, terminal behavior produced by exposure to conditions ("steady states") or with transitions between steady states.

4. What will be the experimental design? Clearly, this matter does not warrant a formulaic answer.

5. Impose experimental conditions. If the concern is with steady state behavior, wait until stability. Assessment of stability typically focuses upon minimal day-to-day fluctuation in behavior, as well as minimal longer-term trends. If the concern is with behavior in transition, observe what factors accelerate or retard transition between one state and the next.

6. Isolate relevant variables, so they are what control the scientific verbal behavior that emerges from the experiment, rather than nonscientific or cultural variables. Establish the functional relation between independent and dependent variables (e.g., Mill's methods, parametric research). Again, this process is not formulaic, but rather one of keeping the control of scientific verbal behavior at a descriptively consistent level.

7. Replicate within and across subjects, to assess reliability and generality. Replication allows the research to meet concerns about such things as a sequence effect, in which an observed effect depends on a particular series of conditions, rather than simply the condition currently in effect. Again, if a sequence effect is relevant, it may be construed as an independent variable in its own right, rather than a nuisance. Although experimenters vary on how to demonstrate that the known and manipulated, rather than unknown and unsystematically encountered independent variables are responsible for the effect, many researchers rely on a discrimination and

reversal. That is, in the presence of one antecedent stimulus (A), one contingency is present, and in the presence of another (B), the contingency is absent. After stable behavior is observed in A, conditions are reversed, such that the contingency formerly in effect in A is not in effect in B, and vice versa. The reoccurrence of the behavior in question constitutes a replication of the effects of the original experimental condition, and an adequate demonstration of experimental control.

Reversibility

As suggested above, many behavioral effects are reversible. That is, the behavior reverts to formerly observed (e.g., baseline) levels when the independent variables or environmental circumstances that produce the effects in question are removed. That is the logic of experimental manipulations that successively impose and remove contingencies to demonstrate control.

To be sure, not all behavioral effects are reversible. However, if behavior does not reverse to baseline levels when baseline contingencies are reinstated, then the irreversibility of a process is a bit of information about the nature of that process. This bit of information needs to be included in the data base of generalizable knowledge, just as much as when the process was reversible.

Nonhuman Subjects

Some behavioral research uses nonhuman subjects, such as rats or pigeons. One legitimate question is how can important knowledge about humans be gained from studying nonhumans? Of course, humans and nonhumans differ appreciably. Humans clearly are capable of more complex behavior than rats or pigeons, and humans can engage in verbal behavior that rats and pigeons cannot. Worth remembering, of course, is that rats' eyesight is not particularly good, although their senses of hearing, touch, smell, and taste are exquisite. Similarly, pigeons' visual abilities correspond fairly closely to humans, although not in binocular capacity, and pigeons' hearing, while adequate, often plays a secondary role to vision when they interact with their environment. Subjects do differ.

An important point is that many sciences have progressed by starting out with simple preparations, and then moved to complex. Physics examined balls rolling down inclined planes or objects falling in space. Laws were expressed in terms of frictionless surfaces or objects falling in a vacuum. It is unlikely much would have been learned by trying to study the movement of a leaf in a windstorm. Behavioral research has employed nonhuman subjects for similar reasons. The subjects represent a simpler preparation. There are no expectancy or demand effects. It is possible to get better control of the environment, the prior history of the subjects, and their genetic endowment. They can be trained to make an easily repeatable, representative response, often for extended periods of time, without a great deal of fatigue. Hence, one can study the rat's lever press or the pigeon's key peck and formulate meaningful conclusions about behavioral interactions with the environment, in the same way that we can make meaningful conclusions about genetics by studying whether peas from particular plants have wrinkled or smooth skins.

Again, the question of the extent to which one can generalize the results from nonhumans to humans is an empirical one. The following example is thoroughly contrived, but perhaps it is adequate to illustrate the point. Suppose a skeptic challenged the use of nonhumans in research. A rejoinder might be to ask the skeptic to eat a cracker that had been treated with a food additive. The additive kept the cracker fresh, but it had caused rapid death in 100% of the rats on whom it had been tested. Chances are the skeptic would say something like, "I know the rat is not the same as a human, but it is enough like a human that the results should be of some concern to humans. After all, rats eat food, metabolize it, drink water, and breathe air. They have brains, lungs, stomachs, and digestive systems. So do humans. If the food additive affects rats that way, a reasonable guess is that it would affect humans similarly. Consequently, the prudent course of action is not to eat it." The skeptic has just made the case. Rats are not just like humans, but they are enough like humans that humans will be better off by taking into account the effects of the food additive on rats. In cases of behavioral research, rats do not necessarily behave just like humans, but they behave enough like a human that humans will be better off by taking into account the effects on rats.

The radical behaviorist also notes that:

> Another common misunderstanding concerns extrapolation from animal to human behavior. Those who study living organisms—say, in genetics, embryology, or medicine—usually start below the human level, and students of behavior have quite naturally followed the same practice. The experimenter needs an organism which is readily available and cheaply maintained. He must submit it to daily regimens, often for long periods of time, confine it in easily controlled environments, and expose it to complex contingencies of reinforcement. Such organisms are almost necessarily simpler than men. Nevertheless, with very few exceptions, those who study them are primarily concerned with human behavior. Very few people are interested in the rat or pigeon for their own sakes....

> Although it is sometimes said that research on lower animals makes it impossible to discover what is distinctly human, it is only by studying the behavior of lower animals that we can tell what is distinctly human. The range of what has seemed to be human has been progressively reduced as lower organisms have come to be better understood. What survives is, of course, of the greatest importance. It must be investigated with human subjects. There is no evidence that research on lower organisms contaminates research on men or that those who study animals can have nothing important to say about men. (Skinner, 1969, pp. 100–101)

Again, research conducted with nonhuman subjects has its place. Not only might the results be applicable to humans, but also the techniques might be helpful in training the scientist to develop a more effective repertoire for future research.

Context of Discovery versus Context of Justification

A classic distinction in the philosophy of science, traceable to the empirical thinking that arose in the 1930s in the era of logical positivism, is that between the context of discovery and the context of justification. The former concerns the source of scientific ideas. The latter concerns how they are evaluated. Many philosophers of science in the logical positivist tradition dismiss scientific concern with the former, saying that only the latter is of scientific concern. For radical behaviorists, both are of concern. Presumably, science no longer seriously tests hypotheses related to phlogiston as a theory of combustion, or a flat earth as a geographical reality. They are dismissed as unscientific, based on their origin. Thus, science has always been intimately concerned with the source of scientific ideas. To say otherwise is to give equal credibility to the ideas of the fool and expert. In regard to the source of ideas in psychology, Skinner pointed out that:

> [T]he reasons for the popularity of cognitive psychology ... have nothing to do with scientific advances but rather with the release of the floodgates of mentalistic terms fed by the tributaries of philosophy, theology, history, letters, media, and worst of all, the English language....
>
> I have accused cognitive scientists, in particular, of misusing the metaphor of storage and retrieval, speculating about internal processes about which they have no reliable information, studying behavior in response to descriptions of experimental settings rather than in response to the settings themselves, studying reports of intentions rather than the behavior intended, attributing behavior to feelings and states of minds instead of the contingencies of reinforcement of which they are current surrogates, and inventing explanatory systems which are admired for a profundity that is better called inaccessibility. (Skinner in Catania & Harnad, 1988, p. 447, 472)

Thus, the radical behaviorist holds that no other science has ever had to move against such a tradition of folklore and superstition. Consequently, it is not surprising that traditional psychologists have put a high price on trying to be factual and objective. They try to be factual and objective by making inferences about mental life on the evidence of publicly observable behavior, in the hope of being recognized as a science. The problem is that they have failed to critically examine their basic assumptions. There is no dimension of mental life about which to make a science. There is certainly private behavior, but it is in a behavioral dimension. There is certainly neuroscience, but that is a different science from behavior analysis in the one dimension. Becoming knowledgeable is not a matter of attaining certain cognitive states, but rather a matter of skilled and highly discriminative repertoires that develop through interaction with the world. To try to develop research methods derived from mentalistic assumptions about a mental dimension in a science of behavior, for the behavior of the subject and the behavior of the scientist, will not be effective.

The alternative is not necessarily to be formulaic in one's approach to science. Indeed, in one description of his own scientific career titled "A Case History in Scientific

Method," Skinner (1956) put his tongue squarely in his cheek and described five "unformalized principles" of scientific practice:

1. When one encounters something interesting, drop everything else and study it.

2. Some ways of doing research are easier than others.

3. Some people are lucky.

4. Apparatuses sometimes malfunction.

5. Serendipity—one may find one thing while looking for something else.

Of course, not all that Skinner contributed about doing science displays the same level of playfulness as the above account. An important point of the "Case History ..." account is that scientists necessarily bring their own unique histories to bear when they seek to examine some subject matter, and that attempts to reconstruct scientific practices in the manner suggested by formal logicians is misleading. Skinner's point was that doing science is behaving, and is usefully formulated in terms of operant contingencies.

In a relevant section toward the end of *Verbal Behavior*, Skinner (1957) offered a more systematic treatment of scientific methodology:

> Logical and scientific verbal behavior differs from the verbal behavior of the layman (and particularly from literary behavior) because of the emphasis on practical consequences.... The test of scientific prediction is often, as the word implies, *verbal* confirmation. But the behavior of both logician and scientist leads at last to effective nonverbal action, and it is here that we must find the ultimate reinforcing contingencies which maintain the logical and scientific verbal community.... Logical and scientific verbal behavior, as well as the practices of the community which shape and maintain it, have been analyzed in *logical and scientific methodology*.... A ... sequence in science might be as follows: (1) relatively abstract responses specifying particular properties of stimuli prove useful, (2) the scientific community arranges contingencies of reinforcement which constrain speakers to respond to isolated properties, and (3) the rules and canons of scientific thinking which govern classification and abstraction are studied to explain the effectiveness of (1) and (2) and possibly to suggest improved behavior and practices.... The techniques of logical and scientific methodology must, of course, be adapted to the phenomena of verbal behavior.... The verbal processes of logical and scientific thought deserve and require a more precise analysis than they have yet received. One of the ultimate accomplishments of a science of verbal behavior may be an empirical logic, or a descriptive and analytic scientific epistemology, the terms and practices of which will be adapted to human behavior as a subject matter. (pp. 429–431, italics in original)

Given that much of science is verbal behavior, the scientific community establishes and refines the contingencies that maintain effective scientific practices. Analysis of these contingencies, with a particular emphasis on analyzing verbal contingencies, will ultimately reveal the processes responsible for effective scientific behavior. These topics are reviewed more closely in the next two chapters on scientific verbal behavior.

Chapter 12 begins with a review of the role of theories in science from the standpoint of radical behaviorism.

TABLE 11–3

The function of science
The point of science ... is to analyze the contingencies of reinforcement found in nature and to formulate rules or laws which make it unnecessary to be exposed to them in order to behave appropriately. (Skinner, 1969, p. 166)

Reasons why scientists conduct scientific research
   a. to evaluate hypotheses
   b. to indulge the investigator's curiosity about nature
   c. to try out a new method or technique
   d. to establish the existence of a phenomenon; and
   e. to explore the conditions under which a phenomenon occurs (from Sidman, 1960).

The goals of a science of behavior according to radical behaviorism

1. To search for order, for lawfulness, for general relations in behavior

2. To start with a description of simple cases and collect facts, then advance to larger systematic arrangements of those facts, where the arrangements include higher-order concepts that aid in organizing the facts

3. To identify what aspects of behavior are significant

4. To identify the variables of which changes in these aspects are a function

5. To identify how the relations among behavior and its controlling variables are to be brought together in a system

6. To identify what methods are appropriate to the study of such a system (from Catania & Harnad, 1988, p. 104)

Traditional Research Methods

1. Define an experimental question to be asked, or a hypothesis to be tested.

2. Define independent and dependent variables.

3. Randomly assign subject or participants to a control group and one or more experimental groups.

4. Expose the experimental group(s) but not control group to some level of the independent variable; measure dependent variable for all subjects.

5. Compute a test statistic that pertains to the difference between the dependent variable of the control group and that of the experimental group(s).

6. If the probability of obtaining the test statistic is greater than some conventionally acceptable level (e.g., .05 or .01), accept a null hypothesis that any difference between groups is the result of chance; if the probability is less, reject the null hypothesis and accept the alternative hypothesis that any difference between groups is the result of the independent variable.

Four Steps of "Strong Inference"

1. Devise competing hypotheses (e.g., with differential predictions) as to why things are the way they are.

2. Devise one or more crucial experiments that will decide among the hypotheses.

3. Carry out the experiments.

4. Recycle and refine based on the outcomes of the experiments and their relation to the hypotheses, such that decisions about the adequacy of the hypotheses become apparent (from Platt, 1964).

Reliability of data
Direct replication

Generality of data
Systematic replication,
Generality across: subjects, species, response classes, settings;
Generality of: variables, methods, processes

Behavior-analytic research methods

1. Select subjects.

2. Determine how the environmental conditions will be controlled.

3. Determine whether interested in steady state or transitional states.

4. Determine the experimental design.

5. Impose experimental conditions. If the concern is with steady state behavior, wait until stability. If the concern is with behavior in transition, observe what factors accelerate or retard transition between one state and the next.

6. Isolate relevant variables. Establish the functional relation between independent and dependent variables.

7. Replicate within and across subjects, to assess reliability and generality.

Reversibility
Will experiment replicate previous data when previous conditions reinstated?

Context of discovery versus context of justification
The former deals with determining the source of a knowledge claim; the second deals with determining its validity.
Traditional methods ignore the context of discovery in favor of justification. Radical behaviorism emphasizes both equally.

REFERENCES

Bakan, D. (1966). The test of significance in psychological research. *Psychological Bulletin, 66,* 423–437.

Catania, A. C., & Harnad, S. (Eds.). (1988). *The selection of behavior: The operant behaviorism of B. F. Skinner: Comments and controversies.* Cambridge: Cambridge University Press.

Chiesa, M. (1994). *Radical behaviorism: The philosophy and the science.* Boston: Authors Cooperative.

Copi, I. (1982). *Introduction to logic* (6th ed.). New York: Macmillan.

Danziger, K. (1990). *Constructing the subject: Historical origins of psychological research.* New York: Cambridge University Press.

Estes, W. K. (1964). All-or-none processes in learning and retention. *American Psychologist, 19,* 16–25.

Feyerabend, P. (1970). Against method: An outline of an anarchistic theory of knowledge. In M. Radner & S. Winokur (Eds.), *Minnesota studies in the philosophy of science, Vol. 4,* pp. 17–130. Minneapolis, MN: University of Minnesota Press.

Fisher, R. A. (1935). *The design of experiments.* London: Oliver & Boyd.

Johnston, J., & Pennypacker, H. (1993). *Strategies and tactics of behavioral research* (2nd edition). Hillsdale, NJ: Erlbaum.

Kuhn, T. S. (1970). *The structure of scientific revolutions.* Chicago: University of Chicago Press.

Lakatos, I. (1970). Falsification and the methodology of scientific research programmes. In I. Lakatos & A. Musgrave (Eds.), *Criticism and the growth of knowledge,* pp. 91–195. Cambridge: Cambridge University Press.

Lykken, D. (1968). Statistical significance in psychological research. *Psychological Bulletin, 70,* 151–159.

Meehl, P. (1967). Theory-testing in psychology and physics: A methodological paradox. *Philosophy of Science, 34,* 103–115.

Meehl, P. (1970). Nuisance variables and the ex post facto design. In M. Radner & S. Winokur (Eds.), *Minnesota studies in the philosophy of science, Vol. 4,* pp. 373–402. Minneapolis, MN: University of Minnesota Press.

Meehl, P. (1978). Theoretical risks and tabular asterisks: Sir Karl, Sir Ronald, and the slow progress of soft psychology. *Journal of Consulting and Clinical Psychology, 46,* 806–834.

Mill, J. S. (1956). *A System of logic* (8th ed.). London: Longmans, Green, and Co. (Original edition published 1843)

O'Donohue, W., & Buchanan, J. A. (2001). The weaknesses of strong inference. *Behavior and Philosophy, 29,* 1–20.

Platt, J. (1964). Strong inference. *Science, 146*, 347–353.

Rozeboom, W. W. (1960). The fallacy of the null-hypothesis significance test. *Psychological Bulletin, 57*, 416–428.

Sidman, M. (1960). *Tactics of scientific research*. New York: Basic Books.

Skinner, B. F. (1945). The operational analysis of psychological terms. *Psychological Review, 52*, 270–277, 290–294.

Skinner, B. F. (1956). A case history in scientific method. *American Psychologist, 11*, 221–233.

Skinner, B. F. (1957). *Verbal behavior.* New York: Appleton-Century-Crofts.

Skinner, B. F. (1969). *Contingencies of reinforcement*. New York: Appleton-Century-Crofts.

Skinner, B. F. (1972). *Cumulative record*. New York: Appleton-Century-Crofts.

Skinner, B. F. (1974). *About behaviorism*. New York: Knopf.

STUDY QUESTIONS

1. State or paraphrase Skinner's (1969) statement about the point of science.

2. Distinguish between science, as represented in the experimental analysis of behavior and applied behavior analysis, and professional practice, as represented in behavior-analytic service delivery. Be sure to mention the roles of (a) research and (b) communication.

3. List five reasons why scientists conduct research according to Sidman (1960).

4. List the six goals of science according to radical behaviorism.

5. Describe the five canons of scientific research according to J. S. Mill.

6. Distinguish between necessary and sufficient conditions.

7. Summarize the six steps of the traditional view of the scientific method.

8. Describe four traditional modes of scientific reasoning, indicating which ones are valid according to the rules of logic. Use the term "falsifiability" and the phrase "affirming the consequent" knowledgeably in your answer.

9. In two or three sentences each, summarize the contributions of the following to the development of hypothetico-deductive methods in science: logical positivism, A. Quetelet, R. A. Fisher.

10. Summarize Platt's (1964) four-step method of strong inference. Summarize any two concerns about this method based on O'Donohue & Buchanan (2001).

11. Compare and contrast the traditional perspective regarding variability or experimental error with the behavior-analytic perspective.

12. Describe how radical behaviorists address the matter of the reliability of data.

13. Distinguish between generality of and generality across.

14. Describe why an analysis employing aggregated data is not always valid.

15. Summarize the seven steps of behavior-analytic research methods.

16. Describe how radical behaviorists address the matter of the reversibility of behavioral processes.

17. List three reasons why meaningful psychological research can be carried out with nonhuman subjects.

18. Distinguish between the contexts of discovery and justification according to the traditional view.

19. Describe how radical behaviorists address this distinction.

12

Scientific Verbal Behavior: Theories

Synopsis of Chapter 12: Chapters 8 and 9 in this section focused on elementary and complex verbal relations, Chapter 10 focused on private events, and Chapter 11 focused on the nature of science and scientific research. Chapter 12 focuses on one form of scientific verbal behavior: theories. Theories are often regarded as the principal vehicle by which scientific knowledge is expressed. A coherent analysis of theorizing is therefore important from anyone's perspective. However, anyone's view of theorizing is derived from the underlying view of verbal behavior, and the subsequent extension of that view to what knowledge means. The present chapter first reviews theories from a traditional viewpoint. It then analyzes theorizing as verbal behavior, and seeks to outline sources of control over that verbal behavior. It proceeds then to an analysis of such representative issues as whether theories are more usefully interpreted from the standpoint of instrumentalism or realism. Throughout, the emphasis is on understanding theorizing as behaving verbally. Once theorizing is understood as behaving verbally, the way is clear to examine the contingencies responsible for the verbal behavior in question, to determine its function as a guide for effective action.

Writing in 1950, Skinner rhetorically posed the question "Are theories of learning necessary?" and suggested the answer was no. Largely because of this article, and because those who study scientific activity typically regard theories as the highest form of scientific activity, a sort of received view has developed among traditional psychologists about Skinner and other radical behaviorists. According to this view, radical behaviorists are no better than scientific Luddites who for some misguided reason insist on an epistemological stance that entails collecting and talking about data in the absence of

265

an organizing theoretical framework. The received view goes on to hold that this stance is clearly unworthy of serious scientific attention, and is to be tolerated only when it doesn't interfere with respectable scientific activity, which as everyone knows, involves proposing theories and then testing hypotheses deduced from the theories. Besides, the received view continues, radical behaviorists are probably engaging in some low-level theorizing anyway, even if they don't know it, and if they don't want to improve their proto-theories by formalizing them according to respectable procedures, so much the worse for the radical behaviorists. Indeed, this view seems especially strong among traditional psychologists, who since the advent of certain developments in scientific epistemology during the 1930s believe they know what merits serious scientific attention in the discipline of psychology, and what merits serious attention is the proposing and testing of theories. One passage that illustrates this received view is from Kendler and Spence (1971):

> [T]he radical positivistic position, at times enunciated by Skinner (1950), [is] that theories are unnecessary. The scientist's task is to manipulate events that are directly observable to discover the facts as they are, and nothing more....
>
> Skinner's atheoretical position has generated much confusion simply because it is itself unclear. It is one thing to state that at a particular time in the history of psychology the systematic collection of data without any theoretical preconceptions, but with a desire to control phenomena, may be more productive than self-conscious efforts to erect theoretical structures that cannot be supported by available empirical evidence. It is quite another thing to state that theories are unnecessary and should be ignored as a scientific goal. Skinner seems to maintain both of these positions, frequently arguing in favor of the latter, but defending it in terms of the former....
>
> In truth, the denial of the significance of the theoretical goal in psychology has been more of a debator's point than a controversy that reflects in actual practice two forms of scientific effort. Skinner himself has theorized extensively, in his efforts both to systematize the variables that determine behavior and to generalize from the operant conditioning situation to all aspects of life. But his theorizing has been covert and thus he has felt no need to defend his speculations. (pp. 21–22)

A second passage that illustrates the received view is from Williams (1986):

> All constructs, including those commonly employed by behavior analysts, are argued to be inherently hypothetical, because they provide a causal basis for extending empirical findings to new sets of variables. Moreover, the constructs employed by radical behaviorists (e.g., "reinforcement") are not qualitatively different from those often employed by cognitivists (e.g., "short-term memory"). The result is that much of the basis for recent criticisms of cognitive psychology by behaviorists disappears. To the extent that differences do remain it is not the qualitative nature of the two enterprises, but instead in attitudes about parsimony in the relation between data and theory.... I claim instead that all theoretical terms, including those commonly used by radical behaviorists who believe themselves to be following Skinner's positivistic dicta, involve the postulation of unobservable entities or processes as causes of behavior. In other words, theory construction inherently entails conjectures about a level of real-

ity not available for direct empirical observation, and the failure of radical behaviorists to appreciate this fact has created a needless schism between themselves and other approaches to psychology. (pp. 111-112)

Notwithstanding the disparaging tenor of the forgoing passages, it turns out that radical behaviorists have commented many times on just these matters. For example, concerning the matter of theories, it can be noted that as early as 1947, Skinner said:

> But the cataloguing of functional relationships is not enough. These are the basic facts of a science, but the accumulation of facts is not science itself. There are scientific handbooks containing hundreds of thousands of isolated facts—perhaps the most concentrated knowledge in existence—but these are not science. Physics is more than a collection of physical constants, just as chemistry is more than a statement of the properties of elements and compounds…. Behavior can only be satisfactorily understood by going beyond the facts themselves. What is needed is a theory of behavior…. [T]heories are based upon facts; they are statements about organizations of facts…. [W]ith proper operational care, they need be nothing more than that. But they have a wider generality which transcends particular facts and gives them a wider usefulness…. [E]xperimental psychology is properly and inevitably committed to the construction of a theory of behavior. A theory is essential to the scientific understanding of behavior as a subject matter. (Skinner, 1972, pp. 301–302, original published 1947)

The bottom line is that if the received view mentioned at the beginning of this chapter, that Skinner and other radical behaviorists eschew theories, is accurate, then the question arises as to how Skinner could have written that "experimental psychology is properly and inevitably committed to the construction of a theory of behavior. A theory is essential to the scientific understanding of behavior as a subject matter." The aim of this chapter is to clarify the radical behaviorist perspective on theories, particularly as expressed in the words of Skinner. The way is then open to clarify the radical behaviorist perspective on explanation, which is addressed in Chapter 13.

THE TRADITIONAL VIEW

A more specific outline of the view held by traditional psychologists is helpful in framing the issues for discussion. The traditional view is largely derived from logical positivism and logical empiricism that began during the 1930s. It may be summarized in the following way (e.g., Moore, 1998):

1. Theories are the ultimate objective of science.   A theory may be regarded as a set of propositions concerning some natural phenomena and consisting of symbolic representations of: (a) observed relations among events, (b) observed variables, mechanisms, and structures underlying observed relations, and (c) inferred or unobserved variables, mechanisms, and structures necessary to complete the account of observed relations. The job of the philosopher of science is (a) to provide

a rational reconstruction of scientific theories in the language of formal logic, (b) to formulate the underlying theoretical laws in a logically consistent manner, and (c) to determine the logical implications of the theories, although strictly speaking the implications are not parts of theories.

2. Theories have two scientific functions.   The first is to promote explanations of observed events. In turn, there are two common types of explanation, instantiation and deduction from a covering law:

   a. Instantiation.   In instantiation, the current observation is regarded as explained when it can be described as a specific instance of a more general expression (e.g., equation or model), with specific values of variables or parameters in the expression. In one common usage, the variables or parameters are "estimated" after the fact, with the result that the statement thereby describes the data in question. In this form of explanation, the mathematical model along with the set of assumptions for its application is often referred to as a theory.

   b. Deduction from a covering law.   In the covering law type of explanation (Hempel & Oppenheim, 1948), the current observation is regarded as explained when its description follows as a valid logical deduction in an argument that has a "covering law" as one premise and a statement of antecedent conditions as another premise. In this form of explanation, also known as the Deductive-Nomological model, the covering law is some reasonably lawlike generalization, often expressed in formal terms and referred to as a theory.

3. The second function of theories is to generate predictions.   In instantiation, the prediction is that future observations will conform to the general expression, allowing for different specific values of variables or parameters. In the covering law approach, explanation, description, and prediction are regarded as symmetrical activities. For example, if the antecedent conditions are described in the past tense, the conclusion or deduction would similarly employ the past tense, and is called an explanation. However, if the antecedent conditions are described in the future tense, as in as-yet-unexamined conditions, the conclusion or deduction would similarly employ the future tense, and is called a prediction. The form of the argument is the same throughout. Predictions are an essential element of a theory, as they can be subjected to empirical test. The hypothetico-deductive technique is then regarded as the engine that drives scientific activity.

4. Theories are necessary for explaining events in two ways:

   a. They cannot be avoided in practice.   According to this argument, one must engage in theoretical activity if one is to truly explain any phenomenon. Anything else is merely description.

b. Theories are uniquely appropriate to the logical processes by means of which humans acquire knowledge. This argument is similar to (a) above, except that this argument concerns assumptions about what knowledge is, and how scientists become knowledgeable, rather than about the subject matter.

5. Theories may be evaluated according to the following criteria:

a. Testability: Can data inconsistent with the theory be specified a priori? Does a method exist for checking the theory against these data? A theory that cannot specify the data and the method by which they are to be checked is regarded as inadequate in principle.

b. Validity: Can the theory adequately account accounting for the observation in question? One theory is regarded as better than another if it provides a better (e.g., better organized, more internally consistent) accounting for the observation. Indeed, scientific activity that is not coordinated with a theory is deemed to be risky at best, or bankrupt otherwise, because the activity is not tied together by a framework that effectively organizes it.

c. Utility: Does the theory synthesize a large number of observations? One theory is regarded as better than another if it synthesizes a larger number of observations.

d. Parsimony: Is the theory simple? Given that two theories are plausible, one theory is regarded as better than another if it is simpler.

e. Heuristic value: Does the theory suggest new lines of research? Can it predict what will happen in as-yet-unexamined situations? One theory is regarded as better than another if it suggests more new lines of research, with novel predictions.

6. Theories consist of three sorts of scientific terms: (a) logical terms, (b) observational terms, and (c) theoretical terms. Logical terms indicate logical operations and relations, such as conjunction, disjunction, subset of, and so on. Observational terms indicate entities and properties directly measured by one's apparatus. Theoretical terms do not refer to anything that is directly observed or measured, but they are nevertheless critical to theorizing. They come in two varieties: (a) intervening variables, and (b) hypothetical constructs. Intervening variables are true logical constructs. They exist only by dint of human verbal creation, and do not refer to anything that exists in the world at large. They are wholly bound by the empirical relations they portray, and they do not allow surplus meaning beyond their systematizing role in a particular scientific statement. They simply summarize existing relations in an economical or shorthand way. Consequently, their operational definitions are said to be "exhaustive." In contrast, hypothetical constructs do refer to entities or processes that exist in some sense in the world at large. They refer to phenomena that are unobserved in

a given setting, but evidence for them could presumably be gathered, given suitable equipment. They are not entirely reducible to empirical terms, and they do allow surplus meaning beyond their role in a particular scientific statement. Consequently, their operational definitions are said to be only "partial" or "incomplete." Again, both varieties of theoretical terms are "unobservable," but the basis for saying they are unobservable differs for the two terms. Intervening variables are unobservable because they do not refer to things that actually exist. Hypothetical constructs presumably refer to things and properties and entities and so on that are not directly measured, but that may be inferred to actually exist on the basis of whatever evidence is available, although they haven't been directly observed. Moreover, because hypothetical constructs are inferred to exist, they presumably have other properties as well.

7. Psychology should formulate theories, and these theories are permitted to have elements that refer to unobservable, inferred phenomena.

8. Technically, most elements that refer to unobservable phenomena in psychological theories should be regarded as hypothetical constructs, rather than intervening variables:

   a. They mediate causality.

   b. They are heuristic, meaning that they stimulate other ideas and other possibilities about variables and relations to examine.

   c. They are parsimonious and simplify the subject matter under consideration. Given m independent variables and n dependent variables, the use of mediating hypothetical constructs means researchers need only explore (m + n) relations, instead of (m x n) relations.

   d. They afford greater degrees of freedom in theory construction.   Recall that hypothetical constructs are only partially defined in terms of observables, whereas intervening variables are exhaustively defined. The "Theoretician's Dilemma" is that, on the one hand, if the intervening variable is not helpful, it would surely not be used, but if it is helpful, it technically is superfluous as it adds nothing beyond what is already available. In neither case is its use justified. The surplus meaning of hypothetical constructs allows theorists to escape from the horns of the Theoretician's Dilemma and are therefore the preferred form of theoretical terms.

9. What if theories are incorrect in some sense (Harré, 1960)? In general, theorists take one of three steps:

   a. Maintain the theory but acknowledge that some findings may differ for an unknown reason.

b. State that the theory has limitations, and that the contrary findings lie outside the domain to which the theory is intended to apply.

c. Modify the theory in such as way as to accommodate the new findings. As Williams (1986) noted, this step is prevalent in much scientific work. Typically, theorists attempt to incorporate apparent disconfirmations by adding auxiliary assumptions to their original theory. The resulting, more elaborate theories are then evaluated not so much by whether they can account for the data (the auxiliary statements almost certainly allow the theorist to do so), but rather by whether the auxiliary assumptions are plausible and worth the loss of parsimony.

10. In sum, according to the traditional view, the important thing is whether a theory allows one to predict an outcome in terms of publicly observable data.   So long as terms or concepts in a psychological theory can be operationally defined, it is perfectly acceptable to appeal to inferred, unobservable terms, even mental or cognitive, and then render them as theoretical. The rationale is that other sciences have incorporated inferred, unobservable variables, mechanisms, and structures as theoretical, so why not psychology? Operational definitions and inferential logic are held to preserve the rigor of the theory. Indeed, appeal to inferred, unobservable terms might even be desirable, because of their heuristic value. At best, in a traditional view Skinner's radical behaviorism is held to be merely descriptive, not explanatory, because it doesn't meet the conventional requirements of a theory as outlined above. Although Skinner's radical behaviorism may try to achieve a theoretical explanation of an event, its statements don't observe conventional requirements, so they can't be seriously considered either theories or explanations. It is better to dismiss them, as well as the radical behaviorism that is responsible for them, entirely.

THEORIES AS VERBAL BEHAVIOR

How, then, do radical behaviorists deal with all these matters? A reasonable place to start is by recognizing that to theorize is to behave verbally, and theories are encountered as products of verbal behavior. Accordingly, the place to start with the analysis of theories is with the contingencies that govern their emission. Skinner (1945) framed the matter in the following way:

> A considerable advantage is gained from dealing with terms, concepts, constructs, and so on, quite frankly in the form in which they are observed—namely, as verbal responses. There is then no danger of including in the concept that aspect or part of nature which it singles out…. Meanings, contents, and references are to be found among the determiners, not among the properties, of response. (p. 271)

In this passage, written at a particular time in a particular context for a particular audience, Skinner eschewed one common approach to theories, according to which: (a) a
theory symbolically postulates, represents, or refers to some part of nature that is
unobservable, perhaps even in principle, but nevertheless inferred to be metaphysically
real and permanent; and (b) if one wishes to analyze scientific activity, one must systematically establish the correspondence between the verbal elements of the theory and
the part of nature identified by the verbal elements. Additional discussion regarding
this point may be found in the section below dealing with positions called
"instrumentalism" and "realism." In any case, suffice it to note at this point that according to Skinner's alternative view, the "meaning" of verbal behavior, including the scientific verbal behavior called "theoretical," was to be found among the independent
variables, rather than the structure of the dependent variable. Thus, the way to begin an
analysis of the impact or meaning of a theory is to assess the factors that cause theorists
to propose their theories in the way that they do, rather than accept that the terms in the
theory refer to real things, and then try to extract meaning from the logical arrangement
of terms in the theory (i.e., from the "properties of response").

Clearly, then, the radical behaviorist position on theories follows from the radical
behaviorist position on verbal behavior. The radical behaviorist position on verbal
behavior is just that—a behavioral position, appealing to behavioral processes—and
not a referential position, appealing to logical or symbolic processes. Most of the criticisms levied against the radical behaviorist position assume that a logical, referential, or symbolic position is correct. According to a referential position, words or
terms should be regarded as constructs that somehow refer to things, events, or properties that either exist independently or via human logical manipulations. Skinner
(e.g., 1957) commented so extensively on the shortcomings of the referential approach that readers are encouraged to consult his writing. Suffice it to say that problems such as the ones Williams (1986) identifies above involve viewing any term as a
"construct" that must have a referent to be meaningful. This stance has been a feature
of the approach that traditional psychology routinely takes to verbal behavior, but
that radical behaviorism never takes, and hence is a source of much confusion for
those who criticize radical behaviorism.

In particular, radical behaviorism rejects the sorts of mentalistic theories that appeal
to unobserved events and entities that take place somewhere else, at some other level of
observation, in a different dimension (neural, psychic, "mental," cognitive, subjective,
conceptual, hypothetical) in which those events and entities must be described in different terms (Skinner, 1950, p.193). Radical behaviorism further rejects the assumption that theorizing in psychology, and psychological knowledge in general, consists in
framing such theories. Indeed, radical behaviorism argues that the assumption that psychological knowledge necessarily consists in the formulation of such theories is a further illustration of the same mentalistic problem. Thus, Skinner put it as follows:

The theories to which objection is raised here are not the basic assumptions essential to any scientific activity or statements that are not yet facts, but rather explanations which appeal to
events taking place somewhere else, at some other level of observation, described in different
terms, and measured, if at all, in different dimensions…. Theory is possible in another sense.
Beyond the collection of uniform relationships lies the need for a formal representation of the
data reduced to a minimal number of terms. A theoretical construction may yield greater generality than any assemblage of facts; such a construction will not refer to another dimensional
system. (Skinner in Catania & Harnad, 1988, p. 77)

A further understanding of the radical behaviorist position on theories may be
gained by examining certain other of Skinner's writings on scientific epistemology,
and in particular, writings in which Skinner used the term *theory*. For instance, in one
article, Skinner (1947/1972) followed an avowedly Machian line of reasoning and
more explicitly outlined three important steps in the development of a theory:

The first step in building a theory is to identify the basic data….

Since we have not clearly identified the significant data of a science of behavior, we do not arrive
well prepared at the second stage of theory building, at which we are to express relations among
data…. A weakness at the first stage of theory construction cannot be corrected at the second….

This step—at the third stage in theory building—can be exemplified by a simple example from
the science of mechanics. Galileo, with the help of his predecessors, began by restricting himself to a limited set of data. He proposed to deal with the positions of bodies at given times,
rather than with their color or hardness or size. This decision, characteristic of the first stage in
building a theory, was not so easy as it seems to us today. Galileo then proceeded to demonstrate the relation between position and time—the position of a ball on an inclined plan and the
time which had elapsed since its release. Something else then emerged—namely, the concept
of acceleration. Later, as other facts were added, other concepts appeared—mass, force, and so
on. Third-stage concepts of this sort are something more than the second-stage laws from
which they are derived. They are peculiarly the product of theory-making in the best sense, and
they cannot be arrived at through any other process.

There are few, if any, clear-cut examples of comparable third-stage concepts in psychology,
and the crystal ball grows cloudy…. When it is possible to complete a theoretical analysis at
this stage, concepts of this sort will be put in good scientific order….

From all of this should emerge a new conception of the individual as the locus of a system of
variables… A proper theory must be able to represent the multiplicity of response systems. It
must do something more: it must abolish the conception of the individual as a doer, as an originator of action. This is a difficult task. The simple fact is that psychologists have never made a
thoroughgoing renunciation of the inner man. He is surreptitiously appealed to from time to
time in all our thinking, especially when we are faced with a bit of behavior which is difficult to
explain otherwise. (pp. 305–308)

The radical behaviorist objection to traditional approaches to theorizing is that many
"theoretical" statements in psychology have not gone through anything remotely re-
sembling a developmental process, three stages or otherwise. Theorists often pride
themselves on their creativity or insight, but what they don't recognize is that the verbal
responses themselves are controlled to a large extent by factors that are cherished for ir-

relevant and extraneous reasons. Their verbal responses are the product of many mentalistic if not dualistic factors; they consist of many unfortunate metaphorical extensions, and so on. The verbal responses appeal to other dimensions at the first and second stages, and consequently get off track. The implication is that as a result of these mentalistic influences, the stimulus control over what are hailed as advanced third-stage activities is suspect. Skinner's (1950) argument was that it was simply not necessary that the first- and second-stage activities be carried out according to a theory. They can "proceed in a rather Baconian fashion" (Skinner, 1969, p. 82). Indeed, as Skinner has noted, it may even be wasteful to conduct research at this level that presumes to test a theory. The appropriate base needs to be established before useful third-step concepts will appear, and in many cases psychology is so contaminated by mentalism that it has not gone through the appropriate prior steps to establish that base.

In a related discussion of these matters, Skinner (1953) endorsed Mach's position that the first laws and theories of a science were probably rules developed by artisans who worked in a given area. As these individuals interacted with nature, they developed skilled repertoires. Descriptions of the effects brought about by relevant practices were then codified in the form of verbal statements that functioned as verbal stimuli, the purpose of which was to occasion effective action. The verbal statements, often taking the form of maxims or other informal expressions (e.g., "rules"), supplemented or replaced private or idiosyncratic forms of stimulus control. The verbal stimuli became public property and were transmitted as part of the culture, enabling others to behave effectively. The first- and second-stage activities of which Skinner talked presumably reflected this sort of activity.

However, science progressed beyond just these lower-level activities, to develop higher- order statements and concepts. A relevant passage is as follows:

> [Science] is a search for order, for uniformities, for lawful relations among the events in nature. It begins, as we all begin, by observing single episodes, but it quickly passes on to the general rule, to scientific law.... As Ernst Mach showed in tracing the history of the science of mechanics, the earliest laws of science were probably the rules used by craftsmen and artisans in training apprentices.... In a later stage science advances from the collection of rules or laws to larger systematic arrangements. Not only does it make statements about the world, it makes statements about statements. (Skinner, 1953, pp. 13–14)

Many scientific laws and theories therefore have the character of statements that specify the relation between responses and their consequences. In this regard, scientific laws and theories are not statements that are obeyed by nature. Rather, scientific laws and theories are statements that exert discriminative control over individuals who need to deal effectively with nature. As Skinner (1969) put it in one place:

> Scientific laws also specify or imply responses and their consequences. They are not, of course, obeyed by nature but by men who deal effectively with nature. The formula $s = \frac{1}{2} gt^2$ does not

govern the behavior of falling bodies, it governs those who correctly predict the position of falling bodies at given times. (p. 141)

Here again are the familiar Baconian and Machian themes about statements that organize observations and facilitate desired outcomes.

Finally, readers may recall the earlier passage from Skinner (1947/1972), in which he emphasized the theme that theories are "based upon facts; they are statements about organizations of facts" (p. 302). Skinner's statements here presumably concern more advanced, third-stage scientific formulations. Skinner's statements are presumably consistent with Russell's (1932) comment that cause and effect statements may turn out to be absent from certain scientific renderings:

> All philosophers, of every school, imagine that causation is one of the fundamental axioms or postulates of science, yet, oddly enough, in advanced sciences such as gravitational astronomy, the word "cause" never occurs. (p. 180)

What was Russell's alternative? In the empiricist tradition of his time, Russell (1932) embraced the position noted earlier by Mach:

> We then considered the nature of scientific laws, and found that, instead of stating that one event A is always followed by another event B, they stated functional relations between certain events at certain times, which we called determinants, and other events at earlier or later times or at the same time. (pp. 207–208)

The early stages of Skinner's intellectual development were much influenced by Russell's epistemology, and Skinner represents a unique blend of Bacon, Mach, and Russell. Skinner's point in his analysis of theories is that statements of facts identifying cause-and-effect relations may well be conspicuous at the first and second stages of theory development, but the terms cause and effect may be absorbed into higher-order, third-stage statements taken as theories because of the verbal processes inherent in their development. Of course, for Russell, mere observation was not always going to be adequate. Observation had to be supplemented by the application of rigorous logic. Hence, Russell (1932) noted, "Whenever possible, logical constructions are to be substituted for inferred entities" (p. 155). For Russell, then, description supplemented by logical or mathematical formulations became the benchmark for scientific theorizing. Although Skinner was much influenced by Russell, Skinner did stop short of embracing formal logic in the same way as Russell.

MULTIPLE CONTROL

To be sure, many sets of variables, rather than just one set of variables, often control the scientific verbal behavior called theoretical. Thus, verbal behavior regarded as theoretical is often under "multiple control" (Skinner, 1957, pp. 227 ff.). As Moore (1981) noted, some of the stimulus control derives from experimental operations and contacts with data. Other control derives from other sources.

For example, some theoretical verbal behavior simply manifests "control by ordinary language habits, extensive chains of familiar intraverbals, and one or another preconception about the inherent nature of scientific explanation" (Day, 1969, p. 323). As Day (1969, p. 319) noted, the traditional conception assumes that the chief function of language is to identify the essential Platonic or Kantian properties in another dimension that endow the things with their inherent identities. This position is clearly evident in Williams (1986), who stated that "theory construction inherently entails conjectures about a level of reality not available for direct empirical observation" (p. 112). At best, such reification and talk of levels of reality only illustrate the "Formalistic Fallacy" of invoking hypothetical constructs, if not outright psychophysical dualism (Skinner, 1969, p. 265).

Other theoretical verbal behavior manifests control by metaphors and social or cultural factors that are cherished for irrelevant and extraneous reasons. For example, memory is traditionally characterized using the metaphor of storage and retrieval. This metaphor is a popular one in the culture, and talk of memory typically assumes that an all-directing inner agent of a mind directs the "encoding" of incoming information, its assignment to some storage location, and its calling up when needed. Currently, the metaphor of computer technology, with basic input-output systems and routines for switching information from one location to another, not to mention short- and long-term storage facilities (volatile versus nonvolatile memory in random-access versus read-only memory of a computer), fits comfortably into traditional verbal behavior about memory. To be sure, organisms are changed by their experiences, but to talk of organisms as storing information or memories or experiences presupposes conceptual schemes grounded in culturally inspired mentalism. For radical behaviorism, the changed organism is what is "stored," not a copy of an event called a memory. The result is that the organism responds differently when stimulated in the future. Physiological processes are, of course, transpiring as the organism is changed, no doubt related to protein synthesis, and traumatic events such as bumps to the head can interrupt the processes. These processes can be investigated using appropriate techniques. Mentalistic talk of minds and copies that are stored and retrieved does little to shed light on those underlying physiological processes.

In sum, behavior analysis is concerned with the contingencies that are responsible for a given instance of verbal behavior, and the contingencies into which the verbal artifact subsequently enters as it exerts discriminative control among those who entertain it. This concern applies to the scientific verbal activity called theorizing just as much as any other kind of verbal activity. The radical behaviorist argument is that to understand the validity of scientific theorizing, one must operationally analyze scientific verbal behavior and strip away any control that arises from these mischievous metaphors and social or cultural factors, leaving only the factors producing such things as manipulation and control. Mathematics can be a particularly effective way to remove superfluous stimulus control arising from inappropriate sources. In keeping with the emphasis on viewing theories as verbal behavior, Skinner (1957) put it as follows:

> The scientific community encourages the precise stimulus control under which an object or property of an object is identified or characterized in such a way that practical action will be most effective.... Generic extensions are tolerated in scientific practice, but metaphorical, metonymical, and solecistic extensions are usually extinguished or punished. Metaphorical extension may occur, but either the controlling property is quickly emphasized by additional contingencies which convert the response into an abstraction or the metaphor is robbed of its metaphorical nature through the advent of additional stimulus control.... In ruling out the effects of other consequences of verbal behavior the contingencies established by the scientific community work to prevent exaggeration or understatement, misrepresentation, lying, and fiction.... Scientific verbal behavior is most effective when it is free of multiple sources of strength; and humor, wit, style, the devices of poetry, and fragmentary recombinations and distortions of form all go unreinforced, if they are not actually punished, by the scientific community.... In general, however, practices are designed to clarify the relation between a verbal response made to a verbal stimulus and the nonverbal circumstances responsible for it. The community is concerned with getting back to the original state of affairs and with avoiding any distortion due to the intervening verbal linkage.... (pp. 419–420)

Figure 12–1 presents the sense of multiple control graphically. In this figure, the contingency is presented for scientific verbal behavior: the discriminative stimulus, the verbal response, and the reinforcer. One source of control arises from operations and contacts with data, and leads to effective prediction and control. Another source of control arises from normative social and cultural traditions, linguistic practices, and metaphors. This source involves social and cultural reinforcement from other members of society for acting in conventional ways. Much scientific verbal behavior is a blend of these two sources. However, within the blend, mentalistic scientific verbal behavior occurs and raises difficulties when the second source outweighs the first.

THEORIES: INSTRUMENTALISM OR REALISM?

Generally, analyses of scientific epistemology recognize two interpretations of how scientific theories are intended to function. The first is instrumentalism. According to this interpretation, theories imply nothing about the world at large. Rather, they are simply convenient, conventionally accepted ways of talking about events. This interpretation is sometimes also called conventionalism. The second is realism. The version of realism of interest here is not an assumption that there is in fact a material, physical

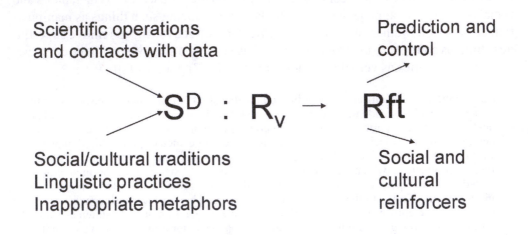

Figure 12.1   The multiple control of scientific verbal behavior.

world that has objects and properties, but rather an assumption that words identify elements of a metaphysical reality that is universal, independent of any object currently under consideration. This interpretation is sometimes also called essentialism. A review of these two interpretations of scientific theories and their relation to behavior analysis is instructive.

Instrumentalism

According to instrumentalism, the goal of science is to generate new concepts that mediate prediction and explanation. Theories and their associated theoretical concepts are therefore conventionally accepted instruments that enable scientists to derive new statements about observables from other statements about observables (Suppe, 1977). Any theoretical concepts included in a theory need not be construed as referring to phenomena that actually exist in the world at large, although they may exist by virtue of human construction. Perhaps the theory states that it is "as if" the phenomena exist, but no other commitment is made. Instrumentalism is linked with the work of Henri Poincaré in the late nineteenth and early twentieth centuries, who argued that scientific laws are rules for successful action (Skinner, 1979, p. 83). Given MacCorquodale and Meehl's (1948) distinction between intervening variables and hypothetical constructs, theoretical concepts in an instrumentalist view of theories are interpreted as intervening variables.

In this view, the important question about a theory concerns its range of application, rather than whether the theory is true or false in the way an empirical proposition is true or false. A theory is regarded as a statement of properties and relations pertaining to a given set of events. The application of a theory to a particular set of events is to be decided on the basis of empirical evidence. Statements about the range of a theory's application can be true or false, but not the theory itself (e.g., Toulmin, 1953; Turner, 1967).

Realism

The second interpretation of theories is realism. Originally, the realists were scholastic philosophers who, while quibbling over the exegesis of Aristotle, held that categories are defined by essential properties that transcend specific instances of the categories. For example, the category of white things is defined as those elements that possess the property of "whiteness." Whiteness is an essence, a "thing" that is known in its own right through experience with white objects. Instances within a category might vary widely, but they were all seen as variants of a single template. Individual variability is explained as the outcome of less fundamental factors—accident, random processes, or other vicissitudes. The origin of the template itself is generally unexplained. The position can be traced back, in some form, to Plato and Parmenides (Palmer & Donahoe, 1992).

The realist interpretation of theories has three premises: (a) the aim of science is to find a true theory or description of the world (and especially of its regularities or "laws"), which shall also provide an explanation of the observable facts; (b) science can succeed in finally establishing the truth of such theories beyond all reasonable doubt; and (c) the best and truly scientific theories describe the "essential properties" of things—the realities that lie beyond appearances; such theories are ultimate explanations, and to find them is the ultimate aim of the scientist (Suppe, 1977).

The realist argues that the goal of science is to discover new concepts that represent real phenomena in nature. In this view, any theoretical concepts included in a theory are construed as real phenomena that actually exist in the world at large, and that may be directly observed or indirectly inferred through their effects (for a brief discussion of realism and "existence claims," see Suppe, 1977, pp. 566–570). Given MacCorquodale and Meehl's (1948) distinction between intervening variables and hypothetical constructs, theoretical concepts in a realist view of theories are interpreted as hypothetical constructs.

Analysis

In the radical behaviorist perspective, the traditional approach and both instrumentalist and realist interpretations of theories and theoretical concepts are troublesome. All entail a tacit commitment to a reference theory of language. That is, all assume that a theoretical term is a thing that must refer or correspond to another thing. For instrumentalism, the thing exists in the mind of the scientist. For realism, the thing exists in the world at large. Given this commitment to a reference theory of language, there is hardly any distinction between instrumentalism and realism, despite what is conventionally regarded as an adequate means for distinguishing between them.

Moreover, the traditional approach and appeals to either instrumentalism or realism are inherently representational. Representationalism holds that immediately given phenomena are representative of events or processes taking place at some other level or in some other dimensional system. Representationalism assumes extra-dimensional processes on the part of the knower are involved in forming or responding on the basis of the representation. The postulation of a theory is the essential means by which the theorist gains access to the other dimension.

As an alternative to the traditional approach, radical behaviorism seeks to distinguish itself from traditional concerns with instrumentalism, realism, and representationalism. It seeks to do so by addressing the assumptions underlying assertions that instrumentalist considerations justify the use of theoretical terms and the disregard of questions of ontology. Presumably, the hypothetical construct is not useful because it affords some unique logico-theoretical insight into another dimension. That kind of insight does not exist for anybody, including those who appeal to hypothetical constructs. There is no such dimension, so there can be no such insight. Similarly, the hypothetical construct is not useful because it correctly takes advantage of the underlying mental processes of the scientist. Those kinds of processes do not exist for anybody either, especially for those who appeal to hypothetical constructs, despite their statements to the contrary. Readers may recall Skinner's comment that "The hypothetico- deductive method and the mystery which surrounds it have been perhaps most harmful in misrepresenting ways in which people think" (Skinner in Catania & Harnad, 1988, p. 102).

Instrumentalism and the use of theoretical concepts are often justified by arguments that knowledge of any sort is actually derived from the manipulation of subjective or cognitive entities in the theorist's mental world, apart from the theorist's behavioral world. Therefore, employing fictions is perfectly acceptable; fictions are all there are for anyone to employ anyway. That is what the human mind creates when it tries to become knowledgeable (e.g., "[O]ne of the components of theory is the generation of useful fictions. That's what theories are about," George Mandler in Baars, 1986, p. 255). The proof of the pudding, so to speak, lies in the ability to mediate prediction.

Radical behaviorism adopts an explicitly pragmatic orientation to the matter of theories and scientific verbal behavior. As is discussed more extensively in Chapter 17, pragmatism is an orientation based on practical outcomes: The significance of a statement is explicitly held to be a function of how well the statement promotes effective action. At first blush, instrumentalism seems equivalent to pragmatism. However, the perspective presented here (which is actually the appropriate interpretation of Skinner's position; cf. Williams, 1986) dissociates pragmatism from instrumentalist justifications of certain kinds of theories, from realism and the use of hypothetical constructs, and from representationalism. The important question about pragmatism may then be phrased in the following way: If a theoretical term promotes effective action, such as prediction and control, on what basis does it do so? The answer does not have anything to do with the logical status of the theoretical term, or with any of the other issues raised by the traditional approach. Terms are not things that correspond to objects in the mind of the scientist or in world at large and that need to be validated through a logical analysis. Theoretical terms are not essentially logical phenomena. They are verbal phenomena. The strict interpretation of instrumentalism would not ask why a term seems to promote effective action, although pragmatism would, and therein lies the distinction between instrumentalism and pragmatism.

Because theoretical terms are verbal rather than logical phenomena, the important issue again concerns the contingencies that are involved in the verbal processes in question. The fundamental question is: "What are the contingencies that control the occurrence of the term, as an instance of verbal behavior?" Thus, one may meaningfully ask: "In what sense is the 'theoretical term' an abstraction, an extended tact, or a constructed tact?" The issue is not simply the percent of variance accounted for in a mathematical model when one envisions the theoretical term as referring to a metaphysical entity. The issue is that if a given theoretical term aids the scientific endeavor, it does so because of its impact on the discriminative repertoires involved. If the term is helpful, it is so because of its contact with the one dimension. Lines of latitude and longitude don't literally exist on the face of the Earth, but rather are tacts constructed on the basis of geographic distances. Their origin is in the one dimension of the world in which any organism lives, not some fanciful other dimension, such as the ones in which the hypothetical constructs of traditional psychology reside. Therefore, a meaningful analysis views the issue as a matter of identifying the stimulus control involved (a) in the provenance of the term as an instance of verbal behavior; and (b) in the application of the term among the scientists for whom it facilitates effective action in the world at large.

Several passages from past and current behavioristic theorists have proposed what appear to be pragmatic positions. For example, Spence (1936) talked about justifying constructs "wholly from the pragmatic standpoint that they serve as an aid to the integration and comprehension of the observed phenomena" (p. 447). Similarly, Amsel (1989) argues that neobehaviorist theoretical terms should be judged "by their success in organizing that segment of the describable world they set out to organize" (p. 59). Killeen (1995) argues from what appears to be a pragmatic perspective when he suggests that the important issue concerning constructs is "whether they pay their way in the cost-benefit ratio of constructs to predictions" (p. 407). However, in the view presented here, any link between these positions and pragmatism is more apparent than real. Rather, these positions reflect instrumentalism and representationalism, rather than pragmatism. They make no effort to operationally analyze the statement to determine the source of control, and to operationally analyze whether the statement could be refined so as to be even more precise. Moreover, when the theorists then embrace a hypothetical-construct interpretation of theoretical terms, which they do when they talk of surplus meaning of the terms, the positions then mischievously shift to realism, and theorists set out in pursuit of all sorts of fanciful processes and entities in other dimensions that are only incidentally related to what might actually be manipulated to control events in the world at large.

A brief examination of research into motivational processes underlying feeding and satiety provides a convenient example. For many years, theorists supposed that one brain region, the lateral hypothalamus (LH), was the brain "center" responsible for eating, and another brain region, the ventromedial nucleus of the hypothalamus (VMH), was the brain "center" responsible for satiety. Initially, these ideas were spawned by empirical findings that lesioning of the LH decreased eating, whereas stimulation increased eating. Similarly, lesioning of the VMH increased eating, whereas stimulation decreased eating. Subsequent research has shown that these ideas were not encouragingly general. For example, if the LH was actually the center that switches on eating, an LH lesion would interfere with the switch, such that eating would not get turned on correctly. Hence, one would expect that rats with lesions to the LH would permanently show a weight reduction. They do not. Similarly, if the VMH was actually the satiety center that switches off eating, a VMH lesion would interfere with the switch, such that eating would not be turned off correctly. Hence, one would expect that subjects such as rats with lesions to the VMH would generally perform an operant response to a much greater extent than control subjects with food as a reinforcer. They do not.

The crucial question concerns the idea of a single localized "center" that controls a motivational process. A center is no doubt a convenient device for representing a motivational process, and many researchers assume there is nothing wrong with postulating such a device as a theoretical entity. Clearly, the various structures of the hypothalamus do respond to levels of blood glucose and hormones emanating from the gut during digestion. Researchers may well have linked their theoretical concepts such as a center to their data, justifying the link by its seeming to organize and represent a valid idea. However, from the radical behaviorist perspective, analysis of verbal behavior would have revealed that it was premature to talk of "centers" in the proposed sense. Rather, talk of a center may ultimately owe its strength to the longstanding cultural concept of an internal, all-powerful regulator, such as a religious soul or the secular equivalent of mind. Recall that Descartes talked of the pineal gland as the portal through which the soul agitated animal spirits to produce voluntary, willful, purposive behavior. Current theorizing speaks of an "executive" in the pre-frontal cortex of the human brain. The point remains that research has subsequently showed the factors controlling eating and satiety are diffuse throughout the brain, with many structures and pathways that are implicated, rather than localized. Lesions and stimulation of the LH and VMH obviously do produce effects, but not because the lesions are interfering with a central controlling entity, just as lesions of the pineal gland obviously do produce effects, but not because the lesions are interfering with the portal through which the soul influences the body.

SUMMARY AND CONCLUSIONS

Clearly, theories are an essential element of the epistemological stance in radical behaviorism, and always have been. However, radical behaviorists view theories as products of verbal behavior. In their worst sense, theories promoted explanations of observed facts that appealed to events taking place somewhere else, at some other level of observation, described in different terms, and measured, if at all, in different dimensions (e.g., Skinner, 1950). In their best sense, theories were abstract, economical descriptions of facts, reduced to a minimal number of terms. They promoted efficiency of practice and simplicity of expression. Theories in their best sense come at the conclusion of a developmental process. They may have begun as laws of craftsmen, then progressed to statements identifying basic data, then to statements of basic relations in the data, and finally to statements about organizations of facts, including higher-order abstractions. Radical behaviorists value operational analyses of theories and other instances of analytic scientific language because they reveal the nature of the contingencies that control scientific verbal behavior, rather than because operational analyses promote agreement among practitioners. In other words, operational analyses reveal the sources of control over the verbal behavior, and from those sources, the possibilities for prediction and control.

Skinner himself stated numerous times that he came to psychology because of the possibilities it offered for understanding distinctly human phenomena, such as knowledge claims. Skinner then extended his ideas on verbal behavior into the realm of logical and scientific behavior and ultimately to the pragmatic stance of radical behaviorism. Skinner spoke disparagingly of the low practical value of much of instantiation and the attendant appeals to mathematical models in many instrumentalist approaches when he said:

> Early techniques available for the study of learning—from the nonsense syllables of Ebbinghaus, through the problem boxes of Thorndike and the mazes of Watson, to the discrimination apparatuses of Yerkes and Lashley—always yielded learning curves of disturbing irregularity. In experiments with these instruments an orderly change in the behavior of a single organism was seldom seen. Orderly processes had to be generated by averaging data, either for many trials or many organisms. Even so, the resulting "learning curves" varied in a disturbing way from experiment to experiment. The theoretical solution to this problem was to assume that an orderly learning process, which always had the same properties regardless of the particular features of a given experiment, took place somewhere inside the organism. A given result was accounted for by making a distinction between learning and performance. Though the performance might be chaotic, the psychologist could continue to cherish the belief that learning

was always orderly. Indeed, the mathematical organism seemed so orderly that model builders remained faithful to techniques which consistently yielded disorderly data. An examination of mathematical models in learning theory will show that no degree of disorder in the facts has placed any restriction on the elegance of the mathematical treatment.... At the moment we make little effective use of empirical, let alone rational, equations.... But the most elementary preliminary research shows that there are many relevant variables, and until their importance has been experimentally determined, an equation which allows for them will have so many arbitrary constants that a good fit will be a matter of course and cause for very little satisfaction. (Skinner in Catania & Harnad, 1988, pp. 82–83, 101)

Thus, for Skinner and radical behaviorism, much of science seeks to generate rules or theories as verbal discriminative stimuli for deriving reinforcers from nature. The entire process is a verbal process, based on a behavioral rather than logical view of verbal behavior. For that matter, what is called a "logical view of verbal behavior" will itself be explained in behavioral terms. In the end, this behavioral view proposes nothing less than the operational analysis of both (a) the nature of the discriminative control over the verbal behavior in question, and (b) the nature of discriminative control exerted by the verbal behavior in question. Analyses of this sort of control reveal the function of theories. Given that the topic of theories has now been reviewed, the next chapter in this section reviews a second form of scientific verbal behavior: explanations.

TABLE 12–1

Traditional view of theories
A set of propositions concerning some natural phenomena and consisting of symbolic representations of :
   a. observed relations among events
   b. observed variables, mechanisms, and structures underlying observed relations
   c. inferred variables, mechanisms, and structures necessary to complete the account of observed relations

Two functions of theories, according to a traditional view
   1. Explain
   2. Predict

Two forms of explanation, according to a traditional view
   1. Instantiation
   2. Covering law model

Five criteria for evaluating theories, according to a traditional view
1. Testability
2. Validity
3. Utility
4. Parsimony
5. Heuristic value

Three sorts of terms in theories, according to a traditional view
1. Logical terms
2. Observational terms
3. Theoretical terms

Two sorts of theoretical terms, according to a traditional view
1. Intervening variables
2. Hypothetical constructs

Radical behaviorist view of a traditional view of theories
Explanations of observed facts that appealed to events taking place somewhere else, at some other level of observation, described in different terms, and measured, if at all, in different dimensions (from Skinner, 1950)

Radical behaviorist view of theories
1. Abstract, economical descriptions of facts, reduced to a minimal number of terms

2. They promote efficiency of practice and simplicity of expression.

3. Theories in their best sense come at the end of a developmental process. They may have begun as laws of craftsmen, then progressed to statements identifying basic data, then to statements of basic relations in the data, and finally to statements about organizations of facts, including higher-order abstractions.

Instrumentalism
The goal of science is to generate new concepts that mediate prediction and explanation. Theories and their associated theoretical concepts are therefore conventionally accepted instruments that enable scientists to derive new statements about observables from other statements about observables. Any theoretical concepts included in a theory need not be construed as referring to phenomena that actually exist in the world at large, although they may exist by virtue of human construction. Perhaps the theory will state it is "as if" the phenomena exist (from Suppe, 1977).

Realism

1. The aim of science is to find a true theory or description of the world (and especially of its regularities or "laws"), which shall also provide an explanation of the observable facts

2. Science can succeed in finally establishing the truth of such theories beyond all reasonable doubt

3. The best and truly scientific theories describe the "essential properties" of things—the realities which lie beyond appearances; such theories are ultimate explanations, and to find them is the ultimate aim of the scientist (from Suppe, 1977).

Pragmatism

The significance of a statement is explicitly held to be a function of how well the statement promotes effective action. Pragmatism is not equivalent to instrumentalism because pragmatism is concerned with operationally analyzing the basis by which the effective action comes about.

REFERENCES

Amsel, A. (1989). *Behaviorism, neobehaviorism, and cognitivism in learning theory: Historical and contemporary perspectives*. Hillsdale, NJ: Erlbaum.

Baars, B. J. (1986). *The cognitive revolution in psychology*. New York: Guilford.

Catania, A. C., & Harnad, S. (Eds.). (1988). *The selection of behavior: The operant behaviorism of B. F. Skinner: Comments and controversies*. Cambridge: Cambridge University Press.

Day, W. F. (1969). Radical behaviorism in reconciliation with phenomenology. *Journal of the Experimental Analysis of Behavior, 12*, 315–328.

Harré, R. (1960). *An introduction to the logic of the sciences*. New York: St. Martin's Press.

Hempel, C. G., & Oppenheim, P. (1948). Studies in the logic of explanation. *Philosophy of Science, 115*, 135–175.

Kendler, H. H., & Spence, J. T. (1971). Tenets of neobehaviorism. In H. H. Kendler & J. T. Spence (Eds.), *Essays in neobehaviorism: A memorial volume to Kenneth W. Spence*, pp. 11–40. New York: Appleton-Century-Crofts.

Killeen, P. R. (1995). Economics, ecologics, and mechanics: The dynamics of responding under conditions of varying motivation. *Journal of the Experimental Analysis of Behavior, 64*, 405–431.

MacCorquodale, K., & Meehl, P. (1948). On a distinction between hypothetical constructs and intervening variables. *Psychological Review, 55*, 95–107.

Moore, J. (1981). On mentalism, methodological behaviorism, and radical behaviorism. *Behaviorism, 9*, 55–77.

Moore, J. (1998). On behaviorism, theories, and hypothetical constructs. *Journal of Mind and Behavior, 19*, 215–242.

Palmer, D. C., & Donahoe, J. W. (1992). Essentialism and selectionism in cognitive science and behavior analysis. *American Psychologist, 47*, 1344–1358.

Russell, B. (1932). *Mysticism and logic*. London: George Allen.

Skinner, B. F. (1945). The operational analysis of psychological terms. *Psychological Review, 52,* 270–277, 291–294.

Skinner, B. F. (1947). Experimental psychology. In W. Dennis (Ed.), *Current trends in experimental psychology,* pp. 16–49. Pittsburgh, PA: University of Pittsburgh Press. Reprinted in Skinner (1972).

Skinner, B. F. (1950). Are theories of learning necessary? *Psychological Review, 57,* 193–216.

Skinner, B. F. (1953). *Science and human behavior.* New York: Macmillan.

Skinner, B. F. (1957). *Verbal behavior.* New York: Appleton-Century-Crofts.

Skinner, B. F. (1969). *Contingencies of reinforcement.* New York: Appleton-Century-Crofts.

Skinner, B. F. (1972). *Cumulative record.* New York: Appleton-Century-Crofts. (Original published in 1947.)

Skinner, B. F. (1979). *The Shaping of a Behaviorist*. New York: Knopf.

Spence, K. W. (1936). The nature of discrimination learning in animals. *Psychological Review, 43,* 427–449.

Suppe, F. (1977). *The structure of scientific theories* (2nd ed.). Urbana, Illinois: University of Illinois Press.

Toulmin, S. (1953). *The philosophy of science*. London: Hutchinson.

Turner, M. B. (1967). *Philosophy and the science of behavior.* New York: Appleton-Century-Crofts.

Williams, B. A. (1986). On the role of theory in behavior analysis. *Behaviorism, 14,* 111–124.

STUDY QUESTIONS

1. In three or four sentences, summarize the traditional, received view of the radical behaviorist philosophy of science.

2. Describe the three elements of a theory from the traditional point of view.

3. List the two function of theories.

4. List the two common types of explanation from the traditional point of view.

5. Describe how theories are related to prediction from the traditional point of view.

6. Describe the five criteria according to which theories may be evaluated from the traditional point of view.

7. Describe the three sorts of scientific terms in theories from the traditional point of view. Be sure to distinguish between intervening variables and hypothetical constructs as examples of theoretical terms.

8. Describe three reasons why hypothetical constructs are the preferred form of theoretical terms from the traditional point of view.

9. Define what is meant by a theory from the radical behaviorist point of view.

10. Describe the three steps to building a theory from the radical behaviorist point of view.

11. Describe the contribution of the concept of "multiple control" to the understanding of scientific verbal behavior.

12. Distinguish between instrumentalism and realism as orientations to scientific theories. Describe two reasons why radical behaviorists don't embrace either one of these orientations.

13. Describe why radical behaviorists find it useful to distinguish between instrumentalism and pragmatism.

13

Scientific Verbal Behavior: Explanations

Synopsis of Chapter 13: The second section of the book deals with the realization of the radical behaviorist program. Accordingly, the chapters in this section have addressed the topics of verbal behavior, private events, scientific methods, and theories. One important topic remains—explanation, which is the subject of Chapter 13. The chapter begins by outlining two traditional approaches to explanation: instantiation and the covering law model. It then examines the relation between description and explanation. The topic of causal explanations is given special attention, particularly concerning a balance between "internal" and "external" factors that participate in the to-be-explained event. A radical behaviorist view of the explanatory process is proposed, and a related form of scientific activity, interpretation, is discussed. Throughout, the chapter emphasizes that to explain is to behave verbally. Given that explanations are products of verbal behavior, that verbal behavior is operant behavior, and that operant behavior is analyzed in terms of contingencies, the topic of explanations may therefore be analyzed from the standpoint of the contingencies that control the verbal behavior in question. For radical behaviorism, explanations are forms of verbal behavior occasioned by functional relations between environment and behavior. Some forms of verbal activity may appear to be explanatory, but their focus on inferred powers and forces from other dimensions detracts from an analysis of those functional relations.

Etymologically, the word explanation is derived from the Latin "explanare," meaning to make plain, or flatten out. Beyond that, the term has been used in many different ways, with many different meanings, by many different theorists. Braithwaite's (1953) definition is representative, although perhaps whimsical:

> An explanation, as I understand the use of the term, is an answer to a 'Why?' question which gives some intellectual satisfaction. (pp. 348–349)

Perhaps the concern with explanation that is most central to science is causal explanation. For example, according to Wallace (1972):

> Scientia est cognitio per causas. [e.g., Science is knowledge through causes.] ... The early understanding of science—from which the modern notion grew—was that it must be concerned with a search for causes. And the explanations for which science was ultimately searching, from its beginnings among the Greeks ..., were causal explanations. (p. 6)

Accordingly, the present chapter focuses on causal explanations. The chapter notes two dominant forms of explanation, primarily in traditional psychology, and offers a contrasting interpretation of various explanatory practices from the standpoint of radical behaviorism.

TWO PROMINENT EXPLANATORY STRATEGIES IN TRADITIONAL NEOBEHAVIORISM

Instantiation

Chapter 12 briefly mentioned the two explanatory strategies that are prominent in much of traditional behavioral science: (a) instantiation, and (b) the covering law or deductive-nomological model (e.g., Kaplan, 1964; Turner, 1967). These two strategies may now be addressed in greater detail. According to the explanatory strategy of instantiation, an event is said to be explained when it can be described using a general proposition, equation, or law, with variables as parameters in the statement. The parameters can then take on different values in different cases (e.g., they can be "estimated" after the fact from obtained data), with the result that the statement thereby symbolically represents the data in question. Explanations by instantiation presumably get their name because the event to be explained is regarded as a particular "instance," providing a concrete realization of the more general and abstract statement. The strategy emphasizes curve-fitting and percentage of variance accounted for by some mathematical statement, equation, or model. Chapter 10 mentioned that this strategy is descended from the basic observational, descriptive nature of science evident in Bacon's inductivism and traditions of Galileo and Newton. It is further related to Comte's positivism of the first half of the nineteenth century, Mill's methods of inductive inference of the middle of the nineteenth century (see Chapter 11), and Mach's descriptive positivism of the later nineteenth century.

The psychophysical law of S. S. Stevens illustrates this explanatory strategy in psychology. As is no doubt known to many readers, Stevens spent much of his scientific career developing and validating a formal mathematical description of the relation between two factors. Chapter 10 briefly considered this topic when it talked of private events and what is popularly regarded as the strength of sensations in a subjective dimension. Standard psychophysical experiments examined the relation between a pair of numerical values. The first value for Stevens was the "objective," physical magnitude of stimuli that were presented to individuals. Examples are the intensity of a light, the weight of an object, the concentration of sugar in a glass of water, the number of abrasive particles per unit of area in sandpaper, or the number of times per second a light flashed, as measured using the instruments of physics. The second value was a verbal report by participants when they were asked to estimate the magnitude of the sensation they experienced when presented with the objective stimulus, presumably derived from some personal scale of such magnitudes. Stevens assumed science could only deal with publicly observable data. The sensation itself was assumed to be part of a subjective dimension and hence unobservable; as a result, the sensation couldn't be directly included as part of science. Stevens restricted his explanation to describing the experimental operations he conducted and the relations among the publicly observable data produced by those operations. The equation that Stevens (1957) developed to describe the data was $\psi = k\,S^n$. This equation takes the form of a power law and is known as the "psychophysical law." In this equation, ø represents the strength of the psychological, subjective sensation, as inferred from the participant's reported numerical estimate; k is an individual difference parameter; S is the actual magnitude of the physical stimulus—measured objectively as the physicist would measure it—and the exponent n is the term that relates the subjective estimate of the stimulus to its objective measure. An event, or any particular instance of data reported from a subject, was described by particular values of the variables, but the form of the equation was what was regarded as important, rather than the particular values of the variables (except perhaps for n, corresponding to the subject's sensitivity to the stimulus in that modality). This work was consistent with Stevens' earlier assertion that "Science seeks to generate confirmable propositions by fitting a formal system of symbols (language, mathematics, logic) to empirical observations" (Stevens, 1939, p. 222).

This general style of research found favor with much of the community of experimental psychologists. The positivistic tradition of describing observable data was well established in science: Newton's laws of motion described the observable relation between force and movement, and Stevens was simply conforming to this tradition. Psychology was regarded as notoriously resistant to mathematization because of the assumption that its subject matter was subjective and unobservable. Stevens' approach meant that such "subjective" topics as sensation could at last be dealt with "scientifically," without resorting to introspection. In short, sensation could now be operationally analyzed in terms of the objective and publicly observable measures in a sensory discrimination procedure. Stevens published four highly influential articles during the 1930s on the new "operational" methodology and its conceptual underpinnings

(Stevens, 1935a, 1935b, 1936, 1939). In fact, E. G. Boring (1950, p. 656) lauded Stevens' for leading the operational movement in the Harvard department and American psychology generally. Indeed, in recognition of Stevens' profound influence, Killeen (1976) extolled the merits of Stevens' methods for the experimental analysis of behavior; for example, in the scaling of reinforcement value.

Covering Law Model

The second kind of explanation involves deductions from a "covering law" (Hempel & Oppenheim, 1948; see also discussions in Pitt, 1988, and Salmon, 1989, which are the basis for most of what follows). According to this kind of explanation, an event is said to be explained when its description follows as a valid deduction in a logical argument in which at least one of the premises is a "covering law" and at least one of the other premises (if there is more than one other premise) is a statement of antecedent conditions. Covering law explanations presumably get their name because the law "covers" the event to be explained by subsuming the event under (e.g., as a logical consequence of) the law. Covering law explanations have several subtypes based on the nature of the covering law, but an exhaustive treatment of all of the subtypes is highly technical and beyond the scope of the present chapter. This strategy is descended from Aristotle's knowledge of the reasoned fact, Hume's demonstrative knowledge, and modern treatments of logic following in the tradition of Mach's and Russell's versions of positivism. It is particularly related to logical positivism's blending of empiricism with formal symbolic logic and hypothetico-deductive techniques, and its desire to unify the methods of scientific procedure.

The logical argument exemplifying explanation as a deduction from a covering law may be summarized as follows (e.g., Turner, 1967, p. 275):

C1, C2, C3, ... Cn	Statement(s) of antecedent conditions
L1, L2, L3, ... Ln	Covering law(s) [Universal/General law(s) or statistical law(s)]
D	Conclusion/Description of event to be explained

The covering law model has the following requirements:

1. One of the premises in the argument must be either a general law, a statistical law, or a "lawlike generalization."

2. The other premise in the argument must have empirical content, such that it is capable of being tested by experiment or observation.

3. The premises must be true or else highly confirmed.

4. The explanation must be a logically valid (in the case of deductions from a general law) or highly probable (in the case of deductions from a statistical law) consequence of the premises.

Suppose one is interested in explaining why a piece of wood floated when it was placed on water. The antecedent condition is that the piece of wood is less dense than water. The covering law is that any solid body that is less dense than a liquid will float when placed on the liquid. The conclusion providing the explanation is the description of the observed state of affairs: that the wood (the solid) floated when placed on the water (the liquid). Consequently, the form of the argument for "explaining" why the wood floated on water is as follows:

Statement of antecedent condition:	Wood is a solid that is less dense than water.
Covering Law:	A solid that is less dense than a given liquid will float on the latter.
Description:	Wood floated on the water.

The covering law model also contributed to explanations in such traditional forms of psychology as neobehaviorism. For example, the noted learning theorist and neobehaviorist Clark Hull sought to devise a hypothetico-deductive system in which behavioral events could be subsumed under an interlocking network of covering laws, much as Euclidean geometry consisted of deductions based on an interlocking network of postulates, axioms, theorems, and corollaries. In one of his seminal papers, Hull (1937) wrote:

1. A satisfactory scientific theory should begin with a set of explicitly stated postulates accompanied by specific or 'operational' definitions of the critical terms employed.

2. From these postulates there should be deduced by the most rigorous logic possible under the circumstances, a series of interlocking theorems covering the major concrete phenomena of the field in question.

3. The statements in the theorems should agree in detail with the observationally known facts of the discipline under consideration…. (p. 5)

In addition, Kendler and Spence (1971) identified the focal importance of deductive processes in neobehavioristic explanations:

The neobehavioristic decision concerning the nature of explanation is, in principle, both clear and simple. Explanation is equated with theoretical deduction: an event is explained by deducing it from one or more general propositions. The deductive process is analogous to mathematical proof although its precision can vary from mathematical verification to the logical use of ordinary language. The constructs used in the theoretical propositions must in some manner be representative of the concepts involved in the events to be explained. In other words the theoretical constructs must be coordinated with the empirical events. (p. 21)

One particularly noteworthy feature of covering law explanations is the symmetry among description, explanation, and prediction. For example, if the conclusion of the argument is expressed in the past tense, the conclusion is in fact a description of what has already been observed, and one says the event has been explained. If the conclusion of the argument is expressed in the future tense, the conclusion is in fact a description of something that has not yet happened but will happen if the designated antecedent conditions prevail, and one says the event has been predicted. Moreover, the positions of (a) the statement of antecedent conditions, and (b) the conclusion, can technically be reversed in the argument with no loss of validity. The covering law model sidesteps these matters by emphasizing simply the logical structure of the argument. However, as is seen below, this symmetry raises a technical question about the relation between explanation and description.

THE RELATION AMONG EXPLANATION, DESCRIPTION, AND THEORY IN BEHAVIOR ANALYSIS

The distinctions and practices of the epistemology of radical behaviorism often do not map neatly onto traditional distinctions and practices. The distinctions and practices of radical behaviorist explanation are no exception. In brief, as with the term "theory," for radical behaviorism to explain an event is to engage in a particular form of verbal behavior related to the event (Catania, 1993). To understand what that form is, and thereby analyze the meaning of explanation, one analyzes the discriminative stimuli that occasion the use of the term and the reinforcers that maintain it.

In the most general and conventional use of the term *explanation*, one labels an instance of verbal behavior as an explanation when it is occasioned by the causal influence of environmental factors on behavior at the level of phylogeny, ontogeny, or culture. Typically, that influence takes the form of a functional relation. For instance, in talking of behavior that developed during an organism's lifetime, Skinner (1964) stated: "When I said 'explanation,' I simply meant the causal account. An explanation is the demonstration of a functional relationship between behavior and manipulable or controllable variables" (p. 102). In other words, one has explained an event when one's verbal behavior is under the discriminative control of the observed functional relation; that is, under the discriminative control of the variables participating in the event and their functional relation to the behavior of interest. Thus, causal explanation plays a central role in Skinner's system, given the fundamental concern with practical outcomes, and causation is expressed as a functional relation, in the fashion of Mach and Russell. In virtually every case, to say that one has explained an event is equivalent to saying one has identified what has caused it. When individuals are asked to explain what they have said, they are typically being asked to specify what has caused them to say what they have said.

As Moore (2000) has reviewed, Skinner's early writing and its self-acknowledged embrace of Baconian induction and Machian positivism created some confusion about the roles of description, explanation, and theory in behavior analysis. For example, Chapter 2 of *The Behavior of Organisms* (Skinner, 1938) opens as follows: "So far as scientific method is concerned, the system set up in the preceding chapter may be characterized as follows. It is positivistic. It confines itself to description rather than explanation" (p. 44). For many years, Skinner's approach was characterized as a "descriptive behaviorism" (e.g., Marx, 1951, p. 439). However, the relation between description and explanation was clarified in Skinner's later writings. For example, Skinner (1957) distinguishes between descriptive and explanatory practices as follows:

> The direction to be taken in an alternative approach is dictated by the task itself. Our first responsibility is simple description: What is the topography of this sub-division of human behavior? Once that question has been answered in at least a preliminary fashion we may advance to the stage called explanation: What conditions are relevant to the occurrence of the behavior—what are the variables of which it is a function? (p. 10)

Thus, for radical behaviorism, description and explanation are not isomorphic, but rather on a continuum of scientific activity.

For radical behaviorism, therefore, an explanation is more than a description. A description might very well be offered on the basis of just a single observation, whereas an explanation is ordinarily never so offered. An explanation of behavior goes beyond a description of behavior by specifying the functional relations between the to-be-explained response and its controlling variables. Explanation therefore involves more complex and presumably abstract stimulus control than does description (Skinner, 1957, Chapter 18). A description might well identify prevailing antecedent conditions and consequent conditions, but not a functional relation per se. The identification and further specification of causes and effects in terms of functional relations constitutes explanation in the ordinary usage of the term. Nevertheless, that specification involves a consistent level of observation and analysis. Behavior in particular is explained at the level of behavior; that is, at the level of the operations and prevailing stimulus conditions that impinge upon the organism. These factors, together with the genetic make-up of the organism that affords responsiveness to these factors, may be considered as responsible for the behavior. Therefore, Skinner argued that one explains behavior by locating it "in a frame of reference provided by the organism itself or by various external objects or fields of force" (Skinner, 1938, p. 6). Chapters 4 and 10 of this book provided further detail on the contribution of physiology and private behavioral events to behavior-analytic explanations.

When Skinner (1938, p. 44) suggested he was interested in description rather than explanation, he was simply indicating that he was subscribing to the Machian preference for formulating observed functional relations in a descriptively consistent manner, and that he was not going to appeal to inferred "powers and forces" from other dimensions, such as the neural or mental dimension, as causes of the observed events. Explanations that take the form of appeals to inferred powers and forces in another dimension are rejected, but not principally for the reason that such powers and forces are unobservable and hence ontologically unsuitable for science, which can only deal with observables. Rather, such fanciful explanations are rejected because there is no other dimension, and searching for powers and forces in another dimension will necessarily interfere with investigations of the dimension in which relevant variables are to be found.

Why are explanations offered? This question is about the factors and relations that occasion and reinforce the verbal behavior of explaining. Again, in conventional usage explanations are offered because they contribute, perhaps only indirectly, to understanding, prediction, and control. In short, an explanation provides the basis for effective interaction with nature. In an extension of the influence of Bacon and Mach, Skinner (1979) spoke about these and other more subtle factors that might maintain the behavior of explaining in a volume of his autobiography:

> I proposed to cover not only how scientists worked but why: "A theory of knowledge should include a theory of motivation to supply a complete description of the phenomena. Not only how do men think? but under what circumstances? ..." (p. 118)

> Was not confirmation the be-all and end-all of science? It was a question concerning my own behavior, and I thought I had an answer: "...What is the motivational substitute for thing-confirmation? Pretty important in teaching method to graduate students. Resulting order instead of confirmation?" My reinforcers were the discovery of uniformities, the ordering of confusing data, the resolution of puzzlement. (p. 282)

In any event, at issue in any analysis of explanation are the contingencies governing the verbal behavior regarded as explanatory (Moore, 1990).

CAUSAL EXPLANATION, PREDICTION, AND DESCRIPTION

As the traditional covering law model of explanation has been presented above, one of its principal features is that it mediates prediction and generally supports the hypothetico-deductive approach to scientific activity. Where does radical behaviorism stand with respect to the important feature of prediction? For radical behaviorism, prediction is certainly important, but because of its practical implications, not because it validates a logical system. Skinner (1953) explicitly acknowledged the importance of prediction as follows:

The scientific "system," like the law, is designed to enable us to handle a subject matter more efficiently. What we call the scientific conception of a thing is not passive knowledge. Science is not concerned with contemplation. When we have discovered the laws which govern a part of the world about us, we are then ready to deal effectively with that part of the world. By predicting the occurrence of an event we are able to prepare for it. By arranging conditions in ways specified by the laws of a system, we not only predict, we control: we "cause" an event to occur or to assume certain characteristics. (pp. 13–14)

Hence, radical behaviorism is not simply interested in post-hoc description. Radical behaviorism is clearly interested in prediction, but by virtue of its implications for practical, direct action, rather than as a property of a logical argument.

To be sure, Skinner was also influenced by Russell, who as discussed in Chapter 12, stated that laws in many mature sciences were not essentially causal in nature (Russell, 1932). One example is the Boyle-Charles gas law, in which various mathematical relations are expressed among pressure, volume, and temperature: $p \times v = kt$, where p is pressure, v is volume, t is temperature, and k is a constant.

In the view presented here, the Boyle-Charles gas law is an example of the second- and third-stage scientific activity described in Skinner (1972) and reviewed in Chapter 12. It is a statement about the organization of facts. The statement is built upon a foundation of identifying basic data and functional relations, and weaknesses at lower levels cannot be corrected at higher levels. Cause and effect statements are clearly relevant during the lower stages. Increasing force over a given area causes pressure to increase, other things (e.g., temperature) being equal at the start of the process. Decreasing the dimensions of a container causes volume to decrease, other things (e.g., pressure) being equal at the start of the process. The gas laws formulate the appropriate relations among these data, but cause and effect statements were involved at some point.

The process of going from first- to second- to third-stage statements provides the foundation for scientific explanations, and the process is not wisely circumvented. Stevens' version of the scientific method in psychology—sometimes called behavioristic because of its commitment to operationism and publicly observable data rather than introspection (e.g., Boring, 1950)—was to describe mathematically the form of the observed relations, but remain silent on an underlying "mechanism" that had produced them. What, then, was the provenance of the data that were being described? Recall that Skinner pointed out that "it was Stevens ... who then continued to believe in the existence of mental life" (Skinner in Catania & Harnad, 1988, p. 217), and "S. S. Stevens has applied Bridgman's principle [of operationism] to psychology, not to decide whether subjective events exist, but to determine the extent to which we can deal with them scientifically" (Skinner, 1969, p. 227). The implication of the operationism of Boring and Stevens, which has dominated traditional psychology for more than 60 years, is that mental processes are causing the behavior, but that psychology as a science cannot deal with the mental processes because they are not publicly observable; instead, psychology must confine itself to events that are accessible to at least two observers, such as by describing the mathematical relation between independent and dependent variables and doing nothing else.

Given that Skinner expressed so much fundamental concern with this form of explanation, one wonders why theorists suggest that there is "much about Stevens of which experimental analysts of behavior would approve" (Killeen, 1976, p. 123). Although Stevens' approach to science may yield certain benefits, presumably those benefits do not follow from the reasons Stevens believed they did. Moreover, there are also liabilities, and from the radical behaviorist perspective those liabilities decidedly outweigh any benefits. The liabilities follow from the realization that there are no such mental causes underlying the observable data as Stevens or any other theorist supposed. Hence, treating observable data as the expression of mental causes leads researchers to neglect the environmental factors that actually cause the observable data.

THE CAUSAL EXPLANATION OF BEHAVIOR

In view of the preceding analyses, it is apparent that a great difference between traditional psychology, on the one hand, and radical behaviorism, on the other, lies in the area of what constitutes a causal explanation of behavior. To be sure, much has been written in philosophy of science about the nature of causal explanation. For example, consider the following passage from Harré (1970):

Scientific knowledge consists of two main kinds of information.

1. Knowledge of the internal structures, constitutions, natures, and so on of things and materials, as various atoms and galaxies, for these are what persist.

2. Knowledge of the statistics of events, of the behavior of persisting things and materials. In this way we discern patterns amongst events. In an explanation we show how the patterns discerned amongst events are produced by the persisting natures and constitutions of things and materials. (p. 125)

Next, consider a statement from Block (1980), who identifies a mode of explanation "that relies on a decomposition of a system into its component parts and the way the parts are integrated with one another" (p. 171).

These two statements represent a traditional orientation to causal explanation. At the heart of these two passages is a distinction between: (a) the "internal" properties of objects that make up the to-be-explained event, and: (b) the relation between the objects themselves that make up the event. According to the traditional orientation, the observed relations are explained in terms of the internal properties. This traditional orientation to causal explanation may now be more closely examined from the standpoint of radical behaviorism.

Radical behaviorism agrees in some ways, but not all, with the traditional orientation to causal explanation. Radical behaviorism agrees that objects participating in an event clearly do have internal properties, and that these properties are relevant to understanding the event being analyzed. Atoms have electrons with certain properties that make them more or less susceptible to forming bonds with other atoms having other properties, for example. Similarly, organisms have various physiological systems, such as sensory systems, motor systems, and neural systems that connect the sensory and motor systems. These systems make it possible for organisms to respond to environmental stimulation and act with respect to features of the environment. For radical behaviorism, the role of physiology in explanations of behavior was outlined in Chapter 4 of the present book. In addition, private behavioral events may well contribute to discriminative control over ongoing behavior, as described in Chapter 10.

However, radical behaviorism disagrees in at least two ways with the traditional orientation. The first way concerns the very nature of the supposed internal information. Is the information based on actual investigatory techniques appropriate to the discipline, or is the information simply an inference about properties that have not themselves been observed? If the former, then there is no problem, as suggested in Chapter 4. Neuroscience can clearly contribute to behavioral explanations and efforts to predict and control. However, in traditional psychology knowledge about supposed "internal structures" is typically only an inference based on the observable behavior of things and events. Radical behaviorists argue that when actual contact is absent or even limited with what is taken to be the first sort of information, the postulations may then be of uncertain and dubious origin. The actual nature of anything internal may be incorrectly cast in terms of metaphors and so on. As discussed in Chapter 12, theories of memory appealing to the metaphor of storage and retrieval are a conspicuous example.

Chapters 4 and 10 also pointed out that radical behaviorism does not conceive of the organism as empty or a black box. Rather, it is traditional psychology that does so, by its constant appeal to inferred, hypothetical, or conceptual inner causes, supposedly on the evidence of observable data. The inadequacy of this inferential strategy is conspicuous. In principle, one cannot ascertain the actual workings of a "black box" by studying only input-output relations, any more than one can ascertain what the lines of code are in a computer program by observing its inputs and outputs. The dominance of explanations in traditional psychology that appeal to inferred powers and forces inside the organism is one of the principal concerns of radical behaviorism. The stimulus control over such language is suspect. An organism obviously has physiological structures that are relevant to its behavior, just as a computer program obviously has lines of code that are relevant to what it does. However, it is clearly not an effective strategy to simply make up causal mentalistic entities inside the skin, assert that they are legitimate because they are theoretical inferences, and by labeling them as theoretical believe one has successfully offered an explanation of the behavior in question. Such a strategy is no more effective than making up causal mentalistic entities inside a computer, asserting that they are legitimate because they are theoretical inferences, and by labeling them as theoretical, believe that one has explained the operation of the computer. One can directly analyze physiological processes inside the skin, instead of treating them as inferred metaphors, just as one can directly analyze lines of computer code, instead of treating them as inferred metaphors. Valid information about internal events may shed a different kind of light on the processes that participate in the event as it is observed externally, but the information does not alter the facts of the event as it is observed externally.

The second way that radical behaviorism disagrees with the traditional orientation is that the supposed internal structures are actually nothing but thinly disguised appeals to causal phenomena from another dimension. Consider how the traditional orientation conceives of the balance between the two sorts of data. Harré (1970) states that the second kind is "produced by" the first kind, and Block (1980) "relies" on the internal information. This position indicates a bias in which internal information is preferred or held to be otherwise superior in an explanation, such that no explanation can respectably be labeled as such unless it includes such internal information. Indeed, part of the criticism of any form of behavioral psychology by traditional psychologists, and as is seen in Chapters 14, 15, and 16 by cognitive psychologists especially, is that any form of behavioral psychology by definition restricts itself to only the second sort of data, which is inadequate. Skinner (1972) commented on the bias toward explanations that appeal to internal causes in the following passage:

> Inner entities do not "cause" behavior, nor does behavior "express" them…. In an acceptable explanatory scheme the ultimate causes of behavior must be found *outside* the organism…. Both sets of facts [physiological and behavioral], and their appropriate concepts, are important—but they are equally important, not dependent one upon the other. Under the influence of a contrary philosophy of explanation, which insists upon the reductive priority of the inner event, many brilliant men who began with an interest in behavior, and who might have advanced our knowledge of the field in many ways, have turned instead to the study of physiology. We cannot dispute the importance of their contributions, we can only imagine with regret what they might have done instead. (pp. 325–326)

Radical behaviorists argue that when traditional psychologists uncritically and inferentially embrace supposed data about internal structures, traditional psychologists have committed themselves to the position where the inferred properties carry the entire burden of causal explanation. In effect, this commitment endows the inferred acts, states, mechanisms, and processes with efficient, homuncular power to cause behavioral events. In addition, the commitment limits the possibilities for prediction and control by foreclosing on the analysis of how environmental circumstances contribute to a given behavioral event. The commitment incorrectly represents the legitimate role of internal variables in causal explanations when those variables are physiological, and it compounds the problem when it conceives of the variables as from the mental dimension.

In a perceptive treatment, Hocutt (1985) discussed the role and status of information about internal properties in explanations when he examined talk about the magnetism of an iron bar:

> One might hold that a bar's being magnetic causes it to attract iron filings…. However, a behaviorist thinks that view a little too crude to capture the complicated truth. On his view, we ought not to say that magnetism causes the bar to attract iron filings; rather, we ought to say that the bar's attracting iron filings is one manifestation of its being magnetic... We ought to say this because, strictly speaking, there is no such entity as magnetism; there are just magnetic entities. So, the cause, strictly so-called, of the bar's attracting filings is not its "magnetism" but either the process (e.g., of shooting electricity through it) that made it magnetic or the proximity of the filings. If we wish, we may say that the magnet attracts iron filings because it is magnetic, but there would be little clear sense in saying that its magnetism causes it to attract iron filings…. [I]t is inaccurate to say that the arrangement of its molecules causes the bar to attract filings. Rather, what causes the bar to attract iron filings, given that it is magnetic, is our placing it close to the filings... (pp. 93–94)

In this passage, Hocutt clearly accepts the applicability of information about the inner state; note that he acknowledges the importance of that information by saying "given that it [the bar] is magnetic." However, he maintains a critical balance between the two sorts of information: Given that the bar has been made magnetic, the cause of the bar's attracting iron filings is to be found in an analysis of its external circumstances—its being placed in proximity to the filings.

With respect to the causal explanation of behavior, the radical behaviorist view is similar to that described by Hocutt (1985). As noted in Chapter 4 of this book, in the radical behaviorist view, two questions are clearly relevant:

1. What are the features of the world with which the person interacts?

2. How does the person's body work when it interacts with those features of the world?

Nevertheless, these two questions are different. An answer to one does not constitute an answer to the other. The first is of concern to psychology. The second is of concern to neuroscience.

As suggested above, radical behaviorism recognizes the importance of understanding the contribution of events going on inside the skin. Some of these events are private, behavioral events, such as: (a) the processes associated with verbal reports of bodily states, and (b) the emission of covert behavior that then contributes to the stimulus control over subsequent behavior.

Other events concern physiology. These events are concerned with the two unavoidable gaps in a behavioral account: within a behavioral event and between behavioral events (see Chapter 4). Information about these events will be provided by physiologists, rather than psychologists, although psychologists will inform the physiologists what to look for.

As Skinner (1969, 1974) has suggested, when the momentary state of an organism can be observed, it may be used to predict behavior, instead of the history responsible for it. When a state can be generated or changed directly, it can be used to control behavior. Only neuroscience can fill those gaps. In doing so, neuroscience completes the account; it does not give a preferred or more fundamental account of the same thing. Moreover, physiological information may have a heuristic value and suggest possibilities for interventions and manipulations, or for prediction and control. In any event, the cooperative action of ethology, neuroscience, and behavior analysis offers great promise for the explanation of human behavior.

EPISTEMOLOGICAL DUALISM AND OTHER MISCHIEVOUS SOURCES OF CONTROL OVER THE VERBAL BEHAVIOR OF THE SCIENTIST

Many discussions of scientific epistemology are dominated by a position that can generically be called "epistemological dualism." Epistemological dualism is roughly the position that the analysis of the knowing process when scientists become knowledgeable must include both physical and mental variables, and hence is dualistic, even though the world at large is not dualistic in the traditional sense of metaphysical dualism. Epistemological dualism is based on the view that words or terms are symbols created in the immediate experience of the scientist; that immediate experience is a mental dimension different from the physical; that it contains things; and that the scientist can create things in it to symbolize or represent the physical, constitutes mentalism. Epistemological dualism is readily identified when behaving scientists describe their own activities in terms of such devices as theoretical constructs, hypothesis testing, traditional covering law models of explanation, and so on. These descriptions tacitly assume that fundamentally mentalistic entities cause the behavior of scientists. Sometimes psychologists who appeal to the epistemological power of theories, logic, and constructs believe they are not mentalistic because they are not bifurcating objects from the world into physical and extra-physical components. However, this belief is in error, because the way that they conceive of the processes by which the scientist becomes knowledgeable makes them epistemological dualists and therefore mentalistic. The root of these problems is the conception of verbal behavior as an essentially referential, symbolic, or representational activity, which is a comprehensively mentalistic conception of verbal behavior.

Interestingly, Skinner elaborated his position in the following passage:

> In 1950 I asked the question Are theories of learning necessary?, and suggested the answer was no.... Fortunately, I had defined my terms. The word theory was to mean "any explanation of

an observed fact which appeals to events taking place somewhere else, at some other level of observation, described in different terms, and measured, if at all, in different dimensions"— events, for example, in the real nervous system, the conceptual system, or the mind. I argued that theories of this sort had not stimulated good research on learning and that they misrepresented the facts to be accounted for, gave false assurances about the state of our knowledge, and led to the continued use of methods which should be abandoned.

A reputation as an antitheorist is easily acquired by anyone who neglects hypothetico-deductive methods. When a subject matter is very large (for example, the universe as a whole) or very small (for example, subatomic particles) or for any reason inaccessible, we cannot manipulate variables or observe effects as we should like to. We therefore make tentative or hypothetical statements about them, deduce theorems which refer to accessible states of affairs, and by checking the theorems confirm or refute our hypotheses. The achievements of the hypothetico-deductive system, where appropriate, have been brilliant. Newton set the pattern in his *Principia*, and the great deductive theorists who follow him have been given a prominent place in the history of science.

Their significance has nevertheless probably been exaggerated, and in part for rather trivial reasons. Unlike direct observation and description, the construction of a hypothesis suggests mysterious intellectual activities.... For one thing, the method tends to be used when it is not needed, when direct observation is not only possible but more effective.... The hypothetico-deductive method and the mystery which surrounds it have been perhaps most harmful in representing ways in which people think. Scientific behavior is possibly the most complex subject matter ever submitted to scientific analysis, and we are still far from having an adequate account of it....

Behavior is one of those subject matters which do not call for hypothetico-deductive methods. Both behavior itself and most of the variables of which it is a function are usually conspicuous. (Responses which are of very small magnitude or difficult to reach are notable exceptions, but the problems they pose are technical rather than methodological.) If hypotheses commonly appear in the study of behavior, it is only because the investigator has turned his attention to inaccessible events—some of them fictitious, others irrelevant. (Skinner in Catania & Harnad, 1988, pp. 101–103).

In this passage, Skinner did two things. First, he acknowledged that in certain instances, what is called the hypothetico-deductive approach can yield positive theoretical contributions. Thus, Skinner cannot be said to be uniformly opposed to that approach, although he did view the process by which the approach made its contributions somewhat differently than does traditional psychology. Second, Skinner nevertheless pointed out that the theorists who have made positive contributions through the hypothetico-deductive approach would not have gone far without a foundation of basic experimental findings. Newton feigned no hypotheses about the existence of fictitious entities from another dimension in his mechanical universe (even though he was ultimately concerned with illustrating how the laws established by his Christian deity were expressed in that universe). The important point is that Newton's verbal behavior was enough under the stimulus control of stage 1 and stage 2 events that an adequate foundation existed for the stage 3 verbal behavior called "theoretical."

In connection with the first point mentioned above, readers may recall Skinner's statement that "The hypothetico-deductive method and the mystery which surrounds it have been perhaps most harmful in representing ways in which people think" (Skinner in Catania & Harnad, 1988, p. 102). In this statement, Skinner was not challenging whether verbal manipulation reveals new relations to be investigated. It clearly can. Rather, he was challenging that one can guarantee something useful comes out of scientific activities taking place at stage 3 just by adhering to the hypothetico-method. To hold that the hypothetico-deductive method guarantees success is an instance of epistemological dualism. The hypothetico-deductive method may produce useful activity or it may not, depending on the stimulus control over the verbal events being manipulated. If the stimulus control is suspect—for example, if the stage 1 and 2 activities have not established the appropriate foundation—then the hypothetico-deductive method will only lead to blind alleys and dead ends. Hence, Skinner's criticism is that the hypothetico-deductive method can be wasteful.

In further analyses, Skinner commented explicitly on the development of quantum mechanics and relativity theory in physics, often held to be the supreme theoretical accomplishment of science. In the passage below, Skinner commented on the verbal behavior of such theorists as Boltzmann, Planck, Einstein, Bohr, and Born, and pointed out that they would not have been able to emit their theoretical verbal behavior if the relevant foundation had not been established earlier:

> I nevertheless reminded my readers that the great theorists would not have got far without experimental science. It is true that Boltzmann, Planck, Einstein, Bohr and Born theorized about "'events taking place somewhere else,' clearly 'at some other level of observation..., described in different terms' and definitely measured in different dimensions' from the experimental setup,' but take the experiments away and they could not have done so. As Nicholas says, "the best theories ever devised on almost every factor by which they can be ranked" were "firmly engaged with a great array of experiments of historic caliber." It is perhaps equally true that there would be no research without theories in the fields represented by scientists of that kind; they are dealing with a world beyond the reach of direct observation. It is also worth asking whether Einstein, Planck, Bohr, and the others discovered a new kind of scientific thinking or whether their science had reached the state at which a new method could be invoked. If the latter is the case, we have to ask whether a science of behavior has reached that stage or whether cognitive science is premature in pretending to have reached it. (Skinner in Catania and Harnad, 1988, p. 125)

Note again the thrust of this passage. Of central importance are the dimensions of theories and explanations. Scientific statements leading to explanations become troublesome when they appeal to different dimensions. Skinner points out that the question of dimensions particularly applies to stages 1 and 2 scientific activity. Assume one goes off searching for the basic data (stage 1) and causal or functional relations (stage 2) in other, fictitious dimensions. Of course, there is no other dimension, so that is not actually where one is searching, but in any case, nothing will be found. One might believe one has found something, but one misses what could be found by looking in the "one" dimension. As Skinner (1957, p. 6) said, "It is the function of an explanatory fiction to allay curiosity and bring inquiry to an end."

What, then, about the third-stage activity, endorsed by Skinner above in connection with theoretical physics, with its apparent appeal to events in other dimensions? What is going on during third-stage activities is the verbal process of abstraction. The verbal process of abstraction does not identify a thing in another dimension, if only because there is no other dimension that contains a thing to be identified, despite appeals to Platonic or Kantian essentialism. Readers may recall Williams' (1986, p. 112) explicit endorsement in Chapter 12 of another "level of reality." Rather, verbal behavior simply comes under the control of certain properties of a class of stimuli. The process of abstraction gives the appearance of a world in a different dimension composed of general idealized properties. Skinner's apparent approval of appeals to other dimensions in theoretical physics may be seen as a rhetorical device to indicate that third-stage concepts have emerged that are more than first- or second-stage statements, just as the verbal process of abstraction is more than the verbal process that results in a tact.

Schnaitter (1986, p. 262) suggested Skinner implicitly rejected explanations appealing to hypothetical entities on the basis of two criteria:

1. The criterion of intraverbal distance. According to this criterion, as the amount of verbal behavior intermediating between the world and a conclusion about the world increases, the opportunity for a faulty inference increases.

2. The criterion of metaphoric contamination. According to this criterion, metaphoric extension invariably leads to misdirection and conceptual error in science.

Again, according to the present perspective, these two criteria apply to ostensible third-stage entities that have been proposed without the benefit of the first two stages. In these instances, the necessary stimulus control may be lacking, and the resulting scientific product is suspect. To be sure, verbal manipulation can generate supplemental stimulus control in efforts to derive more reinforcers from nature. However, such manipulations may be understood in terms of the stimulus control over verbal behavior (Skinner, 1957, Chapter 18), rather than in terms of nomological networks and hypothetical constructs that are held to be distinct from behavior. Moreover, one must be cautious about attempts to manipulate the verbal behavior prematurely, without establishing an adequate foundation in the first two steps.

A case history in chemistry is illustrative. Some two hundred years ago many chemists thought combustion was related to processes involving a magical substance called phlogiston. Phlogiston had a remarkable property: It had a negative weight. This property was hypothesized to account for observations that some substances lost weight when they were burned, whereas other substances gained weight when they were burned. The popular solution of the time was to hypothesize that some substances contained phlogiston. When they burned, they released it and thereby gained weight. The companion hypothesis was that other substances didn't contain phlogiston. When they burned, they gathered free-floating phlogiston from the atmosphere and thereby lost weight. The discovery of oxygen and its relation to combustion put the processes in good order. Oxygen was necessary for combustion. Weight gains could be accounted for in terms of the development of oxides. Weight losses could be accounted for in terms of the release of water vapor or other particles. Inferences about substances with magical properties were not attributable to data at the first and second steps described above. Rather, those inferences were attributable to popular lore and unscientific conceptions of natural processes.

As suggested by the story of phlogiston in chemistry, many sciences are vulnerable to such premature leaps. Given that psychology is burdened by a "vast vocabulary of ancient and non-scientific origin" (Skinner, 1945, p. 271) and that "No other science has ever had to move against such a mass of folklore, superstition, and error" (Skinner, 1969, p. 96), psychology is no exception. Skinner's numerous critical references to cognitive psychology consistently point out how it is related to nonscientific ideas: "Cognitive science is the creation science of psychology, as it struggles to maintain the position of a mind or self" (Skinner, 1990, p. 1209).

To be sure, scientists are not immune from the laws of behavior. Scientists have lived their entire lives in a generally mentalistic culture, and unless appropriate discriminations have been shaped, they may uncritically talk in mentalistic ways about the behavior of others, as well as even their own behavior. Terms relating to general modes of behavior, such as feelings, ideas, thoughts, beliefs, or expectations, and terms relating specifically to scientific epistemology, such as knowing, reasoning, judging, perceiving, or hypothesizing, are often fraught with mentalistic implications. Skinner (1974, p. 214) lists over 60 representative terms that are commonly involved in mentalistic explanations. Because of the mentalistic implications of much of our everyday language, radical behaviorists are wary of the self-descriptive activity of scientists when those scientists come to explain their own scientific behavior. Again, the concern is that attributing the cause of the behavior to factors that turn out to be mentalistic interferes with an appropriate understanding of the operant relations inherent in effective scientific verbal behavior.

INTERPRETATION

Yet to be examined is the matter of interpretation. Interpretation is especially important in connection with understanding the radical behaviorist view of theories and explanations, in light of the strong pragmatic orientation of radical behaviorism. For the radical behaviorist, interpretation is the making sense out of events when those events cannot be further investigated. A representative statement is found in Skinner's (1974) own writing:

> Obviously we cannot predict or control human behavior in daily life with the precision obtained in the laboratory, but we can nevertheless use results from the laboratory to interpret behavior elsewhere.... [A]ll sciences resort to something much like it.... [T]he principles of genetics are used to interpret the facts of evolution, as the behavior of substances under high pressures and temperatures are used to interpret geological events in the history of the earth. (pp. 228–229)

More formally, then, interpretation is the use of scientific terms and principles in talking about facts when too little is known to make prediction and control possible, or when precise manipulation is not feasible (Moore, 1998, p. 231). As suggested in the Skinner (1974) passage above, two examples of interpretation are: (a) the theory of evolution, and (b) the theory of plate tectonics. These theories are interpretations of a vast number of facts, in one case about the origin of species and in another about the nature of the earth's crust. They use terms and principles taken from much more accessible material and from experimental analyses and their technological applications. The basic principles of variation, interaction, and replication can be studied in the laboratory under controlled conditions, but their role in explanations of the evolution of species is interpretation. Similarly, the basic principles governing the behavior of material under high pressure and high temperature can be studied in the laboratory under controlled conditions, but their role in explanations of the formation of surface features of the earth is interpretation (e.g., Skinner in Catania & Harnad, 1988, pp. 207–208).

Once emitted, the interpretive verbal behavior can be confirmed by generating additional discriminative stimuli that increase the probability of the verbal response being emitted as a tact, thereby increasing the probability that any action occasioned by the verbal response will be effective (Skinner, 1957, p. 425). For example, if individuals look up information about some event, they add a textual response to clarify their understanding of the event. If individuals ask an expert, they add an echoic. If individuals manipulate other verbal behavior concerned with the same event, they supplement the interpretation with intraverbals. If individuals use instruments to amplify aspects of the events with which they are concerned, they bring themselves into contact with new stimuli that sharpen stimulus control over their actions, and thereby increase the probability that the interpretation will develop into a tact and occasion future effective behavior.

Interpretation plays a large role in radical behaviorism, as it does in all sciences. Skinner (1957) stated his most important book was *Verbal Behavior*, precisely because it was "an exercise in interpretation rather than a quantitative extrapolation of rigorous experimental results" (p. 11). Most everyday functioning, of course, involves a considerable degree of interpretation, because the knowledge claims of everyday life simply are not typically the result of conducting experiments under carefully controlled conditions. Rather, they are the result of applying what has been learned elsewhere to beneficial effect. As Skinner (1974) put it, "Speculation is necessary, in fact, to devise methods which will bring a subject matter under better control" (p. 17), and that speculation is consistent with the dimensions of known principles and processes.

SUMMARY AND CONCLUSIONS

Just as for theories, the nature of causal explanation is an essential element of the epistemological stance in radical behaviorism, and always has been. Importantly, just as for theories, radical behaviorists view explanations as products of verbal behavior. Analysis of explanations consists of the analysis of the provenance and discriminative function of the verbal behavior regarded as explanatory. Explanations follow from theories, but are more highly evolved statements derived from functional relations. Whereas explanations in traditional psychology took the form of instantiation or deductions from covering laws, radical behaviorism rejects these approaches. To be sure, radical behaviorism is ultimately interested in the description of publicly observable data. Accordingly, some have mistaken the radical behaviorist position as not that much different from traditional positions. The difference is that for radical behaviorism, the description would follow from the identification of basic data and functional relations. To offer a statement as explanatory in the absence of a grounding in the identification of basic data and functional relations is to have invited extraneous control over the verbal behavior in question. Interpretation supplements theoretical and explanatory activity in science, but not at the expense of surrendering contact with the dimensions in which behavior takes place.

Chapter 13 concludes the second section of the book, in which the realization of the radical behaviorist program is outlined. The chapters dealt with verbal behavior, private events, scientific methods, theoretical verbal behavior, and explanatory verbal behavior. The third and final section of the book examines the way that radical behaviorism approaches some selected, traditional topics in philosophical psychology. It begins with Chapter 14 on mentalism.

TABLE 13–1

Traditional explanation—Instantiation
An event is said to be explained when it can be expressed as some specific value of a variable in a general proposition, equation, or law. Explanations by instantiation presumably get their name because the event to be explained is regarded as a particular "instance," providing a concrete realization, of the more general and abstract statement. According to this strategy, then, the aim of science is to devise a

---

general statement with variables as parameters in the statement. The parameters can then take on different values in different cases (e.g., they can be "estimated" after the fact from obtained data), with the result that the statement thereby symbolically describes the data in question. The strategy emphasizes curve-fitting and percentage of variance accounted for by some mathematical statement, equation, or model. This strategy is descended from the basic observational, descriptive nature of science evident in Bacon's inductivism and traditions of Galileo and Newton. It is further related to Comte's positivism, Mill's methods of inductive inference, and Mach's descriptive positivism.

Traditional explanation—Covering law
An event is said to be explained when its description follows as a valid deduction in a logical argument in which at least one of the premises is a "covering law" and at least one of the other premises (if there is more than one other premise) is a statement of antecedent conditions. Covering law explanations presumably get their name because the law "covers" the event to be explained, by subsuming it under (e.g., as a consequence of) the law. Covering law explanations are descended from Aristotle's knowledge of the reasoned fact, Hume's demonstrative knowledge, and modern treatments of logic following in the tradition of Mach's and Russell's versions of positivism. This form of explanation is particularly related to logical positivism's blending of empiricism with formal symbolic logic and hypothetico-deductive techniques, and its desire to unify the methods of scientific procedure.

Radical behaviorist explanation

1. What conditions are relevant to the occurrence of the behavior? What are the variables of which it is a function?

2. "When I said 'explanation,' I simply meant the causal account. An explanation is the demonstration of a functional relationship between behavior and manipulable or controllable variables" (Skinner, 1964, p. 102).

Interpretation
The use of scientific terms and principles in talking about facts when too little is known to make prediction and control possible, or when precise manipulation is not feasible.

REFERENCES

Baars, B. J. (1986). *The cognitive revolution in psychology.* New York: Guilford.
Block, N. (Ed.). (1980). *Readings in philosophical psychology, Vol. 1.* Cambridge, MA: Harvard University Press.

Boring, E. G. (1950). *A history of experimental psychology*. New York: Appleton-Century-Crofts.

Braithwaite, R. B. (1953). *Scientific explanation*. Cambridge: Cambridge University Press.

Catania, A. C. (1993). The unconventional philosophy of science of behavior analysis. *Journal of the Experimental Analysis of Behavior, 60*, 449–452.

Catania, A. C., & Harnad, S. (Eds.). (1988). *The selection of behavior: The operant behaviorism of B. F. Skinner: Comments and controversies*. Cambridge: Cambridge University Press.

Harré, R. (1970). *Principles of scientific thinking*. Chicago, IL: University of Chicago Press.

Hempel, C. G., & Oppenheim, P. (1948). Studies in the logic of explanation. *Philosophy of Science, 115*, 135–175.

Hocutt, M. (1985). Spartans, strawmen, and symptoms. *Behaviorism, 13*, 87–97.

Hull, C. L. (1937). Mind, mechanism, and adaptive behavior. *Psychological Review, 44*, 1–32.

Kaplan, A. (1964). *The conduct of inquiry*. San Francisco, CA: Chandler.

Kendler, H. H., & Spence, J. T. (1971). Tenets of neobehaviorism. In H. H. Kendler & J. T. Spence (Eds.), *Essays in neobehaviorism: A memorial volume to Kenneth W. Spence*, pp. 11–40. New York: Appleton-Century-Crofts.

Killeen, P. R. (1976). The schemapiric view. Notes on S. S. Stevens' philosophy and *Psychophysics*. *Journal of the Experimental Analysis of Behavior, 25*, 123–128.

Marx, M. H. (1951). *Psychological theory*. New York: Macmillan.

Moore, J. (1990). On behaviorism, privacy, and mentalism. *Journal of Mind and Behavior, 11*, 19–36.

Moore, J. (1998). On behaviorism, theories, and hypothetical constructs. *Journal of Mind and Behavior, 19*, 215–242.

Moore, J. (2000). Varieties of scientific explanation. *The Behavior Analyst, 23*, 173–190.

Pitt, J. C. (Ed.). (1988). *Theories of explanation*. New York: Oxford University Press.

Russell, B. (1932). *Mysticism and logic*. London: George Allen.

Salmon, W. (1989). *Four decades of scientific explanation*. Minneapolis, MN: University of Minnesota Press.

Schnaitter, R. (1986). Behavior as a function of inner states and outer circumstances. In T. Thompson & M. D. Zeiler (Eds.), *The analysis and integration of behavioral units*, pp. 247–274. Hillsdale, NJ: Erlbaum.

Skinner, B. F. (1938). *The behavior of organisms*. New York: Appleton-Century-Crofts.

Skinner, B. F. (1945). The operational analysis of psychological terms. *Psychological Review, 52*, 270–277, 291–294.

Skinner, B. F. (1953). *Science and human behavior*. New York: Macmillan.

Skinner, B. F. (1957). *Verbal behavior*. New York: Appleton-Century-Crofts.

Skinner, B. F. (1964). Behaviorism at fifty. In T. W. Wann (Ed.), *Behaviorism and phenomenology*, pp. 79–97. Chicago: University of Chicago Press.

Skinner, B. F. (1969). *Contingencies of reinforcement*. New York: Appleton-Century-Crofts.

Skinner, B. F. (1972). *Cumulative record*. New York: Appleton-Century-Crofts.

Skinner, B. F. (1974). *About behaviorism*. New York: Knopf.

Skinner, B. F. (1979). *The shaping of a behaviorist*. New York: Knopf.

Skinner, B. F. (1990). Can psychology be a science of mind? *American Psychologist, 45*, 1206–1210.

Stevens, S. S. (1935a). The operational basis of psychology. *American Journal of Psychology, 47*, 323–330.

Stevens, S. S. (1935b). The operational definition of psychological concepts. *Psychological Review, 42*, 517–527.

Stevens, S. S. (1936). Psychology: The propadeutic science. *Philosophy of Science, 3*, 90–103.

Stevens, S. S. (1939). Psychology and the science of science. *Psychological Bulletin, 36*, 221–263.

Stevens, S. S. (1957). On the psychophysical law. *Psychological Review, 64*, 153–181.

Turner, M. B. (1967). *Philosophy and the science of behavior*. New York: Appleton-Century-Crofts.

Wallace, W. A. (1972). *Causality and scientific explanation, Vol. 1*. Ann Arbor, MI: University of Michigan Press.

Williams, B. A. (1986). On the role of theory in behavior analysis. *Behaviorism, 14*, 111–124.

STUDY QUESTIONS

1. Describe and give an example of the traditional form of explanation called instantiation.

2. Describe and give an example of the traditional form of explanation called the covering law model.

3. Describe what radical behaviorists mean by explanation.

4. Describe how radical behaviorists view the relation between description and explanation.

5. Describe how radical behaviorists view the relation between prediction and explanation.

6. Describe why some scientific statements (e.g., the gas laws) may not specifically be expressed in terms of cause-and-effect relations.

7. Describe how traditional approaches (Block, Harré) view the contribution of internal components, properties, or parts to explanation.

8. Describe how radical behaviorists view the contribution of internal components, properties, or parts to explanation.

9. Describe what radical behaviorists mean by epistemological dualism, and indicate why it represents a problem.

10. Describe why the dimensions of a scientific explanation are of concern to radical behaviorists.

11. Describe what radical behaviorists mean by interpretation.

Section 3

Comparison and Contrast with Alternative Viewpoints

Chapters 14 through 18 make up Section 3 of this book. These chapters compare and contrast radical behaviorism with alternative conceptual and philosophical viewpoints. Chapter 14 critically examines mentalism, the generic name for the family of traditional internalist positions that appeal to causes from another dimension in behavioral explanations. Chapter 15 takes up one example of mentalism: cognitive psychology. Chapter 16 takes up a second example of mentalism: psycholinguistics. Chapters 17 and 18 address representative topics in philosophical psychology, such as various other intellectual positions nominally identified as behaviorisms, dispositions, mind-body relations, agency, intentionality, intensionality, and pragmatism.

Section 3

Comparison and Contrast with Alternative Viewpoints

14

Opposition to Mentalism

Synopsis of Chapter 14: The first section of this book consisted of six chapters concerned with the foundations of radical behaviorism. These chapters dealt with history, behavior as a subject matter in its own right, categories of behavior, concepts in behavior analysis, and selection by consequences as a causal mode in behavior, across the three levels of phylogeny, ontogeny, and culture. The second section of this book consisted of six chapters that examined the realization of the radical behaviorist program. These chapters dealt with elementary and complex verbal behavior, private behavioral events, the nature of science and scientific methods, and two forms of scientific verbal behavior: theories and explanations. The third section of the book consists of five chapters that compare and contrast radical behaviorism with alternative conceptual and philosophical viewpoints. Chapter 14, the first chapter in the third section, specifically addresses the topic of mentalism. An orientation may be regarded as mentalistic when it holds that an appeal to causal phenomena from an internal dimension is necessary in an explanation of behavior. Mentalism has been, and indeed continues to be, the dominant viewpoint in Western culture. Radical behaviorism is opposed to mentalism. The chapter gives some examples of mentalism, and then considers the source of the explanatory talk called mentalistic. The chapter concludes with an assessment of why mentalism is objectionable to radical behaviorists.

Chapter 1 indicated that an important concept in the analysis of various viewpoints in psychology is mentalism. Mentalism is a particular perspective on the causal explanation of behavior, and this perspective differs significantly from that of radical behaviorism. What, then, is mentalism, and why is radical behaviorism so opposed to it?

A DEFINITION OF MENTALISM

In simple terms, an orientation is mentalistic when it explains behavior by appealing to causal phenomena from an internal dimension. The phenomena are regarded as part of a dimension that is inferred to be inside the organism in some sense, and qualitatively different from the dimension in which behavior takes place, rather than just a subset of that dimension. The dimension is typically referred to using such descriptors as psychic, "mental," cognitive, spiritual, subjective, conceptual, hypothetical, or theoretical. The internal phenomena are typically characterized as acts, states, mechanisms, processes, schemata, representations, expectancies, memory traces, feelings, or comparable sorts of mental or cognitive entities. Skinner has collectively referred to many of these phenomena as "explanatory fictions." Conventional dualism, in which the mind (or some phenomenon from the nonphysical, nonmaterial dimension) is presumed to cause behavior (which is in the physical, material dimension), is probably the most common form of mentalism, but other forms are possible. Whether the other forms of mentalism successfully avoid the scientific liabilities of dualism is a debatable question. Radical behaviorists believe many if not most forms of contemporary psychology are mentalistic by this definition. Regardless of the form, mentalism takes for granted that (a) there are these sorts of mental entities in another dimension, and (b) an explanation of behavior necessarily consists in specifying these entities as causally effective antecedents.

Readers may recall that in Chapter 1, Skinner defined radical behaviorism as a philosophy of science that treated behavior as a subject matter in its own right, apart from explanations that appealed to internal factors, either mental or physiological. Similarly, Skinner (1950) objected to theories that appealed to neural, mental, or conceptual causal entities. At the heart of these statements is a concern about mentalism. In short, explanations that appeal to mental or hypothetical or physiological causal factors are mentalistic. As reviewed in Chapter 13, radical behaviorism seeks explanations at a descriptively consistent level, in terms of functional relations between behavior and environmental variables. Given this approach to explanation, Skinner's objections to explanations that appealed to mental and hypothetical causal factors and his regarding those explanations as mentalistic may not be surprising. However, his objections to explanations that appealed to neural and physiological causal factors and his regarding them as mentalistic may be surprising. As discussed in Chapter 1, an explanatory appeal to neural or physiological variables can be mentalistic in two cases. First, the explanation may invest neural or physiological variables with some kind of internal power or force to cause the behavior in question. Skinner (1950) cited explanations of behavior that appealed to the making and breaking of synaptic connections, the disrupting or reorganizing of electrical fields, or the concentration or diffusing of ions, where these physiological events are taken as the cause of behavior, without any effort to ascertain what had caused the physiological events in question. More contemporary examples are explanations of behavior that appeal to the causal efficacy of brain structures, hormone levels, neurotransmitters, and various other features of neural and physiological functioning. Second, the explanation may invoke neural and physiological factors in an effort to legitimize inferences about mental causes. The physiology may only be a thinly disguised appeal to a dualistic cause from somewhere else.

Thus, the generic term *mentalism* applies to particular types of explanations that cite a wide range of internal factors, and can even include explanations whose principal causal factors are neural or physiological. Of course, neural or physiological factors can be included in another way in explanations, by providing continuity within a behavioral event and between behavioral events. This way was discussed in Chapter 4, and is not mentalistic because there is no appeal to causally effective antecedents from other dimensions.

Mentalism exists in many forms. Therefore, the sense of something being a causally effective antecedent can take many forms. In some cases, perhaps the most common, mentalists hold that the mental factors initiate or originate the behavior. For example, an explanation might state that an individual spontaneously decided to pursue a particular course of action, where the use of "spontaneously" implies a capricious action uncaused by environmental circumstances. In other cases, the mental factors operate the machinery of the body to produce desired ends, and the job of psychology is to determine the nature of the machinery that is available to be operated. This approach is the "ghost in the machine" case, attributable to Descartes. In still other cases, mentalists are concerned with factors or conditions from another dimension that are held to underlie the behavior in question and afford "competence." By competence is meant a supposed underlying capability that enables an organism to behave in a particular way. Developmental psychologists often offer these sorts of explanations, particularly concerning language acquisition in children. In still other cases, the internal phenomena are endowed with homuncular power to cause behavior of a sort that is more properly a sort of behavior that the organism as a whole is doing. This latter sort occurs when the "mind" (or in physiologically tinged instances of mentalism, the brain) is inferred to be the source of making judgments, reaching decisions, weighing alternatives, serving an executive function, choosing, discriminating, perceiving, attributing, expecting, desiring, intending, and so on. The field of cognitive psychology generally, and cognitive neuroscience especially, is unselfconsciously committed to such a viewpoint. For example, in their important review of the philosophical foundations of cognitive neuroscience, Bennett and Hacker (2003) criticize the tendency in cognitive neuroscience to take psychological terms such as those listed above (e.g., judging, deciding, choosing, etc.), which properly characterize the action of the whole organism, as being caused by the action of a part. This tendency constitutes mentalism, if not dualism, and they identify it as the "mereological fallacy."

Many positions in other forms of psychology—such as in social psychology, sensation and perception, personality theory, and even much learning theory such as is represented in mediational neobehaviorism—are substantially if not totally mentalistic, by virtue of their appeal to inner mental causes from another dimension in their explanations. Neither time nor space is available for anything remotely close to an exhaustive listing here of the mentalism in these other forms. In any event, regardless of how mentalists conceive of the causal relation, mentalists typically argue that an appeal to these mental phenomena is *required* to adequately explain at least some, and perhaps all, instances of behavior. Mentalists consider any explanation of behavior to be deficient if it doesn't appeal to these sorts of mental phenomena. Obviously, radical behaviorism is squarely at odds with this entire orientation.

The paragraph above suggested that mediational neobehaviorism was substantially mentalistic. This suggestion may be puzzling to some readers, because historically any given form of behaviorism is supposed to differ from mentalism. The point here is that even though a position might be regarded as nominally behavioristic, radical behaviorists argue that the position might still evidence mentalism. Consider the predominant form of behaviorism, mediational S – O – R neobehaviorism, discussed in Chapter 3. Researchers who work in this tradition are concerned with the internal, unobservable factors that "mediate" the relation between stimulus and response. By *mediation* is meant that external stimuli activate some intervening, internal process or entity that is connected in a complex but systematic way to an eventual response, and the mediating process or entity is the proper focus of psychological science, rather than the actual response. The response is regarded as providing the evidence for the operation of the mediating internal process. Thus, explanations in mediational neobehaviorism emphasize the causal role of this internal, nonbehavioral process or entity, and by this criterion mediational neobehaviorism is mentalistic. Note that the mentalism is not circumvented by claims that the presumed mediators have been operationally defined.

The descriptions above focus on mentalistic descriptions of an observed person's behavior, such as a participant in an experiment. However, as described in Chapter 13 in the discussion of epistemological dualism, mentalism can also be involved in a more subtle way in an explanation. Scientists and researchers may explain their own behavior of explaining in mentalistic terms. Indeed, scientists often appeal to theories, hypotheses, insights, constructs, inferential processes, logic, and so on, as pre-behavioral entities or activities from another dimension that cause the scientist to explain an event correctly. Radical behaviorists argue that the scientific behavior called explaining is in the final analysis operant behavior. As operant behavior, explaining is itself to be explained in terms of contingencies involving various forms of discriminative stimuli and various forms of reinforcers. Mentalism is still a problem when the behavior of the scientist is accounted for in mentalistic terms, even if an explanation of the participant's behavior does not appear to appeal to mental causes.

Note that just saying "mental" words is not by itself mentalistic. Rather, what makes a given statement mentalistic is using mental terms in a causal explanation of behavior. Sometimes, the verbal behavior said to be mentalistic is influenced partially by naturalistic factors, rather than totally by mentalistic factors, but the issue is whether the mentalistic influence predominates. If it does, then it is called mentalistic.

An analogy might be helpful at this point. Often individuals speak of the sun rising in the east and setting in the west. Such a geocentric statement would be the counterpart of a mentalistic explanation in astronomy if the individual is arguing that an ethereal charioteer and a team of winged horses pull the sun from below the eastern horizon of a flat and stationary Earth to start the day, across the sky during the day, and to beyond the western horizon to end the day. In contrast, the statement is not mentalistic if the individual is arguing that the Earth is spinning on its axis and it is a stationary sun that only gives the appearance of rising and setting. Rather, the important issue is the source of control over the verbal behavior called mentalistic.

EXAMPLES OF MENTALISM

Folk Psychology

Once mentalism is recognized, its prevalence in contemporary culture is hard to ignore. Numerous examples may be reviewed here, starting with "folk psychology." Folk psychology is the name given to the conception of humans that is associated with everyday language. For example, everyday language has a large number of conventionally accepted, "common-sense" terms, such as wishes and wants, thoughts and feelings, intentions and beliefs. These terms are held to refer to phenomena in the realm of the mental or the mind. Moreover, the proper understanding or explanation of behavior is assumed to take the form of identifying sensory stimulation, which in turn gives rise to one of the mental states, which may then link to one or more other mental states, which ultimately link to observable behavior. Folk psychology, then, is the everyday mentalism of Western culture. It accepts the terms of everyday language as correctly identifying our underlying psychological functioning, such that those terms should be regarded as having functional or structural referents in the dimension of the mind. Moreover, because they are often present just prior to behavior, the vernacular seizes upon them as causes when an explanation of behavior is sought. An example would be an individual who smells food cooking while walking down the street. The folk psychology account is that the aroma creates a mental state of hunger, which is then linked with the belief that hunger can be assuaged by entering a restaurant, which is then linked with the memory that more favored restaurant A is closed on a particular day, but less favored restaurant B is open, which finally causes the individual to enter restaurant

B. The behavior is explained in such terms as hunger, belief, and memory. The concern is not so much with the publicly observable behavior of entering restaurant B, but rather with the character of the state of hunger, the strength of the belief, and the storage and retrieval processes associated with the memory that restaurant A is closed but B is open. Much of traditional psychology uncritically accepts folk psychology as correctly identifying the phenomena that a science of behavior should address, and then tries to do so.

At issue is not so much whether one can say people wish and want, desire and believe, intend and feel. Of course people can. However, it is another matter to say such things as wishes and wants, desires and beliefs, intentions and feelings exist as entities that people have, that these terms correctly map the underlying reality of human psychological functioning, and that they cause behavior. To be sure, internal phenomena can be involved in psychological explanations. At issue is how the nature and functional role of internal phenomena are formulated, so that effective explanations of behavior arise.

Feelings

Consider "feelings." In a folk psychology account, feelings are regarded as subjective things, inside one's body, that cause subsequent behavior. When individuals are asked why they did something, society readily accepts the statement "Because I felt like it" as an explanation. As recounted in Chapter 10, radical behaviorists argue that what are felt are conditions of the body, and that those conditions are themselves reactions to environmental circumstances. In this view, feelings are themselves dependent variables, rather than independent variables. Some conditions cause the feelings, and some conditions cause the to-be-explained behavior. Sometimes the conditions that cause the feelings are the same as those that cause the behavior, and sometimes the conditions that cause the feelings differ from those that cause the behavior. In any case, if feelings have any relation to an explanation of behavior, one needs to go back far enough in the causal sequence to ask what caused the feelings. In particular, the circumstances that caused the feelings are what are functionally related to behavior, rather than the feelings themselves. Analysis of the causal sequence is unfinished if it doesn't trace back to those antecedent conditions. At best, the feelings are intermediate by-products of the circumstances that cause behavior, and a particular feeling may not be functionally related at all to a person's eventual behavior, despite societal tendencies to attribute causality to feelings.

Beliefs

Consider "beliefs." Beliefs are another integral element of folk psychology. Commonly, beliefs are viewed as mental states that cause behavior. Radical behaviorists argue that beliefs are comments on the strength of behavior. That is, if one believes that x is the case, the probability is high that one will frequently act in ways consistent with x being the case. For example, one will state that x is the case. Thus, beliefs may be understood as statements about behavior, rather than mental states that cause behavior (since there are no mental states anyway). As with feelings, one is obliged to identify where the beliefs come from. Again, to talk of beliefs is to be concerned with the strength of the dependent variable, rather than an independent variable.

Intentionality

Consider "intentionality." The traditional concept from folk psychology is that behavior is "purposive." In addition, behavior is said to reflect the notion of agency. That is, persons don't simply act in a mechanical way. Rather, they have conceptions and can state that their actions will achieve some purpose. In short, this conception holds that humans are active agents who make independent contributions to their own behavior, not mechanical automata that merely react to pushes and pulls from environmental stimulation. In regard to this conception, radical behaviorists agree that behavior is not a mechanical process. Indeed, operant behavior, with its emphasis on the consequences of behavior, is the very field of purpose. Behavior is with respect to the environment, as implied by the notion of a contingency with the elements of a discriminative stimulus and consequence. However, behavior analysts argue that any apparent role of a pre-existing conception is simply the discriminative effect of one's own verbal behavior. This form of verbal regulation is itself attributable to contingencies in the lifetime of the individual in question. Thus, the individual represents a unique history of interaction with the environment as well as a specific genetic endowment, and so clearly the individual is contributing something to the explanation of behavior. Attributing behavior to various internal entities of uncertain origin is both mischievous and deceptive.

Day (1976) characterized mentalism in the following passage, also linking it to the folk psychology of Western culture:

> At heart, behaviorists mean by mentalism a conception of the nature of man that is tacitly assumed or taken for granted to be true and that is deeply ingrained in our culture as part of Western civilization…. From the Greeks we have it that the most important thing about a human being is his capacity for rationality: man is a rational animal. Yet the concept of rationality can not go very far by itself in enabling us to make sense of behavior. The mentalistic outlook involves a complete system of primitive psychology. Our rationality consists of our making use of *ideas* in a fashion that is *logically satisfactory*; our words have meaning because they are external symbols of our ideas; and all it takes for communication to be successful is to speak distinctly with words the other person is familiar with; behavior is rational if it follows a decision reached as a result of clear thinking; action following a *decision* manifests the human capacity for *choice;* it is up to the individual as an *autonomous agent* to act on his decision or not; he makes his choices and acts on his decisions according to his *will*; his will is *free*, since, as I have said, it is up to the individual to act on his own decision or not; however, man's freedom carries

with it the *responsibility* each person must bear for the consequences of his acts, and hence we are appropriately liable to the judgment of others and subject to their *condemnation* and *blame* (or approval, as the case may be). And so the primitive psychological account goes on. (p. 539)

In this passage, Day linked mentalism to the familiar picture of the human condition that has emerged in Western civilization. This picture includes the basis for jurisprudence, government, and organized religion. Consequently, it is little wonder that mentalism is so prevalent in contemporary society.

Intelligence

Consider "intelligence." In a traditional view, intelligence is regarded as some mental attribute, distributed across the population in a normal, bell-shaped curve. A lucky few have a lot, an unlucky few have only a little, but most have an intermediate amount. Tests reveal how much an individual possesses, and whether it is composed of subcategories of intelligence. For radical behaviorists, contingencies associated with our linguistic practices and cultural assumptions lead us to say a person does something intelligently, then does something that shows intelligence, and finally has intelligence. Through a series of word-to-word linkages and other socially mediated relations, a term that started as an adverb ("intelligently"), describing the efficiency and accuracy of a response in the behavioral dimension, is converted to a noun ("intelligence"), naming an entity in a supposed mental dimension that caused the response. The whole process subscribes to normative cultural traditions, according to which inner entities from another dimension cause behavior. All this is mentalism. Comparable arguments can be made for many other terms from the lexicon of traditional psychology.

To be sure, as Chapter 10 outlined, part of the environment with which individuals interact is private, and individuals may sometimes engage in covert operant behavior, but privacy and covertness are concerned with how many people have access to the phenomena in question, not whether the phenomena are in another dimension. There is only one dimension. Although publicly observable events are certainly the key to understanding all forms of behavior, including covert, radical behaviorism is not limited to only the publicly observable aspects of the one dimension. However, for radical behaviorists, private stimuli gain their influence through interactions with the environment; their origins are not simply declared to be innate or emergent. Again, Skinner (e.g., 1953, 1969) wrote a great deal about the importance of a naturalistic understanding of the participation of private behavioral events in contingencies; for example, in chapters on thinking, recall, and problem-solving. Consequently, readers may refer to Skinner's arguments in addition to the coverage in this book. It is simply wrong to claim that for radical behaviorists, explanations can include only publicly observable factors.

The "Copy Theory"

Early versions of behaviorism, such as classical S – R behaviorism reviewed in Chapter 2, sought to be objective and describe behavior in mechanistic terms. An important principle was linear, antecedent causation, in which causal efficacy was bound up in a prior stimulus that was temporally and spatially contiguous with the response. When it became apparent that this model wasn't satisfactory—for example, for reasons related to the variability and spontaneity of behavior—some behaviorists adopted the S – O – R approach of mediational neobehaviorism. A popular version of the mediational approach is one in which the organism is presumed to take in the environment, transform it, create a representation of it, and then respond with respect to the transformed representation, rather than to the environment itself. This version is often referred to as "the copy theory," in the sense that the organism is making a copy of its world, and is another instance of mentalism.

Zuriff (1985, p. 161) has outlined the main features of the copy theory, which are paraphrased below:

1. Behavior is typically not in one-to-one correspondence with the environment.

2. Because behavior is typically not in one-to-one correspondence with the environment, there must be something else with which it is in one-to-one correspondence, and that something else is an internal representation of the environment.

3. The organism must engage in some internal processes and operations by which it transforms input from the environment into an internal representation, accesses the representation, and subsequently behaves.

4. An adequate theory of behavior must identify the features of the processes and operations by which the organism transforms and represents the environment.

Zuriff (1985) goes on to cite numerous examples from the literature that testify to the popularity of the copy theory:

> The statement that the world as we know it is a representation is ... a truism—there is really no way it can be wrong.... We can say in the first place, then, that knowing necessarily involves representation. (Attneave, 1974, p. 493)

> We have no direct, immediate access to the world, nor to any of its properties.... Whatever we know of reality has been mediated, not only by the organs of sense but by complex systems which interpret and reinterpret sensory information. (Neisser, 1967, p. 3)

> Mentalists are committed to the view that the behavior of an organism is contingent upon its internal states—in particular, upon the character of its subjective representation of the environment. (Fodor, Bever, & Garrett, 1974, p. 506)

> The human organism responds primarily to cognitive representations of its environments rather than to those environments per se. (Mahoney, 1977, p. 7)

Noteworthy in all these examples is the continued commitment to the doctrine of contiguous antecedent causation. When the external environment wouldn't do, an internal copy was invented to preserve the notion of a causal stimulus that was contiguous with the response. Indeed, the link between mediational neobehaviorism and cognitive psychology is apparent. Left unexamined is the question of who sees the copy. Although mentalists typically deny they appeal to extra-physical factors and relations, the answer to the question of who sees the copy seems not to differ from long-standing doctrines of the soul. Secularizing the soul by saying "mind" or physiologizing it by saying "brain" does not change the mentalistic commitment to internal causes from another dimension.

The "Medical Model" of Abnormality

The mentalistic outlook pervades a great many aspects of psychological thinking. Consider the "Medical Model" of abnormality. The medical model is:

1. A general orientation to the problem of abnormality in which:
   a. unusual behaviors (bizarre, extreme, disturbing) are viewed as symptoms
   b. of an underlying mental pathology (some category from DSM-IV)
   c. caused by an underlying internal or mental entity, state, or condition (biological: chemical imbalance, brain injury; psychological: weak ego, defective personality, faulty cognitive perception, etc.)

2. In the same way that:
   a. unusual medical conditions (cough, fever, sore throat) are viewed as symptoms
   b. of an underlying medical pathology (cold, flu, pneumonia)
   c. caused by an underlying medical entity or condition (bacteria, virus)

3. In each case, the task of the specialist is to infer the nature of the underlying pathology and the underlying cause on the basis of the evidence provided by the symptoms.

The medical model approach predominates in the field of abnormal psychology. The mentalism in the medical model approach is the postulation of the underlying internal or mental entity, state, or condition as the cause of the pathology. Following from traditional personality theory, the medical model approach is concerned with identifying the internal components which, when they function abnormally, constitute the cause of the abnormal behavior. This entire orientation, of course, is mentalistic. The practice was derived from the unsophisticated, mentalistic diagnostic practices of medicine beginning in the late 1800s, since the early workers in the field of abnormal behavior came from medicine. Consequently, those workers simply applied their practices. Absent is the recognition that any instance of abnormal behavior could be caused by anything other than a faulty internal phenomenon.

Freud

Finally, the positions of two prominent figures in psychology may be mentioned as examples of mentalism: Sigmund Freud and Jean Piaget. Freud was clearly an acute observer of the human condition. Nevertheless, the way he conceived of personality structures, psychosexual drives, and the interplay between a presumed mental life and developmental experiences was obviously mentalistic. For Freud, one could simply not understand or explain behavior without appealing to such factors. In his defense, Freud did conceive of the drives as biologically based and instinctive, but the origins and dimensions of the other factors, such as personality components, were uncertain.

Piaget

Similarly, Piaget proposed an elaborate system of childhood cognitive development. This system appealed to various mental acts and structures that Piaget sought to incorporate into a developmental ("genetic") scheme. No doubt, most readers have heard of his system of cognitive development in terms of sensorimotor, pre-operational, concrete operational, and formal operational stages. Piaget appealed to active mental processes by which a child organized information in characteristic ways at each stage. There are schemata that represent the "cognitive structures" at particular ages and in turn allow a child to accomplish certain tasks. If these schemata are not present, one must wait until they are before the child can meaningfully engage in some task. All this is simply mentalism. What is at issue is the behavioral repertoire of the developing child. Any benefit of a Piagetian analysis is that it identifies certain experiences and certain elements of a behavioral repertoire as modal prerequisites for future elements. The liability of a Piagetian analysis is that it neglects to systematically identify what can be done to facilitate the development of that repertoire.

Again, the mentalism in such statements is ultimately objectionable because of the source of the talk of the inner entities in the explanation. Analysis of the source would reveal it lies predominantly in cultural tradition and social practice, rather than observation of natural events. If the source of the talk about internal acts, states, mechanisms, processes, and so on in the explanation is not critically examined, the possibilities for prediction and control are not assessed, and the possibilities for improving the human condition remain untouched.

Review

Given that much of psychology is mentalistic, examples of mentalism may be found in virtually any traditional text in psychology. The important question concerns the source of the mentalistic causal entities spoken about: Are they from another dimension? Where did they come from: innate, acquired, emergent, developmental? Just calling them theoretical or inferential or hypothetical or logical constructs or "it is 'as if' they exist" won't suffice, without critically examining the source of control over their emission. Instances of mentalistic verbal behavior need to be examined on a case-by-case basis to determine the source of their control. One instance of verbal behavior may be mentalistic because it is controlled by one set of factors, and another instance may be mentalistic because it is controlled by another set of factors, but ultimately mentalism of any sort forecloses analysis of the functional relation between behavior and environment.

As suggested earlier, some mentalists are unselfconsciously dualists who talk of a formal ontological distinction between mind and matter, or physical and nonphysical, and who reject determinism. However, other mentalists claim that they reject dualism. They claim to be as committed to materialism and physicalism as scientists in other disciplines, such as physics and chemistry, and they embrace determinism. For radical behaviorists, the question is what factors control the verbal behavior in question, rather than ontology per se. If the verbal behavior of those who assert they are not dualists is controlled by many of the same factors of language use and social or cultural tradition as those who are dualists, then their verbal behavior is just as troublesome as that of those who subscribe to a dualistic ontology. The verbal behavior may only exhibit epistemological dualism, as noted in the last chapter, but it remains a dualism.

SOURCES OF CONTROL OVER MENTALISTIC TALK

As implied above, it is not enough to simply say that radical behaviorists oppose mentalism. Without getting too far ahead in the story, suffice it to say that radical behaviorists have the same obligation to critically analyze mentalism and account for the phenomena that the mentalist tries to account for, as they do any other approach to psychology.

In the final analysis, mentalism is an explanatory practice, and hence verbal behavior. More specifically, it is a particular way of attempting to explain behavior. Mentalistic verbal behavior is not of concern to radical behaviorists simply because it purports to refer to subjective, mentalistic entities from another dimension, which aren't acceptable in a scientific explanation because they are not publicly observable. There is no such other dimension, and there are no such entities. Therefore, mentalistic verbal behavior can't literally be referring to that dimension or those entities. At issue in analyses of mentalism and the problems it creates are the factors that cause mentalism. In the present view, all verbal behavior, even that which is called mentalistic, is a function of naturalistic factors that exist in space and time, in the physical and material dimension. The task is to determine what those factors are. Thus, radical behaviorists hold that even mentalistic verbal behavior may be analyzed in terms of the contingencies that promote it.

Accordingly, the next question is: Where does mentalistic talk come from? Actually, this question is not really specific enough, as there are in a sense two questions involved. The initial question is: What do mentalists say is the origin of these causal mental phenomena? The second is: What do behavior analysts say is the origin of talk of these causal mental phenomena? The initial question is addressed first. According to mentalists, the causal internal phenomena are sometimes regarded as innate or developmental or emergent, but often their origin is simply left unspecified. The ambiguity about their origin and nature was one of the factors that led Skinner (1971) to talk in terms of "autonomous man." Perhaps in recognition of the ambiguity of the origins of these mental phenomena, recent versions of the position known as "Evolutionary Psychology," advanced by such contemporary authors as Steven Pinker, attempt to link mental factors to evolution and genetics, particularly in the case of verbal behavior. For many radical behaviorists, a closer examination of the facts suggests Pinker's position is biologically implausible.

What, then, do radical behaviorists say is the origin of these causal mental phenomena? Again, as there is literally no mental dimension, there are literally no mental entities that participate in contingencies that cause people to engage in mentalistic verbal behavior. Therefore, to ask about the sources of mentalistic explanations is to ask about the contingencies in the natural world that cause speakers to talk in mentalistic ways.

In brief, mentalism may be understood as arising from our conventional linguistic practices, as they are embedded in a matrix of prevailing cultural assumptions. In particular, conventional word usage gives rise to unfortunate metaphors and other sources of extraneous influence. Even though he was one of the original S – O – R mediational theorists, Woodworth (1921) commented insightfully on conventional linguistic practices in the following way:

> Instead of "memory," we should say "remembering"; instead of "thought" we should say "thinking"; instead of "sensation" we should say "seeing, hearing", etc. But, like other branches, psychology is prone to transform its verbs into nouns. Then what happens? We forget that our nouns are merely substitutes for verbs, and go hunting for the things denoted by the nouns; but there are no such things, there are only the activities that we started with, seeing, remembering, and so on.

> Intelligence, consciousness, the unconscious, are by rights not nouns, nor even adjectives or verbs; they are adverbs. The real facts are that the individual acts intelligently—more or less so—acts consciously or unconsciously, as he may also act skillfully, persistently, excitedly. It is a safe rule, then, on encountering any menacing psychological noun, to strip off its linguistic mask, and see what manner of activity lies behind. (pp. 5–6)

Two passages from Skinner's writings also illustrate this source of mentalism. Here is the first:

Turning from observed behavior to a fanciful inner world continues unabated. Sometimes it is little more than a linguistic practice. We tend to make nouns of adjectives and verbs and must then find a place for the things the nouns are said to represent. We say that a rope is strong, and before long we are speaking of its strength. We call a particular kind of strength tensile, and then explain that the rope is strong because it possesses tensile strength. The mistake is less obvious but more troublesome when matters are more complex. There is no harm in saying that a fluid possesses viscosity, or in measuring and comparing different fluids or the same fluid at different temperatures on some convenient scale. But what does viscosity mean?.... The term is useful in referring to a characteristic of a fluid, but it is nevertheless a mistake to say that a fluid flows slowly because it is viscous or possesses a high viscosity. A state or quality inferred from the behavior of a fluid begins to be taken as a cause.

Consider now a behavioral parallel. When a person has been subjected to mildly punishing consequences in walking on a slippery surface, he may walk in a manner we describe as cautious. It is then easy to say that he walks with caution or that he shows caution. There is no harm in this until we begin to say that he walks carefully because of his caution....

The extraordinary appeal of inner causes and the accompanying neglect of environmental histories and current setting must be due to more than a linguistic practice. I suggest that it has the appeal of the arcane, the occult, the hermitic [sic], the magical—those mysteries which have held so important a position in the history of human thought. It is the appeal of an apparently inexplicable power, in a world which seems to lie beyond the senses and the reach of reason. It is the appeal still enjoyed by astrology, numerology, parapsychology, and psychical research. (Skinner, 1974, pp. 165–166, 169)

Here is the second:

We have not advanced more rapidly to the methods and instruments needed in the study of behavior precisely because of the diverting preoccupation with a supposed or real inner life....

It is easier to make the point in the field of medicine. Until the present century very little was known about bodily practices in health and disease from which useful therapeutic practices could be derived. Yet it should have been worthwhile to call in a physician. Physicians saw many ill people and should have acquired a kind of wisdom, analyzed perhaps but still of value in prescribing simple treatments. The history of medicine, however, is largely the history of barbaric practices—bloodlettings, cuppings, poultices, purgations, violent emetics—which much of the time must have been harmful. My point is that these measures were not suggested by the intuitive wisdom acquired from familiarity with illness; they were suggested by theories, theories about what was going on inside the ill person. Theories of mind have had a similar effect, less dramatic, perhaps, but quite possibly far more damaging.... But philosophy and psychology have had their bleedings, cuppings, and purgations too, and they have obscured simple wisdom. They have diverted wise people from a path that would have led more directly to an eventual science of behavior.... We have been misled by the almost instinctive tendency to look inside any system to see how it works, a tendency doubly powerful in the case of behavior because of the apparent inside information supplied by feelings and introspectively observed states. Our only recourse is to leave that subject to the physiologist, who has, or will have, the only appropriate instruments or methods. (Skinner, 1978, pp. 77, 81)

Ultimately, mentalistic explanations are supported by the social reinforcement inherent in conceiving of the causes of behavior in culturally approved ways. Skinner wrote extensively about the influence of these contingencies, for example, in his book *Beyond Freedom and Dignity*, and in such articles as "Why I Am Not A Cognitive Psychologist" (Skinner, 1977). Unfortunately, because of these strong verbal and cultural contingencies, mentalism and the accompanying appeal to another dimension have always been the dominant orientation in contemporary society, as evidenced in our general cultural outlook.

THE HISTORICAL ORIGIN OF MENTALISM

An examination of the critical literature reveals much that has been written about the historical traditions underlying mentalism. Two examples are provided here, one by J. R. Kantor and the other by Skinner.

J. R. Kantor

Although not a radical behaviorist, the interbehaviorist J. R. Kantor has provided some fiery language excoriating the mentalistic and dualistic traditions in Western culture:

> Dualism may be traced back to the Hellenistic era of our history. At that time through the speculations of the early church fathers, the neoplatonic philosophers like Plotinus, and later Saint Augustine, the "ideal" world was constructed to contrast with the ordinary everyday one. Anguished by the destruction of the grand and glorious Greek and Roman worlds they created the eternal world of spirit. In that transcendental world was concentrated all that was ultimate, truly real, indestructible and perfect. Moreover, the transcendent world afforded an escape from evil and thralldom. The voluble men of the Hellenistic period and beyond made full use of the extrapolative function of speech to recreate the world to match their heart's desire. Students of philosophy are aware of the successive transformations of cosmic spirit into individual soul, which through various metamorphoses became mind, self, the unconscious, the transcendental unit of apperception, the apperception mass, consciousness, sensation, emotion, mental state, mental image, and so on.

> The persistence of philosophical institutions is truly remarkable. When philosophers recently increased their appreciation of the futility of the venerable metaphysics whose speculations have no secure starting place, nor any attainable goal, they did not liquidate that metaphysics but instead developed a variant of it in the guise of analytical and linguistic philosophy. Analytic philosophers instituted a scrutinizing search into the language of philosophy for ways and means of discovering the intrinsic meaning of words and phrases. But they retained the old assumptions of universality, absoluteness, certainty, a priority, and the mind-body dichotomy. Forgetting that terms or words are artifacts produced by various interactions of particular persons, they reify them and endow them with transcendental "meaning." ....

> The implied transcendence here is perhaps better seen when analytic philosophy is carried over into the psychological field. We cannot miss the fanfare that is now being heard in the domain of psycholinguistics. Perhaps the loudest noise is made by those who seek a mystic source for the behavior of children when they learn to speak and continue the behavior when they become adults. It is loudly proclaimed that the speaking process is not a matter of learning at all but the

innate operation of soul. Speaking correctly or grammatically is a power innate in the mind. For corroboration they resort to the writings of the early philosophers who taught the doctrine of psychic intuition in the seventeenth century, for example, Descartes, and the Commonsense Realists of the eighteenth century, for example, Thomas Reid and his followers.

Now, who can ignore the fact that a radical revolution is in order? If we hope to develop an authentic philosophy, the sort that is basic to a valid logic of science and which can serve as an aid to thinking scientific psychology, we must destroy the old transcendental way of thinking, and replace it with a valid philosophy. (Kantor, 1981, pp. 114–116)

B. F. Skinner

Skinner's own version of historical and cultural events responsible for mentalism is more abbreviated, although it too appeals to historical and cultural traditions:

A rough history of the idea is not hard to trace. An occasional phrase in classic Greek writings which seemed to foreshadow the point of view need not be taken seriously. We may also pass over the early bravado of a La Mettrie who could shock the philosophical bourgeoisie by asserting that man was only a machine. Nor were those who simply preferred, for practical reasons, to deal with behavior rather than with less accessible, but nevertheless acknowledged, mental activities close to what is meant by behaviorism today.

The entering wedge appears to have been Darwin's preoccupation with the continuity of the species. In supporting the theory of evolution, it was important to show that man was not essentially different from the lower animals—that every human characteristic, including consciousness and reasoning powers, could be found in other species. Naturalists like Romanes began to collect stories which seemed to show that dogs, cats, elephants, and many other species were conscious and showed signs of reasoning. It was Lloyd Morgan, of course, who questioned this evidence with his Canon of Parsimony. Were there not other ways of accounting for what looked like signs of consciousness or rational powers? Thorndike's experiments at the end of the nineteenth century were in this vein.... Thorndike remained a mentalist, but he greatly advanced the objective study of behavior which had been attributed to mental processes.

The next step was inevitable: if evidence of consciousness and reasoning could be explained in other ways in animals, why not also in man? And if this was the case, what became of psychology as a science of mental life? It was John B. Watson who made the first clear, if rather noisy, proposal that psychology should be regarded simply as a science of behavior. He was not in a very good position to defend it. He had little scientific material to use in his reconstructions. He was forced to pad his textbook with discussions of the physiology of the receptor systems and muscles and with physiological theories which were at the time no more susceptible to proof than the mentalistic theories they were intended to replace. A need for "mediators of behavior which might serve as objective alternatives to thought processes led him to emphasize subaudible speech. The notion was intriguing, because one can usually observe oneself thinking in this way, but it was by no means an adequate or comprehensive explanation. He tangled with introspective psychologists by denying the existence of images. He may well have been acting in good faith, for it has been said that he himself did not have visual imagery; but his arguments caused unnecessary trouble. The relative importance of a genetic endowment in explaining behavior proved to be another disturbing digression.

All this made it easy to lose sight of the central argument—that behavior which seemed to be the product of mental activity could be explained in other ways.... But introspection was already being taken seriously. The concept of a science of mind in which mental events obeyed mental laws had led to the development of psychophysical methods and to the accumulation of facts which seemed to bar the extension of the principle of parsimony. What might hold for animals did not hold for men because men could see their mental processes.

Curiously enough, part of the answer was provided by the psychoanalysts, who insisted that, although a man might be able to see some of his mental life, he could not see all of it. ... [Freud] nevertheless contributed to the behavioristic argument by showing that mental activity did not, at least, require consciousness....

But that was not the whole answer. What about the part of mental life which a man can see? It is a difficult question, no matter what one's point of view, partly because it raises the question of what seeing means and partly because the events seen are private. The fact of privacy cannot, of course, be questioned. Each person is in special contact with a small part of the universe enclosed within his own skin.... The importance assigned to this kind of world varies. For some, it is the only world there is. For others, it is the only part of the world which can be directly known. For still others, it is a special part of what can be known.... (Skinner, 1969, pp. 223–226)

SUMMARY AND CONCLUSIONS: BEHAVIOR-ANALYTIC OBJECTIONS TO MENTALISM

In conclusion, why do radical behaviorists find mentalism so objectionable? At the outset, it should be noted that for most of society and traditional psychology, mentalistic explanations aren't in the least objectionable. Indeed, mentalistic explanations are preferred. Therefore, any movement in psychology like behavior analysis that objects to mentalism is likely to be viewed as some sort of bizarre aberration. No doubt, the sometimes skeptical reception of behavior analysis in society, and perhaps also the controversial opinion that many hold of Skinner himself, testify to this difficulty.

Skinner (1969) described the difficulty of contrasting the mental with the physical in the following passage:

It is a little too simple to paraphrase the behavioristic alternative by saying that there is indeed only one world and that it is the world of matter, for the word "matter" is then no longer useful. Whatever the stuff may be of which the world is made, it contains organisms (of which we are examples) which respond to other parts of it and thus "know" it in a sense not far from "contact." Where the dualist must account for discrepancies between the real world and the world of experience, and the Berkeleyan idealist between different experiences, the behaviorist investigates discrepancies among different responses.

It is no part of such an investigation to try to trace the real world into the organism and to watch it become a copy. (pp. 248–249)

Many think the radical behaviorist objection to mentalism is based on ontological or metaphysical grounds. That is, many think radical behaviorists object to mentalism primarily because it purports to refer to entities that literally exist in another dimension, which are not publicly observable and hence can't be part of a respectable scientific explanation. Although issues related to ontology are clearly involved in the radical behaviorist position on mentalism, radical behaviorists do not necessarily object to talk that appeals to phenomena that are not publicly observable. After all, in some instances radical behaviorists appeal to private events, and those events, by definition, are not publicly observable.

It is probably more appropriate to say that radical behaviorism objects to mentalism for two interrelated reasons, and the reasons are of equal status. The first reason is ontological, but with a slightly different interpretation than that expressed in the paragraph above. Radical behaviorists reject that there is another dimension. Consequently, entities that are talked about as being in another dimension do not literally exist. It is not that they exist but cannot be talked about, but that they do not exist at all. They are explanatory fictions. Talk of such entities is attributable to social and cultural factors, as reviewed earlier in this chapter.

The second reason is that mentalism is unpragmatic. Mentalistic statements and appeals to various explanatory fictions from the mental dimension are substantially under the control of incidental factors, cherished for irrelevant and extraneous reasons. Because of this sort of control, mentalistic statements interfere with an effective understanding of behavior. That is, in the radical behaviorist view, the problem is that mentalism induces people to search for the wrong causes of, and to accept incorrect answers about, the causes of behavior. Radical behaviorists argue that mentalism exerts these harmful effects because it obscures important details, it misrepresents the facts to be accounted for, it impedes the search for genuinely relevant variables, it allays curiosity by getting people to accept the postulation of fictitious entities as explanations, and it generally gives false assurances about the state of our knowledge. Moreover, it leads to the continued use of scientific techniques that should be abandoned, for example, because they are wasteful and ineffective. Humans then needlessly suffer from many conditions that can be corrected.

Thus, radical behaviorists are concerned about mentalism because mentalistic positions interfere with the effective prediction, control, and explanation of behavior. Mentalistic statements and the explanatory fictions to which they appeal lead people to believe that behavior is not an orderly subject matter in its own right, and if they want to look for some causal entity, in whatever sense of causal they might choose, they should look for it in the mental dimension. Regrettably, this whole approach is doomed to failure. To repeat, there is no other dimension, and appeals to explanatory fictions are ineffective and irrelevant. It is an inescapable fact that behavior is related in an orderly way to genetics and contingencies at the level of phylogeny, ontogeny, and the culture. Under the influence of mentalism, people neglect what would be more effectively undertaken to improve the human condition; namely, the analysis of the relation between behavior and contingencies at the level of phylogeny, ontogeny, and the culture. Again, Skinner's (1971) arguments against "autonomous man" and traditional doctrines of "free will" show how troublesome the neglect of contingencies is. Although mental talk may appear to successfully explain behavior, any success is only an illusion. Any apparent success of a mental explanation is related to other factors, rather than its literal mentalism. As Skinner (1974) put it: "We must remember that mentalistic explanations explain nothing" (p. 230). The elements of mentalistic explanations are the legacy of cultural dualism, and portraying them as legitimate because they are "theoretical" is counterproductive.

As recounted in this chapter, mentalism exists in many branches of psychology. The next two chapters continue to examine the relation between radical behaviorism and alternative viewpoints by looking at two influential forms of mentalism in contemporary psychology: cognitive psychology (Chapter 15) and psycholinguistics (Chapter 16).

TABLE 14–1

Mentalism
An orientation may be regarded as mentalistic when it directly or indirectly admits an appeal to internal phenomena (i.e., from another dimension) in a causal explanation of behavior. The internal phenomena are typically characterized as acts, states, mechanisms, processes, schemata, representations, memory traces, feelings, or comparable sorts of mental or cognitive entities. The phenomena are regarded as part of a dimension that is inferred to be inside the organism in some sense, and qualitatively different from the dimension in which observable behavior takes place, rather than just a subset of that dimension. The dimension is typically referred to using such descriptors as psychic, "mental," spiritual, subjective, conceptual, hypothetical, theoretical, or cognitive. Conventional dualism, in which the mind (or some phenomenon from the nonphysical, nonmaterial dimension) is presumed to cause behavior (which is in the physical, material dimension), is probably the most common form of mentalism, but other forms are possible.

Folk psychology
The name given to the conception of humans that is associated with the conventionally accepted, "common-sense" terms of everyday language, such as wishes and wants, thoughts and feelings, intentions and beliefs.

Sources of control over mentalistic verbal behavior
1. Inappropriate metaphors
2. Conventional linguistic practices
3. Social-cultural traditions

Radical behaviorist objections to mentalism

1. Based on pragmatism—mentalism interferes with effective prediction and control of behavior.
2. Mentalism obscures important details.
3. Mentalism misrepresents the facts to be accounted for.
4. Mentalism impedes the search for genuinely relevant variables.
5. Mentalism allays curiosity by getting people to accept the postulation of fictitious entities as explanations
6. Mentalism gives false assurances about the state of our knowledge.
7. Mentalism leads to the continued use of scientific techniques that should be abandoned, such as the hypothetico-deductive method, because they are wasteful and ineffective.

REFERENCES

Attneave, F. (1974). How do you know? *American Psychologist, 29*, 493–499.

Bennett, M. R., & Hacker, P. M. S. (2003). *Philosophical foundations of neuroscience*. Oxford: Blackwell.

Day, W. F. (1976). The case for behaviorism. In M. H. Marx & F. E. Goodson (Eds.), *Theories in contemporary psychology*, pp. 534–545. New York: Macmillan.

Fodor, J., Bever, T., & Garrett, M. (1974). *The psychology of language*. New York: McGraw-Hill.

Kantor, J. R. (1981). *Interbehavioral philosophy*. Chicago, IL: Principia Press.

Mahoney, M. (1977). Reflections on cognitive-learning trend in psychotherapy. *American Psychologist, 32*, 5–13.

Neisser, U. (1967). *Cognitive psychology*. New York: Appleton-Century-Crofts.

Skinner, B. F. (1950). Are theories of learning necessary? *Psychological Review, 57*, 193–216.

Skinner, B. F. (1953). *Science and human behavior*. New York: Free Press.

Skinner, B. F. (1969). *Contingencies of reinforcement*. New York: Appleton-Century-Crofts.

Skinner, B. F. (1971). *Beyond freedom and dignity*. New York: Knopf.

Skinner, B. F. (1974). *About behaviorism*. New York: Knopf.

Skinner, B. F. (1977). Why I am not a cognitive psychologist. *Behaviorism, 5*, 1–10.

Skinner, B. F. (1978). *Reflections on behaviorism and society*. Englewood Cliffs, NJ: Prentice-Hall.

Woodworth, R. S. (1921). *Psychology* (rev. ed.). New York: Henry Holt.

Zuriff, G. E. (1985). *Behaviorism: A conceptual reconstruction*. New York: Columbia University Press.

STUDY QUESTIONS

1. In about three or four sentences, define what radical behaviorists mean by mentalism.

2. Define what is meant by "folk psychology."

3. Describe how radical behaviorists view the relation between feelings and an explanation of behavior.

4. Define what radical behaviorists mean by beliefs.

5. Define intentionality and agency.

6. Describe what radical behaviorists mean by the medical model of abnormality.

7. In three or four sentences, describe the contingencies radical behaviorists say are responsible for mentalistic talk.

8. In three or four sentences, describe why radical behaviorists find mentalism objectionable. Use the term pragmatic knowledgeably in your answer.

15

The Challenge of
Cognitive Psychology

Synopsis of Chapter 15: The chapters in the third section of the book compare and contrast radical behaviorism with alternative conceptual and philosophical viewpoints. Chapter 14 dealt with mentalism. Chapter 15 specifically addresses the relation between radical behaviorism and one form of mentalism, cognitive psychology. The chapter examines the nature of cognitive orientations, their history, and then critically analyzes some common assumptions among cognitivists about the ways that cognitivism differs from behaviorism. The analysis concludes that the assumptions are incorrect for two reasons. First, cognitive psychology is actually an extension of mediational neobehaviorism, rather than a revolutionary alternative. Therefore, cognitive psychology and mediational neobehaviorism are more alike than different. Second, radical behaviorism differs in other ways from both mediational neobehaviorism and cognitive psychology. The present argument is that the differences between Skinner's radical behaviorism and cognitive psychology lie in the respective conceptions of verbal behavior, which in turn give rise to different conceptions regarding the causal explanation of behavior. For cognitive psychology, the position on explanation is an unselfconsciously explicit mentalism, which radical behaviorism rejects. The chapter concludes that because of its commitment to mentalism, cognitive psychology cannot be considered as complementary to radical behaviorism.

Readers will recall that an orientation is mentalistic when its explanations of behavior appeal to internal causal phenomena (e.g., acts, states, mechanisms, processes, entities) from another dimension (e.g., mental, psychic, conceptual, hypothetical, spiritual). Appeals to neural and physiological factors can also be mentalistic when they endow those factors with homuncular power to cause behavior, or when they act as proxies for causal entities from another dimension. Mentalistic orientations argue that explanations must do so to be regarded as adequate. They further argue that because radical behaviorism does not do so, it is inadequate. Radical behaviorism disagrees with the entire range of mentalistic assertions about causal explanations and the elements appropriate to them. The present chapter continues the examination and evaluation of mentalistic orientations by focusing specifically on the challenge of cognitive psychology.

THE NATURE OF COGNITIVE SYSTEMS

Cognitive psychology exists in many varieties. Given this diversity, the present discussion speaks of "cognitive orientations," "cognitive systems," and cognitivism more generally, rather than characterizes the many individual varieties. In general, cognitive orientations emphasize traditional rationalist doctrines in the sense of Plato and Kant, in which the mind is endowed with certain innate functional properties and capabilities. Accordingly, cognitive orientations emphasize an abstract description of the functional properties of internal acts, states, mechanisms, structures, processes, and systems that are said to enable organisms to behave as they do in a given context. Cognitive orientations are further agent-oriented and intentional, in the sense that they are concerned with the self-regulating capabilities that achieve desired end states. Finally, they are less interested, if at all, in the analysis of an actual instance of performance and the identification of particular environmental factors that participate in that instance.

Cognitive systems tend to have the following elements (adapted from Norman, 1981):

1. One or more sets of receptors, by means of which an organism receives information about the world.

2. One or more sets of effectors, by means of which an organism acts upon the world.

3. One or more sets of structures and processes, by means of which an organism: (a) identifies and interprets information received by its receptors, (b) assesses the functional relevance of internal states produced by the information, (c) controls the actions to be performed by its effectors, (d) allocates resources when demands exceed what can immediately be done, and (e) stores and retrieves records of past actions, outcomes, and other relevant experiences, so that the organism can achieve its goals.

Elements 1 and 2 are not remarkable, as they could be elements of virtually any psychological system. What distinguishes cognitivism is the appeal to the structures and processes with the kind of properties stated in 3 above. These structures and processes give cognitive psychology its name, and the different emphases regarding those structures and processes give rise to the many varieties of cognitive psychology. For example, the statements relating to the "Copy Theory" in Chapter 13 on mentalism are consistent with the kind of structures and processes outlined in 3 above. Cognitivists base their argument for these structures and processes on the following considerations (e.g., Norman, 1981):

1. Because resources of the system are necessarily finite, there are times when demands exceed what can be accomplished; therefore, an organism must possess some means of intelligently allocating resources and intelligently synchronizing steps to meet the demands.

2. Because the system will need to make intelligent adjustments, there must be a set of basic operations and instructions, feedback mechanisms, and an executive to oversee system functioning, particularly concerning the regulation of internal states produced by the information the organism receives.

3. The executive must have metaknowledge, or a superordinate level of knowledge in which the executive is capable of observing itself, inferring relations among the concepts it possesses and the events it experiences, and then adjusting its functioning based on feedback from past actions.

The computer and associated information processing systems are often regarded as offering a suitable metaphor for the working of what are presumed to be the underlying mental processes. The computer metaphor is predicated more at the level of the operating system, or a set of instructions that sets up internal functional states. It is not necessarily predicated on any particular program written in any particular programming language. In addition, there is a principle of "multiple realizability." According to this principle, the internal functional states within any particular computer, or even between different computers (e.g., an Apple Macintosh versus a Windows-based computer), may be realized in different ways in their respective central processing units and other components, although in the end the same function may be accomplished with each set of hardware.

Philosophical functionalism is the dominant stance on the mind-body problem and philosophy of mind for cognitive psychology (see Block, 1980; Dennett, 1978; Fodor, 1968). Modern philosophical functionalism regards itself as a coherent materialist philosophy of mind that is concerned with the functional design features of the mechanisms that accomplish the psychologically interesting work of organisms. In keeping with the principle of multiple realizability, the functional design is independent of whatever specific hardware or structures may realize that design, although appeal to various metaphors may be used to give the design some understandable context. The principal feature is the appeal to causal "mental states" that are definable in terms that do not mention physics or chemistry, as would presumably be required by physicalistic definitions of operationism and logical positivism. Rather, the causal mental states are defined in terms of their functional contribution in the chain of events in question, in the same way that internal states of the computer may be defined in terms of their functional contribution to what the computer accomplishes.

PRECURSORS

Cognitive psychology is a relative newcomer to the intellectual scene, but its impact has been remarkable. It unselfconsciously prides itself on its embrace of mentalism and its departure from what it regards as established traditions in psychology. Precursors of cognitive psychology include post-WW II developments in information and communication theory, cybernetics, mathematics and computer technology, and verbal learning traditions (Gardner, 1985). Historically, the date of birth of cognitive psychology is sometimes taken to be September 11, 1956, which is the date of the Symposium on Information Theory at MIT at which several revolutionary papers were presented (Gardner, 1985, p. 28). The decade of the 1960s witnessed the founding of the Harvard Center for Cognitive Studies and the publication of two significant books: *Plans and the Structure of Behavior* (Miller, Galanter, & Pribram, 1960) and *Cognitive Psychology* (Neisser, 1967). The decade of the 1970s witnessed the infusion of financial support from the Sloan Foundation, as well as an increase in the number of textbooks and journals on cognitive psychology (Knapp, 1986). Although Leahey (1992) has challenged whether these events should genuinely be termed a revolution, clearly a sea change in professional psychology was well underway.

Cognitive psychology views itself as the antithesis of behaviorism, and even casual observers of the contemporary scene can scarcely miss the tension between cognitive psychology and behaviorism (see Moore, 1984; Schnaitter, 1987). A conspicuous aspect of this tension is the set of claims by cognitivists that behaviorism is entirely inadequate and that appeal to cognitive processes is necessary for the proper understanding of human behavior and experience. The following passages from advocates of cognitive psychology appear to illustrate this orientation:

> Cognitivism in psychology and philosophy is roughly the position that intelligent behavior can (only) be explained by appeal to internal "cognitive processes." (Haugeland, 1981, p. 243)

> Any psychology, therefore, that fails to talk about mental events and processes will not be remotely adequate. The transformations which take place between our ears are the missing links needed to account for the regularities between stimuli and responses. The behaviorist's tactic of only attending to lawlike connections between observable events is comparable to resting satisfied with the knowledge that the Big Bang is responsible for the present state of the cosmos and not giving a hoot about what has gone on in between. (Flanagan, 1984, p. 243)

The assertions that intelligent behavior can "only" be accounted for by appealing to cognitive processes, and that behaviorists of any stripe, presumably including radical behaviorists,"only" attend to observable events, are ample testimony to the strong feelings involved.

Although occasionally cognitivists may acknowledge that behaviorism contributed to the development of a scientific psychology by calling for experimental data rather than introspection, in general cognitivists currently argue that behaviorism has out-lived any usefulness it may have once had, and that it is now manifestly necessary to move beyond it. The argument is predicated on the position that after a certain point in the development of a science, advances come from the theoretical postulation of phe-nomena that aren't publicly observable. Cognitivists hold that behaviorism is restricted to variables and factors that are only directly observable, and thus can only go so far in its contributions. What is necessary, according to cognitivists, is the theoretical investi-gation of unobservable structures, processes, and systems, in a fashion that is common to other sciences. With its investigation into atomic and sub-atomic particles, physics is often cited as an example. Indeed, the cognitivist argument goes, only by theorizing, testing, and refining hypotheses about underlying, unobservable cognitive phenomena can scientific psychology provide an appropriate understanding of the human condi-tion. Moreover, the cognitivist argument goes, postulation of unobservable cognitive phenomena has a heuristic function, and suggests new avenues of investigation and new insights into the human condition. Such investigations are held to be the unique outcome of postulating unobservables, and thus couldn't possibly come about by re-maining at the level of observables. Without considering these cognitive phenomena, scientific psychology is left with the behavioristic view of the human condition: me-chanical, associative, and not conforming to what is plainly evident, namely, that an ex-planation in terms of observables alone will not be adequate.

To be sure, radical behaviorists do not shrink from the battle. For example, Skinner (1987) "accused" cognitive scientists of half a dozen improprieties, including flooding the literature with metaphysical speculation that was inimical to science. He further asked for behaviorism to be brought "back from Devil's Island to which it was trans-ported for a crime it never committed," and that psychology be allowed to become once again a behavioral science (p. 111).

Given these frequently held positions, Table 15.1 presents a fairly common division of the field of psychology. According to such a division, one might suspect that cogni-

TABLE 15.1

A Common View of the Fields of Psychology

Cognitive Psychology	Behaviorism
Anderson	Watson
Norman	Tolman
Simon	Hull
Neisser	Spence
Mandler	Skinner
Chomsky	
Fodor	
Dennett	

tive psychology is to be clearly distinguished from any form of behaviorism, exemplified by any practitioner.

SOME COMMON ASSUMPTIONS ABOUT THE RELATION BETWEEN BEHAVIORISM AND COGNITIVE PSYCHOLOGY

In keeping with the preceding brief review, many authoritative sources (e.g., Baars, 1986; Flanagan, 1984; Gardner, 1985) in cognitive psychology assume that cognitive psychology differs from any form of behaviorism in the following ways:

1. Behaviorism is primarily concerned with publicly observable phenomena, presumably because of some link with logical positivism, whereas cognitive psychology is free from the restrictions of logical positivism and is thereby free to offer theories and explanations involving internal and unobservable underlying processes.

2. Because of its concern with publicly observable phenomena, behaviorism is primarily descriptive, with a corresponding limitation in the scope of its theories and explanations; whereas cognitive psychology is more theoretically inclined and therefore can offer more appropriate explanations.

3. Theoretical concepts in cognitive psychology aren't linked to publicly observable phenomena in the same way that theoretical terms in behaviorism are. For example, cognitive psychology tends to view mental states in terms of their functional properties, instead of envisioning them as minuscule versions of publicly observable stimuli and responses. Therefore, theoretical concepts in cognitive psychology have greater power, with the result that theories and explanations in cognitive psychology are superior to those in behaviorism.

These three assumptions touch on quite a number of important matters, such as the nature of theories and explanations, the relation between description and explanation, the nature of theoretical concepts, and the use of theoretical concepts in theories and explanations. Readers may recall that earlier chapters have reviewed how radical behaviorism deals with many of these matters. Sections of this chapter and future chapters continue to do so. In any case, the validity of each of these three assumptions may now be analyzed. Given that cognitive psychology assumes these differences distinguish cognitive psychology from any form of behaviorism, the next section of this chapter analyzes how these assumptions relate to the dominant form of behaviorism: mediational neobehaviorism. Following sections of the chapter analyze the relation between cognitivism and radical behaviorism.

1. BEHAVIORISM IS CONCERNED WITH OBSERVABLE PHENOMENA, BY VIRTUE OF ITS RELATION WITH LOGICAL POSITIVISM

The first assumption is that any form of behaviorism is restricted to dealing with publicly observable behavior because it embraces logical positivist philosophy. Smith (1986) notes that the relation between mediational neobehaviorism and logical positivism is complex; the two are not necessarily isomorphic. Importantly, logical positivism was intensely and explicitly interested in phenomena that weren't publicly observable, such as those in relativity theory and quantum mechanics. In addition, mediational neobehaviorism was certainly concerned with phenomena that weren't publicly observable, such as Tolman's cognitive maps, as well as Hull's oscillation factors and afferent neural interactions. Thus, despite the frequency with which cognitive psychology links any form of behaviorism to logical positivism, this assumption simply doesn't apply to mediational neobehaviorism.

Indeed, the following passage from a mediational neobehaviorist illustrates the point:

> It has never been debatable—certainly not among neobehaviorists—that explanations should involve constructs [representing nonbehavioral states and processes that go on inside organisms].... And it is really not debatable either that stimulus-response theory refers, as it did in Hull's 21 papers in *Psychological Review* ..., as well as his *Principles of Behavior* (1943), to hypothetical states and processes that "go on inside organisms." ... The fact is that for the present S – R theorist, as I think for Hull and certainly for Spence, the mediating machinery defined as hypothetical Ss and Rs are no more or no less permissible, and no more or no less observable, than are the cognitive constructs the "emergent behaviorists" are now willing to permit... It is an essential contradiction to refer to models of observables; and as I indicated earlier, such a characterization of S – R models does not fit the neobehaviorism of Hull, Spence, Miller, or Mowrer—or any other version of neobehaviorism, including my own. (Amsel, 1989, pp. 50–51, 71)

To be sure, the use of the passage above to support the present point was not in keeping with Amsel's agenda. In particular, Amsel argued that the neobehavioristic approach to dealing with unobservables is preferable to the cognitive approach because the concepts of the neobehavioristic approach are derived from physiology (p. 41) and classical conditioning (pp. 72–73), whereas the concepts of the cognitive approach are typically not so derived. In Amsel's view, these differences contribute to the fundamental difference between the two approaches. Suffice it to say that the explicit focus on the importance of unobservables in explanations, evidenced in the passage above, implies that neobehaviorism was always concerned about the question of underlying processes. Thus, the present point is that to characterize neobehaviorism as only being concerned with observables, and cognitive psychology as being liberated so that it can be concerned with unobservables, is manifestly incorrect. Amsel's quotation above so readily illustrates the present point that it is difficult not to call it to the reader's attention.

2. BEHAVIORISM IS DESCRIPTIVE, WHEREAS COGNITIVE PSYCHOLOGY IS THEORETICAL AND EXPLANATORY

The following passages from Baars (1986) evidence this second assumption:

> Cognitive psychologists also have a claim about the domain of scientific psychology—essentially, it is that psychologists observe behavior in order to make inferences about underlying factors that can explain the behavior. They agree with behaviorists that the data of psychology must be public, but the purpose of gathering this data is to generate theories about unobservable constructs, such as "purposes" and "ideas," which can summarize, predict, and explain the data....

> We have defined cognitive metatheory as a belief that psychology studies behavior in order to infer unobservable explanatory constructs, such as "memory," "attention," and "meaning." A psychological theory is a network of such constructs, serving to summarize empirical observations, predict new results, and explain them in an economical way. Like behaviorism, cognitive psychology is primarily a metatheory for psychology, one that simply encourages psychologists to do theory... No longer is it thought necessary for theoretical constructs to resemble visible stimuli and responses, or to adhere to rigid conceptions of theoretical parsimony... By the same token cognitive psychology is an act of imagination that permits wider latitude in imagining explanations for behavior. Whereas behaviorism taught psychologists to respect empirical evidence, the cognitive metatheory may make it possible to do good theory. (pp. 7, 144–145)

As implied in the Amsel (1989) passage above, mediational neobehaviorism made liberal use of unobservable theoretical constructs. The whole history of "learning theory." from Tolman to Hull to Spence, is ample testimony to this liberal use. Again, despite Baars' (1986) insights, this second assumption simply doesn't apply to mediational neobehaviorism.

3. BEHAVIORIST THEORETICAL CONCEPTS ARE INADEQUATE BECAUSE THEY ARE DEFINED IN TERMS OF PUBLICLY OBSERVABLE STIMULI AND RESPONSES

Chapter 3 pointed out that mediational neobehaviorists began to appeal to mediating, organismic variables in their explanations during the 1930s. Consequently, psychological terms were taken to refer to or symbolically represent these organismic variables as instances of inferred, unobservable underlying processes and entities that mediated the relation between stimulus and response. At the heart of this trend was the conventionally accepted, but often unstated, position that language is essentially a symbolic, referential activity. Cognitive psychology also shares the position that language is essentially a symbolic, referential activity. Chapters 8 and 9 argued that at heart language is essentially not such an activity for anybody, but for the sake of argument, the present discussion is going to grant the assumption for rhetorical purposes, to permit an analysis of the coherence of the third assumption from the standpoint of mediational neobehaviorism.

To return to the analysis, the mediating terms in neobehaviorism were then made scientifically respectable through the use of operational definitions. However, an unresolved issue at the time was whether the terms were exhaustively or partially defined. To recapitulate the debate, if the terms were exhaustively defined by their role in an equation or scientific statement (the intervening variable interpretation), they didn't refer to something that existed in the world at large. They did not have surplus meaning. In contrast, if they were only partially defined in terms of public observations (the hypothetical construct interpretation), they could refer to something that existed in the world at large. They did have surplus meaning.

By the late 1940s, most mediational neobehaviorists regarded their theoretical terms as hypothetical constructs, meaning that those terms did refer to something that existed in the world at large, and the referent did have any number of other properties (e.g., see discussion of Tolman, 1949, in Chapter 3). This distinction is relevant to evaluating the coherence of this third assumption because cognitivists tend to assume that behaviorist theoretical terms and concepts are intervening variables, and have no other properties. Thus, when mediational neobehaviorists defined their mediating theoretical terms and concepts by relating them to observable stimuli and responses, those definitions established the conditions of use for the theoretical terms. The definitions didn't equate the theoretical concepts with stimuli and responses. The concepts could have other properties, including the mental. In short, the criticisms of behaviorist theoretical concepts by cognitivists may possibly be justified, given an intervening variable interpretation of those theoretical concepts. However, the dominant interpretation in mediational neobehaviorism is in fact a hypothetical construct interpretation. The hypothetical construct interpretation admits surplus meaning. Thus, an assumption that the difference between mediational neobehaviorism and cognitive psychology is attributable to the ways their respective theoretical concepts are defined is not supported. Indeed, given that the respective conceptions of theoretical concepts do not differ, any contention that explanations in cognitive psychology are superior because they adhere to a superior conception of theoretical concepts is not coherent, by their own standards.

RECONSIDERING THE RELATION

Cognitive psychologists typically assert that the three assumptions above distinguish cognitive psychology from any form of behaviorism. As has been shown, the three assumptions don't apply to presumed differences between cognitive psychology and even mediational neobehaviorism, let alone radical behaviorism. In fact, the analysis of the assumptions leads to an entirely different and quite startling conclusion regarding the relation between cognitive psychology and mediational neobehaviorism: Cognitive psychology is in fact the direct linear successor of mediational neobehaviorism, rather than its so-called revolutionary replacement. This conclusion follows because in a hypothetical construct interpretation of theoretical terms, which mediational neobehaviorism embraces, the theoretical terms of mediational neobehaviorism and the various mental acts, states, mechanisms, or processes of cognitive psychology do not in fact differ.

The following passages from Thomas Leahey, historian of psychology, support the present argument that contemporary cognitive psychology, which explains behavior by appealing to mental states, really does not differ appreciably from mediational neobehaviorism, which explains behavior by appealing to its own set of theoretical terms:

> Although it was a major theoretical position in the 1950s, mediational behaviorism ultimately proved to be only a bridge linking the inferential behaviorialism of the 1930s and 1940s—Hull's and Tolman's theories—to the inferential behavioralism of the 1980s: cognitive psychology … [note: According to Leahey, behavioralism may be defined as the attempt to predict, control, explain, or model behavior, and to do so one may or may not refer to conscious or unconscious mental processes. Behavioralism is aimed at behavior; consciousness—the mind—is not the object of study, although it may be called on to explain behavior.] The mediationalists' commitment to internalizing S–R language resulted primarily from their desire to achieve theoretical rigor and to avoid the apparently unscientific character of "junkshop psychology." In essence, lacking any other language with which to discuss the mental processes in a clear and disciplined fashion, they took the only course they saw open to them. However, when a new language of power, rigor, and precision came along—the language of computer programming—it proved easy for mediational psychologists to abandon their mediating response life raft for the ocean liner of information processing. (2000, p. 479)

> The explication of the information-processing "paradigm" by Lachmann et al. makes clear that information-procesing psychology is a form of behaviorism with strong affinity to all but radial behaviorism. … In short, although Lachmann et al. specifically deny it, information processing adopted a modified logical positivism than neobehavioralism. (2000, p. 508)

> Although it's quite different from radical behaviorism, information-processing psychology is a form of behavioralism. It represents a continuing conceptual evolution in the psychology of adaptation. … Herbert Simon, one of the founders of modern information-processing psychology, revealed the continuity of information processing with behavioralism, and even its psychology, revealed the continuity of information processing with behavioralism, and even its affinity with behavioralism. … Information-processing psychologists share many important behaviorist assumptions: atomism, associationism, and empiricism. On the philosophical side, information processing espouses materialism, holding that there is no independent Cartesian soul, and positivism, continuing to insist on operationalizing all theoretical terms (2000, p. 510).

Thus, the present argument is that the relation between cognitive psychology and traditional mediational neobehaviorism is entirely different from that portrayed in much of the contemporary literature, particularly by those who favor cognitive psychology (e.g., Baars, 1986; Flanagan, 1984; Gardner, 1985). Indeed, the present argument is that cognitive psychology is essentially consistent with mediational neobehaviorism. They are consistent because they subscribe to the same interpretation of theoretical terms. If the commonly asserted differences between cognitive psychology and behaviorism, at least traditional mediational neobehaviorism, don't in fact exist, and cognitive psychology is in fact consistent with mediational neobehaviorism, what, then, can be said about the differences between cognitive psychology and Skinner's radical behaviorism, which differs significantly from mediational neobehaviorism?

The present argument is that the differences between Skinner's radical behaviorism and cognitive psychology lie in the respective conceptions of verbal behavior, which in turn give rise to different conceptions regarding the causal explanation of behavior. Cognitive psychology embraces a referential, symbolic view of verbal behavior. According to this view, terms and concepts used in psychological explanations are presumed to refer to underlying psychological structures and processes. Importantly, those structures and processes are in an internal dimension that differs from the behavioral dimension. This explanatory strategy is mentalism. Chapter 14 reviewed what mentalism is, the problems it creates, and how radical behaviorism rejects mentalism in all its forms.

Nevertheless, subtle confusions still exist. Again, an important confusion concerns the use of theoretical terms. The analysis above of the relation between cognitive psychology and mediational neobehaviorism emphasizes the similar views of theoretical terms held in cognitive psychology and mediational neobehaviorism. The similar views are predicated on a referential, symbolic theory of language. As identified many times in this book, one of the features that distinguishes radical behaviorism from virtually any other position in psychology, including cognitive psychology and mediational neobehaviorism, concerns verbal behavior, and particularly scientific verbal behavior such as "theoretical terms." Chapters 8 and 9 emphasized that radical behaviorism embraces a behavioral, rather than a referential, symbolic theory of verbal behavior. Chapter 12 outlined how this view of verbal behavior relates to theories, and chapter 13 outlined how it relates to scientific explanations. Accordingly, radical behaviorism does not distinguish between observational and theoretical terms in theories and explanations. Again, to talk of a distinction between observational and theoretical terms is to accept a referential, symbolic theory of language that radical behaviorism rejects. In the final analysis, radical behaviorism is therefore simply not concerned with traditional problems regarding supposed differences between theoretical terms of any interpretation, and whether one set of terms is logically superior to another (cf. Zuriff, 1985). Radical behaviorists don't even subscribe to the referential, symbolic theory of language upon which the traditional discussion is based, in either cognitive psychology or mediational neobehaviorism. Attempts to cast radical behaviorist-analytic terms and concepts as belonging in one or another of the traditional categories of scientific terms, and radical behaviorist theories and explanations as being versions of one or another of the traditional categories of scientific practice, are fundamentally mistaken. Indeed, no one's verbal behavior, including that of cognitive psychologist or media-

TABLE 15–2
A Revised View of the Fields of Psychology

Classical S – R Behaviorism	Mediational S – O – R Neobehaviorism	Cognitive Psychology	Radical Behaviorism
Watson	Tolman Hull Spence	Anderson Norman Simon Neisser Mandler Chomsky Fodor Dennett	Skinner

tional neobehaviorist, is a referential, symbolic activity. Thus, the third assumption about differences mentioned earlier, that theoretical terms in cognitive psychology are supposedly superior and so the theories and explanations in cognitive psychology are superior, is simply wrong on all counts.

Overall, with respect to an earlier division of the house, the division presented in Table 15–2 now seems rather more appropriate. According to Table 15–2, such mediational neobehaviorists as Tolman, Hull, and Spence may legitimately be considered as forerunners of cognitive psychology, or at least anticipating some elements of what would become cognitive psychology, rather than behaviorists in any meaningful Skinnerian sense (e.g., "In addition to the stimulus, I had called the conditions of which reflex strength was a function 'third variables,' but Tolman called them 'intervening.' That may have been the point at which the experimental analysis of behavior parted company from what would become cognitive psychology" (Skinner, 1989, p. 109). No doubt, some readers, especially cognitivists and neobehaviorists, will balk at such an unconventional assertion and dismiss it as preposterous and uninformed. Again, the magnitude of the differences between either cognitive psychologists or mediational neobehaviorists, on the one hand, and radical behaviorists, on the other hand, when viewed from the perspective of radical behaviorism, should not be underestimated.

THE NATURE OF THE DIFFERENCES

Much of Skinner's writing late in his career addressed the nature of the differences between radical behaviorism and cognitivism and why these differences are important. For radical behaviorists, much of the control over cognitive verbal behavior arises from social-cultural traditions, rather than contacts and operations with data. A relevant feature of cognitive orientations is that of autonomy, as in the traditional conception of the individual in Western civilization. In other words, the individual is held to possess inner qualities that make its behavior independent of any influence of the occasions in which it occurs: "Behavior starts within the organism.... Cognitive scientists make the person an initiator when they adopt the paradigm of information processing" (Skinner, 1987, p. 94). The notion of an executive that oversees the structures and processes of cognitive systems described at the outset of this chapter is clearly a commitment to traditional ideas. In Skinner's (1990) view, just as biology has had to overthrow any influence of creationism, so must psychology overthrow any influence of cognitive psychology.

Cognitive psychologists may believe they are addressing legitimate topics of psychological inquiry that are inside an organism, but to the extent they are addressing anything relevant, in actuality they are addressing other matters, transformed from the description of behavior or the occasions in which it occurs. The metaphor of storage and retrieval is a case in point. Because of the influence of social-cultural traditions, descriptions of the properties of behavior and its relation to the environment are transformed into nouns, and cognitive psychologists set off looking for the things the nouns are said to represent. As reviewed earlier in this book, representations of events aren't encoded, stored, and then retrieved. Rather, the organism is changed by its experiences. The changed organism then responds differently to stimuli than previously. The physiological processes involved in these behavioral processes are worthy topics of investigation, but in terms of physiology, rather than in terms of the metaphors that cognitive psychology deploys. As indicated earlier in this chapter, Skinner (1987) accused cognitive psychology of multiple improprieties, including: (a) misusing the metaphor of storage and retrieval; (b) conducting research by presenting participants with descriptions of events and asking for verbal reports of what they would do, rather than examining actual behavior in actual settings; (c) perpetuating the cultural tradition that feelings and mental states may legitimately be taken as causes of behavior; (d) inventing explanatory systems with honorific but spurious appeals to other dimensions; and (e) relaxing standards of thinking by employing characteristics of dualistic metaphysics, literature, and the vernacular, rather than science. To be sure, radical behaviorism does entail interpretation that might be called speculation, but the interpretation is guided and constrained by established principles. Interpretation in radical behaviorism clearly differs from the speculation in cognitive psychology grounded only in the cultural traditions of folk psychology.

ARE BEHAVIORISM AND COGNITIVE PSYCHOLOGY COMPLEMENTARY?

Although interesting and sophisticated, the arguments offered by contemporary cognitive psychology against the adequacy of behaviorism generally or Skinner's radical behaviorism particularly have very little to do with the actual radical behaviorist position. As reviewed above, Skinner's radical behaviorism differs from other forms of behaviorism, such as mediational neobehaviorism, in several important ways. For example, radical behaviorism does not appeal in any significant explanatory sense to intervening variables, hypothetical constructs, or other sorts of theoretical terms that are operationally defined with respect to publicly observable behavior. As reviewed in Chapter 10, Skinner's radical behaviorism is willing to include private behavioral events, which are by definition accessible only to one person. Again, the position against which mentalists seem to be arguing is classical S – R behaviorism or an early form of mediational behaviorism, rather than radical behaviorism. Indeed, Skinner's differences with respect to both early S – R behaviorism and later forms of mediational S – O – R neobehaviorism are as great as those with respect to positions more conventionally cast as mentalistic, such as cognitive psychology and psycholinguistics.

An important issue is whether cognitive psychology can be regarded as complementary to Skinner's radical behaviorism. Chapter 4 pointed out that radical behaviorism and a theoretical neurophysiology concerned with the structure and function of the central nervous system are clearly complementary sciences. The question is whether cognitive psychology is a theoretical neurophysiology concerned with filling the "unavoidable gaps" in a behavioral account? Will the two "gaps" in a behavioral account be filled by anything remotely similar to the various conceptual acts, states, mechanisms, processes, structures, and entities of contemporary cognitive psychology? Radical behaviorists think not (e.g., "The cognitive constructs give physiologists a misleading account of what they will find inside," Skinner, 1978, p. 111; see additional discussion of this point in Marr, 1983, p. 12; Schnaitter, 1984, p. 7). Thus, because contemporary cognitive psychology attributes causal efficacy to acts, states, mechanisms, or processes from a mental dimension, typically derived from folk psychology, it is not complementary with behavior analysis.

Wessells states that there are very great differences between cognitivists and behaviorists regarding goals and conceptions of explanation, and that in order to achieve extensive cooperation between behaviorists and cognitivists, these differences will have to be reconciled.

> [T]he principal aim of cognitive psychology is to explain behavior by specifying on a conceptual level the universal, internal structures and processes through which the environment exerts its effects. (Wessells, 1981, p. 167)

> The trouble is, for cognitivists, functional relations between environment and behavior are not explanatory... No amount of order among observables will satisfy the desire to discover the internal processes through which the environment influences behavior. (Wessells, 1982, p. 75)

Wessells' points are well taken, but merit clarification. From the radical behaviorist perspective, as well as Leahey (2001), cognitive psychology is actually not very different from mediational neobehaviorism. The very great differences lie between radical behaviorism, on the one hand, and both cognitive psychology and mediational neobehaviorism, on the other. Radical behaviorism rejects them both, and on similar grounds.

SUMMARY AND CONCLUSIONS

In conclusion, the present argument is that the differences between Skinner's radical behaviorism and cognitive psychology lie in the respective conceptions of verbal behavior, which in turn give rise to different conceptions regarding the causal explanation of behavior. For radical behaviorism, explanations specify functional relations between behavior and environment. For cognitive psychology, explanations postulate unobserved acts, states, mechanisms, processes, and entities, which operate from mental, psychic, or conceptual dimensions to cause behavior. Why should the differences between these conceptions be cause for concern?

One reason relates to practical action. Closer analysis suggests that much of contemporary psychology is at best a kind of sophisticated census-taking, where mentalists study behavior engendered in our culture by common contingencies. The behavior in question is then named. After the behavior has been named, some causal entity, existing in a neural, mental, or conceptual dimension, is assumed to cause the behavior. As Skinner noted many times, the problem is that the resulting theories of behavior are misleading and vague, they obscure important details, they are wasteful, they allay curiosity by getting us to accept fictitious way stations as explanatory, they impede the search for relevant environmental variables, they misrepresent the facts to be accounted for, they give us false assurances about the state of our knowledge, and they lead to the continued use of scientific techniques that should be abandoned. Thus, in this view, mentalism and cognitive psychology actually interfere with effective prediction, control, and explanation of events, notwithstanding arguments to the contrary, precisely because they lead investigators to search for things in another dimension, irather than analyze contingencies in the behavioral dimension (Moore, 1990).

A second reason concerns an even larger issue: the culture. At issue is whether cognitive psychology is an essentially conformist doctrine that supports the decidedly mentalistic if not dualistic institutions and practices that prevail in our Western culture in the form of folk psychology (Skinner, 1971). Alternative cultural practices that will improve the quality of life need to be implemented. However, to do so means that the cultural obstacles supported by mentalism and cognitive psychology must be overcome. The concerns are serious. Psychology can make a contribution. From the point of view of Skinner's behaviorism, the problem is that psychology has never been behavioristic enough.

Another branch of psychology that is largely mentalistic is psycholinguistics, in which the processes underlying language are assumed to be mental or cognitive, as opposed to behavioral. This form of mentalism is the subject of Chapter 16.

TABLE 15-3

Cognitive psychology
Orientations to psychology that emphasize an abstract description of functional properties of "mental" acts, states, mechanisms, structures, processes, and systems that are said to enable organisms to behave as they do in a context. Thus, cognitive orientations are less interested in the analysis of an actual instance of performance and the identification of particular factors that participate in that instance. Cognitive orientations further emphasize Kantian rationalism and the a priori. They adopt a top down, design stance. Moreover, they are at once intentional and agent-oriented.

Elements of cognitive systems
1. Affectors
2. Effectors
3. Mediating structures and processes that: (a) identify and interpret information; (b) allocate affector, effector, and information processing resources according to the demands on organism, particularly concerning the regulation of internal states produced by the information the organism receives; and (c) control actions to be performed.

Philosophical functionalism
A philosophical approach that appeals to causal "mental states" that are definable in terms that do not mention physics or chemistry, as would presumably be required by physicalistic definitions of operationism and logical positivism. Rather, the causal mental states are defined in terms of their functional contribution in the chain of events in question.

Three criticisms of behaviorism by cognitivists
1. Behaviorism is only concerned with observables, because of its link with logical positivism, whereas cognitive psychology is liberated to theorize about unobservables.
2. Behaviorism is descriptive, whereas cognitive psychology is theoretical and explanatory.

---

3. Behaviorist theoretical terms are inadequate because they are defined with respect to publicly observable phenomena

Skinner's accusations against cognitive psychology

1. Cognitive psychology is the creationism of behavioral science.
2. Cognitive psychology misuses the metaphor of storage and retrieval.
3. Cognitive psychology conducts research by presenting participants with descriptions of events and asking for verbal reports of what they would do, rather than examining actual behavior in actual settings.
4. Cognitive psychology perpetuates the cultural tradition that feelings and mental states may legitimately be taken as causes of behavior.
5. Cognitive psychology invents explanatory systems with honorific but spurious appeals to other dimensions.
6. Cognitive psychology employs relaxed standards of thinking characteristic of dualistic metaphysics, literature, and the vernacular, rather than science (from Skinner, 1987).

REFERENCES

Amsel, A. (1989). *Behaviorism, neobehaviorism, and cognitivism in learning theory: Historical and contemporary perspectives*. Hillsdale, NJ: Erlbaum.

Baars, B. J. (1986). *The cognitive revolution in psychology*. New York: Guilford.

Block, N. (Ed.). (1980). *Readings in philosophical psychology, Vol. 1*. Cambridge, MA: Harvard University Press.

Dennett, D. (1978). *Brainstorms*. Montgomery, VT: Bradford Books.

Flanagan, O. J. (1984). *The science of mind*. Cambridge, MA: MIT Press.

Fodor, J. A. (1968). *Psychological explanations*. New York: Random House.

Gardner, H. (1985). *The mind's new science*. New York: Basic Books.

Haugeland, J. (1981). *Mind design*. Cambridge, MA: MIT Press.

Hull, C. L. (1943). *Principles of behavior*. New York: Appleton-Century.

Knapp, T. J. (1986). The emergence of cognitive psychology in the latter half of the twentieth century. In T. J. Knapp & L. C. Robertson (Eds.), *Approaches to cognition: Contrasts and controversies*, pp. 13–35. Hillsdale, NJ: Erlbaum.

Leahey, T. H. (2000). *A history of psychology*. Upper Saddle River, NJ: Prentice-Hall.

Marr, M. J. (1983). Memory: Metaphors and models. *The Psychological Record, 33*, 12–19.

Miller, G. A., Galanter, E., & Pribram, K. (1960). *Plans and the structure of behavior*. New York: Holt, Rinehart, and Winston.

Moore, J. (Ed.). (1984). On cognitive and behavioral orientations to the language of behavior analysis: Why be concerned over the differences? *Psychological Record, 33*, 3–30.

Moore, J. (1990). On mentalism, privacy, and behaviorism. *Journal of Mind and Behavior, 11*, 19–36.

Neisser, U. (1967). *Cognitive psychology*. New York: Appleton-Century-Crofts.

Norman, D. A. (Ed.). (1981). *Perspectives in cognitive science*. Hillsdale, NJ: Erlbaum.

Schnaitter, R. M. (1984). Skinner on the "mental" and the "physical." *Behaviorism, 12*, 1–14.

Schnaitter, R. M. (1987). Behaviorism is not cognitive and cognitivism is not behavioral. *Behaviorism, 15*, 1–11.

Skinner, B. F. (1971). *Beyond freedom and dignity*. New York: Knopf.

Skinner, B. F. (1978). *Reflections on behaviorism and society.* Englewood Cliffs, NJ: Prentice-Hall.

Skinner, B. F. (1987). *Upon further reflection.* Englewood Cliffs, NJ: Prentice-Hall.

Skinner, B. F. (1989). *Recent issues in the analysis of behavior.* Columbus, OH: Merrill.

Skinner, B. F. (1990). Can psychology be a science of mind? *American Psychologist, 45,* 1206–1210.

Smith, L. D. (1986). *Behaviorism and logical positivism.* Stanford, CA: Stanford University Press.

Tolman, E. C. (1949). Discussion (from interrelationships between perception and personality: A symposium). *Journal of Personality, 18,* 48–50.

Wessells, M. G. (1981). A critique of Skinner's view of the explanatory inadequacy of cognitive theories. *Behaviorism, 9,* 153–170.

Wessells, M. G. (1982). A critique of Skinner's views on the obstructive character of cognitive theories. *Behaviorism, 10,* 65–84.

Zuriff, G. E. (1985). *Behaviorism: A conceptual reconstruction.* New York: Columbia University Press.

STUDY QUESTIONS

1. Describe the three sets of elements that cognitive systems are said to possess (e.g., Norman, 1981). Describe three considerations upon which the requirement for cognitive systems is said to be based.

2. List four milestones in the development of cognitive psychology.

3. Describe why cognitive psychologists argue that behavioral psychology has outlived any contributions it once might have made to scientific psychology.

4. Describe three common assumptions about the relation between behaviorism and cognitive psychology. Describe how radical behaviorism argues that these assumptions apply to mediational neobehaviorism rather than radical behaviorism.

5. Describe how viewing theoretical terms as hypothetical constructs, rather than intervening variables, enables one to view cognitive psychology as the successor to mediational neobehaviorism, rather than its successor.

6. Describe how radical behaviorists view the supposed complementarity between radical behaviorism and cognitive psychology.

16

The Challenge of Psycholinguistics

Synopsis of chapter 16: The third section of the book compares and contrasts radical behaviorism with alternative conceptual and philosophical viewpoints. Chapter 14 examined mentalism. Chapter 15 specifically examined the relation between radical behaviorism and one form of mentalism: cognitive psychology. Chapter 16 continues the theme of the third section by examining the relation between radical behaviorism and a second form of mentalism: the cognitive orientation underlying psycholinguistics. The chapter presents the general view of language according to psycholinguistics, which differs considerably from the operant behavioral view outlined in Chapters 8 and 9 of the present book. The chapter then critically analyzes two common charges that psycholinguists level against the adequacy of behavioral approaches, among which they include radical behaviorism. The first is that sequential processes cannot explain language. The second is that environmental factors do not significantly influence the development of verbal behavior. As with other criticisms directed at the radical behaviorist position, the two charges are based on a set of faulty assumptions. Consequently, the charges simply do not pertain to radical behaviorism. Whether they apply to mediational neobehaviorism is even questionable. The chapter next examines the particular criticisms that the linguist Noam Chomsky has directed against a behavioral, empirical approach to language. A review of Chomsky's criticisms indicates that they also don't apply to radical behaviorism. The chapter concludes that a cognitive orientation to psychology generally and psycholinguistics particularly reveals the unfortunate influence of mentalistic causes from another dimension, rather than a concern with the operant contingencies that underlie verbal behavior.

Another area of psychological study in which cognitivism is influential is psycholinguistics, or the study of the psychological processes underlying language acquisition and use. The present chapter continues the critical examination and evaluation of mentalistic orientations by focusing specifically on the challenge of psycholinguistics.

PSYCHOLINGUISTICS AND LANGUAGE

According to many psycholinguists, the explanation of language should emphasize the underlying cognitive structures that make it possible to speak grammatically and syntactically correct sentences, rather than "learning experiences." Any learning experiences are incidental at best. These structures that underlie language are regarded as cognitive or mental, rather than behavioral. Moreover, the structures are innate. The structures have uniquely evolved for language, rather than for general purpose forms of intellectual activity. Humans inherit these structures by virtue of being human, and the structures distinguish humans from nonhumans. Any analysis that doesn't recognize the innateness of the mental structures that give humans the propensity for language isn't remotely adequate. The human brain, or some module(s) thereof, is assumed to be a language organ that has evolved to process language in the same way that the human stomach is assumed to be a digestive organ that has evolved to process food. The primary concern is to understand a cognitive system that affords competence, rather than to identify environmental factors or relations that might determine any instance of linguistic performance.

Language should therefore be construed as a system whereby mental activity is transformed into words and grammatically or syntactically correct utterances according to a set of "rules." The rules are prescriptions for the functioning of the innate structures. A commonality in languages across different cultures, or a universal, is typically taken as evidence for the position. A commonality may take several forms. For example, no language forms questions by simply reversing the order of words within a sentence (Pinker, 1994, p. 233). Subjects precede objects in almost all languages, and verbs and their objects tend to be adjacent. If the order of a language is Subject-Object-Verb, it will usually have question words at the end of a sentence; if the order is Subject-Verb-Object, it will have question words at the beginning. If a language has nasal vowels, it will have non-nasal vowels. If a language has a word for purple, it will also have one for red. If a language has a word for leg, it will also have one for arm. Understanding language consists in knowing how mental representations are transformed into sentences according to linguistic rules. Pinker (1994) summarizes the position in the following passage:

> All languages have a vocabulary in the thousands or tens of thousands, sorted into part-of-speech categories including noun and verb. Words are organized into phrases according to the X-bar system (nouns are found inside N-bars, which are found inside noun

phrases, and so on). The higher levels of phrase structure include auxiliaries ..., which signify tense, modality, aspect, and negation. Nouns are marked for case and assigned semantic roles by the mental dictionary entry of the verb or other predicate. Phrases can be moved from their deep structure positions, leaving a gap or "trace," by a structure-dependent movement rule, thereby forming questions, relative clauses, passives, and other widespread constructions. New word structures can be created and modified by derivational and inflectional rules. Inflectional rules primarily mark nouns for case and number, and mark verbs for tense, aspect, mood, voice, negation, and agreement with subjects and objects in number, gender, and person. The phonological forms of words are defined by metrical and syllable trees and separate tiers of features like voicing, tone, and manner and place of articulation, and are subsequently adjusted by phonological rules. Though many of these arrangements are in some sense useful, their details, found in language after language but not in any artificial system like FORTRAN or musical notation, give a strong impression that a Universal Grammar, not reducible to history or cognition, underlies the human language instinct. (pp. 237–238)

Consider the nonsense sentence "Colorless green ideas sleep furiously." According to psycholinguists, that this sentence can be produced testifies to the prevalence of rules: It conforms to standard principles of sentence construction, even if it doesn't make sense. Consider the sentence "This sentence is false." Again, it conforms to the principles of sentence construction, even if it is internally inconsistent and incoherent. Consider the sentence "They are eating apples." According to psycholinguists, this sentence cannot be understood on the basis of the sequence of words that gives it its form. It could be a description of either a bowl of apples on a table, or the actions of individuals consuming some fruit. However, psycholinguists argue, the sentence can be understood if one knows the grammatical function of "eating." If it is an adjective describing the apples, then the former interpretation is correct. If it is the present participle of the verb to eat, then the latter interpretation is correct. Hence, psycholinguists argue, to try to understand language without understanding the operation of the structures that produce and process language will not do.

Earlier, Chapter 8 of this book mentioned that psycholinguists make two broad charges against the adequacy of any behavioral explanation of language. The first concerns the view that a linear, sequential process underlies language. Psycholinguists charge that sequential processes cannot reasonably explain the production and understanding of grammatically and syntactically correct sentences in a linguistically competent speaker. The second charge concerns the role of the environment in linguistic development. Psycholinguists charge that direct interaction with the environment cannot reasonably explain the development of such linguistic processes as grammar and syntax. It follows that any position committed to a sequential or environmental view, as psycholinguists assume any form of behaviorism is—including radical behaviorism, by virtue of being a behaviorism—cannot possibly be adequate. These two charges may now be examined in greater detail.

THE CHARGE THAT SEQUENTIAL PROCESSES CANNOT ADEQUATELY EXPLAIN LANGUAGE

The first charge that psycholinguists level against behavioral explanations is that behaviorists assume people speak in sentences because one word of a sentence becomes "associated" with the next in a simple linear sequence through the action of some environmental event such as reinforcement. According to this charge, word #1 in a sentence should be construed as evoking word #2, word #2 as evoking word #3, and so on, according to a linear chaining process. To be sure, this charge is not entirely without foundation. For instance, classical S – R behaviorists such as Watson appealed to simple, "single-stage" S – R mechanisms to explain various complex, temporally extended behavioral phenomena, including language. With regard to language, these accounts held that saying one word constitutes a stimulus for saying the next, and so on, until the entire utterance is completed. The process is essentially a left-to-right (for English speakers), linear chaining process. To illustrate, consider Watson (1913): "The hypothesis that all of the so-called 'higher thought' processes go on in terms of faint reinstatements of the original muscular act (including speech here) and that these are integrated into systems which respond in serial order (associative mechanisms) is, I believe, a tenable one" (p. 174). In addition, consider Watson (1930):

> Suppose you read from your little book (your mother usually sets an auditory pattern), 'Now—I—lay—me—down—to—sleep.' The sight of "now" brings the saying of 'now' (response 1), the sight of 'I,' the response of saying of 'I' (response 2) and so on throughout the series. Soon the mere saying of 'now' becomes the motor (kinaesthetic) stimulus for saying 'I.' (p. 235)

More advanced versions of this account explained sentence construction by suggesting that some classes of words (e.g., nouns) had a high conditional probability of evoking other classes of words (e.g., verbs). In any event, there are numerous reasons to question the adequacy of this sort of mechanical, linear chaining approach as the single account of all forms of complex behavior, including language. As mentioned in Chapter 5, Lashley (1951) reviewed one line of evidence in his classic paper on the problem of serial order in behavior. A representative example is that finger movement in typing exceeds the capability of the relevant neurophysiology to give the requisite feedback. If such was the case, then neither could the speaking of words be regarded as simple "beads on a chain," emitted according to a serial process. As Lashley (1951) put it:

> From such considerations, it is certain that any theory of grammatical form which ascribes to it direct associative linkage of the words of the sentence overlooks the essential structure of speech. The individual items of the temporal series do not in themselves have a temporal "va-

lence" in their associative connections with other elements. The order is imposed by some other agent. This is true not only of language, but of all skilled movements or successions of movements. (p. 116)

Chapter 3 of this book pointed out that when the S – R, linear chaining approach of classical behaviorism to complex, temporally extended behavior proved inadequate, as it had by the 1930s, behaviorism entered its second phase. The second phase was that of mediational S – O – R neobehaviorism. During this phase, many behaviorists sought to augment their basic approach by intercalating unobserved mediating "organismic" variables between publicly observable stimulus and response. One example of the attempt to apply the mediational model to the general problem of language learning was Mowrer (1960). In Mowrer's view, a conditioned stimulus leads to a broad affective state, such as relief, fear, hope, or disappointment, based on the relation between the conditioned stimulus and an unconditioned stimulus. The mediating state then ultimately determines the overt response.

Note that according to Mowrer (1960), the "meaning" of a stimulus is determined through its role in a conditioning operation: "When a formerly neutral or indifferent stimulus is associated with a significant (reinforcing) one, the first stimulus takes on a representational function, coming to mean or stand for the second one. This moving forward in time of a part of the reaction evoked by a biologically important situation, so that the organism can make an anticipatory response of either an approach or avoidant nature, is clearly one of Nature's most ingenious inventions" (p. 124). Of particular importance in Mowrer's analysis is that the internal sensations created by responding to the word (e.g., by reading or saying it) come to function as a conditioned stimulus. That is, these sensations acquire the same affective connotations as the unconditioned stimulus with which they were originally associated. Moreover, they mediate further responses involving the word. Consider the children's rhyme "Tom, Tom, the piper's son, stole the pig and away he run." Mowrer reviews what he takes as the processes involved in learning an entire sentence about Tom, such as "Tom is a thief":

> Let us assume that John is telling Charles that: Tom is a thief. It is clear that for the intended effect to be produced by this sentence, Charles must already know Tom and must know about thieves and thievery. In other words, Charles must already have meanings attached to the words, Tom and Thief. What, then, is the function of the sentence, "Tom is a thief"? Most simply and most basically, it appears to be this. "Thief" is a sort of "unconditioned stimulus"—we shall later want to qualify this term, but for the moment it will suffice—a sort of "unconditioned stimulus" which can be depended upon to call forth an internal reaction which can be translated into, or defined by, the phrase, "a person who cannot be trusted," one who "takes things, steals." When, therefore, we put the word, or sign, "Tom" in front of the sign "thief," ... we create a situation from which we can predict a fairly definite result. On the basis of the familiar principle of conditioning, we would expect that some of the reaction evoked by the second sign, "thief," would be shifted to the first sign, "Tom," so that Charles, the hearer of the sen-

tence, would thereafter respond to the word, "Tom," somewhat as he had previously responded to the word, "thief." ....

The notion ... is that the sentence is, pre-eminently, a conditioning device, and that its chief effect is to produce new associations, new learning, just as any other paired presentation of stimuli may do.

By first order conditioning some part of the total reaction elicited by real thieves is shifted to the word, "thief"; and by second order conditioning of the type provided by the sentence, this same reaction ... gets further transferred or shifted to the word "Tom." (pp. 139–140, 141–142, 144)

To this point Mowrer's account is functionally similar to such single-stage accounts as Watson's (1930). Recognizing the shortcomings of these accounts, Mowrer then advanced the notion of the internal mediating state:

Instead of r_t, the thief-meaning, getting connected directly to the word, "Tom," and more or less replacing the r_T reaction, we may infer that r_t will be conditioned rather to the reaction—or more accurately, to the stimuli or sensations produced by the reaction—which the word "Tom" produces, namely r_T. This internal reaction, or meaning, thus becomes ... a mediating response ....

The essence of the argument advanced up to this point is that the subject-predicate complex which we call a sentence is, in effect, simply an arrangement for conditioning the meaning reaction produced by the predicate to the interoceptive stimulation aroused by the meaning reaction elicited by the sentence subject. (pp. 146–147)

Thus, sentences were devices for expanding meanings, and meanings were the internal affective states produced by conditioned stimuli, through their relation with unconditioned stimuli.

In any case, psychologists working in the area of language during the 1950s and 1960s began to reach more and more conclusions that they believed seriously challenged the adequacy of the traditional mediational approach, even allowing for more sophisticated mediators. For example, in an influential article, Fodor (1965) critically examined the adequacy of the mediational approach based on Mowrer (1960). As Fodor (1965) put it, the mediational approach interposed

s-r chains of any desired length between S's and R's that form the observation base of ... [mediational] theory. Though this constitutes a proliferation of unobservables, it must be said that the unobservables postulated are not different in kind from the S's and R's in terms of which single-stage theories are articulated. It follows that, though [mediational theorists] are barred from direct, observational verification of statements about mediating responses, it should prove possible to infer many of their characteristics from those that S's and R's are observed to have. (p. 77)

Fodor then goes on to point out that if mediational theory is to have any explanatory force, each mediating response can be tied to one, and only one, overt response. However, this one-to-one correspondence is difficult to accept if the mediators are the broad, affective sorts of reactions Mowrer presumed them to be. Moreover, if a one-to-one correspondence does hold, Fodor (1965) argued that

> the only distinction that can be made between mediational and single-stage views is that, according to the former but not the latter, some of the members of the stimulus-response chains invoked in explanations of verbal behavior are supposed to be unobserved. But clearly this property is irrelevant to the explanatory power of the theories concerned....
>
> If this argument is correct, it ought to be the case that, granting a one to one correspondence between r's and R's, anything that can be said on the mediation-theoretic view can simply be translated into a single-stage language. (pp. 80–81)

Ultimately, Fodor concluded that an account based on this interpretation of mediation is seriously deficient (see also Fodor, 1983, pp. 22–38, for a related analysis using the language of "association" instead of the language of mediation).

In addition, Bever, Fodor, and Garrett (1968) pointed out that language comprehension shows recursive properties, where once an individual has learned a language, the individual exhibits an ability to understand combinations of sentences on the basis of hierarchical transformations. This feature challenges the sequential account of sentence structure appealing to conditional probabilities of some words following others, mentioned earlier. For example, a sentence stating that "The canary sang" may be combined with another sentence stating that "The cat ate the canary." The result is "The canary that the cat ate sang." One can then add "The cat grinned." The transformed sentence now becomes "The canary that the cat that grinned ate sang." That individuals can understand such recursive transformations is difficult if not impossible to reconcile with a linear chaining account of language, where words that are subjects of sentences have a high probability of evoking words that are verbs of sentences, which in turn have a high probability of evoking words that are objects of the verb, and so on (see also Catania, 2007, p. 286).

Research in linguistics and psycholinguistics during the 1950s, 1960s, and 1970s provided empirical evidence directed against the S – O – R mediational approach, at least as psycholinguists conceived of that approach. Two examples illustrate the point. The first example is Fodor and Bever (1965). These researchers had subjects listen to sentences on a tape recorder. One sentence might be "In her hope of marrying Anna was surely impractical" and another, "Your hope of marrying Anna was surely impractical." Occasionally, a click was superimposed on the sentence. In the sentences above, the click occurred precisely in the middle of the word "Anna." In fact, when the researchers prepared the sentences, only the tapes that gave the first and second words for tape 1 and the first word for tape 2 were different; the tapes that gave the words after "hope of marrying..." were identical for both sentences. The results showed that subjects had considerable difficulty indicating the precise point at which the click occurred. In general, the results indicated that subjects reported the click as having "migrated" to the nearest boundary between major syntactic units of the sentence, rather than at its actual location. In the first sentence, the click was heard as having migrated to a location earlier in the sentence than it actually occurred, before "Anna," at the boundary between the introductory clause and the subject. In the second sentence, the click was heard as having migrated to a location later in the sentence than it actually occurred, after "Anna," at the boundary between the prepositional phrase that is part of the subject of the sentence and the verb of the sentence. The results of having the same click in the same word migrate to an earlier location in one sentence and a later location in another sentence are clearly inconsistent with a simple, left-to-right, linear account of verbal behavior based on associations and mediators.

Another example is Bransford and Franks (1971). These researchers first presented subjects with numerous sentences, each of which expressed several propositions. One sentence might be "The ants were in the kitchen," and another might be "The ants ate the sweet jelly." Then, the researchers presented subjects with a mixture of the original sentences and test sentences. The test sentences were similar to the original sentences, in that they contained some of the propositions from the prior sentences, but they were not identical to the prior sentences. An example of a test sentence might be "The ants in the kitchen ate the sweet jelly." The researchers asked the subjects to judge whether they had seen the test sentences before. The subjects showed almost no ability to discriminate the new sentences from the old and judged that all sentences were equally familiar. However, the subjects could readily discriminate new sentences from old when the new sentences expressed new propositions but with the same words. The researchers concluded that when the subjects heard the original sentences, they abstracted the propositions and remembered them. They did not simply remember what propositions they had heard in what sentences, or indeed, what words they had heard. Such results are clearly inconsistent with a simple, left-to-right, linear account of verbal behavior based on associations and mediators.

In summary, one of the main objectives of the psycholinguistic movement was to displace extant neobehavioral models of language, as a glance at the literature from linguistics and psycholinguistics of the 1960s will attest (see Baars, 1986). The argument was that if language essentially conforms to such a sequential, mechanical process, how would one explain that speakers can readily understand transformed or recursive sentences. To throw covert associative factors into the mix as theoretical behavioral mechanisms that supposedly link the elements of the sequential approach doesn't help, the charge goes, because the mediating associative factors can't correct the fundamental assumptions that are faulty to begin with. Psycholinguists point out that because of the variability, complexity, and novelty of language, one cannot reasonably say that language generally occurs according to a sequential chaining process. Consequently, the charge goes, a behavioral or even empirical approach is entirely wrong and must be abandoned.

How do radical behaviorists reply to this first charge?

A RADICAL BEHAVIORIST REPLY TO A CHARGE BASED ON SEQUENTIAL ANALYSES AND MEDIATION

Radical behaviorists point out two features of the first charge, and that neither applies to radical behaviorism. The first feature concerns the nature of the theoretical entities proposed as mediators by neobehavioristic accounts. Worth noting is that most of the criticism arising from psycholinguists is based on an interpretation of theoretical terms and processes as intervening variables, rather than hypothetical constructs. For example, Jenkins characterized neobehavioristic mediational theory as "really an attempt to build on the stimulus-response theory, to permit invisible things like internal stimuli and responses, but to be very explicit about these intervening variables. The hidden parts were all little s's and r's" (as cited in Baars, 1986, pp. 240–241). Jenkins was here interpreting theoretical terms as intervening variables as he argued against mediational approaches. Similarly, Fodor's (1965) attack against mediational approaches was based on an intervening variable interpretation of the mediating responses. He talked in terms of a one-for-one correspondence between the mediating response and the eventual overt response.

Readers may recall that intervening variables require exhaustive definition, whereas hypothetical constructs do not. Thus, hypothetical constructs admit surplus meaning in a way that intervening variables do not. It follows that when cognitivists reject mediational theories of neobehaviorists, the form of mediation the cognitivists are rejecting is based on an intervening variable interpretation of the mediating entities and processes. To be sure, the mediating theoretical terms of some neobehaviorists were intervening variables. However, given that most of the theoretical terms deployed in mediational neobehaviorism were hypothetical constructs, rather than intervening variables, the cognitive rejection of neobehaviorism seems to miss the mark. Readers may also recall Amsel (1989) explicitly acknowledged that neobehaviorist theoretical terms referred to "non-behavioral" "hypothetical states and processes that 'go on inside organisms'" (p. 50). As with general forms of cognitive psychology outlined in Chapter 15, the point remains that ironically, given a hypothetical construct interpretation of mediation, no qualitative inconsistency exists between the theoretical approach taken by mediational neobehaviorists and the theoretical approach taken by psycholinguists, which involves hypothetical "rules and representations." The internal phenomena of the psycholinguists are generally orders of magnitude more complex than most of the hypothetical constructs of the neobehaviorists, but by and large they do not differ in kind from those that are most frequently deployed by the neobehaviorists.

Again, the present argument is not that mediational models are acceptable to radical behaviorism if they appeal to hypothetical constructs as opposed to intervening variables. Rather, the present argument is that radical behaviorism does not subscribe to a mediational explanatory model of any sort, regardless of whether the mediators are viewed as intervening variables or hypothetical constructs (cf. Zuriff, 1985, pp. 85-87). To be sure, grammar and syntax do need to be explained. Skinner (1957) did so with his concept of autoclitic activity. As described in Chapter 8, autoclitics are supplemental forms of verbal behavior that depend on the relations that produce elementary verbal behavior and modify the effects of that verbal behavior. When a speaker tacts who does what to whom, the speaker emits words in a particular order, according to the conventional practices of the verbal community. The ordering process is conventionally called "syntax," and is one example of autoclitic activity. When the speaker indicates how many individuals are involved in the action, and whether the action took place in the past, is currently taking place, or is expected to take place in the future, the speaker applies endings and tags to the elementary verbal operants in the statement, again according to the conventional practices of the verbal community. The correspondence that is thereby established among elementary verbal operants is called "agreement" in case, tense, number, voice, and so on. The resulting agreement is conventionally called "grammar," and is another example of autoclitic activity. Importantly, autoclitics are themselves fostered by contingencies: The verbal community delivers reinforcers when speakers provide additional information about their statements and the conditions that determine them. Consequently, an explanation in terms of contingencies differs conspicuously from explanations appealing to either the innate, transformational rules of psycholinguists or the hypothetical covert associative mediators of neobehaviorists.

The second feature of the charge is that it assumes a linear chaining process with unobservable associative mediators generally underlies all behavioral accounts of verbal behavior. As noted, although accounts offered by early S – R behaviorists such as Watson did appeal to a linear chaining process, and in modern accounts some forms of verbal behavior might involve a linear chaining process (e.g., intraverbals), most forms of verbal behavior according to radical behaviorism do not involve a linear chaining process. Thus, although radical behaviorism agrees that verbal behavior doesn't occur according to a chaining process with mediators of any sort, it disagrees that radical behaviorism is committed to a chaining process as a general account. Thus, the first charge simply doesn't apply for a second reason.

How, then, do radical behaviorists explain the experimental data that psycholinguists cite to support their position? Radical behaviorists point to perceptual processes as well as stimulus generalization. Individuals have lived a considerable period of time in a linguistic environment by the time they serve as subjects in experiments. Their prior experiences shape their perception of auditory stimulation, just as their experiences would shape their perception of visual information. Radical behaviorists talk of (classically) conditioned seeing and operant seeing (Skinner, 1953, Chapter 17), and the auditory phenomena may have their counterparts in conditioned hearing and operant hearing. One hears the click as having migrated to a boundary of a syntactical unit because one has learned to interpret the auditory stimulation of a sentence in terms of its functional elements. Presumably, a click superimposed onto a string of nonsyntactic auditory information would not be interpreted as having migrated anywhere. Similarly, generalization takes place when similar words (e.g., ants, in the kitchen) are part of two comparably formulated sentences. The process of generalization links the sentences, such that their content becomes related. The finding is for an average subject. It is conceivable that the finding is not inevitable for someone who had been trained as an expert listener, and would be prepared to treat the two sentences as independent.

THE CHARGE THAT DIRECT INTERACTION WITH THE ENVIRONMENT CANNOT ADEQUATELY EXPLAIN THE DEVELOPMENT OF SUCH LINGUISTIC PROCESSES AS GRAMMAR AND SYNTAX

This second charge against the adequacy of behavioral explanations assumes a behavioral account must be committed to the view that speech or language develops only through the process of direct reinforcement. The problem with this assumption, according to psycholinguists, is that language develops so fast in children, and when it appears is so rich and complex, that environmental factors could not possibly be responsible. For example, at a year and a half, a child might have a vocabulary of 25 words, and at 6 years, 15,000 words. The increase is about 10 per day. Moreover, the number of sentences is infinite, and children can produce sentences of remarkable complexity and novelty without those sentences having been emitted and then reinforced in the past. Psycholinguists charge there is no evidence to support the behaviorist claim that direct stimulus "feedback" from the environment plays a significant and meaningful role in the development of such linguistic processes in children (e.g., by virtue of stimulus control and reinforcement), in contrast to the "independent contribution of the organism." Thus, psycholinguists argue that learning experiences are far too messy and unstructured to provide a meaningful basis for understanding the rapid acquisition and richness of a child's vocalizations. Hence, the development of linguistic processes must be relatively independent of environmental influence.

This second charge is sometimes called "the poverty of the stimulus" argument, according to which the stimulus circumstances are held to be too impoverished to account for the undeniable richness of verbal expression. In other words, environmental stimulation "underdetermines" behavior. Thus, the charge goes, stimulus conditions don't completely determine verbal behavior, and any account that appeals to stimulus conditions (as any form of behaviorism does, including radical behaviorism, by virtue of being a behaviorism) is necessarily impoverished. Consequently, the charge goes, a behavioral approach is wrong and must be abandoned. Instead of looking for environmental determinants of performance, psycholinguists argue that language can only be understood as a result of innate, cognitive mechanisms. The appropriate explanation of verbal behavior must emphasize these factors, rather than any influence of the environment.

To the extent that the second charge is based on empirical data, psycholinguists often appeal to Brown's (1958, 1973) analyses of mother-child interactions; psycholinguists claim that these analyses show the mother does not systematically reinforce a child's verbal responses. Therefore, some other process is responsible for language acquisition, and that process must be cognitive. For example, according to Brown (1973):

> In sum, then, we do not presently have evidence that there are selection pressures of any kind operating on children to impel them to bring their speech into line with adult models. (p. 412)

Brown further argues that "there is no clear evidence at all that parental frequencies [of interaction, such as reinforcement] influence the order of development of the forms we have studied. I am prepared to conclude that frequency is not a significant variable" (p. 368). The alternative, according to Brown, is that "children work out rules for the speech they hear" (p. 412). These rules "describe what people know, not what they do" (Miller, 1981, p. 89).

How do radical behaviorists reply to this second charge?

A RADICAL BEHAVIORIST REPLY TO THE CHARGE THAT DIRECT INTERACTION WITH THE ENVIRONMENT CANNOT ADEQUATELY EXPLAIN THE DEVELOPMENT OF SUCH LINGUISTIC PROCESSES AS GRAMMAR AND SYNTAX

The second charge is slightly more complex than the first, and consequently the radical behaviorist reply is slightly more complex than the first. The second charge entails three related assumptions:.

1. First, the charge assumes that reinforcement of verbal behavior is accomplished through a mechanism of reinforcement related to drive reduction, and if there has not been drive reduction, then reinforcement could not be involved. Radical behaviorism replies to this assumption by noting that although some conceptions of reinforcement in the past did appeal to drive reduction, the radical behaviorist conception does not.

2. Second, the charge assumes that the only form of reinforcement in verbal behavior is unconditioned reinforcement. Radical behaviorism replies to this assumption by noting that modern behavioral approaches involve conditioned reinforcement much more than unconditioned reinforcement.

3. Third, the charge assumes that the stimulus control by antecedent circumstances cannot be a complex process, individually determined by one's prior experiences. Radical behaviorism replies to this assumption by emphasizing the complexity of stimulus control, in which novel features of the environment combine to occasion novel verbal responses. There will be generalization and abstraction, based not only on observed features of the environment but also on subtle relations among features of the environment and the speaker's own verbal behavior, both prior and ongoing. In addition, the study of equivalence relations and other verbal relations demonstrated under the rubric of Relational Frame Theory shows how verbal behavior can develop rapidly in the absence of direct reinforcement. Although radical behaviorism agrees with the first part of the charge—that verbal behavior does develop very rapidly in children—it disagrees with the second part—that radical behaviorism is committed to the view that verbal behavior develops only through the direct action of reinforcement. Not every response develops because it was directly reinforced in the past. Rather, some verbal behavior develops indirectly, but still as the result of environmental and not mental influences.

Interestingly, Moerk (1990, 1992) has reanalyzed the mother-child interactions reported in Brown (1958, 1973). In distinct contrast to Brown's conclusions, Moerk found that: (a) the child's responses to the maternal utterances often incorporated linguistic improvements that had been modeled by the mother; and (b) probabilities of certain responses by the child given maternal utterances surpassed chance, thereby indicating a preceding learning history in which the mother's utterance, correcting or expanding on the child's earlier utterance, exerts both a discriminative (i.e., stimulus control) and a reinforcing effect. As Salzinger (1994) has pointed out, whereas Brown failed to find a statistically significant correlation between general frequencies of parental input and the child's order of acquisition for the 14 earliest phonemes, Moerk found impressively high correlations when cause and effect data from adjacent time periods were related. In short, Moerk found that the mother was intensively modeling the verbal response in question shortly before the child produced it, which certainly is a significant environmental influence.

Moerk also found evidence that the mother shaped appropriate grammatical utterances of the child. If the child said something that was almost correct, the mother would respond positively and then present a discriminative stimulus in the form of the fully correct response, all in a way that was appropriate to the age of the child. In one sequence of 38 episodes, the mother provided missing elements, such as prepositions in prepositional phrases, in 33. To be sure, the child would often be able initially to echo the mother's correct response, but would then return to an incorrect form. In such cases, the mother would correct, and the correct form would re-emerge after the child had experienced a relatively large number of corrections. When the child did not acquire "fell" as the past tense of "to fall," but instead persisted in "falled," Moerk found that in over 20 hours of exchanges, the parents uttered "fell" only 10 times, using instead "did fall" or "is falling." Why did the child use "falled," given that the child never heard the parents say "falled" and the child never received reinforcement from the parents when the child said "falled"? Presumably, the response of adding "-ed" to form the past tense of verbs was acquired independently as autoclitic behavior and then generalized, as Skinner (1957, Chapter 13) discussed in conjunction with such grammatical tags. Thus, the child did not receive the same kind of modeling for the past tense of some verbs as for the acquisition of other verb forms. Apparently, Brown based his rejection of the influence of reinforcement on language acquisition on an all-or-nothing process in which only the entirely correct response could be followed by only unconditioned reinforcement based on drive reduction. Salzinger points out that Brown apparently did not consider as relevant the possibility of shaping or of using conditioned reinforcement, where an approximation to the correct form was followed with a reinforcing consequence that was simple parental attention. Overall, Moerk concludes that environmental circumstances, such as parental modeling as a discriminative stimulus and attention as a reinforcing consequence, are intimately involved in language acquisition.

In sum, radical behaviorists accept that verbal behavior may develop very quickly for children, and in many cases without the direct action of the environment. However, the rapid development does not negate the possibility that behavioral processes such as stimulus control and reinforcement are at work in ways that psycholinguists don't recognize. These processes may operate indirectly, rather than directly. In fact, an intensive examination of the interactions between caregivers and developing infants yields further information about the interactive processes in which reinforcement contributes to language development in children, despite claims to the contrary by many psycholinguists.

CHOMSKY VERSUS BEHAVIOR ANALYSIS

At this point, it is useful to acknowledge the enormous impact of Noam Chomsky in the development of cognitive orientations generally and psycholinguistics especially, even though Chomsky is often quick to dissociate himself from professional activity in much of contemporary psychology, including much of contemporary cognitive psychology and psycholinguistics. Chomsky was relatively unknown until one of his early works was reviewed in the journal *Language*. Interestingly, that work was essentially notes from the classes he had been teaching at the Massachusetts Institute of Technology. His first formal book, written earlier during the 1950s, was too far ahead of other developments in the field to attract attention from domestic publishers, and was ultimately published in Europe almost 20 years later. The publication of his critical review (Chomsky, 1959) of Skinner's (1957) *Verbal Behavior* brought him to the attention of the scientific community. Thus, Chomsky quickly became a leading figure in the new discipline, in both its constructive aspects and its highly critical attacks against behavioral and learning theory explanations of language (see also Palmer, 2006).

In brief, Chomsky argued against interpreting language in terms of any kind of empirically oriented conditioning model, no matter how sophisticated. As Zuriff (1985, pp. 130–149) has written, Chomsky's argument has several components. First, Chomsky argued that the complexity and novelty of language were so great that no possible conditioning experience could account for it. Second, appeals to any form of linear sequencing, even if they included mediators, were inadequate. Third, theories concerning language needed to distinguish competence, or what the speaker knows about language and is capable of demonstrating, from performance, or what is realized in actual episodes of speaking and understanding. Fourth, having made the competence-performance distinction, theories needed to place a higher priority on issues of competence. Fifth and finally, Chomsky felt human physiology was innately "hard-wired" to produce sentences that were grammatically and syntactically correct, by virtue of cognitive functions that were in keeping with the deep structure of language. As Chomsky (1990) himself later put it, whereas behaviorists would contend that language is a system of habits, dispositions, and abilities, he would contend that language is a computational rule system of some sort, such that knowledge of language is knowledge of the rule system. Whereas behaviorists would contend that language is acquired by conditioning, training, or general learning mechanisms, he would contend that language is acquired through an innate language acquisition device; this device determines possible rules and modes of interaction. Whereas behaviorists would contend that language use is the exercise of an ability, much like any other skill, he would contend that the use of language is rule-governed behavior; rules form mental representations, and the speakers and listeners then parse sentences and systematically search through the rule system of the language in question in order to generate and understand the sentence.

In brief, Chomsky argues that language is most profitably understood in terms of certain elements of Platonic, Cartesian, and Kantian rationalism and nativism, as opposed to the classical empiricism of Locke, Hume, and Mill, and any empirical trends represented in certain twentieth century forms of behaviorism. Overall, he argues that sentence structure, grammar, and syntax are not acquired through interactions with the environment, according to any kind of sequential or associative or mediational conditioning model, regardless of how sophisticated the model generating the language was. Rather, a child is born with a perfect knowledge of universal grammar. This knowledge consists in a set of fixed cognitive functions that are consistent with the deep structure of language. The child then uses these functions as it acquires language. Chomsky believed human physiology is innately "hard-wired" to produce sentences that are grammatically and syntactically correct, by virtue of these functions. The functions constitute an "independent contribution of the organism," and any theoretical position that does not take them into account and give them priority over any kind of environmental influence is hopelessly inadequate. Some examples from Chomsky's writings illustrate this sentiment:

> The normal use of language is innovative, in the sense that much of what we say ... is entirely new, not a repetition of anything that we have heard before and not even similar in pattern.... But the normal use of language is not only innovative and potentially infinite in scope, but also free from the control of detectable stimuli, either external or internal. It is because of this freedom from stimulus control that language can serve as an instrument of thought and self-expression. (1972, pp. 11–12)

> No doubt what the organism does depends in part on its experience, but it seems to me entirely hopeless to investigate directly the relation between experience and action.... An attempt ... to study directly the relation of behavior to past and current experience is doomed to triviality and scientific insignificance. (1975, pp. 16–17)

In fact, for Chomsky interpreting any kind of complex human behavior in empirical terms that appeal to any determining environmental influence is hopelessly inadequate. Language happens to be an especially good example.

Chomsky's (1959) review crystallized many of the thoughts of psycholinguists, and is often regarded as one of the most influential papers in the history of psychology. Unquestioningly, more have read Chomsky's review of Skinner's book than have read Skinner's book itself.

Skinner himself never responded to the review. That he never responded is taken by many to mean that Chomsky's critical comments are in fact unanswerable and therefore essentially valid. Skinner (1972) describes his reaction to Chomsky and his review in the following passage:

> Let me tell you about Chomsky. I published *Verbal Behavior* in 1957. In 1958 I received a 55-page typewritten review by someone I have never heard of named Noam Chomsky. I read half a dozen pages, saw that it missed the point of my book, and went no further. In 1959, I received a reprint from the journal *Language*. It was the review I had already seen, now reduced to 32 pages in type, and again I put it aside. But then, of course, Chomsky's star began to rise. Generative grammar became the thing—and a very big thing it seemed to be. Linguists have always managed to make their discoveries earthshaking. In one decade everything seemed to hinge on semantics, in another decade on the analysis of the phoneme. In the sixties, it was grammar and syntax, and Chomsky's review began to be widely cited and reprinted and became, in fact, much better known than my book.

> Eventually the question was asked, why had I not answered Chomsky? My reasons, I am afraid, show a lack of character. In the first place I should have had to read the review, and I found its tone distasteful. It was not really a review of my book but of what Chomsky took, erroneously, to be my position. I should also have had to bone up on generative grammar, which was not my

field, and to do a good job I should have had to go into structuralism, a theory which Chomsky, like Claude Levi-Strauss, acquired from Roman Jakobson. According to the structuralists we are to explain human behavior by discovering its organizing principles, paying little or no attention to the circumstances under which it occurs. If anything beyond structure is needed by way of explanation, it is to be found in a creative mind—Levi-Strauss's savage mind or Chomsky's innate rules of grammar. (Compare the recent analysis of Shakespeare's sonnet "Th' expence of spirit" by Jakobson and Jones with my earlier analysis in *Verbal Behavior*. Where Jakobson and Jones confine themselves to the structure or pattern of the poem as it appears to the reader, I used the same features to illustrate the behavior processes of formal and thematic strengthening which, to put it roughly, made words available to the poet as he wrote.) No doubt I was shirking a responsibility in not replying to Chomsky, and I am glad an answer has now been supplied by Kenneth MacCorquodale in the *Journal of the Experimental Analysis of Behavior*. (pp. 345–346)

Thus, readers misunderstand the situation if they take the absence of a response from Skinner to imply the charges that Chomsky and other psycholinguists have laid at the doorstep of radical behaviorism are so essentially valid as to be irrefutable. As Skinner noted above, MacCorquodale (1970) did offer a behavior-analytic reply to Chomsky's charges. Interestingly, MacCorquodale's reply was originally sent to *Language*, the very journal that had published Chomsky's review, but it was rejected (Catania, 1997, p. 967). So much for scholarly open mindedness and the politics of the discipline. How then did MacCorquodale reply to Chomsky?

MacCorquodale's (1970) reply to Chomsky took the form of restating Chomsky's comments in the form of three criticisms, and then systematically assessing their validity. MacCorquodale (1970) stated Chomsky's first criticism of Skinner's approach as follows: "Verbal Behavior is an untested hypothesis which has, therefore, no claim upon our credibility" (p. 84). With regard to this criticism, MacCorquodale suggested that Chomsky was apparently looking for a more traditional neobehavioristic approach, such as the logical analysis of postulated entities and constructs. When Chomsky didn't see it, he rejected what was offered out of hand. Chomsky failed to grasp the significance of Skinner's functional approach to contingencies among stimuli, reinforcement, and behavior, as well as the concern with probability as a fundamental dependent variable. MacCorquodale pointed out that Skinner readily acknowledged that the emphasis in his book was on "an orderly arrangement of facts, in accordance with a formulation of behavior derived from an experimental analysis of a more rigorous sort. The present extension to verbal behavior is thus an exercise in interpretation rather than a quantitative extrapolation of rigorous experimental results" (Skinner, 1957, p. 11). This emphasis was entirely in keeping with Skinner's approach to theorizing, which Chomsky didn't grasp.

MacCorquodale (1970) stated Chomsky's second criticism of Skinner's approach as follows: "Skinner's technical terms are mere paraphrases for more traditional treatments of verbal behavior" (p. 88). With regard to this criticism, MacCorquodale pointed out that for Chomsky, many of Skinner's analytical concepts were simply inadequate versions of concepts that were already available. For example, where Skinner used "stimulus control," Chomsky would have had Skinner use the more traditional mentalistic term "reference." The point, of course, was that Skinner was trying to avoid using the same old vocabulary with its mentalistic connotations. Chomsky was especially bothered by the term *reinforcement*. He devoted a portion of the review to attacking the drive-reduction view of reinforcement, as if by destroying that view, he was discrediting any analysis that happened to use the term reinforcement. Interestingly, Chomsky (1959, p. 39) even acknowledged that Skinner rejected a drive-reduction view, but then Chomsky proceeded to refute this view anyway. To be sure, reinforcement as drive reduction is inadequate, which is presumably why Skinner never embraced that approach to reinforcement in the first place, so Chomsky's criticisms are about a behaviorism to which Skinner does not subscribe. On Chomsky's (1959) view, Skinner's notion of reinforcement means that cutting one's finger should be reinforcing (p. 37), and that the effects of reinforcement should be to make someone shout more frequently and in a higher pitched voice (p. 52). Apparently, Chomsky failed to appreciate a functional view of reinforcement, and his comments are striking in their fatuousness.

MacCorquodale (1970) stated Chomsky's third criticism of Skinner's approach as follows: "Speech is complex behavior whose understanding and explanation require a complex, mediational, neurological-genetic theory" (p. 90). With regard to this criticism, MacCorquodale indicated that for Chomsky, Skinner's basic explanatory system was just too simple to account for the complexity of the domain it was intended to handle. For example, in discussing the mand, Chomsky questions how someone would know whether or how to reinforce "relevantly." Dennett (1978, p. 67) makes an analogous point. MacCorquodale then suggested that Skinner's analysis is intended to deal with the variables that control the behavior of the speaker, rather than the behavior of the listener. What Chomsky didn't appreciate was the fundamental nature of Skinner's functional analysis: If the verbal behavior specifies some characteristic consequence, and if the speaker was indeed speaking under the functional control of a motivational condition (e.g., deprivation, aversive stimulation) relevant to this consequence, then the delivery of the characteristic consequence will strengthen the particular response of the speaker, such that it will occur again under the appropriate conditions. Moreover, Skinner makes much use of multiple control to account for complex cases. Figures of speech, extensions, supplemental stimulation, thinking, editing, logical and scientific verbal behavior, are all treated with a descriptively consistent set of principles. In place of this sort of functional analysis, Chomsky (1959) suggested: "We must attribute an overwhelming influence on actual behavior to ill-defined factors of attention, set, volition, and caprice" (p. 30). Just how "volition" and "caprice" are to be accommodated in a deterministic science is not immediately clear.

Overall, MacCorquodale concluded that Chomsky's review did not constitute a critical analysis of Skinner's approach. Chomsky expected a formal, logical approach to language, and when he did not find it, rejected a combination of outdated, stereotyped preconceptions about the sequential analyses of mediational behaviorism. What was actually there, of course, was a sparkling example of Skinner's unique analytical and interpretive approach. Chomsky's disparaging dismissal was off the mark (Palmer, 2006).

SUMMARY AND CONCLUSIONS

In conclusion, one can ask, as in Chapter 15: Why should the differences between cognitive and radical behaviorist conceptions of verbal behavior be cause for concern?

Early in this chapter, the sentences "Colorless green ideas sleep furiously" and "This sentence is false" were presented. For radical behaviorists, the critical question is: What caused the production of these sentences? Perhaps the sentences were emitted as mands, reinforced by the way they amused or perplexed listeners. Alternatively, the sentences may have been constructed by simply sequencing words of particular grammatical categories. Each word may have been drawn from a pool of other words of the same grammatical category, much like slips of paper with words on them are drawn from various baskets, each of a separate grammatical category. When Chomsky constructed the "Colorless green ideas ..." sentence in 1957, he presumably did so for the professional social reinforcement of illustrating a point, rather than in conventional interpersonal discourse about the world with another human. In other words, he was not tacting anything. Thus, regardless of what Chomsky was up to, the origin of the sentence is fully understandable in terms of contingencies.

The sentence "They are eating apples" was also presented. As before, the question is what caused the production of the sentence? Was the speaker tacting the bowl of fruit or the actions of individuals eating fruit? Some contingency caused the speaker to generate the sentence in the way it was generated. What was the contingency? An analysis in terms of contingencies reveals the meaning of the sentence.

The point here concerns a causal analysis. The differences between cognitive and behavioral orientations to verbal behavior are of concern because the causal analysis of the behavioral approach leads directly to significant practical implications. Psycholinguistics has little to say about how to create an environment that will cause a child to speak or read. It has little to say about how to implement effective language rehabilitation programs, for example, for a child who is autistic or an adult who has suffered an unfortunate brain injury or stroke. Psycholinguistics may seek to defend its position by saying that it is interested in competence rather than performance. However, even if this defense were reasonable, one still needs to account for what causes performance, since performance is what matters in human social interaction. Miller (1981) was exactly wrong: The critical question is exactly what speakers do. Speakers do what they know.

That psycholinguistics has little to say about practical implications is indicative of its foundations. Those foundations are in the mentalistic if not dualistic social-cultural matrix that underlies cognitive orientations generally. The foundations are removed from the world of behavior and analysis of the circumstances in which it occurs, and entail appeals to other dimensions. The liabilities of these orientations clearly are troublesome.

The preceding three chapters have reviewed very strong positions in contemporary thought: mentalism, cognitive psychology, and psycholinguistics. Despite the strong reception given to these positions, radical behaviorism argues that much of the support for them is illusory. Although the positions claim to be able to account for important phenomena that any form of behaviorism—including radical behaviorism—cannot, a closer analysis indicates that radical behaviorism can indeed explain the very activity that mentalistic positions say it can't. The remaining two chapters in this section of the book address a series of representative topics in philosophical psychology, to show how radical behaviorism accommodates those topics.

TABLE 16.1

Psycholinguistics
The study of the psychological processes underlying language acquisition and use.

Explanation of language according to psycholinguistics
1. Innate structures have evolved to process language in humans according to rules.
2. What needs to be explained is competence, or what a language user knows, not performance.
3. The relevant consideration is the independent contribution of the organism, not learning experiences.

According to psycholinguistics, can sequential, linear processes explain language acquisition and use?
1. No
2. Verbal processes occur much too fast.
3. Much grammatical and syntactical evidence suggests sentences are not organized sequentially, such that word #1 evokes word #2 and so on, even if mediators are assumed.

Radical behaviorist position on sequential, linear processes
1. Radical behaviorism agrees that sequential, linear processes cannot explain language acquisition and use.

---

2. The mediators employed by many neobehavioristic approaches were not what psycholinguists assumed them to be.
3. In any case, even though neobehaviorism appealed to mediators, radical behaviorism has not appealed to sequential, linear processes as a general account of language, even with mediating entities.
4. Even though radical behaviorism agrees that sequential, linear processes cannot explain language acquisition and use, it does not accept the mentalistic alternative advocated by psycholinguistics.

According to psycholinguistics, is the development of linguistic processes relatively independent of environmental influence and learning experiences?
1. Yes.
2. Word and sentence acquisition occur much too rapidly to be explained by the direct action of reinforcement.
3. The "Poverty of the Stimulus" argument: Stimulus conditions are not rich enough to explain the complexity and novelty of linguistic processes. Stimulus conditions and learning experiences underdetermine language.

Radical behaviorist position on the development of linguistic processes
1. Modern conceptions of reinforcement do not ordinarily appeal to drive reduction.
2. Modern behavioral approaches involve conditioned reinforcement at least as much as unconditioned reinforcement.
3. Not every instance of verbal behavior occurs because it has previously been reinforced, as research into equivalence relations, stimulus generalization, and multiple control shows.
4. Analysis of developmental data in children nevertheless reveals significant environmental influence in language development, such as from parents.

Chomsky's criticisms of empirically oriented accounts of language
1. Language is so complex and novel that environmental experiences cannot possibly account for it.
2. Linear sequencing models are hopelessly inadequate.
3. Competence needs to be distinguished from performance.
4. Competence is what is critical, rather than performance.
5. Human neurophysiology is "hard-wired" to produce sentences that are grammatically and syntactically correct, according to cognitive functions that are consistent with the deep structure of language.

> *MacCorquodale's rebuttal of Chomsky's criticisms*
> 1. Chomsky failed to understand Skinner's functional analysis based on operant contingencies.
> 2. Chomsky failed to appreciate the complex nature of reinforcement.

REFERENCES

Amsel, A. (1989). *Behaviorism, neobehaviorism, and cognitivism in learning theory: Historical and contemporary perspectives*. Hillsdale, NJ: Erlbaum.

Baars, B. J. (1986). *The cognitive revolution in psychology*. New York: Guilford.

Bever, T., Fodor, J., & Garrett, M. (1968). A formal limitation of associationism. In T. R. Dixon & D. L. Horton (Eds.), *Verbal behavior and general behavior theory,* pp. 582–585. Englewood Cliffs, NJ: Prentice-Hall.

Bransford, J. D., & Franks, J. J. (1971). The abstraction of linguistic ideas. *Cognitive Psychology, 2,* 331–350.

Brown, R. A. (1958). *Words and things*. Glencoe, IL: Free Press.

Brown, R. A. (1973). *A first language: The early stages*. Cambridge, MA: Harvard University Press.

Catania, A. C. (1997). An orderly arrangement of well-known facts: B. F. Skinner's *Verbal Behavior. Contemporary Psychology, 42,* 967–970.

Catania, A. C. (1998). *Learning* (4th interim ed.). Cornwall-on-Hudson, NY: Sloan Publishing.

Chomsky, N. (1959). Review of Skinner's *Verbal Behavior. Language, 35,* 26–58.

Chomsky, N. (1972). *Language and mind*. New York: Harcourt Brace Jovanovich.

Chomsky, N. (1975). *Reflections on language*. New York: Pantheon.

Chomsky, N. (1990). On the nature, use, and acquisition of language. In W. Lycan (Ed.), *Mind and cognition: A reader,* pp. 627–646. Cambridge, MA: Blackwell.

Dennett, D. (1978). *Brainstorms*. Montgomery, VT: Bradford Books.

Fodor, J. A. (1965). Could meaning be an r_m? *Journal of Verbal Learning and Verbal Behavior, 4,* 73–81.

Fodor, J. A. (1983). *Modularity of mind*. Cambridge, MA: MIT Press.

Fodor, J. A., & Bever, T. G. (1965). The psychological reality of linguistic segments. *Journal of Verbal Learning and Verbal Behavior, 4,* 414–420.

Lashley, K. (1951). The problem of serial order in behavior. In L. A. Jeffress (Ed.), *Cerebral mechanisms in behavior,* pp. 112–146. New York: Wiley.

MacCorquodale, K. (1970). On Chomsky's review of Skinner's *Verbal Behavior. Journal of the Experimental Analysis of Behavior, 13,* 83–99.

Miller, G. A. (1981). *Language and speech*. San Francisco: Freeman.

Moerk, E. L. (1990). Three-term contingency patterns in mother-child verbal interactions during first-language acquisition. *Journal of the Experimental Analysis of Behavior, 54,* 293–305.

Moerk, E. L. (1992). *First language: Taught and learned*. Baltimore, MD: Brookes.

Mowrer, O. H. (1960). *Learning theory and the symbolic processes*. New York: Wiley.

Palmer, D. C. (2006). On Chomsky's appraisal of Skinner's *Verbal Behavior*: A half century of misunderstanding. *The Behavior Analyst, 29,* 253–267.

Pinker, S. (1994). *The language instinct*. New York: Harper Collins.

Salzinger, K. (1994). The LAD was a lady, or the mother of all language learning: A review of Moerk's *First Language: Taught and Learned. Journal of the Experimental Analysis of Behavior, 62,* 323–329.

Skinner, B. F. (1953). *Science and human behavior.* New York: Macmillan.
Skinner, B. F. (1957). *Verbal behavior.* New York: Appleton-Century-Crofts.
Skinner, B. F. (1972). *Cumulative record.* New York: Appleton-Century-Crofts.
Watson, J. B. (1913). Psychology as the behaviorist views it. *Psychological Review, 20,* 158–177.
Watson, J. B. (1930). *Behaviorism* (rev. ed.). New York: Norton.
Zuriff, G. E. (1985). *Behaviorism: A conceptual reconstruction.* New York: Columbia University Press.

STUDY QUESTIONS

1. Describe how cognitive psychologists argue against S – R mediational accounts of verbal behavior. Incorporate one piece of experimental evidence that is often cited to support the argument.

2. Describe five of Chomsky's argument against interpreting language in terms of any kind of empirically oriented conditioning model, regardless of how sophisticated the model is (e.g., as presented in Zuriff, 1985).

3. Describe the argument by traditional psycholinguists that sequential analyses, including those that appeal to covert mediational processes, cannot adequately explain the production and understanding of grammatically and syntactically correct sentences in a linguistically competent speaker. Describe how radical behaviorists respond to this argument.

4. Describe the argument by traditional psycholinguists that environmental stimuli underdetermine verbal behavior, and that the development of verbal behavior in children shows that reinforcement is not involved in any significant way. Describe how radical behaviorists respond to this argument, and include the differences between the investigations of R. Brown and E. Moerk in your answer.

5. Summarize the main features of MacCorquodale's (1970) rebuttal to Chomsky's (1959) critical review of Skinner's (1957) *Verbal Behavior.*

17

Radical Behaviorism and Traditional Philosophical Issues—1

Synopsis of Chapter 17: The chapters in the third section of the book compare and contrast radical behaviorism with alternative conceptual and philosophical viewpoints. The topics considered to this point are mentalism (Chapter 14), cognitivism (Chapter 15), and psycholinguistics (Chapter 16). Chapter 17 is the first of two chapters that examines a series of topics more directly related to philosophical psychology. It begins by analyzing four forms of philosophical psychology that are often associated with behaviorism: logical behaviorism, conceptual analysis, metaphysical behaviorism, and methodological behaviorism. An early and later form of methodological behaviorism are noted. Importantly, the later from is identified as having become orthodox in behavioral science, and as having inspired a particular set of experimental and theoretical practices. Radical behaviorism notes that these practices are linked to mentalism, even though methodological behaviorists ostensibly remain silent on the mental. The chapter then moves to a consideration of pragmatism as a truth criterion, where pragmatism implies fruitfulness in practical outcomes of both verbal and nonverbal behavior. Given that pragmatism implies successful action, pragmatism is entirely consistent with the radical behaviorist conception of reinforcement: The evaluation of whether a given activity or verbalization is useful is therefore whether it leads to reinforcing consequences. Other orientations, including traditional and cognitive orientations, may be analyzed from a pragmatic perspective to assess whether they contain any "kernel of truth" that might lead to effective, practical action. However, because of the preponderance of mentalistic control over traditional and cognitive orientations, the prospects of finding anything useful are regrettably low.

Despite the longstanding reservations of radical behaviorists, mental terms prevalent in philosophy have played a significant role in traditional explanatory schemes in Western culture. This chapter continues the analyses begun in the third section by addressing the way that radical behaviorism addresses important philosophical issues in psychology, such as the place of mental terms in a science of behavior.

FORMS OF PHILOSOPHICAL PSYCHOLOGY CARRYING THE DESIGNATION "BEHAVIORISM"

A common understanding among philosophers is that behaviorism of any stripe takes mental or psychological terms to refer to either behavior or dispositions to engage in behavior, rather than mental phenomena per se. By "behavior" here is meant publicly observable behavior, intersubjectively verifiable on the basis of direct observation that can be agreed upon by at least two people. By "disposition" here is meant a robust conditional probability to engage in some particular form of behavior, given some particular form of antecedent stimulation. Indeed, the designation "philosophical behaviorism" is the generic designation often used in contemporary discussions among speakers of English for positions that translate mental or psychological terms into publicly observable behavior or dispositions to engage in publicly observable behavior. Thus, to the extent radical behaviorism is a behaviorism, a common although erroneous understanding is that it also must entail translating all mental terms into publicly observable behavior or dispositions.

To be sure, radical behaviorists agree that some orientations nominally identified as instances of behaviorism do adopt the characteristics ascribed to them by philosophers, and that these other orientations do take mental terms to refer to dispositions. Moreover, there are instances in which radical behaviorism itself interprets certain terms as dispositions. However, radical behaviorism does not take all mental terms to refer to dispositions. Thus, radical behaviorists disagree with philosophical treatments that lump radical behaviorism with those other orientations simply because all happen to be labeled with the term *behaviorism*. The net result is that radical behaviorism disagrees just as much with orientations that equate all mental terms with dispositions as it does with the more conspicuous forms of mentalism. Four examples of philosophical behaviorism are reviewed, in an effort to clarify how they relate to radical behaviorism: logical behaviorism, conceptual analysis, metaphysical behaviorism, and methodological behaviorism.

LOGICAL BEHAVIORISM

One of the important philosophical traditions in the twentieth century is Anglo-Germanic empiricism. Chapter 3 noted that this tradition spawned an exceptionally influential movement in the first quarter of the century known initially as logical positivism and somewhat later as logical empiricism. Logical behaviorism represents the application by the logical positivists of verificationism and physicalism to psychology.

In its simplest form, logical behaviorism holds that psychological terms shouldn't be taken to refer to mental phenomena per se. Mental phenomena aren't directly, publicly observable and can't be measured using the instruments of physics, for purposes of verification and agreement. Psychological terms must be like terms in all other domains in science. They must be taken to refer to either: (a) phenomena that can be measured using the instruments and concepts of physics, and through being measured, verified and agreed upon; or (b) logical or mathematical entities inferred or constructed from the public observations. Logical behaviorism therefore argued that psychological terms must be taken to refer to either: (a) publicly observable behavior or (b) measured physiological states correlated with publicly observable behavior, or (c) dispositions to engage in publicly observable behavior. Indeed, when possible, dispositions were even to be reduced to measures of underlying physiological states. As noted in Chapter 3, the logical positivists were familiar with Watson's behaviorism by virtue of Bertrand Russell's treatment of it in one of his publications, and believed its commitment to objectivity meant they had less work to do to secure the requisite meaningfulness of its terms. However, logical behaviorism was relatively tolerant when it came to choice of language, and it didn't matter which school of psychology one embraced—structuralism, functionalism, Freudian, behavioral—so long as the terms deployed in that form could ultimately be verified in physical terms. Overall, logical behaviorism was more a linguistic recommendation or a semantic thesis for achieving meaningfulness than an assertion of fact regarding which school of psychology was correct. Although in principle logical behaviorism could remain silent on whether a mental dimension actually existed, it generally conceded a mental dimension did exist, even at the same time it insisted that the meaning of psychological terms had to be expressed in physical, rather than mental terms. Rudolf Carnap (1932–1933/1959) and Carl Hempel (1935/1949) were two figures who vigorously articulated the position of logical behaviorism.

CONCEPTUAL ANALYSIS

A second orientation, or perhaps more accurately collection of positions, is known as analytical behaviorism or conceptual analysis. The positions arose when the principles of analytical philosophy or ordinary language philosophy were applied to psychology. Again, a common denominator among these positions is that mental terms should be taken to refer to dispositions. Any distinctions among the positions turn more on such factors as different time frames and the involvement of different individuals than on the few concerns that weren't shared. The designation conceptual analysis is used here.

The background of this orientation is as follows. In the early 1930s the logical positivist movement began to come under intense political pressure from the Nazi political system. This pressure forced many of the logical positivists to leave continental Europe for more intellectually hospitable circumstances, particularly in the United States and England. The United States was a suitable choice because of its traditions of empiricism and pragmatism. In addition, the principle of "operationism" as espoused by the physicist P. W. Bridgman (1928) was becoming influential in the United States, and this principle was thoroughly in keeping with the logical positivist orientation. England was similarly a good choice because empiricism, logic, and the study of language were already well linked in England before World War I, owing in various ways to such distinguished figures as Russell and his logical atomism, Russell and Whitehead and their work on the formal logic of mathematics, and G. E. Moore and his common-sense philosophy. In the period between World Wars I and II, the emigrating logical positivists joined with this existing and certainly compatible English tradition. The English philosopher A. J. Ayer became a prominent representative of logical positivism in England during this time.

In addition, the philosopher Ludwig Wittgenstein began teaching at Cambridge in 1929. As mentioned in Chapter 3, Wittgenstein was an intellect of monumental proportions whose early work was seminal in the founding of logical positivism in the early 1920s. However, during the mid-1920s Wittgenstein began to depart from his earlier position, resulting in renewed interest in various philosophical matters that concerned language, meaning, and how persons learn to speak about themselves and the world at large. He taught at Cambridge until 1947, when he retired because of failing health, ultimately dying from cancer in 1951. Although Wittgenstein published relatively little during his lifetime, especially during his Cambridge years, his students took copious notes from his lectures. These notes along with his own lecture notes were the principal sources of numerous works published posthumously.

In the rich intellectual environment established by logical positivism, Wittgenstein, and the indigenous English logico-empirical tradition, Gilbert Ryle and John Austin founded the position that is referred to here as conceptual analysis. Similar to logical positivism and logical behaviorism, conceptual analysis views philosophy not as the propounding of theories about nature, but rather as an activity of clarifying and sharpening the meaning of ordinary language and correcting misuses of it, though this process may well reveal theories underlying the use of language (Lyons, 1980). On the whole, conceptual analysis is less concerned with formal logic and the specific application of the logical analysis of language to science and scientific method than was logical positivism. Conceptual analysis is also less concerned about measures of physiological states, although it is not opposed to measuring them. For conceptual analysis, then, the important activity consists in mapping the logical geography of all concepts used in language, and especially mental concepts. As did logical behaviorism, conceptual analysis holds that mental terms refer either to behavior or dispositions to behave. As before, by *behavior* is meant publicly observable behavior, and by *dispositions* is meant conditional probabilities of engaging in publicly observable behavior, given certain forms of antecedent stimulation. However, whereas the logical positivists held this position because of a commitment to physicalism and establishing truth by agreement, conceptual analysts such as Gilbert Ryle and John Austin, who were markedly influenced by Wittgenstein, held the position on a slightly different basis.

An important feature of analytic philosophy is the rejection of solipsism and all its implications. In general, *solipsism* is the thesis that one can only know one's own private, mental world of thoughts and sensations. The external, physical world cannot be known directly, and may not even exist. Solipsism then tries to understand all human activity in terms of this model. As discussed in the paragraph below, of special concern is the application of solipsism to language. Solipsism has a long history, but owes much in Western thought to the influence of Descartes.

Conceptual analysis argues that solipsism and the entire Cartesian model are based on the myth of a "ghost in a machine." The ghost is the mind or soul, which is presumed to operate the machinery of the body. Interestingly, when the Cartesian model is applied to language, the model assumes that language of any sort must be based on some mental entity (e.g., mind, soul) that observes mental events in a private, subjective dimension, and then causes the resulting language. In other words, the model assumes that language comes about when (a) an observer (b) reports veridically on (c) some designated property of an event being observed. The important concern for conceptual analysis was whether this solipsistic, observational model for language could be applied meaningfully to psychological terms.

Many proponents of conceptual analysis believed it could not, for essentially two reasons. The first was that to accept this solipsistic model constitutes a "category mistake" (Ryle, 1949). The second was that to accept this solipsistic model constitutes an acceptance of the possibility that individuals must have developed a private language that they use to describe their own privately registered experiences; Wittgenstein (1953/1973) has argued against the possibility of a purely private language arising in this sense. These two reasons may now be examined.

Ryle's argument that the traditional Cartesian position represents a "category mistake" is roughly as follows. According to Place (1999, p. 374), conceptual analysis as a technique for elucidating word meaning rests on the principle that the meaning of a word or expression is the contribution it makes to meanings of those (meaningful) sentences in which it occurs. This principle is derived from the work of such logicians and philosophers as Frege (1884/1960) and Wittgenstein (1922/1974), among others. Therefore, an effective way to study word meanings is to contrast the kinds of sentence in which the word or expression can meaningfully occur with those in which its insertion makes nonsense. A conceptual analysis is carried out by substituting words that are supposed to be of the same logical category. If the words are indeed of the same logical category, then they ought to function equivalently in the same context, and the resulting sentence should be meaningful. If they do not so function and the sentence is not meaningful, then they are not of the same category, and knowledge claims involving these words can be rejected.

A frequently quoted illustration is that of the foreign visitor to Oxford who was shown classrooms, laboratories, the library, playing fields, museums, scientific departments, administrative offices, and so on (Ryle, 1949, p. 16). The individual then asked to see "the University." In so doing, the individual made a category mistake, that of mistaking a part for the whole, by treating "the University" as an instance of the same category as classrooms, libraries, and laboratories (i.e., a part), when actually it is of a different category (i.e., a whole; see other examples in Schnaitter, 1985, p. 146).

On the basis of such analyses of ordinary language, analytic philosophers argue that traditional psychology makes a category mistake when psychological terms, in particular verbs, are used to designate specially observed mental activities taking place in a special domain apart from the behavioral world. Analytic philosophers argue that such words actually relate to the probability or to a particular way of engaging in publicly observable behavior. In this regard, Place (1999, pp. 367–368) points out that Ryle distinguished among three types of psychological verbs: (a) dispositional verbs (Ryle, 1949, pp. 116–135); (b) activity verbs (Ryle, 1949, pp. 135–149); and (c) achievement verbs (Ryle, 1949, pp. 149–153). A category mistake would consist in taking a verb as belonging to one category when it actually belongs to another. For example, suppose one "believes" that London is the capital of England. If the word "believes" really is an activity verb, in the sense implied by the solipsistic, observational Cartesian doctrine of the "ghost in the machine," then it would make sense to hold that just as one can begin to whistle or stop on demand, where "whistle" is a noncontroversial activity verb, so also should one be able to begin to "believe" or stop on demand. But this locution doesn't make sense. Beliefs just aren't the sort of things that are observed to be switched on and off on demand, as is whistling. Hence, Ryle argued that "believe" is not an activity verb, but rather a dispositional verb. The word indicates a disposition of speakers who say they "believe" to assert that "London is the capital of England," with a high probability, in a loud voice, and in a wide variety of circumstances. Comparable arguments can be made for the use of such terms as "knowing" and "understanding." Ryle's (1949) expert application of this technique was the *reductio ad absurdum* argument, showing that many uses of psychological terms as activities in our everyday language were muddled. The uses were derived from the solipsistic, observational Cartesian doctrine, and just didn't make sense. A conceptual analysis of word usage would therefore establish a sound, coherent approach to language.

The second reason for rejecting the official Cartesian doctrine of the "ghost in the machine" is Wittgenstein's argument against the possibility of a "private language"

(1953/1973, paragraph 242 ff.). The Cartesian doctrine is that any time anyone speaks, the speaker is technically not talking about the world itself, but rather the copy or sensation of the world as registered in the speaker's mind. In this view, the basis for language is something internal and private. Wittgenstein's argument against this doctrine is based on the concept of a "language game." According to this concept, language is like a game that is played between two or more people, according to a shared set of rules. The rules are the conventional practices followed in the community that speaks the language. It follows then that speakers are not able use a particular word in connection with some event that is not accessible in principle to anyone else because language involves a give and take between speakers and listeners. In the case of private copies or sensations, listeners would simply not know what event speakers were talking about.

Place (1993, pp. 28–29; see also Zuriff, 1985, pp. 128–131) has framed this argument in the following way. If, as the traditional subjectivist theory implies, the statements that are made about the public world are derived from observations of one's private sensory experiences, then the language in which these statements are formulated must consist of words that derive their meaning from what has been called "private ostensive definition," in which speakers resolve to use a particular word to denote a kind of experience which they are currently undergoing, without coming to any agreement with other persons as to the correctness and consistency of this usage. But, as Wittgenstein points out, no one else can learn the language whose words derive their meaning in this way, because no one else can have the experiences to which a particular name has been assigned. It follows that there is no possible way in which such private observation sentences could provide a basis for the kind of knowledge that is public and communicable, and that language cannot be generally construed as a phenomenon in which speakers are presumed to be observing and then describing their own subjective sensory experiences. Thus, the account on which rests the traditional subjectivist theory of everyday Western culture, typically referred to as "folk psychology," is not tenable.

As intriguing as such arguments are, what remained unresolved was why individuals would say something that manifested a category mistake. In other words, if the task of philosophy was to make sense out of language, shouldn't philosophy be able to account for the reasons why individuals said anything, even if what they said was not in the form that philosophy preferred, such as a category mistake? If logical analysis was the way to determine the meaning of an utterance, and if someone said something that didn't respect logic, was the statement meaningless? Why would individuals say something that was meaningless? Early on, the logical positivists distinguished between the cognitive significance and emotional significance of statements. Suppose a speaker said, "I am anxious" What was a listener to make of the statement? Only statements that were reducible via the techniques of formal symbolic logic to the bedrock language of physics had cognitive significance. Could the speaker's statement be verified by counters, dials, or pointers, preferably activated by events in the speaker's nervous system? If so, the statement had the requisite cognitive significance. It was meaningful and warranted serious attention; it was a statement of fact. If the statement could not be so reduced, it possessed only emotional significance; it was a statement only of value or personal taste. It was dismissed as psychological or worse—metaphysical and meaningless. Yet, why would someone say something that was meaningless by this criterion? Interestingly, Russell (1926, p. 116) rejected as illusory the distinction between the emotional and logical use of words. Skinner read Russell's piece early in his career, and has always pointed out the great impact of Russell on his intellectual development. Unfortunately, such questions remained unanswered.

In any case, staying within the confines of the questions that these forms of philosophical psychology engaged, an important consideration now is: How far can one extend the interpretation that subjective or mental terms only refer to dispositions to engage in publicly observable phenomena? For example, what do individuals mean when they say they are in pain? Is it the case that subjective or mental terms are meaningful only to the extent they refer to the public circumstances, such as publicly observable behavior? When speakers report they are in pain, are they reporting that they have observed in themselves a disposition to moan and groan, and not that they are experiencing some kind of private sensation, because there is no basis for the putative private meaning of the term? As discussed in Chapter 15, cognitive psychologists and philosophical functionalists reject this position out of hand. Whether anyone has ever held such an extreme position is not clear, but is it even a defensible position to hold?

METAPHYSICAL BEHAVIORISM

One solution to these problems is to argue that the only things that merit scientific investigation are those that are publicly observable and measurable. In this test, psychological theories and explanations can include only publicly observable phenomena, because they are the only things that are real, in the sense that they are the only things that are measurable, countable, or recordable on dials, pointers, or meters. Things purportedly going on inside the skin can only be addressed as matters of physiology. If they can't be addressed as matters of physiology, they are held not to exist at all. This position is called metaphysical behaviorism.

In certain respects, Watson's uncompromising rejection of such supposedly mental phenomena as consciousness was a metaphysical behaviorist stance. For example, Heidbreder (1933) emphasized that for Watson, consciousness was simply

> a "plain assumption." It cannot be proved by any scientific test, for consciousness cannot be seen, nor touched, nor exhibited in a test-tube. Even if it exists it cannot be studied scientifically, because admittedly it is subject only to private inspection. Finally, a belief in the mental is allied to modes of thinking that are wholly incompatible with the ways of science. It is related

to the religious, the mystical, and the metaphysical interpretations of the world. The notion of consciousness is the result of old wives' tales and monks' lore, of the teachings of medicinemen and priests. Consciousness is only another name for the soul of theology, and the attempts of the older psychology to make it seem anything else are utterly futile. To admit the mental into science is to open the door to the enemies of science–to subjectivism, supernaturalism, and tendermindedness generally. (p. 235)

The question that arose from metaphysical behaviorism was again whether the import of all phenomena that aren't publicly observable should be dismissed. In other words, if the existence of mental phenomena is denied because they are unobservable, is the existence of everything that is unobservable, including sensations, feelings, and other unobservable personal experiences, to be denied? Some metaphysical behaviorists did in fact go this route and deny the relevance of anything that wasn't publicly observable; for example, experiences commonly regarded as private or subjective. They held rigorously to the position that only the publicly observable can be part of psychological science. Nevertheless, leaving aside the question of whether something is mental, aren't there profound implications of denying the relevance, if not the existence, of things that are not publicly observable? What if their public observation simply awaits better measuring equipment? Again, these matters remained unresolved.

METHODOLOGICAL BEHAVIORISM

One last term may now be considered in connection with the discussion of various forms of behaviorism and philosophical matters: methodological behaviorism. *Methodological behaviorism* is again a generic term that applies to a family of positions nominally designated as behavioral. It is usually contrasted with radical behaviorism, and as shall be seen, correctly so. Methodological behaviorism is also linked with mentalism, although the link is not obvious. Finally, methodological behaviorism is a form of philosophical behaviorism that embraces many of the philosophical features of logical behaviorism, conceptual analysis, and sometimes even metaphysical behaviorism. However, it goes beyond these positions by incorporating procedural features, such as those pertaining to how research should be carried out in light of the associated philosophical commitments.

The principal thesis of methodological behaviorism is that the only data that psychology can directly consider if it seeks to be a science and engage in epistemologically respectable activity are public data. In other words, psychology can't directly consider private data. The core assumption is that science entails objective and empirical measures of phenomena, so that its statements and analytic concepts can be agreed upon. Thus, methodological behaviorism represents a formal and strategic agreement to regard the relation between publicly observable stimulus variables and publicly observable behavior as the appropriate subject matter for psychology as a science.

That the aim of science was to describe publicly observable data followed from such historical figures as Galileo and Newton. Moreover, it was certainly consistent with positivism. Methodological behaviorism first appeared as a relatively formal position in psychology during the first quarter of the twentieth century. Recall that much of the psychology of the time focused on the structure and contents of mental life (i.e., "consciousness") as revealed through introspection. Unfortunately, the development of a coherent science of mental life was proving intractable. Concepts in psychology so conceived were beset by problems of ambiguity and lack of clarity. Workers in psychology wanted "a fresh set of concepts derived from a direct analysis of ... newly emphasized data" (Skinner, 1945, p. 292).

Methodological Behaviorism: The Early Form

The exposition here suggests there were early and late forms of methodological behaviorism, and presents examples of these forms. In addition, a significant term in the definition of methodological behaviorism presented above is "directly." The point is that over the years, methodological behaviorists subscribed to the principal thesis for several different reasons, based on how they interpreted the proscription against commenting directly on private data, and it is useful to view their positions in context.

Some early methodological behaviorists were metaphysical behaviorists. They interpreted the proscription against speaking directly about the mental to mean that since the mental did not exist, obviously one couldn't speak directly about it. Again, one example was John B. Watson, whose version of metaphysical behaviorism has already been discussed.

Other early methodological behaviorists interpreted the proscription against speaking about the mental somewhat differently. Consequently, they argued on somewhat different grounds. For these methodological behaviorists, a science could only deal with things that were publicly observable and objective. Behavior was publicly observable and objective. In contrast to metaphysical behaviorism, this form tacitly assumed the mental actually did exist, and might have the characteristics ascribed to it, including being a cause of behavior. However, conscious experience was not publicly observable. Hence, psychology as a science had to deal with behavior as a subject matter, rather than conscious experience. These early methodological behaviorists rejected introspection as a methodology because it was not appropriate to the subject matter of publicly observable behavior. Introspection may well have been an appropriate methodology for conscious experience, but conscious experience could no longer be a legitimate subject matter for psychology as a science, given the commitments to objectivity and agreement. Experimentation rather than introspection was necessary to secure the relation between the publicly observable variables and publicly observable behavior.

In short, these early methodological behaviorists simply suggested that if they were to pay attention to the "mental" at all, it required another mode of analysis, such as philosophical. If pushed further, these methodological behaviorists said that anything gained by considering private data can just as easily or acceptably be gained by speaking only of public data. Those who promoted this view variously subscribed to parallelism or the double-aspect view of the mind-body relation, which are described in Chapter 18.

Max Meyer's often-cited book, *The Psychology of the Other-One* (Meyer, 1922), represents one instance of early methodological behaviorism that took this stance. Here Meyer attempted to present the case in an introductory-level book for psychology as an objective, positivistic science of behavior concerned with measurable properties. Part of the impetus behind the book was to rid psychology as a science of the legacy of structuralism, introspection, and a concern with the contents of consciousness. A representative passage from early in the book provides the flavor of Meyer's (1922) approach:

> In times past one used to turn to psychology books when he wanted to learn something about his Self—his Soul.... Modern science owes its triumphs to the fact that it has learned to restrict itself to describing merely that which one can measure. The psychology of the Other-one follows the same road. Why should Robinson Crusoe, wanting information [on Friday], use the antiquated, the sterile method?.... Crusoe's desire to know as much ... as possible about his man Friday cannot be satisfied by the psychology of Selves. He needs the psychology of the Other-one. He needs the psychology which applies sense organs to the object of study, compares what the sense organs perceive, counts and—leaves the question whether Friday has a Self, a Soul, a Mind, a Consciousness to the single being whom it might concern, to Friday. (pp. 3, 4)

As had Watson before him, Meyer attempted to call attention to the pragmatic issue that science was primarily concerned with phenomena that could be touched and measured. Conscious experience could not be measured as such. Accordingly, psychology needed to deal with what it could touch and measure: behavior. Psychology had to rule consciousness and mind out of bounds, not so much because they didn't exist, but rather because they could not be reached by methods whose products could be measured and agreed upon. Introspection was largely irrelevant to psychology as a scientific method. Here the mental was ignored on procedural grounds, rather than on the metaphysical or ontological grounds that it had been for Watson.

A final and enormously influential example of early methodological behaviorism is the Harvard psychologist S. S. Stevens, who was supported by E. G. Boring, also from the Harvard department. In Stevens' view, the task of a science of behavior was simply to describe the relation–the preferred form of the description was quantitative—between publicly observable stimulus inputs and behavioral outputs. Nothing was formally or explicitly said about what caused the input to be related to the output in the observed way. This approach was held to be consistent with the highest traditions of empiricism and positivism. Stevens wrote numerous articles seeking to clarify the new methodology during the 1930s, in addition to conducting laboratory research in psychophysics, and was widely regarded as one of the most influential experimental psychologists in the discipline for over 30 years.

Skinner (1953) commented critically on this early form of methodological behaviorism in the following way:

> Modern science has attempted to put forth an ordered and integrated conception of nature. Some of its most distinguished men have concerned themselves with the broad implications of science with respect to the structure of the universe. The picture which emerges is almost always dualistic. The scientist humbly admits that he is describing only half the universe, and he defers to another world—a world of mind or consciousness—for which another mode of inquiry is assumed to be required. Such a point of view is by no means inevitable, but it is part of the cultural heritage from which science has emerged. It obviously stands in the way of a unified account of nature. (p. 258)

At first blush, this early form of methodological behaviorism was not without some virtue: By focusing on only publicly observable variables, its statements were clearly objective and clearly generated agreement. It therefore represented some improvement over introspection. However, the virtue was more apparent than real. For instance, how can this form of methodological behaviorism account for introspective statements? One doesn't have to accept the validity of all introspective statements to recognize that some are valid. People think, they label pains as sharp or dull, and they describe sensations and feelings inside their bodies. According to what processes do such descriptions come about? In equating privacy with the mental, and then not commenting directly on the mental, weren't methodological behaviorists ignoring something that was relevant to human life? Ironically, methodological behaviorists had painted themselves into a corner. According to their own assumptions, they couldn't directly comment on introspective statements. If they tried to comment anyway, they weren't confining themselves to publicly observable data. Of course, even the most ardent of them strayed from their corner and made statements about mental causes, although they tended to demur when challenged about them.

Methodological Behaviorism: The Later Form

As a result of such problems, the early form of methodological behaviorism was eventually abandoned. Methodological behaviorism then morphed into a second, later form. This form interpreted the proscription against commenting directly on private data in another sense. This form of methodological behaviorism avoided commenting directly on private data but did comment *indirectly* on private data. These methodological behaviorists rendered private variables as theoretical terms (e.g., intervening variables, hypothetical constructs) with suitable operational definitions and other features of a newly emerging scientific method. This form shows the considerable influence of logical positivism and the principle of operationism as they began to become prominent in the 1930s. This later form was in fact the foundation of S – O – R mediational neobehaviorism, in which the referents of the mental terms were unselfconsciously engaged indirectly, as mediating theoretical terms, rather than directly, as observational terms or introspections about the supposed contents of consciousness. In this regard, the dispositions of the various philosophical positions were incorporated as one example, but by no means the only example, of a mediating theoretical concept. Thus, mediational S – O – R neobehaviorism emerged as the preferred format for pursuing the thesis of methodological behaviorism, with the result that mediational S – O – R neobehaviorism and methodological behaviorism are now largely synonymous.

The later form has come to predominate in the field, as a sort of professional methodological orthodoxy. It goes well beyond any concerns that Skinner voiced early in his career about how S. S. Stevens and E. G. Boring ostensibly restricted their attention to publicly observable data. It includes a whole set of epistemological principles, as well as prescriptions for research practices based on these principles. In this regard, Day (1983) argued:

> Methodological behaviorism involves a widely accepted professional orientation towards how one should conduct psychological research in general. Verbalizations of this orientation amount to a crude kind of philosophy of science…. It is similar in ways to a kind of naive realism, and it is at least historically derived from logical positivism, operationism, and the behaviorism of the 1940's…. (p. 91)

Day (1983) goes on to suggest that Skinner himself often restricted his own usage of the term *methodological behaviorism,* with the result that Skinner's various treatments of the issue didn't readily reflect a conventional professional orientation toward research methodology:

> Skinner's conception of methodological behaviorism is so narrow that for him simply to make a distinction between methodological and radical behaviorism is for him not to engage at all the complete set of professional practices and beliefs that are now orthodox in most psychology departments. (p. 97)

The salient features of these orthodox practices and beliefs constituting the later form of methodological behaviorism may be outlined in the following way (e.g., Day, 1976; 1983, pp. 91–92; Moore, 1981, p. 64):

1. That scientific knowledge is gained from conducting carefully controlled research that manipulates publicly observable stimulus and response variables;

2. That this research uses objective research procedures and impartial tests of statistical inference to evaluate predictions of theories;

3. That scientific knowledge is intrinsically different from and superior to common sense knowledge, by virtue of being logically derived from publicly observable stimulus and response variables according to objective research procedures;

4. That claims to scientific knowledge involve constructing logical domains, within which the logical properties of symbolic entities and mathematical formulae are to be established; generalized mathematical formulae accounting for a suitably high percent of the variance or logically valid deductions from the theories may be taken as explanations of the event under consideration;

5. That permissible elements in claims to scientific knowledge are publicly observable stimulus and response variables, as independent and dependent variables, along with any inferred, mediating "theoretical" variables that can be operationally defined in terms of publicly observable variables;

6. That causal processes are to be accommodated according to a linear chain model:

$$S \Rightarrow O \Rightarrow R$$

in which the middle term identifies the operationally defined, mediating organismic variables;

7. That the claims to scientific knowledge concern a virtually limitless variety of "psychological" states or processes that are inferred to be causally effective antecedents; these states and processes are instances of the mediating organismic variables; they are not publicly observable but are nevertheless the presumed causes of behavior; and

8. That the claims to scientific knowledge involving these psychological states and processes generally have their source in the mentalistic conceptual system commonly employed in our culture; the use of a prescribed methodology assures that claims to scientific knowledge appealing to these causal states may be taken as satisfactory.

In short, roughly during the second quarter of the twentieth century, psychologists borrowed techniques from philosophy and operationism to legitimize what they were doing anyway. The various orientations that existed in psychology then coalesced into one version or another of mediational S – O – R neobehaviorism, supported by methodological behaviorism. As a result, a wide variety of terms, from the inferred organismic variables to the mental, were incorporated as mediating theoretical terms and given suitable operational definitions in terms of publicly observable stimulus or response variables. Dispositions similarly came to be regarded as examples of the mediating, organismic variables. The experimental method was understood as the testing of theories about psychological states and processes, assessing the reliability of findings by comparing the results from one or more experimental groups with control groups, and so on. Problems with methodological and epistemic underpinnings of psychology were regarded as resolved.

The bottom line is that methodological behaviorism has become the dominant position in contemporary behavioral science. Indeed, as early as the mid-twentieth century Bergmann (1956) said in his canonical statement on methodological behaviorism, "Virtually every American psychologist, whether he knows it or not, is nowadays a methodological behaviorist" (p. 270). Interestingly, cognitive psychology is tightly linked to methodological behaviorism as well. For example, George Mandler, a prominent cognitive psychologist, echoes Bergmann's methodological behaviorism in the following passages:

> [N]o cognitive psychologist worth his salt today thinks of subjective experience as a datum. It's a construct.... Your private experience is a theoretical construct to me. I have no direct access to your private experience. I do have direct access to your behavior. In that sense, I'm a behaviorist. In that sense, everybody is a behaviorist today. (Mandler in Baars, 1986, p. 256)

> We [cognitive psychologists] have not returned to the methodologically confused position of the late nineteenth century, which cavalierly confused introspection with theoretical processes and theoretical processes with conscious experience. Rather, many of us have become methodological behaviorists in order to become good cognitive psychologists. (Mandler, 1979, p. 281)

Thus, methodological behaviorism is the very foundation of orthodox contemporary psychology, and the extensiveness of its impact should not be underestimated. Ironically, it is intimately associated with cognitive psychology, when behaviorism and the mentalism of cognitive psychology are supposedly mutually exclusive (Fodor, 1968).

METHODOLOGICAL BEHAVIORISM AND THE ONTOLOGICAL STATUS OF THE "MENTAL"

In light of methodological behaviorism, what then can be said about the ontological status of mental concepts qua mental in philosophical psychology, given that mental concepts had historically and foundationally played such a major role in the science? Recall that for logical positivism and logical behaviorism, one could safely remain silent on the ontological status of the mental. Similarly, according to methodological behaviorism, one could no longer appeal directly to mental concepts qua mental. However, the distinction in philosophy of science between observational and theoretical terms meant that the mental could be treated as a theoretical concept. Again, theorists assumed that the mental actually did exist, and had the characteristics ascribed to it. As before, there was no direct appeal to the mental, which is consistent with the thesis of methodological behaviorism, although one can point to the indirect appeal to the mental, via the theoretical concept.

Radical behaviorism hadn't really developed in the first quarter of the twentieth century, when the early form of methodological behaviorism was influential. However, radical behaviorism had a lot to say about the second, later form. In particular, radical behaviorists argue that although it may not be obvious, the later form of methodological behaviorism is mentalistic in two ways. The first way it is mentalistic concerns the subject's behavior. Methodological behaviorists can propose all sorts of causal entities, especially mental or cognitive, and then designate them as "theoretical" factors that can be operationally defined in terms of publicly observable variables. By so doing, the later form of methodological behaviorism achieved a degree of consensus that contributed to its popularity, but avoided a charge that it was directly mentalistic. However, methodological behaviorists are still attributing the cause of the subject's behavior to mental entities. Indeed, Skinner (1974) commented that "Most methodological behaviorists granted the existence of mental events while ruling them out of [direct] consideration" (p. 13). Day (1983) summarized the case against methodological behaviorism as follows:

> Methodological behaviorism relies on the model of antecedent causation almost universally. Thus in methodological behaviorism it is commonly taken that any hypothesized or inferred psychological processes or states are the presumed causes of behavior. This is mentalism. The hypotheses involving these antecedently causal psychological processes and states generally have their source in the conceptual system employed in our culture. Thus there is in orthodox experimental psychology no resistance at all to these "very old ideas" which it is the business of radical behaviorism to challenge. (p. 92)

The second way the later form of methodological behaviorism is mentalistic concerns the scientist's behavior. The scientist was held to become knowledgeable through the appeal to the theoretical concept. In other words, the theoretical concept was taken to be a hypothetical or conceptual device from another dimension that had the ability to cause behavior, in this case the behavior of the scientist when it came to correct explaining, predicting, or controlling. This view represents a mentalistic cause of the scientist's behavior, and is an instance of epistemological dualism. Scientific epistemology is portrayed as the product of a mental process, apart from the world of behavior. A naturalistic science of behavior is compromised.

In principle, methodological behaviorism attempts to remain ontologically neutral. That is, methodological behaviorism nominally takes no stand on monism, materialism, or dualism. It simply tries to emphasize that whatever one proposes must ultimately be decided in terms of publicly observable data.

In practice, however, the issue is not so clear. Once theoretical terms are interpreted as hypothetical constructs, any statement of methodological behaviorism becomes fragile indeed. For example, Bergmann's (1956) classic article rejected the metaphysics of "interacting minds," but the interaction was what he rejected, not the dualism of mental and physical. Bergmann adopted a version of psychophysiological parallelism that fully endorsed minds and mental phenomena that were qualitatively different from publicly observable behavior. To do otherwise was "silly," and "a lot of patent nonsense" (Bergmann, 1956, p. 266). Indeed, Natsoulas (1984) points out that Bergmann: (a) admits mental episodes that are different from physical episodes (p. 52), (b) admits mental causes for behavior (p. 63); and (c) concedes that mental variables may legitimately be invoked to explain behavior (p. 64). Moreover, Natsoulas (1983) discusses extensively "the mind-body dualism of methodological behaviorism" (p. 13) and how methodological behaviorism considers "conscious content to be mental as distinct from physical" (p. 5). Thus, methodological behaviorism hardly guarantees that science is free from one sort of ontological commitment or another, and is hardly a coherent stance in professional psychology. It is simply another form of mentalism.

Indeed, over the years, the theorist Sigmund Koch has written scathing indictments of the intellectual bankruptcy of the methodological behaviorist position: "I think that for both metaphysical and methodological variants of behaviorism (and I am not convinced that the methodological variety is quite so 'uncontaminated' with metaphysics as stereotype would have it), the following can be said: These are essentially irrational positions ... which cannot be implemented without brooking self-contradiction" (Koch, 1964, p. 6). In other words, a science of behavior cannot be considered as internally consistent if it admits some relevant variable exists, but then refuses to directly incorporate that variable into its formulations. Radical behaviorists agree with Koch that methodological behaviorism is incoherent. However, it disagrees with Koch about the solution. Koch's solution is to abandon the thesis of methodological behaviorism and directly incorporate unobservables as mental. Radical behaviorists argue that the appropriate solution is to abandon any conception of unobservables as mental. To the extent that talk of unobservables is talk of behavioral variables, those variables may then be directly incorporated as private.

PRAGMATISM

An enduring question in philosophical circles is how to assess the truth value of an idea, concept, or statement. As seen below, radical behaviorism embraces a pragmatic theory of truth, as opposed to a correspondence or coherence theory.

A correspondence theory is based on reference: The truth value of a statement is a function of the extent to which the statement can be shown to agree, refer, match, or correspond to some publicly observable set of facts or state of affairs. Interestingly, this position assumes that facts are things that have an independent existence, and what language does is to apprehend and express those facts.

A coherence theory is based on logic: The truth value of a statement is a function of how well the statement accords with other statements in a logical network of statements. Interestingly, this position is almost an idealism. It played a large part in the position advocated by the logical positivists, whose all-encompassing embrace of logic was predicated on an assumption that the world had some sort of ideal structure that could be revealed and expressed through logic.

A pragmatic theory is based on practical outcomes: The truth value of a statement is a function of how well the statement promotes effective, practical action. It is derived from the American pragmatism of C. S. Peirce, William James, and John Dewey, although the details of their positions differed slightly, and is ably reviewed in Zuriff (1985).

From the perspective of radical behaviorism, matters of effective action, success, usefulness, efficiency, expedience, workability, or producing practical consequences all pertain to the degree that reinforcing consequences follow from the verbal behavior in question. In other words, these matters all pertain to the degree that verbal behavior functions as antecedent stimulation that mediates reinforcement. Skinner expressed this sentiment in the following passages:

> The ultimate criterion of goodness of a concept is not whether two people are brought into agreement but whether the scientist who uses the concept can operate successfully upon his material—all by himself if need be. What matters to Robinson Crusoe is not whether he is agreeing with himself but whether he is getting anywhere with his control over nature. (1945, p. 291)

> The extent to which the listener judges [a verbal response] as true, valid, or correct is governed by the extent to which comparable responses have proved useful in the past. (1957, p. 427)

> [A] proposition is "true" to the extent that with its help the listener responds effectively to the situation it describes. (1974, p. 242)

Indeed, correspondence and coherence theories may be interpreted as less effective derivations of pragmatism, rather than separate categories. The importance of correspondence theory is that it emphasizes the extent to which the verbal behavior in question evidences the tact relation, although correspondence theory is ordinarily expressed in quite different terms. Similarly, the importance of coherence theory is that it emphasizes autoclitic and intraverbal support, as well as the generic nature of verbal responses, although again coherence theory is ordinarily expressed in quite different terms.

PRAGMATISM AND SCIENTIFIC VERBAL BEHAVIOR

According to William James (1892), the aim of science is to predict and control:

> All natural sciences aim at practical prediction and control and in none of them is this more the case than psychology today. We live surrounded by an enormous body of persons who are most definitely interested in the control of states of mind, and in incessantly craving for a sort of psychological science which will teach them how to *act*. What every educator, every asylum su-

perintendent, asks of psychology is practical rules. Such men care little or nothing about the ultimate philosophic grounds of mental phenomena, but they do care immensely about improving the ideas, dispositions, and conduct of the particular individuals in their charge. (p. 148)

This view was subsequently endorsed by Watson (1913), who held that psychology's "theoretical goal is the prediction and control of behavior" (p. 158). The notion of prediction and control, or perhaps influence more generally, emphasizes direct actions that have a practical effect. Language provides discriminative stimulation to guide such behavior. Its truth value is assessed in terms of the practical action it occasions.

As noted earlier in Chapter 12, the pragmatic conception of truth is similar to another position in the philosophy of science called instrumentalism. Instrumentalism holds that scientific verbal behavior need not be examined to determine whether it is true or false. Rather, the central question is the degree to which the verbal behavior mediates accurate predictions. Pragmatism is similar to instrumentalism by pointing out that terms do not necessarily stand in a one-for-one relation with metaphysically real aspects of nature. It is further similar in emphasizing the practical function of language, with regard to effective action. Where they differ is that pragmatism calls for an analysis of the basis on which a statement works when it does. In contrast, instrumentalism stops short of doing so. The pragmatist asks if theory yields useful knowledge, why? If in the name of pragmatism scientists simply use the theoretical term and never ask the next question, scientists blind themselves to ever finding out more.

Typically, however, scientists always want to find out more. If scientists so ask, they are tacitly assuming there is more to be found. Thus, instrumentalism is the antithesis of scientific progress. One doesn't gain knowledge by assuming knowledge is adventitious outcome of manipulating fictions. To argue for instrumentalism is to argue for explanatory fictions and to go off in search of metaphorical mental way stations. Scientists operate much more practically. Fictions and metaphors mislead and distort eventually. Indeed, the techniques of science are designed to promote supplemental control that reduces the metaphorical nature of statement (Skinner, 1957, pp. 419–420). Instrumentalism is based on the view that any knowledge is actually derived from the manipulation of subjective or cognitive entities, in a mental world apart from a behavioral world. Therefore, it is perfectly acceptable to employ fictions, because fictions are all there is for anyone to employ. That's what the human mind creates when it tries to become knowledgeable. This entire perspective is mentalism, and comprehensively misrepresents what knowledge is. The passage below by the noted cognitive psychologist George Mandler is a conspicuous illustration of mentalism based on instrumentalism:

I think the major problem in behaviorism was the fear of theory. I have a rather peculiar view of that. I think that what characterized American psychology and American science through the

19th and into the 20th century was an antitheoretical point of view. I include Hull in this. Now what do I mean by that? I mean that one of the components of theory is the generation of useful fictions. That's what theories are about. Here was this great deductive theory that Hull had proposed, but when Hull generated fictions he was so afraid of generating real fictions, that his fictions had the names of observable events—little internal responses, and little stimuli. The fear of theory. (George Mandler in Baars, 1986, p. 255)

In contrast, radical behaviorism calls for the operational analysis of scientific verbal behavior. Such an analysis assesses: (a) the discriminative control over the utterance of the verbal behavior, as the contingencies act on the speaker; and (b) the discriminative control that the verbal behavior exerts, as it participates in subsequent contingencies that act on the listener. Therein lies the pragmatic function of scientific verbal behavior. Skinner expressed his pragmatic orientation in the three passages below:

We may quarrel with any analysis which appeals to ... an inner determiner of action, but the facts which have been represented with such devices cannot be ignored. (Skinner, 1953, p. 284)

No entity or process which has any useful explanatory force is to be rejected on the ground that it is subjective or mental. The data which have made it important must, however, be studied and formulated in effective ways. (Skinner, 1964, p. 96)

It is often said that an analysis of behavior in terms of ontogenic contingencies "leaves something out of account," and this is true. It leaves out of account habits, ideas, cognitive processes, needs, drives, traits, and so on. But it does not neglect the facts upon which these concepts are based. It seeks a more effective formulation of the very contingencies to which those who use such concepts must eventually turn to explain their explanations. (Skinner in Catania & Harnad, 1988, p. 390)

Day (1969) also adopted a pragmatic stance in one of his seminal articles on radical behaviorism:

[I]n the last analysis the radical behaviorist is committed to an exceedingly liberal position with respect to the verbal behavior of his professional colleagues. Admittedly, the reliance upon a speculative epistemology is deplorable, especially when unrecognized or unintended, but objection is ultimately to be raised only on pragmatic grounds. Anyone is basically free to speak as he does. A man says what he can say; he says what he does say, and all this is in principle acceptable to the radical behaviorist, since whatever is said is as such a manifestation of complex human functioning and is consequently the legitimate object of behavioral investigation. In responding to professional language, the radical behaviorist has his own new course to follow: he must attempt to discover the variables controlling what has been said. Even the most mentalistic language is understandable and valuable in this sense. (p. 320)

In a pragmatic view, then, topics for scientific investigation can come from any one of a number of sources: "hunches," the breakdown of one's apparatus, convenience, luck, serendipity. One must recognize that something acts to generate these topics, and that they do not spring full-blown from the forehead of Zeus. In any case, by recognizing that the topics are derived from the way the scientist comes into contact with nature, one can then proceed to investigate them in an orderly and effective way.

The difficult question, of course, is whether radical behaviorists will find it worthwhile to continually assess stimulus control over the mentalistic language found in most instrumentalist or realist theories involving cognitive theoretical constructs. Day (1969) seemed to argue that they will. At issue is whether the time given to such a task would be better used by simply attempting to move forward on one's own, and by attempting to discover new facts and relations. Admittedly, the question is not any easy one. From the standpoint of Skinner's radical behaviorism, scientific language is often under multiple control of both (a) operations and contacts with data, and (b) social-cultural traditions. Thus, despite its inclinations, even the most mentalistic sounding theory might contain something of value. The value would derive from the theory's implicit contact with operations and data, rather than its unfortunate embrace of social-cultural traditions. On the one hand, if behavior analysts entertain the mentalistic theory, then they run the risk of finding out later that time and resources have been wasted by entertaining something trivial at best. On the other hand, if behavior analysts reject the mentalistic theory, then they risk missing something of genuine value, even though the value is not what the mentalist thinks it is. In one instance, Skinner was not very optimistic about the prospects of finding anything useful in cognitive psychology. When asked about how broad he thought a student's training in psychology should be, Skinner replied:

> If I were to design a course for students who did not have to answer someone else's final examinations, who were genuinely interested in understanding human behavior, and who wanted to be effective in dealing with it, I should not bother with ordinary learning theory, for example. I would eliminate most of sensory psychology and I would give them no cognitive psychology whatsoever. I would include very little of mental measurement or testing. My students would never see a memory drum. They would study a bit of perception, but in a different guise. I don't mean that I want a narrow curriculum. I want students to know some history and some literature. And other sciences. I would much rather see a graduate student in psychology taking a course in physical chemistry than in statistics. And I would include other sciences, even poetry, music, and art. Why not? (Skinner in Evans, 1976, p. 93)

In another instance, Skinner (1969, pp. 93–94) suggested that an emphasis on basic dimensions would help in making such decisions. Graphs in the research related to the theory should not ordinarily show changes in behavior from trial to trial, in terms of time or number of errors required to reach a criterion, or in terms of amount remembered. In addition, dimensions are probably suspect if the work was done with mazes, jumping stands, or memory drums. Perhaps the choice will also involve the "track record" of individual scientists in individual laboratories. The behavior analyst may occasionally miss something relevant by following these guidelines, but in the long run would presumably be further ahead.

TABLE 17–1

Philosophical behaviorism
The generic designation for positions that take mental or psychological terms to refer to publicly observable behavior or dispositions to engage in publicly observable behavior.

Logical behaviorism
An early form of philosophical behaviorism in which psychological terms were taken to refer to either: (a) publicly observable behavior, or (b) measured physiological states correlated with publicly observable behavior, or (c) dispositions to engage in publicly observable behavior. Two advocates were Rudolf Carnap and Carl Hempel.

Conceptual analysis
A later form of philosophical behaviorism based on Ryle's arguments concerning category mistakes and Wittgenstein's anti-private language argument.

Metaphysical behaviorism
The position that psychological theories and explanations can include only publicly observable phenomena, because they are the only things that can be measured, counted, or recorded on dials, pointers, counters, or meters, and are therefore the only things that really exist. Things inside the skin can only be addressed as matters of physiology, if they are held to exist at all.

Methodological behaviorism (early form)
The only data that psychology can directly consider if it seeks to be a science and engage in epistemologically respectable activity are public data. In particular, psychology can't directly consider private data, such as those coming from introspective reports. It must therefore ignore or disregard private data. Consciousness can't be a direct part of science because it is not public, so it doesn't matter whether it exists. Many versions of the position assume that an adequate explanation can be secured without admitting mental phenomena; they are unnecessary, even though they exist.

Methodological behaviorism (later form)
Private data can be admitted indirectly as mediating theoretical concepts (e.g., intervening variables, hypothetical constructs), to the extent that they can be suitably operationally defined in terms of publicly observable measures. This later form was in fact the foundation of S – O – R mediational neobehaviorism, in

which the referents of the mental terms were unselfconsciously engaged indirectly, as mediating theoretical terms, rather than directly, as observational terms or introspections about the supposed contents of consciousness. The dispositions of the various forms of philosophical behaviorism were incorporated as one example, but by no means the only example, of mediating theoretical terms.

Features of the later form of methodological behaviorism

1. That scientific knowledge is gained from conducting carefully controlled research that manipulates publicly observable stimulus and response variables;

2. That this research uses objective research procedures and impartial tests of statistical inference to evaluate predictions of theories;

3. That scientific knowledge is intrinsically different from and superior to common sense knowledge, by virtue of being logically derived from publicly observable stimulus and response variables according to objective research procedures;

4. That claims to scientific knowledge involve constructing logical domains, within which the logical properties of symbolic entities and mathematical formulae are to be established; generalized mathematical formulae accounting for a suitably high percent of the variance or logically valid deductions from the theories may be taken as explanations of the event under consideration;

5. That three sorts of elements are permissible in claims to scientific knowledge; the first is a publicly observable stimulus variable, as an independent variable; the second is a publicly observable response variable, as a dependent variable; the third is an inferred, "theoretical" variable that can be operationally defined in terms of publicly observable stimulus and response variables and that mediates the relation between the independent and dependent variables;

6. That causal processes are to be accommodated according to a linear chain model:

$$S => O => R$$

in which the middle term identifies the operationally defined, mediating organismic variables;

7. That the claims to scientific knowledge concern a virtually limitless variety of "psychological" states or processes that are inferred to be causally effective antecedents; these states and processes are instances of the mediating organismic variables; they are not publicly observable but are nevertheless integral to the causal analysis of behavior; and

8. That the claims to scientific knowledge involving these psychological states and processes generally have their source in the mentalistic conceptual system commonly employed in our culture; the use of objective research methods assures that claims to scientific knowledge appealing to these causal states may be taken as satisfactory.

Two ways that the later form of methodological behaviorism is mentalistic

1. The mediating theoretical concept used to account for the observed behavior is typically mental in nature, notwithstanding its operational definition.
2. The commitment to the mediational model involving theoretical concepts is a commitment to a mentalistic view of epistemology on the part of the scientist in the account of scientific behavior.

Pragmatism
The truth value of a statement is a function of how well the statement promotes effective action.

Chapter 17 considered a series of positions in philosophical psychology and topics related to those positions. However, some important topics remain. Those topics are addressed in chapter 18.

REFERENCES

Baars, B. J. (1986). *The cognitive revolution in psychology*. New York: Guilford.

Bergmann, G. (1956). The contribution of John B. Watson. *Psychological Review, 63*, 265–276.

Bridgman, P. W. (1928). *The logic of modern physics*. New York: Macmillan.

Catania, A. C., & Harnad, S. (Eds.). (1988). *The selection of behavior: The operant behaviorism of B. F. Skinner: Comments and controversies*. Cambridge: Cambridge University Press.

Day, W. F. (1969). Radical behaviorism in reconciliation with phenomenology. *Journal of the Experimental Analysis of Behavior, 12*, 315–328.

Day, W. F. (1976). The case for behaviorism. In M. H. Marx & F. E. Goodson (Eds.), *Theories in contemporary psychology*, pp. 534–545. New York: Macmillan.

Day, W. F. (1983). On the difference between radical and methodological behaviorism. *Behaviorism, 11*, 89–102.

Evans, R. I. (1976). *The making of psychology*. New York: Knopf.

Fodor, J. A. (1968). *Psychological explanation*. New York: Random House.

Frege, G. (1960). *The foundations of arithmetic*. New York: Harper. (Original edition published 1884.)

Heidbreder, E. (1933). *Seven psychologies*. New York: The Century Co.

James, W. (1892). A plea for psychology as a "natural science." *Philosophical Review, 1*, 146–153.

Koch, S. (1964). Psychology and emerging conceptions of knowledge as unitary. In T. W. Wann (Ed.), *Behaviorism and phenomenology*, pp. 1–45. Chicago: University of Chicago Press.

Lyons, W. (1980). *Gilbert Ryle: An introduction to his philosophy*. Atlantic Highlands, NJ: Humanities Press.

Mandler, G. (1979). Emotion. In E. Hearst (Ed.), *The first century of experimental psychology*, pp. 275–321. Hillsdale, NJ: Erlbaum.

Meyer, M. (1922). *The psychology of the other-one*. Columbia, MO: Missouri Book Co.

Moore, J. (1981). On mentalism, methodological behaviorism, and radical behaviorism. *Behaviorism, 9*, 55–77.

Natsoulas, T. (1983). Perhaps the most difficult problem faced by behaviorism. *Behaviorism, 13*, 1–26.

Natsoulas, T. (1984). Gustav Bergmann's psychophysiological parallelism. *Behaviorism, 12*, 41–69.

Place, U. T. (1993). A radical behaviorist methodology for the empirical investigation of private events. *Behavior and Philosophy, 20–21*, 25–35.

Place, U. T. (1999). Ryle's behaviorism. In W. O'Donohue & W. F. Kitchener (Eds.), *Handbook of behaviorism*, pp. 361–398. San Diego, CA: Academic Press.

Russell, B. (1926). Review of *The Meaning of Meaning. Dial, 81*, 114–121.

Ryle, G. (1949). *The concept of mind*. London: Hutchison.

Schnaitter, R. (1985). The haunted clockwork: Reflections on Gilbert Ryle's *The concept of mind. Journal of the Experimental Analysis of Behavior, 43*, 145–153.

Skinner, B. F. (1945). The operational analysis of psychological terms. *Psychological Review, 52*, 270–277, 291–294.

Skinner, B. F. (1953). *Science and human behavior*. New York: Macmillan.

Skinner, B. F. (1957). *Verbal behavior*. New York: Appleton-Century-Crofts.

Skinner, B. F. (1964). Behaviorism at fifty. In T. W. Wann (Ed.), *Behaviorism and phenomenology*, pp. 79–97. Chicago: University of Chicago Press.

Skinner, B. F. (1969). *Contingencies of reinforcement*. New York: Appleton-Century-Crofts.

Skinner, B. F. (1974). *About behaviorism*. New York: Knopf.

Watson, J. B. (1913). Psychology as the behaviorist views it. *Psychological Review, 20*, 158–177.

Wittgenstein, L. (1973). *Philosophical investigations* (3rd ed.). Englewood Cliffs, NJ: Prentice-Hall. (Original edition published in 1953; trans. by G. E. M. Anscombe)

Wittgenstein, L. (1974). *Tractatus Logico-Philosophicus*. New York: Routledge. (Original edition published in 1922; trans. by D. F. Pears and B. F. McGuiness)

Zuriff, G. E. (1985). *Behaviorism: A conceptual reconstruction*. New York: Columbia University Press.

STUDY QUESTIONS

1. Describe two reasons why the radical behaviorist position on private events is not equivalent to mentalism.

2. Describe the position known as logical behaviorism.

3. Describe the position known as conceptual analysis.

4. Describe Ryle's argument concerning a category mistake.

5. Describe Wittgenstein's anti-private language argument.

6. Describe the position known as metaphysical behaviorism.

7. Describe eight features of the position known as methodological behaviorism.

8. Describe two ways that methodological behaviorism is nevertheless mentalistic, despite its attempts to remain ontologically neutral.

9. Distinguish among correspondence, coherence, and pragmatism as orientations for assessing the truth value of statements.

10. Distinguish between instrumentalism (or conventionalism) and realism (or essentialism) in regard to scientific verbal behavior.

11. Describe why radical behaviorists argue that pragmatism is not equivalent to instrumentalism.

12. Describe why radical behaviorism looks to pragmatism, rather than ontology, for assessing the merit of scientific statements.

18

Radical Behaviorism and Traditional Philosophical Issues—2

Synopsis of Chapter 18: Chapter 17 was the first of two chapters to examine a series of topics related to philosophical psychology. It dealt with four forms of philosophical psychology related to behaviorism, and was particularly concerned with a position called methodological behaviorism. Further, it examined truth criteria, focusing on pragmatism. Chapter 18 is the second of two chapters that examines topics related to philosophical psychology. It begins with a review of traditional positions on the mind-body relation, and then assesses these traditional positions from the standpoint of radical behaviorism, offering an alternative position based on a thoroughgoing behaviorism. The chapter continues by examining the assumptions, particularly frequent among philosophers and cognitivists, that any form of behaviorism renders mental terms as dispositions to behave, that this rendering is inadequate, and that any form of behaviorism is therefore inadequate. Although radical behaviorism does in some instances invoke dispositions, it views them as aspects of the dependent variable, rather than independent or theoretical, mediating variables. Consequently, any implication that radical behaviorism is inadequate because it generally views mental terms as dispositions is wide of the mark. The chapter concludes by examining mechanistic analyses, intentionality, and intensionality. Radical behaviorism conceives of behavior as something that is carried out with respect to the environment. It therefore includes the environment at every step in its analyses. Mechanistic approaches involving fixed relations and transfers of energy play no role in radical behaviorist analyses. Operant behavior, for example, is the very field that purposive analyses seek to address, unfortunately in mentalistic terms. Intensionality and agency may be seen as implications of the generic basis of behavior, rather than as reflections of causal entities from other dimensions.

A time-honored distinction in psychology as well as philosophy is the relation between mind and body. To the radical behaviorist, this distinction is troublesome, as it implies there is a metaphysical legitimacy to distinguishing between: (a) a mind in the mental dimension, and (b) behavior in the physical, material dimension. Ontologically speaking, any phenomena associated with the mental dimension are held to be of a different "stuff" from objects in the physical, material dimension. Radical behaviorists don't ordinarily enter into this kind of ontological debate. Entering into the debate implies that there are actually two such dimensions, and that the business of a science is to deal with only the material dimension and either ignore what is presumed to be another dimension, or else surrender it to another mode of inquiry. Radical behaviorists view the entire debate as simply the legacy of dualistic social-cultural factors, rather than anything observational. That is, to speak of a mind in this way is tantamount to speaking in ways ultimately derived and institutionalized from religious doctrines of the soul or other sorts of transcendental entities, even if secularized over the ages.

MIND AND BODY

Nevertheless, if any feature of traditional, mentalistic psychology is well ensconced in contemporary life, it is that of the mind. Psychology is often defined in textbooks as the study of behavior and mental life, and an explanation of behavior is assumed to follow from an explanation of how the mind works. Mind is often defined informally as "what the brain does," in an effort to anchor the definition of mind in the legitimacy of neuroscience. That the definitions and assumptions are uncritical is revealed when one tries to understand how one might influence the other. If the two—mind and behavior—are from different dimensions, how do they interact? How can one affect the other? That there can be an interaction between (a) the body and (b) whatever the use of mind refers to suggests they are part of the same dimension, not different dimensions, else how could one influence the other?

In many ways, a discussion of the mind-body problem is linked to discussions of mentalism, private events, the nature of behavior, and the relation between neuroscience and behavior analysis. In other words, the questions that theorists are asking may well be important ones, but because of the influence of decades if not centuries of social-cultural tradition, the theorists are led astray.

The following section briefly notes the principal theories of the relation between mind and body, simply to provide a complete picture of what traditional psychology thinks is important. Readers may recognize that there is some overlap between the theories, and that the theories arose from concerns that are not current. In particular, early theories tended to arise from religious concerns, whereas later theories arose from philosophical analyses.

Idealism

One early theory is idealism. This theory assumes that only the mental dimension of the mind exists. To talk of a physical reality that differs from a mental reality is not meaningful, as the very idea of physical reality is held to be something that exists in one's mind. An advocate of this theory was the empiricist George Berkeley (1685–1753).

Materialism

A counterpart to idealism is a strict materialism. This theory assumes that only the material dimension exists. An advocate of this theory was Thomas Hobbes (1588–1679), who was sometimes also called an empiricist. For example, Hobbes conceived of "mental experience" as nothing but matter in motion, caused by material properties of objects in the environment pressing against the sense organs.

Interactionism and Epiphenomenalism

Other theories recognize an ontological distinction between mind and body or mind and matter. Two such theories are interactionism and epiphenomenalism. Interactionism is a theory attributable to Réné Descartes (1596–1650). It assumes there are two irreducibly distinct dimensions, of both the mind and body, and that events in each can influence the other. Descartes had an interesting conjecture of how they interacted: through the body's pineal gland, which served as sort of a portal for events in one dimension to influence the other. The full version of Descartes' story is beyond the scope of the present analysis. Suffice it to say that Cartesian dualism has been extraordinarily influential in the history of psychology, as well as contemporary Western culture.

Epiphenomenalism is the theory that there are indeed two different dimensions, but the relation between the two differs from that in interactionism. According to epiphenomenalism, the relational is unidirectional, from the body to the mind, rather than bidirectional, as it is in interactionism. An advocate of this theory was the English biologist Thomas Huxley (1825–1895).

Parallelism

Parallelism is the theory that there are two irreducibly distinct dimensions, but they do not interact. According to this theory, there are two independent dimensions that are harmoniously correlated by an omniscient, omnipotent God. Events in one dimension run parallel with events in the other, but never interact. The standard analogy is to two clocks that show the same time. An advocate of this theory is Gottfried Leibniz (1646–1716).

Double-Aspect Theory

A theory that is related to parallelism is the double-aspect theory. According to this theory, mind and body are simply two different aspects of the same person, or two different ways of looking at a person, in the same way that heads and tails are simply two different aspects of the same coin, or the same coin seen in two different ways. The complete description of a person, just as the complete description of a coin, is to be found by including both aspects. Thus, the complete person is neither totally mind nor totally body. The early version of this theory was proposed by Benedict Spinoza (1632–1677), but it has been resurrected by some modern philosophers, such as Peter Strawson (1919– 2006).

Mind-Brain Identity Theory

Mind-brain identity theory is the stance that mental terms and processes deployed in folk psychology denote the same thing as physiological terms referring to brain activities. The comparable statement in chemistry is that water (folk chemistry) is the same thing as H_2O (scientific chemistry), or in physics that lightning (folk physics) is the same thing as electrical discharge (scientific physics). Thus, identity theory holds that mental states and processes (folk psychology) are identical to brain states and processes (scientific psychology). One is reducible to the other, without remainder. Unlike logical behaviorism, identity theory is an assertion of factual relation, rather than a linguistic recommendation for achieving meaningfulness.

An important feature of this stance is that it postulates a one-for-one relation between: (a) the type of talked about mental state, and (b) the type of perhaps an as-yet-undiscovered neural state. This position is known as "type-identity physicalism." Consider the phenomenon of pain. Strictly speaking, identity theory only seems to allow for the sense of being in pain as the activation of neural fibers in the brain at stereotaxic coordinates x-y-z, or of having a belief as the activation of neural fibers in the brain at another set of coordinates. At issue then are several questions: (a) Could one be in pain if other fibers were active? (b) Even if these fibers were active, could one not be in pain? (c) Could another individual be experiencing pleasure with activation of fibers at that same set of coordinates? In other words, the stance seems committed to equating a type of mental experience with a rather prescribed type of brain activity, and differentiating types of mental experiences in terms of the correlated types of brain activities.

Eliminative Materialism

Eliminative materialism is in some ways a successor to identity theory. Eliminative materialism is the proposition that the brain states and processes identified in folk psychology simply do not exist. They are either mistakes or the result of confused thinking. Rather, the talk of mental states so common in folk psychology should be replaced with talk of the neurophysiological activity of the brain. Thus, eliminative materialism goes further than identity theory, which accepts talk of mental states but equates them with brain states, by holding that all talk of mental states will need to be eliminated and replaced entirely by talk of brain neurophysiology. Whether eliminative materialism represents a later form of metaphysical behaviorism is often debated.

Functionalism

Functionalism is the doctrine that mental states are not defined with respect to their neural make-up, as in identity theory or eliminative materialism. Rather, they are defined with respect to how they function, or their causal role, in the behavioral system in question. Thus, to be in pain is not defined with respect to the activation of certain neural fibers. Rather, it is defined as itself being caused by some sort of, say, tissue damage, which in turn causes a belief that one is injured and that one should do something about it, which in turn gives rise to the action of applying an antiseptic, bandage, and possibly pain reliever, which actions are taken because one believes they will begin to resolve the problem. Functionalists would accept that although an instance of being in pain entails neural activation, the essential feature of functionalism is how the state of being in pain causally links with other states and eventually with behavior, rather than the neural activation per se. Indeed, functionalists subscribe to the thesis of multiple realization, which holds that the brain state in question can be realized in different ways within an organism or across different organisms. Given this thesis, functionalists argue that it doesn't make sense to hold that one and only one pattern of neural activation at some set of stereotaxic coordinates represents the meaning of a mental term, as in identity theory. Thus, one could be in pain if a wide variety of fibers were active, not just those at a particular set of stereotaxic coordinates. In addition, one might not be in pain even if these fibers were active. Finally, another individual could be experiencing pleasure, rather than pain, with activation of fibers at the same set of coordinates. Technically, functionalism also admits dualism, as functionalism doesn't rule out the possibility that nonphysical states could play a functional role and enter into a behavioral sequence. Functionalism is the currently most prominent philosophy of mind, although several related varieties of functionalism exist. Functionalism is also considered to be the basis for cognitive psychology. Functionalism accepts a position called "token-identity physicalism," which accepts that instances of mental states such as being in pain have physical properties, but rejects "type-identity physicalism," which defines classes of those states in terms of those physical properties.

Machine-State Functionalism

To further understand functionalism, one additional example may be reviewed, called "Machine-State Functionalism." According to machine state functionalism, any organism that can be said to have a mind can be compared to a machine that operates according to something like the following instruction:

> If the machine is in state S-1, and receives input I-1, generate output O-1 and go into state S-2 (and so on, for some specified number of states, inputs and outputs)

One variation of this mechanism and the associated instructions is that the outputs and transitions to a subsequent state may be probabilistic, rather than certain, but the principle remains the same.

In either case, the important feature of this organism is that its "mental states" can be conceptualized and described in terms of "machine states." The states are computed from the prior state and the input. The correspondence is shown in a "machine-state table." Each entry in the machine-state table identifies the relation among: (a) the internal state of the machine, (b) input while in that state, and (c) output while in that state. In other words, each entry identifies how inputs will affect the organism's mind, and its subsequent behavior. Functionalists argue that these relations are more than simple behavioral dispositions because they entail the internal state of the organism, in addition to just inputs and outputs. By so doing, functionalism regards itself as having overcome a shortcoming of behaviorism, which functionalism believes would only recognize a disposition to yield an output given an input.

One example that has been used to illustrate machine-state functionalism is that of a vending machine that dispenses soft drinks contingent on the insertion of a series of coins. Each coin may be regarded as an input, which in turn produces the next internal state of the machine. Now suppose an individual has inserted some subset of the required amount of coins, but then runs out of coins before the necessary amount has been entered. The individual walks away, and the next individual comes up to the machine a few minutes later. In order to predict or understand what will happen when the next individual starts to insert coins, functionalists argue that one needs to know what state the machine is in, as a function of having earlier received some of the coins necessary to produce a soft drink. Each state in the process can be viewed as being computed from the way the input affects the prior state.

RADICAL BEHAVIORIST PERSPECTIVE ON THE MIND-BODY PROBLEM AND PHILOSOPHY OF MIND

The older positions on the mind-body problem were intended to resolve problems brought about by conceiving of a mental world that differed from a physical, material world. The positions provided by classical, medieval, renaissance, and early modern philosophers tried to reconcile these problems by postulating one or the other "stuff" as dominant or prior. Mid-twentieth century and contemporary philosophers continued in this same tradition, pursuing the S – O – R model of human behavior. These philosophers postulated a model in which there are stimulus inputs, a behavioral output, and then some sort of processing that takes place in between, to mediate the relation between S and R. As part of the continuation of this S – O – R tradition, much of contemporary philosophy of mind remains committed to the proposition that verbal behavior reflects the mediating mental or cognitive activity in a mental dimension that differs from the behavioral dimension. This view not only perpetuates the doctrine of mental causes of behavior, but creates a false impression about the nature and contribution of verbal behavior to the full range of human activity, science included.

More recent positions such as eliminative materialism appear to avoid many of the aforementioned problems, but raise others. For example, eliminative materialism is a reductionist position. It assumes that there is public behavior and physiological activity, but not private or covert behavior as discussed in Chapter 10 on Private Events. Eliminative materialism denies covert behavior, and relegates anything internal to physiology. To be sure, physiology participates in all behavior, but to reduce covert behavior to physiology is just as troublesome as reducing overt behavior such as lever pressing to physiology. Just as the analysis of a lever press is not reducible to the biochemistry of the contraction of *biceps femoris*, neither is "thinking" reducible to the biochemistry of cortical structures and pathways. The reduction misrepresents the behavioral origins and character of the event in question. In this regard, eliminative materialism perpetuates the doctrine that only publicly observable phenomena can count as behavior. As discussed in Chapter 10, although much behavior is publicly observable, not all behavior is. To fail to view some covert behavior as behavior relegates it to a status suggesting that its origins cannot be influenced by antecedent circumstances, which is one of the principal liabilities of mentalism.

In general, radical behaviorism rejects the entire set of premises upon which the various mind-body theories are based. As noted numerous times throughout this chapter, the very idea of a mind that differs from behavior was brought about by social-cultural traditions. However, there may clearly be relevant elements in a behavioral sequence that do not involve publicly observable stimuli and responses. At issue for radical behaviorism is what occasions the use of a mental term. For radical behaviorism there is not one and only one thing that occasions the use of a mental term. There are several, and they may function alone or in combination.

When one talks of mental acts, states, mechanisms, processes, or entities, what, then, is responsible for such talk? If an explanation does appeal to causal phenomena from the mental dimension, then radical behaviorists argue that one needs to analyze that explanation so as to determine whether it is occasioned by one or more of the following factors, and make the accompanying decisions regarding its nature and suitability:

1. Processes or relations that are actually in the behavioral dimension, whether publicly observable or private. In this case, the purported mental phenomenon is appropriate for analysis as a private behavioral phenomenon. In this view, any explanation involving a private behavioral phenomenon needs to be further connected, at least in principle, with the public processes or relations that are responsible for the private phenomenon exerting an effect in the current instance; or

2. Neural, muscular, or hormonal processes, in which case the mental term is appropriate for neuroscience, but only in a limited way for psychology; strictly speaking, the physiological states do not cause the behavior in question in the same sense as do environmental variables, but rather provide the context in which environmental variables function; or

3. Complex social-cultural epistemological preconceptions, in which case the term is a fanciful explanatory fiction (e.g., from "folk psychology"), and is of interest only in regard to the social and cultural conditions that promote its use, rather than as a genuinely explanatory term. No such mental dimension exists, and no such causal mental phenomena exist in this dimension. Talk of such causal phenomena in a mental dimension is occasioned by other factors, rather than those that cause behavior, and is cherished for irrelevant and extraneous reasons.

As an exercise, the example of machine-state functionalism, reviewed earlier, may be examined. As Schnaitter (1986) has outlined, the claims of superiority by machine-state functionalism are exceedingly curious to the radical behaviorist. Most particularly, the "machine-state table" may be understood as simply a history of the environmental operations that have been performed on the machine. In other words, the machine-state table catalogs the interactions that have taken place between the machine and the environment. The "state" of the soft drink machine is isomorphic with the insertion of coins. To say the internal states are computational is to say no more than the states are orderly with respect to those environmental operations. Radical behaviorism would point to whatever phylogenic or ontogenic relations are responsible for the relation between states and whatever "inputs" or other factors will alter those states, so that subsequent inputs have different effects. One can predict whether a given coin will yield a soft drink if one knows the environmental operations that have been performed on the machine, in terms of how many coins have already been inserted. One can compensate for possibly inadequate information about environmental operations by knowing its "internal state." Neither sort of information is superior to the other. However, for the information on the internal state to be valid, it needs to be gathered by independent means, not inferred on the basis of external observations.

Schnaitter (1987) has pointed out that radical behaviorism "presupposes inner states, and is inconceivable without them" (p. 64; see also Schnaitter, 1986, p. 256 n3). To be sure, Skinner's own writings testify to the relevance of understanding the internal state of the organism:

> This does not mean, of course, that the organism is conceived of as actually empty, or that continuity between input and output will not eventually be established. (Skinner, 1972, p. 269)

> What an organism does will eventually be seen to be due to what it is, at the moment it behaves. (Skinner, 1974, p. 249)

> It is a given organism at a given moment that behaves, and it behaves because of its "biological equipment" at that moment. (Skinner in Catania & Harnad, 1988, p. 301)

> I agree that at any given moment a person's behavior is due to the state of his body at that moment ... (Skinner in Catania & Harnad, 1988, p. 327)

In a common example, food will typically serve as the reinforcer for the operant response of an organism when it is hungry, so hunger is an internal state that is clearly relevant to prediction and control of behavior. Of course, food is not a reinforcer for an individual who is anorexic, and sweet-tasting consumables may reinforce a response even when the individual is not deprived. Schnaitter's (1986) alternative statement of the response-reinforcer relation is significant: An environmental event is a reinforcer just in case the organism is in a state such that the event in question alters the future probability of responses on which it has been contingent, other things being equal; the organism moves in and out of that state by manipulating other antecedent environmental conditions, such as prior access to the putative reinforcer. Indeed, Skinner stated that "Reinforcement is another concept which depends on the state of the organism which, unfortunately, we must leave to the physiologist, who has or will have the appropriate techniques and methods" (Skinner in Catania & Harnad, 1988, p. 423). Elsewhere, however, Skinner cautions that even though it is possible "some single state of the organism will eventually be identified that is correlated with all the so-called manifestations of hunger, ... until then it seems wise to deal with each one of them as it is observed and to deal with it as a function of an environmental variable" (Skinner in Catania & Harnad, 1988, p. 438). Assigning motivational properties to inferred mediating states in the absence of direct physiological evidence has traditionally proved troublesome.

Similarly, the kind of output produced by a given input can be clearly related to an organism's hormonal state. Birds may not build nests unless sufficient levels of reproductive hormones are present. Indeed, Chapter 4 noted the whole relation between neuroscience and behavior analysis is a pragmatic matter of understanding the internal state and workings of the body, so that if knowledge of the internal state is available, prediction and control can be predicated on this knowledge. The problem is that often the requisite knowledge of the internal state is inadequate or inferential and therefore not available. Consequently, one deals with the knowledge that is available, namely, the knowledge of inputs and outputs. Moreover, any knowledge of the function of internal states is achieved by manipulating inputs and outputs, so the knowledge of internal states is not necessarily propadeutic to prediction, control, or explanation.

Suppose one wants to account for why an individual would take an umbrella after looking at the weather forecast. The functionalist argues that a behaviorist would say taking an umbrella is a disposition that follows from reading the weather forecast. The functionalist holds this account unsatisfactory. The functionalist regards "wanting to stay dry" as the initial internal state, and "believing it will rain" as the subsequent internal state, given the input of reading the weather forecast. The individual then takes an umbrella, following from this chain of internal states. In contrast, the radical behaviorist would appeal to the reinforcement of avoiding becoming wet, and the establishing operation provided by the threatening weather forecast. The umbrella is taken because it is available and in good working order, thereby increasing the likelihood of avoiding becoming wet, given a forecast of impending rain. Any appeal to an internal state or belief as an entity is mischievous and gratuitous. Certainly the functionalist has not specified where the internal state has come from; if it has come from prior experience, then the cause of taking an umbrella may be traced back to those earlier experiences, just as the cause of the soft drink machine dispensing a soft drink when an individual inserts fewer than the specified number of coins may be traced back to the insertion of some prior number of coins. Of course, the radical behaviorist may well agree that the individual who takes an umbrella may well emit a chain of covert responses that contributes to taking the umbrella. If so, these responses are within the behavioral dimension. The conditions responsible for their origin and contribution to the current episode may be readily understood in terms of operant contingencies.

AN INTERPRETATION OF DISPOSITIONAL APPROACHES FROM THE STANDPOINT OF RADICAL BEHAVIORISM

Chapter 17 suggested that from the point of view of philosophy, behaviorism is the position that mental states or psychological terms generally should be taken to refer to observable behavior or to dispositions to engage in such behavior, where dispositions would be interpreted as a theoretical term. Philosophers inclined toward cognitive psychology or other mentalistic orientations make some of their strongest arguments against the adequacy of behaviorism by questioning the theoretical interpretation of mental states as "dispositions," which are then operationally defined with respect to publicly observable phenomena such as behavior or neural states. Two such arguments may now be examined.

Dispositions and Putnam's Spartans

The first is the "perfect actor" counterexample, generally attributed to the philosopher Hilary Putnam (see Putnam, 1980). Suppose that talk of pain is held to be meaningful only when there is some publicly observable pain-related behavior, or only when some set of neural fibers is firing. Now suppose that there is a world populated by a race of particularly stalwart Spartans, who when they have pains do not act like it. Analogous cases might be actors who act like they are in pain when they really are not, or those who are in pain but are paralyzed and cannot act at all. A related case concerns the firing of a given set of neural fibers that could conceivably be associated with pain for one individual but pleasure for another.

In such cases, the presence or absence of pain is not systematically related to the presence or absence of observable pain behavior or the firings of particular neural fibers. Thus, mentalists argue that behaviorism is incorrect when it asserts that talk of pain is meaningful only with reference to some publicly observable, pain-related behavior, or the firing of some particular set of neural fibers. Cognitive psychologists argue that instances of mental states (i.e., tokens) are surely physical. Thus, they argue that being in pain might well mean the individuals are engaging in some form of behavior, or that some nerve fibers are firing. However, they argue that classes of mental states (i.e., types) cannot be individuated by their physical properties. They can be realized in multiple forms, not just one form. Thus, they argue that one cannot generally characterize pain in terms of one class of behavior, or the firing of one class of nerve fibers. Rather, cognitivists argue, types of mental states are individuated by their function, rather than by their physical properties. Cognitivists further argue that when behaviorists talk of mental states and then operationally define those states in terms of physical properties such as behavior or neural firings, behaviorists make a commitment to distinguishing types of mental phenomena by their physical properties, which is false. Therefore, cognitivists argue, behaviorism is false and untenable (see Block, 1980).

Dispositions and Chisholm's Infinite Regress

The second argument is generally attributed to the philosopher Roderick Chisholm (see Chisholm, 1957). According to this argument, treating mental terms as dispositions to engage in observable behavior only creates an endless chain of such dispositions. For example, suppose being in pain from a headache is taken to mean nothing but having a disposition to take an aspirin. A disposition to take aspirin causes one to take the aspirin only if one also has the desire to get rid of the headache, the belief that the aspirin exists, the belief that taking aspirin reduces headaches, and so on. Since mental states interact in generating behavior, the argument goes, it is necessary to construe psychological explanations in terms of causal sequences of mental events and processes (e.g., Fodor,

1981). Cognitivists argue that the problem with viewing mental states as dispositions to behave is that the behavior in question never gets explained. Thus, cognitivists argue against troublesome circumlocutions to observable behavior, as in (they presume) any kind of behaviorism. Instead, they advocate direct appeals to the causal efficacy of underlying mental states.

Relevance of the Two Arguments to Mediational Neobehaviorism

The two arguments above against the adequacy of behaviorism are predicated on certain assumptions about the nature and role of dispositions in behavioral explanations. As sophisticated as the arguments appear to be, they actually have little to do with current forms of behaviorism, whether mediational or radical. Recall that mediational behaviorists interpret most theoretical terms as hypothetical constructs, rather than as intervening variables. Thus, an interpretation of dispositions as hypothetical constructs allows dispositions to exercise surplus meaning. In this view, behavior should be regarded as the evidence for using the term, not the exclusive and exhaustive referent of the term. Worthy of note is that the logical positivist Carnap (1956) framed the problem as follows:

> In a way similar to the philosophical tendencies of empiricism and operationism, the psychological movement of Behaviorism had, on the one hand, a very healthful influence because of its emphasis on the observation of behavior as an intersubjective and reliable basis for psychological investigations, while, on the other hand, it imposed too narrow restrictions. First, its total rejection of introspection was unwarranted.... Secondly, Behaviorism in combination with the philosophical tendencies mentioned led often to the requirement that all psychological concepts must be defined in terms of behavior .... [T]he interpretation of a psychological concept as a theoretical concept, although it may accept the same behavioristic test procedure based on S and R, does not identify the concept (the state or trait) with the pure disposition....
>
> The distinction between intervening variables and theoretical constructs, often discussed since the article by MacCorquodale and Meehl, seems essentially the same or closely related to our distinction between pure dispositions and theoretical terms. "Theoretical construct" means certainly the same here as "theoretical term", viz., a term which cannot be explicitly defined even in an extended observation language, but which is introduced by postulates and not completely interpreted. (pp. 70–71, 73)

Carnap's terminology differs slightly from that used by MacCorquodale and Meehl (1948) and from that used in the present chapter. For example, he uses "pure disposition" to imply an intervening variable that is exhaustively defined in terms of publicly observable measures. Similarly, he uses "theoretical term" and "theoretical construct" to imply a hypothetical construct that is only partially interpreted in terms of publicly observable measures. Nevertheless, allowing for these differences, his usage of the term *disposition*, when interpreted as a hypothetical construct, can "mean" (i.e., refer to) virtually anything, including a mental state in the same sense as cognitive psychology, and not simply something that is publicly observable.

Relevance of the Two Arguments to Radical Behaviorism

Given that arguments against the adequacy of behaviorism are predicated on the nature and role of dispositions, what, then, does radical behaviorism say about dispositions? Interestingly, the term "disposition" does not occur very often in Skinner's writings. When it does, the usage differs appreciably from the conventional treatment ("An angry man, like a hungry man, shows a disposition to act in a certain way," Skinner, 1953, p. 168; "A disposition to perform behavior is not an intervening variable; it is a probability of behaving," Skinner in Catania & Harnad, 1988, p. 360). By itself, of course, the term *disposition* is a perfectly reasonable *descriptive* term relating to the strength of a response. As a descriptive term, it pertains to the dependent variable, rather than a mediating variable. To say that individual W "believes" X is the case is presumably to say that W is disposed to state, or has a high probability of stating, that X is the case of acting in ways consistent with X being the case, and so on. One's degree of "belief" is identical with the probability that one will take action with respect to what is believed in (Skinner, 1957, pp. 159 ff.). This probability is itself a function of various conditions, such as the precision of discriminative stimulus control, the certainty of reinforcement, and so on. As suggested in Skinner's quote above, certain conditions contribute to the establishment of the disposition in the first place. Therefore, dispositional analyses are sometimes useful in countering mentalistic and mediational explanations of behavior.

The important question concerns a causal explanation of behavior. If dispositions are invoked in causal explanations, they either become mentalistic causes in their own right (as in, "He acted *because* of his beliefs"; see discussion in Schnaitter, 1985, pp. 146–147), or else they become treated as another sort of intervening theoretical term, as they did eventually for Carnap (1956). Thus, dispositions are not spatio-temporal elements that are themselves manipulated in any direct, pragmatic sense of a functional relation. Consequently, analyses couched in terms of dispositions may obscure more pragmatic concerns with the spatio-temporal elements that participate in contingencies, with respect to which a causal explanation in terms of manipulable variables is sought (e.g., Hocutt, 1985). Behavior analysts find fault with Ryle's (1949) view that "the explanation is not of the type 'the glass broke because a stone hit it,' but more nearly of the different type 'the glass broke when the stone hit it, because it was brittle'" (p. 50). Behavior analysts suggest that the statement ought more effectively to take the form "*Given that the glass was brittle*, it broke when it was hit by the stone." This locution has the virtue of identifying the cause of the glass's being brittle as its molecular structure, or the manufacturing processes that are responsible for that structure. The locution then indicates that the glass actually broke when it was hit by the stone.

With respect to psychology, behavior analysts find fault with explanations taking the form "the pigeon pecked the key when it was exposed to the contingency, because it was hungry." As before, the statement is perhaps acceptable as an illustration of a simple descriptive statement, but the difficulty comes when one pursues a causal explanation. The risk is that invoking the disposition of "hunger" will elevate hunger to the status of an internal entity that can be taken as a solely sufficient cause of publicly observable behavioral events such as pecking a response key. Behavior analysts suggest that an answer to the question of why the pigeon pecked the key ought more effectively to take the form "*Given that the pigeon was hungry*, it pecked the key when it was exposed to the contingency." This locution has the virtue of identifying the cause of the pigeon's being hungry as the establishing operation of food deprivation, which in turn produced certain changes in blood glucose. The locution then indicates that the pigeon actually pecked the key when it was exposed to the contingency. Consequently, psychological explanations in radical behaviorism reflect more pragmatic concerns with the spatio-temporal elements that participate in contingencies, with respect to which the causal explanation is more effectively sought (Moore, 1999).

In this regard, Place (1999) has recently argued that analytic philosophy should recognize that it in fact has treated dispositions as causal entities:

> Had [Ryle] realized that the natural partner for his hypothetical analysis of dispositional statements is the counterfactual theory of causal necessity (the thesis that to say that A was the cause of B is to say that if A had not existed as and when it did, B would not have existed when and as it did), he would have had to accept that not only are dispositions causes of their manifestations (for if the glass had not been brittle as it was, it would not have broken when struck by the stone) but that without such a dispositional cause, no mere juxtaposition of substances, no mere striking of a stone against a pane of glass, can have an effect. (pp. 388–389)

Unfortunately, this move elevates the disposition to the status of a conceptual cause and opens the door to mentalism.

For radical behaviorism, then, the term *disposition* can be used in several different senses. One is the straightforward phylogenic sense. Pigeons are disposed to peck, rather than swim, because during the course of evolution a particular muscular structure and a particular way of interacting with the environment have been selected. Fish are disposed to swim but not peck, because a different muscular structure and a different way of interacting with the environment have been selected. If there is further concern with the microstructure, one can say that the genetic structure of a pigeon differs from that of a fish.

A second and related sense is motivational. Suppose pigeons are deprived of food and made hungry (i.e., an establishing operation). The pigeons are thereby disposed to peck, rather than remain immobile. Equivalently, one might say the motivative operation of food deprivation evokes pecking. As before, this mode of interaction with the environment as a function of the internal metabolic economy of the pigeon has been selected and differentially replicated. If there is further concern with the microstructure, one can say the physiological state of a hungry pigeon differs from that of a satiated pigeon.

A third sense is ontogenic. This sense implies existence of stimulus control by virtue of experiences the pigeon has had during its lifetime. One would say that hungry pigeons are disposed to peck in the presence of a green light instead of a red light because during the pigeon's lifetime food has been the consequence of pecking in the presence of green but not red. The pigeon's nervous system has evolved in such a way as to be sensitive to these sorts of environmental experiences. Thus, one can say that the probability of behavior increases in the presence of certain antecedent circumstances when the behavior has in the past had particular consequences, given those antecedent circumstances. If there is concern with the microstructure, one can say that the physiological state of a pigeon that has been trained to peck in the presence of green but not red differs from its physiological state when it has been trained differently, or from that of another pigeon that has been trained differently.

In summary, the cognitive arguments against the adequacy of behaviorism based on dispositional analyses don't necessarily apply to the dominant form of behaviorism, mediational neobehaviorism. Moreover, the arguments apply even less to radical behaviorism, which has an entirely different conception of the nature and role of dispositions. Therefore, cognitive arguments based on dispositions are simply irrelevant.

MECHANISTIC ANALYSES AND INTENTIONALITY

The concept of a machine has long been attractive to some scientists as they seek to explain a natural phenomenon without appealing to mental factors. Machines, or mechanisms in general, are objective and don't depend on the particular tastes or inclinations of the scientist doing the describing. They are relatively unambiguous in the way they operate, and scientists who appeal to them can't be accused of slipshod or subjective thinking.

An appeal to mechanistic principles was aligned with the natural sciences in the late nineteenth century, as scientists of that era sought to investigate nature's mysteries. In particular, it was thought that ever closer observation and measurement of nature was the key to scientific progress, in keeping with prevailing trends toward empiricism and objectivity in science. Thus, biology, chemistry, and physics sought increasingly accurate explanations of their subject matter through increasingly accurate observations and measurements of their subject matter. If an explanation of an event was found wanting, it was because the scientists hadn't observed the event closely enough or measured it carefully enough, such that they could come up with the mechanism at work.

A mechanism seems especially attractive to scientists who are interested in objectively explaining human behavior. Human behavior has long been thought to be a subject matter for which an explanation required an appeal to subjective or mental factors and relations, not directly or publicly observable in the same sense as physical or material factors and relations. The problem was that such explanations were criticized for being at odds with more conventional explanations in science, of the type that entailed physical and material factors and relations.

Therefore, one solution was to formulate an explanation in terms of a mechanism that did precisely the things that needed to be explained. However, as a mechanism the device didn't involve any appeal to subjective or mental factors and relations. This approach simply disregarded the original problem: namely, how to determine whether what were cast as subjective or mental factors and relations were actually involved in favor of parallelism. If a machine could be built that did the same thing, one needn't bother with the question of whether subjective or mental factors and relations were involved. Indeed, to be concerned with such "metaphysical" factors and relations was regarded as unscientific. Thus, mechanistic explanations assume a functioning organism can be compared to a machine, and that an organism's behavior is completely explicable in terms of the laws of physical mechanics and the exchange of energy as calculated in physics.

Consider a thermostat. The device is at heart a feedback or cybernetic mechanism, in which input is processed and compared with some set point. Activity continues until the set point is reached, when the activity ceases. A heat-sensing device on the thermostat reads the ambient temperature periodically. The furnace continues to operate until the ambient temperature reaches the prescribed point, at which the furnace is shut off. The mechanism simulates what is called purposive or intentional activity. In other words, the mechanism duplicates what in mental language is called its purpose or aim: the achievement of an end state or outcome: namely, the desired temperature, but without appeal to mental language. Because it doesn't appeal to mental language, the endeavor is widely regarded as in keeping with the highest traditions of scientific explanation. If neurophysiological correlates can be proposed for the various components of the mechanism, hypothetical or not, the mechanism is even better.

Although not widely recognized, a mechanistic explanation runs contrary to behavior-analytic explanatory practices. It acknowledged there was in fact a world beyond the reach of science in which causal forces were at work, and that the best science could do was mimic this world without actually engaging it. It left science as at best an approximation to an understanding of nature. An analysis of the disparity begins in an interesting way with the philosopher Franz Brentano (1838–1917). Brentano proposed that intentionality was the mark of the mental. In other words, Brentano proposed that human actions are directed toward something: they have an object. Standard examples are: (a) to think, which implies one is thinking of something; (b) to believe, which implies one is believing that P is the case; or (c) to wish, which implies one is wishing for something. Notwithstanding its mentalistic language, Brentano's proposal has considerable application in the behavior-analytic approach to explanation. As does behavior analysis, Brentano's proposal rejects mechanistic explanation. It suggests behavior has a "meaning" that is not readily accommodated by mechanistic forms of explanations. For behavior analysis as for Brentano, talk of meaning is perfectly respectable. However, for behavior analysis that meaning is to be found among the determiners, not the properties of response. A relevant passage in the behavior analytic literature is from Skinner (1974):

> Meaning is not properly regarded as a property either of a response or a situation but rather of the contingencies responsible for both the topography of behavior and the control exerted by stimuli. To take a primitive example, if one rat presses a lever to obtain food when hungry while another does so to obtain water while thirsty, the topographies of their behaviors may be indistinguishable, but they may be said to differ in meaning: to one rat pressing the lever "means" food; to the other it "means" water. But these are aspects of the contingencies which have brought behavior under the control of the current occasion. Similarly, if a rat is reinforced with food when it presses the lever in the presence of a flashing light but with water when the light is steady, then it could be said that the flashing light means food and the steady light means water, but again these are references not to some property of the light but to the contingencies of which the lights have been parts.
>
> The same point may be made, but with many more implications, in speaking of the meaning of verbal behavior. The over-all function of the behavior is crucial. In an archetypal pattern a speaker is in contact with a situation to which a listener is disposed to respond but with which he is not in contact. A verbal response on the part of the speaker makes it possible for the listener to respond appropriately. For example, let us suppose that a person has an appointment, which he will keep by consulting a clock or a watch. If none is available, he may ask someone to tell him the time, and the response permits him to respond effectively….
>
> The meaning of a response for the speaker includes the stimulus which controls it (in the example above, the setting on the face of a clock or watch) and possibly aversive aspects of the question from which a response brings release. The meaning for the listener is close to the meaning the clock face would have it is were visible to him, but it also includes the contingencies involving the appointment, which make a response to the clock face or the verbal response probable at such a time… .
>
> One of the unfortunate implications of communication theory is that the meanings for speaker and listener are the same, that something is made common to both of them, that the speaker conveys an idea or meaning, transmits information, or imparts knowledge, as if his mental possessions then become the mental possessions of the listener. There are no meanings which are the same in the speaker and listener. Meanings are not independent entities. (pp. 90–92)

Brentano's proposal is more often associated with varieties of humanistic or phenomenological psychology than behavior analysis, and correctly so. These varieties, drawing additional support from Kant, hold that humans are agents who have conceptions of themselves as they exist in the world, and how they interact with the world.

These varieties reject mechanical, efficient cause explanations in favor of teleological, intentional, final-cause explanations.

Behavior analysis joins with humanistic and phenomenological psychology in rejecting mechanistic explanations, but does not join with them in other ways, such as their embrace of agency or of teleological, final-cause explanations. The notion of agency is surely complex, but is dealt with in behavior analysis by recognizing it is the organism that is behaving, and the organism brings a variety of factors to the behavioral event in question. It brings its physiology and history surely. Humans may also engage in covert behavior, some of which may be verbal and some of which may involve specifying the contingencies that are in force, as in verbally regulated behavior. These are naturalistic factors and relations, but are mistakenly assumed in the other varieties of psychology to require another mode of analysis, one which appeals to other dimensions. Why are the assumptions mistaken? For radical behaviorists, the answer is to be found in the influence of past centuries of mentalistic social-cultural tradition concerning inner causes.

As Skinner put it, operant behavior is the very field of purpose. Operant behavior occurs with respect to the reinforcer, and is usefully formulated in the three terms of the operant contingency. It is not simply behavior that mechanically unfolds in response to pushes and pulls from the environment. Innate behavior might be characterized to be of that sort, but clearly operant behavior is not.

The noted learning theorist and neobehaviorist C. L. Hull (e.g., 1943) explicitly and unselfconsciously favored mechanistic explanations. He specified the relevant mechanism by suggesting that if a response is made in the presence of some antecedent stimulus setting, and the response is then closely followed by the reduction of a drive state, the tendency of the antecedent stimulus to evoke the response in question is increased. The mechanism emphasized two sorts of temporal relations: (a) the response made in the presence of the antecedent stimulus, and (b) the temporal contiguity between the response and any ensuing drive reduction. Hull sought to anchor his theories to descriptions of the operating characteristics of a conceptual nervous system, and to give the endeavor some scientific credibility by the use of mathematics to express the characteristics. However, the rigor was more apparent than real. He had little actual knowledge of such a nervous system. Rather, he simply inferred those characteristics from the observable behavior it was intended to explain, a circular approach if there ever was one. In the end, Hull's mechanistic approach failed.

INTENSIONALITY

Hand in hand with intentionality, mentioned earlier in Chapter 14, is intensionality. In logic, intensionality is usually contrasted with extensionality. A set of items is defined extensionally by listing all its members. Extensional definitions refer to those items. In contrast, a set of items is defined intensionally by specifying a property for being a member of the set. Intensionality is also commonly said to be concerned with an implication of meaning or content. In an intensional view, to say item X is a member of a set implies it has the necessary property to be included in the set. In addition, to say item X is a member of a set means that it has the same defining property as every other member of the set.

How do these terms relate to the analysis of behavior, as opposed to logic? The point of view to be taken here suggests that whereas intentionality is concerned with the end or outcome of the behavior, intensionality is concerned with the means of securing that outcome. The concept of intensionality implies that insofar as an individual's behavior can be said to be intentionally driven—that is, insofar as the individual is an agent and has some conception of what the individual is seeking to accomplish—the behavior is also intensionally driven. In other words, the individual also has some conception of what it must do or how it must act to accomplish that outcome. And what it must do is not always the same; perhaps it must do X on one occasion, and X' on another. In regard to behavior, intensionality is therefore concerned with defining the behavior in terms of the property that meets the intention. Again, to invoke intensionality is to invalidate mechanistic explanations of behavior. A mechanistic explanation has no place for intensionality. If mechanistic explanations are to make sense, they must hold that behavior is relatively fixed and invariable, in the sense that the mechanical release of a spring is fixed and invariable. Consequently, in a mechanistic view behavior can be explained without recourse to such conceptions as intentionality and intensionality.

The noted learning theorist and neobehaviorist E. C. Tolman (e.g., 1948) sought to counter the mechanical explanations of behavior promoted by Hull and his disciples. Tolman emphasized that behavior was docile: that is, flexible. To cite a well-known example in Tolman's way of thinking, a rat learned a "cognitive map" of a maze. The implication is that if Tolman blocked one path to the goal box of the maze, the rat would readily take another path. In other words, to Tolman the ability of the rat to adjust its behavior in the face of the obstacle showed that its behavior was not so restricted that it learned one thing and one thing only, to be evoked by the prevailing stimuli in the environment. The empirical basis for a rat's adjusting its behavior to blocked paths in a maze was a robust research area for many years, and the full story is quite complex. Suffice it to say that the rat didn't always act in the way Tolman argued it should, at least not without additional factors coming into play. These additional factors indicate that Tolman's explanations, despite their laudable rejections of a mechanistic approach, were not entirely satisfactory either.

As with many other terms, there are both good and bad things to be taken from the term intensionality. Radical behaviorism makes sense out of the import of intensionality by pointing to the generic nature of operant behavior: that is, operant behavior is not of a fixed form, mechanically "stamped in" by some environmental process. To take a canonical example, when a rat learns to press a lever, it is the class of responses called "lever pressing" that is strengthened. Lever pressing with the right paw is not necessarily strengthened to the exclusion of lever pressing with the left paw, or both paws for that matter. Any form of behavior that satisfies the operant contingency is strengthened. The form is flexible, in the sense that it can vary within the boundaries of the class from instance to instance. Thus, radical behaviorism engages the sense of intensionality by rejecting the mechanical strengthening of a single, stereotyped form of behavior (e.g., through reinforcement), and pointing out the generic, functional, and relational nature of behavior. As with all analyses, radical behaviorism rejects the appeal to a dimension, such as a logical dimension, beyond the one in which the behavior takes place. Given the necessary history, individuals are able to state what circumstances are causing them to engage in the behavior in question, and the verbalizations then exert discriminative control. But all these events are in the physical, material, behavioral dimension, not in another dimension whose contents are simply expressed in behavior.

SUMMARY AND CONCLUSIONS

The vocabulary of philosophy is laden with cognitive and mentalistic terms, testifying to the pervasive influence of mentalism. Much of contemporary philosophy is opposed to the tradition established by logical positivism, and often assumes that all forms of behaviorism follow from logical positivism. Although logical positivism did clearly influence mediational neobehaviorism, any link between logical positivism and radical behaviorism is minimal. Ironically, many of the criticisms contemporary philosophy lays at the doorstep of both logical positivism and mediational neobehaviorism don't actually apply. Moreover, there is a significant kinship between cognitive orientations that appeal to mental states and mediational neobehaviorism. Radical behaviorism differs appreciably from all these other approaches. In particular, radical behaviorism does not grant the status to dispositions that critics say radical behaviorism does. The underlying issue is the conception of verbal behavior. Much of contemporary philosophy, cognitive psychology, and mediational neobehaviorism simply take for granted that verbal behavior is a logical, symbolic activity that refers to other things, and that the way to analyze verbal behavior is to determine what those other things are. In contrast, radical behaviorism analyzes the contingencies responsible for the verbal behavior. Some of the cognitive and mental terms portray fictions, in the sense that they are controlled by extraneous factors. Others are occasioned by irrelevant relations. A few may have some grain of truth, and an operational analysis of the contingencies responsible for them puts things in good order.

TABLE 18–1

Idealism
A mind-body position that assumes only the mental dimension of the mind exists.

Materialism
A mind-body position that assumes only the material dimension of the body exists.

Interactionism
A mind-body position that assumes there are two irreducibly distinct dimensions, of both the mind and body, and that events in each can influence the other.

Epiphenomenalism
A mind-body position that assumes there are two irreducibly distinct dimensions, of both the mind and body, and that events of the body can influence the mind, but events of the mind cannot influence the body.

Parallelism
A mind-body position that assumes there are two irreducibly distinct dimensions, of both the mind and body, but there is no interaction between the dimensions.

Double-aspect theory
A mind-body position that assumes there are two irreducibly distinct dimensions, of both the mind and body, but they are simply two different aspects of the same person, or two different ways of looking at the same person, in the same way that heads and tails are simply two different aspects of the same coin, or two different ways of looking at the same coin.

Mind-brain identity theory
A mind-body position that assumes mental terms and processes deployed in folk psychology denote the same thing as physiological terms referring to brain activities.

Eliminative materialism
A mind-body position that assumes the mental states and processes identified in folk psychology simply do not exist. They are either mistakes or the result of confused thinking. Rather, the talk of mental states so common in folk psychology should be replaced with talk of the neurophysiological activity of the brain. Thus, eliminative materialism goes further than identity theory, which accepts talk of mental states, but equates them with brain states by holding that all talk of mental states will need to be eliminated and replaced entirely by talk of brain neurophysiology.

Functionalism
A mind-body position that assumes mental states are not defined with respect to their neural make-up, as in identity theory or eliminative materialism. Rather, they are defined with respect to how they function, or their causal role, in the behavioral system in question.

Machine-state functionalism
A mind-body position that assumes any organism that can be said to have a mind can be compared to a machine that operates according to a set of instructions for moving from one state to the next.

Radical behaviorist interpretation of what occasions mental talk
   1. Processes or relations that are actually in the behavioral dimension, whether publicly observable or private, and suitable for a science of behavior.
   2. Neural, muscular, or hormonal processes, and suitable for neuroscience.
   3. Complex social-cultural epistemological preconceptions or inappropriate linguistic metaphors, in which case the term is a fanciful explanatory fiction (e.g., from "folk psychology"), and is of interest only in regard to the social and cultural conditions that promote its use, rather than as a genuinely explanatory term.

Cognitive arguments against dispositional analyses:
   1. Publicly observable behavior may not correlate with the putative disposition.
   2. The origin of the disposition is not explained.

Radical behaviorist perspective on dispositional analyses:
   1. Dispositions have a legitimate descriptive but not explanatory function.
   2. Dispositions can be used in the sense of phylogeny, motivation, or to characterize the effect of experiences during the lifetime of an organism.

Mechanism
A mind-body position that assumes a functioning organism can be compared to a machine, and that behavior is completely explicable in terms of the laws of physical mechanics and the exchange of energy as calculated in physics.

Intentionality
The thesis that an instance of behavior possesses a particular property: namely, the property of being organized toward achieving some formulated purpose, end, or goal. The behaving organism is therefore an agent in the behavior in question,

rather than a passive automaton stimulated by the environment in a brute force, mechanical way.

Intensionality
Given that behavior is intentional rather than mechanical, and that the behaving organism is an agent in its behavior, the behaving organism is further cast as having a conception of the intentional organization of behavior, such that it has a choice of which response alternatives it can deploy to achieve the purpose.

Type-identity physicalism
Particular instances of phenomena have physical properties, and classes or types of phenomena are defined by their physical properties. Mental states are regarded as having physiological properties, and classes or types of those states are defined in terms of those physiological properties.

Token-identity physicalism
Particular instances of phenomena have physical properties, but classes or types of phenomena are defined by criteria other than their physical properties. Mental states are regarded as having physiological properties, but classes or types of those states are defined in terms of their causal function, rather than their physiological properties.

REFERENCES

Block, N. (Ed.). (1980). *Readings in philosophical psychology, Vol. 1*. Cambridge, MA: Harvard University Press.

Carnap, R. (1956). The methodological character of theoretical concepts. In H. Feigl & M. Scriven (Eds.), *Minnesota studies in the philosophy of science, Vol. 2*, pp. 33–76. Minneapolis, MN: University of Minnesota Press.

Catania, A. C., & Harnad, S. (Eds.). (1988). *The selection of behavior: The operant behaviorism of B. F. Skinner: Comments and controversies*. Cambridge: Cambridge University Press.

Chisholm, R. (1957). *Perceiving*. Ithaca, NY: Cornell University Press.

Fodor, J. A. (1981). *Representations: Philosophical essays on the foundations of cognitive science*. Cambridge, MA: MIT Press.

Hocutt, M. (1985). Spartans, strawmen, and symptoms. *Behaviorism, 13*, 87–97.

Hull, C. L. (1943). *Principles of Behavior*. New York: Appleton-Century.

MacCorquodale, K., & Meehl, P. (1948). On a distinction between hypothetical constructs and intervening variables. *Psychological Review, 55*, 95–107.

Moore, J. (1999). The basic principles of behaviorism. In B. Thyer (Ed.), *The philosophical legacy of behaviorism,* pp. 41–68. London: Kluwer.

Place, U. T. (1999). Ryle's behaviorism. In W. O'Donohue & W. F. Kitchener (Eds.), *Handbook of behaviorism*, pp. 361–398. San Diego, CA: Academic Press.

Putnam, H. (1980). Brains and behavior. In N. Block (Ed.), *Readings in philosophical psychology, Vol. 1*, pp. 24–36. Cambridge, MA: Harvard University Press.

Ryle, G. (1949). *The concept of mind*. London: Hutchison.

Schnaitter, R. (1985). The haunted clockwork: Reflections on Gilbert Ryle's *The Concept of Mind*. *Journal of the Experimental Analysis of Behavior, 43*, 145–153.

Schnaitter, R. (1986). Behavior as a function of inner states and outer circumstances. In T. Thompson & M. D. Zeiler (Eds.), *The analysis and integration of behavioral units,* pp. 247–274. Hillsdale, NJ: Erlbaum.

Schnaitter, R. (1987). Knowledge as action: The epistemology of radical behaviorism. In S. Modgil & C. Modgil (Eds.), *B. F. Skinner: Consensus and controversy,* pp. 57–68. Philadelphia, PA: Falmer Press.

Skinner, B. F. (1953). *Science and human behavior*. New York: Macmillan.

Skinner, B. F. (1957). *Verbal behavior*. New York: Appleton-Century-Crofts.

Skinner, B. F. (1972). *Cumulative record*. New York: Appleton-Century-Crofts.

Skinner, B. F. (1974). *About behaviorism*. New York: Knopf.

Tolman, E. C. (1948). Cognitive maps in rats and men. *Psychological Review*, 55, 189–208

STUDY QUESTIONS

1. Distinguish between idealism and materialism as positions on the relation between mind and body .

2. Distinguish among parallelism, interactionism, and epiphenomenalism as positions on the relation between mind and body .

3. Distinguish among identity theory, eliminative materialism, and functionalism as positions on the relation between mind and body .

4. Describe three classes of factors that from the perspective of radical behaviorism contribute to talk of mental acts, states, mechanisms, processes, or entities.

5. Describe Putnam's "perfect actor" argument as to why mental states should not be rendered as dispositions to engage in publicly observable behavior.

6. Describe Chisholm's infinite regress argument as to why mental states should not be rendered as dispositions to engage in publicly observable behavior.

7. Describe how radical behaviorism interprets dispositions. Include in your answer three senses in which the term disposition might reasonably be used.

8. Describe why mechanistic explanations run contrary to behavior-analytic explanatory practices, even though radical behaviorism does not embrace teleological, final-cause explanations.

9. Describe how radical behaviorism accommodates the traditional concepts of intentionality and intensionality.

Section IV

Conclusion

19

Radical Behaviorism as Epistemology

Synopsis of Chapter 19: This book is organized into three sections. The chapters in the first section were concerned with the foundations of radical behaviorism. The chapters in the second section were concerned with the realization of the radical behaviorist program. The chapters in the third section compared and contrasted radical behaviorism with alternative viewpoints. Throughout, the book focused on understanding the foundation of radical behaviorism as the philosophy of a science of behavior. The book has now come full circle. Chapter 19 begins with the question: How, then, shall a genuine behaviorism be understood? Radical behaviorism does not take behavior as evidence or a manifestation of mental causes, in order to claim that it follows a respectable methodology. Rather, it deals with functional relations between environment and behavior. Importantly, neither environment nor behavior stops at the skin. The chapter emphasizes that in the radical behaviorist view, talk in traditional psychology of mental causes may itself be analyzed to reveal sources of control that lie in historical tradition and cultural practices, rather than in anything related to prediction and control. The chapter then considers radical behaviorism as epistemology. It outlines how a thoroughgoing, radical behaviorism allows one to profitably engage the question of knowledge. For radical behaviorism, knowledge implies a developed repertoire of operant behavior, and within human operant behavior, verbal behavior. Analyses in terms of underlying contingencies of reinforcement provide insight into all aspects of the human condition, and provide the most direct route to a successful science of human life.

An important argument of this book is that radical behaviorism differs just as much from other positions conventionally known as behavioristic as it does from positions conventionally known as mentalistic. Most other positions conventionally known as behavioristic are forms of mediational S – O – R neobehaviorism and subscribe to methodological behaviorism. In fact, an argument of this book is that mediational and methodological behaviorism share critical features of positions more conspicuously recognized as mentalistic, despite the occasional denials of mediational neobehaviorists, methodological behaviorists, and mentalists.

THE DEFINITION OF A GENUINE BEHAVIORISM

How, then, is it useful to define a genuine behaviorism? Consider the generic statement below, modified from Addis (1982) and Bergmann (1956):

> Behaviorism is a viewpoint that assumes that it must be possible, in principle, to secure an adequate explanation of behavior, including verbal behavior in humans, in terms of present and past behavioral, physiological, and environmental variables, in ways that do not require a direct appeal to phenomena in a mental dimension. The conception of a "mental dimension" used in this statement is of a dimension that is held to be qualitatively distinct from the behavioral dimension (e.g., mental, psychic, spiritual, conceptual, hypothetical), and not just a subdomain of it. The conception of "phenomena in a mental dimension" used in this statement is of phenomena (e.g., acts, states, mechanisms, processes, structures, or entities) that are held to be qualitatively distinct from the behavioral, physiological, and environmental variables of a behavioral dimension, and not just a subset of them.

Does this statement adequately define behaviorism? From the perspective of the present book, the statement above does *not*. Although Cartesian interactionism is disqualified as a behaviorism because it requires a direct appeal to causal mental phenomena, the definition is decidedly ambiguous when it comes to other positions. Two critical terms in the definition are "require" and "direct." Consider first the use of the term "require." The definition does not *require* appeals to mental events, but it does *admit* them. For example, the definition admits parallelism as a form of behaviorism because it holds that phenomena in the mental dimension are just as valid a basis by which to predict and understand behavior as are events in the behavioral dimension. On this basis, those who are parallelists could and do claim to be behaviorists.

The problem is that there is no mental dimension, and psychologists who think they can adequately explain behavior by appealing to phenomena in a mental dimension are gravely mistaken. Explanations of events reflect the functional role of factors that participate in the event. Since there is no mental dimension, purported phenomena in a purported mental dimension cannot be what is influencing the explanation of the behavioral event. Rather, the explanation is a function of other factors, such as the social-cultural traditions that have institutionalized mentalism. As such, the explanation will necessarily omit the consideration of some relevant present or past behavioral, physiological, and environmental variable.

Consider next the use of the term "direct." Logical behaviorism and various forms of methodological behaviorism such as mediational S – O – R neobehaviorism don't appeal directly to mental events, and hence would seem to count as a behaviorism by the definition above. However, they do appeal *indirectly* to mental events through the use of hypothetical constructs. Consider also conceptual analysis. This position does not rule out the possibility that events in a mental dimension cause behavior, even though conceptual analysis holds that psychological terms do not identify anything pertaining to the process. Chapter 17 has already reviewed how troublesome these various positions are, and how radical behaviorism differs from them. Hence, the generic definition above would allow one to group many positions conventionally known as behavioral, ranging from parallelism to mediational neobehaviorism to analytical behaviorism, with radical behaviorism under a common heading. Clearly a definition that allows one to do so is not adequate.

What is an alternative definition that appropriately disambiguates the several possible interpretations of behaviorism? Consider the following extended statement:

Behaviorism is a viewpoint that assumes that it must be possible, in principle, to secure an adequate causal explanation of behavior, including verbal behavior in humans, in terms of present and past behavioral, physiological, and environmental variables, in ways that reject either a direct or indirect appeal to causal phenomena in a mental dimension. The conception of a "mental dimension" used in this statement is of a dimension that is held to be qualitatively distinct from the behavioral dimension (e.g., mental, psychic, spiritual, conceptual, hypothetical), and not just a subdomain of the behavioral dimension. The conception of "causal phenomena in a mental dimension" used in this statement is of phenomena (e.g., acts, states, mechanisms, processes, structures, or entities) that are held to be qualitatively distinct from the behavioral, physiological, and environmental variables of a behavioral dimension, and not just a subset of them. The mental dimension is rejected because it does not exist, and therefore when one talks of mental phenomena, one is actually not talking about phenomena from another dimension at all. Rather, any talk appealing to this dimension and these sorts of causal phenomena is occasioned by (a) social-cultural traditions or spurious social factors; (b) physiological factors; (c) the relation between publicly observable behavior and present and past behavioral, physiological, and environmental variables; or (d) private behavioral events. In the first case, the talk is not functionally related to any factors in space and time that can be manipulated to affect behavior. Rather, the talk illustrates only unwarranted metaphors from language patterns or fictional distortions that are cherished for irrelevant and extraneous reasons. In the second, the talk is functionally related to organized physiological systems that are the province of neuroscience and its methods. In the third, the talk is functionally related to how various circumstances affect the probability of engaging in behavior. In the fourth, the talk is functionally related to felt conditions of the body or covert operant behavior, as those conditions or behavior are situated in a context. The conditions of the body or covert operant behavior assume the form they do, and acquire the behavioral effect they do, by virtue of public relations.

However tortuous, this definition offers some possibility of identifying a genuine behaviorism that differs from ersatz versions that have emerged as intellectual compromises since the second quarter of the twentieth century. The definition explicitly rejects mentalism and methodological behaviorism. Instead, it calls for the analysis of verbal behavior ostensibly concerned with the mental, but in terms of naturalistic contingencies that operate in space and time.

To be certain, an approach emphasizing publicly observable factors was thought to safeguard the scientific character of psychology against the vagaries of introspectionism and a concern with consciousness. However, history reveals that the particular way publicly observable factors were emphasized has been troublesome. Skinner (1945, p. 292) explicitly charged over 60 years ago that traditional psychology has only preserved the old explanatory fictions unharmed—in some cases quite unselfconsciously—instead of dispensing with them. Mediational neobehaviorism has continued to preserve those fictions. Cognitive orientations project themselves as being liberated from the restrictions of behaviorism, but the lack of any practical import testifies to the manifest bankruptcy, rather than self-proclaimed richness, of their endeavors. Cognitive psychology is a conceptual and logical extension of the mediational approach of neobehaviorism. The root of the trouble across all these positions is the conception of language as a logical, symbolic process instead of a behavioral process. By properly understanding language as verbal behavior, one can properly understand a genuine behaviorism and how it contributes to a genuine behavioral epistemology.

RADICAL BEHAVIORISM AS AN EPISTEMOLOGY

Radical behaviorism may therefore be understood as the unique epistemological position arising from the perspective of B. F. Skinner. It began in the second quarter of the twentieth century, as Skinner pursued his interests in the empirical study of behavior. Skinner came to psychology with a background in literature and the arts, although with a decidedly objective, empirical perspective. Before entering graduate school, his interests were stimulated by certain writings of Francis Bacon, Ivan Pavlov, Bertrand Russell, and John B. Watson. While Skinner was in graduate school, his research interests were influenced by William Crozier, Jacques Loeb, Rudolf Magnus, and William Sherrington, and his theoretical, philosophical, and conceptual interests by Percy Bridgman, Ernst Mach, and Henri Poincaré. After graduate school, Skinner worked on his own research program and applied his objective, empirical perspective to analyses of his own behavior as a scientist, as well as the behavior of his subjects. As these analyses proceeded, he also developed a unique perspective on verbal behavior, applying it again to himself as well as others.

Radical behaviorism grew from the conception of behavior as a subject matter in its own right. According to this conception, behavior was functionally related to the environmental circumstances in which it occurred. It was not merely evidence to justify inferences about supposedly underlying entities from neural, mental, or conceptual dimensions, which traditional accounts took as the true causes of behavior. Not only were there classes of behavior that were elicited by the presentation of stimuli, but also there were classes of behavior that were important because of their consequences. The unit of analysis for these latter classes involved three terms: (a) the antecedent setting that was correlated with (b) the response that produced (c) the consequence. The three-term unit of analysis was called a contingency of reinforcement, and the behavior in question was called operant behavior. The relevant causal mode was selection by consequences, just as in other areas of biological science. The operant approach differed in both style and substance from mediational approaches that were deemed behavioral, such as those of Hull, Tolman, and Spence.

The extension of the operant approach to verbal behavior represented a further step in the development of radical behaviorism. The conception of verbal behavior as operant behavior opened up a uniquely human activity to meaningful scientific analysis, and further dispelled the mentalistic idea that the individual was an initiator or originator.

The operant approach to verbal behavior was then extended to matters with which only the behaving individual was in contact. The extension to these matters addressed time-honored topics that were thought to be suitable only for another mode of analysis: the mental, the cognitive, the subjective. By rendering these topics as behavioral and examining the source of control over verbal behavior about these topics, it became apparent that radical behaviorism encompassed what was traditionally encompassed under the heading of epistemology: the nature and limits of knowledge. Not only did radical behaviorism encompass epistemology, but it also took the lead in understanding what knowledge was, how it came about, and how to improve the human condition by making humans even more knowledgeable. Thus, radical behaviorism represents nothing less than a thoroughgoing, naturalistic epistemology, grounded in fundamental principles of behavior and extended in an operant approach to verbal behavior.

Skinner testified repeatedly to his early interest in epistemology when he described how he came to behaviorism:

> The first thing I can remember happened when I was only twenty-two years old. Shortly after I was graduated from college Bertrand Russell published a series of articles in the old *Dial* magazine on the epistemology of John B. Watson's *Behaviorism*. I had had no psychology as an undergraduate but I had a lot of biology, and two of the books which my biology professor had put into my hands were Loeb's *Physiology of the Brain* and the newly published Oxford edition of Pavlov's *Conditioned Reflexes*. And now here was Russell extrapolating the principles of an objective formulation of behavior to the problem of knowledge! (Skinner, 1972, p. 103)

> I was drawn to psychology and particularly to behaviorism by some papers which Bertrand Russell published in the *Dial* in the 1920s and which led me to his book *Philosophy* (called in England *An Outline of Philosophy*), the first section of which contains a much more sophisticated discussion of several epistemological issues raised by behaviorism than anything of John B. Watson's. (Skinner, 1978, p. 113)

> I came to behaviorism, as I have said, because of its bearing on epistemology, and I have not been disappointed. (Skinner, 1978, p. 124)

I also planned to observe the history of science as it unfolded and, following Francis Bacon a little too closely, to take all knowledge to be my province. (Skinner, 1979, pp. 49–50)

First, however, a word about sources. The commitment to behaviorism that sent me from college to graduate study in psychology was at the time no better supported than my commitment in high school to the theory that Francis Bacon wrote the works of Shakespeare. I had taken my college degree in English Language and Literature with a minor in Romance Languages and was hoping to be a writer. An important book for writers at that time was *The Meaning of Meaning* by C. K. Ogden and I. A. Richards (1923). Bertrand Russell reviewed it for a literary magazine called the *Dial*, to which I subscribed, and in a footnote he acknowledged his indebtedness to "Dr. Watson," whose recent book *Behaviorism* (1925) he found "massively impressive." I bought Watson's book and liked its campaigning style. Later I bought Russell's *Philosophy* (1927), in which he treated a few mentalistic terms in a behavioristic way. Although I had never had a course in psychology, I became an instant behaviorist.… (Skinner, 1989, pp. 121–122)

In other writing, Skinner explicitly framed knowledge in behavioral terms in the following ways:

A knowledge of history ... is simply a verbal repertoire ... . Knowledge is a repertoire of behavior. (Skinner, 1953, p. 409)

Men are part of the world ... their "knowledge" is their behavior with respect to themselves and the rest of the world. (Skinner, 1957, p. 451)

The world which establishes contingencies of reinforcement of the sort studied in an operant analysis is presumably "what knowledge is about." A person comes to know that world and how to behave in it in the sense that he acquires behavior which satisfies the contingencies it maintains. (Skinner, 1969, p. 156)

Knowledge is action rather than sensing, and ... formulation of knowledge should be in terms of behavior. (Skinner, 1972, p. 255)

We know algebra ... in the sense of possessing various forms of behavior with respect to [it]. (Skinner, 1974, p. 138)

The important point to be taken from these several passages is that for radical behaviorism, questions about epistemology are simply questions about the behavior of individuals said to know something. Moreover, the behavioral processes that promote what is called "knowledge" are equally applicable to the individuals who are said to know themselves:

A science of behavior must consider the place of private stimuli as physical things, and in so doing it provides an alternative account of mental life. The question, then, is this: What is inside the skin, and how do we know about it? The answer is, I believe, the heart of radical behaviorism. (Skinner, 1924, pp. 217–218)

Thus, there is no primacy or privilege as Descartes would have had it about self-knowledge. Rather, the self is just one more object of knowledge. Is it correct to assume that radical behaviorism, by virtue of being classed as a behaviorism, actually denies that when a person is "thinking" or that when a person senses one sort of pain and labels it as sharp and senses another but labels it as dull, little if anything of psychological significance is involved? Does radical behaviorism hold that such matters must be analyzed through non-scientific means? Does radical behaviorism argue that if such matters are to be addressed, they can only be addressed *indirectly* through the verbal intermediaries, or by pointing to the publicly observable behavioral surrogates that are asserted to be the measures of the internal states? Most assuredly, radical behaviorists answer no to all such questions.

 Given that radical behaviorism may be construed as an epistemological stance, the following statements summarize the sense of radical behaviorism as epistemology. The statements are presented as a sequence of relatively small steps, from simple to more substantive concerns:

1. The most significant and relevant form of human behavior said to show scientific knowledge is operant behavior, which is analyzed in terms of contingencies of reinforcement that control both the verbal and nonverbal operant behavior of the scientist.

    1.1 Scientific knowledge does not differ in principle from any other kind of knowledge, although the contingencies that control the scientific behavior said to show knowledge may be more refined.

    1.2 Knowledge is power, and the fundamental issue is the extent to which claims of scientific knowledge function as forms of discriminative stimulation that contribute to effective action with respect to the environment.

2. Claims of scientific knowledge (e.g., theories, explanations) and the terms or concepts therein are instances of verbal behavior; they are always and have only ever been matters of differential behavior in differential circumstances. Any such claims of scientific knowledge may therefore be analyzed in terms of contingencies of reinforcement that control the verbal behavior in question of the scientist.

    2.1 The same principles that apply to understanding the sources and development of operant behavior in general apply to understanding the sources and development of (verbal) behavior said to show scientific knowledge.

    2.2 The sophisticated (verbal) behavior said to show scientific knowledge develops and is maintained through the action of environmental consequences, which select its most effective forms.

3. Some elements of knowledge claims may well be accessible only to one individual. Those elements may be parts of the contingencies controlling the behavior of the scientist doing the speaking or of the person being spoken about. Although

others may have dealt with these elements by inference, to the one individual they are not inferential and are not appropriately regarded as such. The origin and subsequent functional role of these private elements may ultimately be traced back to the effect of public contingencies in the environment, meaning that an appeal to private, covert behavioral elements in specific instances is consistent with the overall thesis of analyzing knowledge claims in terms of operant behavior controlled by contingencies of reinforcement.

4. Accounting for knowledge claims is not a matter of appealing to unobservable acts, states, mechanisms, processes, structures, or entities elsewhere, in some other dimension, at some other level (e.g., neural, mental, cognitive, conceptual, psychic, hypothetical, subjective), for which observable behavior is the license that makes such appeals scientifically respectable. These other statements need to be critically examined on a case-by-case basis to determine the extent of their net value as knowledge claims, rather than literally accepted. To argue in favor of the literal acceptance of such appeals is to invite control by linguistic traps, unwarranted metaphors, grammatical habits, and otherwise mischievous and deceptive contingencies of social reinforcement and general cultural traditions.

5. Historical attempts to rationally reconstruct the grounds for scientific activity and knowledge claims in terms of logical, symbolic, or representational processes of the scientist were incorrect on two counts. First, these attempts implicitly entailed appeals to activity in other dimensions on the part of the scientist, if not also the subject. Second, the attempts explicitly drew attention away from the analysis of the contingencies that actually controlled the verbal and nonverbal behavior of the scientist.

6. Ultimately, knowledge claims are part of a culture and function to promote the welfare and survival of the culture. A culture that has not convinced its members to work for its welfare and survival is not likely to survive.

Taken together, these statements reveal how a causal analysis of the verbal behavior of the scientist illustrates radical behaviorism as a thoroughgoing, behavioral epistemology at work.

Thus, radical behaviorism as an epistemology takes its departure from the pragmatic stances of Bacon and Mach. In addition, following Russell's early treatment, it is based on a causal, behavioral conception of verbal behavior. Following Watson, it views behavior as a subject matter in its own right, to be explained without appealing to events in other dimensions, such as the neural, mental, or conceptual dimensions. Knowledge and meaning are therefore behavioral matters, to be analyzed in terms of operant contingencies of reinforcement. What is important is how features identified in the study of epistemology function in one's life. If one can account for scientific verbal behavior, one has accomplished one of the major goals in an analysis of behavior. If one can account for how one comes to know oneself, one has accomplished another. Radical behaviorism may ultimately be understood as the set of guidelines for carrying out these several tasks according to thoroughgoing behavioral principles.

For radical behaviorism, then, questions of knowing are always and have only ever been questions about events and relations in the behavioral dimension. As such, the questions fall squarely within the purview of a science of behavior. The fundamental thesis of radical behaviorism is that a valid conception of what knowledge means and how it is to be achieved is of immense benefit to humankind. Moreover, this conception will be based on behavioral principles, rather than supposed mental principles. In one of his autobiographical statements, Skinner (1967) commented:

> To me behaviorism is a special case of a philosophy of science which first took shape in the writings of Ernst Mach, Henri Poincaré, and Percy Bridgman.... Behaviorism is a formulation which makes possible an effective experimental approach to human behavior. It is a working hypothesis about the nature of a subject matter. It may need to be clarified, but it does not need to be argued. I have no doubt of the eventual triumph of the position–not that it will eventually be proved right, but that it will provide the most direct route to a successful science of man. (pp. 409–410)

Just so.

TABLE 19–1

Definition of behaviorism
A viewpoint that assumes that it must be possible, in principle, to secure an adequate causal explanation of behavior, including verbal behavior in humans, in terms of present and past behavioral, physiological, and environmental variables, in ways that reject any sort of appeal, however indirect, to causal phenomena in a mental dimension. The conception of a "mental dimension" used in this statement is of a dimension that is held to be qualitatively distinct from the behavioral dimension (e.g., mental, psychic, spiritual, conceptual, hypothetical), and not just a subdomain of the behavioral dimension. The conception of "causal phenomena in a mental dimension" used in this statement is of phenomena (e.g., acts, states, mechanisms, processes, structures, or entities) that are held to be qualitatively distinct from the behavioral, physiological, and environmental variables of a behavioral dimension, and not just a subset of them. The mental dimension is rejected because it does not exist, and therefore when one talks of mental phenomena one is actually not talking about phenomena from another dimension at all. Rather, any talk appealing to this dimension and these sorts of causal phenomena is occasioned by (a) social-cultural traditions or spurious social factors; (b) physiological

factors; (c) the relation between publicly observable behavior and present and past behavioral, physiological, and environmental variables; or (d) private behavioral events.

Knowledge
Differential behavior in differential circumstances, as a function of exposure to environmental events. To say that individual A is more knowledgeable than individual B is to say that A's behavior is more differentiated across a wider variety of circumstances, as a function of exposure to environmental events.

REFERENCES

Addis, L. (1982). Behaviorism and the philosophy of the act. *Nous, 16*, 399–420.

Bergmann, G. (1956). The contribution of John B. Watson. *Psychological Review, 63*, 265–276.

Ogden, C. K., & Richards, I. A. (1923). *The meaning of meaning*. London: Longman.

Russell, B. (1927). *Philosophy*. London: George Allen and Unwin.

Skinner, B. F. (1945). The operational analysis of psychological terms. *Psychological Review, 52*, 270–277, 290–294.

Skinner, B. F. (1953). *Science and human behavior*. New York: Macmillan.

Skinner, B. F. (1957). *Verbal behavior*. New York: Appleton-Century-Crofts.

Skinner, B. F. (1967). B. F. Skinner (An autobiography). In E. G. Boring & G. Lindzey (Eds.), *A history of psychology in autobiography, Vol. 5*, pp. 387–413. New York: Appleton-Century-Crofts.

Skinner, B. F. (1969). *Contingencies of reinforcement*. New York: Appleton-Century-Crofts.

Skinner, B. F. (1972). *Cumulative record*. New York: Appleton-Century-Crofts.

Skinner, B. F. (1974). *About behaviorism*. New York: Knopf.

Skinner, B. F. (1978). *Reflections on behaviorism and society*. Englewood Cliffs, NJ: Prentic-Hall.

Skinner, B. F. (1979). *The shaping of a behaviorist*. New York: Knopf.

Skinner, B. F. (1989). *Recent issues in the analysis of behavior*. Columbus, OH: Merrill.

Watson, J. B. (1925). *Behaviorism*. New York: Norton.

STUDY QUESTIONS

1. Define behaviorism in a way that is acceptable to radical behaviorism.

2. List three individuals who stimulated Skinner's interests before he entered graduate school.

3. List three individuals who stimulated Skinner's research interests while he was in graduate school.

4. List three individuals who stimulated Skinner's theoretical, philosophical, and conceptual interests while he was in graduate school.

5. State the name of the English philosopher who sought to extrapolate the principles of Watson's objective formulation of behavior to the problem of knowledge, and in so doing, captured Skinner's interest.

6. State or paraphrase one of Skinner's statements in which knowledge is framed in behavioral terms.

7. Describe the continuity among operant behavior, verbal behavior, and scientific behavior.

8. Describe how a valid conception of: (a) what knowledge means, and (b) how it is to be achieved will be based on behavioral principles emphasizing the three-term contingency of reinforcement.

Acknowledgments

Portions of this book have appeared in material previously published by the author and edited for the current presentation. Permission to use this material is gratefully acknowledged.

From the *Journal of Mind and Behavior*:
Moore, J. (1990). On mentalism, privacy, and behaviorism. *Journal of Mind and Behavior, 11*, 19–36.
Moore, J. (1996). On the relation between behaviorism and cognitive psychology. *Journal of Mind and Behavior, 17*, 345–368.
Moore, J. (1998). On behaviorism, theories, and hypothetical constructs. *Journal of Mind and Behavior, 19*, 215–242.
Moore, J. (2005). Some historical and conceptual background to the development of B. F. Skinner's "radical behaviorism" – Part 2. *Journal of Mind and Behavior, 26*, 95–124.
Moore, J. (2005). Some historical and conceptual background to the development of B. F. Skinner's "radical behaviorism" – Part 3. *Journal of Mind and Behavior, 26*, 137–160.

From *The Psychological Record*:
Moore, J. (2002). Some thoughts on the relation between behavioral neuroscience and behavior analysis. *The Psychological Record, 52*, 261–280.

From *Behavior and Philosophy*:
Moore, J. (2001). On psychological terms that appeal to the mental. *Behavior and Philosophy, 29*, 167–186.

From Chase, P., & Lattal,K. (Eds.). (2003). *Behavior theory and philosophy.* Dordrecht, NL: Kluwer.

Moore, J. (2003). Explanation and description in traditional neobehaviorism, cognitive psychology, and behavior analysis. In P. Chase & K. Lattal (Eds.), *Behavior theory and philosophy* (pp. 13–39). Dordrecht, NL: Kluwer.

From *European Journal of Behavior Analysis*:

Moore, J. (2000). Behavior analysis and psycholinguistics. *European Journal of Behavior Analysis, 1*, 5–22.

Moore, J. (2001). On distinguishing methodological from radical behaviorism. *European Journal of Behavior Analysis, 2*, 221–244.

From *The Analysis of Verbal Behavior*

Moore, J. (2000). Words are not things. *The Analysis of Verbal Behavior, 17*, 143–160.

From *The Behavior Analyst*:

Moore, J. (2003). Behavior analysis, mentalism, and the path to social justice. *The Behavior Analyst, 26*, 181–193.

From Athabasca University:

Moore, J. (1998). Behaviorism tutorial (on-line). Available: http://psych.athabascau.ca/html/Behaviorism/. Copyright © 1998, Athabasca University. Reproduced with permission.

Name Index

Subject Index